Succeeding in Business™ with Microsoft® Office Access 2003:
A Problem-Solving Approach

"With knowledge comes opportunity,
with opportunity comes success."
— Anonymous

Karin Bast
University of Wisconsin, La Crosse
Leon Cygman
DeVry University
Gerard Flynn
Pepperdine University
Rebekah Tidwell
Lee University

THOMSON
COURSE TECHNOLOGY

Australia • Canada • Mexico • Singapore • Spain • United Kingdom • United States

Succeeding in Business™ with Microsoft® Office Access 2003:

A Problem-Solving Approach

by Karin Bast, Leon Cygman, Gerard Flynn, and Rebekah Tidwell

Managing Editor
Rachel Goldberg

Senior Product Manager
Kathy Finnegan

Developmental Editors
Jessica Evans & Lisa Ruffolo

Contributing Authors
Joesph A. Adamski, Jessica
Evans & Lisa Ruffolo

Series Consultants
Frank Akaiwa & Bill Littlefield

Senior Product Manager
Amanda Shelton

Product Manager
Brianna Hawes

Associate Product Manager
Shana Rosenthal

Marketing Manager
Joy Stark

Production Editor
Jennifer Goguen

Composition
Digital Publishing Solutions

Text Designer
Tim Blackburn

Cover Designer
Steve Deschene

Brief
Contents

Table of **Contents**

Preface

THE SUCCEEDING IN BUSINESS™ SERIES

Because you're ready for more.

Increasingly students are coming into the classroom with stronger computer skills. As a result, they are ready to move beyond "point and click" skills and learn to use these tools in a way that will assist them in the business world.

You've told us you and your students want more: more of a business focus, more realistic case problems, more emphasis on application of software skills and more problem-solving. For this reason, we created the **Succeeding in Business Series.**

The **Succeeding in Business Series** is the first of its kind designed to prepare the technology-savvy student for life after college. In the business world, your students' ability to use available tools to analyze data and solve problems is one of the most important factors in determining their success. The books in this series engage students who have mastered basic computer and applications skills by challenging them to think critically and find effective solutions to realistic business problems.

We're excited about the new classroom opportunities this new approach affords, and we hope you are too. We look forward to hearing about your successes!

The Succeeding in Business Team
www.course.com/succeeding
CT.succeeding@thomson.com

GETTING THE MOST OUT OF *SUCCEEDING IN BUSINESS WITH MICROSOFT OFFICE ACCESS 2003*

Succeeding in Business with Microsoft Office Access 2003 expects more from your students. Whether they were introduced to basic Office skills in another course, or you expect that they have learned them on their own, chances are students will need to refresh their skills before they delve into the challenging problem-solving this series requires.

To meet this need, Thomson Course Technology is proud to offer the *Succeeding in Business Skills Training CD* for Microsoft Office Access 2003, powered by SAM. You will find this CD in the back of this book.

The Access Skills Training CD offers training in a simulated environment on the exact skills needed to face the real-world business problems this textbook presents. The CD ensures students have the tools they need to be successful in their studies. Using the Access Skills Training CD, students can:

- Ensure they have mastered the prerequisites of the course.
- Refresh their knowledge of computer skills they learned in another course or on their own.
- Receive additional "granular" skills-based training as they move through the more complex skills and concepts covered in the textbook.

Students can use the Access Skills Training CD both before they begin and during their studies with the Succeeding in Business series. A relevant list of related skills (indicated by the SAM icon at right) is provided in the Introduction Chapter and prior to each chapter level. This enables students to self-assess their knowledge and use the Access Skills Training CD to refresh or expand their skills. We recommend students use this list and their Training CD to review the mechanics behind the skills that will be covered in more depth in the texts.

THE SUCCEEDING IN BUSINESS INSTRUCTOR RESOURCES

A unique approach requires unique instructor support; and we have you covered. We take the next step in providing you with outstanding Instructor Resources—developed by educators and experts and tested through our rigorous Quality Assurance process. Whether you use one resource or all the resources provided, our goal is to make the teaching and learning experience in your classroom the best it can be. With Course Technology's resources, you'll spend less time preparing, and more time teaching.

To access any of the items mentioned below, go to www.course.com or contact your Course Technology Sales Representative.

INSTRUCTOR'S MANUAL

The instructor's manual offers guidance through each level of each chapter. You will find lecture notes that provide an overview of the chapter content along with background information and teaching tips. Also included are classroom activities and discussion questions that will get your students thinking about the business scenarios and decisions presented in the book.

EXAMVIEW® TEST BANK

ExamView features a user-friendly testing environment that allows you to not only publish traditional paper and LAN-based tests, but also Web-deliverable exams. In addition to the traditional multiple-choice, true/false, completion, short answer, and essay, questions, the **Succeeding in Business** series emphasizes new critical thinking questions. Like the textbook, these questions challenge your students with questions that go beyond defining key terms and focus more on the real word decision making process they will face in business, while keeping the convenience of automatic grading for you.

STUDENT DATA FILES AND SOLUTION FILES

All student data files necessary to complete the hands-on portion of each level and the end-of chapter material are provided along with the solutions files.

ANNOTATED SOLUTION FILES AND RUBRICS

Challenging your students shouldn't make it more difficult to set grading criteria. Each student assignment in your textbook will have a correlating Annotated Solution File that highlights what to look for in your students' submissions. Grading Rubrics list these criteria in an auto-calculating table that can be customized to fit the needs of your class. Electronic file format of both of these tools offers the flexibility of online or paper-based grading. This complete grading solution will save you time and effort on grading.

POWERPOINT PRESENTATIONS

The PowerPoint presentations deliver visually impressive lectures filled with the business and application concepts and skills introduced in the text. Use these to engage your students in discussion regarding the content covered in each chapter. You can also distribute or post these files for your students to use as an additional study aid.

FIGURE FILES

Every figure in the text is provided in an easy to use file format. Use these to customize your PowerPoint Presentations, create overheads, and many other ways to enhance your course.

SAMPLE SYLLABUS

A sample syllabus is provided to help you get your course started. Provided in a Word document, you can use the syllabus as is or modify it for your own course.

SUCCEEDING IN BUSINESS SERIES WALK-THROUGH

The Succeeding in Business approach is unique. It moves beyond point-and-click exercises to give your students more real-world problem solving skills that they can apply in business. In the following pages, step through *Succeeding in Business with Microsoft Office Access 2003* to learn more about the series pedagogy, features, design, and reinforcement exercises.

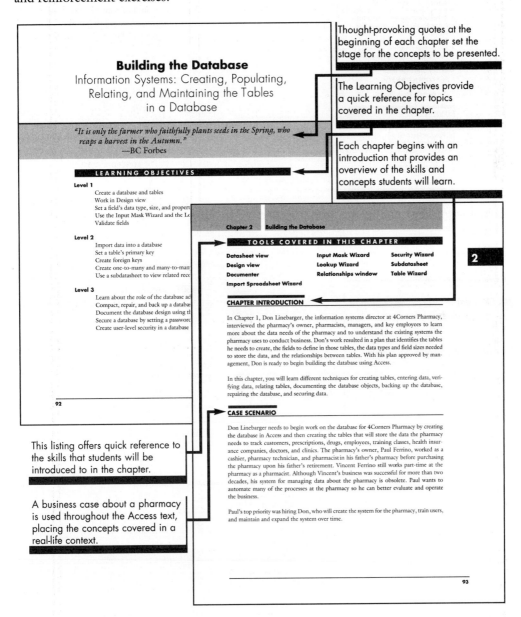

Thought-provoking quotes at the beginning of each chapter set the stage for the concepts to be presented.

The Learning Objectives provide a quick reference for topics covered in the chapter.

Each chapter begins with an introduction that provides an overview of the skills and concepts students will learn.

Building the Database
Information Systems: Creating, Populating, Relating, and Maintaining the Tables in a Database

"It is only the farmer who faithfully plants seeds in the Spring, who reaps a harvest in the Autumn."
—BC Forbes

LEARNING OBJECTIVES

Level 1
Create a database and tables
Work in Design view
Set a field's data type, size, and propert
Use the Input Mask Wizard and the Lc
Validate fields

Level 2
Import data into a database
Set a table's primary key
Create foreign keys
Create one-to-many and many-to-man
Use a subdatasheet to view related rece

Level 3
Learn about the role of the database ad
Compact, repair, and back up a databa:
Document the database design using tl
Secure a database by setting a passwor
Create user-level security in a database

92

Chapter 2 | Building the Database

TOOLS COVERED IN THIS CHAPTER

Datasheet view	Input Mask Wizard	Security Wizard
Design view	Lookup Wizard	Subdatasheet
Documenter	Relationships window	Table Wizard
Import Spreadsheet Wizard		

2

CHAPTER INTRODUCTION

In Chapter 1, Don Linebarger, the information systems director at 4Corners Pharmacy, interviewed the pharmacy's owner, pharmacists, managers, and key employees to learn more about the data needs of the pharmacy and to understand the existing systems the pharmacy uses to conduct business. Don's work resulted in a plan that identifies the tables he needs to create, the fields to define in those tables, the data types and field sizes needed to store the data, and the relationships between tables. With his plan approved by management, Don is ready to begin building the database using Access.

In this chapter, you will learn different techniques for creating tables, entering data, verifying data, relating tables, documenting the database objects, backing up the database, repairing the database, and securing data.

CASE SCENARIO

Don Linebarger needs to begin work on the database for 4Corners Pharmacy by creating the database in Access and then creating the tables that will store the data the pharmacy needs to track customers, prescriptions, drugs, employees, training classes, health insurance companies, doctors, and clinics. The pharmacy's owner, Paul Ferrino, worked as a cashier, pharmacy technician, and pharmacist in his father's pharmacy before purchasing the pharmacy upon his father's retirement. Vincent Ferrino still works part-time at the pharmacy as a pharmacist. Although Vincent's business was successful for more than two decades, his system for managing data about the pharmacy is obsolete. Paul wants to automate many of the processes at the pharmacy so he can better evaluate and operate the business.

Paul's top priority was hiring Don, who will create the system for the pharmacy, train users, and maintain and expand the system over time.

93

This listing offers quick reference to the skills that students will be introduced to in the chapter.

A business case about a pharmacy is used throughout the Access text, placing the concepts covered in a real-life context.

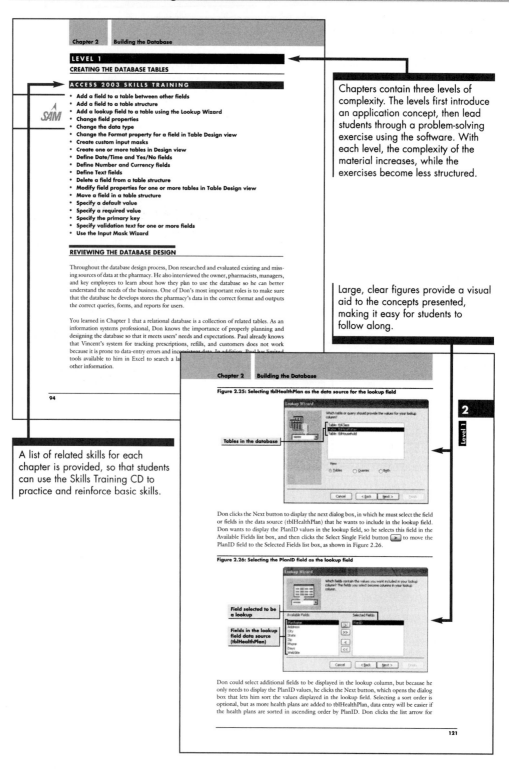

Chapters contain three levels of complexity. The levels first introduce an application concept, then lead students through a problem-solving exercise using the software. With each level, the complexity of the material increases, while the exercises become less structured.

Large, clear figures provide a visual aid to the concepts presented, making it easy for students to follow along.

A list of related skills for each chapter is provided, so that students can use the Skills Training CD to practice and reinforce basic skills.

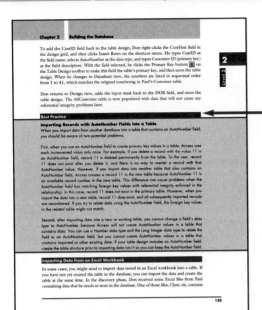

Best Practice boxes offer tips to help students become more efficient users of the application.

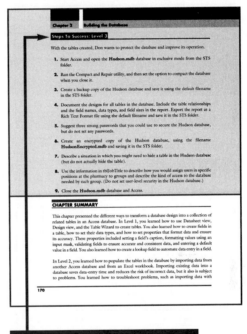

How To boxes offer a quick reference to the steps needed to complete certain tasks.

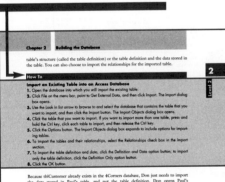

Steps to Success activities within each level offer students the opportunity to apply the skills they have learned before moving to the next level.

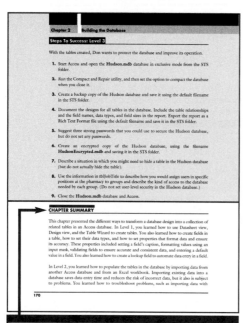

The Chapter Summary provides a brief review of the lessons in the chapter.

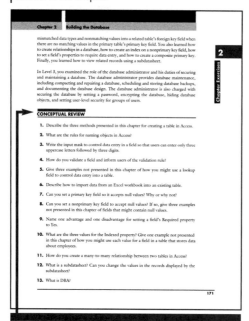

Conceptual Review questions provide a brief review of key concepts covered throughout the chapter.

Business-focused case problems provide additional practice for the problem-solving concepts and skills presented in each level.

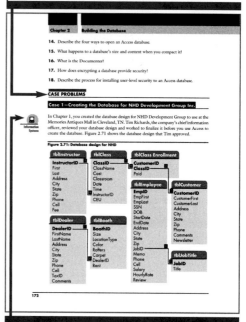

Each case problem focuses on a specific business discipline, such as accounting, information systems, marketing, sales, and operations management. Marginal icons representing each discipline make it easy to see which disciplines are covered in each case problem.

ABOUT THE AUTHORS

Leon Cygman
DeVry University
Leon Cygman has an MBA majoring in Information Systems and is currently pursuing his PhD in Electronic Commerce. He has been instructing post secondary mathematics and computer applications for over 20 years. He has also been involved with curriculum design and has developed several online courses. Leon owns and operates a consulting company which specializes in advising small businesses on how to effectively leverage the Internet and computer information systems to their strategic advantage. Leon is a licensed private pilot and an avid backgammon player.

Karin Bast
University of Wisconsin, La Crosse
Karin Bast teaches at the University of Wisconsin-La Crosse in the Information Systems department (part of the College of Business). Her academic background consists of a BA in Mathematics and Psychology from the University of Minnesota-Minneapolis and an MBA from the University of Wisconsin-La Crosse. Her business career began as the Minneapolis manager of a branch of a computer time-sharing company. For more than 20 years she had her own consulting firm, advising small- and medium-sized businesses on systems development, software selection, application and training, and strategic planning. During her 18 years of teaching she has taught the introductory course in information systems as well as other courses in information and network management. She also has done PC and network support for the College of Business and led the campus-wide faculty development program. Her favorite hobbies are playing golf and reading mysteries.

Gerard Flynn
Pepperdine University
Gerard Flynn holds an MBA and is the technology training manager for Pepperdine University in Malibu, California, where he teaches a variety of classes, including Microsoft Access, Excel, Outlook, PowerPoint, Word, and Computer Science for Business Majors. Flynn is committed to improving efficiency in the workplace by making computer programs accessible to everyone.

Rebekah Tidwell
Lee University
Rebekah Tidwell is currently a part-time professor at Lee University in Cleveland, Tenessee and a freelance writer for Course Technology. She has also taught at East Tennessee State University, Tusculum College, and Carson Newman College. She has instructed Computer Info Systems, Database Development, Database Design, Systems Development and Design, Web Development and Design, and just about every course in between. She is a publisher of numerous papers and Course Instructor Manuals, as well as Course Technology's Visual Basic for Applications for Microsoft Office text. She enjoys painting, bicycling, scuba diving, swimming, and antiquing in her spare time.

AUTHOR ACKNOWLEDGEMENTS

The authors would like to express our gratitude for the opportunity to work on this book. A project of this magnitude requires the assistance and input of many people. We are thankful for the invaluable feedback from all the reviewers whose comments helped guide this book from inception to completion.

In addition, we realize that Course Technology placed a great deal of confidence in our ability to produce this problem-solving approach to teaching Access. We feel honored to be a part of this new series that will surely be a great success. We would like to take this opportunity to express our gratitude to key members of the team at Course Technology:

> **Rachel Goldberg, Senior Managing editor:** Thank you for placing your confidence in us and for encouraging us along the way.
> **Brianna Hawes, Product Manager:** Thank you for your attention to scheduling and your unending patience through numerous delays. Throughout the process, it was always good to know that we could count on you for quick and accurate responses.
> **Joy Stark, Marketing Manager:** We believe this is a book that will alter, for the good, the way Access is taught in the future. Thank you for selling our ideas and getting the word out about this new book.
> **Jennifer Goguen, Production Editor:** Thank you for all your contributions to this endeavor.
> **Jessica Evans and Lisa Ruffolo, Development Editors:** Your numerous hours and willingness to help each of us as we struggled to find the right approach did not go unnoticed. You went above and beyond the call of duty in this endeavor. Your hard work and expertise contributed immeasurably to the success of this work. For all your efforts, we are extremely grateful and we want you to know that it was a pleasure and honor to work with you.
> **Bill Littlefield and Frank Akaiwa, Series Consultants:** We believe that this new approach to presenting Access will provide a foundational understanding of the concepts which students can apply to many of their own future projects. Thank you for your ideas and expertise that have brought this series to fruition.
> **Christian Kunciw, John Freitas, Susan Whalen, and Serge Palladino, QA Testers:** Thank you for you attention to detail that made it possible for us to "get it right".
> **Shana Rosenthal and Karen Lyons, Associate Production Managers:** Thank you for all your contributions to this effort.

— Karin Bast
— Leon Cygman
— Gerard Flynn
— Rebekah Tidwell

I would like to thank my husband for being my biggest supporter throughout my career and for dragging we away from the computer screen occasionally for a game of golf during the writing of this book. I would also like to acknowledge the efforts of Tim Schuldt, graduate assistant, for helping to create the data for the 4Corners Pharmacy database.
— **Karin**

In addition to the people listed above, to whom I owe a huge debt of gratitude, I'd like to recognize the work of the other three authors, Gerard, Rebekah and Karin with whom I've formed a special friendship and common bond.

I also want to acknowledge the three most important women in my life; my mother, Mina and my daughter, Toby who encouraged my efforts in this project and Vivian, who become my wife during the writing of this book, who edited every word and who was very understanding of the many long hours I spent in its creation.
— **Leon**

Theresa, for your ceaseless devotion to me as I wrote this book, you win the Wife of the Year award 2005. I love you more than anything in the world; you are the Brett Favre of womanhood. John Dylan, Caitlin Jolie, Grace Gabriella: may the road rise to meet you, the wind be always at your back, the sun shine warm upon your face, and may this book sell really well.
— **Gerard**

I have had the pleasure of working on behalf of Course Technology for many years. My experience has always been pleasant and I consider it honor to be entrusted with such a task as this book. I am especially grateful for Brianna, Jess, and Lisa with whom I have worked most closely and who have been extremely helpful and supportive.

In every endeavor, every challenge, every joy, and every heartbreak, there has been one steady force in my life, my husband, Gene. I can barely remember a time before I had him at my side. I am so thankful for the hundreds of cups of coffee you brought to my desk, for your patience and attention as I read manuscripts to you that you knew nothing about, and for your encouragement when I was ready to give up. You ARE the wind beneath my wings.
— **Rebekah**

Introduction to Data Management with Microsoft Access 2003

"To succeed in life in today's world, you must have the will and tenacity to finish the job."
—Chin-Ning Chu

LEARNING OBJECTIVES

Introduce the company used in this book

Identify how an organization manages data

Describe how problem solving is presented in this book

Understand the roles of data consumers in an organization

Determine how data is interlinked throughout an organization

Understand the current deficiencies in an organization's data

Introduce the companies used in this book's end-of-chapter case problems

ABOUT THIS BOOK AND MICROSOFT OFFICE ACCESS 2003

Traditional study of computer applications has mostly involved acquiring skills related to an application's features and functions. Although this approach is important in teaching the mechanics required to perform certain tasks, it does not address *when* a particular tool is most appropriate or *how* it should best be utilized in solving a specific problem.

Although this book focuses on learning how to organize data using Microsoft Office Access 2003, the concepts and tasks presented in this book could apply to other database programs as well. Access is a relational database program in which data is stored in tables that are related to each other using relationships. You will learn about tables and relationships in Chapters 1 and 2, but the idea is important, because these tables can store a great deal of related information in one location and display the information in many ways. Access stores information in one database and lets the user manipulate that information to see as much or as little of it as is desired and in many ways. For example, Access can provide you with a list of employees living in certain cities or a report that shows sales organized and totaled by product category.

What is information and where does it come from? The term "information" can mean many things to different people. For the purpose of this discussion, **information** is defined as data that is organized in some meaningful way. **Data** can be words, images, numbers, or even sounds. Using data to make decisions depends on an organization's ability to collect, organize, and otherwise transform data into information that can be used to support those decisions—a process more commonly referred to as **analysis**. A **data consumer** is a person in an organization who transforms data into information by sorting, filtering, or performing calculations on it to perform this analysis.

The amount of information available can overwhelm many decision makers as they try to determine which sets of data and information are important and which should be ignored. The result is a complex world in which decision makers can no longer rely on intuition and back-of-the-envelope calculations to make effective decisions; they need tools that support decision making and help to solve problems.

CASE SCENARIO

The problems to be solved in this book are presented within the context of the fictional company 4Corners Pharmacy, which is so named because it is located in southwestern Colorado on the border of the four corners connecting the states of Arizona, Colorado, New Mexico, and Utah. This case scenario is used to provide real-world business examples to illustrate the lessons in each chapter; it is not based on real people or events. You will be guided through the solutions to solve realistic business problems for various people working for this company. These "employees" represent a variety of business functions: accounting, finance, human relations, information systems, marketing, operations management, and sales. Context is an important factor to consider when solving the problems in this book. The following background on 4Corners Pharmacy gives you perspective on the situations that you will encounter throughout this book.

The Company

Vincent Ferrino opened 4Corners Pharmacy in 1989. Over the years, Vincent's business evolved from a small "mom and pop" corner drugstore to the busiest pharmacy in the area. Vincent's son, Paul Ferrino, has worked at the pharmacy in different capacities since 1990. After graduating with a degree in pharmacy and becoming licensed by the state of Colorado, Paul worked as a pharmacist in his father's store, and then took two years off to earn an MBA from Thunderbird University in Arizona. When Vincent decided to retire, he sold the store to Paul but continues to work as a part-time pharmacist.

Paul envisions expanding his father's business to take advantage of the growing pharmaceutical industry. Paul was encouraged recently by a study indicating that 44% of Americans take prescription drugs on a regular basis. He sees the trend increasing as more baby-boomers get older and need an increasing number of prescriptions as life expectancy and medical invention increase. Although he was a shrewd and successful businessperson, Vincent ran the day-to-day operations of the business with little help from computers, primarily because he was never trained to use them and never realized the benefits they could offer his business. Consequently, the pharmacy's recordkeeping, although meticulous and professional, is inefficient. Maintaining the growing business using mostly manual systems is becoming more costly as additional people are hired to meet stricter industry regulations regarding the Health Insurance Portability and Accountability Act (HIPAA) and because of state regulations that affect the sale, storage, and dispensing of prescription drugs. Although Paul succeeded in automating some of the pharmacy's data management in Excel workbooks, he knows that a more substantial change is needed to properly maintain and store data about the business.

Key Players

Paul Ferrino—Pharmacist and Owner

Paul began working as a pharmacist at 4Corners Pharmacy in January 1990, and bought the store from his father in May 2006. Paul is the head pharmacist and, as such, he manages a dedicated and capable group of experienced pharmacists, pharmacy technicians, and sales assistants. Paul's vision for the pharmacy is to continue his father's lifelong pledge of providing excellent customer service and "giving back" to the community. Vincent regularly sponsored and underwrote local events for kids and senior citizens, which resulted in several community service awards for Vincent and multiple wins in the "best pharmacy" category by a reader's poll sponsored by the local newspaper. The pharmacy also earned three awards from the local Chamber of Commerce. Although there are other big chain drugstores in the area, Vincent has managed to hang on to generations of customers because of his community involvement and excellent rapport with his customers. Paul is dedicated to continuing his father's traditions.

Donald Linebarger—Information Systems Director

After purchasing the store, Paul's first order of business was hiring someone who could overhaul the pharmacy's manual recordkeeping systems. Don Linebarger worked for many years as a systems analyst for a large business in the area. He was the perfect choice to work at 4Corners Pharmacy because he is capable and experienced, but also because he has been a satisfied customer of 4Corners Pharmacy for many years. After developing the system for 4Corners Pharmacy, Don will train employees to use it, perform system maintenance and make any necessary changes, and maintain all of the records necessary for the business. He will also work to improve relationships with doctors, a source of many of the pharmacy's customers, and to develop greater knowledge of existing customers to anticipate their needs and generate more business.

Maria Garcia—Human Resources Manager

Maria Garcia has been the human resources manager at 4Corners Pharmacy since 2004. She is responsible for interviewing and hiring employees; maintaining data about certifications for pharmacists and pharmacy technicians; monitoring attendance and sick days; and maintaining and administering company benefits, including life and health insurance, 401(k) programs, and bonuses.

Elaine Estes—Store/Operations Manager

Elaine Estes has worked at 4Corners Pharmacy since 1995. During this time, she has been the store's general manager and operations manager. Elaine maintains the inventory of prescription and nonprescription items, places orders for additional stock, and disposes of drugs when they are stocked past their expiration dates. Elaine also supervises the 4Corners Pharmacy staff and reports their achievements and any problems to Maria.

Company Goal: Expand Operations into Other Areas

The strength of 4Corners Pharmacy has always been Vincent's dedication to his customers and his community. Paul wants to continue this tradition by sponsoring local events and ensuring that his customers and their families never have a reason to seek another pharmacy. Paul also wants to open a second store in Colorado by the end of the year, possibly by acquiring an existing business. With the addition of another store on the horizon, Paul needs to ensure that the database created to run 4Corners Pharmacy is easily expanded and adapted as necessary to run the operations at a second location.

How Is Access Used at 4Corners Pharmacy?

Employees at 4Corners Pharmacy will use Access in many ways to assist them with the daily operations of the pharmacy. Specific examples of how a database will improve store operations and customer service are as follows:

Accounting

- **Accounting**
  As the store manager, Elaine needs reports that detail how much inventory remains for each prescription and nonprescription item in the store. She also needs to know the value of the existing inventory for insurance purposes. Access can compute information about sales and produce it in a report that is current and easy to read.

Finance

- **Finance**
  Elaine and Paul need to ensure that the pharmacy's bottom line is healthy. As a result, Access must produce reports that detail the pharmacy's sales figures, salary commitments, and similar financial data to determine the financial health of the pharmacy.

Human Resources

- **Human Resources**
  As the human resources manager, Maria needs to manage all of the data about employees. Some of this data is descriptive, such as the employee's name and address. Other data is sensitive, such as the employee's Social Security number, salary, and information about job performance, and needs to be protected from unauthorized access. Maria can use Access to manage data about employees and ensure that sensitive data is protected from fraud and abuse.

Information Systems

- **Information Systems**
  Don's goal for the new database at 4Corners Pharmacy is to produce a system that meets user needs, stores and manages the correct information, displays it in the correct format, and is easy for employees to use. He will use the tools available in Access to secure, back up, and maintain the database to ensure that it is properly protected from unauthorized access, loss, and failure. Don will also add Web functionality to the system so that customers can use the pharmacy's database to update their information, display a list of their current prescriptions, and obtain general drug information.

Marketing

- **Marketing**
  As the store's marketing contact, Elaine works with an outside advertising agency to produce the store's weekly advertising inserts in the local newspaper. Elaine can use Access to determine how store items are selling and determine which products to add to the store's advertising. She can also use Access to produce reports about the buying behavior and demographic data for 4Corners Pharmacy customers. Although this data exists within the pharmacy, it is not currently organized in a format that makes it easy to analyze for determining market trends and buying behavior by demographic group.

Management

- **Operations Management**
  Elaine needs a way to know which drugs to order from suppliers and in what quantities. She frequently evaluates the store's inventory for low drug volumes and expired drugs. Customer health is of great importance to the pharmacy. Although no one has ever been injured as a result of pharmacist negligence at 4Corners Pharmacy, increased federal

regulations and legal liability issues mandate that pharmacy employees are properly certified and diligently inform customers of dosage instructions, possible side effects, and adverse interactions for each prescription sold. The pharmacy keeps meticulous records about pharmacist certifications, and pharmacists and pharmacy technicians diligently inform their customers about the drugs they dispense, but with the increase in hiring and the possible expansion of the company, Don wants formal processes in place to track these things.

- **Sales**

  Customers are also data consumers at the pharmacy. They receive data from the pharmacists detailing drug information and potential interactions. Some customers participate in flexible spending accounts (FSAs) that allow them to pay for prescriptions with pre-tax dollars. Participating customers frequently request a list of the prescriptions ordered by their households on a quarterly or annual basis. Access can manage these requests by creating reports of all drugs ordered by a single customer or household.

All of these business areas are related, just as the tables in the database are related. For example, when a customer fills a prescription, it affects different parts of the database as shown in Figure 1.

Sales

Figure 1: Data to store in the database at 4Corners Pharmacy

1. Doctor writes a prescription for patient. Doctor and clinic data is stored in the database.

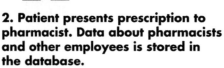

2. Patient presents prescription to pharmacist. Data about pharmacists and other employees is stored in the database.

3. Pharmacy staff enters customer, insurance, and prescription data into the database.

4. Pharmacist fills prescription. The database records the prescription and reduces the drug inventory by the correct amount.

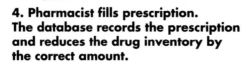

5. Customer picks up prescription and makes payment. The database stores the cost and price of the drug, which are used to generate the profit amount.

The customer requests the prescription, either by presenting a written order from a doctor to a pharmacist or asking for a refill of an existing prescription. The pharmacist adds this request to the system by getting the required information to fill it, including information about the drug, customer, customer's health plan, and so on. The prescription also affects the inventory that is tracked by operations and the profile of buying behavior that is tracked for marketing purposes. Eventually, the prescription affects the pharmacy's financial health by contributing revenue and profit to the store. In Chapter 1, you will learn how 4Corners Pharmacy manages its data and create a plan for storing this data in a database.

MANAGING DATA FOR THE ORGANIZATION

All organizations must deal with how to best collect, store, and manage their data. There are several problems at 4Corners Pharmacy. First, not all data is gathered for managers to make informed business decisions. For example, marketing data is scarce and dispersed throughout the organization. Several departments import and export data to each other and then maintain that data separately, resulting in errors and redundancy of data. The operations department, for example, manages inventory based on data imported from the pharmacists, but this data is not updated on a regular basis, resulting in orders placed too early, too frequently, or not frequently enough. Moreover, redundancy occurs in the customer list as each customer is listed with his own address, despite the fact that several people might live at the same address. Therefore, if one person submits a change of address or phone number, this data is not updated for people living in the same household. This problem leads to erroneous data that might result in undelivered mail sent to customers from 4Corners Pharmacy or the pharmacist not being able to reach a customer because of an incorrect phone number.

The business motivation for gathering all the data used in 4Corners Pharmacy and storing it in one relational database is to save time and money and to prevent errors and redundancy. But why is using a database program such as Access a superior method for organizing data? Why not use Excel to manage this data? After all, it is possible to sort, filter, and manipulate a significant amount of data in an Excel worksheet. There are many benefits to using a relational database to address the data deficiencies at 4Corners Pharmacy. First, the pharmacy produces too much data to effectively store in an Excel workbook. 4Corners Pharmacy gathers data about employees, customers, drugs, health plans, and doctors, each of which is its own unique category and should have its own worksheet. It would be difficult to list all the pharmacy's employees, customers, and prescribing doctors in one Excel worksheet, much less all the drug and health plan data. Excel is limited in the structure of its data; you cannot easily manage all of this data in one workbook, but you can do so in one database. A database might contain dozens of tables, just as an Excel workbook might contain dozens of worksheets. However, through a process of relating tables to each other, you can join together multiple tables in Access if they share common data and then query those tables as though they were one big table, presenting a huge advantage over managing data in multiple worksheets in Excel. For example, 4Corners Pharmacy will use three tables to store and manage data about employees, customers, and doctors; a table to store and manage data about prescriptions that pharmacists fill for customers; and a table to store and manage data about the drugs prescribed, such as the drug's name, dosage, expiration date, cost, and so on. All of these tables have a relationship that connects them to the others, as shown in Figure 2.

Figure 2: Interlinked data at 4Corners Pharmacy

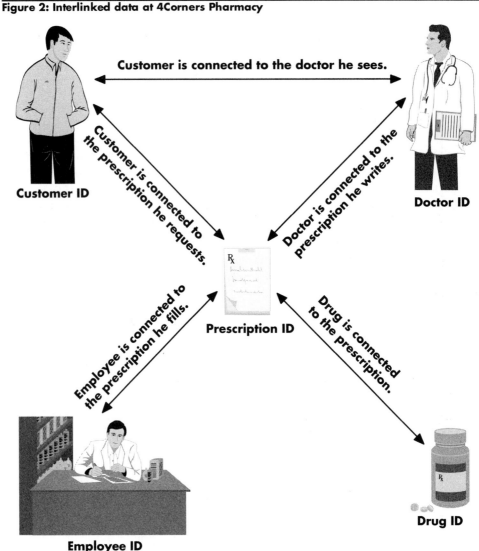

Customer is connected to the doctor he sees.

Customer is connected to the prescription he requests.

Doctor is connected to the prescription he writes.

Employee is connected to the prescription he fills.

Drug is connected to the prescription.

Customer ID

Doctor ID

Prescription ID

Employee ID

Drug ID

Figure 2 shows that a customer fills a prescription written by a doctor for a drug, and then a pharmacist fills the prescription. In the database, the customer's data is stored in a table that stores information about all customers. The prescription table contains data about prescriptions and a reference to the customer table (such as a customer identification number) to indicate the customer who purchased the prescription. The prescription table contains a reference (such as a prescription identification number) to the table that stores data about pharmacists, a reference to which pharmacist filled the prescription, and a reference (such as a drug identification number) to the table that stores data about drugs. Finally, the doctor table contains a reference to the prescription table, indicating which doctor wrote the prescription.

The benefit of designing tables and then creating relationships between them is that you are able to retrieve the data stored in these tables easily and quickly. For example, you can select any prescription and find out which doctor wrote it, which pharmacist filled it, and which customer purchased it. This type of querying simply isn't possible in Excel.

PROBLEM SOLVING IN THIS BOOK

Throughout this book, you will be presented with various problems to solve or analyses to complete using different Access tools. Each chapter in this book presents three levels of problem solving with Access. Level 1 deals with basic problems or analyses that require the application of one or more database tools, focusing on the implementation of those tools. However, problem solving not only requires you to know *how* to use a tool, but, more importantly, *why* or *when* to use *which* tool. So, with Level 2 the problems and analyses presented increase in complexity. By the time you reach Level 3, the complexity increases further, providing you with opportunities for more advanced critical thinking and problem solving.

In the hands-on portions of each chapter—the "Steps To Success" sections at the end of each level and the Case Problems at the end of each chapter—the degree of complexity increases, matching how the material is presented in each level. In addition, while the complexity *increases*, the structure of the problem to be solved *decreases* in the hands-on sections for each level. Figure 3 illustrates this approach to problem solving in this book.

Figure 3: Pedagogical model for problem solving

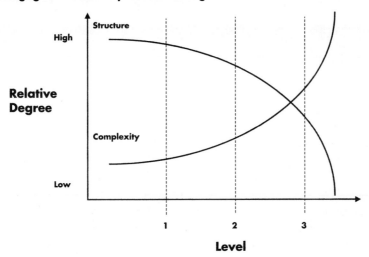

In this model, structure can be thought of as the way that various parts of a problem are held or put together. In a highly structured situation, almost every part of the problem is defined, and it is up to you to put the last few pieces in place to reach a solution. As the amount of structure is reduced, you need to understand more of the pieces and how they fit together to reach a solution. As structure is further reduced (more missing pieces of the puzzle) and complexity is increased (more pieces to understand), the difficulty of solving the problem increases. You can measure this difficulty in the time, number of steps, and decisions required to reach a solution. The goal is to increase your problem-solving skills while moving you toward an environment that is more like the real business world you will encounter during internships and upon graduation from college.

Steps To Success Exercises

As you read each level in a chapter, you will see how business problems are evaluated and solved at 4Corners Pharmacy using a database. At the end of each level, you will complete the exercises in the Steps To Success section to reinforce what you learned in the level. However, to ensure that you have a way to practice everything you learned in each level, the Steps To Success exercises are completed in a separate database for a similar business, Hudson Bay Pharmacy, which has slightly different data needs and requirements. The Hudson Bay Pharmacy is located in Edmonton, Alberta (Canada). This pharmacy has similar needs to those of 4Corners Pharmacy, but because Canada has different require-ments for the data it collects about employees and drugs, you will need to develop the database with these needs in mind. You will create this database in the Steps To Success exercises in Level 1 of Chapter 2, and then do all subsequent work for the Steps To Success exercises in your copy of the database. This approach makes it possible for you to develop a database from scratch and practice everything you learned in the chapter in your copy of the database. Because the database has slightly different requirements, you will be faced with decisions and problems that are unique to that database but are not specifically taught in the levels.

Working with SAM

This book assumes that you are already familiar with some of the more fundamental skills in Access, such as entering records into a datasheet, navigating a datasheet, and creating simple queries and forms. Depending on your skill level and working knowledge of Access, you might want to use the SAM Training product before you begin Chapter 1. (See the Preface section of this book or ask your instructor for more information about SAM.) The following is a list of prerequisite skills for which SAM Training is available; your instructor might have other requirements as well:

- Close Access
- Create a new database
- Create forms using the Form Wizard
- Create queries using wizards

- Delete records from a table using a datasheet
- Edit records from a table using a datasheet
- Enter records into a datasheet table
- Enter records using a form
- Open a form
- Open Access objects in the appropriate views
- Open an existing database
- Order records in Datasheet view
- Preview a report
- Preview the contents of a table
- Print a report
- Print specific pages of a report
- Resize to best fit
- Start Access
- Use Access Help
- Use navigation controls to move among records in a form
- Use navigation controls to move among records in a table
- Use the New Record button to add a record
- Use Undo and Redo
- Work with the Task Pane

In addition to these prerequisite skills, additional SAM skills are listed at the beginning of each level. These skills correspond to the material presented in that level, and give you a chance to practice the "mechanics" before you start applying the skills to solve problems. If you are using SAM Training with this book, it is recommended that you check each list of SAM skills before beginning work on a particular level. In this way, you can take advantage of the SAM Training to come up to speed on any of those skills and be better prepared to move forward in the chapter.

CHAPTER SUMMARY

This chapter detailed the purpose of this book—using Access to organize data efficiently and solve business problems effectively. It outlined the case that will be used throughout the chapters in this book and presented the data consumers of the pharmacy, while discussing how data is interlinked throughout the organization and how to determine current deficiencies in data availability in the organization.

The method of teaching problem solving in this book was also discussed. Each chapter is organized into three levels of problem solving with Access, and the material presented increases in complexity from one level to the next. The hands-on sections present problems that increase in complexity and decrease in structure, providing more challenging problems for you to solve and analyses to perform as you move from level to level.

CONCEPTUAL REVIEW

1. What is a data consumer? Who are the data consumers at your school, job, or internship?

2. What data do administrators require to support decision making about faculty, courses, and students at your school?

3. How is data related throughout your school, job, or internship?

4. What are some examples of data deficiencies that might occur at your school, job, or internship?

END-OF-CHAPTER CONTINUING CASE PROBLEMS

At the end of each chapter, there are three Case Problems that let you apply the skills that you learned in the chapter to problems faced by different kinds of businesses. All three Case Problems put you in the position of working for the company and making decisions about how to best store, analyze, and manage the data for the business. Instead of asking you to perform certain skills to arrive at a result, these Case Problems ask you to analyze a situation, evaluate the choices, and determine the correct way to reach a certain goal.

Although all three Case Problems are challenging, they are structured so that the first Case Problem provides the most structure and requires skills learned in all of Level 1 and some of Level 2 as necessary to complete the tasks. Case Problem 2 is less structured and requires skills learned in all of Levels 1 and 2. The third Case Problem is the most challenging, as it requires you to evaluate a problem and make most of the decisions to solve it. This Case Problem requires skills from all three levels in the chapter, and as such, it is the most comprehensive.

As you work through the chapters in this book, you should complete the same Case Problem in each chapter using the database you first create in Chapter 2. For example, when you begin working in Chapter 3, you will open the database you created in Chapter 2 and continue your work.

Case Problem 1: NHD Development Group Inc.

NHD Development Group Inc. develops commercial properties throughout the United States. Tim Richards, the company's chief information officer, is charged with scouting prospective projects and evaluating current ones. He has identified a current investment, a series of shopping malls that sell antiques, as being deficient in reporting financial returns, making it difficult to determine their profitability. Consequently, he seeks to design a database that manages the mall's data and produces the reports he needs. Tim chose a mall in Tennessee as a pilot project. If successful at this southern mall, NHD will use the database at other malls in the investment portfolio. Your assistance is required to create objects within the database and to produce the financial reports required by the business.

Case Problem 2: MovinOn Inc.

MovinOn Inc. is a moving and storage company based in the northwestern United States. Having grown from a start-up venture consisting of one vehicle and one warehouse in Oregon, the company is burgeoning into other states and is outgrowing its paper-based recordkeeping system. The CEO of MovinOn Inc., David Bowers, hired an information systems manager to design a database to manage employee, driver, customer, and order data. Your assistance is required to design the objects in the database so that the present inefficient system is replaced and reliable upon implementation. You will also assist in securing the database so that the company's data is not accidentally or maliciously deleted.

Case Problem 3: Hershey College Intramural Department

Hershey College is a four-year liberal arts college in Hershey, Pennsylvania. Having received a grant to promote health and wellness, the college seeks to expand the athletic and fitness offerings by creating an intramural department. The college appointed Marianna Fuentes, an assistant coach for the women's basketball team, as the intramural department's director. She needs to build and maintain a database of teams, coaches, and captains so that she can report information about the department's popularity and usage to grant administrators and the college administration. It is important that her participation reporting is accurate, professional, and timely, as the grant will not be renewed without it. Because the intramural department is new, Marianna's challenge is to develop a system from scratch without the benefit of evaluating an existing system. Your assistance is required to design this database.

Preparing to Automate Data Management
Information Services: Gathering Data and Planning the Database Design

"You can use all the quantitative data you can get, but you still have to distrust it and use your own intelligence and judgment."
—Alvin Toffler

LEARNING OBJECTIVES

Level 1

Discover and evaluate sources of existing business data

Research sources of missing or incomplete data

Assign data to tables and use field types and sizes to define data

Level 2

Understand relational database objects and concepts

Create table relationships

Understand referential integrity

Level 3

Learn the techniques for normalizing data

Evaluate fields that are used as keys

Test the database design

CHAPTER INTRODUCTION

The first step in planning a database is to gather existing data, determine the desired output, confirm that you have all the fields required to produce that output, and obtain data that you are missing. Existing data within an organization might be stored using paper forms, Microsoft Excel workbooks, Microsoft Word documents, or other applications.

This chapter details the process that you should follow prior to creating a database. The first step, the **discovery phase**, includes gathering all existing data, researching missing and incomplete data, and talking with users about their data output needs. Subsequent steps in the process include putting data into groups, called tables; identifying unique values for each record in those tables; and designing the database to produce the desired output. It is then imperative to test the new database prior to its implementation. Designing the database requires knowledge of database concepts, which are introduced in this chapter. Figure 1.1 illustrates the steps followed in the database design process and highlights the first step, the discovery phase.

Figure 1.1: Database design process: the discovery phase

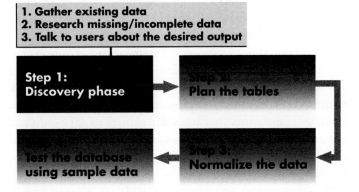

CASE SCENARIO

Creating a database is a significant undertaking that requires careful planning, organization, and management. In many cases, it takes several weeks or even months to identify the data that an organization needs to collect and then determine how managers and employees will enter and use that data to assist them in the organization's day-to-day operations and long-term planning. The 4Corners Pharmacy is an existing business, and you have already learned that Vincent Ferrino's system for managing the prescription, inventory, employee, and other data for the pharmacy is lacking in several respects. Paul Ferrino's vision for the pharmacy, which he now owns, is to convert all of the existing paper and spreadsheet systems to a database. By doing so, Paul will realize many benefits, such as more accurate and consistent data and the ability to track inventory and customer buying habits.

LEVEL 1

EXAMINING EXISTING AND MISSING SOURCES OF DATA

DISCOVERING AND EVALUATING SOURCES OF EXISTING DATA

One of the first tasks of creating a database is to identify the information that the organization needs to manage and organize. This task might take several days to several months and might involve interviewing department heads and other key employees to understand the data they collect and the way they use it. You might find that some departments manage their data in paper files or in computerized records. In larger organizations, data might be stored in different computerized systems. Regardless of the current data storage method, it is important to take the time to understand not only what data is collected, but also how that data is used.

As you collect information from the organization's key players, you might begin to see patterns that indicate how to organize the data. For example, you might see that the organization manages data about customers, employees, and products. Different departments might use this data in different ways and employees might need different levels of access to this data, depending on the departments in which they work and their positions in the company. For example, a manager of an order department needs information about products and customers, but not about employees; a human resources manager needs information about employees, but not about products; a customer service representative needs information about products and orders, but not about employees; and so on. In addition to needing different kinds of data, some employees might need more detailed information than others. An assistant in the human resources department might need a list of employees working in the organization, but only the human resources manager should be able to obtain a list of employees and their salaries.

You can use a **database management system**, or **DBMS**, to manage data. There are several DBMSs, including Oracle, ColdFusion, Microsoft Access, and MySQL. Each of these DBMS programs has specific advantages that benefit different organizations, depending on the kind and amount of data they store. For example, very large organizations will benefit from the power of Oracle or ColdFusion to manage large amounts of data on a network or in a Web site. Smaller organizations might choose to use Access because this DBMS, part of the Microsoft Office suite of programs, is fairly easy to use and quite powerful, but does not require extensive programming knowledge. Some businesses might choose MySQL, an open source program that is available for free. MySQL, however, requires programming expertise in Structured Query Language (SQL), the language used by most DBMSs. You will learn about SQL in Chapter 3.

Because the 4Corners Pharmacy is a small business, the company's information systems director, Don Linebarger, selected Access as the DBMS to manage the pharmacy's database. As the business grows in the future, Don might choose another DBMS, but for now, Access will handle the pharmacy's data management needs.

Before he gets started, Don needs to determine how the pharmacy collects and stores data about prescription transactions, drug inventories, customers, and employees. Don also needs to determine if there are other data needs at the pharmacy that are currently going unfulfilled or about which he is not informed. After extensive consulting with Vincent and Paul Ferrino, Don learns that data is managed in many ways and realizes that entering customer data at 4Corners Pharmacy is a manual and time-consuming process. When new customers visit the pharmacy to fill a prescription, they complete a customer information form by hand. A pharmacy technician enters the information into an Excel workbook. Figure 1.2 shows the pharmacy's customer information form.

Figure 1.2: Customer information form used by 4Corners Pharmacy

CUSTOMER INFORMATION

Thank you for choosing 4Corners Pharmacy. Please fill out this form so that we can assist you promptly.

Name:	Birth Date:
Address:	
Social Security Number:	
Home Phone Number:	Fax Number:
E-mail Address:	
Gender: Male Female	Marital Status (circle one): Single Married Widowed Divorced
Employer:	Occupation:
Primary Care Physician:	Physician's Phone Number:
Emergency Contact:	Relationship to Patient:
Emergency Contact's Phone Number:	Spouse's Name:
Allergies:	
Prefer child proof caps? Y N	

HEAD OF HOUSEHOLD

(Complete this section only if someone other than the customer is financially responsible.)

Name:	Social Security Number:
Address:	
Home Phone Number:	Work Phone Number:

INSURANCE INFORMATION

Insurance Plan:	
Insurance Plan Phone Number:	Insurance ID Number:
Subscriber's Name:	Subscriber's Employer:

I authorize the release of any medical information necessary to process my claim and payment of benefits to 4Corners Pharmacy.

_____   _____

Signature of Customer/Responsible Party   **Date**

After entering the data from the customer information form into the workbook, the technician stores the form in a filing cabinet in one of 26 file folders arranged by the first letter of the customer's last name. This system makes it difficult to find individual customer information later when forms require an update, such as a change of address, a change in insurance information, or a new drug allergy. Vincent's original objective was to have one row in the worksheet for each customer, as shown in Figure 1.3.

Figure 1.3: Customer data maintained in an Excel workbook

One row for each customer

	A	B	C	D	E	F	G	H
1	SSN (Last 4)	First Name	Last Name	Birthdate	Address	City	State	Zip
2	0424	Gaetano	Feraco	7/4/1946	19504 Lowell Boulevard	Aneth	UT	84510
3	0849	Scott	Prager	8/27/1951	2510 West 108th Avenue	Pleasant View	CO	81331
4	0975	Isabel	Lopez	8/30/1949	6969 South Valmont Road	Montezuma Creek	UT	84534
5	0979	Geoffrey	Baaz	12/31/2001	1233 Myrna Place	Kirtland	NM	87417
6	1064	Sonia	Cardenas	4/12/1968	16455 Warren Avenue	Chinle	AZ	86547
7	1068	Gina	Mercado	6/17/1979	240 South Monaco Parkway	Cortez	CO	81321
8	1168	Ted	Sabus	12/11/1954	460 West Pioneer Road	Dolores	CO	81323
9	1329	Daniel	Cardenas	5/12/2002	16455 Warren Avenue	Chinle	AZ	86547
10	1395	Josefina	Hernandez	6/30/1978	411 Mariposa Street	Flora Vista	NM	87145
11	1422	Chloe	Feraco	6/1/1946	19504 Lowell Boulevard	Aneth	UT	84510
12	1486	Oksana	Lapshina	4/29/1957	5171 Idylwild Creek Road	Yellow Jacket	CO	81335
13	1689	Gloria	Fernandes	5/1/1979	1011 East Bayaud Avenue	Flora Vista	NM	87415
14	2197	Christina	Hargus	2/14/1998	5465 South Nelson Circle	Shiprock	NM	87420
15	2215	Maria	Gabel	8/12/1980	4255 Kittredge Street	Lewis	CO	81327
16	2243	Anders	Aannestad	9/11/1974	1279 Cherokee Avenue	Farmington	NM	87499
17	2253	Steven	Nguyen	10/12/1976	9874 South Main Street	Blanding	UT	84511
18	2797	Jessica	Cortez	8/13/1978	3663 South Sheridan Boulevard	Kayenta	AZ	86033
19	2943	Rose	Baaz	4/12/1970	1233 Myrna Place	Kirtland	NM	87417
20	3623	Kimberley	Schultz	1/16/1969	411 East Cornish Court	Chinle	AZ	86507
21	3650	Adriana	Woltere	4/22/1952	14444 North Tamarac Street	Cortez	CO	81321

4Corners Customers

Don knows from experience that this recordkeeping system is error-prone, as it is possible to store two records for the *same* customer without realizing the mistake. For example, if a customer has a formal name and a nickname or goes by a middle name, it might be possible to store two separate records for the same individual without realizing that these records are for the same person. This problem might also occur if the person who entered the record misspelled a customer's name on one or more occasions. This phenomenon is known as **data duplication**, and it is undesirable because additional space is required in the database to store extra records, which leads to inconsistent and inaccurate data. For example, a pharmacist might indicate that the customer named John W. Jackson has a drug allergy, but the record for J. William Jackson—the same person but with a different version of his name—might not indicate this important fact. This situation might not seem important for billing or correspondence issues, but a serious error occurs when the pharmacist accesses the duplicate customer record that does *not* include the important information about the customer's drug allergy and gives the customer a prescription to which he is allergic. Don's first order of business is to work to avoid data duplication in the database.

In addition to deleting duplicate records for customers, Don also notes that he needs to find a way to group and store the address and phone information for people in the same household, thereby reducing the amount of space required to store this information. This repetition is known as **data redundancy** and is to be avoided. When one member of a household reports a new address or change of insurance that also affects other people in the household, the database must update the records for everyone affected by the change. Figure 1.4 shows the customer data shown in Figure 1.3, but it is sorted alphabetically by last name.

Figure 1.4: Sorted customer data illustrates data duplication and errors

Daniel and Danny Cardenas are the same person

Baaz address listed twice

	A	B	C	D	E	F	G	H
1	SSN (Last 4)	First Name	Last Name	Birthdate	Address	City	State	Zip
2	2243	Anders	Aannestad	9/11/1974	1279 Cherokee Avenue	Farmington	NM	87499
3	8848	Dusty	Alkier	4/5/1940	3046 West 36th Avenue	Aneth	UT	84510
4	0979	Geoffrey	Baaz	12/31/2001	1233 Myrna Place	Kirtland	NM	87417
5	2943	Rose	Baaz	4/12/1970	1233 Myrna Place	Kirtland	NM	87417
6	6282	Byron	Buescher	6/1/1944	4165 Umatilla Avenue	Pleasant View	CO	81331
7	1064	Sonia	Cardenas	4/12/1968	16455 Warren Avenue	Chinle	AZ	86547
8	1329	Daniel	Cardenas	5/12/2002	16455 Warren Avenue	Chinle	AZ	86547
9	1329	Danny	Cardenas	5/12/2002	16455 Warren Avenue	Chinle	AZ	86547
10	4293	Jonathan	Cardenas	8/22/2004	16455 Warren Avenue	Chinle	AZ	86547
11	9189	Albert	Cardenas	10/14/1965	16455 Warren Avenue	Chinle	AZ	86547
12	5229	Dana	Coats	8/16/2002	126 Valley View Road	Shiprock	NM	87420
13	8361	Dallas	Coats	10/31/1972	5541 East Zuni Street	Shiprock	NM	87420
14	9493	Octavia	Coats	6/30/1976	5541 East Zuni Street	Shiprock	NM	87420
15	2797	Jessica	Cortez	8/13/1978	3663 South Sheridan Boulevard	Kayenta	AZ	86033
16	5569	Malena	D'Ambrosio	4/15/1980	10555 East Circle Way	Montezuma Creek	UT	84534
17	0424	Gaetano	Feraco	7/4/1946	19504 Lowell Boulevard	Aneth	UT	84510
18	1422	Chloe	Feraco	6/1/1946	19504 Lowell Boulevard	Aneth	UT	84510
19	1689	Gloria	Fernandes	5/1/1979	1011 East Bayaud Avenue	Flora Vista	NM	87415
20	4484	James	Fernandes	2/18/1977	1011 East Bayaud Avenue	Flora Vista	NM	87415
21	2215	Maria	Gabol	8/12/1980	4255 Kittredge Street	Lewis	CO	81327

4Corners Customers

Old address for Dana Coats

Don spots several errors when the data is arranged in this different way. For example, Don suspects that Daniel and Danny Cardenas might be the same person. Although it is possible that two similarly named boys live in Chinle, Arizona, a closer look reveals that they share the same date of birth and address. Don imagines that the first record is the boy's formal name and the second is his nickname. Further evidence supports Don's belief: Daniel and Danny share the same last four digits of their Social Security numbers. Don must devise a way to eliminate this repetition while at the same time preserving the customer's prescription history.

Don also notices cases of data redundancy. For example, there are two records for people with the last name Baaz, and both people share the same address. As mentioned earlier, this duplication consumes a great deal of space in the database—it would be more efficient and require less space in the database to store the address for the Baaz family just once.

Don also notices that there are three records for people with the last name Coats. Don scrutinizes these records and suspects that Dallas and Octavia must have informed the pharmacy of an address change at some point, but failed to identify Dana Coats, who is listed as having a different address, as their daughter. No child of Dana's age lives alone, yet her address appears to suggest that she does.

Concerned that other errors might exist in the 4Corners Pharmacy recordkeeping system, Don asks Paul about the method he uses to manage new prescriptions and prescription refills that are brought to the pharmacy by customers or that are phoned in or faxed from doctors' offices. Paul explains that prescriptions are logged in a separate worksheet for each day the pharmacy is open. For each prescription filled by the pharmacy, the worksheet contains one row that includes the customer's first and last names, address, phone number, and insurance information; the prescription number, drug name, instructions, fill date, expiration date, and number of refills authorized by the physician; and the prescribing physician's name, address, clinic affiliation, and phone number. Figure 1.5 shows the worksheet from January 2, 2008.

Figure 1.5: Prescription data managed in an Excel workbook

	A	B	N	O	P
	First Name	Last Name	PrescriptionID	Name	Instructions
2	Anders	Aannestad	2	Myobuterol	1 teaspoon every 4 hours
3	Dusty	Alkier	4	Dseurton	2 pills every 12 hours
4	Dusty	Alkier	5	Clonazepam	2 pills every 6 hours with food
5	Anders	Anestad	72	Syocil	2 pills every 6 hours with food
6	Anders	Annestad	60	Phalastat	3 teaspoons full every 6 hours
7	Daniel	Cardenas	61	Myobuterol	1 teaspoon every 4 hours
8	Octavia	Coats	56	Myobuterol	1 teaspoon every 4 hours
9	Octavia	Coats	70	Tvalaxec	1 teaspoon every 6 hours
10	Christina	Hargus	47	Ampicillin	1 pill every 4 hours
11	Paula	Hargus	55	Montelukast sodium	2 pills daily
12	Isabel	Lopez	10	Phalastat	3 teaspoons full every 6 hours
13	Steven	Nguyen	52	Didanosine	2 pills every 4 hours with food
14	Scott	Prager	19	Cefixime	1 pill every 5 hours with food
15	Jennifer	Ramsey	3	Nvalax	2 pills daily
16	Shannon	Sabus	18	Rivastigmine tartrate	2 pills every 6 hours with food
17	Ted	Sabus	24	Acebutolol hydrochloride	2 pills daily
18	Marisella	Velasquez	33	Quentix	2 pills every 8 hours
19	Marisella	Velasquez	63	Tolbutamide	2 pills every 6 hours
20	Kevin	Wachter	39	Myobuterol	1 teaspoon every 4 hours
21	Adriana	Walters	14	Didanosine	2 pills every 4 hours with food

Anders Aannestad is listed three times

Jan. 2, 2008 Prescriptions

Don sorted the worksheet by last name and in doing so notices that Anders Aannestad is listed three times, with three different spellings of his last name due to typographical errors or illegible penmanship on a written or faxed prescription. Don also realizes that the table is unwieldy because it spans 27 columns and requires hiding columns or frequent scrolling to see the details of a given prescription, such as which doctor prescribed which drug for which customer.

Don hides 11 columns of customer address and insurance information so he can see prescription details. An audit of this customer address and insurance information reveals additional errors. Figure 1.6 shows another view of the prescription worksheet from January 2, 2008, with the customer health plan identification numbers displayed.

Figure 1.6: Prescription data with address and insurance plan errors

	A	B	C	D	E	F	G
1	First Name	Last Name	Address	City	State	Zip	PlanID
2	Anders	Aannestad	1279 Cherokee Avenue	Farmington	NM	87499	498-1112-A
3	Dusty	Alkier	3046 West 36th Avenue	Aneth	UT	84510	A089
4	Dusty	Alkier	3046 West 36th Avenue	Aneth	UT	84510	A098
5	Anders	Anestad	1279 Cherokee Avenue	Farmington	NM	87499	498-1112-A
6	Anders	Annestad	1279 Cherokee Avenue	Farmington	NM	87499	498-1112-A
7	Daniel	Cardenas	16455 Warren Avenue	Chinle	AZ	86547	498-1112-A
8	Octavia	Coats	5541 East Zuni Street	Shiprock	NM	87420	OP-87-A087
9	Octavia	Coats	5541 East Zuin Street	Shiprock	NM	87420	OP-87-A087
10	Christina	Hargus	5465 South Nelson Circle	Shiprock	NM	87420	OP-87-A087
11	Paula	Hargus	5465 South Nelson Circle	Shiprock	NM	87420	OP-87-A087
12	Isabel	Lopez	6969 South Valmont Road	Montezuma Creek	UT	84534	2B8973AC
13	Steven	Nguyen	9874 South Main Street	Blanding	UT	84511	498-1112-A
14	Scott	Prager	2510 West 108th Avenue	Pleasant View	CO	81331	4983
15	Jennifer	Ramsey	4775 Argone Circle	Chinle	AZ	86547	498-1112-A
16	Shannon	Sabus	460 West Pioneer Road	Dolores	CO	81323	4983
17	Ted	Sabus	406 West Pioneer Road	Dolores	CO	81323	4983
18	Marisella	Velasquez	54213 Oak Drive	Kirtland	NM	87417	000H98763-01
19	Marisella	Velasquez	54213 Oak Drive	Kirtland	NM	87417	000H98763-01
20	Kevin	Wachter	2931 East Narcissus Way	Montezuma Creek	UT	84534	A089
21	Adriana	Wolters	14444 North Tamarac Street	Cortez	CO	81321	4983

Misspelled address — Incorrect plan ID

Jan. 2, 2008 Prescriptions

Incorrect street number

Figure 1.6 shows multiple data-entry errors and some design problems that create redundant data. The address data for each customer is redundant in the Prescriptions worksheet; these addresses already exist in the Customers worksheet shown in Figure 1.4. This problem is compounded when data-entry mistakes are made. In looking at the data shown in Figure 1.6, Don sees that Octavia Coats lives on either Zuni or Zuin Street, that Shannon and Ted Sabus live in house number 460 or 406, and that Dusty Alkier's health insurance is a plan with the identification number A089 or A098.

Don continues examining the Prescriptions worksheet by scrolling and hiding columns as necessary and notes the many mistakes it contains. Figure 1.7 details the last of Don's sleuthing. Marisella Velasquez's doctor is named either Chinn or Chin, and the phone number of Octavia Coats's doctor ends with the digits 1879 or 1897. These problems are probably the result of typographical errors.

Figure 1.7: Prescription data with doctor name and telephone errors

Incorrect phone number for this doctor

	B	N	O	U	V	AA
1	Last Name	PrescriptionID	Name	DoctorLast	ClinicName	DoctorPhone
2	Aannestad	2	Myobuterol	Gramann	Connley Memorial Clinic	(928) 488-1741
3	Alkier	4	Dseurton	Allen	San Juan County Clinic	(505) 884-0542
4	Alkier	5	Clonazepam	Allen	San Juan County Clinic	(505) 884-0542
5	Anestad	72	Syocil	Gramann	Connley Memorial Clinic	(928) 488-1741
6	Annestad	60	Phalastat	Gramann	Connley Memorial Clinic	(928) 488-1741
7	Cardenas	61	Myobuterol	Deleon	Chinle Memorial Clinic	(928) 888-4178
8	Coats	56	Myobuterol	Escalante	Northwest New Mexico Area Clinic	(505) 545-1879
9	Coats	70	Tvalaxec	Escalante	Northwest New Mexico Area Clinic	(505) 545-1897
10	Hargus	47	Ampicillin	Escalante	Northwest New Mexico Area Clinic	(505) 545-1879
11	Hargus	55	Montelukast sodium	Escalante	Northwest New Mexico Area Clinic	(505) 545-1879
12	Lopez	10	Phalastat	Jurski	Blanding City Clinic	(435) 887-1818
13	Nguyen	52	Didanosine	Zamarron	Blanding City Clinic	(435) 887-1818
14	Prager	19	Cefixime	Wilson	Sodt Memorial Clinic	(435) 189-9874
15	Ramsey	3	Nvalax	Loke	University of Northern Arizona Clinic	(928) 449-4174
16	Sabus	18	Rivastigmine tartrate	Trevino	Dolores LaPlata Memorial Clinic	(970) 429-7475
17	Sabus	24	Acebutolol hydrochloride	Huddleston	St. Thomas Clinic	(970) 898-4788
18	Velasquez	33	Quentix	Chinn	San Juan County Clinic	(505) 884-0542
19	Velasquez	63	Tolbutamide	Chin	San Juan County Clinic	(505) 884-0542
20	Wachter	39	Myobuterol	Zamarron	Blanding City Clinic	(435) 887-1818
21	Walters	14	Didanosine	Huddleston	St. Thomas Clinic	(970) 898-4788

Jan. 2, 2008 Prescriptions

Incorrect spelling of this doctor's last name

Don sees some very serious problems with the current process of logging prescriptions using this system. First, there is no method to control the duplication of data. If a customer fills three prescriptions on the same day, there will be three rows in the worksheet—one row for each prescription filled. The name, address, and phone number can vary in each of these three rows because there is no built-in method in a worksheet to prevent this problem from occurring. It is possible to have similar variances in the doctor's name, address, clinic affiliation, and phone number. Second, data is difficult to track and aggregate. For example, because the pharmacy creates new worksheets for each day's prescriptions, pharmacists would need to know the original fill date for a prescription to find out how many refills the doctor authorized. Aggregating data by customer, doctor, or drug would also be difficult.

After finishing his exploration of the current system, Don asks Paul for other changes that he wants to make and data that he wants to store in the future that is lacking in the current system. Paul tells Don that he wants to eliminate the paper registration forms; make it easier to update customer information; have quick access to a customer's prescription history (without searching a paper file); print a list of drug names; create a way to ensure that the person entering the customer's information inquired about the customer's allergies, that the pharmacist explained interactions with other drugs, and that the pharmacist provided counseling about using the drug to the customer; and print a list of doctors and their contact information.

In talking with the pharmacy staff, Don also learns that in the past it has been difficult to generate items for the marketing person, such as mailing labels for customers and doctors, so that the pharmacy can send notices to customers and doctors about events at the pharmacy, such as drug recalls or local health fairs. Don also learns from the pharmacy technicians that some customers have requested year-end reports identifying all of the prescriptions and their total cost for each family member so they can reconcile their insurance statements and produce the total prescription drug costs to use when reconciling their prescription costs with Flexible Spending Accounts (FSAs) provided by their employers. Because the current system has no way to account for this data, this need is going unmet.

After examining the pharmacy's records and discovering all of the problems with data-entry errors and data duplication, Don moves on to look at how Vincent manages the pharmacy's inventory of prescription drugs. He talks with Vincent about his method for tracking the value and number of each item in inventory and the system he uses for reordering out-of-stock items, evaluating items that do not sell well and discontinuing them, and making sure that items on sale are stocked in appropriate quantities before the sale is advertised. Figure 1.8 shows the worksheet that Vincent uses to track prescription drug inventory.

Figure 1.8: Prescription drug inventory data

	A	B	C	D	E	F	G	H	I
1	UPN	Name	Generic	Description	Unit	Dosage	DosageForm	Cost	Price
2	247	Acebutolol hydrochloride		Arthritis	Pill	400	mg	$0.55	$1.10
3	732	Albuterol Sulfate	Yes	Asthma	Pill	2	mg	$0.30	$0.95
4	741	Almotriptan	Yes	Conjunctivitis	Pill	6.25	mg	$0.14	$0.87
5	102	Ampicillin	Yes	Antibiotic	Pill	250	mg	$0.75	$1.45
6	224	Avatocin		Allergies	Pill	100	mg	$0.65	$1.40
7	524	Cefixime	Yes	Antihistamine	Pill	400	mg	$0.95	$1.60
8	398	Clonazepam		Epiliepsy	Pill	4	mcg	$0.65	$1.20
9	452	Diazapam	Yes	Anxiety	Pill	5	mg	$0.45	$1.12
10	878	Didanosine	Yes	Sinus infection	Pill	200	mg	$0.65	$1.12
11	256	Dseurton	Yes	High blood pressure	Pill	175	mg	$0.60	$1.20
12	311	Dyotex		Tonsillitis	Bottle	2	tsp	$0.25	$1.05
13	412	Epronix		Pain	Pill	500	mg	$0.85	$1.50
14	467	Glimepiride	Yes	Diabetes	Pill	2	mg	$0.25	$0.90
15	587	Haloperidol		Diuretic	Pill	6	mcg	$0.70	$1.30
16	644	Hyometadol		Asthma	Bottle	2	tsp	$0.65	$1.35
17	289	Levothyroxine	Yes	Thyroid disorders	Pill	25	mg	$0.70	$1.40
18	642	Montelukast sodium	Yes	Acne	Pill	10	mcg	$0.32	$0.90
19	828	Myobuterol	Yes	Antibiotic	Bottle	1	tsp	$0.55	$1.60
20	711	Nvalax	Yes	Depression	Pill	200	mg	$0.30	$0.90
21	852	Oxaprozin	Yes	Anti-inflammatory	Pill	1200	mg	$0.60	$1.25
22	366	Phalastat		Allergies	Bottle	1	tsp	$0.75	$1.60

Drugs

Because the data in this worksheet isn't connected to the systems that the pharmacists and cashiers use to sell prescription drugs and other items, sales volume cannot be calculated electronically. Indeed, Vincent has always performed a bimonthly hand count of inventory, and then built temporary columns in Excel to determine costs and profits. Don suspects that it would be difficult to use this worksheet to determine how much inventory exists for any given item in the store or prescription drug in the pharmacy, and imagines that it is unlikely that Vincent could accurately account for any product in stock. Thus, not only is it difficult to determine the quantity or volume of drugs in stock and the overall value of the inventory, there is no way to determine which items sell well and which sell poorly. Consequently, Don guesses that reordering occurs only when a pharmacist or other employee notices that a product's inventory is low or nonexistent. Don wants the database to address all of these problems by providing timely and accurate information about sales volume, inventory levels, and drug expiration dates. Furthermore, he wants to incorporate a list of interactions, pregnancy risks, and suppliers of each drug in the inventory, as presently these must be cross-referenced with data found online or in proprietary databases.

Vincent explains to Don that his system has worked fine for the nearly two decades in which he has been in business. However, Don knows that Paul wants to automate all of the business processes that must occur to run the pharmacy. As a pharmacist working for his father's company, Paul knows that Vincent's systems do not work well enough to ensure timely and accurate information. Paul also knows that his father's systems contain many errors.

Don moves to his examination of the employee records by talking with Maria Garcia, who manages all of the pharmacy's employment records, including applications, employee reviews, benefits, certifications, training, and salary and tax-related information. Maria tells Don that as the pharmacy grows, it is becoming increasingly difficult to manage employee records. Currently, she maintains employee data in paper forms and in three programs. As shown in Figure 1.9, Maria uses Microsoft Outlook contacts to maintain employee address and telephone information.

Figure 1.9: Employee contact information in Outlook

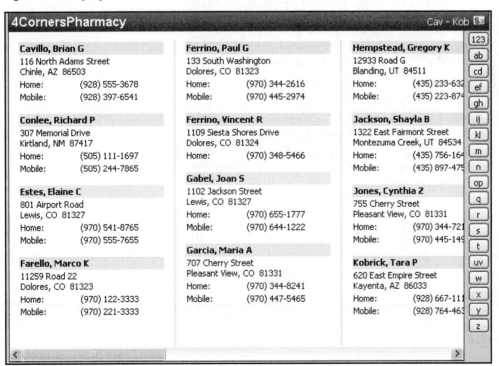

Maria uses Excel for tracking key employee dates, such as date of birth, hire date, termination date, and date of the employee's last personnel review. Maria also uses Excel for recording salary data. Because this worksheet contains sensitive information—in addition to salaries the table lists employee Social Security numbers—Maria keeps this file in its own workbook and has protected it with a password that only she knows. Figure 1.10 shows Maria's Excel workbooks.

Figure 1.10: Employee date and salary data in Excel workbooks

	A	B	C	D	E	F
1	First Name	Last Name	Birth Date	Hire Date	End Date	Review Date
2	Brian	Cavillo	8/14/1970	6/14/2005		7/19/2008
3	Richard	Conlee	3/1/1971	1/29/1992		3/17/2008
4	Elaine	Estes	5/1/1969	5/18/1995		1/15/2009
5	Marco	Farello	12/16/1974	11/22/2001		4/18/2008
6	Paul	Ferrino	7/4/1962	1/29/1990		
7	Vincent	Ferrino	4/2/1939	2/15/1989		
8	Joan	Gabel	9/12/1968	1/22/2002	5/31/2004	
9	Maria	Garcia	12/29/1971	10/11/2004		10/3/2008
10	Gregory	Hempstead	2/14/1975	9/12/2005		11/20/2007
11	Shayla	Jackson	9/28/1978	6/14/2000		4/2/2008
12	Cynthia	Jones	10/6/1958	3/14/1993		12/7/2008
13	Tara	Kobrick	7/30/1976	10/15/1999	6/15/2005	
14	Dora	Langston	10/14/1978	6/14/2006		2/20/2008
15	Anthony	Laporte	11/24/1975	4/5/2001		4/16/2008
16	Dominque	Latour	6/20/1977	8/14/2005		10/3/2008
17	Darnell	Lightford	4/5/1977	9/10/2005		7/21/2007
18	Donald	Lineharger	2/28/1968	5/30/2006		11/15/2007

Employees

Employee date data

	A	B	C	D	E
1	First Name	Last Name	SSN	Salary	HourlyRate
2	Brian	Cavillo	711-56-6444		$8.17
3	Richard	Conlee	968-96-3214		$12.00
4	Elaine	Estes	545-98-0000	$50,000.00	
5	Marco	Farello	885-00-7777		$11.00
6	Paul	Ferrino	953-23-3639	$135,000.00	
7	Vincent	Ferrino	998-01-5466	$35,000.00	
8	Joan	Gabel	901-88-3636		$10.75
9	Maria	Garcia	701-05-2465	$65,250.00	
10	Gregory	Hempstead	701-12-2765		$7.40
11	Shayla	Jackson	998-36-4789		$6.88
12	Cynthia	Jones	000-23-3655	$65,000.00	
13	Tara	Kobrick	728-12-3465		$11.00
14	Dora	Langston	718-78-4111		$11.15
15	Anthony	Laporte	727-65-5752		$8.00
16	Dominque	Latour	926-95-4878		$7.70
17	Darnell	Lightford	512-00-8899		$7.50
18	Donald	Lineharger	707-55-7541	$72,000.00	

Salary

Employee salary data

In addition to using Outlook and Excel, Maria keeps several employee records in Word, including a list of bilingual employees at 4Corners Pharmacy. If a bilingual employee is not on duty, pharmacists can refer to this list and call these employees when Spanish-speaking customers request assistance. She also keeps a Word document to track absenteeism. Although absenteeism is not a large problem at 4Corners Pharmacy, Maria is aware that Paul plans to expand the company and documentation should be in place as the employee base grows. Figure 1.11 shows both of these documents.

Figure 1.11: Bilingual employees and absentee report

4Corners Pharmacy Bilingual Employees

Name	Language	Proficiency
Joan Gabel	Spanish	Fluent
Maria Garcia	Spanish	Fluent
Darnell Lightford	Spanish	Fluent

4Corners Pharmacy Absentee Report

Name	Date	Absent/Tardy
Dominque Latour	9/28/07	Tardy
Shayla Jackson	10/15/07	Absent
Gregory Hempstead	11/14/07	Tardy

Maria is also responsible for monitoring staff development, a time-consuming task. Each pharmacist and pharmacy technician must maintain the proper license and certification as mandated by Colorado state law. Maria is responsible for ensuring that employees take the required classes to maintain their certifications. In addition, she must manage the employee performance reviews, which occur every 90 days, six months, or 12 months for employees, depending on their job titles and the number of years they have worked at the pharmacy. She also serves as the pharmacy's benefits coordinator and manages requests for sick days and vacation, extended leaves of absence, pension benefits, and life insurance benefits.

Although Maria's various documents and workbooks seem to manage the information she needs, Don worries that these systems will not work well if the pharmacy grows as expected and adds additional stores and employees. Don sees that Maria could also benefit from storing and managing personnel data in a database.

After talking extensively with Vincent, Paul, and Maria, Don took a few days to talk to other employees in the store to understand and view the data that they use and need to perform their jobs. Upon concluding his discovery phase of the database design process, Don learned many things. First, there are many paper-based and handwritten methods of gathering data at 4Corners Pharmacy that use various forms, faxes, and memos. Second, many employees copy and paste data from one worksheet to another or import and export data from one program to another, thereby creating redundant data. This process occasionally leads to errors. Finally, Don suspects that the pharmacy is not collecting data that it needs to produce reports for outside consultants, such as the value of inventory in the pharmacy for insurance purposes or the value of business capital for local taxing authorities.

Don also sees that some data collected by the customer information form (Figure 1.2), such as insurance information, is never recorded in detail. As the business grows, it will be important to automate all of the processes at the pharmacy. Don knows that a DBMS will serve this function better than hiring a large staff of people to manage the growing data needs of 4Corners Pharmacy and that using a DBMS will make Paul's business run smoother and more efficiently.

Concluding the first part of the discovery phase, Don details his findings to Paul. Table 1.1 lists the expectations of the database as Don understands them.

Table 1.1: Preliminary database expectations for 4Corners Pharmacy

Department	Expectation
Pharmacy	• Eliminate paper forms. • Provide quick access to prescription history. • Print list of drug names. • Ensure pharmacist consulted with customer about dosage instructions, allergies, and interactions. • Print doctor contact information.
Marketing	• Print customer mailing labels. • Print doctor mailing labels. • Use customer data to gather data information on customer buying habits.
Operations	• Track inventory. • Identify poor-selling items.
Human Resources	• Monitor staff development. • Confirm certifications. • Create employee performance reviews.
Customers	• Print a year-end report of all prescriptions purchased by individual or household.
Accounting and Finance	• Determine profit and loss for individual sale items. • Value the store's inventory. • Track the business profit.

Best Practice

Combating "Scope Creep" During the Database Design Process

During the discovery phase of the database design process, it is necessary to interview as many members of the organization as possible to learn about all sources of input and desired output. This process might result in a large "wish list." At 4Corners Pharmacy, Paul asks Don if it is possible to include legal, tax, and investment data in the DBMS. Don informs Paul that while it is *possible* to do this, it would require a great deal more work, be significantly more expensive, and lie outside the scope of the original project, which is creating a database to manage day-to-day store operations. As a result, Paul and Don agree on the scope and deliverables of the project—managing customer and prescription data, managing personnel data, tracking buying behavior, and evaluating inventory. The exact specifications of the project—how much it costs, when it is delivered, and what exact output is expected—will be negotiated after Don concludes the database design process. During the planning stage, it is important to manage expectations early and agree on project specifications, as Don has done. Otherwise, the project can become unmanageable.

Now that Don has identified the existing sources of data and has interviewed many of the employees at the pharmacy, he turns his attention to another important part of the discovery phase—researching sources of missing data.

RESEARCHING SOURCES OF MISSING DATA

Don's efforts have identified the data collected by 4Corners Pharmacy and have given him a chance to evaluate how employees and managers use it. Another important part of the discovery phase is determining data that is missing and identifying the sources you can use to obtain that missing data. This part of the process is often difficult because you must ask the right questions of the right people to get the right answers. In interviews with key employees and managers, it is best to ask questions such as "What else would you like to know about the data?" and similarly worded inquiries. You might find that employees need to know certain things about the data that the current system cannot provide.

In his conversations with employees, Don learned a great deal about the kind of data that the DBMS must collect, organize, and manage. He also learned about data that various departments and employees want to collect but are not collecting presently. For example, Maria needs to obtain certain data about employee training and classes, but has no way to do so. She also wants to have an electronic record of the classes that employees have taken and need to take, a way to determine which employees are bilingual, and scanned images of important employment documents such as the driver's licenses of employees who are authorized to make pharmacy deliveries.

Best Practice

Determining Output

When interviewing members of an organization during the discovery phase of database design, listen closely to their needs. Few people are familiar with database concepts. Consequently, they will speak of needing lists, reports, files, printouts, records, and other terms. Your job is to translate those needs into database deliverables. You will learn database terms later in this chapter, but it is important to remember that no one will direct you to "employ the 'and' logical operator in conjunction with the 'or' logical operator in a select query to list the customers in Colorado who are allergic to aspirin." People don't talk that way. They will say: "I need a printout of every customer who can't take aspirin and who's either been a customer for a long time or who spends a lot of money at the pharmacy. I want to send these customers a free sample of a new aspirin substitute." It becomes your job to translate this information into database commands. You will learn how to work in a database as you complete this book.

ASSIMILATING THE AVAILABLE INFORMATION AND PLANNING THE DATABASE

Databases are not created in a vacuum; it is essential to interview employees, managers, and potential users of the database to learn how data is gathered and stored in an organization and to seek feedback regarding what output and functionality they want to obtain from the database. After gathering this information, you will better understand which users require access to which data, how that data should be stored and formatted, and how to organize the data into logical groups.

Now that Don has completed his interviews with the various managers and key employees at 4Corners Pharmacy, he is ready to start planning the database. His notes include sample documents showing how and which data is currently stored, data that should be collected but currently is not, and information that suggests possible additions and desires from future users of the system. With all of this information, Don has a good understanding of how 4Corners will store, manage, and use the data it collects, so he is ready to move into the next phase of database development—planning the database design.

The first step in database design is to determine the best way to organize the data that you collected in the discovery phase into logical groups of fields. These logical groups of fields are known as entities. An **entity** is a person, place, thing, or idea. In a database, a **field** (or **column**) is a single characteristic of an entity. For example, the fields to describe a customer would be ones such as first name, last name, address, city, state, and so on. When all the fields about an entity are grouped together, they create **record** (or **row**). A **table** (also called a **relation**) is a collection of records that describe one entity. A **database** is a collection of one or more tables.

When a database contains related tables through fields that contain identical data, the database is called a **relational database**. For example, a table that stores customer data might be named Customer and contain a field that stores unique identification numbers for each customer; this field might be named Customer ID. To relate customers to the sales representatives who represent them, the database might also contain a table named Rep that includes information about sales representatives. To relate the Customer and Rep tables to each other so you can determine which representative represents which customers, the Rep table would also contain a field named Customer ID and this field would contain identical values in both tables. You will learn more about tables and relationships later in this chapter.

EVALUATING FIELD VALUES AND ASSIGNING APPROPRIATE DATA TYPES

After identifying the fields that describe the data that will be stored in the tables in the database, the next step is to determine the data type to assign to each field. A database stores data in different ways; a **data type** determines how to store the data in the field.

Some fields store text values, such as a person's name; other fields store numbers, such as zip codes, phone numbers, or dollar amounts. A database might also store objects such as pictures or fields that contain hyperlinks to Internet or file locations. Table 1.2 describes the different data types that you can assign to fields. DBMSs use different names for some data types. In Table 1.2, Access data type names are listed in the first column; when other DBMSs use a different data type name, it is noted in parentheses. For example, the Text data type used in Access is called a Char data type in other DBMSs.

Table 1.2: Common data types and their descriptions

Data Type	Description	Example
Text (Char)	Text or alphanumeric combinations of data and numbers that are not used in calculations	Names, addresses, phone numbers, Social Security numbers, and zip codes
Memo	Long passages of data containing text and alphanumeric characters	Employee review information and detailed product descriptions
Number (Decimal)	Numbers that are used in calculations	Currency values, number ordered, and number of refills
Date/Time (Date)	Dates or date and time combinations	Inventory expiration dates and birth dates
Currency (not available in all DBMSs)	Monetary amounts	Item cost and item price
AutoNumber (not available in all DBMSs)	An automatically generated number that produces unique values for each record	Any number that is necessary to uniquely identify records, such as a customer ID number or product ID number that is not assigned by another method
Yes/No (not available in all DBMSs)	A field value that is limited to yes or no, on or off, and true or false values	Responses to indicate whether child-proof caps are requested or whether the employee is CPR certified (both require yes or no responses)
OLE Object (not available in all DBMSs)	Linked or embedded objects that are created in another program	Photographs, sounds, documents, and video
Hyperlink (not available in all DBMSs)	Text that contains a hyperlink to an Internet or file location	Web pages, e-mail addresses, and files on network or workstation
Lookup Wizard (not available in all DBMSs)	A field that lets you look up data in another table or in a list of values created for the field	Predefined list of drug codes, categories of information, and state abbreviations

How do you determine which data type to assign each field? Doing so depends on what function you want to derive from that data, because each data type has different properties. For example, 4Corners Pharmacy requires name and address data for employees, customers, and doctors. Don will create separate tables for each of these entities. Within each table, he will create fields for first names, last names, street addresses, cities, states, and zip codes. The data stored in each field and its intended use determine what data type to assign to the field.

The Text and Memo Data Types

Don will assign the **Text** data type to the fields that store a person's name, because names are composed of letters, but he will also assign the Text data type to the street address as it is often an alphanumeric combination. A zip code is a number, but this number is not used in calculations—you would never add, subtract, multiply, or divide one customer's zip code by another or use it in any other calculation, so the appropriate data type is Text.

Maria wants to enter comments about disciplinary actions for employees in the database. Don will need to create a field in the Employee table for this and assign it the **Memo** data type as this data type can store long passages of text. You might wonder how much longer the Memo data type is than the Text data type and whether you should assign the Memo data type to all fields requiring textual entries. The Text data type stores a maximum of 255 characters, whereas the Memo data type stores a maximum of 65,535 characters. Maria could write a 15-page evaluation in a Memo field and have plenty of room to spare. So why not assign the Memo data type to every field containing text? A primary goal in designing a database is to keep it small by assigning the data type to each field that is large enough to hold the data required in that field without wasting additional space. Thus, names, addresses, descriptions, and so on generally require the Text data type, whereas notes, comments, and journal entries generally require the Memo data type. Because it is the most commonly assigned data type, the Text data type is the default for all fields created in an Access database.

The Number Data Type

Don will also create a table to store the details for every prescription filled at 4Corners Pharmacy, including the number of prescriptions filled for each customer and the number of refills authorized by the doctor. Don will assign the **Number** data type to these fields because Paul will want to use them to calculate how many prescriptions were filled in a given period or perhaps to calculate the average refill allowance per drug type. The Number data type stores both positive and negative numbers in a field (although the pharmacy probably will not need to store negative numbers) containing up to 15 digits. A simple way to remember the purpose of the Number data type is that it is for numbers that you need to use in calculations. As mentioned earlier, data such as telephone numbers, Social Security numbers, and zip codes, despite their appearance and the fact that most people identify these values as numbers, are not used in calculations and are not assigned the Number data type, but rather the Text data type.

The Currency Data Type

Another important consideration is that monetary values are not assigned the Number data type, as you might expect. Despite the fact that these amounts are numbers and are used in calculations, fields storing monetary data are assigned the **Currency** data type, which by default includes two decimal places and displays values with a dollar sign. Thus, Don will assign the Currency data type to fields that store the costs and prices for drugs and the salaries and wages for employees.

Best Practice

Avoiding Storing Calculated Fields in Tables

Although it is important to assign the Number data type to fields containing values that you will use in calculations, it is important not to include calculated fields in your tables. That is, you must avoid creating fields to store data such as a person's age or GPA, since a person's age is valid for only one year and a person's GPA is good for only one semester. Many amateur database developers include calculated fields such as these in their tables, but soon find themselves having to update fields or correct static values that have changed. To avoid this problem, you should include the raw numbers from which such things as age and GPA are calculated, such as a date of birth or a grade and the credit hours earned, respectively, and calculate an age or GPA when you need to do so. You will learn more about performing calculations on Number fields later in this book.

The Date/Time Data Type

Don will include a field in the Employee and Customer tables to store a person's date of birth. He will assign this field the **Date/Time** data type. By default, fields assigned the Date/Time data type display values in the format mm/dd/yyyy, but they can also include the time in different formats. Dates can be used in calculations if necessary to calculate the number of days between a starting date and an ending date, or to determine a person's age. Just like other data types, Don can change the default formatting of the Date/Time data type to display date and time values in different ways.

The AutoNumber Data Type

The **AutoNumber** data type is unique to Access; it is a number automatically generated by Access that produces unique values for each record. This data type is useful when you need to distinguish two records that share identical information. For example, two prescriptions of the same drug, in the same amount, filled on the same day might be entered into a Prescription table. It would be difficult to tell these prescriptions apart, but if assigned the AutoNumber data type, this unique value created for each record would differentiate them. The AutoNumber field produces values of up to nine digits.

The Yes/No Data Type

The **Yes/No** data type is assigned to those fields requiring a yes/no, true/false, or on/off answer and takes up one character of storage space. Don will assign the Yes/No data type to the field in the Customer table that indicates whether the customer prefers child proof caps on prescription bottles. The Yes/No field will make data entry easy; a user only needs to click the check box to place a check mark in it to represent a "yes" value. Using a check box also saves space, as each field takes only one character of space compared to the 16 characters that would be required to type the words "child proof caps."

The OLE Object Data Type

The **OLE object** data type is used to identify files that are created in another program and then linked or embedded in the database. (OLE is an abbreviation for object linking and embedding.) Don might use this data type if he needs to link an employee's record to a scanned image of the employee driver's license that Maria might have on file for delivery personnel.

The Hyperlink Data Type

The **Hyperlink** data type is assigned to fields that contain hyperlinks to Web pages, e-mail addresses, or files that open in a Web browser, an e-mail client, or another application when clicked. Don can use this data type when creating fields that link to Web sites for health plans or doctors.

The Lookup Wizard Data Type

The **Lookup Wizard** data type creates fields that let you look up data in another table or in a list of values created for the field. Don could use the Lookup Wizard in a Customer table to display the two-letter abbreviations for each state so the user could choose the correct state from a drop-down menu. A lookup field accomplishes two things—it makes data entry easy and ensures that valid data is entered into the field. The user cannot misspell the state and cannot enter more or fewer letters than are available in the drop-down menu. For example, if you have the lookup table store state values, you won't have mistakes such as a user entering the abbreviation for Mississippi as MI when in fact that abbreviation is for Michigan. In addition, you won't have an erroneous entry of DA, which isn't an allowable value because it's not a valid abbreviation for a state. In this case, did the user mean to type DE for Delaware or DC for Washington, DC? Is this a typo that you need to correct or is this abbreviation for something else? Lookup fields are also good for controlling inconsistent data. Without them, users might erroneously enter DA as indicated earlier. Were Don to search later for all customers from Delaware, find customers with state abbreviations of DA, because he would not know to look for them. Thus, a state field is an ideal candidate for a lookup field.

Selecting the Correct Data Type

Choosing the appropriate data type for each field in a table is essential for two reasons. First, it helps store the correct data in the correct format while using the least amount of space. Second, it eases data entry and interactivity with data because choosing certain data types results in user-friendly interactive features, such as drop-down menus, check boxes, and hyperlinks. Choosing the appropriate data type also lets you correctly manipulate the data. For example, if the pharmacy decides to start a customer loyalty program in which the pharmacy rewards longtime customers who spend a set amount at the pharmacy by giving them a coupon to save 10% off their next pharmacy purchase, Don will need a way to calculate the sum of all orders placed by each customer. If the database can calculate the total for each pharmacy order, Don can use it to create yearly or monthly totals by customer. If this field uses the Text data type, these calculations would not be possible because a database cannot perform calculations on text values, even if they contain numbers. If this field uses the Currency data type, then these calculations are possible.

Data types are important not only for manipulating data, but also for entering data into the database. A Memo field accepts a large amount of text—even an essay, if desired—whereas the default Text data type accepts up to 255 characters (a few sentences). For example, Maria might want to include a field in a table that identifies the various training classes and describes the content of the classes. To accomplish this goal, she might need to use a field with the Memo data type to have room to include a complete course description that includes the course objectives, prerequisites, and requirements.

The Yes/No and Lookup Wizard data types ease data entry by controlling what data a user can enter into a field. The Yes/No data type only accepts the values "yes" and "no." This restriction is valuable for answering such questions as "Did the pharmacist ask the customer about her allergies?" In this case, the pharmacist simply clicks the check box to indicate that he asked the question. Either the pharmacist followed or did not follow the procedures—there is no other choice for this field. The Yes/No data type provides a nice audit trail in this case.

What happens when the answer is not always yes or no? What if the answer could be "undetermined," "undecided," or "maybe?" If any of these answers are possible—however rare—then you should not use the Yes/No data type because the allowable responses—yes or no—would be inaccurate.

The Lookup Wizard data type also ensures accurate data, but can be more flexible than the Yes/No data type. For example, if the majority of 4Corners Pharmacy customers reside in the four nearby states of Colorado, Utah, New Mexico, and Arizona, it might be convenient to list those four states in a lookup field that provides a drop-down menu allowing the pharmacist to choose among them. The menu saves a great deal of typing for the pharmacist and ensures that the state abbreviations are entered correctly and in the appropriate format into the State field. For any other values, such as CA for a customer from California, the default is to let a user override the lookup field values by typing the value CA directly into the field. If you need to prohibit a user from overriding the lookup field values—perhaps the pharmacy cannot accept out-of-state patients, for example—you could set the field's properties to forbid new values. You will learn more about data validation and other field properties in Chapter 2.

Assigning the Correct Field Size for Text Fields

As mentioned earlier, it is important to consider field size when assigning data types and to minimize the space reserved for each record by assigning the smallest data type that will store your data. For example, to store the two-letter abbreviation for a state instead of the state's full name, you would need to create a field with the Text data type and a field size of two characters. In this case, the field size not only saves space, but also prohibits someone from entering "Cal," "Cali," "Calif," or "California" instead of "CA" into the field. Any value *except* CA would pose problems later when Don tried to search for customers from CA.

It is important to be conservative when assigning field sizes, but not too conservative. For example, how many spaces should be allowed for a person's last name? Upon first consideration you might choose a field size of 10 or 12 characters and safely store the names "Jefferson" (requiring nine characters) or "O'Callaghan" (requiring 11 characters). But what happens when you try to store the names "Thangsuphanich," "Traiwatanapong," or "Jefferson-O'Callaghan," which requires 21 characters (nine characters in Jefferson, one character for the hyphen, and 11 characters for O'Callaghan)? Storing a last name with 21 characters in a field designed to store 12 characters would result in almost half of the name being truncated, or cut off. On the other hand, you would not want to leave the last name field at the default 50 or at the maximum of 255 characters as these field sizes would waste space and violate a cardinal rule of database design. A good compromise is to define fields that store last names with 30 to 40 characters.

Assigning the Correct Field Size for Number Fields

Just as you must be aware of preserving storage space when assigning the Text data type, you must also be conservative when assigning the Number data type, as there are seven choices for Number field sizes. Table 1.3 describes the different field sizes for fields with the Number data type.

Table 1.3: Field sizes for the Number data type

Field Size	Values Allowed	Decimal Precision	Storage Size
Byte	0 to 255 (excludes fractions)	None	1 byte
Integer	–32,768 to 32,767 (excludes fractions)	None	2 bytes
Long Integer	–2,147,483,648 to 2,147,483,647 (excludes fractions)	None	4 bytes
Single	$-3.402823E^{38}$ to $-1.401298E^{-45}$ for negative values and from $1.401298E^{-45}$ to $3.402823E^{38}$ for positive values	7	4 bytes
Double	$-1.79769313486231E^{308}$ to $-4.94065645841247E^{-324}$ for negative values and from $4.94065645841247E^{-324}$ to $1.79769313486231E^{308}$ for positive values	15	8 bytes

Table 1.3: Field sizes for the Number data type (cont.)

Field Size	Values Allowed	Decimal Precision	Storage Size
Decimal	-10^{28-1} through 10^{28-1}	28	12 bytes
Replication ID	Globally unique identifiers (GUID) are used to identify replicas, replica sets, tables, records, and other objects	N/A	16 bytes

To determine the correct field size, you must evaluate the data stored in a Number field just as you would evaluate the data stored in a Text field. For example, Don might assign the Number data type to a Dependents field in the Customer table and then set the field size to Byte. A Byte field stores only positive numbers up to 255. Because a customer cannot have a negative number of dependents, a fractional number of dependents, or more than 255 dependents, this is the correct field size because it stores the correct data using the least amount of space possible.

It is important to choose the correct data type prior to entering data into a table. Although it is possible to change a field's data type after entering data into a table, you might lose some of the data if you decrease a field size because you might truncate any existing data that requires more space than the revised field size allows.

DIVIDING THE EXISTING AND MISSING DATA INTO TABLES

The discovery phase now over, Don must create the tables to be used in the 4Corners Pharmacy database. Figure 1.12 details the four steps involved in this process.

Figure 1.12: Database design process: planning the tables

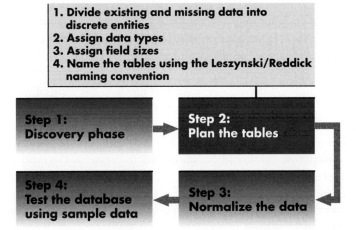

1. Divide existing and missing data into discrete entities
2. Assign data types
3. Assign field sizes
4. Name the tables using the Leszynski/Reddick naming convention

Step 1: Discovery phase

Step 2: Plan the tables

Step 3: Normalize the data

Step 4: Test the database using sample data

Tables are the single most important component of the database; the other objects in a database could not even exist without being based on tables. A database might have only one table with only one field and only one record in it, such as your first name. Such a database wouldn't be terribly useful, but it would still be a database. Most databases contain multiple tables and hundreds or even thousands of records.

In the discovery phase, Don interviewed 4Corners Pharmacy employees so he could understand the desired database output. Now he needs to divide the existing and missing data into discrete entities, break those entities into smaller fields that describe some attribute, assign data types to these fields, modify the field sizes as necessary, and then name each table according to standard conventions.

Don focuses first on the employee data that Maria collects because it is currently the most fragmented. Recall that Maria keeps personnel records in Outlook, Excel, Word, and on paper, with much of the data, such as the employee's name, appearing in all of these sources. Don lists the data necessary to create the desired output that Maria identified about employees in the discovery phase:

- Name
- Age
- Years with company
- Address
- Position
- Job description
- Pay rate
- Annual review
- Training classes attended
- Other information (such as whether the employee is bilingual and attendance information)
- Prescriptions filled (if the employee is a pharmacist or pharmacy technician)

The amateur database designer might be tempted to list these fields and move on. Don, however, is a seasoned veteran who knows that brainstorming like this is just the first step in creating a table. He must now step back and analyze five things.

1. Don did not include all the data necessary to produce the desired output from his initial discovery phase. Maria needs to print telephone lists of bilingual employees so that if no bilingual pharmacists were on duty and a Spanish-speaking customer required assistance, the staff could call an off-duty colleague to assist with the translation. This telephone list would be impossible to create as Don did not include a phone number in his initial field list. Thus, it is imperative to review the desired output and then ensure that you have the necessary data to produce it. Don expands the list to include one field for telephone number and another field for cell phone number, as most employees have both.

2. Don did not identify a field that he could use as a primary key. A **primary key** is one field (or perhaps a combination of fields) that creates a unique value in each record so you can identify each record in the table. The employees at 4Corners Pharmacy have unique last names, and at first it appears that the last name will uniquely identify each record. However, if a second employee with the last name "Garcia" is hired, there would be no way to use the last name field to distinguish between two employees with that last name. In addition, if Paul opens additional stores, the likelihood of having employees with the same name increases. To create a unique value in each employee's record, Don could expand the list to include the employee's Social Security number. However, because of new privacy laws, Don decides instead to create an Employee ID field, into which he will enter a unique value for each employee, and selects this field as the primary key.

3. The fields Don listed are too broad. Although it is possible to store a person's first and last names in one field (Name), by doing so you would limit what you could do with the data. For example, Maria sends quarterly updates to all employees informing them of how many sick days and holidays they have accrued. Recently learning how to perform a mail merge in Word, Maria wants to customize the contents of the letter to include individualized names. But as listed in Don's brainstorming list, Name is only one field. If Maria used the Name field in the mail merge, the salutation would read "Dear Maria Garcia," which would have an impersonal effect, the exact opposite of Maria's intention of writing the more customary and personal "Dear Maria." Thus, Don decides that the Name field should be broken down into at least two fields to store the first name and last name. Indeed, he could break down the Name field further, including additional fields to store the employee's title, middle name, suffix, and preferred name. For the Employee table, Don includes fields for first name, middle initial, and last name. Following this principle, Don also divides the address into multiple fields (address, city, state, and zip code) and the pay rate into multiple fields (salary and hourly rate).

4. After expanding as many fields as possible into discrete units, Don identifies a fourth problem with the proposed fields in the Employee table: age is a static number. If stored as a whole number, it will become outdated within a year. You will remember from the earlier discussion about data types that age and other calculated fields should never be stored in a table. Rather, good database design includes birth date fields. By storing a person's birth date, you can calculate the person's age by subtracting the birth date from today's date. Don changes the Age field to Date of Birth and then changes the Years with company field, another value that he can calculate, to Start Date and End Date.

5. The fifth and final problem with the proposed fields for the Employee table is that some break the cardinal rule of relational database design—avoiding data redundancy. The Employee table includes fields for job description and training classes attended. Although this data describes employees, these fields belong in two separate tables to prevent data redundancy. For example, 14 employees might attend the same training class. If the training class information appears in the Employee table, Maria would need to add the class to the record for each employee who attended the class, as shown in Figure 1.13.

Figure 1.13: Employee training data

	A	B	C	D
1	First Name	Last Name	Class	Date
2	Amy	Urquiza	Adult CPR	6/20/2004
3	Tara	Kobrick	Adult CPR	4/10/2004
4	Joan	Gabel	Adult CPR	2/6/2004
5	Rachel	Thompson	Adult CPR	3/17/2004
6	Tara	Kobrick	Adult CPR Recertification	4/12/2005
7	Louis	Moreno	Adult CPR Recertification	4/1/2006
8	Paul	Ferrino	Adult CPR Recertification	2/5/2007
9	Virginia	Sanchez	Adult CPR Recertification	6/1/2007
10	Virginia	Sanchez	Adult CPR Recertification	6/29/2008
11	Rachel	Thompson	Adult CPR Recertification	3/16/2005
12	Amy	Urquiza	Adult CPR Recertification	6/21/2005
13	Amy	Urquiza	Adult CPR Recertification	3/10/2006
14	Dora	Langston	Adult CPR Recertification	6/15/2006
15	Dora	Langston	Adult CPR Recertification	3/5/2007
16	Vincent	Ferrino	Adult CPR Recertification	2/2/2005
17	Vincent	Ferrino	Adult CPR Recertification	4/2/2007
18	Vincent	Ferrino	Adult CPR Recertification	4/5/2008
19	Marco	Farello	Adult CPR Recertification	2/1/2006
20	Dora	Langston	Child/Infant CPR	6/9/2004
21	Marco	Farello	Child/Infant CPR	1/30/2004

Redundant data: "Adult CPR Recertification" appears 14 times

Employee Training

Typing the same information into each employee's record is a waste of time for Maria and exactly what Don seeks to avoid by designing a relational database. Retyping "Adult CPR Recertification" 14 times is inefficient and could result in inconsistent data. Don is glad that he spotted this redundancy now and knows that this is why the brainstorming component of database design is imperative and often time-consuming, but well worth the effort. By foreseeing this potential redundancy, Don will avoid it by creating a separate table to store data about the class descriptions, cost, provider, and any other pertinent data.

Don also recognizes that the Position field contains repetitive data because multiple employees can share the same job title, so he creates a table to store information about positions held by employees. He also needs a way to identify which employee filled which prescription, so he creates another table to store information about prescriptions.

As you can see, Don's brainstorming about employees resulted in the creation of three additional tables and several more fields. Don will complete this brainstorming process for each table that he creates, making sure to include all necessary fields, identify primary keys, break broad fields into smaller discrete components, avoid calculated fields, and avoid data redundancy. He will create as many tables as necessary to avoid repeating any information in the database. The result of Don's brainstorming is shown in Table 1.4, with the fields for the Employee table and their corresponding data types.

Table 1.4: Field names and data types for the Employee table

Field Name	Data Type
Employee ID	Number
First Name	Text
Middle Initial	Text
Last Name	Text
Social Security Number	Text
Date of Birth	Date/Time
Start Date	Date/Time
End Date	Date/Time
Address	Text
City	Text
State	Text
Zip	Text
Memo	Memo
Phone	Text
Cell	Text
Salary	Currency
Hourly Rate	Currency
Review	Date/Time

The data about training classes attended, job positions, and prescriptions filled, which originally appeared in the Employee table, will become fields in their own tables.

Naming Conventions

After brainstorming the employee fields and grouping them together, Don must name the table. Database tables must have unique names and follow established naming conventions for the DBMS in which they are stored. Some general rules for naming objects (including tables) are as follows:

- Object names cannot exceed 64 characters, although shorter names are preferred.
- Object names cannot include a period, exclamation point, accent grave, or brackets.
- Object names should not include spaces. Most developers capitalize the first letter of each word when a table name includes two words, such as EmployeeTraining.

In general, field names follow the same naming rules. For example, in the Employee table, Don will change the field name First Name (which includes a space) to FirstName.

Most database developers also follow established naming conventions, in which a prefix (also called a tag) precedes the object name to define it further. Instead of naming the table Employee, Don uses the Leszynski/Reddick naming conventions shown in Table 1.5 and names the table tblEmployee.

Table 1.5: Leszynski/Reddick naming conventions for database objects

Database Object	Prefix	Example
Table	tbl	tblEmployee
Query	qry	qryPharmacists
Form	frm	frmCustomer
Report	rpt	rptBilingualPharmacists
Macro	mcr	mcrUpdateClasses
Module	bas	basInventory

Some developers use a prefix to identify the fields in a table, as well, such as changing the field name LastName to txtLastName to identify the field as having the Text data type. Don decides not to use this convention because it will increase the time it takes to type the field names.

Although it will take some time to build all the tables, Paul is encouraged by the benefits that a DBMS will offer the pharmacy. Don interviewed as many key players at 4Corners Pharmacy as possible, gathered the existing data, researched any sources of missing data, and talked to users about desired output. He and Paul agreed on expectations, and then Don began planning the tables by dividing existing and missing data into discrete entities, naming the fields, and assigning data types to these fields.

Steps To Success: Level 1

After concluding the discovery phase of database design, Don began brainstorming about the tables he needs to create and which specific fields within those tables are necessary to capture all data required for the desired output he identified. Don created tblEmployee. He asks you to create the table designs for the remaining tables in the database by grouping the existing and missing data he identified into tables, creating field names and data types, and naming the fields and tables according to the standards he established.

On a piece of paper, complete the following:

1. Plan the tables needed in the 4Corners Pharmacy database using the information Don garnered during the discovery phase.

2. Name each table according to its contents and the Leszynski/Reddick naming conventions.

3. List the fields in each table.

4. Designate data types for each field in each table.

5. Look at the plan you created for the 4Corners Pharmacy and look for any missing or incomplete data. What other changes would you suggest making, and why?

LEVEL 2
UNDERSTANDING AND CREATING TABLE RELATIONSHIPS

UNDERSTANDING RELATIONAL DATABASE OBJECTS

Although tables store the data in a DBMS, users can view the data in tables by opening the table or by creating other objects. The four main objects in a database are tables, queries, forms, and reports.

Tables

You learned in Level 1 that the data in a relational database is stored in one or more tables. You can view the data in a table by opening it and scrolling through its records. However, most of the time you will use one of the three other main database objects—queries, forms, and reports—to display the data from one or more tables in a format that matches your needs.

Queries

A **query** is a question that you ask about the data stored in a database, such as "Which customers live in Colorado?" You could generate a list of customers by scrolling through the records in tblCustomer or by sorting the records alphabetically by state, but with many customers, this process could take a lot of time and is only a temporary rearrangement of the data in the table. If you use a query to find the answer to this question, you can save the query in the database and use it again to list the customers who live in Colorado because the query object searches each record in tblCustomer and lists in the results each one with the value CO (the state abbreviation for Colorado) in the State field. The query results look similar to a table, with fields displayed in columns and records displayed in rows. (This arrangement of data in Access is called a **datasheet**.) There are three different kinds of queries: select queries, action queries, and crosstab queries.

The **select query** is the most commonly used query. As the name suggests, data is selected from the table on which the query is based (also called the **base table** or the **underlying table**), and is displayed in a datasheet. A query can select basic information or very specific information. For example, a select query might select all customers who live in Colorado. A more specific select query might select all customers who live in Colorado, are older than 55, and live in the 81323 zip code. When you run a select query, the query results are dynamic; that is, if every customer living in Colorado moves to another state, the datasheet will display no matching records the next time you run a query that selects customers living in Colorado. On the other hand, if 1,000 new Colorado customers were entered into tblCustomer, running a query that selects customers living in Colorado would display 1,000 new records.

A two-way relationship exists between a table and queries that are based on the table. As you just learned, records are "pulled" from the table upon which a query is based and displayed in a datasheet. You can also use a query to "push" data into the table using the query. For example, if a pharmacist viewing a query that selects customers living in Colorado changes the value in the State field from CO to AZ for a customer, the customer's record is updated in tblCustomer. When he runs the query again, that customer's record will no longer appear in the query results because it no longer satisfies the requirements for being included. If a pharmacist accidentally deletes a record from the query results, that record is also deleted from tblCustomer.

An **action query**, as its name implies, performs an action on the table on which it is based. Some action queries let you select specific records in a table and update them in some way, such as increasing the cost of every drug purchased from a specific supplier by 10%. Other action queries let you select data from one table and append (add) it to another table; you can use this type of query to create a new table or add records to an existing table. You can also use an action query to delete records from a table, such as deleting all customer records from a table when the customer's account has been inactive for a specific length of time.

A **crosstab query** performs calculations on the values in a field and displays the results in a datasheet. A crosstab query might sum the values in a field to create a total or select the maximum or minimum value in a field. You will learn more about queries in Chapter 3.

Forms

A **form** is used to view, add, delete, update, and print records in the database. A form can be based on a table or a query. A form might also have a two-way relationship with a table because changing the data displayed in a form might update the data in the table on which the form is based, depending on how the form was created. Often a form displays many or all the fields from the table on which it is based, and you can enter data into the form to add a record to the table. A form based on tblClinic is shown in Figure 1.14.

Figure 1.14: Form based on a table

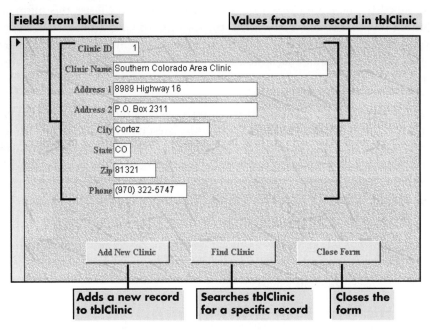

Fields from tblClinic   Values from one record in tblClinic

Clinic ID	1
Clinic Name	Southern Colorado Area Clinic
Address 1	8989 Highway 16
Address 2	P.O. Box 2311
City	Cortez
State	CO
Zip	81321
Phone	(970) 322-5747

Add New Clinic   Find Clinic   Close Form

Adds a new record to tblClinic   Searches tblClinic for a specific record   Closes the form

Don could use the clinic information form he obtained during the discovery phase to create its database counterpart so the pharmacy staff can add a new clinic to the database using the form object. If the clinic's information changes, an employee could update fields as necessary by displaying the form again and using it to find and view the clinic's data, and then make the necessary changes. You will learn more about forms in Chapter 4.

Another benefit of using a form to display data is that the interface is more attractive than the table datasheet, and you can customize a form's appearance with instructions and command buttons. The command buttons shown in Figure 1.14 change the form's function to add a new clinic, find an existing clinic, and close the form. As a result, even the least experienced user of a database feels confident when entering or viewing data. Forms are also used as a type of welcome menu to your database; when used in this capacity, a form is called a switchboard. A **switchboard** is a form that might be displayed when you open a database and provides a controlled method for users to open the objects in a database. Users click buttons to open existing objects, which is more user friendly than using the database interface. You will learn how to create and use a switchboard in Chapter 6.

Reports

A **report** is a formatted presentation of data from a table or query that is created as a printout or to be viewed on screen. A report might contain an employee telephone directory, inventory summaries, or mailing labels. Some reports are simple to create, such as generating telephone lists. Other types of reports, such as inventory summaries, are more complicated because they might display data in ways not available by using other database objects. For example, Don needs to create a report for Paul that details customer expenditures grouped by the city in which the customer lives. Paul will use this information for marketing purposes so he knows where the majority of his customers live. Paul also needs reports showing the pharmacy's daily, monthly, quarterly, and yearly revenues. If Paul opens one or more additional stores, he'll need this same information, but grouped by location.

The data displayed by a report is usually based on a query, although you can also base a report on a table. Reports are dynamic, reflecting the latest data from the object on which they are based. However, unlike forms, you can only view the data in a report; you cannot change the data or use a report to add a new record. The amount of data in a report varies—a report might list the top five best-selling drugs at 4Corners Pharmacy or all customers at the pharmacy who take a certain drug. When a report exceeds more than one page, the user must use the page navigation features to view the pages on screen. Figure 1.15 shows a report that displays the accounts receivable data for customers with outstanding balances.

Figure 1.15: Accounts receivable report

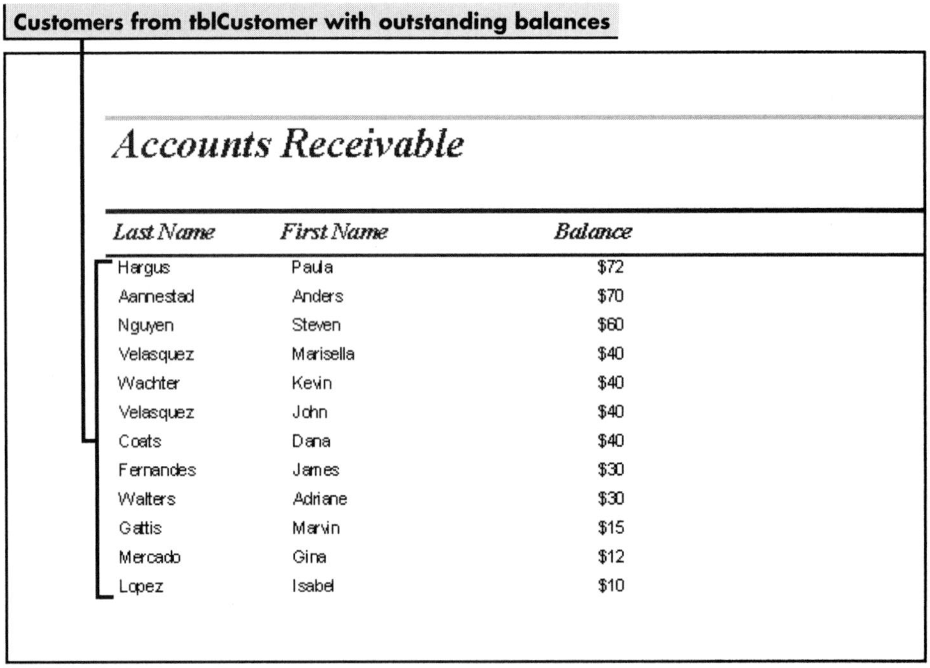

Customers from tblCustomer with outstanding balances

Accounts Receivable

Last Name	First Name	Balance
Hargus	Paula	$72
Aamestad	Anders	$70
Nguyen	Steven	$60
Velasquez	Marisella	$40
Wachter	Kevin	$40
Velasquez	John	$40
Coats	Dana	$40
Fernandes	James	$30
Walters	Adriane	$30
Gattis	Marvin	$15
Mercado	Gina	$12
Lopez	Isabel	$10

The report shown in Figure 1.15 is based on the query shown in Figure 1.16. As you can see, the data in the report and query are the same, but the report format makes the data easier to read. The report contains a title to identify its contents. You can also add page numbers, headers, and footers to a report. You will learn more about reports in Chapter 5.

Figure 1.16: Query datasheet

tblCustomer Query

First Name	Last Name	SumOfBalance
Paula	Hargus	$72.00
Anders	Aannestad	$70.00
Steven	Nguyen	$60.00
Marisella	Velasquez	$40.00
Kevin	Wachter	$40.00
John	Velasquez	$40.00
Dana	Coats	$40.00
James	Fernandes	$30.00
Adriane	Walters	$30.00
Marvin	Gattis	$15.00
Gina	Mercado	$12.00
Isabel	Lopez	$10.00

Other Database Objects

Most users interact mostly with the tables, queries, forms, and reports in a database, but you might also use three other objects. A **page**, also called a **data access page**, is a Web page that lets you view and interact with data stored in an Access database. A data access page is an HTML document that is stored outside the database, usually in a shared network folder or on a server that is connected to the Internet. All data access pages let you view the data in the object on which the data access page is based; in some cases, you can also add and delete records from the underlying object. Figure 1.17 shows a data access page with information about doctors who have written prescriptions filled at 4Corners Pharmacy.

Figure 1.17: Data access page

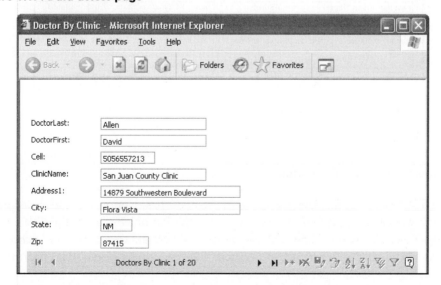

A **macro** is a set of instructions that you specify to automate certain database tasks. A macro might contain instructions to open a specific form or query in the database when you click a command button on a form. A macro can also contain instructions to close an object, find a record, print an object, or close Access. You will learn more about using and creating macros in Chapter 6.

A **module** is another object that contains instructions to automate a database task. Modules are written in **Visual Basic for Applications (VBA)**, the programming language for Microsoft Office programs, including Access. A macro usually automates a simple task, such as opening or closing a form. A module performs more sophisticated actions, such as verifying the data entered into a field before storing it in the database. You will learn more about modules in Chapter 7.

UNDERSTANDING RELATIONAL DATABASE CONCEPTS

The worksheet and other systems used by the pharmacy indicate that Vincent is not familiar with a relational database, but rather with a **flat file database**, a simple database that contains a single table of information. A relational database contains multiple tables to store related information. When most people are faced with a task that requires some kind of data management, they often open Excel and start entering data into a worksheet with columns to define the different fields for each row in the worksheet. Figure 1.18 shows a flat file database that Vincent created using Excel.

Figure 1.18: Flat file database that includes rows for new records

Redundant and inconsistent data for people living in the same household

First Name	Last Name	Address	City	State	Zip	PlanID
Christina	Hargus	5465 South Nelson Circle	Shiprock	NM	87420	OP-87-A087
Paula	Hargus	5465 South Nelson Circle	Shiprock	NM	87420	OP-87-A087
Isabel	Lopez	6969 South Valmont Road	Montezuma Creek	UT	84534	2B8973AC
Steven	Nguyen	9874 South Main Street	Blanding	UT	84511	498-1112-A
Scott	Prager	2510 West 108th Avenue	Pleasant View	CO	81331	4983
Jennifer	Ramsey	4775 Argone Circle	Chinle	AZ	86547	498-1112-A
Shannon	Sabus	460 West Pioneer Road	Dolores	CO	81323	4983
Ted	Sabus	406 West Pioneer Road	Dolores	CO	81323	4983
Marisella	Velasquez	54213 Oak Drive	Kirtland	NM	87417	000H98763-01
Marisella	Velasquez	54213 Oak Drive	Kirtland	NM	87417	000H98763-01
Kevin	Wachter	2931 East Narcissus Way	Montezuma Creek	UT	84534	A089
Adriane	Walters	14444 North Tamarac Street	Cortez	CO	81321	4983
Adriane	Walters	14444 North Tamarac Street	Cortez	CO	81321	4983

Redundant data for the same customer

Figure 1.18 shows a flat file database in which each new prescription was added in a new row in the worksheet. This method creates at least three problems. First, the pharmacist wastes time by entering the name, address, phone number, and data for each prescription the customer fills. Notice that Adriane Walters filled two prescriptions. The pharmacist entered Adriane's name, address, and health plan information into both records, even though this data is the same for both records.

Second, and more important, this process is prone to errors. Notice that Ted and Shannon Sabus, who filled prescriptions on the same day, seem to be related but live in different house numbers, suggesting that one or both of these house numbers contains an error. Such errors are common occurrences in flat file databases because of the amount of data repetition and data redundancy.

Third, what if Adriane or the Sabuses move or change health plans? The pharmacist would need to locate every row in the flat file database containing this data for these customers and change the corresponding data—another waste of time and another opportunity for inconsistent data to occur. You might think that a solution to this problem is to add columns to the worksheet, instead of rows, as shown in Figure 1.19.

Figure 1.19: Flat file database with columns for new prescriptions

First Name	Last Name	PrescriptionID	Name	PrescriptionID	Name	PrescriptionID
Shannon	Sabus	18	Rivastigmine tartrate			
Ted	Sabus	24	Acebutolol hydrochloride			
Marisella	Velasquez	33	Quentix	63	Tolbutamide	
Kevin	Wachter	39	Myobuterol			
Adriane	Walters	14	Didanosine	36	Almotriptan	

This is a clever solution as the name, address, phone number, and health plan data do not repeat. If this design were adopted, 4Corners Pharmacy could track all prescriptions in one worksheet instead of creating a new worksheet daily to detail each day's prescriptions. Although this method will work for some time, the table will become too large after months and years of adding new columns. In addition, Excel limits the number of columns in a worksheet to 256, and it is unlikely that someone would scroll 256 columns to find all prescriptions filled for a customer. Moreover, this system would only work if the customer has the same doctor write all his prescriptions, for each row includes a field for prescribing doctor. If Adriane is prescribed migraine medicine from a general practitioner and eye drops from an ophthalmologist, then the pharmacy could not use this table, or would need to modify it to include a prescribing doctor field for each prescription. This field would contain duplicate data for most customers, thereby defeating the purpose of the new design.

What if you attempt to solve these problems by creating two workbooks to store orders? One workbook would store customer data and the other workbook would store prescription data, as shown in Figure 1.20.

Figure 1.20: Storing customer and prescription data in separate workbooks

First Name	Last Name	Telephone	Date of Birth	Gender	Balance	ChildCap	PlanID	HouseID
Anders	Aannestad	(505) 499-6541	9/11/1974	M	$35.00	FALSE	498-1112-A	9
Dusty	Alkier	(435) 693-1212	4/5/1940	M	$0.00	FALSE	A089	10
Rose	Baaz	(505) 477-8989	4/12/1970	F	$0.00	TRUE	OP-87-A087	3
Geoffrey	Baaz	(505) 477-8989	12/31/2001	M	$0.00	TRUE	OP-87-A087	3
Byron	Buescher	(970) 119-3474	6/1/1944	M	$0.00	FALSE	4983	18
Albert	Cardenas	(928) 551-5547	10/14/1965	M	$0.00	TRUE	498-1112-A	4
Sonia	Cardenas	(928) 551-5547	4/12/1968	F	$0.00	TRUE	498-1112-A	4
Daniel	Cardenas	(928) 551-5547	5/12/2002	M	$0.00	TRUE	498-1112-A	4
Jonathan	Cardenas	(928) 551-5547	8/22/2004	M	$0.00	TRUE	498-1112-A	4
Dallas	Coats	(505) 312-6211	10/31/1972	M	$0.00	TRUE	OP-87-A087	21
Dana	Coats	(505) 312-6211	8/16/2002	F	$20.00	TRUE	OP-87-A087	21
Octavia	Coats	(505) 312-6211	6/30/1976	F	$0.00	TRUE	OP-87-A087	21
Jessica	Cortez	(928) 644-1674	8/13/1978	F	$0.00	FALSE	498-1112-A	17
Malena	D'Ambrosio	(435) 444-1233	4/15/1980	F	$0.00	FALSE	2B8973AC	6
Chloe	Feraco	(435) 777-3244	6/1/1946	F	$0.00	FALSE	000H98763-01	23
Gaetano	Feraco	(435) 777-3244	7/4/1946	M	$0.00	FALSE	000H98763-01	23
James	Fernandes	(505) 988-6547	2/18/1977	M	$30.00	FALSE	OP-87-A087	22
Gloria	Fernandes	(505) 988-6547	5/1/1979	F	$0.00	FALSE	OP-87-A087	22
William	Gabel	(970) 223-4156	7/4/1980	M	$0.00	FALSE	4983	8

Customers

PrescriptionID	UPN	Quantity	Unit	Date	ExpireDate	Refills	AutoRefill	RefillsUsed
1	224	1	mg	9/10/2007	6/10/2008	2	TRUE	0
2	828	1	ml	12/15/2007	12/11/2008	3	FALSE	1
3	711	1	mg	6/21/2008	7/30/2008	5	FALSE	0
4	256	1	mg	1/10/2008	10/24/2008	2	TRUE	0
5	398	1	mg	9/10/2007	9/12/2008	3	TRUE	1
6	121	1	mg	4/26/2008	8/30/2008	4	TRUE	0
7	932	1	ml	1/24/2008	9/22/2008	2	TRUE	1
8	523	1	ml	1/29/2008	6/14/2008	3	FALSE	1
9	311	1	ml	9/24/2007	11/25/2008	4	TRUE	0
10	366	1	ml	3/14/2008	7/26/2008	3	TRUE	0
12	444	1	mg	2/24/2007	1/20/2008	4	TRUE	0
13	642	1	mg	4/12/2007	2/11/2008	3	TRUE	0
14	878	1	mg	5/16/2008	12/12/2008	2	FALSE	0
15	852	1	mg	4/11/2008	11/20/2008	3	TRUE	0
16	654	1	mg	1/22/2007	1/8/2008	3	FALSE	0
17	398	1	mg	4/15/2007	6/11/2008	4	TRUE	1
18	972	1	mg	5/5/2007	6/7/2008	4	TRUE	2
19	524	1	mg	4/28/2007	2/20/2008	4	TRUE	1
20	741	1	mg	6/14/2007	1/2/2008	3	TRUE	1

Prescriptions

Customers are listed only once in the Customers workbook, and all prescriptions filled for those customers are listed in the Prescriptions workbook. There is no longer a need to create daily worksheets to track the prescriptions filled each day. Given that Excel has 65,526 rows, these workbooks could last for some time, and it seems that you have solved the problems caused by using a flat file database. However, there is no indication of which customer purchased which prescription. The only way to distinguish customers is by name, and the workbooks do not share any common fields. Although pharmacists might be able to distinguish customers by name for the time being, what would happen if there were two customers named John Smith? You might suggest that you could distinguish the John Smiths by their addresses. But what if the two people named John Smith are father and son, both sharing the same address, telephone number, and doctor? There would be no way to distinguish the customers and no way to know who ordered which prescriptions, as the workbooks lack a unique identifying value for each customer and prescription.

Professional relational database design requires that every table has a primary key field that stores unique values. To satisfy this requirement, a new column named CustID is added to the Customers workbook. In Figure 1.21, Daniel Cardenas has the CustID 9. No one else has this number, ever had this number, or ever will have this number, except for Daniel Cardenas. It uniquely identifies his record in the table.

Figure 1.21: Customer data with CustID column added

CustID values uniquely identify each customer

CustID	First Name	Last Name	Telephone	Date of Birth	Gender	Balance	ChildCap	PlanID	HouseID
18	Anders	Aannestad	(505) 499-6541	9/11/1974	M	$35.00	FALSE	498-1112-A	9
19	Dusty	Alkier	(435) 693-1212	4/5/1940	M	$0.00	FALSE	A089	10
5	Rose	Baaz	(505) 477-8989	4/12/1970	F	$0.00	TRUE	OP-87-A087	3
6	Geoffrey	Baaz	(505) 477-8989	12/31/2001	M	$0.00	TRUE	OP-87-A087	3
27	Byron	Buescher	(970) 119-3474	6/1/1944	M	$0.00	FALSE	4983	18
7	Albert	Cardenas	(928) 551-5547	10/14/1965	M	$0.00	TRUE	498-1112-A	4
8	Sonia	Cardenas	(928) 551-5547	4/12/1968	F	$0.00	TRUE	498-1112-A	4
9	Daniel	Cardenas	(928) 551-5547	5/12/2002	M	$0.00	TRUE	498-1112-A	4
10	Jonathan	Cardenas	(928) 551-5547	8/22/2004	M	$0.00	TRUE	498-1112-A	4
30	Dallas	Coats	(505) 312-6211	10/31/1972	M	$0.00	TRUE	OP-87-A087	21
31	Dana	Coats	(505) 312-6211	8/16/2002	F	$20.00	TRUE	OP-87-A087	21
32	Octavia	Coats	(505) 312-6211	6/30/1976	F	$0.00	TRUE	OP-87-A087	21
26	Jessica	Cortez	(928) 644-1674	8/13/1978	F	$0.00	FALSE	498-1112-A	17
14	Malena	D'Ambrosio	(435) 444-1233	4/15/1980	F	$0.00	FALSE	2B8973AC	6
35	Chloe	Feraco	(435) 777-3244	6/1/1946	F	$0.00	FALSE	000H98763-01	23
36	Gaetano	Feraco	(435) 777-3244	7/4/1946	M	$0.00	FALSE	000H98763-01	23
33	James	Fernandes	(505) 988-6547	2/18/1977	M	$30.00	FALSE	OP-87-A087	22
34	Gloria	Fernandes	(505) 988-6547	5/1/1979	F	$0.00	FALSE	OP-87-A087	22
16	William	Gabel	(970) 223-4156	7/4/1980	M	$0.00	FALSE	4983	8

Assigning a primary key to the Customers workbook reduces the amount of data repetition and the number of errors. For example, a pharmacist could identify Daniel Cardenas and Danny Cardenas by sorting the records by customer ID number—both records have the CustID 9. Don could then remove the duplicate record, which he discovered in his research of existing data at 4Corners Pharmacy, and implement ways to avoid redundancy prior to entering customer data in order to prevent duplicate records from occurring. Thus, assigning a primary key to the Customers workbook helps pharmacists distinguish customer records, but, even so, problems will remain in the flat file database design because the customer and prescription workbooks do not share any common fields.

Although the Prescriptions workbook includes a PrescriptionID (uniquely identifying each prescription) and the Customers workbook includes a CustID (uniquely identifying each customer), there is no way to know which prescription belongs to which customer, or vice versa. A solution is to add the CustID field to the Prescriptions workbook and assign each prescription to its customer. Figure 1.22 shows the Prescriptions workbook with the CustID field added to it. Now it is possible to associate a customer with his prescriptions using the CustID. For example, CustID 9 was prescribed PrescriptionID 16 on 1/22/2007.

Figure 1.22: Prescription data with CustID column added

CustID 9 (Daniel Cardenas)

PrescriptionID	CustID	UPN	Quantity	Unit	Date	ExpireDate	Refills	AutoRefill	RefillsUsed
1	17	224	1	mg	9/10/2007	6/10/2008	2	TRUE	0
2	18	828	1	ml	12/15/2007	12/11/2008	3	FALSE	1
3	23	711	1	mg	6/21/2008	7/30/2008	5	FALSE	0
4	19	256	1	mg	1/10/2008	10/24/2008	2	TRUE	0
5	19	398	1	mg	9/10/2007	9/12/2008	3	TRUE	1
6	34	121	1	mg	4/26/2008	8/30/2008	4	TRUE	0
7	14	932	1	ml	1/24/2008	9/22/2008	2	TRUE	1
8	16	523	1	ml	1/29/2008	6/14/2008	3	FALSE	1
9	21	311	1	ml	9/24/2007	11/25/2008	4	TRUE	0
10	37	366	1	ml	3/14/2008	7/26/2008	3	TRUE	0
12	1	444	1	mg	2/24/2007	1/20/2008	4	TRUE	0
13	38	642	1	mg	4/12/2007	2/11/2008	3	TRUE	0
14	25	878	1	mg	5/16/2008	12/12/2008	2	FALSE	0
15	27	852	1	mg	4/11/2008	11/20/2008	3	TRUE	0
16	9	654	1	mg	1/22/2007	1/8/2008	3	FALSE	0
17	4	398	1	mg	4/15/2007	6/11/2008	4	TRUE	1
18	3	972	1	mg	5/5/2007	6/7/2008	4	TRUE	2
19	28	524	1	mg	4/28/2007	2/20/2008	4	TRUE	1
20	31	741	1	mg	6/14/2007	1/2/2008	3	TRUE	1

PrescriptionID 16

Sorting the Prescriptions worksheet by CustID, rather than by PrescriptionID, reveals that CustID 9 had two prescriptions filled at 4Corners Pharmacy: Prescription IDs 16 and 61, filled on 1/22/2007 and 3/16/2007, respectively, as shown in Figure 1.23. The CustID field is called a common field in this case because it is appears in the Customers and Prescriptions workbooks. A **common field** is a field that appears in two or more tables and contains identical data to relate the tables. The common field is a primary key in the first table. The common field is called a **foreign key** in the second table.

Figure 1.23: Prescription data sorted by CustID column

PrescriptionID	CustID	UPN	Quantity	Unit	Date	ExpireDate	Refills	AutoRefill	RefillsUsed
12	1	444	1	mg	2/24/2007	1/20/2008	4	TRUE	0
24	1	247	1	mg	1/16/2008	12/18/2008	4	TRUE	0
57	1	102	1	mg	5/2/2008	10/30/2008	3	TRUE	0
40	2	524	1	mg	11/22/2007	6/18/2008	2	TRUE	0
18	3	972	1	mg	5/5/2007	6/7/2008	4	TRUE	2
51	3	644	1	ml	1/17/2008	12/1/2008	3	TRUE	0
17	4	398	1	mg	4/15/2007	6/11/2008	4	TRUE	1
52	4	878	1	mg	6/13/2008	12/12/2008	2	TRUE	0
42	5	452	1	mg	6/14/2007	9/1/2008	3	FALSE	0
64	5	224	1	mg	4/29/2008	10/4/2008	3	TRUE	1
43	6	311	1	ml	7/27/2007	1/21/2008	3	FALSE	0
21	7	587	1	mg	8/12/2007	3/15/2008	3	FALSE	1
35	7	102	1	mg	1/3/2008	12/31/2008	3	TRUE	0
41	8	398	1	mg	5/16/2007	7/11/2008	4	TRUE	0
16	9	654	1	mg	1/22/2007	1/8/2008	3	FALSE	0
61	9	828	1	ml	3/16/2007	4/15/2008	4	TRUE	1
44	10	932	1	ml	9/24/2007	4/16/2008	3	TRUE	0
45	11	732	1	mg	8/14/2007	7/31/2008	4	TRUE	0
55	11	642	1	mg	7/8/2007	1/6/2008	4	TRUE	0

CustID 9 (Daniel Cardenas) filled two prescriptions

The solutions to overcoming the limitations of a flat file database are as follows:

- Create separate tables for each entity.
- Assign a primary key to each table, using either a field that already uniquely identifies each record or an AutoNumber field that generates a unique number.
- Include a common field in the related table that identifies which records match.

Figure 1.23 shows that CustID 9 filled two prescriptions with the Prescription IDs 16 and 61. However, there's no easy way to determine the identity of CustID 9. Unless the pharmacist recalls that CustID 9 is Daniel Cardenas, he would have to cross-reference the Customers workbook to identify CustID 9. You cannot overcome this limitation of a flat file database because there is no way to view data from multiple workbooks at the same time. The solution is to create a relational database.

CREATING TABLE RELATIONSHIPS

By now you see the limitations of a flat file database and are familiar with the objects in a relational database and have a good idea of how they interact: tables store the data, queries display subsets of data from the tables in response to a command that asks a question, forms present an interface to enter data into tables and view individual records, and reports produce aesthetically pleasing views and printouts of data pulled from tables or queries. Although a relational database might consist of just one table and several interrelated objects, a database usually consists of at least *two* related tables. You might wonder why you need to create these relationships. You need to create relationships between tables so that you can take advantage of these interrelated objects. Remember that the goal in good database design is to create separate tables for each entity, ensure that each table has a primary key, and use a common field to relate tables. Relational databases overcome the limitations of flat file databases. If you relate two (or more) tables, you can query them as though they are one big table, pulling as much or as little data as you need from each table.

The question then arises: how do the tables know that they are related? They know they are related if they share a common field and you create a join between them. A **join** specifies a relationship between tables and the properties of that relationship. How do you create table relationships? The first step is to decide which type of relationship you need to create: one-to-many, one-to-one, or many-to-many.

One-to-Many Relationships

Most tables have a **one-to-many relationship** (abbreviated as **1:M**), in which one record in the first table matches zero, one, or many records in the related table. For example, one customer can fill zero, one, or many prescriptions at 4Corners Pharmacy; one teacher can have zero, one, or many students; and one realtor can list zero, one, or many homes for sale. In a one-to-many relationship, the **primary table** is on the "one" side of the relationship and the **related table** is on the "many" side of the relationship. For example, at 4Corners Pharmacy, tblCustomer is the "one" table and tblRx is the "many" table because one customer might fill zero, one, or many prescriptions. Figure 1.24 illustrates the one-to-many relationship between customers and prescriptions.

Figure 1.24: One-to-many relationship between customers and prescriptions

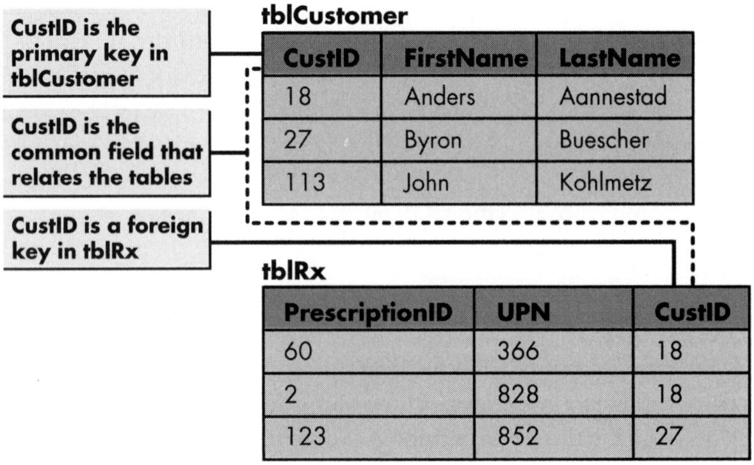

In Figure 1.24, CustID 18 (Anders Aannestad) has two prescriptions with the PrescriptionIDs 60 and 2, CustID 27 (Byron Buescher) has one prescription (PrescriptionID 123), and John Kohlmetz, a new customer at 4Corners Pharmacy, has not yet filled a prescription, and, therefore, has no related records in tblRx.

One-to-One Relationships

A **one-to-one relationship** (abbreviated as **1:1**) exists when each record in one table matches exactly one record in the related table. For example, Paul seeks to expand part of his business by selling large quantities of drugs to hospitals. Each hospital has a physical mailing address to use when delivering prescriptions. However, some hospital clients have their accounts payable operations off-site, with separate billing addresses. To store the physical and billing addresses of the hospitals, Don could create one table to store the name and physical address of each hospital and another table to store the billing address for each hospital. These two tables have a one-to-one relationship in which each hospital has one physical address that matches exactly one billing address and one billing address matches exactly one physical address, as shown in Figure 1.25.

Figure 1.25: One-to-one relationship between physical and billing addresses

tblHospital

HospitalID	Name	Address	City	State	Zip
1	County	123 Main	Chinle	AZ	86547
2	St. John's	555 Maple	Blanding	UT	84512
3	Bellview	2121 Chestnut	Farmington	NM	87499

tblHospitalBilling

HospitalID	BillingAddress	City	State	Zip
1	2727 Jefferson	Chinle	AZ	86544
2	8292 Brady	Blanding	UT	84518
3	3230 Bradford	Farmington	NM	87492

HospitalID 1 has exactly one matching record

One-to-one relationships are used infrequently because it is often possible to combine the data in the related tables into one table. Another example of a one-to-one relationship is using two tables to store employee data—one table might contain basic employee data, such as name and address information, and the other table might contain sensitive information, such as psychiatric evaluations. In this case, the sensitive data isn't stored with address information, but kept in a separate table and matched to the primary employee table via a one-to-one relationship.

Many-to-Many Relationships

A **many-to-many relationship** (abbreviated as **M:N**) occurs when each record in the first table matches many records in the second table, and each record in the second table matches many records in the first table. For example, Maria needs to print a class roster for the instructor of the CPR class so employees can sign it to verify their attendance. At the same time, Maria wants to print a report of all the classes that Richard Conlee has attended in the previous year so that she can evaluate Richard's certification status as a pharmacy technician for his next annual review. To be able to print Richard's certification records, Maria needs the database to have a relationship between tblEmployee and tblClass, but what is the nature of that relationship? The classes will go on perfectly fine if Richard never registers for one of them, and Richard will be fine if he never takes a class, thus there is no one-to-many or one-to-one relationship. Maria needs a way to produce the class roster and Richard's attendance report, but these tables are not related. Don can create a third, intermediary table (named tblEmployeeTraining), called a **junction table**, that contains the primary keys from tblEmployee and tblClass. The tblEmployeeTraining table lets you create two one-to-many relationships between the two primary tables (tblEmployee and tblClass) and the related table (tblEmployeeTraining). The tblEmployeeTraining table exists only as a conduit so that data can be retrieved from the primary tables. Figure 1.26 shows this many-to-many relationship. The result is the ability to query both tables as though they are one big table. Now, Maria can display only those classes that Richard or any other employee has taken, and she can display all employees who have taken a specific class, such as Child/Infant CPR.

Figure 1.26: Many-to-many relationship between employees and classes

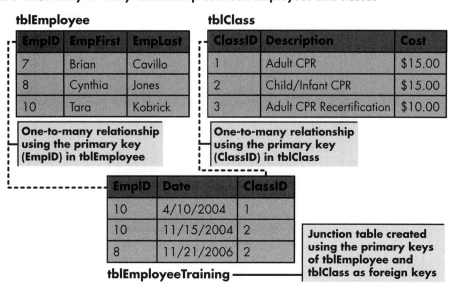

UNDERSTANDING REFERENTIAL INTEGRITY

Now that you know the three types of relationships that you can create in a relational database, it is important that you understand how to create them properly. By now you are familiar with the importance of including a primary key in each table to ensure that the table does not contain duplicate records. The database also prohibits users from failing to enter a value in the primary key field because doing so would risk data duplication. How would you differentiate customers if the CustID field contains no value? When a field does not contain a value, either because that value is unknown or inapplicable, it is called a **null value**. Including a primary key field in a table ensures **entity integrity**, a guarantee that there are no duplicate records in a table, that each record is unique, and that no primary key field contains null values.

Entity integrity specifies that the primary key value must not repeat in the primary table; that is, Tara Kobrick is EmpID 10, and no other employee can have that EmpID. However, her EmpID can repeat in the related tblEmployeeTraining table. Indeed, you would expect to see Tara's EmpID number in tblEmployeeTraining because Tara has taken several training classes. This common field, shared by both the primary and related tables, is called the foreign key in the related tblEmployeeTraining table.

Referential integrity is the rule that if the foreign key in one table matches the primary key in a second table, the values in the foreign key must match the values in the primary key. When the database does not enforce referential integrity, certain problems occur that lead to inaccurate and inconsistent data. For example, in tblDrug the primary key is the UPN field, which is a universal drug identifier for prescription drugs. The record for the drug Phalastat has a UPN value of 366. No other record in tblDrug can have a UPN value of 366 because it is this record's primary key value and duplicate values are not allowed in the primary key field. The pharmacy filled three prescriptions for this drug to customers with CustIDs 18, 22, and 37. The one-to-many relationship between tblCustomer and tblRx relates these records to each other, making it possible to determine which customers filled prescriptions for which drugs.

Suppose that the drug manufacturer for Phalastat changes the drug formulation and issues a new UPN code—367—for it. The pharmacy would need to update its database to use the new code. This UPN doesn't exist in tblDrug, so it would be an allowable primary key value because it meets the requirement of being unique. At first, it might seem like this change is possible.

However, if the pharmacy changes Phalastat's UPN value from 366 to 367, then there no longer exists a drug in the database with the UPN value 366. Yet Customers 18, 22, and 37 were prescribed drug 366 and remain in the database with that designation. Were they to seek a refill, or worse yet—become allergic to drug 366—there would be no way to identify which drug they were prescribed. The prescription records would become **orphaned** as the UPN primary key was changed in the primary table, but the corresponding foreign keys in the related table were not. There would no longer be a match between the primary key in the primary table and the foreign keys in the related table, resulting in orphaned records. Enforcing referential integrity prevents this data loss. Figure 1.27 illustrates this referential integrity error.

Figure 1.27: Referential integrity errors

tblDrug

UPN	Name
367	Phalastat
566	Quentix
972	Rivastigmine tartrate

UPN is changed from 366 to 367 in tblDrug

tblRx

PrescriptionID	UPN	CustID
60	366	18
50	366	22
49	366	22
10	366	37

UPN is NOT changed in tblRx, orphaning four records

tblCustomer

CustID	CustFirst	CustLast
18	Anders	Aannestad
22	Josefina	Hernandez
37	Isabel	Lopez

Customers prescribed the drug with UPN 366 cannot receive refills as there no longer is a drug with UPN 366

Another reason to enforce referential integrity is to prevent orphaned related records if the record in the primary table is deleted. For example, identity theft is discovered on occasion at 4Corners Pharmacy; in two cases, a customer used fake identification to obtain restricted prescription drugs. When Paul is informed of such occurrences—usually by the health plan that refuses to pay for such charges—he is obligated to turn over the prescription data to the FBI. After doing so, he no longer wants to retain this data in his database as he cannot collect on the accounts and does not want to keep the record of fictitious customers. Consequently, he is inclined to delete the customer's name, address, and entire record from the database. If he does so, however, the customer's corresponding prescriptions will remain in the database. These prescriptions will become orphaned, appear to belong to no one, and will confuse auditors trying to reconcile the pharmacy's accounts receivable.

A third reason to enforce referential integrity is to make it impossible to add records to a related table that does not have matching records in the primary table. An inexperienced or hurried technician might add prescriptions to tblRx for a new customer that she did not first enter into tblCustomer, resulting in orphaned records in tblRx because it would contain prescriptions that would not belong to a customer.

The results of all three scenarios lead to inconsistent data, which relational databases should be designed to avoid. By enforcing referential integrity, however, you can prohibit changing the primary key of the records in the primary table if matching records exist in the related table, deleting records in the primary table if matching records exist in the related table, and adding records to the related table if no matching record exists in the primary table.

Overriding Referential Integrity

Referential integrity is the rule that makes it possible for a DBMS to prevent records from being orphaned if a user attempts to change a primary key or delete a record in a table that has matching records in another table. But there are times when you might want to override referential integrity to intentionally change a primary key or delete a parent record. Some DBMSs let you change the way that the DBMS handles these types of changes so that changes to the primary key value in a record that has matching records in a related table are also made to the foreign key in the matching records. For example, if a pharmacy technician changes the UPN from 366 to 367 in tblDrug, then records in tblRx would be orphaned because the drug with the UPN 366 no longer exists.

In some DBMSs, including Access, you can choose the option to **cascade updates**, which permits a user to change a primary key value so that the DBMS automatically updates the appropriate foreign key values in the related table. In this case, when the pharmacy changes the UPN value of 366 to 367, the records for the customers with CustIDs 18, 22, and 37 will still indicate that they were prescribed the drug because the DBMS will update the UPN values in the records for these customers by changing it from 366 to 367. Figure 1.28 shows how cascade updates works.

Figure 1.28: Cascade updates

tblDrug

UPN	Name
367	Phalastat
566	Quentix
972	Rivastigmine tartrate

UPN is changed from 366 to 367 in tblDrug

tblRx

PrescriptionID	UPN	CustID
60	367	18
50	367	22
49	367	22
10	367	37

Cascade updates option changes the UPN for matching records in tblRx from 366 to 367

What if the drug manufacturer for the drug Phalastat discontinues it because a risk of heart attack has been identified? In this case, the pharmacy might want to delete the drug from the database to discontinue it. When the pharmacy tries to delete the record from tblDrug with the UPN 366, the DBMS will not permit the deletion because there are related records in tblRx. However, if the DBMS has the **cascade deletes** option enabled, the DBMS will permit the deletion of the record from tblDrug. In addition, the DBMS also deletes the related records from tblRx. Before enabling the cascade deletes option, it is a good idea to verify that you really want to delete all data for this drug and all related data from the database. A better method might be to leave the drug in the database so the customer's prescription records aren't deleted with it. If you delete Phalastat from the database, the database will show that CustIDs 18, 22, and 37 *never* received it. Figure 1.29 shows how the cascade deletes option works.

Figure 1.29: Cascade deletes

tblDrug

UPN	Name
~~366~~	~~Phalastat~~
566	Quentix
972	Rivastigmine tartrate

The record for UPN 366 is
deleted from tblDrug

tblRx

PrescriptionID	UPN	CustID
~~60~~	~~366~~	~~18~~
~~50~~	~~366~~	~~22~~
~~49~~	~~366~~	~~22~~
~~10~~	~~366~~	~~37~~

Cascade deletes option deletes
all matching records in tblRx

You will learn more about creating relationships and referential integrity in Chapter 2.

Steps To Success: Level 2

You have learned a great deal about database objects, concepts, and table relationships, all requisite knowledge for planning a relational database. Now it is time to consider which database objects are required for the 4Corners Pharmacy database and how to relate the tables.

On a piece of paper, complete the following:

1. Although the 4Corners Pharmacy database might ultimately include additional tables, it will include tables for the following entities: customers, prescriptions, drugs, doctors, clinics, employees, job titles, and training classes. Given these tables, describe five queries, two forms, and three reports that managers at the pharmacy might create and describe how they would use them in the pharmacy's day-to-day operations.

2. What are some examples of flat file databases that you have used? How would a relational database simplify the work you needed to complete?

3. What primary keys might you assign to tables that store data about the following entities: customers, prescriptions, drugs, doctors, clinics, employees, job titles, and training classes? Describe why and how you chose the primary key for each table.

4. Suppose that tblDoctor includes the fields DoctorID, DoctorFirst, DoctorLast, and Phone; and tblClinic includes the fields ClinicID, ClinicName, Address, City, State, Zip, and Phone. Is there a common field? Is there a foreign key? What kind of relationship might you create between these two tables?

5. Paul wants to monitor refills. He wants to use the UPN field to query which drugs are refilled most often. (For example, Paul wants to know how many times the drug Phalastat, with UPN 366, was refilled and by whom.) At the same time, he needs to determine which employees filled a given prescription. (For example, customer

Marvin Gattis was prescribed Hyometadol on 7/7/2007, his doctor authorized five refills, and Mr. Gattis has refilled this prescription three times.) Suppose that tblRx lists every prescription that every customer has filled at 4Corners Pharmacy and contains the following fields: PrescriptionID, UPN, Quantity, Date, Refills, Instructions, CustID, and DoctorID. Also suppose that tblEmployee lists every employee working at 4Corners Pharmacy and contains the following fields: EmpID, FirstName, LastName, DOB, SSN, Address, City, State, and Zip. What would you do to create a relationship between these two tables so that Paul can query them to answer his questions? Identify the primary and foreign keys necessary to create this relationship. Would you use the cascade updates and cascade deletes options? Why or why not?

LEVEL 3

IDENTIFYING AND ELIMINATING DATABASE ANOMALIES BY NORMALIZING DATA

NORMALIZING THE TABLES IN THE DATABASE

By now you are familiar with database concepts and how to create tables and relationships between them. You have learned that good database design seeks to avoid data redundancy and inconsistent data. Now you will learn the specific rules for ensuring a good database design using a process called **normalization**. Figure 1.30 details the third step of the database design process and illustrates how normalization fits into the plan.

Figure 1.30: Database design process: normalizing the data

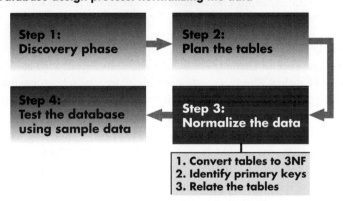

Normalization has three goals. First, normalization reduces the space required to store data by eliminating duplicate data in the database (with the exception of duplicate data in the foreign key fields). Second, normalization reduces inconsistent data in the database by storing data only once, thereby reducing the chance of typographical, spelling, and transposition errors and other inconsistent data that you discovered in the flat file databases you viewed in Level 2. Finally, normalization reduces the chance of deletion, update, and insertion anomalies. The data shown in Figure 1.31 is not normalized (also called **unnormalized data**) and exhibits all three anomalies.

Figure 1.31: Data with anomalies

Deleting Connie Nader's record creates two deletion anomalies because she is the only cashier and the only employee enrolled in the Yoga class; deleting her record also deletes the job title and class information

Adding a new job title or class creates an insertion anomaly because there must first be an employee with that title or taking the class, which is not possible until you add the title or class

EmpID	EmpFirst	EmpLast	SSN	Title	Description	DateAttended
15	Connie	Nader	705-19-1497	Cashier	Yoga	1/23/2007
21	Dora	Langston	718-78-4111	Technician	Nutritional Supplements	9/1/2007
21	Dora	Langston	718-78-4111	Technician	First Aid	6/12/2006
3	Virginia	Sanchez	921-23-3333	Technician	Defibrillator Use	1/25/2005
17	Rachel	Thompson	928-98-4165	Technician	Defibrillator Use	5/2/2004
13	Paul	Ferrino	953-23-3639	Owner	Child/Infant CPR Recertification	6/15/2008
27	Vincent	Ferrino	998-01-5466	Pharmacist	Child/Infant CPR Recertification	5/21/2008
14	Richard	Conlee	968-96-3214	Technician	Child/Infant CPR Recertification	11/15/2006
2	Marco	Farello	885-00-7777	Technician	Child/Infant CPR Recertification	1/15/2006
3	Virginia	Sanchez	921-23-3333	Technician	Child/Infant CPR Recertification	5/15/2006
8	Cynthia	Jones	000-23-3655	Pharmacist	Child/Infant CPR	11/21/2006
2	Marco	Farello	885-00-7777	Technician	Child/Infant CPR	1/30/2004
10	Tara	Kobrick	728-12-3465	Technician	Child/Infant CPR	11/15/2004
21	Dora	Langston	718-78-4111	Technician	Child/Infant CPR	6/9/2004
13	Paul	Ferrino	953-23-3639	Owner	Adult CPR Recertification	2/5/2007
27	Vincent	Ferrino	998-01-5466	Pharmacist	Adult CPR Recertification	2/2/2005
27	Vincent	Ferrino	998-01-5466	Pharmacist	Adult CPR Recertification	4/2/2007
27	Vincent	Ferrino	998-01-5466	Pharmacist	Adult CPR Recertification	4/5/2008
12	Louis	Moreno	666-16-7892	Pharmacist	Adult CPR Recertification	4/1/2006

Changing the Child/Infant CPR class description in the record for Cynthia Jones creates an update anomaly in three other records

A **deletion anomaly** occurs when a user deletes data from a database and unintentionally deletes the only occurrence of that data in the database. In Figure 1.31, Connie Nader is the only cashier at 4Corners Pharmacy and the only employee who took the Yoga class. Deleting her record also deletes the Cashier title and the Yoga class from the database, making it appear as though her title and the Yoga class never existed. An **update anomaly** occurs when, due to redundant data in a database, a user fails to update some records or updates records erroneously. For example, in Figure 1.31, changing the description for the course titled "Child/Infant CPR" in the record for Cynthia Jones leaves inconsistent data in the other records for employees who took this class and creates corrupted data. An **insertion anomaly** occurs when a user cannot add data to a database unless it is preceded by the entry of other data. In Figure 1.31, an insertion anomaly occurs if you try to add a new class. You cannot add a class unless an employee has registered for it, but how is this possible for a new class? As you can see, it is important to avoid creating anomalies in a database; normalization seeks to avoid these problems.

The goal of normalization is to split tables into smaller related tables to avoid creating anomalies. To understand normalization, you must first understand **functional dependency**, because it will help you analyze fields within tables and help you decide if they need to be split into smaller tables. A column in a table is considered functionally dependent on another column if each value in the second column is associated with exactly one value in the first column. Given this definition and after viewing Figure 1.31, it appears that the SSN field is functionally dependent on the EmpID field. Dora Langston's Social Security number (718-78-4111) is associated with exactly one EmpID, 21. It would appear that the Title field, however, is not functionally dependent on the EmpID field because there are multiple records that are associated with the title Technician, for example. Consequently, the Title field becomes a prime candidate for its own table. Your goal should be to use your knowledge of functional dependency to test the columns in the tables that you create, identify columns that are not functionally dependent, and consider moving those columns to their own tables.

Before doing this, however, you must be aware of a partial dependency. In tables in which more than one field is needed to create a primary key, a **partial dependency** occurs when a field is dependent on only part of the primary key. When a primary key uses two or more fields to create unique records in a table, it is called a **composite primary key** (or a **composite key**). Figure 1.32 shows a conceptual diagram of the fields in a proposed tblClassesAttended which indicates which employee took which classes on which dates.

Figure 1.32: tblClassesAttended table design

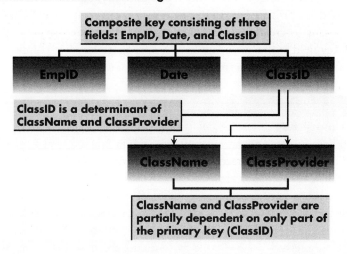

The EmpID field cannot be the table's primary key because an employee can take many classes and, therefore, would have many records in the table. The Date field cannot be the table's primary key because it will contain repeating data if more than one class is taught on the same date or if more than one employee attends the same class on the same date— both of which are likely occurrences. The ClassID field cannot be the table's primary key because it will contain repeating data if more than one employee attends the same class.

Neither the ClassName nor ClassProvider fields can be the table's primary key because they also contain repeating data. Thus, you must create a composite key to create unique values for the records in this table. In some cases a composite key consists of two fields, but this table requires the combination of three fields—EmpID, Date, and ClassID—to create unique records in the table.

Notice the arrows pointing from ClassID to the ClassName and ClassProvider fields. This structure indicates that ClassID is a determinant of the other two fields. A **determinant** is a field or collection of fields whose value determines the value in another field. This determinant relationship between fields is the inverse of dependency, as ClassName and ClassProvider are dependent on ClassID. However, this relationship exhibits a partial dependency, for the two fields are dependent on only part of the composite key. Your goal should be to rid your tables of partial dependencies to avoid anomalies. The solution, again, is to create a separate tblClass table and then create a relationship between tblClass and tblClassesAttended using the common field, ClassID.

Other kinds of keys exist, as well. A **natural key** is a primary key that details an obvious and innate trait of a record. For example, the UPN field in tblDrug is a unique value for each drug sold, and is, therefore, a natural key for the table. Other examples of natural keys include Social Security numbers for people and International Standard Book Numbers (ISBNs) for books. When a natural key exists, it is easy to identify and use as a primary key.

Sometimes, however, a table does not contain a natural key, and no field or combination of fields can be used as a primary key. In these cases, you can create an **artificial key**, a field whose sole purpose is to create a primary key. Artificial keys are usually visible to users. A third type of key field is the surrogate key. A **surrogate key** is a computer-generated primary key that is usually invisible to users.

Best Practice

Choosing a Primary Key

After completing data normalization, you must then assign primary keys to your tables. This is easy to do if a natural key exists, such as a SSN, PIN, or ISBN in your table. If it does not, which field should be the primary key: an artificial key or a composite key? There is no definitive answer, but a best practice is to consider possible negative consequences of creating a composite key. If the composite key comprises more than two fields, as was shown in tblClassesAttended in Figure 1.32, you might want to choose an artificial key, because three fields will be consumed in every table that includes the three-field composite key as a foreign key, wasting significant database space. In addition, primary keys cannot be null. This might prove frustrating if you are trying to enter a record, but lack the values to enter in one or more of the three fields that the composite key comprises. You will not be able to enter a record unless you have all three fields. Consequently, think twice before creating composite keys and consider using artificial keys instead.

Having a good grasp of the fundamental concepts of how fields interact as determinants, dependents, and in composite primary keys is essential to combating anomalies in relational table designs. After you understand these concepts, you are prepared to normalize the tables. Normalization requires a series of steps, each one building on the previous. These steps are called normal forms, or first, second, and third normal forms, sometimes abbreviated as 1NF, 2NF, and 3NF. Three other increasingly more sophisticated normal forms exist, but most database developers agree that they are rarely necessary and might lead to diminished functionality in a database because they make it run slower.

First Normal Form

When a field contains more than one value, it is called a **repeating group**. A table is in **first normal form (1NF)** if it does not contain any repeating groups. Table 1.6 shows a table that violates 1NF rules because the Description field contains more than one value in some cases, creating unnormalized data. Marco Farello, for instance, has taken five classes, all of which reside in the Description field. The repeating groups in this table would make it difficult to filter or query this table to determine which employees have taken which classes.

Table 1.6: Unnormalized data contains repeating groups

EmpID	EmpFirst	EmpLast	SSN	Description	DateAttended	Provider
14	Richard	Conlee	968-96-3214	Child/Infant CPR Recertification	11/15/2006	Red Cross
2	Marco	Farello	885-00-7777	Child/Infant CPR Child/Infant CPR Recertification Adult CPR Recertification	1/30/2004 1/15/2006 2/1/2006	Red Cross Red Cross Red Cross
13	Paul	Ferrino	953-23-3639	Adult CPR Recertification Child/Infant CPR Recertification	2/5/2007 6/15/2008	Red Cross Red Cross
27	Vincent	Ferrino	998-01-5466	Adult CPR Recertification Adult CPR Recertification Adult CPR Recertification Child/Infant CPR Recertification	2/2/2005 4/2/2007 4/5/2008 5/21/2008	Red Cross Red Cross Red Cross Red Cross
1	Joan	Gabel	901-88-3636	Adult CPR	2/6/2004	Red Cross
8	Cynthia	Jones	000-23-3655	Child/Infant CPR	11/21/2006	Red Cross

A seemingly good solution might be to remove the repeating groups and instead create new rows for each class attended, as shown in Table 1.7.

Table 1.7: Unnormalized data contains repeating rows

EmpID	EmpFirst	EmpLast	SSN	Class Description	Date Attended	Provider
14	Richard	Conlee	968-96-3214	Child/Infant CPR Recertification	11/15/2006	Red Cross
2	Marco	Farello	885-00-7777	Child/Infant CPR	1/30/2004	Red Cross
2	Marco	Farello	885-00-7777	Child/Infant CPR Recertification	1/15/2006	Red Cross
2	Marco	Farello	885-00-7777	Adult CPR Recertification	2/1/2006	Red Cross
13	Paul	Ferrino	953-23-3639	Adult CPR Recertification	2/5/2007	Red Cross
13	Paul	Ferrino	953-23-3639	Child/Infant CPR Recertification	6/15/2008	Red Cross
27	Vincent	Ferrino	998-01-5466	Adult CPR Recertification	2/2/2005	Red Cross
27	Vincent	Ferrino	998-01-5466	Adult CPR Recertification	4/2/2007	Red Cross
27	Vincent	Ferrino	998-01-5466	Adult CPR Recertification	4/5/2008	Red Cross
27	Vincent	Ferrino	998-01-5466	Child/Infant CPR Recertification	5/21/2008	Red Cross
1	Joan	Gabel	901-88-3636	Adult CPR	2/6/2004	Red Cross
8	Cynthia	Jones	000-23-3655	Child/Infant CPR	11/21/2006	Red Cross

You already know, however, that repeating data by adding records in this fashion is called data redundancy and is inefficient, wastes space, and can lead to errors. Marco Farello now has three records, all of which repeat his EmpID, EmpFirst, EmpLast, and SSN. Table 1.7 violates normalization rules because of this repetition. What can be done, then, to make this table conform to 1NF? The answer is to create two tables: one for employees and one for classes. Examples of what these tables might look like are shown in Tables 1.8 and 1.9.

Table 1.8: Employee data in 1NF

EmpID	EmpFirst	EmpLast	SSN
1	Joan	Gabel	901-88-3636
2	Marco	Farello	885-00-7777
3	Virginia	Sanchez	921-23-3333
8	Cynthia	Jones	000-23-3655
10	Tara	Kobrick	728-12-3465

Table 1.8: Employee data in 1NF (cont.)

EmpID	EmpFirst	EmpLast	SSN
12	Louis	Moreno	666-16-7892
13	Paul	Ferrino	953-23-3639
14	Richard	Conlee	968-96-3214
15	Connie	Nader	705-19-1497
17	Rachel	Thompson	928-98-4165
19	Amy	Urquiza	728-65-6941
21	Dora	Langston	718-78-4111
27	Vincent	Ferrino	998-01-5466

Table 1.9: Class data in 1NF

ClassID	Description	EmpID	DateAttended	Provider
1	Adult CPR	1	2/6/2004	Red Cross
1	Adult CRP	10	4/10/2004	Red Cross
1	Adult CPR	17	3/17/2004	Red Cross
1	Adult CPR	19	6/20/2004	Red Cross
2	Child/Infant CPR	2	1/30/2004	Red Cross
2	Child/Infant CPR	8	11/21/2006	Red Cross
2	Child/Infant CPR	10	11/15/2004	Red Cross
2	Child/Infant CPR	21	6/9/2004	Red Cross
3	Adult CPR Recertification	2	2/1/2006	Red Cross
3	Adult CPR Recertification	3	6/1/2007	Red Cross
3	Adult CPR Recertification	3	6/29/2008	Red Cross
3	Adult CPR Recertification	10	4/12/2005	Red Cross
3	Adult CPR Recertification	12	4/1/2006	Red Cross
3	Adult CPR Recertification	13	2/5/2007	Red Cross
3	Adult CPR Recertification	17	3/16/2005	Red Cross
3	Adult CPR Recertification	19	6/21/2005	Red Cross
3	Adult CPR Recertification	19	3/10/2006	Red Cross
3	Adult CPR Recertification	21	6/15/2006	Red Cross
3	Adult CPR Recertification	21	3/5/2007	Red Cross

Table 1.9: Class data in 1NF (cont.)

ClassID	Description	EmpID	DateAttended	Provider
3	Adult CPR Recertification	27	2/2/2005	Red Cross
3	Adult CPR Recertification	27	4/2/2007	Red Cross
3	Adult CPR Recertification	27	4/5/2008	Red Cross
4	First Aid	21	6/12/2006	Red Cross
5	Defibrillator Use	3	1/25/2005	Johnston Health Systems
5	Defibrillator Use	17	5/2/2004	Johnston Health Systems
6	Child/Infant CPR Recertification	2	1/15/2006	Red Cross
6	Child/Infant CPR Recertification	3	5/15/2006	Red Cross
6	Child/Infant CPR Recertification	13	6/15/2008	Red Cross
6	Child/Infant CPR Recertification	14	11/15/2006	Red Cross
6	Child/Infant CPR Recertification	27	5/21/2008	Red Cross
7	Nutritional Supplements	21	9/1/2007	Food Co-op
8	Yoga	15	1/23/2007	Yoga Center

The employee training class data now satisfies the requirements for 1NF. This was accomplished by creating two tables—a primary Employee table and a related Class table. These tables share a common field, EmpID, which creates a relationship between them.

Second Normal Form

To ensure that a table is in **second normal form (2NF)**, the table must be in 1NF and must not contain any partial dependencies on the composite primary key. Tables that are in 1NF and contain a primary key with only one field are automatically in 2NF because no other field in the table can be dependent on only a portion of the primary key. The data shown in Table 1.9 violates 2NF rules because the description of the class is dependent not just on the ClassID, but also on the EmpID and DateAttended; the combination of ClassID, EmpID, and DateAttended is the table's composite primary key. If left as is, this table might include inconsistent data, such as the misspelling of "Adult CRP" in the second record. To convert this table to 2NF, it is necessary to break it into two tables: one table listing the classes offered and another table listing the classes taken. Tables 1.10 and 1.11 show these changes.

Table 1.10: ClassesOffered table in 2NF

ClassID	Description	Provider
1	Adult CPR	Red Cross
2	Child/Infant CPR	Red Cross
3	Adult CPR Recertification	Red Cross
4	First Aid	Red Cross
5	Defibrillator Use	Johnston Health Systems
6	Child/Infant CPR Recertification	Red Cross
7	Nutritional Supplements	Food Co-op
8	Yoga	Yoga Center

Table 1.11: ClassesTaken table in 2NF

ClassID	EmpID	Date Attended
1	1	2/6/2004
1	10	4/10/2004
1	17	3/17/2004
1	19	6/20/2004
2	2	1/30/2004
2	8	11/21/2006
2	10	11/15/2004
2	21	6/9/2004
3	2	2/1/2006
3	3	6/1/2007
3	3	6/29/2008
3	10	4/12/2005
3	12	4/1/2006
3	13	2/5/2007
3	17	3/16/2005
3	19	6/21/2005
3	19	3/10/2006
3	21	6/15/2006
3	21	3/5/2007

Table 1.11: ClassesTaken table in 2NF (cont.)

ClassID	EmpID	Date Attended
3	27	2/2/2005
3	27	4/2/2007
3	27	4/5/2008
4	21	6/12/2006
5	3	1/25/2005
5	17	5/2/2004
6	2	1/15/2006
6	3	5/15/2006
6	13	6/15/2008
6	14	11/15/2006
6	27	5/21/2008
7	21	9/1/2007
8	15	1/23/2007

The data shown in Tables 1.10 and 1.11 is in 2NF—notice that the ClassesTaken table is a junction table that creates a many-to-many relationship between the ClassesOffered table (Table 1.10) and the Employee table (Table 1.8). As a result, you can query these tables as though they are one big table and do so from two perspectives. You can list all the classes taken by a single employee, or produce a report for a single class, listing all those employees who attended a class on a given day.

Third Normal Form

For a table to be in **third normal form (3NF)**, it must be in 2NF and the only determinants it contains must be candidate keys. A **candidate key** is a field or collection of fields that could function as the primary key, but was not chosen to do so. Table 1.10 is in 2NF, but one problem remains. ClassID is the primary key, but Description and Provider are **nonkey fields**, fields that are not part of the primary key. A **transitive dependency** occurs between two nonkey fields that are both dependent on a third field; tables in 3NF should not have transitive dependencies. The Provider field gives more information about the Description field, so you might think that it is important to keep this field in this table. You might also think that Table 1.10 is pretty small as it is and appears to cause little harm other than having the "Red Cross" provider repeating a few times. The truth is, however, that this table is in jeopardy of a deletion anomaly. The Provider is at the mercy, if you will, of the Class to which it is assigned. If you delete ClassID 5 (Defibrillator Use) from this table, you would also delete Johnston Health Systems from the database. Johnston Health Systems might offer other classes that employees might attend in the future, but if the single present occurrence of the Defibrillator Use class is removed from this database, Johnston Health Systems is also removed. Consequently, to put the data in 3NF, it is necessary to break it, once again, into two smaller tables. The result, as shown in Tables 1.12 and 1.13, is two tables: one solely for class titles and one solely for providers.

Table 1.12: ClassesOffered table in 3NF

ClassID	Description	ProviderID
1	Adult CPR	3
2	Child/Infant CPR	3
3	Adult CPR Recertification	3
4	First Aid	3
5	Defibrillator Use	2
6	Child/Infant CPR Recertification	3
7	Nutritional Supplements	1
8	Yoga	4

Table 1.13: Provider table in 3NF

ProviderID	Provider
1	Food Co-op
2	Johnston Health Systems
3	Red Cross
4	Yoga Center

You can see that data normalization requires creating additional tables so that normalization rules are not violated.

Best Practice

Testing the Database Using Sample Data
After normalizing your data and assigning primary keys, you might think that your work is done in the database design process. Figure 1.33 shows that there is one major step left: testing the database using sample data.

Figure 1.33: Database design process: testing the database

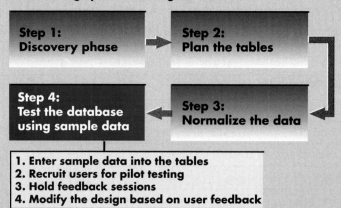

1. Enter sample data into the tables
2. Recruit users for pilot testing
3. Hold feedback sessions
4. Modify the design based on user feedback

You should, of course, test it yourself, but as Figure 1.33 suggests, the best practice to follow is to recruit pilot testers, hold feedback sessions, modify the design and functionality using the recommendations given during feedback sessions, and *then* unveil the finished database. Getting criticism from third parties is invaluable as the more eyes and hands that scrutinize and investigate your database, the better it will perform after modifications made from the pilot testers.

Steps To Success: Level 3

After learning how Don will normalize the data in the 4Corners Pharmacy database, you have gained a deeper understanding of how to pare down tables so that anomalies do not occur. This process requires ensuring that groups do not repeat in columns, such as avoiding a Dependents field that stores the names of two people. Breaking the data into two tables—HeadOfHousehold and Dependent—satisfies the requirement for 1NF. After doing that, however, it is important to analyze the resultant tables for violations of 2NF. Does data repeat within the same column? For example, in the Dependent table, is the same doctor listed multiple times? Breaking the data into two tables—Dependent and Doctor—satisfies the requirement for 2NF. Converting tables to 3NF is also important and requires diligence to make sure that every column is dependent on the primary key and not on another column.

On a piece of paper, complete the following:

1. Figure 1.34 contains anomalies or potential anomalies.

Figure 1.34: Flat file database with anomalies

PrescriptionID	RefillDate	UPN	Name	CustID	FirstName	LastName	EmpID	EmpFirst	EmpLast	Title
1	12/11/2007	224	Avatocin	17	Maria	Gabel	2	Marco	Farello	Technician
2	4/14/2008	828	Myobuterol	18	Anders	Aannestad	2	Marco	Farello	Technician
2	6/1/2008	828	Myobuterol	18	Anders	Aannestad	8	Cynthia	Jones	Pharmacist
3	7/1/2008	711	Nvalax	23	Jennifer	Ramsey	17	Rachel	Thompson	Technician
4	6/21/2008	256	Dseurton	19	Dusty	Alkier	8	Cynthia	Jones	Pharmacist
5	1/12/2008	398	Clonazepam	19	Dusty	Alkier	2	Marco	Farello	Technician
5	3/11/2008	398	Clonazepam	19	Dusty	Alkier	17	Rachel	Thompson	Technician
6	6/3/2008	121	Tolbutamide	34	Gloria	Fernandes	3	Virginia	Sanchez	Technician
6	8/25/2008	121	Tolbutamide	34	Gloria	Fernandes	17	Rachel	Thompson	Technician
7	5/14/2008	932	Tvalaxec	14	Malena	D'Ambrosio	8	Cynthia	Jones	Pharmacist
8	3/18/2008	523	Xeroflarol	16	William	Gabel	12	Louis	Moreno	Pharmacist
8	6/1/2008	523	Xeroflarol	16	William	Gabel	12	Louis	Moreno	Pharmacist
9	4/14/2008	311	Dyotex	21	Cesar	Lopez	3	Virginia	Sanchez	Technician
9	10/11/2008	311	Dyotex	21	Cesar	Lopez	2	Marco	Farello	Technician
10	3/11/2008	366	Phalastat	37	Isabel	Lopez	2	Marco	Farello	Technician
10	6/21/2008	366	Phalastat	37	Isabel	Lopez	14	Richard	Conlee	Technician
13	11/1/2007	642	Montelukast sodium	38	Oksana	Lapshina	3	Virginia	Sanchez	Technician
13	1/3/2008	642	Montelukast sodium	38	Oksana	Lapshina	12	Louis	Moreno	Pharmacist
14	9/29/2007	878	Didanosine	25	Adriane	Walters	14	Richard	Conlee	Technician
15	6/10/2007	852	Oxaprozin	27	Byron	Buescher	3	Virginia	Sanchez	Technician
16	4/22/2007	654	Warfarin Sodium	9	Daniel	Cardenas	8	Cynthia	Jones	Pharmacist
16	11/13/2007	654	Warfarin Sodium	9	Daniel	Cardenas	8	Cynthia	Jones	Pharmacist
17	11/16/2007	398	Clonazepam	4	Steven	Nguyen	17	Rachel	Thompson	Technician
17	2/14/2008	398	Clonazepam	4	Steven	Nguyen	14	Richard	Conlee	Technician

Ultimately, Paul wants to query this table to answer the following questions:

a. What prescriptions did Marco Farello fill?

b. Which employees processed refills for Anders Aannestad?

c. Which employees processed refills for PrescriptionID 17?

2. Create as many tables as necessary to normalize this data to 3NF.

CHAPTER SUMMARY

This chapter presented some of the fundamental concepts you need to understand when planning an Access database. In Level 1, you learned that the discovery phase of database planning takes a great deal of work and requires researching existing sources of data within an organization, researching sources of missing data, and interviewing users about desired output. The next step is to assimilate your findings by grouping fields into tables, assigning data types to fields, choosing appropriate field sizes, and assigning standardized names to the tables.

Level 2 covered database objects and concepts. You learned that there are seven types of objects in an Access database, four of which—tables, queries, forms, and reports—were discussed at length. Tables hold data, queries display subsets of data in response to a question about the data, forms provide an electronic interface for entering data into tables while at the same time allowing you to view records in the tables, and reports allow you to organize data in a custom or standard format for on-screen display or in a printout. After learning about database objects, you learned about how a flat file database leads to inconsistent and redundant data; the importance of creating primary keys, foreign keys, and common fields in tables; and the process of creating relationships between tables in a relational database, including one-to-many, one-to-one, and many-to-many. You also learned about referential integrity and how it works to prevent deletion, update, and insertion anomalies in the database.

In Level 3, you studied the process of normalizing data, which requires putting tables in first normal form by removing repeating groups, then putting tables in second normal form by eliminating partial dependencies, and then putting tables in third normal form by eliminating transitive dependencies. You also learned that is important to assign primary keys and how to distinguish between natural, artificial, and surrogate keys. Finally, you learned that testing a database before implementation and seeking feedback from a pilot group is the best way to make modifications to a database before implementing the final version.

CONCEPTUAL REVIEW

1. Name and describe the four steps in the database design process.

2. What are data duplication and data redundancy, and how do you work to remove these problems from a database?

3. What is scope creep?

4. What are some of the considerations you must evaluate about the data before assigning it a field data type and size?

5. What is the difference between the Text and Memo data types, and how would you use each one?

6. What is the difference between the Number and Currency data types, and how would you use each one?

7. Should you store calculated fields in a database? Why or why not? If you should not, what data can you store in place of a calculated field?

8. Why and when should you use the Lookup Wizard data type? Give two specific examples not described in the book.

9. What are three general rules about naming objects in a database?

10. What are the four main database objects, and how is each one used?

11. What are the three types of queries you can use, and what does each one accomplish?

12. What are three limitations associated with using flat file databases for data management?

13. What is a primary key? What is a foreign key? How do these keys work together in a database?

14. Which of the following pairs of entities would require a one-to-one, one-to-many, and many-to-many relationship? Describe your answer.

    a.   Customers and orders

    b.   States and state capitals

    c.   College students and classes

15. What is entity integrity? What is referential integrity? Should you enforce referential integrity in a database all the time? Why or why not?

16. Name and describe the three types of anomalies that can occur in a database.

17. What is the goal of normalization? Name and describe the three normal forms.

18. What is a determinant? A partial dependency? A transitive dependency?

CASE PROBLEMS

Case 1 – Creating the Database Design for NHD Development Group Inc.

NHD Development Group Inc. builds, leases, and manages shopping centers, convenience stores, and other ventures throughout the country. Last year, NHD purchased several antique malls in the southeastern United States. The antique malls have shown potential for a good financial return over time. Tim Richards is the chief information officer for NHD. Tim's responsibility is to provide information to the board of directors so it can make strategic decisions about future development ventures.

Information Systems

Most of the antique malls do their bookkeeping on paper, and Tim is concerned that the data he needs from the antique malls will not be easy to obtain. Because of the paper-based systems, Tim expects it to be difficult to obtain items such as total sales, total commissions, dealer sales, and staff expenses such as salaries. Tim believes that by creating a specialized database for the antique mall managers to use, he can ensure that the data he needs will be easy for managers to create and maintain. The antique malls will be able to use the database to create the reports he needs so he can easily demonstrate the financial health of the malls to the board.

The antique malls are housed in large buildings that are owned by the parent company, NHD. The buildings are divided into booths that are rented to dealers, who then fill the booths with inventory that is sold to customers. A dealer might be a small company or an individual. It is each dealer's responsibility to manage its own inventory; the mall does not maintain an inventory list for the dealers. As the dealer sells items from its inventory, the mall records the dealer number and the price of each item using the information on the item's price tag. At the end of the month, the mall generates a list of total sales for each dealer, computes the mall's commission, deducts the dealer's rent for booth space, and then issues the dealer a check for the remaining amount.

Tim determined that the database must manage sales, booths in the mall, dealers that rent the booths, and mall employees. At the end of each month, the database must be able to produce a complete list of sales by dealer. In addition, the database must calculate the commission on the sales, subtract the dealer's rent, and determine the profit amount for each dealer.

Some malls also offer classes to their customers. Because the classes provide customers with a reason to return to the mall, NHD will encourage all malls to offer classes. Tim suggests that the database should store information about the classes offered, their instructors, and the customers who enroll in the classes. Instructors are not employees of the mall; rather, they are freelance instructors who are paid from the fees customers pay to take the courses. Customers can sign up for more than one class; payments for course fees are collected at enrollment or on the first day of class. The database needs to manage data about the customers who take these courses, including their name, the course(s) in which they enroll, and the payment of course fees.

Tim has discussed his goals with the board and it has agreed to go forward with developing a database. Tim suggested selecting one mall to serve as a six-month pilot for the project, allowing him to design and test the database before using it elsewhere. Tim selected the Memories Antique Mall in Cleveland, TN, for the pilot project. The mall's manager, Linda Sutherland, has managed the mall for many years and is excited about replacing the mall's manual systems with a database. After meeting with Linda to discuss the database, Tim asks her to provide him with all of the existing documents that she uses to run the mall so he can examine them and use them to better understand the data he needs to collect.

In this chapter, you will begin the discovery and planning phases of creating a database for NHD. You will use the documents that Linda provides to develop a database design. After completing the database design, Tim will review it and provide feedback that you will use to create the database in Chapter 2.

Complete the following:

1. Linda gave you the form shown in Figure 1.35, which the mall uses to collect data about customers who enroll in classes. On paper, design a customer table based on this form. Notice that the form does not contain a place for a customer identification number. Rather, the paper documents are currently filed alphabetically according to the customer's name. You know that you will need an identification number to uniquely identify customers. Be certain to add this field to your table design. Your table design should include field names, data types, field properties (as necessary), and field descriptions.

Figure 1.35: Customer information form

2. Linda gave you the form shown in Figure 1.36, which she uses to obtain information about dealers. On paper, design a dealer table based on this form. Your table design should include field names, data types, field properties (as necessary), and field descriptions. Be certain that each dealer is uniquely identified.

Figure 1.36: Dealer information form

Memories Antique Mall
Dealer Information Form

Name: _Marcia Tyler_

Address: _9800 Harbor Lane_

City: _Cleveland_ State: _TN_ Zip: _37364_

Phone: _(423) 890-8788_ Cell Phone: _(423) 645-8900_

Tax ID: _34 -5690654_

Comments: _Call cell phone first. Up to 15% discount is approved._

3. After meeting with Linda, she tells you that she needs to manage the booths, their sizes, and their monthly rental amounts. She currently keeps this information on a piece of paper that she posts on the bulletin board in her office. Create the booth table using the information in the map shown in Figure 1.37. Linda tells you during your interview with her that she also needs to store data about the booth's location (outside perimeter, inside perimeter, or aisle), its color (green, tan, yellow, or white), which dealer rents the booth (or which booths are vacant), and whether the booth has rafters above it and carpeting.

Figure 1.37: Map of the Memories Antiques Mall

A-16 12x8 $175	A-15 12x8 $175	A-14 12x10 $230	A-13 12x10 $230	A-12 12x18 $310	A-11 12x18 $310	A-10 12x10 $230	A-09 12x10 $230	A-08 12x10 $230	A-07 12x12 $290

A-17 12x8 $175

A-18 12x12 $290

A-19 12x18 $310

A-20 12x18 $310

B-12 8x12 $175

B-11 8x12 $175

B-13 8x12 $175

C-13 8x16 $150

B-14 8x10 $120

C-14 8x20 $200

B-15 8x10 $120

C-15 8x20 $200

B-10 8x10 $120

B-09 8x10 $120

C-12 8x16 $150

C-06 8x8 $90

C-07 8x8 $90

C-11 8x8 $90

C-08 8x8 $90

C-09 8x8 $90

Front Counter

C-10 8x8 $90

B-08 8x10 $120

B-07 8x8 $105

B-06 8x8 $105

C-05 8x8 $90

B-05 8x8 $105

C-04 8x8 $90

B-04 8x8 $105

C-03 8x8 $90

B-03 8x10 $120

C-02 8x8 $90

B-02 8x10 $120

C-01 8x8 $90

B-01 8x10 $120

A-06 12x18 $310

A-05 12x12 $290

A-04 12x12 $290

A-03 12x12 $290

A-02 12x18 $310

A-01 12x18 $310

4. Linda uses the spreadsheet shown in Figure 1.38 to collect personal data about the mall's employees.

Figure 1.38: Personal data about employees

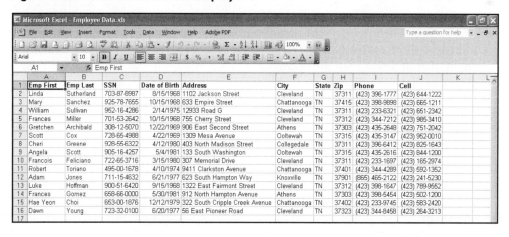

She uses the spreadsheet shown in Figure 1.39 to collect other data about employees, including their hire date, last personnel review date, and salary. Use these spreadsheets to design an employee table. Your table design should include field names, data types, field properties (as necessary), and field descriptions. Be certain that each employee is uniquely identified and that you eliminate redundant data.

Figure 1.39: Employee history and salary data

	A	B	C	D	E	F	G	H	I	J	K
1	Emp First	Emp Last	Start Date	End Date	Position	Memo	Salary	Hourly Rate	Review Date		
2	Linda	Sutherland	2/15/2002		Manager		$67,000.00				
3	Mary	Sanchez	6/15/2005		Accounting		$35,500.00		5/31/2008		
4	William	Sullivan	5/23/2004		Maintenance			$9.25	3/1/2008		
5	Frances	Miller	3/22/2004		Sales			$12.50	4/1/2008		
6	Gretchen	Archibald	1/5/2000	5/16/2004	Maintenance			$9.25			
7	Scott	Cox	4/19/2003	4/22/2005	Sales			$15.50			
8	Cheri	Greene	8/5/2005		Assistant Manager		$35,500.00		1/15/2009		
9	Angela	Scott	9/22/2005		Sales			$15.00	2/1/2008		
10	Francois	Feliciano	7/16/2004		Sales			$16.00	5/1/2008		
11	Robert	Toriano	9/16/2004		Administrative Assistant			$15.50	6/1/2008		
12	Adam	Jones	10/12/2005		Sales			$15.00	6/1/2008		
13	Luke	Hoffman	11/16/2004	2/22/2007	Sales			$15.50			
14	Frances	Gomez	5/31/2006		Administrative Assistant	Speaks fluent Spanish		$12.00	11/1/2008		
15	Hae Yeon	Choi	12/15/2007		Administrative Assistant			$13.50	3/1/2009		
16	Dawn	Young	1/16/2004		Sales			$15.50	12/15/2008		
17											

5. Linda also needs to maintain data about the classes taught at the mall and the instructors who teach these classes. For instructors, she needs to store the instructor's personal information (name, address, phone number, and cell phone number) and the fee that the instructor charges for teaching a class. Design a table that maintains information about instructors. Be certain that each instructor is uniquely identified.

6. Linda needs to maintain information about the classes that instructors teach at the mall. Currently, classes do not have an identification number, and, as such, Linda has a hard time distinguishing different classes with the same class name. For example, the mall offers three "Tattered Treasures" classes, all taught by the same instructor, but the only difference between the classes is the date they occur. Linda wants to distinguish the classes better, and store the class name, cost, classroom in which it is taught, date and time, and the instructor. Classrooms at the mall have a single-digit room number. Recently, the local community college approved some of the mall's classes for continuing education units (CEU) in certain fields, so Linda also needs to indicate whether the classes qualify for credit. Design a table to store this information for Linda.

7. Finally, you need a table that maintains data about class enrollments, including the customer, class, and payment information. Customers can sign up for more than one class. Customers can pay their class fees when they enroll in the class or on the first day of class. Be certain you have a way to indicate the customer's payment status (paid or not paid) for each class.

8. For each table you designed, use a piece of paper to sketch the table design so that you can enter five sample records into it. After creating five records, determine

whether you need to make any adjustments in your table designs so that each table is in third normal form. For example, is the job title repeated in the table that stores data about employees? What field will you use as the primary key in each table, or do you need to create a field to use as the primary key? If you need to make any changes to your table designs, do so on your paper and add the necessary documentation to the existing table designs.

9. Review each table design to ensure you have created all of the necessary fields and that they have the correct data type and field size. Be certain that you have designated a primary key field in each table and that your primary key field will contain unique values for each record.

10. Draw arrows to indicate the fields that will form the relationships in the database.

11. If your instructor asks you to turn in your database design, keep a copy for yourself as you will need it to develop the database in subsequent chapters.

Case 2—Creating the Database Design for MovinOn Inc.

MovinOn Inc. is a moving company that provides moving and storage services in Washington, Oregon, and Wyoming. MovinOn provides a truck, driver, and one or more moving assistants to move residential and commercial items from one location to another within the defined coverage area. In addition to moving services, the company provides temporary and long-term storage in its warehouses. MovinOn's customers are commercial and residential. Some of the storage warehouses are climatically controlled for customers who need to store items that are sensitive to extreme temperatures.

Information Systems

The business started in 1990 with a single truck and a single warehouse in Oregon. Due to a very satisfied clientele, the company has grown over the years into a much larger business. Currently, MovinOn has one warehouse in each state it services and is working on a merger with another company that offers similar services in different service areas. When the merger is complete, MovinOn will acquire additional storage warehouses, trucks, and employees and will expand its operations into different states.

David Bowers is the general manager of MovinOn. In the past, David managed the business using a combination of spreadsheets and paper forms. However, with a merger in the company's future, David needs to expand his system to manage data better. David recently hired Robert Iko, an information systems specialist, to recommend and implement a new plan for managing the company's data.

Robert's first task is to understand the current system and its limitations by talking extensively with David about data management and user needs. David explains that the office in each state accepts reservations for moving and storage services by completing a form that includes the customer's name, address, phone number, and the job's details. Jobs that involve trucking items from one location to another or from an outside location to a storage unit in a warehouse are maintained in a filing cabinet that is organized by customer name. Leases for storage space are stored alphabetically in a separate filing cabinet for each warehouse. All of the forms are stored in the on-site offices at the warehouse from which they were purchased. Unfortunately, David admits that forms are often lost or misplaced and sometimes contain inaccurate or missing data. In addition, when a customer requires the services of another warehouse, a MovinOn employee has to copy the customer's record and send it to the second warehouse so that it is on file at the second location. David wants the new system to be capable of sharing data between the three warehouses and any warehouses that the company acquires in the future so that it is easy for the company to share and maintain data.

Each warehouse has its own manager, office staff, and moving assistants. Drivers are contract employees and can work for any warehouse. David wants the new system to manage employee data, including personal information, salary information, and work performance. In addition to managing personnel data, David also wants to use the new system to manage information about drivers, including their personal information and driving records. The system also needs to store information about the trucks and vans that MovinOn owns and operates.

Finally, the system must maintain data about customers who utilize moving and storage services. Some customers might require storage in more than one location. When there is a request for services, the request is recorded on a form. Any request constitutes a "job" in the lingo of the company—a job must include all the pertinent data, including information about the customer, the originating location, the destination location, and the estimated mileage and weight of the load.

Robert gathered a collection of documents during the discovery phase that will help you design the database. You need to be certain that every data item in the existing documents is also represented in the tables in your design. In this chapter, you will begin the discovery and planning phases of creating a database for MovinOn. You will use the documents that Robert provides to develop a database design. After completing the database design, Robert will review it and provide feedback that you will use to create the database in Chapter 2.

Complete the following:

1. Robert gave you the form shown in Figure 1.40, which collects data about employees. In addition to storing the data shown in Figure 1.40, Robert also needs to identify the warehouse in which the employee works. On paper, design an employee table based on this form. The table design for all tables that you create should include field names, data types, field properties (as necessary), and field descriptions. Remember that each table must have a primary key field.

Figure 1.40: Employee information form

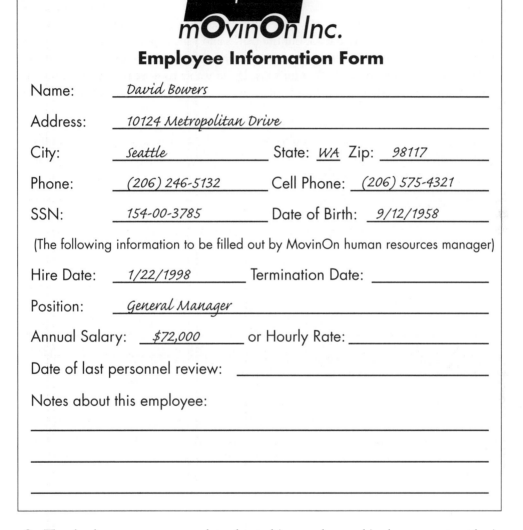

mOvinOn Inc.

Employee Information Form

Name: _David Bowers_

Address: _10124 Metropolitan Drive_

City: _Seattle_ State: _WA_ Zip: _98117_

Phone: _(206) 246-5132_ Cell Phone: _(206) 575-4321_

SSN: _154-00-3785_ Date of Birth: _9/12/1958_

(The following information to be filled out by MovinOn human resources manager)

Hire Date: _1/22/1998_ Termination Date: _____

Position: _General Manager_

Annual Salary: _$72,000_ or Hourly Rate: _____

Date of last personnel review: _____

Notes about this employee:

_____

_____

_____

2. The database must manage data about drivers, who are hired on a contract basis. Design a table that stores information about drivers. The table should include the same information stored for employees, except for an indication about the warehouse in which the driver works, in addition to storing the following additional information:

- Drivers are not paid an hourly rate or salary; they are paid based on the number of miles driven for any job. The payment for a job is determined by multiplying the rate per mile by the number of miles for the job.

- MovinOn rates drivers based on their safety records, successful on-time deliveries, and other factors. The company's rating system uses the values A, B, C, D, and F to rate drivers, with A being the highest rating and F being the lowest rating. (You do not need to worry about how MovinOn assigns ratings to drivers; you only need to store the driver's rating.)

3. Design a table that stores data about the trucks and vans owned by MovinOn. Each vehicle has a unique identification number appearing on the vehicle in the format TRK-001 for trucks or VAN-009 for vans. David wants to store the vehicle's license plate number, number of axles, and color.

4. Design a table that stores data about warehouses using the data shown in Figure 1.41. The warehouse identification number is the two-letter state abbreviation in which the warehouse is located followed by a dash and then a number. For example, the warehouse in Wyoming is WY-1.

Figure 1.41: Data about warehouses

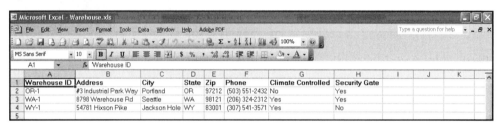

5. Currently, information about storage units is stored in an Excel workbook; a portion of this data is shown in Figure 1.42. Use this information to help you design a table that manages data about the storage units.

Figure 1.42: Data about storage units

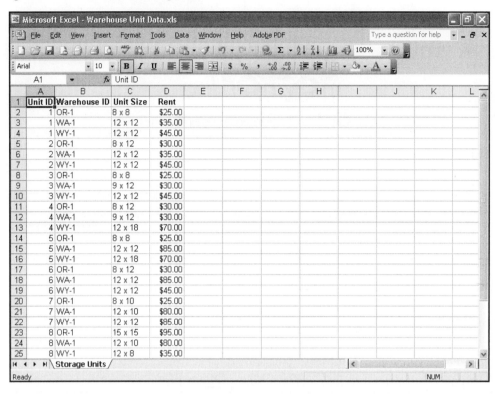

6. You also need to manage data to indicate which customer rents which unit. David wants to store the date the lease started and ended on each unit in each warehouse. For current customers, the ending lease date will be null. Design a table that manages data about unit rentals.

7. You have learned that data pertaining to moving jobs is actually accumulated in two steps. When the customer requests a job, the administrative assistant from the warehouse that will perform the services fills out the form shown in Figure 1.43. This form is considered a "job order."

Figure 1.43: Job order information form

mOvinOn Inc.

Job Order Information Form

Customer: _____Piazza Real Estate_____

Move Date: _____9/5/2008_____

Address Moving **FROM**: _____1789 Eighth Avenue_____

_____Spokane, WA_____

Address Moving **TO**: _____7899 Grandview Apt #5_____

_____Pullman, WA_____

Estimated Mileage: _____60_____ Estimated Weight: _____1250 lbs_____

Do you need packing service?   Yes _____X_____ No _____

Do you need us to move any heavy items (such as a piano or freezer)?

Yes _____X_____ No _____

Do you need to store any items?   Yes _____ No _____X_____

8. David needs to store the following data about customers: company name (for commercial customers only), the job contact's name, and the address, city, state, zip code, and phone number. Design a customer table using this information.

9. The administrative assistant uses a scheduling program to manage and assign vehicles and drivers for moving jobs, and then this information is entered into the database. Upon completion of a job, the database must store the details about the job, including the customer, truck or van used, driver, actual mileage, and actual weight. This step is considered to be the "job detail." David wants to store job detail data separately from job order data. Design a table that manages the job detail information.

10. For each table you designed, use a piece of paper to sketch the table design so that you can enter five sample records into it. After creating five records, determine

whether you need to make any adjustments in your table designs so that each table is in third normal form. If you need to make any changes to your table designs, do so on your paper and add the necessary documentation to the existing table designs.

11. Review each table design to ensure you have created all of the necessary fields. Be certain that you have designated a primary key field in each table and that your primary key field will contain unique values for each record.

12. Draw arrows to indicate the fields that will form the relationships in the database.

13. If your instructor asks you to turn in your database design, keep a copy for yourself as you will need it to develop your database in subsequent chapters.

Case 3—Creating the Database Design for Hershey College

Information Systems

Hershey College is a small liberal arts college in Hershey, Pennsylvania. Because student enrollment at Hershey College is small, the college participates competitively only in football and basketball. However, the athletic department has been encouraging the college for the past several years to develop an intramural department. The athletic department has conducted research showing that people who exercise regularly have fewer instances of heart disease, osteoporosis, and other illnesses. After receiving a large cash endowment for the development of the intramural department, the college's board of directors agreed to its creation. The board also met with student leadership at the college and by mutual agreement implemented a small activity fee that all students will pay with their tuition to provide funding for the intramural department's activities. The primary goal of the intramural department is to encourage students to participate in sports and activities that promote good health and strong bodies. In addition, many studies have shown that students who are actively involved in sports or other extracurricular activities are less likely to participate in undesirable activities.

The intramural department will offer organized sports leagues for interested students. The department will create schedules for each sport, assign players to teams, provide a coach and a student captain, and manage the team's playing locations. The department will also offer sports equipment that teams can check out and use for practice and games.

Part of the mandate set by the board for the intramural department is to demonstrate that students are using its services by participating on teams and using equipment. The intramural department must provide reports each semester documenting which sports were offered, how many students participated in them, and other information as requested by the board. Admission counselors will also use these reports to show prospective students that there are many opportunities to participate in sports at the college.

Chapter Exercises

1

The college has appointed Marianna Fuentes as the director of the intramural department. Marianna has hired you to develop and maintain the database that will manage the departmental activities and produce the required reports. Because the intramural department is new, Marianna is not yet certain of the data the department needs to collect and manage. Initially, she wants the database to manage data about each sport offered by the intramural department (including team assignments, coaches, and scheduling), the students who sign up for sports teams, and the equipment.

Because you are the only person responsible for the database, there is a lot of responsibility on your shoulders to provide a database that works well for the department. In this chapter, you will begin the discovery and planning phases of creating a database for the intramural department. You will use the information that Marianna provides to develop a database design. After completing the database design, Marianna will review it and provide feedback that you will use to create the database in Chapter 2.

Complete the following:

1. Marianna decides that the best way to get started planning the database is to prepare a list of all the data items that are needed to support the department. Table 1.14 shows her list, which she asks you to use when planning the database. You will need to identify the data to collect, group fields into tables, normalize the data, and relate the tables.

Table 1.14: Intramural department information needs

Item	Description
Students: We need to store information about students who participate on teams and the sports in which they participate, including the team. Students can sign up for more than one sport.	
ID number	Student and faculty IDs at Hershey are five digits.
Name	First and last names.
Phone	Home phone number, cell phone number.
Waiver	Students must sign a waiver to play on a team; we must have this document on file.
Academic eligibility	Students must be academically eligible to play sports by maintaining a C or better grade point average; we must check eligibility at registration.
Sports	
Name	Sports include basketball, football, ping pong, pool, soccer, softball, swimming, tennis, track, and wrestling.
Coach	Each sport has an assigned coach. We need to know the coach's name, office number (such as JK-18), phone number, and cell phone number. A person can coach one or more teams over one or more seasons.
Minimum and maximum players	Each sport has a designated minimum and maximum number of players.

Table 1.14: Intramural department information needs (cont.)

Item	Description
Begin Date	The date each sport begins.
Notes	A place to record notes about each sport.
Equipment: Teams or coaches check out the equipment they need for their sport's practice sessions. Some sports, such as wrestling, do not have equipment.	
ID number	Equipment is assigned an ID number using a sport abbreviation and a number (BAS = basketball, FTBL = football, PNG = ping pong, POOL = pool table, SOC = soccer, SOF = softball, TEN = tennis, and WRES = wrestling). For example, BAS-1 is a basketball. Some equipment ID numbers indicate a collection of items. For example, BAS-BAG-3 is three basketballs.
Description	A description of the equipment.
Storage building	The building where the equipment is stored, such as SB-1.
Fields: Different courts, fields, and tables are available for practice and games.	
ID number	Courts, fields, and tables are assigned ID numbers. For example, BAS-CRT-1 is a basketball court, SOC-FLD-2 is a soccer field, and POL-TBL-2 is a pool table.
Type	Identify the court, field, or table type (basketball, softball, and so on).
Maintenance Contact	Each court, field, and table has an assigned maintenance person, who manages and resolves problems with the court, field, or location. We will need to know the maintenance person's name, phone number, and office number.
Season	The seasons each field is available for use by a team (some fields are unavailable off-season for maintenance purposes). The seasons are fall and spring; some sports run year-round, in which case the season is "always."
Teams: For each team, we need to know the team number, captain, sport name, location where games are played, and the equipment needed for the game.	

2. For each table you identified, determine the data type to assign to each field, and which fields to use as the primary key.

3. For each table you designed, use a piece of paper to sketch the table design so that you can enter five sample records into it. After creating five records, determine whether you need to make any adjustments in your table designs so that each table is in third normal form. If you need to make any changes to your table designs, do so on your paper and add the necessary documentation to the existing table designs.

4. Use arrows to indicate the relationships between tables and the relationship types. Indicate which fields are involved in the relationship and determine how to maintain data integrity.

5. If your instructor asks you to turn in your database design, keep a copy for yourself as you will need it to develop your database in subsequent chapters.

Building the Database
Information Systems: Creating, Populating, Relating, and Maintaining the Tables in a Database

"It is only the farmer who faithfully plants seeds in the Spring, who reaps a harvest in the Autumn."
—BC Forbes

LEARNING OBJECTIVES

Level 1

Create a database and tables
Work in Design view
Set a field's data type, size, and properties
Use the Input Mask Wizard and the Lookup Wizard
Validate fields

Level 2

Import data into a database
Set a table's primary key
Create foreign keys
Create one-to-many and many-to-many relationships
Use a subdatasheet to view related records in a table

Level 3

Learn about the role of the database administrator
Compact, repair, and back up a database
Document the database design using the Documenter
Secure a database by setting a password, encrypting data, and hiding objects
Create user-level security in a database

TOOLS COVERED IN THIS CHAPTER

Datasheet view	**Input Mask Wizard**	**Security Wizard**
Design view	**Lookup Wizard**	**Subdatasheet**
Documenter	**Relationships window**	**Table Wizard**
Import Spreadsheet Wizard		

CHAPTER INTRODUCTION

In Chapter 1, Don Linebarger, the information systems director at 4Corners Pharmacy, interviewed the pharmacy's owner, pharmacists, managers, and key employees to learn more about the data needs of the pharmacy and to understand the existing systems the pharmacy uses to conduct business. Don's work resulted in a plan that identifies the tables he needs to create, the fields to define in those tables, the data types and field sizes needed to store the data, and the relationships between tables. With his plan approved by management, Don is ready to begin building the database using Access.

In this chapter, you will learn different techniques for creating tables, entering data, verifying data, relating tables, documenting the database objects, backing up the database, repairing the database, and securing data.

CASE SCENARIO

Don Linebarger needs to begin work on the database for 4Corners Pharmacy by creating the database in Access and then creating the tables that will store the data the pharmacy needs to track customers, prescriptions, drugs, employees, training classes, health insurance companies, doctors, and clinics. The pharmacy's owner, Paul Ferrino, worked as a cashier, pharmacy technician, and pharmacist in his father's pharmacy before purchasing the pharmacy upon his father's retirement. Vincent Ferrino still works part-time at the pharmacy as a pharmacist. Although Vincent's business was successful for more than two decades, his system for managing data about the pharmacy is obsolete. Paul wants to automate many of the processes at the pharmacy so he can better evaluate and operate the business.

Paul's top priority was hiring Don, who will create the system for the pharmacy, train users, and maintain and expand the system over time.

LEVEL 1

CREATING THE DATABASE TABLES

ACCESS 2003 SKILLS TRAINING

- **Add a field to a table between other fields**
- **Add a field to a table structure**
- **Add a lookup field to a table using the Lookup Wizard**
- **Change field properties**
- **Change the data type**
- **Change the Format property for a field in Table Design view**
- **Create custom input masks**
- **Create one or more tables in Design view**
- **Define Date/Time and Yes/No fields**
- **Define Number and Currency fields**
- **Define Text fields**
- **Delete a field from a table structure**
- **Modify field properties for one or more tables in Table Design view**
- **Move a field in a table structure**
- **Specify a default value**
- **Specify a required value**
- **Specify the primary key**
- **Specify validation text for one or more fields**
- **Use the Input Mask Wizard**

REVIEWING THE DATABASE DESIGN

Throughout the database design process, Don researched and evaluated existing and missing sources of data at the pharmacy. He also interviewed the owner, pharmacists, managers, and key employees to learn about how they plan to use the database so he can better understand the needs of the business. One of Don's most important roles is to make sure that the database he develops stores the pharmacy's data in the correct format and outputs the correct queries, forms, and reports for users.

You learned in Chapter 1 that a relational database is a collection of related tables. As an information systems professional, Don knows the importance of properly planning and designing the database so that it meets users' needs and expectations. Paul already knows that Vincent's system for tracking prescriptions, refills, and customers does not work because it is prone to data-entry errors and inconsistent data. In addition, Paul has limited tools available to him in Excel to search a large worksheet to find related records and other information.

After careful analysis and preparation, Don formulated the database design for Paul's approval. Don reviews the database design with Paul to ensure that it is correct and meets the needs of the pharmacy. To make the design easier to understand, Don begins by presenting some of the table designs to Paul. Figure 2.1 shows the table that stores customer data, including the customer's name, address, phone number, date of birth, gender, balance, preference for child-proof caps, insurance plan, household, and allergies. The table that stores customer information is linked to the table that stores the details about the customer's prescriptions, to the table that stores the details about the customer's health plan, and to the table that stores the details about the customer's household. These links are made by creating foreign keys in the related tables.

Figure 2.1: Data stored about customers

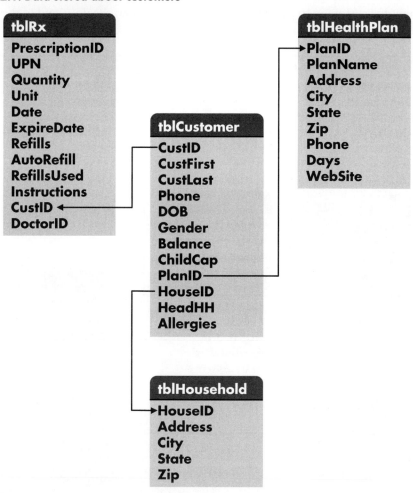

Don used the Leszynski/Reddick guidelines for naming database objects and created four tables: tblCustomer, tblRx, tblHousehold, and tblHealthPlan. When tblCustomer is linked to the related tables tblRx, tblHousehold, and tblHealthPlan, Don can retrieve detailed information about each customer and the prescriptions they have filled, the household to which they belong, and the health plan that covers them. These related tables will also enable him to list all the customers within a household and determine which drugs are being prescribed to which customers.

Figure 2.2 shows the table that stores prescription data, including the prescription's identification number, UPN, quantity ordered, unit of measurement, fill date, expiration date, refills authorized, preference for automatic refills, number of refills used, and the prescribing instructions. In addition, tblRx stores the identification numbers of the customer and the prescribing doctor. The table that stores prescription information is linked to the table that stores the details about the prescribing doctor, to the table that stores details about the customer, to the table that stores details about the drug, and to the table that stores information about refills using foreign keys in the related tables.

Figure 2.2: Data stored about prescriptions

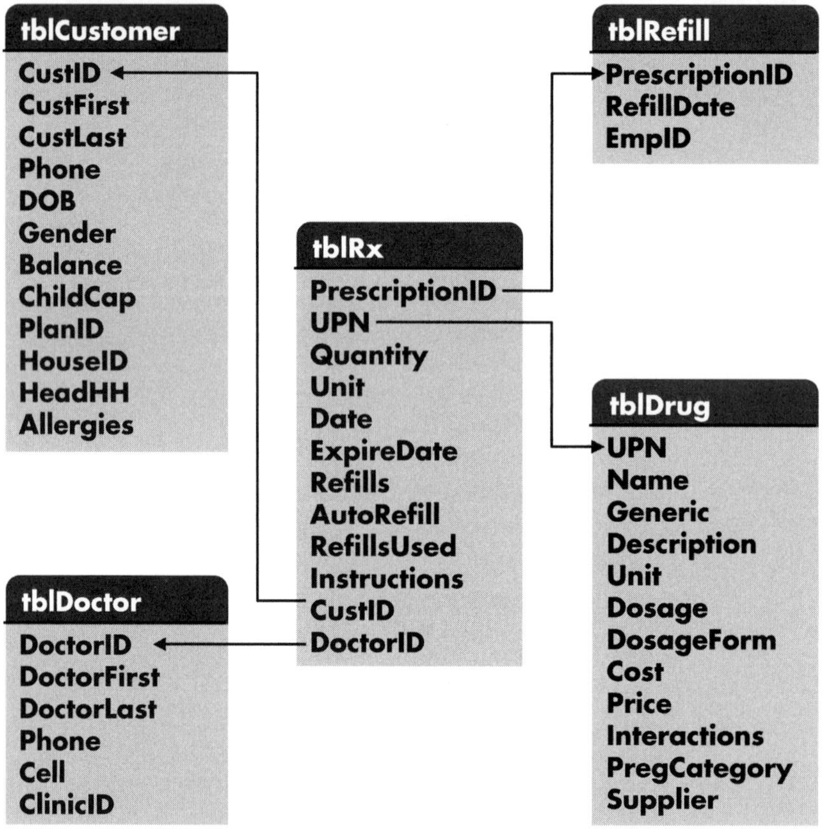

Figure 2.3 shows the table that stores data about employees at the pharmacy, including the employee's identification number, first name, middle initial, last name, Social Security number, date of birth, start date, termination date (if applicable), address, city, state, zip code, job identification number, phone number, cell phone number, salary or hourly rate of compensation, and next personnel review date. In addition, there is a field to store miscellaneous information about the employee, such as being part-time or bilingual. The table that stores employee information is linked to the table that stores the details about the employee's training, to the table that stores information about the refills that the employee has filled, and to the table that identifies the different job titles at the pharmacy.

Figure 2.3: Data stored about employees

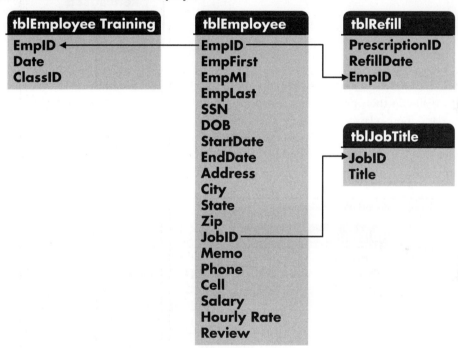

Figure 2.4 shows the table that stores data about doctors, including the doctor's identification number, first and last names, phone number, cell phone number, and the identification number of the clinic at which the doctor works. The table that stores doctor data is linked to the table that stores details about the clinic at which the doctor works and to the table that stores details about prescriptions the doctor has written.

Figure 2.4: Data stored about doctors

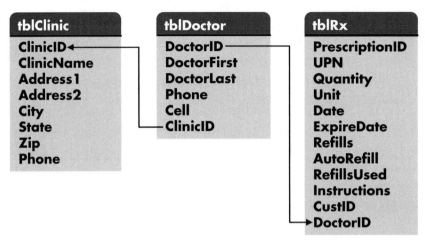

Figure 2.5 shows the table that stores data about the classes that pharmacy employees must take to maintain their professional certifications and other classes of interest. The table stores data about classes, including the class identification number, description, cost, renewal requirement (in years), and provider. In addition, there is a field to indicate whether the class is required. The table that stores data about classes is linked to the table that stores details about the employees who took the classes.

Figure 2.5: Data stored about classes

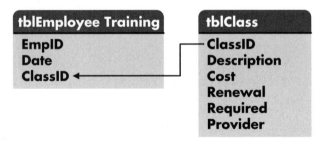

As is customary in the design process, Paul and Don agreed to limit the scope of the new system to managing data about customers, prescriptions, drugs, employees, training classes, doctors, and clinics. As the pharmacy's staff and managers begin using the system, Paul and Don might reevaluate it and add additional functionality, such as managing the inventory of nonprescription items. If Paul opens additional pharmacy locations in the future, he and Don might plan for the system to go on a network so it is possible for employees and managers at each location to share data and other resources across a network.

The entire database design appears in Figure 2.6.

Figure 2.6: Database design for 4Corners Pharmacy

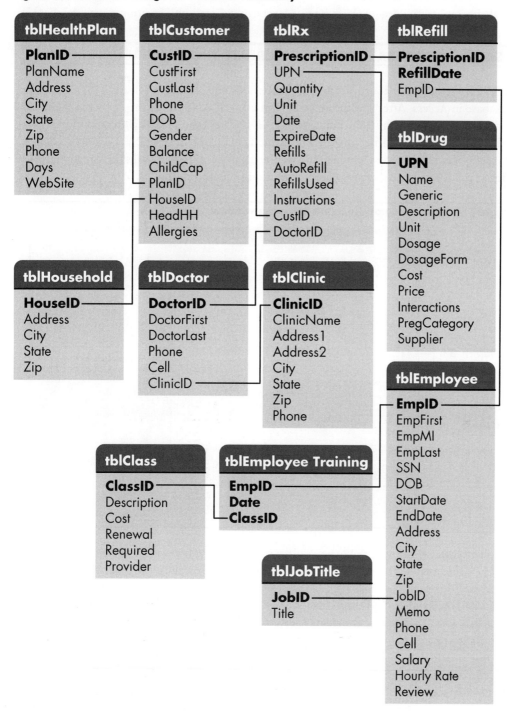

Paul is satisfied that the database will collect and manage the correct data, so he gives his final approval to the design. Don begins by starting Access and creating a new database.

USING THE DATABASE DESIGN TO CREATE THE DATABASE

After receiving Paul's approval on the database design, Don's first task is to create the database in Access. After starting Access, Don clicks the New button 🗋 on the Standard toolbar, which opens the New File task pane. Don clicks the Blank database option, types the database name 4Corners in the File name text box of the File New Database dialog box, chooses a file location in which to save the database, and then clicks the Create button. Figure 2.7 shows the 4Corners database in the Database window.

Figure 2.7: 4Corners database in the Database window

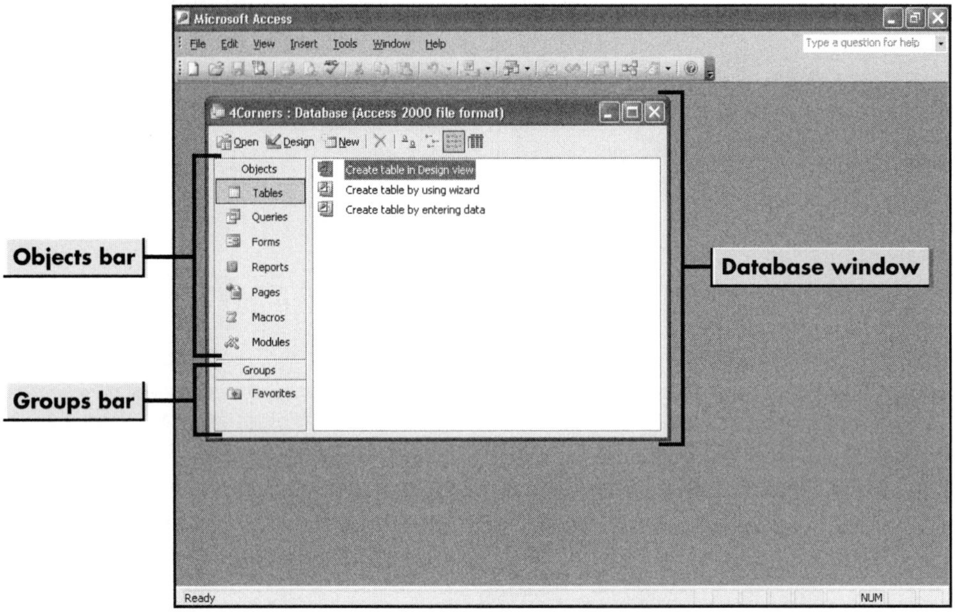

The **Database window** is the main control panel for the database. By clicking the buttons on the **Objects bar**, you can create, open, design, and view all of the objects stored in the database. For example, clicking the Tables button on the Objects bar shows the table objects in the database and shortcuts for creating tables. The **Groups bar** lets you organize database objects and create shortcuts for working with them, making it easier to access the information you need.

Because tables store all of the data in a database, you must create them before any of the other database objects. You can create a table by entering data in Datasheet view, using a wizard, or designing a table in Design view. The method that you select depends on the kind of data that you are ready to organize in a table and your own work preferences. Don will use each of these methods to create the tables in the 4Corners database.

CREATING A TABLE BY ENTERING DATA

The first table that Don creates is the one that stores the details about the different health plans to which customers subscribe. Because he already has a printout with the data for several health plans, he decides to create this table by entering data. Don double-clicks the Create table by entering data option in the Database window to open the datasheet shown in Figure 2.8.

Figure 2.8: Datasheet view

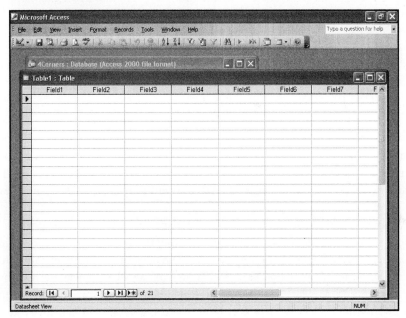

This view of the data in a table is called **Datasheet view**; it shows the table's records in rows and the table's fields in columns. When you are working in a table, the window that opens is called the Table window. The **Table window** indicates the table's name; in this case, the table name is given a default name, Table1, because Don hasn't saved it yet. The table includes default field names, such as Field1 and Field2, because Don hasn't defined the fields yet. When creating a table by entering data, you just start entering the data. Figure 2.9 shows the datasheet after entering the data for six health plans. Don maximized the Table window so he can see more of the datasheet, and he resized the fields so he can see all of the table's fields on the screen at the same time. Some of the records contain a field that does not contain any values because these values are unknown or unavailable.

Figure 2.9: Datasheet with the records for six health plans

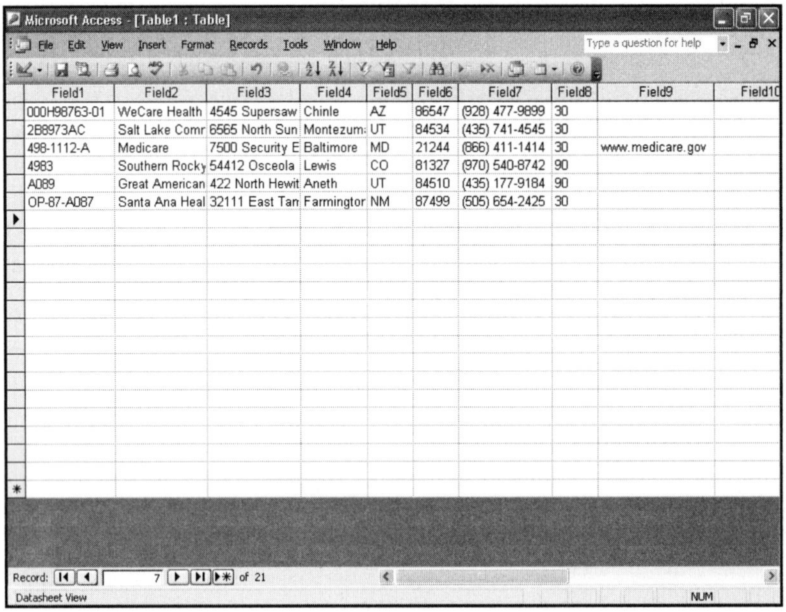

As Don was entering records, Access added a hidden AutoNumber field to the datasheet. Each record that Don entered has a unique value in the hidden _ID field. The datasheet has blank rows for additional records (up to the record with the _ID field value of 21); this is the default datasheet size when creating a table by entering data in Datasheet view.

Now that Don has entered the data for the health plans about which he already has information, he needs to save the table as an object in the 4Corners database and define the fields. Don clicks the Save button 🖫 on the Table Datasheet toolbar, types tblHealthPlan in the Table Name text box of the Save As dialog box, and then clicks the OK button. Because there is no primary key field in the tblHealthPlan table, a warning box opens and asks if Don wants to create a primary key. Don decides not to create a primary key now, so he clicks the No button. To define the fields in a table, Don changes to Design view by clicking the View button for Design view 🗹 on the Table Datasheet toolbar. Figure 2.10 shows Design view for tblHealthPlan.

Figure 2.10: Design view for tblHealthPlan

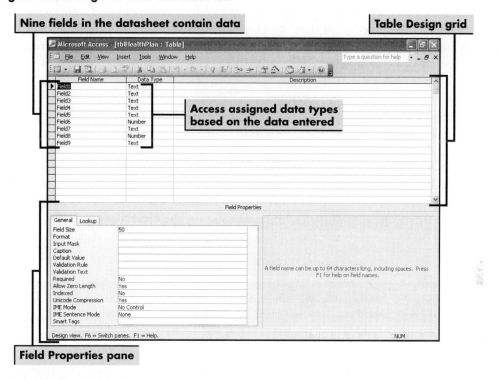

WORKING IN TABLE DESIGN VIEW
====

Don uses **Design view** to define the table's fields and the field properties and rearrange the order of fields as necessary. The top part of Design view is called the **Table Design grid** (or the **design grid**); this area includes the Field Name, Data Type, and Description columns. Each row in the Table Design grid is a field in the table. The bottom part of Design view is called the **Field Properties pane**; this area displays the field properties for the selected field. You can select a field by clicking the field in the Table Design grid. When a field is selected, an arrow appears in the current row. In Figure 2.10, the first field (Field1) is selected.

Next, Don needs to rename the default field names to match the ones in his table design by selecting each field name and typing the new value. Most DBMSs, including Access, have specific rules that you must follow when naming fields and database objects. The following rules apply to naming Access objects:

- Names can contain up to 64 characters.
- Names can contain any combination of letters, numbers, spaces, and special characters, except a period (.), an exclamation point (!), an accent grave (`), and square brackets ([and]).
- Names cannot begin with a space.

In addition to these rules, some organizations establish standards for naming objects and fields. Some organizations might include acronyms or abbreviations in field names to make them shorter. At 4Corners Pharmacy, for example, the field that stores a person's date of birth is abbreviated as "DOB," and field and object names that contain multiple words are capitalized but do not contain any spaces (such as the table name tblHealthPlan or the field name ClinicName).

After changing the default field names, Don defines the data type and field properties for each field. To change the data type, he clicks the right side of the Data Type text box for the field to display a list of all the data types for Access, and then he clicks the desired data type. After selecting a data type, the Field Properties pane changes to display properties associated with the selected data type. Don knows that Text fields can contain a maximum of 255 characters and that there are different field sizes for numeric fields. To save space in the database and improve its performance, Don can use the **Field Size property** to limit the number of characters to store in a Text field or the type of numeric data to store in a Number field.

Best Practice

Setting the Field Size Property for Text and Number Fields Correctly

Choosing the correct Field Size property for a Text or Number field is easy when you have sample data to examine. For Text fields, you can examine the existing data and count the number of characters in the longest field value. For example, the longest address in the sample data might be 29 characters. In this case, you can set the Field Size property for the Address field to 30 or 40 characters to provide enough room for even longer addresses. You can increase the size of a field after designing it, but it is always better to set the field size correctly from the start. If the field size is too small, users might not be able to enter complete data into a field without resizing it in Design view. Depending on the database configuration, users might not be able to make this type of change, in which case the field entry will be incomplete.

Another problem with resizing fields later occurs when the field is involved in one or more relationships. For example, if an EmployeeID number is originally set as a Text field that stores three digits and the company hires 1,000 people, necessitating a four-digit EmployeeID, then the field isn't long enough to store the employee with EmployeeID 1000. If the EmployeeID field is a primary key with a foreign key in a related table, Access prohibits you from changing the field size unless you delete the relationship. In this case, you would need to change the field size in the primary and foreign keys, and then re-create the relationship.

The same problem can occur with Number fields. The values that Access can store in a Number field with the Byte field size are different than the values it can store in a Number field with the Double field size. AutoNumber fields store data using the Long Integer field size. Relationships between fields with the AutoNumber and Number data types must have the same field size, Long Integer, to create the relationship.

When setting field sizes, be certain to consider the data you have from the discovery phase, and then to create a reasonable margin of error to avoid setting the field size so it cannot store values in the future.

Although he can change field options after creating them, Don knows that if the field size is too small, data might be truncated, and if set too long, valuable space might be wasted. The default field size for a Text field is 50 characters; a Text field can store 0 to 255 characters. Don changes the default field size for Text fields to match his table design. For the Days field, which is a Number field, Don changes the field size from the default of Long Integer to Byte as this field will store whole numbers such as 30 and 90.

Adding Descriptions to Fields in Table Design View

Some developers like to use the optional **Description property** for a field to document its contents, such as identifying a field as a primary or foreign key or providing users with instructions about entering values into the field, for example, adding a description of "Must be M or F" in a field that requests a person's gender. When a database is being developed by a team, using the Description property is an important part of documenting the table designs and providing clear instructions for users. Don knows that the Description property is important and adds descriptions to each field in the table to document their contents.

The last thing that Don does is to select the PlanID field and set it as the table's primary key. With the field selected, he clicks the Primary Key button 🔑 on the Table Design toolbar. Access adds a key symbol to the PlanID row to indicate this field as the table's primary key. Figure 2.11 shows the completed table design for tblHealthPlan.

Figure 2.11: Table design for tblHealthPlan

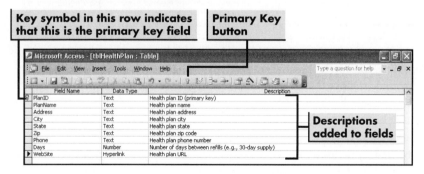

Don finished one table's design and entered data into it. He decides to use another method to create the second table in the database, which will store data about households.

CREATING A TABLE USING THE TABLE WIZARD

The second table that Don will create, tblHousehold, stores the HouseID, address, city, state, and zip code for customers living in the same household (at the same address). Because this table has fields that are commonly used, Don decides to use the Table Wizard to create it. The **Table Wizard** includes sample tables for business and personal needs with fields that you can select and modify to create your own tables. An advantage of using the Table Wizard is that the sample tables and fields already have properties set that might work well in your database or that are easily changed to accommodate your specific data needs. To start the Table Wizard, Don returns to the Tables object in the Database window, and then double-clicks the Create table by using wizard option. The Table Wizard starts, as shown in Figure 2.12.

Figure 2.12: Table Wizard

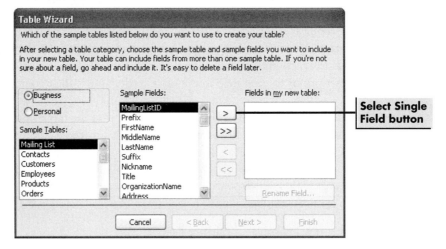

The Business option button is selected by default and displays a list of tables and fields that are commonly used in business situations. Don clicks Customers in the Sample Tables list box. By scrolling the contents of the Sample Fields list box, Don sees that the fields he needs for tblHousehold are included, even though he needs to rename a few of the fields so they match his table design. The first field, CustomerID, is selected by default. To add this field to his new table, Don clicks the Select Single Field button $\boxed{>}$ to add it to the Fields in my new table list box. Because this field isn't named correctly for his purposes, Don clicks the Rename Field button and types HouseID. He repeats the process to add the BillingAddress, City, StateOrProvince, and PostalCode fields to his new table; the fields are now named Address, City, State, and Zip. He clicks the Next button, and then renames the table to tblHousehold, as shown in Figure 2.13.

Figure 2.13: Naming the table and selecting a primary key

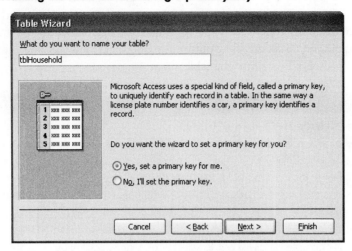

Finally, because household identification numbers are unique, Don will use the HouseID field as the table's primary key. He selects the option to assign a primary key himself, chooses the HouseID field, selects the option to have Access assign consecutive numbers to records, indicates that this table isn't related to any other table yet, and then selects the option to modify the table design after the wizard closes. Figure 2.14 shows the table design for tblHousehold.

Figure 2.14: tblHousehold in Design view

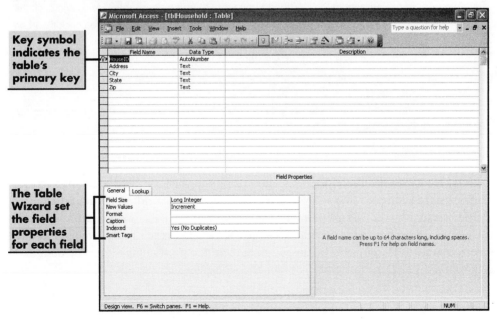

Each field has the correct name and data type and the key symbol in the row for the HouseID field indicates that this field is the table's primary key. Don changes the field size for each field to match his table design and adds field descriptions to document the fields. Don saves the table and clicks the View button for Datasheet view 🗔, and then he enters the pharmacy's household data into the table.

How To

Use the Table Wizard to Create a Table

1. On the Tables object in the Database window, double-click the Create table by using wizard option. The Table Wizard starts.

2. Click the Business or Personal option button to select the category in which the desired table might appear, and then use the Sample Tables and Sample Fields list boxes to find a table that closely meets your needs.

3. Click the sample table to display the sample fields for the selected table.

4. Click a field in the Sample Fields list box to select it, and then click the Select Single Field button ⟨ > ⟩ to add it to the Fields in my new table list box. Repeat this step as necessary to add all of the desired fields to the new table. To add all fields to the Fields in my new table list box, click the Select All Fields button ⟨ >> ⟩. To remove a selected field from the Fields in my new table list box, click the Remove Single Field button ⟨ < ⟩ (to remove all fields, click the Remove All Fields button ⟨ << ⟩.

5. To rename a field, select the field in the Fields in my new table list box, click the Rename Field button, and then type a new field name. After selecting and renaming the fields to include in the table, click the Next button.

6. Type the desired table name in the "What do you want to name your table?" text box, click the option button that identifies how you want to set the table's primary key, and then click the Next button. (If you choose to set the primary key yourself, use the next dialog box to identify the primary key field and the type of data it will store, and then click the Next button.)

7. If necessary, define the relationship that the new table has with other tables in the database, and then click the Next button.

8. Select the option to modify the table design (open it in Design view), enter data directly into the table (open it in Datasheet view), or enter data into the table using a form the wizard creates for you (a form), and then click the Finish button.

Creating a table with the Table Wizard is a good method when the table you want to create already exists as a sample table and you can accept the default field properties assigned to the fields created by the wizard or easily change them. Just like any other table, you can use Design view to change the fields and their properties. However, most developers prefer to create a table in Design view because it gives them the most control over the design.

CREATING A TABLE IN DESIGN VIEW

The remaining tables that Don needs to create have specific requirements that would make it difficult for him to create them in Datasheet view or by using a wizard. The third way to create a table is in Design view. To create a table in Design view, click the Design button on the Database window, or double-click the Create table in Design view option on the Tables object in the Database window to open the Table window in Design view. Just like when creating a table in Datasheet view, the table's default name is Table1; however, the table has no fields until you define them by entering the field names, data type, and properties.

Don uses Design view to create the next table, which stores data about the classes that employees must take to maintain their professional certifications. He begins by entering the first field name, ClassID, and then he presses the Tab key to move to the Data Type text box. If the ClassID field is the Text data type, Don could press the Tab key to move to the Description text box because Text is the default data type. However, the ClassID field is a Number field, so he must change the data type. Clicking the list arrow for the Data Type text box opens a list of data types, or he can type the first letter of the desired data type to select it. Don types "n" and selects the Number data type, presses the Tab key to move to the Description text box, and then types this field's description. The default field size for the Number data type is Long Integer, and Don accepts the default. Don knows that it is a good idea to use Long Integer as the field size for primary key fields to prevent referential integrity errors later when attempting to relate Number fields to AutoNumber fields. Because this field is the table's primary key, Don clicks the Primary Key button 🔑 on the Table Design toolbar, which adds a key symbol to the left of the field name, indicating that this field is the table's primary key. Don does not need to make any other changes to this field, so he presses the Tab key to move to the Field Name text box for the next field. Don creates the other fields in the table and sets their properties. When he is finished, he saves the table using the name tblClass. Figure 2.15 shows the table design.

Figure 2.15: Table design for tblClass

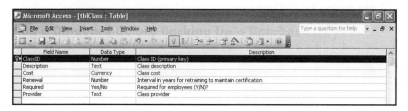

EVALUATING AND TESTING THE TABLE DESIGN

After creating and saving the table design for tblClass, Don switches to Datasheet view, and begins entering the data for this table using the information provided to him by the human resources manager, Maria Garcia. Don enters the value 1 in the ClassID field, presses the Tab key to move to the Description field and types this value, presses the Tab key, and then types 15 in the Cost field. Because the Cost field uses the Currency data type, Access changes the value 15 to $15.00. He presses the Tab key, types 0 in the Renewal field, presses the Tab key and presses the Spacebar to enter a check mark into the Required field, which has the Yes/No data type, and then presses the Tab key and types "Red Cross" in the final field for the first record. To move to the next record, Don can press the Enter key or the Tab key. By moving to the next record, Access saves the record in the table; to cancel the record, Don would press the Esc key. After saving the table for the first time, the only time that Don needs to save the table again is when he makes changes to its design (such as changing a field property in Design view) or to its layout (such as increasing or decreasing a field's width in the datasheet). If you make these kinds of changes to a table and try to close it, Access prompts you to save the table.

Recall from Chapter 1 that data types are necessary to ensure that each field in a table collects the correct values. In theory, you could use the Text data type for any field, but then you would lose the capability to perform calculations on numbers, the flexibility that a Yes/No field provides, the ability to include hyperlinks in a table, and so on.

Now the database contains three tables. Don continues working by creating the table that stores data about customers. He opens the Table window in Design view and enters the field names, data types, and descriptions for each field in the table's design. He also uses the Field Properties pane to set the properties for fields that do not use the default settings. To make his work go faster, he presses the F6 key to move between the design grid and the Field Properties pane. After creating all of the fields and defining their properties, Don selects the CustID field and sets it as the table's primary key, and then saves the table as tblCustomer. Figure 2.16 shows the table's design.

Figure 2.16: Table design for tblCustomer

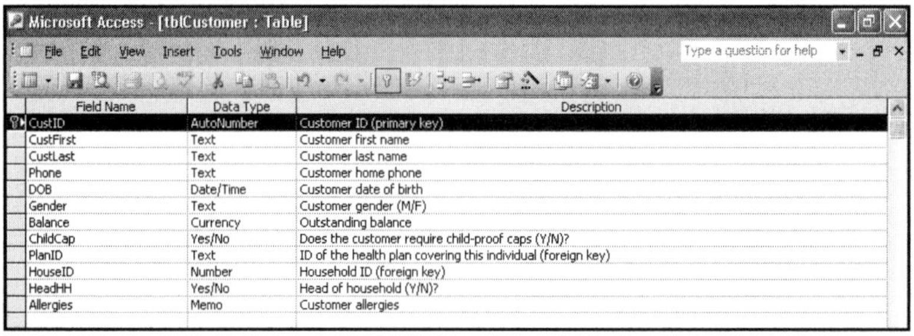

Don changes to Datasheet view and begins entering the data for the first customer, shown in Figure 2.17. (Some of the record has scrolled to the left side of the screen.)

Figure 2.17: tblCustomer with one record entered

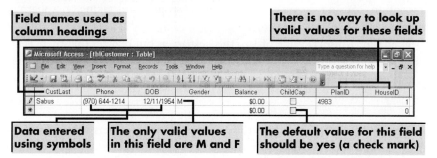

As Don is entering the data, he notices several potential problems:

- The field names are used as the column heading names in the datasheet; for example, "CustFirst" and "CustLast" are the column headings for the fields a pharmacy technician or pharmacist uses to enter the customer's first and last names. Don considers the fact that these field names, although correct, will not be the best ways to identify the information in each field, especially when this data is used in a query, form, or report.
- The Phone field values include telephone numbers. Don entered the phone number using a common format for displaying phone numbers in which the area code appears in parentheses, followed by a space and the seven-digit phone number. He entered the phone number in this way so that it would be displayed with this format each time it appears in a query, form, or report. However, he is concerned that other users won't follow this approach, resulting in inconsistently formatted data. In addition, there is no way to ensure that users enter all 10 digits of the customer's phone number.
- Don entered the DOB (date of birth) field value in a common date format in which the month, date, and year are separated by slash characters. He also entered the year as four digits. This field name is abbreviated, and there is no way to ensure that users enter birth dates in this format, nor is there a way to ensure that users enter four-digit years. If users enter two-digit years, there might be problems later if it becomes necessary to perform calculations with dates, such as determining whether a customer is 18 years old.
- Don entered the uppercase letter "M" in the Gender field to indicate that this customer is a male. However, he realizes that he could have typed q or 9 in this field, either accidentally or on purpose. This problem can lead to inaccurate data.
- The pharmacy's policy about child-proof caps is to give them to all customers unless they specifically request regular caps, so the default value for the ChildCap field should be "yes." To order regular caps for prescription bottles, the user would click the check box or press the Spacebar to remove the check mark and change the value to "no."
- Don entered the plan ID 4983 in the PlanID field to indicate that this customer is insured by Southern Rocky Mountains Health Plan. Knowing that plan ID numbers are

often complicated, Don determines that he needs a way to ensure that the plan ID is accurate. For example, a plan ID number might contain commonly mistyped characters, such as reading a zero and typing a capital "O" or reading a lowercase "l" and typing the digit 1. In these cases, the health plan would reject the plan ID number and reject the prescription, causing inconvenience to the customer and taking the pharmacist's time to discover and correct the error.

- Don assigned the HouseID value of 1 to this customer, but realizes that there is no way to determine which HouseIDs correlate with which households without reviewing the data in another table. He needs a way to ensure that the HouseID is correct for all members of a household.

Before entering additional records into tblCustomer, Don considers the potential problems he identified and decides to stop entering records and use the tools available in Design view to set the fields' properties to ensure that the data entered is clearly labeled, accurate, and consistent.

Displaying Descriptive Field Names Using the Caption Property

The first item on Don's list is to ensure that the field names are displayed in clear, simple language so their function is obvious in a table's datasheet and in queries, forms, and reports. Don could edit the field names in Design view, but the naming conventions for field names might prevent him from being able to use the field identifiers that he wants. Instead of changing the field names, Don can use the **Caption property** for a field to change the way the field name is displayed. The Caption property specifies how a field name will appear in different database objects; the default Caption property is the field name for all data types unless you change it. For example, instead of seeing "CustFirst" in a table datasheet, Don wants users to see "First Name." Setting the Caption property properly can turn abbreviated field names into meaningful identifiers that make data entry easier.

How To

Change a Field's Caption Property
1. If necessary, change to Design view, and then select the field that you want to change.
2. Click the Caption text box in the Field Properties pane.
3. Type the caption. See Figure 2.18.

Figure 2.18: Caption property changed for the CustID field

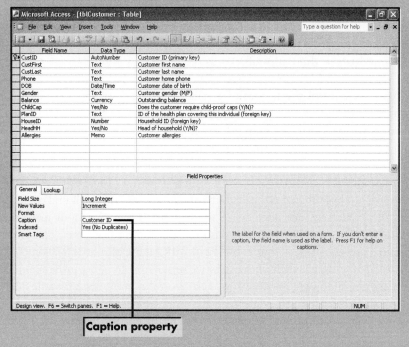

Caption property

4. Save the table design.

Figure 2.19 shows part of the datasheet for tblCustomer after Don changed the Caption property for several of the fields from the default field names to more meaningful descriptions.

Figure 2.19: Datasheet with captions and resized columns

Captions

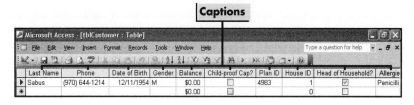

The next item on Don's list is to change the way data is formatted.

Formatting Field Values Using an Input Mask

Don wants the phone number and date of birth for each customer to be formatted the same way; he wants phone numbers in the format (970) 644-1214 and dates of birth in the format 12/11/1954. When Don entered the first record in tblCustomer, he typed the parentheses, space, and dash character in the phone number and the slashes in the date of birth. However, he realizes that other users might not enter these characters correctly, which could result in inconsistently formatted data. In addition, Don knows that by typing the parentheses, space, and dash and slash characters in these fields, these characters must be stored in the database, which requires additional space. The amount of space needed to store these characters in one record isn't significant, but the amount of space required for hundreds or thousands of records is.

In Access, you can control the format of a value by creating an input mask. An **input mask** is a predefined format that you can apply to a field so that its values are displayed using the format you specified. For example, a user might enter a customer's phone number as 9706441214, and this value is stored in tblCustomer. However, when you view the table datasheet or a query, form, or report that includes this value, you see it with the input mask that you defined, such as (970) 644-1214 or 970-644-1214 or 970.644.1214. The input mask supplies these characters, called **literal characters**, but the literal characters are not stored in the database, nor does a user need to type them. An input mask not only works to format data correctly, but it also ensures that all of the necessary data is entered. If a user tries to enter the phone number 6441214 without the area code 970 or 970kajfjfjf, he receives an error message when trying to move to the next field because the input mask only accepts 10-digit numbers. In Access, you can create an input mask for a field by using the **Input Mask Wizard**, which guides you through the necessary steps for creating an input mask and lets you enter sample values to ensure the correct results.

Don changes to Design view for tblCustomer, selects the Phone field in the design grid, and then clicks the Input Mask text box in the Field Properties pane. To create an input mask, Don can type it directly into the Input Mask text box, or he can click the Build button [...] that appears on the right side of the Input Mask text box when he clicks the text box. Because using the Input Mask Wizard is easier, he clicks the [...] button, clicks the Yes button to save the table design, and starts the wizard. Don selects the option to format the phone numbers in the format (970) 644-1214; selects the default placeholder character of an underscore, which appears when the user is entering a value into this field in Datasheet view; and then selects the option so users enter only the value into the field and not the literal characters. Figure 2.20 shows the input mask that the Input Mask Wizard created for the Phone field.

Figure 2.20: Input mask created for the Phone field

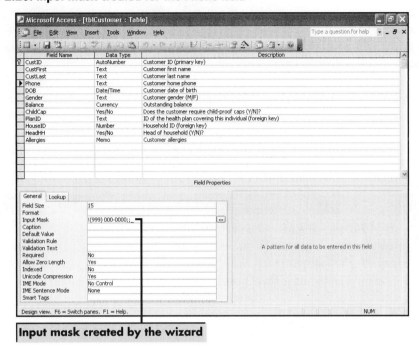

Input mask created by the wizard

Table 2.1 lists some characters that you can use in an input mask and explains their meanings.

Table 2.1: Input mask characters and descriptions

Character	Description
0	Required entry of a digit from 0 to 9
9	Optional entry of a digit from 0 to 9 or a space
L	Letter entry required
?	Letter entry optional
>	Entry that converts all characters following the > to uppercase
!	Entry that causes characters entered into the input mask to fill from right to left rather than from left to right

The input mask shown in Figure 2.20 includes other characters that indicate how to store the input mask in the table, how to display the input mask when a user is entering a value into it, and the identification of literal characters. The two semicolons (;;) near the end of the input mask specify not to store the literal characters in the input mask in the database. Other possible values for storing literal characters are ;1; (do not store literal characters) and ;0; (store the literal characters). Literal characters are generally not stored with the data and are used only to enhance the readability of the information. However, they should be stored if they are an essential part of the data.

The underscore at the end of the input mask specifies to use an underscore when the user is entering a value into the input mask to indicate the current character and total number of characters that the user must enter. Other possible values for the placeholder are #, @, !, $, %, and *. Other characters in the input mask, such as backslashes, quotation marks, and spaces, indicate the literal characters displayed by the input mask.

Because customers can live in multiple states and have different area codes, Don wants to ensure that employees always enter the customer's seven-digit phone number and the three-digit area code. To ensure this data entry, Don changes the 999 in the input mask, which specifies an optional data entry, to 000, which ensures that employees must enter the area code.

How To

Create an Input Mask Using the Input Mask Wizard

1. Click the field in Design view for which you want to create the input mask, click the Input Mask text box in the Field Properties pane, and then click the Build button [...] that appears to the right of the Input Mask text box to start the Input Mask Wizard. See Figure 2.21.

Figure 2.21: Input Mask Wizard

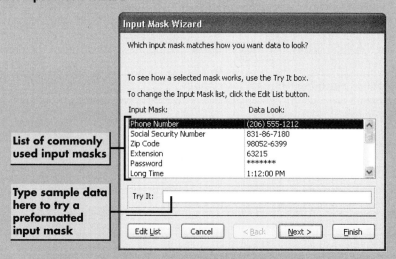

List of commonly used input masks

Type sample data here to try a preformatted input mask

2. Select the input mask that is best suited for the field, use the Try It text box if necessary to test the input mask using your own data, and then click the Next button.

3. If necessary, change the input mask shown in the Input Mask text box and change the placeholder character to use. (*Note:* You do not need to add quotation marks, semicolons, or backslashes to the input mask at this time; Access adds them for you.) If necessary, use the Try It text box to test the revised input mask using your own data, and then click the Next button.

4. If necessary, choose the option that specifies how you want to store literal characters, and then click the Next button.

5. Click the Finish button.
6. Click any other text box in the Field Properties pane to display the completed input mask, and then save the table design.

2

Now users must enter 10 digits in the Phone field; the input mask rejects attempts to store letters, symbols, and incomplete phone numbers. In addition, the input mask does not store the literal characters, which results in the phone numbers being stored using less space in the database.

To ensure that customers' birth dates are formatted consistently and entered properly, Don uses the Input Mask Wizard to create an input mask for the DOB field so that it only accepts digits and displays slashes and four-digit years. The input mask he created for the DOB field is 00/00/0000;;_. This input mask accepts only digits, does not display the literal characters, and ensures that users must enter two-digit months and dates, four-digit years, and complete dates. Because all digits are required, users must enter single-digit month abbreviations and single-digit dates using the leading zero (for example, entering "01" for January and "07" to indicate the 7th day of the month). Requiring input in this manner ensures that all digits are entered into the DOB field for each customer.

Don's next change is to prevent users from entering inaccurate data into the Gender field.

Validating Fields to Ensure Accurate and Consistent Data

Don wants to ensure that the Gender field can contain only the uppercase letter M (for male) or the uppercase letter F (for female). He defined the Gender field using the Text data type and a field size of one character. However, Don notices that a user can type any single character into that field, which could lead to incorrect data.

In Access, you can specify restrictions on the data that users can enter into a field by creating a validation rule. A **validation rule** compares the data entered by the user against one or more valid values that the database developer specified using the Validation Rule property for the field. The **Validation Rule property** specifies the valid values that users can enter into the field. If a user attempts to enter an invalid value, the **Validation Text property** for the field opens a dialog box with a predefined message that explains the valid values. For the Gender field, the only valid values are M and F. Don selects the Gender field's Validation Rule property and enters the validation rule as M or F. When he clicks another property text box, Access changes the validation rule to "M" Or "F" because the values are stored in a Text field and text values must be enclosed within quotation marks. To help users understand the valid values for the Gender field, Don clicks the Validation Text property text box, and then types "Value must be M or F." to specify the valid values. Don also uses the Input Mask property to convert all entries in this field to uppercase by entering the input mask >L. Figure 2.22 shows the completed validation rule, validation text, and input mask for the Gender field. When a user enters an m or f into the Gender field for a customer, Access stores the value as M or F. However, if a user enters any other value, Access opens a dialog box with the message specified in the Validation Text property. The user reads the message, clicks the OK button to close the dialog box, and then can enter a valid value in the Gender field and continue data entry for the customer.

Figure 2.22: Validation rule and validation text entered for the Gender field

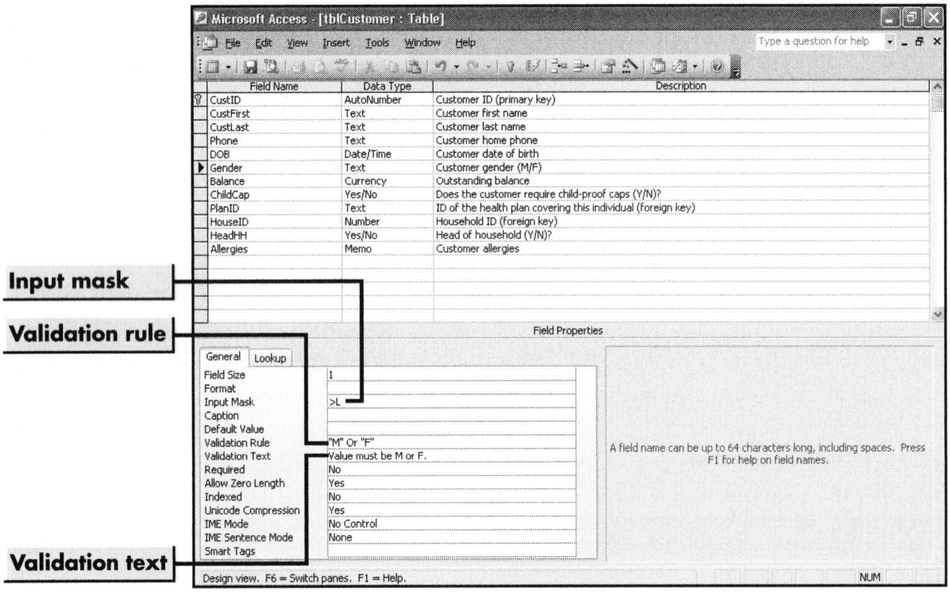

Table 2.2 describes some other validation rules and validation text that you can specify for a field. In the first example, valid values are specified using the In operator and typing valid values within parentheses and separated by commas. The second example uses "Is Not Null" to specify that the field cannot accept null values. The third and fourth examples use comparison operators to specify valid date and numeric values. (You will learn more about operators in Chapter 3.)

Table 2.2: Sample validation rules and validation text

Sample Validation Rule	Sample Validation Text
In('CO', 'AZ', 'NM', 'UT')	The state must be CO, AZ, NM, or UT.
Is Not Null	You must enter a value in this field.
>#01/01/1980#	The date must be later than January 1, 1980.
>=21 And <100	The value must be greater than or equal to 21 and less than 100.

The next item on Don's list is to implement a way to set the default value for using child-proof caps on prescription bottles to "yes."

Automating Data Entry by Using a Default Field Value

According to the pharmacy's policy, all prescriptions are dispensed with child-proof caps unless the customer requests regular caps. This means that the value of the ChildCap field should be set to "Yes" for all prescriptions and changed to "No" only when the client requests a regular cap. By specifying a default value for the ChildCap field, Don can save data-entry time for the user and ensure that all customers receive child-proof caps unless they do not want them. The **Default Value property** enters a default value into any type of field except for an AutoNumber field. To accept the default value specified in the Default Value property, the user simply tabs through the field during data entry. If the user needs to change the default value, he can type the new value. Because the ChildCap field is a Yes/No field, Don needs to specify "Yes" as the field's default value. He clicks the ChildCap field in the design grid, clicks the Default Value property text box in the Field Properties pane, and then types Yes, as shown in Figure 2.23.

Figure 2.23: Default value entered for the ChildCap field

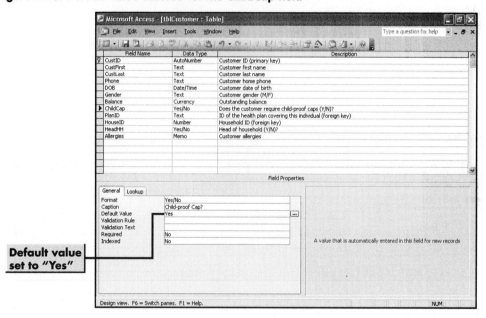

Last on Don's list is to implement a way to ensure that the health plan ID and house ID values for customers are accurate and easy to enter.

Automating Data Entry by Using a Lookup Field

As Don was entering the first record in tblCustomer, he realized that it would be possible for a user to enter a plan ID number for the customer's health plan that is not in tblHealthPlan. He also realized that the user would need a separate method to determine whether the customer belongs to an existing household in the database. Don can solve both of these problems by creating a **lookup field**, which lets the user select a field value from a list of existing field values stored in the database or from a list of values that he specifies when he creates the lookup field. For example, instead of entering the PlanID 4983 for a customer, Don would click this PlanID from a list of PlanIDs stored in tblHealthPlan; instead of entering the HouseID 1, Don would select this household's address by matching it to a list of addresses stored in tblHousehold. Both of these changes to the table design require that the tables on which you will perform the lookup already exist. For example, if the customer resides at a new household that is not yet stored in tblHousehold, the user would need to enter the household information before entering the customer's information so that the household would already exist.

To add a lookup field to a table, you change the field's data type to Lookup Wizard, but the field still stores the data that you specified when you created the field. For the first lookup field, Don selects the PlanID field in the design grid of tblCustomer, clicks the Data Type text box list arrow, and then clicks Lookup Wizard in the menu that opens. The Lookup Wizard starts, as shown in Figure 2.24.

Figure 2.24: Using the Lookup Wizard to specify the lookup column

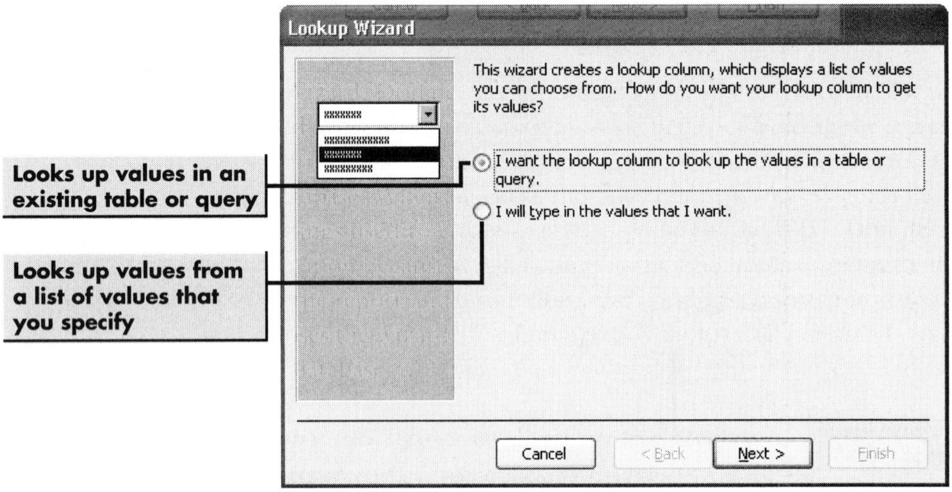

Two types of lookup fields are available. The first type lets you look up field values in another table or query; use this method when the data you want to look up already exists in the database. The second type lets you enter a list of values that you want to permit in the field; use this method when you want to supply a list of valid values for the data entered into the field that are not stored elsewhere in the database.

Don selects the option to look up the data in an existing table or query and clicks the Next button. The database contains three table objects, so he needs to select one of these tables as source of the values he wants to look up. The lookup data for the PlanID field is stored in tblHealthPlan, so he selects this table, as shown in Figure 2.25.

Figure 2.25: Selecting tblHealthPlan as the data source for the lookup field

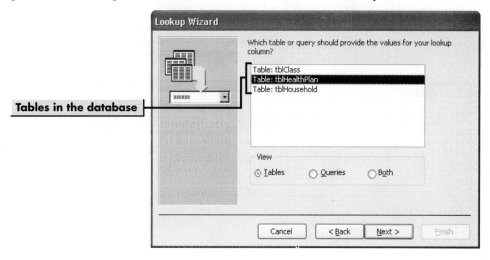

Tables in the database

Don clicks the Next button to display the next dialog box, in which he must select the field or fields in the data source (tblHealthPlan) that he wants to include in the lookup field. Don wants to display the PlanID values in the lookup field, so he selects this field in the Available Fields list box, and then clicks the Select Single Field button (>) to move the PlanID field to the Selected Fields list box, as shown in Figure 2.26.

Figure 2.26: Selecting the PlanID field as the lookup field

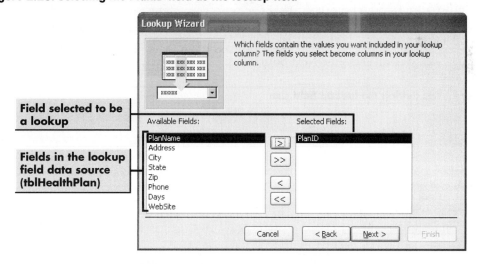

Field selected to be a lookup

Fields in the lookup field data source (tblHealthPlan)

Don could select additional fields to be displayed in the lookup column, but because he only needs to display the PlanID values, he clicks the Next button, which opens the dialog box that lets him sort the values displayed in the lookup field. Selecting a sort order is optional, but as more health plans are added to tblHealthPlan, data entry will be easier if the health plans are sorted in ascending order by PlanID. Don clicks the list arrow for the first list box, and then clicks PlanID to select this field. The button to the right of the first list box displays the label "Ascending," which indicates that the values in the lookup field will be displayed in alphabetical or numerical order. You can also display values in descending order by clicking this button, in which case it displays the label "Descending." Figure 2.27 shows the PlanID field sorted in ascending order.

Figure 2.27: PlanID sorted in ascending order

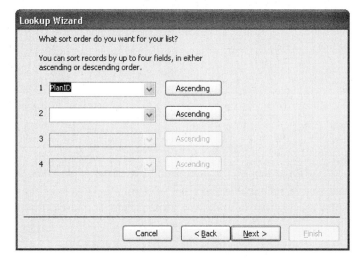

Don clicks the Next button and sees how the lookup field will display existing values in the PlanID field in tblHealthPlan. In some cases, you might need to click and drag the right side of the column to increase or decrease its width so that the data in the lookup field is displayed correctly and completely. The default field size is acceptable, as shown in Figure 2.28, so Don clicks the Next button.

Figure 2.28: Setting the lookup field size

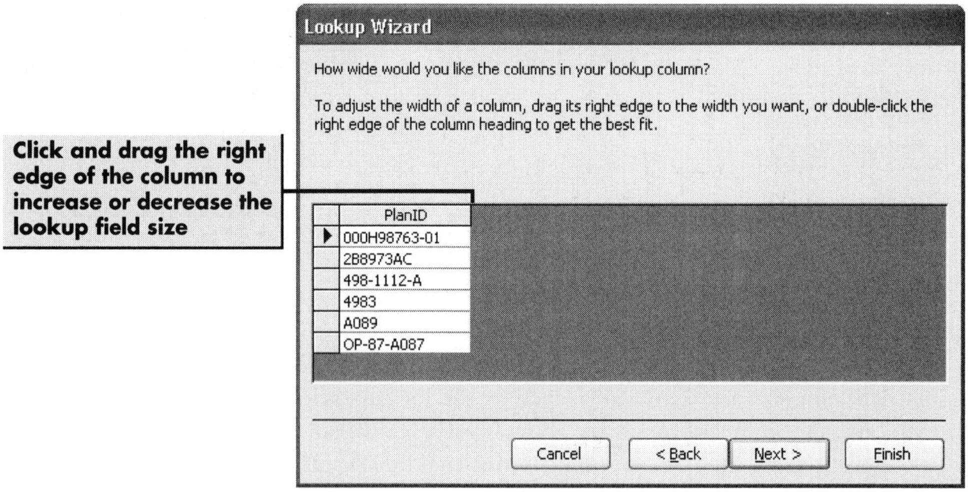

Click and drag the right edge of the column to increase or decrease the lookup field size

In the final dialog box, you can accept the default label for the lookup field (which is the lookup field's name) or specify a new one. Don clicks the Finish button to accept the default name, PlanID, and the Lookup Wizard closes. A dialog box opens and asks him to save the table design, and then the lookup field is created in tblCustomer. Don changes to Datasheet view for tblCustomer, and then clicks the PlanID field for the first record. The lookup field displays the PlanID values from tblHealthPlan, as shown in Figure 2.29. Now users can select the correct PlanID from this list by clicking it.

Figure 2.29: Lookup field values for the PlanID field

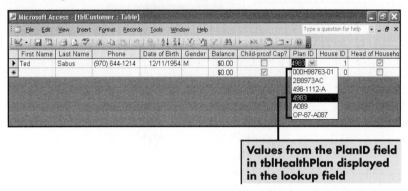

Values from the PlanID field in tblHealthPlan displayed in the lookup field

Don follows the same procedure to create a lookup field for the HouseID field in tblCustomer that displays the HouseID values from tblHousehold. However, in this case, Don wants to display two fields in the lookup field, not just one like in the PlanID field. Displaying only the HouseID field values won't provide enough information for the user entering a record in tblCustomer to determine which household to select because the HouseID stores values in the format 1, 2, 3, and so on. The user needs to enter the HouseID value from tblHousehold into the HouseID field in tblCustomer, but the user determines the correct HouseID based on the complete street address. Because households are unique, displaying the street address will be sufficient information to select the correct household for a new customer. To select more than one field's values in the lookup field, Don adds the HouseID and Address fields to the Selected Fields list box in the Lookup Wizard, as shown in Figure 2.30.

Figure 2.30: HouseID and Address fields added to the Selected Fields list box

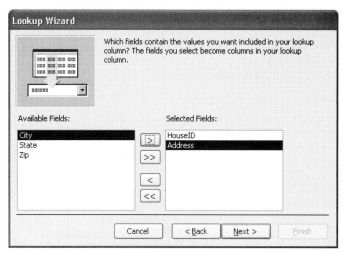

To make values easier to find, Don sorts the lookup field values in ascending order by address, and then removes the check mark from the Hide key column (recommended) check box to display the HouseID and Address values in the lookup field so users entering customer records can select the correct household using either value. Don increases the size of the Address field and decreases the size of the HouseID field so the lookup field will display the complete field values, selects the HouseID as the value to store in the HouseID field in tblCustomer (see Figure 2.31), and then accepts the default lookup field name of HouseID.

Figure 2.31: Selecting the option to store HouseID values in the HouseID field in tblCustomer

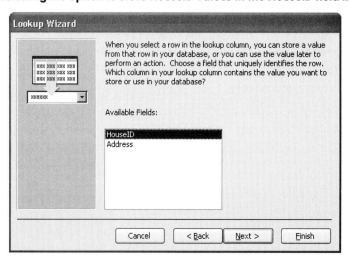

After saving tblCustomer, the lookup field will display data from the HouseID and Address fields stored in tblHousehold. Figure 2.32 shows the lookup field for the HouseID field.

To select a household for the customer, the user clicks the correct one from the list, based on a known HouseID field value or the street address. The values are sorted in ascending order by street address and users can scroll the values using the scroll bar on the lookup field. When the user selects a value in the lookup column, the HouseID value is stored in the HouseID field in tblCustomer.

Figure 2.32: Lookup field values for HouseID

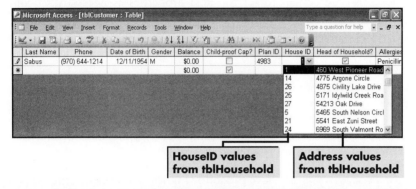

HouseID values from tblHousehold

Address values from tblHousehold

How To

Change or Delete a Lookup Field

1. In the Database window, click the Relationships button ⬚ on the Database toolbar. The Relationships window opens.

2. Right-click the join line that connects the lookup field to the table in which you created it.

3. Click Delete on the shortcut menu.

4. Click the Save button ⬚ on the Relationship toolbar.

5. Close the Relationships window.

6. Open the table in Design view that contains the field that you want to change to a lookup field, create the lookup field again, and then save the table design.

Steps To Success: Level 1

Don just received a request from Paul Ferrino to develop a database for a new pharmacy that Paul is opening in Edmonton, Alberta, Canada. Because the data collected about customers, employees, and drugs is slightly different in Canada, Don decides to create the databases simultaneously, but separately, so he can account for the individual differences in each version. Don wants you to create the database for Hudson Bay Pharmacy and the following tables using the information you learned in Chapter 1 and Level 1: tblClass, tblCustomer, tblHealthPlan, tblHousehold, tblJobTitle, tblDoctor, tblDrug, tblEmployee, and tblRx. (You will create the tblClinic, tblRefill, and tblEmployeeTraining tables in the Level 2 Steps To Success exercises.) Don provides you with additional information so you will know how to account for the differences in the Canadian version of the database.

Complete the following:

1. Start Access and create a new database named **Hudson.mdb** in the STS folder.

2. Use the information provided in Level 1 of this chapter to create the following tables in the database using any method you choose: tblClass, tblCustomer, tblHealthPlan, and tblHousehold. Be certain that each table includes a primary key and the necessary fields. Also, be certain to set the field properties as necessary to collect the correct data. Fields should include appropriate captions and field descriptions. These tables have the same requirements as the ones in the 4Corners database, with the following exceptions:

    a. Canadian addresses include a street address, city, province, and postal code. Provinces are abbreviated using two uppercase letters. Add properties to the Prov fields so that the data entered by the user is converted to uppercase letters. Also, make sure that users cannot enter digits or any other characters except letters into the Prov field.

    b. Postal codes in Canada have the following format: uppercase letter, number, uppercase letter, space, number, uppercase letter, number (for example, T6H 8U7). Add properties to the PostalCode fields to ensure that data entry into this field is accurate and correctly formatted.

3. Change the PlanID field in tblCustomer to a lookup field that displays the PlanID and PlanName values from tblHealthPlan but stores only the PlanID values. Sort values in ascending order by PlanID and adjust the lookup column widths as necessary to display the values that will be stored in these fields.

4. Change the HouseID field in tblCustomer to a lookup field that displays the HouseID and Address values from tblHousehold but stores only the HouseID values. Sort values in ascending order by Address.

5. Use Datasheet view and the data shown in Table 2.3 to create tblJobTitle. JobIDs are whole numbers and the Title field stores 30 characters. Use the Description property to document each field.

Table 2.3: Data for tblJobTitle

JobID	Title
1	Owner
2	Pharmacist
3	Technician
4	Cashier
5	Manager

6. Examine tblDoctor shown in Figure 2.2, and then start the Table Wizard. Use a template to create tblDoctor. DoctorID numbers are assigned sequentially by Access as you enter records into the table. The tblDoctor table is not related to any other database table yet (you will create relationships in the next level). The fields for the doctor's first name and last name should store 30 characters each. The fields that store phone numbers should store 15 characters each and format values in the following format and require entry of area codes: (###) ###-####. The ClinicID field is a foreign key to tblClinic, which you will create in the next level. (*Hint:* Create this field in Design view, and not with the Table Wizard.) Store ClinicID values as long integers. Use the Description property to document each field and enter appropriate captions to fields that require them.

7. Use Design view and the following information to create tblDrug shown in Figure 2.2. Make sure that the table includes a primary key and the necessary fields. Also, make sure that you set the field properties as necessary to collect the correct data. Fields should include appropriate captions and field descriptions.

- Canadian drugs do not have UPNs. Instead, drugs are uniquely identified using a Drug Identification Number (DIN). The DIN is a unique, eight-digit value that identifies each drug sold in Canada. DINs are not used in calculations.
- Drug names do not exceed 30 characters.
- Generic drugs are indicated by selecting a check box.
- Descriptions are alphanumeric values that might exceed 255 characters. The Description field collects data about the drug, such as counterindications, generic equivalents, and recommended dosages.
- The Unit field stores information about the unit of measure for a drug, such as pill or bottle, and requires 10 characters.
- The Dosage field stores information about the drug's strength and requires 10 characters. The Dosage field is not used in calculations.
- The DosageForm field stores information about the unit of measure for the drug strength, such as mg (for milligrams) or mcg (for micrograms). Dosage abbreviations do not exceed 20 characters.
- The Cost and Price fields store the cost and price, respectively, for one unit of the drug. The Canadian government regulates the prices that pharmacies can charge for drugs so pharmacies cover their overhead costs by charging a separate dispensing fee of $10–$12 per prescription. Dispensing fees are determined by the pharmacy and set individually for each drug.
- The Interactions field stores information about possible drug interactions and possible reactions. This field's data might exceed 255 characters.
- Canada does not track pregnancy risk categories like pharmacies in the United States.
- The Supplier field identifies the drug company or manufacturer from which a drug was purchased. Supplier names do not exceed 50 characters.

8. Use Design view and the following information to create tblEmployee shown in Figure 2.3. Make sure that the table includes a primary key and the necessary fields. Also, make sure that you set the field properties as necessary to collect the correct data. Fields should include appropriate captions and field descriptions.

- EmpIDs are assigned by the pharmacy using unique numbers. EmpIDs will be used to relate tables in the database.
- The EmpFirst and EmpLast fields will not exceed 30 characters each. The EmpMI field stores up to two characters.
- Canada issues Social Insurance numbers (SINs) instead of Social Security numbers. A SIN is a nine-digit number displayed with the following format: ###-###-###.
- The DOB (date of birth), StartDate, EndDate, and Review fields should store two-digit months and dates and four-digit years in the format ##/##/####.
- Make sure that the table stores a province (Prov) and postal code (PostalCode) for employees instead of a state and zip code.
- JobID is a foreign key in tblJobTitle. This field stores values as long integers.
- The Memo field stores other information about the employee that might exceed 255 characters.
- The Phone and Cell fields should store 15 characters in the format of (###) ###-####. Area code entry is required.
- Employees are paid an annual salary or an hourly rate.

9. Use Design view and the following information to create tblRx shown in Figure 2.2. Make sure that the table includes a primary key and the necessary fields. Also, make sure that you set the field properties as necessary to collect the correct data. Fields should include appropriate captions and field descriptions.

- PrescriptionIDs are assigned by Access as records are added to the table.
- The DIN is a unique, eight-digit value that identifies each drug sold in Canada. DINs are not used in calculations.
- The Quantity field stores the amount of medication dispensed and it is a numeric field that might contain decimal places.
- The Unit field stores information about the unit of measure for a drug, such as pill or bottle, and requires 10 characters.
- The Date and ExpireDate fields store the date of the prescription and the prescription's expiration date, respectively. Both fields should store two-digit months and dates and four-digit years in the format ##/##/####.
- The Refills field indicates the number of refills authorized by the prescribing doctor.
- The AutoRefill field indicates the customer's preference (yes or no) for automatic refills. The default value is not to order auto refills unless requested by the customer.
- The RefillsUsed field stores the number of refills a customer has used.

- The Instructions field stores medication directions and will not exceed 50 characters.
- The CustID field is a foreign key in tblCustomer and the DoctorID field is a foreign key in tblDoctor. Both fields store numbers.

10. You will enter data into these tables and create the relationships between tables in the next level. Close the **Hudson.mdb** database and Access.

LEVEL 2

POPULATING AND RELATING THE DATABASE TABLES

ACCESS 2003 SKILLS TRAINING

- **Create a database with at least one many-to-many relationship**
- **Create a database with at least one one-to-many relationship**
- **Create a one-to-many relationship using the Relationships window**
- **Enforce referential integrity in a one-to-many relationship**
- **Import a table from another Access database**
- **Import structured data into Access tables**
- **Join a table**
- **Specify a required value**
- **Specify referential integrity options**
- **Use subdatasheets**

CREATING ADDITIONAL TABLES FOR 4CORNERS PHARMACY

While you were working on creating the database and tables for the Hudson Bay Pharmacy, Don created the tblJobTitle, tblDoctor, tblDrug, tblEmployee, and tblRx tables in the 4Corners database. The table designs and properties he used in these tables appear in Tables 2.4 through 2.8.

Table 2.4: Table design for tblJobTitle

Field Name	Data Type	Description	Field Size	Properties
JobID	Number	Job ID (primary key)	Long Integer	Caption: Job ID
Title	Text	Job title (e.g., owner, pharmacist, technician, cashier, manager)	30	

Table 2.5: Table design for tblDoctor

Field Name	Data Type	Description	Field Size	Properties
DoctorID	Number	ID of prescribing doctor (primary key)	Long Integer	Caption: Doctor ID
DoctorFirst	Text	Doctor first name	30	Caption: First Name
DoctorLast	Text	Doctor last name	30	Caption: Last Name
Phone	Text	Doctor phone number	15	Input mask: !\(000") "000\-0000;;_
Cell	Text	Doctor cell phone number	15	Input mask: !\(000") "000\-0000;;_
ClinicID	Number	Clinic ID (foreign key)	Long Integer	Caption: Clinic ID

Table 2.6: Table design for tblDrug

Field Name	Data Type	Description	Field Size	Properties
UPN	Text	Drug ID (primary key)	3	Input mask: 000
Name	Text	Drug name	30	
Generic	Yes/No	Is this the generic (Y/N)?		Caption: Generic?
Description	Memo	Description of drug, counterindications, generic equivalent, and recommended dosage		
Unit	Text	Unit of measure of drug (pill, bottle)	10	
Dosage	Text	Strength of drug (e.g., 30)	10	
DosageForm	Text	Unit of measure	20	Caption: Dosage Form
Cost	Currency	Cost per unit		
Price	Currency	Retail price per unit		
Interactions	Memo	Interactions of drugs and possible reactions		
PregCategory	Text	Pregnancy risks	1	Input mask: >L Caption: Pregnancy Category Validation rule: In ('A','B','C','D','X') Validation text: Invalid pregnancy category. Valid values are A, B, C, D, or X.
Supplier	Text	Name of drug supplier	50	

Table 2.7: Table design for tblEmployee

Field Name	Data Type	Description	Field Size	Properties
EmpID	Number	Employee ID (primary key)	Long Integer	Caption: Employee ID
EmpFirst	Text	Employee first name	30	Caption: First Name
EmpMI	Text	Employee middle initial	2	Caption: Middle Initial
EmpLast	Text	Employee last name	30	Caption: Last Name
SSN	Text	Employee Social Security number	9	Input mask: 000\-00\-0000;;_
DOB	Date/Time	Employee date of birth		Input mask: 00/00/0000;;_ Caption: Date of Birth
StartDate	Date/Time	Employee hire date		Input mask: 00/00/0000;;_ Caption: Start Date
EndDate	Date/Time	Employee termination date		Input mask: 00/00/0000;;_ Caption: End Date
Address	Text	Employee address	30	
City	Text	Employee city	30	
State	Text	Employee state	2	
Zip	Text	Employee zip code	10	
JobID	Number	Employee job ID (foreign key)	Long Integer	Caption: Job ID
Memo	Memo	Other information about the employee		
Phone	Text	Employee home phone	15	Input mask: !\(000") "000\-0000;;_
Cell	Text	Employee cell phone	15	Input mask: !\(000") "000\-0000;;_
Salary	Currency	Employee salary		
HourlyRate	Currency	Employee hourly rate (for non-salaried employees)		Caption: Hourly Rate
Review	Date/Time	Date of next review		Input mask: 00/00/0000;;_

Table 2.8: Table design for tblRx

Field Name	Data Type	Description	Field Size	Properties
PrescriptionID	AutoNumber	Prescription number (primary key)		Caption: Prescription ID
UPN	Text	Drug ID (foreign key)	3	Input mask: 000

Table 2.8: Table design for tblRx (cont.)

Field Name	Data Type	Description	Field Size	Properties
Quantity	Number	Prescription quantity	Long Integer	
Unit	Text	Unit of measure	10	
Date	Date/Time	Date prescription was written		Input mask: 00/00/0000;;_
ExpireDate	Date/Time	Date prescription expires		Input mask: 00/00/0000;;_ Caption: Expire Date
Refills	Number	Number of refills allowed	Integer	Caption: Refills Authorized
AutoRefill	Yes/No	Does customer want auto refills (Y/N)?		Caption: Auto Refill?
RefillsUsed	Number	Number of refills used	Integer	Caption: Refills Used
Instructions	Text	Instructions for prescription	50	
CustID	Number	Customer ID (foreign key)	Long Integer	Caption: Customer ID
DoctorID	Number	Doctor ID (foreign key)	Long Integer	Caption: Doctor ID

POPULATING THE DATABASE TABLES

The 4Corners database now contains nine tables. The next step is to load the tables with data, also known as populating the database. Don could enter records into each table by typing in Datasheet view. However, because much of the data he needs to load is stored in sources found during the discovery phase, Don can import this data into the tables. There are several ways to import data into a database. Don will use two of them, which include copying and pasting records from another database table and importing data from an Excel workbook.

Copying Records from One Table to Another

Before he hired Don, Paul started working on a database and entered his customer data into a Customer table. Don knows that he can import Paul's existing data into tblCustomer as long as the structures of the two tables are identical. Two tables have identical structures if they have the same number of fields and those fields have the same data types and field sizes. For example, you cannot copy the contents of a Text field with a field size of 50 into a Text field with a field size of 10, nor can you copy a Number field with the Long Integer field size into a Number field with the Byte field size. Similarly, you cannot copy Text fields into Number fields, and so on.

If tblCustomer did not already exist in the 4Corners database, Don could import Paul's table design and the data it contains in one step. When you import a table from another database, instead of just the records it contains, you have the option of importing the table's structure (called the table definition) or the table definition and the data stored in the table. You can also choose to import the relationships for the imported table.

How To

Import an Existing Table into an Access Database

1. Open the database into which you will import the existing table.

2. Click File on the menu bar, point to Get External Data, and then click Import. The Import dialog box opens.

3. Use the Look in list arrow to browse to and select the database that contains the table that you want to import, and then click the Import button. The Import Objects dialog box opens.

4. Click the table that you want to import. If you want to import more than one table, press and hold the Ctrl key, click each table to import, and then release the Ctrl key.

5. Click the Options button. The Import Objects dialog box expands to include options for importing tables.

6. To import the tables and their relationships, select the Relationships check box in the Import section.

7. To import the table definition and data, click the Definition and Data option button; to import only the table definition, click the Definition Only option button.

8. Click the OK button.

Because tblCustomer already exists in the 4Corners database, Don just needs to import the data stored in Paul's table, and not the table definition. Don opens Paul's Customer.mdb database, opens the Customer table in Datasheet view, and then confirms that the structures of the two tables are exactly the same. Then he selects all of the records except for the one with CustomerID 1 because he already entered this record into the table. Don clicks the Copy button [image] on the Table Datasheet toolbar, closes the Customer database, clicks the Yes button to keep the data he copied on the Clipboard, and then opens tblCustomer in the 4Corners database in Datasheet view. He clicks the second record in the datasheet, clicks Edit on the menu bar, and then clicks Paste Append. Don was expecting the data to appear in the tblCustomer datasheet, but instead he receives a message that the values aren't appropriate for the input mask. Don clicks the OK button in the dialog box, and then clicks the No button to cancel importing the records from the Customer database. Don opens the Customer table in the Customer database again and examines the data. He realizes that some of the values in the DOB field have only a single digit in the month value, such as the digit 4 for April instead of the digits 04. Because the input mask on the DOB field in tblCustomer requires entry of a two-digit month and date, Don must delete the input mask from the DOB field, temporarily, to be able to copy and paste the customer records. He changes to Design view for tblCustomer, selects and deletes the input mask for the DOB field, and then saves the table and changes back to Datasheet view. He clicks the second record again, and then tries to paste the copied records. This time, he is successful. A message indicates that he is going to paste 40 records, which is correct, so he clicks the Yes button. The records now appear in tblCustomer, as shown in Figure 2.33.

Figure 2.33: Imported worksheet data

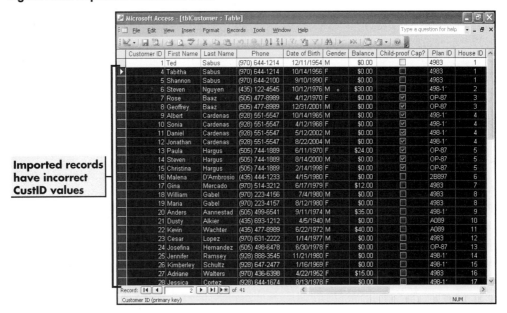

Imported records have incorrect CustID values

Don immediately sees a problem. In Paul's Customer table, the records were added to the table using sequential values with CustIDs 1 through 41. Don's examination of the data he imported shows that the records with CustIDs 2 and 3 were imported with the CustIDs 4 and 5, and the remaining records were renumbered after that. Don realizes that the AutoNumber records 2 and 3 were used when he tried to import the data and received an error message about the input mask. Once an AutoNumber record number is used, it becomes unavailable in the table, even if you delete the record. Right now, Don cannot add back or renumber the records to use CustIDs 2 and 3. Because the CustID is used as a foreign key in another table in the database, this problem will result in two orphaned records in the related table and data integrity errors on every record except the first record because the wrong customer number will exist in the related records. Don must correct this problem before continuing, or the data will not be correct.

To correct errors with AutoNumber field record numbers that should be incremented sequentially, you must delete the AutoNumber field from the table, and then add it back. If the CustID field was related to other tables in the database, Don would need to use the Relationships window to delete the relationship before he could delete the field. Because the CustID field is not yet used in any relationships, he can delete the field without making any changes in the Relationships window. Don right-clicks the CustID field in Design view, and then clicks Delete Rows on the shortcut menu. A message box opens and asks if he wants to permanently delete the selected field and its data, and he clicks the Yes button. Because CustID is the table's primary key, another message box opens asking Don to confirm the deletion, and he again clicks the Yes button. The CustID field is deleted from the table design.

To add the CustID field back to the table design, Don right-clicks the CustFirst field in the design grid, and then clicks Insert Rows on the shortcut menu. He types CustID as the field name, selects AutoNumber as the data type, and types Customer ID (primary key) as the field description. With the field selected, he clicks the Primary Key button [🔑] on the Table Design toolbar to make this field the table's primary key, and then saves the table design. When he changes to Datasheet view, the numbers are listed in sequential order from 1 to 41, which matches the original numbering in Paul's Customer table.

Don returns to Design view, adds the input mask back to the DOB field, and saves the table design. The tblCustomer table is now populated with data that will not cause any referential integrity problems later.

Best Practice

Importing Records with AutoNumber Fields into a Table

When you import data from another database into a table that contains an AutoNumber field, you should be aware of two potential problems.

First, when you use an AutoNumber field to create primary key values in a table, Access uses each incremented value only once. For example, if you delete a record with the value 11 in an AutoNumber field, record 11 is deleted permanently from the table. To the user, record 11 does not exist after you delete it, and there is no way to reenter a record with that AutoNumber value. However, if you import data into another table that also contains an AutoNumber field, Access creates a record 11 in the new table because AutoNumber 11 is an available record number in the *new* table. This difference can cause problems when the AutoNumber field has matching foreign key values with referential integrity enforced in the relationship. In this case, record 11 does *not* exist in the primary table. However, when you import the data into a new table, record 11 *does* exist, and all subsequently imported records are renumbered. If you try to relate data using the AutoNumber field, the foreign key values in the related table might not match.

Second, after importing data into a new or existing table, you cannot change a field's data type to AutoNumber because Access will not create AutoNumber values in a table that contains data. You can use a Number data type and the Long Integer data type to relate the field to an AutoNumber field, but you cannot create AutoNumber values in a table that contains imported or other existing data. If your table design includes an AutoNumber field, create the table structure prior to importing data into it so you can keep the AutoNumber field.

Importing Data from an Excel Workbook

In some cases, you might need to import data stored in an Excel workbook into a table. If you have not yet created the table in the database, you can import the data and create the table at the same time. In the discovery phase, Don received some Excel files from Paul containing data that he needs to store in the database. One of those files, Clinic.xls, contains data about the clinics that employ the doctors who write prescriptions for 4Corners Pharmacy customers. Don decides to create tblClinic by importing the data from the Excel file.

When you import data stored in an Excel workbook into a database, you need to review the contents of the workbook to understand how it is arranged. In most worksheets, the first row of data contains column headings that define the data in each column. If the column heading names comply with the rules for naming fields in Access, Access uses them as field names when you import the data. Figure 2.34 shows the Clinic.xls workbook in Excel. Paul inserted column headings that are valid Access field names, so these column headings will become the field names in tblClinic. If Don wanted to change any existing column headings to different names or to make them comply with the field naming rules in Access, he would make these changes in the worksheet before importing the data into Access.

Figure 2.34: Clinic worksheet data in Excel

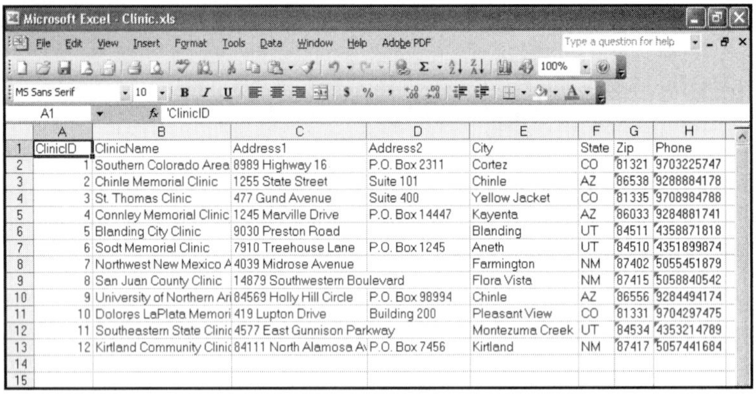

If the worksheet does not contain any column headings, or if the existing column headings violate Access field naming rules, Access assigns generic field names.

Access can import most data from a worksheet, with a few exceptions. It cannot import graphics, such as chart objects. Cells that contain formulas are imported as numbers, without the formulas, and hyperlinks are imported as text data. Access automatically assigns a data type to each column of data it imports by evaluating the data in the first 25 rows of the worksheet. For example, if the data in a column contains text values, Access assigns the Text data type to the field.

Access imports data in columns exactly as they are arranged in the worksheet. If you want to arrange the fields in a different way, you can rearrange the columns in the worksheet to meet your requirements. For example, the worksheet might list a customer's last name first. If you want the database to organize the fields so that the customer's first name comes first, you would need to move the FirstName column in the worksheet so it appears to the left of the LastName column. However, after importing the data, you can always rearrange the fields in the design grid of Table Design view like you would for any other table.

You can use Access to import specific data saved in a workbook. In most cases, you will import the data stored in a single worksheet, but you can also import named ranges of data. For example, if you only want to import the records in the range A2:H3 of the Clinic worksheet, you could specify a name for this range in the worksheet and specify it when you import the data, and Access would import the column headings as field names and the data in rows 2 and 3 and columns A through H of the worksheet.

After examining the worksheet, Don determines that it is properly organized with appropriate field names. He closes the workbook, clicks File on the menu bar in the Access Database window, points to Get External Data, and then clicks Import. The Import dialog box opens. Don selects the folder or drive that contains the workbook, changes the Files of type list arrow to display Microsoft Excel files, and then double-clicks Clinic.xls to select it and to start the Import Spreadsheet Wizard shown in Figure 2.35.

Figure 2.35: Import Spreadsheet Wizard

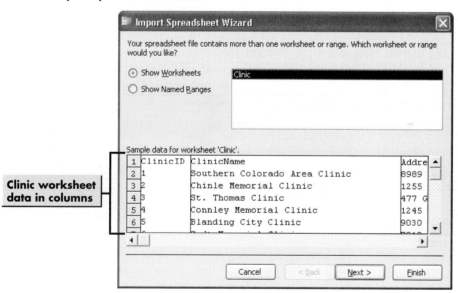

Don wants to import the data stored in the Clinic worksheet, which is the selected option. (If the workbook contained other worksheets, they would be listed in the list box.) If Don wants to select a named range in the worksheet, he would click the Show Named Ranges option button to display the ranges. Don clicks the Next button to accept these settings, and the second dialog box opens, as shown in Figure 2.36.

Figure 2.36: Identifying column headings in the worksheet

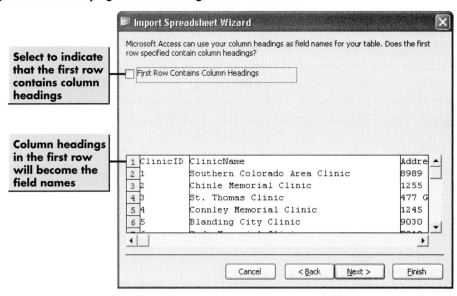

In this dialog box, you specify whether the first row of the worksheet contains column headings. Don selects the First Row Contains Column Headings check box to select it, indicating that the data in the first row should become the field names in the imported table. He clicks the Next button, which opens the third dialog box, shown in Figure 2.37.

Figure 2.37: Choosing the location for the imported data

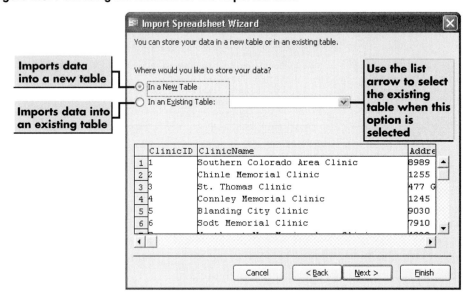

In this dialog box, you must choose the location to store the imported data. You can store it in a new table (the default option) or in an existing database table, in which case you must specify the table name. Don accepts the default option to store the data in a new table, and then clicks the Next button to open the fourth dialog box, shown in Figure 2.38.

Figure 2.38: Specifying information about the columns

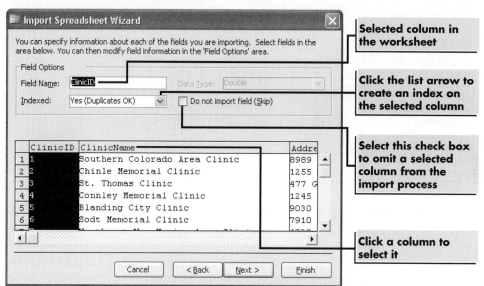

In this dialog box, you can change the default field names and indexing requirements for each field by selecting the field in the table. (Use the scroll bars to examine fields to the right and below the default values.) If the worksheet from which you are importing data is set up correctly, you usually will not need to make any changes in this dialog box. Don accepts the default settings, and then clicks the Next button to open the fifth dialog box, shown in Figure 2.39.

Figure 2.39: Setting a primary key field

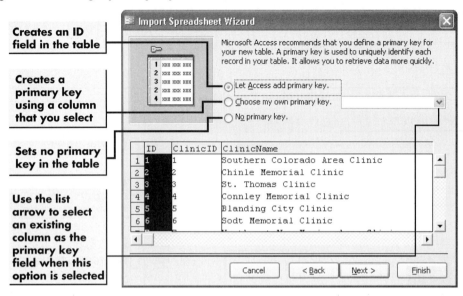

In this dialog box, you can choose a primary key field from the existing worksheet columns, let Access select a primary key (by adding an AutoNumber field to the imported table), or specify that the data contains no primary key. The default option adds an ID field to the table design. Because the worksheet already contains unique values in the ClinicID field, Don clicks the Choose my own primary key option button, and then selects ClinicID using the list box to the right of this option button. He clicks the Next button to open the final dialog box, changes the table name to tblClinic, and then clicks the Finish button. Access creates tblClinic in the 4Corners database and loads it with data. Don clicks the OK button to close the dialog box that opens to tell him that the data was imported, and then the Import Spreadsheet Wizard closes.

Don could use tblClinic as it contains a valid table structure and data. However, the table design that Access created from the imported data most likely does not match the exact table design that Don prepared for this table. To finish creating the table, Don opens tblClinic in Design view so he can verify the field properties for each field in the table and make any necessary changes. The first field, ClinicID, has the Number data type, which is correct. All of the other fields are Text fields, but Access set their field sizes to 255 characters. Because Don knows that the Text field sizes are too long, he changes the field sizes to match his table design. In addition, he adds field descriptions to all fields, captions to the ClinicID, ClinicName, Address1, and Address2 fields, and an input mask to the Phone field. If the table needs to contain any foreign keys, Don would need to add those fields to the table design. He saves the table and closes it. Because he decreased the field sizes for all of the Text fields, a dialog box opens and warns him about potential data loss in one or more fields. Don clicks the Yes button to finish saving the table, knowing that none of the existing data will be truncated by the new field sizes.

Don uses the Import Spreadsheet Wizard to import the existing data into tblDoctor, tblDrug, tblEmployee, tblJobTitle, and tblRx.

How To

Import Spreadsheet Data into an Existing Table

1. Create and save the table in Access, and then close it.

2. Examine the source data and make sure that the columns are arranged in the same order as the fields in the table, make any necessary changes, and then close the spreadsheet file.

3. In the Access Database window, click File on the menu bar, point to Get External Data, and then click Import. The Import dialog box opens.

4. Browse to the folder or drive that contains the file to import, change the Files of type list arrow to find the source data, select the source file, and then click the Import button. The Import Spreadsheet Wizard opens.

5. If necessary, select the worksheet or named range that contains the data to import, and then click the Next button.

6. If necessary, click the First Row Contains Column Headings check box to indicate that the first row in the source file contains headings, and then click the Next button.

7. Click the In an Existing Table option button, click the list arrow, click the table into which to import the data, and then click the Next button.

8. Click the Finish button.

9. Click the OK button to close the wizard.

WORKING WITH PRIMARY AND FOREIGN KEYS

Don's table designs include primary key fields that will contain values that uniquely identify each record in the tables. The table designs also include foreign key fields as necessary to join tables to each other to create the relationships in the database. A primary key and its foreign key counterparts must have the same data type and field size and the fields must contain identical values—you cannot relate fields that have different data types, field sizes, and values. Also, if referential integrity is set, a primary key value must exist before entering a corresponding record. For example, you must enter a new household into tblHousehold before you can add a new customer who lives in that household to tblCustomer.

The primary objective of creating a primary key field in a table is to prevent users from entering duplicate records into the table, but it also has other advantages. When a field has no value—a value that is unknown or unavailable or just missing—it is called a **null value**. A user cannot enter a null value into a primary key field because the primary key field is *required* for data entry and *cannot* store a null value. For example, if a user enters a drug into tblDrug but does not specify a UPN field value, Access has no way to uniquely identify each record in tblDrug. However, in some cases, you might want nonprimary key fields to store null values. For example, in tblDrug, the PregCategory field indicates the risk of using the drug during pregnancy; "A" indicates safe usage and "X" indicates a strong likelihood that the drug will cause birth defects. Most drug manufacturers assess their products for risk during pregnancy, but some drugs have unknown drug risks. In this case, the pharmacist doesn't enter a value in the PregCategory field—the risk is simply unknown.

You don't need to specify that primary key values are required in a table; this occurs automatically by setting a field as a table's primary key. By default, nonprimary key fields can store null values. You can, however, use the **Required property** for a nonprimary key field to ensure that users enter a value into the field. For example, Don could set the CustFirst and CustLast fields in tblCustomer so that users must enter values into these fields to add a customer's record to the table. To set the Required property, select the field in Design view and then change its value in the Required property text box from "No" to "Yes" (without the quotation marks). You must be careful about requiring data entry into a field, however. What if you require data entry in the Address field, but the customer has just moved and doesn't yet have an address to give? If you require data entry in the Address field, you cannot enter the customer's information in tblCustomer.

The primary key field also works to make data retrieval faster. When you specify a field as a table's primary key, Access creates an index for the primary key field. An index in a database is similar to an index that you find in a published book. When you need to find a specific topic in a book, you can find the topic in the book's index and obtain a list of the page numbers on which the topic appears so you can find them quickly. In a database, an **index** is a list maintained by the database (but hidden from users) that associates the field values in the indexed field with the records that contain the field values. You might think of a database index as a small table containing values from a table and record numbers that reference those values. An index does not contain an entire record—it only contains the field from the record and a pointer to the record number.

As the pharmacy grows, more records will be added to the tables and additional tables might be added to the database structure. As the number of records and the complexity of the database increases, the efficiency of the database will decrease. Don knows that employees will use certain tables and fields more often than others. For example, the pharmacy staff will use tblCustomer on a regular basis to manage data about the pharmacy's customers. In the first year alone, tblCustomer might grow in size to include thousands of records. Don also knows that the data in tblCustomer will be used many times by other tables, queries, and reports. Don decides to change the table structure to increase the performance of tblCustomer, which, in turn, will increase the speed of the entire database.

Creating an Index

Don anticipates that the pharmacy staff might need to search tblCustomer frequently to find customers by using their last names. To increase the speed at which Access searches tblCustomer, Don can create an index on the CustLast field. To create an index in a table, open the table in Design view, select the field to index, and then click the Indexed property. You can create an index for any field, except for fields with the Memo, Hyperlink, and OLE

Object data types. When you click the Indexed property for a field, three options appear in a menu, as shown in Figure 2.40.

Figure 2.40: Creating an index for a nonprimary key field

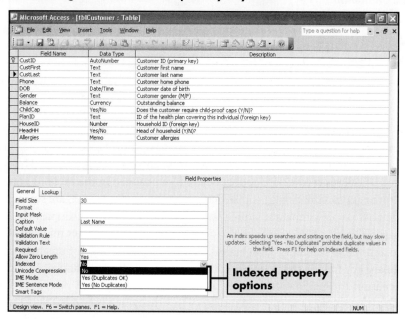

The first option, which is the default option for nonprimary key fields, is "No." The No option means that there is no index for the field. The second option, "Yes (Duplicates OK)," creates an index for the field that accepts and stores duplicate values. Because it is likely that some customers of the pharmacy will have the same last names, using the Yes (Duplicates OK) option permits users to enter duplicate last names into this field. The third option is "Yes (No Duplicates)," which is the default option for primary key fields. You can set this option for nonprimary key fields to control data entry. For example, because U.S. citizens have unique Social Security numbers, two employees in tblEmployee cannot have duplicate Social Security numbers. By setting the SSN field to Yes (No Duplicates), Access prevents duplicate values from being stored in the SSN field.

To view the indexes created in a table, click the Indexes button 📇 on the Table Design toolbar. Figure 2.41 shows the Indexes window for tblCustomer. There are five indexes in this table—two for CustID (the table's primary key), one each for the HouseID and PlanID fields, which are foreign keys, and the one Don just set for the CustLast field. You can add indexes to the Indexes window by typing an index name, field name, and the sort order. You can delete an index by right-clicking the index name, and then clicking Delete Rows on the shortcut menu.

Figure 2.41: Indexes window for tblCustomer

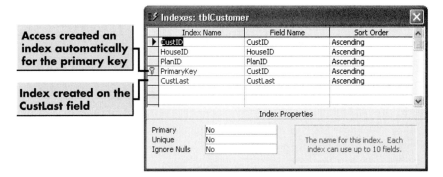

Access created an index automatically for the primary key

Index created on the CustLast field

Don can create indexes for as many fields as necessary to optimize searches in the database. When you create an index, the records are indexed when you save the table. The index is updated automatically as records are added, deleted, or changed in the table. If you specify a sort order for an index (the default sort order is ascending), the records are sorted as well. In a small database, you might not notice the time and computer resources required to sort records using an index. However, as the database grows, the indexes might slow down the database and make searching take longer. Another disadvantage of creating an index on a nonprimary key field is that it increases the size of the database and slows down the database because it must update the index as users add, change, and delete records. To overcome these drawbacks, you can add indexes as needed when improved performance is necessary, and delete indexes to increase speed and reduce file size. For example, Don could add an index prior to running a query or report and then remove the index to reduce the size of the database and to improve efficiency when updating.

CREATING ONE-TO-MANY RELATIONSHIPS BETWEEN TABLES

In Chapter 1, you learned how to relate tables in a database using primary key and foreign key fields. In Access, you define table relationships in the Relationships window or when you create a lookup field that searches the records in another table. To open the Relationships window, click the Relationships button ![icon] on the Database toolbar in the Database window. Figure 2.42 shows the Relationships window for the 4Corners database.

Figure 2.42: Relationships window

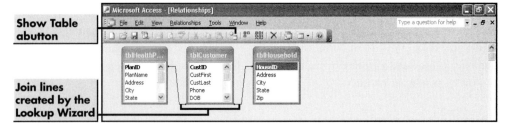

Show Table abutton

Join lines created by the Lookup Wizard

The Relationships window contains the field lists for three tables—tblHealthPlan, tblCustomer, and tblHousehold. Don can use the mouse pointer to resize the field lists to display all of the fields in each table. He can also drag the field lists to new positions to better illustrate the relationships. Because Don created lookup fields in tblCustomer to look up fields in tblHealthPlan and tblHousehold, there are two existing relationships in the database. These relationships appear as join lines that connect the tables to each other. The other tables in the database do not appear in the Relationships window because they do not contain any lookup fields and also because Don has not added them to the window yet.

You learned in Chapter 1 that a relationship has certain properties associated with it. The relationship has a certain type, such as one-to-many, one-to-one, or many-to-many, and certain attributes that specify how to manage changes when records are updated or deleted. To view the properties for a relationship, you can right-click the join line, and then click Edit Relationship on the shortcut menu. Don right-clicks the join line between tblHealthPlan and tblCustomer and opens the Edit Relationships dialog box shown in Figure 2.43.

Figure 2.43: Edit Relationships dialog box

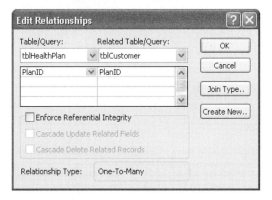

The Edit Relationships dialog box shows the relationship between the primary table tblHealthPlan and the related table tblCustomer, which resulted when Don created the lookup field for PlanID. The relationship type, one-to-many, indicates that one PlanID in the primary table is related to zero, one, or many PlanIDs in the related table (tblCustomer). Don enforces this rule by clicking the Enforce Referential Integrity check box to add a check mark to it. Because a PlanID value in tblHealthPlan might change as a result of a new plan number from an insurance company, Don needs to make sure that changes to the PlanIDs in tblHealthPlan are updated in the related records, so he clicks the Cascade Update Related Fields check box to select it. Don does not, however, want to delete all related records if a PlanID is deleted from tblHealthPlan, so he does not select the Cascade Delete Related Fields check box. After making these changes, Don clicks the OK button to make the changes, and then he clicks the Save button 🖫 on the Relationship toolbar to save the changes in the database. The Relationships window shows a one-to-many relationship between the PlanID field in tblHealthPlan to the PlanID field in tblCustomer. A "1" appears on the "one" side of the relationship and an infinity symbol appears on the "many" side of the relationship. Don edits the relationship created by the lookup field between tblHousehold and tblCustomer to enforce referential integrity and cascade updates as well. The Relationships window appears in Figure 2.44.

Figure 2.44: Relationships window after creating two 1:M relationships

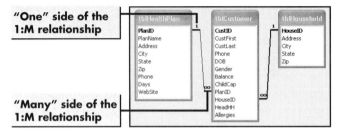

Now Don needs to add the remaining tables to the Relationships window and create the relationships between the appropriate tables using his database design. He clicks the Show Table button 🔲 on the Relationship toolbar to open the Show Table dialog box, clicks tblClass in the Tables list, and then clicks the Add button. The tblClass table is added to the Relationships window. He repeats this process to add tblClinic, tblDoctor, tblDrug, tblEmployee, tblJobTitle, and tblRx to the Relationships window, and then clicks the Close button to close the Show Table dialog box. He resizes the field lists to display all fields in each new table and rearranges the field lists so that related tables are next to each other, as shown in Figure 2.45, to make it easier to create the relationships. Notice that the primary key fields in each table appear in bold type, making it easy to identify the primary key in each table.

Figure 2.45: Relationships window after adding, resizing, and repositioning the database tables

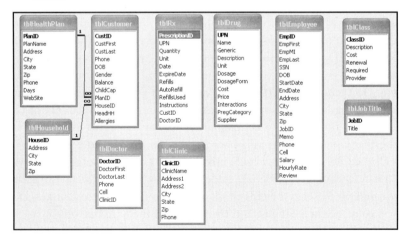

Now Don can start creating the relationships between tables. The first one that Don creates is the one-to-many relationship between tblDoctor and tblRx. A primary key field and the corresponding foreign key field are not required to have the same field name, but the values in the primary key and foreign key fields must match exactly to create the relationship. You can create the relationships by dragging the primary key field from the primary table to the foreign key field in the related table. When you release the mouse button, the Edit Relationships dialog box opens, into which you specify the relationship properties. Don drags the DoctorID field from tblDoctor to the DoctorID field in tblRx, and then releases the mouse button. The Edit Relationships dialog box opens, and he clicks the check boxes to enforce referential integrity and cascade update related fields. After clicking the Create button, the one-to-many relationship between doctors and prescriptions is created. Don also creates the one-to-many relationships between the tblJobTitle and tblEmployee tables, between the tblDrug and tblRx tables, and between the tblCustomer and tblRx tables and then selects the options to enforce referential integrity and cascade update related fields. The Relationships window now looks like Figure 2.46.

Figure 2.46: Relationships window after creating 1:M relationships

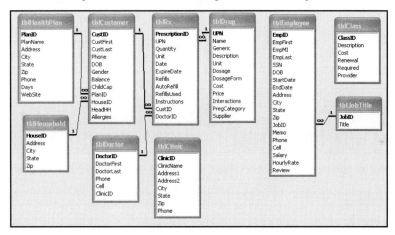

Don sees that he has not yet related the tblClinic and tblDoctor tables. He drags the ClinicID field from tblClinic to the ClinicID field in tblDoctor, and selects the options to enforce referential integrity and to cascade updates. This time, however, instead of creating the one-to-many relationship, Don sees the error message shown in Figure 2.47.

Figure 2.47: Error message about mismatched data types

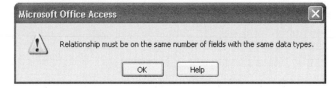

Don knows that this error message indicates that he is trying to join tables with fields that do not have the same data type or field size. He clicks the OK button to close the message box, clicks the Cancel button to close the Edit Relationships dialog box, and then saves the Relationships window and closes it. He opens tblClinic in Design view and sees that the primary key field, ClinicID, has the Number data type and the Double field size. He then remembers how this problem occurred—when he created the table by importing data, Access assigned this field a data type and field size based on the data he imported. He accepted the default field size, Double, and saved the table. However, the ClinicID field in tblDoctor uses the Long Integer field size. The different field sizes caused the error message, so Don changes the field size of ClinicID field in tblClinic to Long Integer, saves tblClinic, clicks Yes in the message box informing him that some data might be lost, and then returns to the Relationships window. This time, he is able to create the one-to-many relationship between tblClinic and tblDoctor, as shown in Figure 2.48.

Figure 2.48: Relationships window with 1:M relationships created

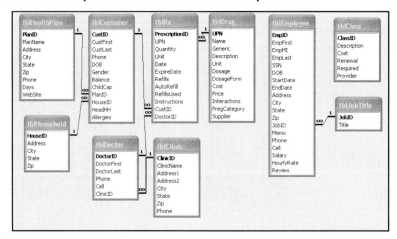

Don looks at the Relationships window and sees that he has no way to relate employees to the classes they take, because there are no common fields between tblEmployee and tblClass. To create this relationship, he needs to create another table in the database that he can use to create a many-to-many relationship.

Best Practice

Troubleshooting Referential Integrity Errors

Relating tables in the Relationships window is usually a smooth process, but you might encounter a few potential problems, especially when you have imported existing table designs and data into your database.

Figure 2.47 showed the error message that opens when the values in the primary key and foreign key fields do not match. This error usually means that you are attempting to relate fields with dissimilar data types or field sizes. This error is common when relating Number and Text fields with different field sizes. If you get this error, open the primary table and the related table in Design view and then compare the primary key and foreign key fields, and change one or both fields so the data types and field sizes match.

Figure 2.49 shows another error that you might see when attempting to relate tables in the Relationships window. In this case, Access cannot create the relationship because it would create orphaned records in the primary or related table.

Figure 2.49: Error message about referential integrity violation

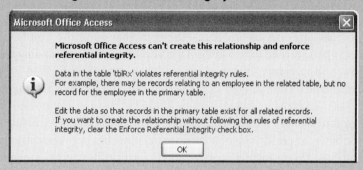

If you receive this error message, it is more difficult to correct the problem because you must compare the primary key values in the primary table to the foreign key values in the related table and identify values in the first table that do not match the second table. To enforce referential integrity and create the relationship, there must be a primary key value in the primary table for every foreign key value in the related table. Correcting this error usually involves adding a missing record to the primary table that matches an existing record in the related table.

CREATING A MANY-TO-MANY RELATIONSHIP BETWEEN TABLES

Don's database design includes creating tblEmployeeTraining, which is a junction table to create the many-to-many relationship between employees and classes. Don creates this table in Design view, as shown in Figure 2.50. Notice that the primary key of tblEmployeeTraining is the combination of all three fields in the table.

Figure 2.50: Table design for tblEmployeeTraining

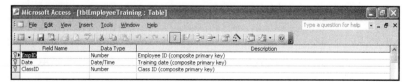

How To

Create a Composite Primary Key

1. In Design view, click in the row for the first field that will become the composite key.

2. Press and hold the Ctrl key, and then click the second field that will become the composite key. If necessary, continue holding the Ctrl key and click any other fields that will become the composite key.

3. When all fields in the composite key are selected, release the Ctrl key.

4. Click the Primary Key button 🔑 on the Table Design toolbar.

5. Save the table.

An employee can take any class on any date—the combination of the EmpID, Date, and ClassID creates a unique record in this table. Don adds tblEmployeeTraining to the Relationships window, and rearranges the field lists so he can see all of the fields in each table and so that related tables are arranged next to each other. To create the many-to-many relationship between employees and classes, he starts by creating the one-to-many relationship between tblClass and tblEmployeeTraining and enforces referential integrity and cascades updates. Then he creates the one-to-many relationship between tblEmployee and tblEmployeeTraining. The result is a many-to-many relationship between employees and classes, as shown in Figure 2.51.

Figure 2.51: Relationships window after creating an M:N relationship

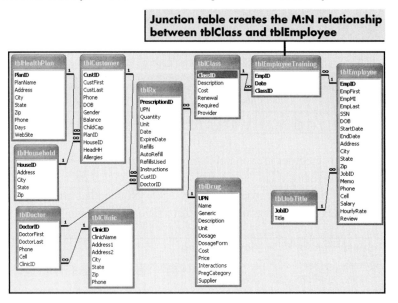

Don needs to add one more table to the database, tblRefill, which will store data about prescription refills, the customers who request them, and the employees who fill them. He returns to Design view and creates tblRefill, as shown in Figure 2.52.

Figure 2.52: Table design for tblRefill

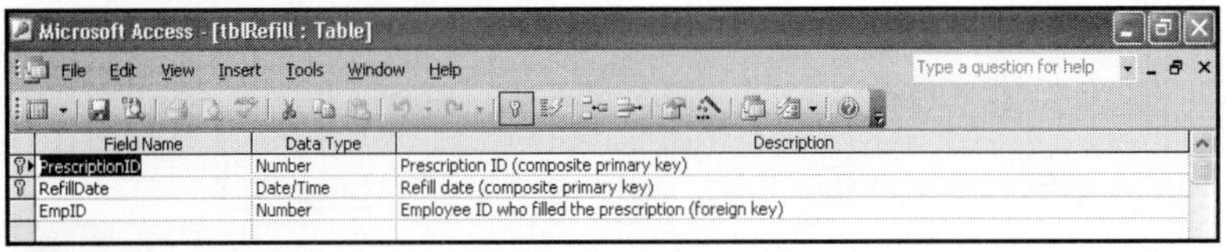

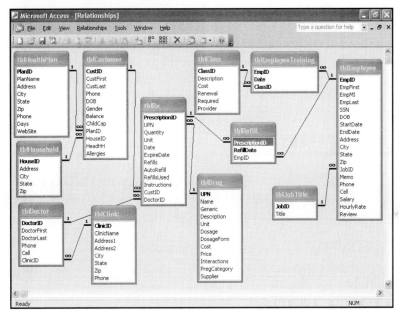

After creating and saving tblRefill, Don adds it to the Relationships window and creates the one-to-many relationship between tblRx and tblRefill and the one-to-many relationship between tblEmployee and tblRefill. Now there is a many-to-many relationship between employees and prescriptions. The final Relationships window appears in Figure 2.53.

Figure 2.53: Completed Relationships window

Now that Don has created all of the relationships in the database, he imports the existing data he has from the discovery phase into tblEmployeeTraining and tblRefill. The database is now fully populated.

USING A SUBDATASHEET TO VIEW RELATED RECORDS

After importing data into a database, it is a good idea to open each table in Datasheet view and check the data for any problems. Don checks each table, including tblHousehold, by opening it in Datasheet view. Because of the relationship Don created between the tblHousehold and tblCustomer tables, a plus box ➕ appears to the left of the HouseID value in each record. He clicks the plus box in the first record, which opens the subdatasheet shown in Figure 2.54.

Figure 2.54: Customer data shown in a subdatasheet

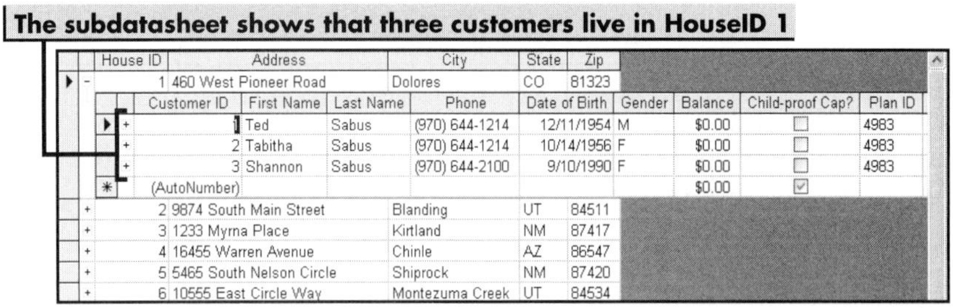

The subdatasheet shows that three customers live in HouseID 1

House ID	Address	City	State	Zip					
1 460 West Pioneer Road	Dolores	CO	81323						
Customer ID	First Name	Last Name	Phone	Date of Birth	Gender	Balance	Child-proof Cap?	Plan ID
1 Ted	Sabus	(970) 644-1214	12/11/1954	M	$0.00	☐	4983
2 Tabitha	Sabus	(970) 644-1214	10/14/1956	F	$0.00	☐	4983
3 Shannon	Sabus	(970) 644-2100	9/10/1990	F	$0.00	☐	4983
(AutoNumber)					$0.00	☑	
2 9874 South Main Street	Blanding	UT	84511						
3 1233 Myrna Place	Kirtland	NM	87417						
4 16455 Warren Avenue	Chinle	AZ	86547						
5 5465 South Nelson Circle	Shiprock	NM	87420						
6 10555 East Circle Way	Montezuma Creek	UT	84534						

When Don clicks the plus box for a record in a table that has a one-to-many relationship, the **subdatasheet** displays records from the related table. In Figure 2.54, Don uses the subdatasheet to see that the customers living in HouseID 1 are Ted, Tabitha, and Shannon Sabus. You can display and hide the subdatasheet for any record in the primary table by clicking the plus box. In addition, you can use the subdatasheet to make changes to the related records, and the subdatasheet will display those changes. The changes are also made in the related table.

Steps To Success: Level 2

In the Steps To Success for Level 1, you created the database for Hudson Bay Pharmacy and created the table designs for nine tables: tblClass, tblCustomer, tblDoctor, tblDrug, tblEmployee, tblHealthPlan, tblHousehold, tblJobTitle, and tblRx. The only table that contains data at this point is tblJobTitle. Don asks you to create the remaining tables in the database (tblClinic, tblEmployeeTraining, and tblRefill) and to populate the database with data using various sources that he has provided to you. You will also need to relate the appropriate tables to each other.

Complete the following:

1. Start Access and open the **Hudson.mdb** database from the STS folder.

2. Populate the existing database tables as follows. The files you need are saved in the Chapter 2 folder.

   a. Use the file **hbpClass.xls** to populate tblClass.

   b. Use the file **hbpCust.xls** to populate tblCustomer.

   c. Use the file **hbpHhold.xls** to populate tblHousehold.

   d. Use the file **hbpHPlan.xls** to populate tblHealthPlan.

e. Use the file **hbpRx.xls** to populate tblRx.

f. Use the file **hbpDrug.xls** to populate tblDrug.

g. Use the file **hbpEmp.xls** to populate tblEmployee.

h. Copy and paste the records in the Doctor table in the **hbpDoc.mdb** database into tblDoctor in the **Hudson.mdb** database.

3. Create tblClinic by importing data from the file **hbpClin.xls**. Be certain the table meets the following requirements:

- The ClinicID field is the table's primary key.
- The ClinicName cannot exceed 50 characters.
- The Address1, Address2, and City fields cannot exceed 40 characters.
- The default value for the Prov field is "AB" and all values entered into this field must be uppercase and two characters in length.
- Values in the PostalCode field must appear in the following format: uppercase letter, number, uppercase letter, space, number, uppercase letter, number (for example, T6H 8U7).
- The Phone field stores 15 characters, displays values in the format of (###) ###-####, and area code entry is required.
- All fields must have appropriate captions and field descriptions.

4. Create tblEmployeeTraining using the following information:

- The EmpID and ClassID fields store numbers with no decimal places and are foreign keys.
- The Date field stores the date of the training session. Display the date using the format ##/##/####.
- Set the composite primary key, add captions to appropriate fields, and add appropriate field descriptions to all fields.
- Use the **hbpEmpTr.xls** file to populate the table.

5. Create tblRefill using the following information:

- The PrescriptionID and the EmpID fields store numbers with no decimal places and are foreign keys.
- The RefillDate field stores the date the prescription was refilled. Display the date using the format ##/##/####.
- Set the composite primary key, add captions to appropriate fields, and add appropriate field descriptions to all fields.
- Use the **hbpRef.xls** file to populate the table.

6. Create an index on the CustLast field in tblCustomer and on the Name field in tblDrug.

7. Create the appropriate relationships in the database.

8. Close the **Hudson.mdb** database and Access.

LEVEL 3

MAINTAINING AND SECURING A DATABASE

ACCESS 2003 SKILLS TRAINING

- **Add permissions to databases**
- **Compact on close**
- **Create a single field index**
- **Create multiple field indexes**
- **Open a database in exclusive mode**
- **Remove a password**
- **Set database encryption**
- **Set passwords for databases**
- **Use database tools to compact a database**
- **Use the Documenter**

THE DATABASE ADMINISTRATOR ROLE

The 4Corners database now contains 12 related tables that store the data needed to dispense prescriptions to customers of the pharmacy. Don populated the tables with the existing data he gathered during the discovery phase. It might be tempting to think that the database is "finished" at this point, but it is not. Don knows that there are other tasks he needs to complete before bringing the database online for users. These tasks include securing the database, backing up and restoring the database, archiving data, and compacting and repairing the database. He also needs to document the database design for himself and other database users. Collectively, these tasks are known as maintaining a database. Most organizations assign these tasks to **database administration**, also known as **DBA**. In many organizations, DBA is a group that is responsible for designing, maintaining, and securing the database. In other organizations, DBA is an individual who is charged with these tasks; sometimes, this individual is called the **database administrator**. At 4Corners Pharmacy, Don is the database administrator. The database administrator sets the security and other features of a database in addition to setting options for individual users and groups of users.

When you open an Access database, the default option is to open it so that it is available to other users should they choose to open the same database at the same time. To change the way you open a database, click the Open button 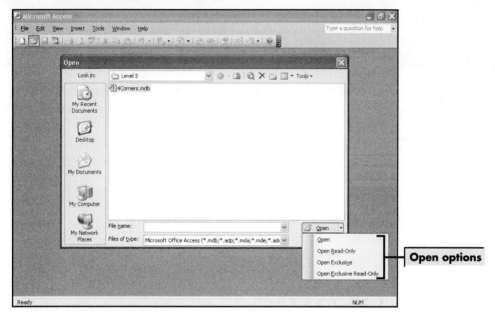 on the Database toolbar, and then click the list arrow for the Open button in the Open dialog box, as shown in Figure 2.55.

Figure 2.55: Open dialog box in Access

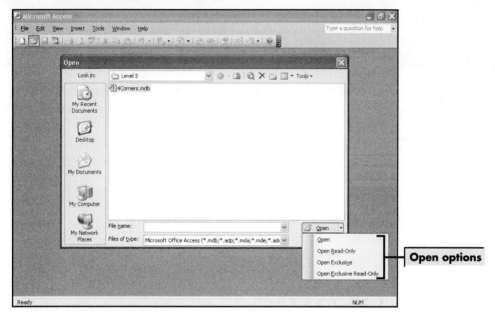

You can open an Access database in four ways:

- **Open mode** allows multiple users to open and use the database at the same time. This is the default option for opening a database.
- **Open Read-Only mode** allows multiple users to open a database, but they cannot write any information to the database, such as adding or changing records or creating new objects. Users are limited to viewing existing data only.
- **Open Exclusive mode** opens the database so that all users except for the current user are locked out from opening and using the database at the same time. A database administrator uses this option to open the database prior to setting a password or database security.
- **Open Exclusive Read-Only mode** opens the database so that all users except for the current user are locked out, but the current user can only view the data in the database.

As the database administrator, Don must open the database with exclusive access prior to performing database maintenance and security tasks to prevent other users from accessing the database while he performs this work. Don knows that there are no other users accessing the database, so he can perform some of these tasks now. He begins by opening the database in exclusive mode.

Open a Database in Exclusive Mode

1. Start Access, and then click the Open button 📂 on the Database toolbar. The Open dialog box opens.
2. Use the Look in list arrow to browse to and select the database you want to open.
3. Click the list arrow for the Open button.
4. Click Open Exclusive.

With all other users locked out from the 4Corners database, Don can maintain the database and set the security options. First, he will compact, repair, and back up the database.

COMPACTING AND REPAIRING A DATABASE

As users work in a database by adding and deleting records and objects, the size of the database increases and decreases. However, the space created by deleting a record or object is not automatically recovered for use by records and objects that users add to the database. Just like any other computer file, a database becomes large with blocks of unused space. These unused areas can ultimately increase the database size and make it inefficient. The process of recovering unused space in a database is known as compacting the database. When you **compact** a database, the data and objects in the database are reorganized and unused spaces are reassigned and deleted. The end result is usually a database with a decreased file size and improved efficiency.

Don has two options for compacting the database. He can do it manually by clicking Tools on the menu bar in the Database window, pointing to Database Utilities, and then clicking Compact and Repair Database. Access closes the database, compacts it, and also repairs the database. When Access finishes the compact and repair utilities, it reopens the database. Don can also set the database to compact the database each time it closes by clicking Tools on the menu bar in the Database window, clicking Options, and then clicking the General tab, as shown in Figure 2.56.

Figure 2.56: Setting the Compact on Close option

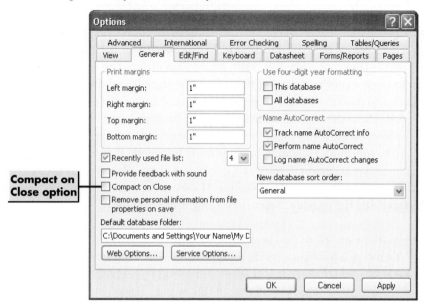

Compact on
Close option

To compact the database when it closes, Don clicks the Compact on Close check box to select it. After clicking the OK button, Access compacts the database each time it is closed. However, setting the Compact on Close option does not also repair the database. Don selects the Compact on Close option, but also decides to run the Compact and Repair utility periodically to repair any problems in the database. He can also use the Compact and Repair utility any time that there is a problem in the database. Don notices that the 4Corners database was just over one megabyte in size before he compacted it manually. After compacting, the database size decreased to 432 KB, which is less than half the original size.

Don's next task is to back up the database so he has another copy of it in case of damage or loss.

Best Practice

Compacting a Database Before Backing Up a Database

Even if you have been compacting a database on a regular basis, either by running the Compact and Repair Database utility or by setting the Compact on Close option, it is a good idea to compact the database immediately prior to performing a backup. When you back up a database, any unused areas become a part of the backup file. By compacting the database first, you might reduce the size of the backup file because these unused spaces are not included in it.

BACKING UP A DATABASE

Now that Don has compacted the database, he wants to create a backup copy. **Backing up** a database creates a copy of the database that you can restore in the event of a loss. A loss might be a power failure or hard disk crash, a user who maliciously or accidentally deletes database objects, or any other situation that affects the records and objects in the database. Most database administrators perform regular database backups for each day the database is used. A good rule of thumb is to schedule database backups based on the amount of data loss that you can manage. If you cannot manage reentering all of the transactions completed in a week's time, you should schedule backups more frequently than once a week. It is not uncommon for an organization to back up a database nightly, after all users have completed their work. Don will schedule a backup of the 4Corners database at midnight each night, so that the most data the pharmacy ever risks losing is the data for one day.

After creating a backup copy of the database, it is important to store the copy in a fireproof location, preferably at a location outside the pharmacy. In most cases, a backup is created on external media, such as a CD, DVD, or external hard drive. Many organizations store multiple backup copies of their databases indexed by date at alternate facilities. For such an organization, a fire might destroy the entire building, but the organization does not lose its business data as well.

To back up the database, Don clicks Tools on the menu bar in the Database window, points to Database Utilities, and then clicks Back Up Database. The default backup database name is the original database name, followed by the current date. You can accept this default filename or create a new one. Clicking the Save button closes the database and begins the backup. Depending on the size of the database, it might take anywhere from a few minutes to several hours to complete the task. When the backup utility is complete, Access reopens the database.

The backup copy of the database is a copy that you can open just like any other Access database. In the event of loss in the master copy of the database, Don could install the backup copy. In this case, he would need to identify any changes that were made between the time of the loss in the original database and the time he installed the backup copy because the backup might not contain all of the data he needs to restore.

The next task Don wants to complete is to document the database objects so he has a record of each table, including the fields in the table and their properties.

DOCUMENTING THE DATABASE DESIGN

After finishing the initial database design, it is a good idea to document the design so you have it for future reference. In Access, the **Documenter** tool produces a report of every object or just selected objects in a database. Don wants to document all of his table designs. Because tables are the only objects in the current database, he will select the option to document every object when he runs the Documenter. To run the Documenter, Don clicks Tools on the menu bar, points to Analyze, and then clicks Documenter. The Documenter dialog box shown in Figure 2.57 opens.

Figure 2.57: Documenter dialog box

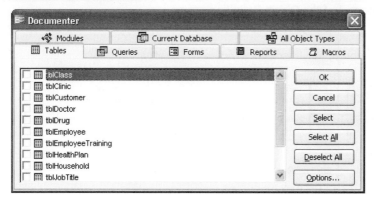

The tabs at the top of the Documenter dialog box let you sort objects by type. The All Object Types tab includes all objects in the current database. Selecting the Current Database tab lets you document the properties of objects or the relationships of objects that you select. Because the database contains only tables, Don clicks the Select All button on the Tables tab, which adds a check mark to each table's check box. Clicking the Options button opens the Print Table Definition dialog box shown in Figure 2.58.

Figure 2.58: Print Table Definition dialog box

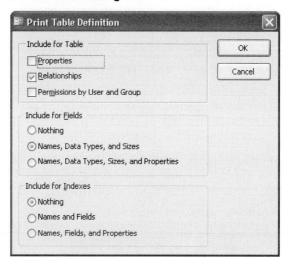

The options in the Print Table Definition dialog box let you specify what to document for each table. You can include table properties, relationships, and permissions; names, data types, field sizes, and field properties for fields; and names, fields, and properties for indexes. Don wants to include the table relationships and names, data types, and field sizes for fields, so he selects these options. When he clicks the OK button in the Documenter dialog box, Access creates an Object Definition report. The first page of this report appears in Figure 2.59.

Figure 2.59: Page 1 of the Object Definition report

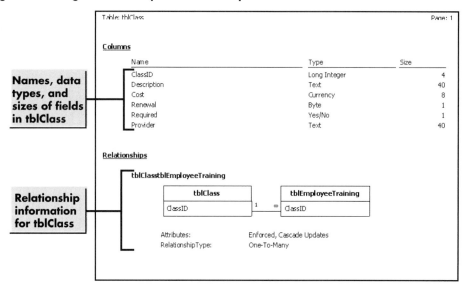

Don can use the Print button 🖶 on the Print Preview toolbar to print the report so he can file it away in a safe place. He can also use the Export command on the File menu to save the report as a file. If he needs to run this report again, he would need to run the Documenter again and select the desired options.

SECURING A DATABASE FROM UNAUTHORIZED USE

Even though Don will create regular backup copies of the database, it is still very important to plan for and prevent data loss in the first place. One of Don's most important tasks is to protect the database from unintentional or malicious damage. Access includes several tools that let you control access to a database. In most cases, the database administrator must open the database with exclusive access prior to setting some of the features that protect the database. These tools are setting a database password, encrypting the database, and hiding the database objects.

Using a Password to Protect a Database

Don knows that it is his job to protect the pharmacy's data, but a bigger responsibility is for the pharmacy to protect its customers' and employees' data. The 4Corners database stores personal information about customers and employees, such as Social Security numbers, phone and address information, salary data, and prescription information. The potential exists for an employee to use information in the database inappropriately or for a hacker to gain access to the database and use it in an identity theft scheme. Don knows that the pharmacy is responsible for maintaining and protecting private information and that customers must feel confident that the pharmacy is taking steps to protect their data from fraud and abuse.

The easiest way to secure a database from unauthorized use is to set a password. A **password** is a collection of characters that a user types to gain access to a file. When a database administrator sets a database password, users cannot open the database file in Access unless they provide the correct password. As long as the database administrator and users who know the password protect it from being known by unauthorized users, the password can adequately protect the database.

Don might want to set a password for the 4Corners database. The database is already open in exclusive mode, so he clicks Tools on the menu bar of the Database window, points to Security, and then clicks Set Database Password. The Set Database Password dialog box shown in Figure 2.60 opens.

Figure 2.60: Set Database Password dialog box

To set a database password, Don would type a password in the Password text box, press the Tab key, and then type the same password in the Verify text box. When he clicks the OK button, Access requests the password from the next user who attempts to open the database. If the user fails to provide the correct password in the Password Required dialog box that opens, Access does not open the database. Don can give the password to users as necessary to provide them with the ability to open the database. At this time, Don decides not to set a password until he brings the database online for employee use. The password will prevent customers and vendors who are in the store from being able to access the database. He is confident that the password will protect the pharmacy's data.

Best Practice

Choosing a Strong Password
When creating a password for a database, it is important to select a password that is easy to remember so it is easy to use. However, some users choose passwords that are easy to remember but are also very easy for another person to guess, such as the name of a

pet, child, or spouse or a date of birth or anniversary. Security experts suggest that users create **strong passwords**, which are character strings that contain at least seven characters consisting of combinations of uppercase and lowercase letters, numbers, and symbols. Random collections of characters are much harder to guess or break because the combination of characters is not a word. In any program that requests a password, choose a strong password in favor of one that is a simple word. Even if your password is 5&uJK#8, you will learn it quickly if you type it frequently.

Encrypting a Database to Prevent Unauthorized Use

Don knows that a password will provide users with the access to the database that they need and prevent unauthorized users from accessing it. However, the password won't protect the database in the event that someone steals the file and tries to open it with a program other than Access. Although an Access database is designed to be opened by the Access program, it is possible to open the database using other programs. For example, if you attempt to open an Access database in Microsoft Word, the resulting document would be difficult to read but it still might be possible to decipher some of the information stored in the database file.

One way to stop programs other than Access from opening a database file is to encrypt or encode the database. **Encrypting** a database (also known as **encoding** a database) converts the data in the database into a format that is readable only by Access. If a user tries to open the database with a word-processing program, the data will be scrambled and unintelligible. Although encrypting the database prevents other programs from opening it, the encryption is transparent to users who open the database using Access.

Don knows that it is a good idea to encrypt the database, especially when it is stored on a network, to prevent other programs from being able to access it. With the database open in exclusive mode, he clicks Tools on the menu bar, points to Security, and then clicks Encode/Decode Database. Access closes the 4Corners database, and then opens the Encode Database As dialog box. Don can use the 4Corners.mdb filename for the encrypted version of the database, in which case Access will encrypt the file and save it by overwriting the existing file. He could also choose an alternate filename for the encrypted version so that the two copies are separate. Don decides to encrypt the 4Corners database, so he clicks the database filename, and then clicks the Save button. A message box asks if he wants to replace the existing file, and he clicks the Yes button. After a few seconds, Access opens the encrypted version of the 4Corners database. The database still functions the same, although data will be encrypted as users add and update records and objects. Sometimes Access requires a lot of processing time to encrypt data as users update the database. If Don experiences performance issues as a result of the encryption, he might choose to **decrypt** (or **decode**) the database, which cancels the encryption. While the database is encrypted, if someone tries to open this file with any program besides Access, the data will be unintelligible.

Hiding Database Objects from Users

Don designed the 4Corners database so that all objects in a database are accessible to all users through the Database window. As the database administrator, Don is skilled at manipulating database objects for the benefit of users. Casual users who do not have Don's experience can damage the database by unintentionally altering an object's design or by deleting an object entirely. Another simple technique to add some security to the database is to hide objects from being displayed in the Database window. These objects are still part of the database and interact with other objects but are not visible to the casual user. The advantage of hiding objects is that the user will not be able to accidentally or intentionally damage the database. Unfortunately, revealing a hidden object is not difficult and a user who knows Access or how to use the Access Help system could learn how to reveal hidden objects.

Don might protect the data in tblEmployee, which contains employees' Social Security numbers and salary information, from being viewed by the store's staff. To hide tblEmployee, Don selects it in the Database window, and then clicks the Properties button 🖼 on the Database toolbar. The Properties dialog box for the object opens. Figure 2.61 shows the Properties dialog box for tblEmployee.

Figure 2.61: Properties dialog box for tblEmployee

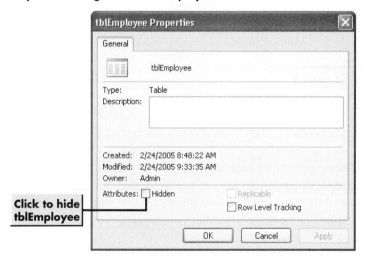

To hide tblEmployee, Don clicks the Hidden check box to select it. When he clicks the OK button, tblEmployee will not appear on the Tables object in the Database window. Maria Garcia, the pharmacy's human resources manager, will need to access this table. Don can show her how to reveal hidden objects by clicking Tools on the menu bar in the Database window, clicking Options, and then clicking the View tab in the Options dialog box. If Maria clicks the Hidden objects check box to select it, tblEmployee will be visible in the Database window again. Figure 2.62 shows tblEmployee after showing hidden objects.

Figure 2.62: Database window after revealing hidden objects

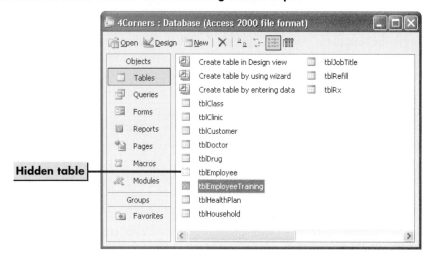

Hidden database objects remain visible unless you remove the check mark from the Hidden objects check box in the Options dialog box. To permanently restore a hidden object, open the Properties dialog box for the object, and then clear the Hidden check box.

Don decides not to hide database objects because Access has better and more secure techniques for hiding objects from users. In Chapter 6, you will learn more about hiding objects from users.

USER-LEVEL SECURITY

The methods that Don has explored thus far protect the database before it is opened and used. He also needs to protect the database while it is in use. The ideal way to protect the database is to create user-level security. **User-level security** establishes specific levels of access to the database objects for individual groups of users. Security is accomplished by setting **permissions** that specify the level of access for each user and group of users. Permissions are granted by the database administrator so that users and groups of users can create the objects, delete and change existing objects, and so on. A user's level of security depends on the access the user needs to perform his job. For example, a cashier requires a different level of access to a database than a person in a management position.

User-level security is implemented by defining groups of users, assigning permissions to groups, and then assigning individuals to those groups. Individuals access the database using passwords assigned to them by the database administrator. Access uses a **workgroup information file** to define user groups, usernames, and user passwords. The database administrator usually assigns users to groups based on their job function so that each user is granted access to the parts of the database that they need to carry out their job functions.

By default, two groups are in the workgroup information file: administrators and users. Don can alter the permissions of the user group and modify their rights so that they have viewing access to objects and have the ability to change specific settings. He can define different groups with different levels of permissions so one group can access a particular set of objects and another group can access a different set of objects. If Don requires more control over a group of users, he can create a new group and then add users to it.

To define user-level security in a database, Don needs to reopen the database with shared access and then run the Security Wizard. To start this wizard, he clicks Tools on the menu bar in the Database window, points to Security, and then clicks User-Level Security Wizard. When he runs this wizard for the first time, he is prompted to create a workgroup information file, as shown in Figure 2.63.

Figure 2.63: Security Wizard

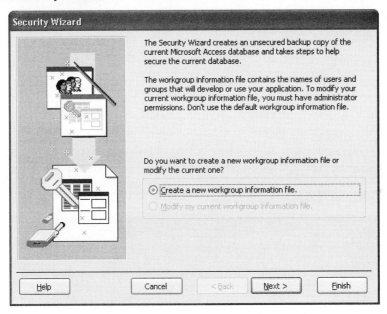

On subsequent uses, Don can modify the workgroup information file. After clicking the Next button, the Security Wizard displays the next dialog box (see Figure 2.64), which Don uses to set the name and workgroup ID for the workgroup information file. The **workgroup ID (WID)** is a unique character string of 4 to 20 characters that identifies the workgroup.

Figure 2.64: Defining the workgroup ID

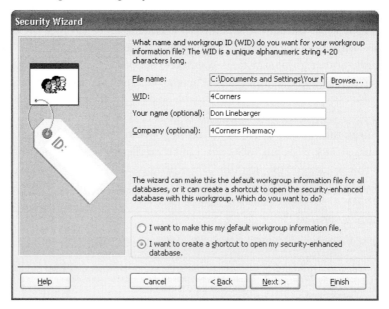

Don clicks the Next button to open the dialog box in which he chooses which database objects to secure. By default, all current and future database objects will be secured, which means that users will need permission to access any object in the database. You can exclude objects from security, but this approach is not recommended. Don accepts the default settings and clicks the Next button to open the dialog box shown in Figure 2.65.

Figure 2.65: Setting permissions for a group

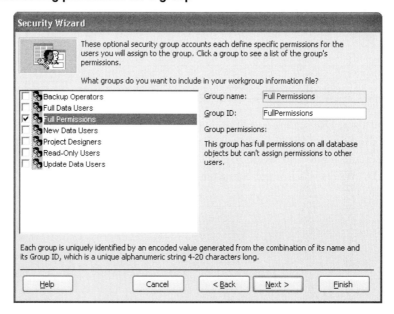

In this dialog box, you set the group name and ID for each group that you want to create. As the database administrator, Don needs full permissions to the database, so he creates a group to have full permissions. He clicks the Next button, chooses the option to skip granting the Users group some permissions, and the next dialog box opens, in which Don can start adding users to the WID. Access automatically adds the administrator of the computer (in Don's case, the administrator is named "Your Name") to the WID. Don sets his password, and then needs to set his **personal ID (PID)**, which is a 4 to 20 character string value that identifies Don as a user. He changes his PID to 4CPAdministrator, as shown in Figure 2.66.

Figure 2.66: Defining a user's personal ID

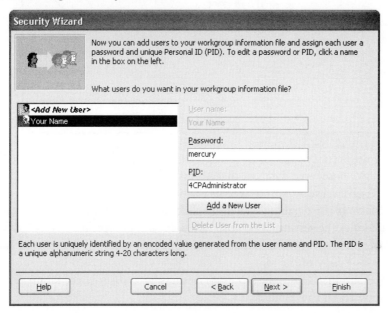

Now Don clicks the Add a New User button, and then he adds himself to the group. Don clicks the Add This User to the List button, and then clicks the Next button to open the next dialog box, in which Don assigns himself to the Full Permissions groups, as shown in Figure 2.67.

Figure 2.67: Assigning users to groups

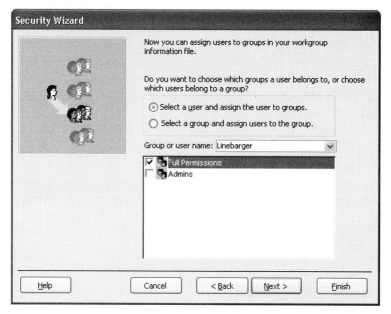

Before closing the Security Wizard, Don needs to specify the filename and location for the backup copy of the unsecured database that Access will create before enhancing the current database with user-level security. He accepts the default name, 4Corners.bak, and stores it in the same folder as the database. When he clicks the Finish button, Access generates a report that identifies the settings used to create users and groups in the WID. Don needs to print and keep this information because it will be important if he needs to re-create the WID. Don prints a copy of the report and also follows the on-screen instructions to save it as a snapshot, and then closes the wizard. The message box shown in Figure 2.68 opens with information about the database.

Figure 2.68: Message box after adding user-level security to a database

After clicking the OK button, Access closes. To reopen the database, Don must use the shortcut that Access created on the Windows desktop. After double-clicking the shortcut, Access starts and opens the Logon dialog box shown in Figure 2.69.

Figure 2.69: Logon dialog box

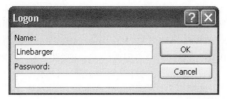

Because Don is the database administrator, he needs to assign the appropriate permissions to employees who will use the database. By logging on to the database as the administrator (instead of with the account he created for himself), Don can create new user accounts and assign users to groups by clicking Tools on the menu bar in the Database window, pointing to Security, and then clicking User and Group Accounts. Don uses the dialog box shown in Figure 2.70 to make these changes.

Figure 2.70: User and Group Accounts dialog box

If Don needs to create new groups, he can run the Security Wizard again and choose the option to modify the current workgroup information file and create new users and groups. Don will create user accounts and groups with different levels of access to the database so that some employees can view data, others can update data, and some have full access and can create and delete objects. The user-level security will ensure that users must log on to the database and the permissions granted to these users will grant and restrict access to the database as needed so they can complete their work at the pharmacy.

Steps To Success: Level 3

With the tables created, Don wants to protect the database and improve its operation.

1. Start Access and open the **Hudson.mdb** database in exclusive mode from the STS folder.

2. Run the Compact and Repair utility, and then set the option to compact the database when you close it.

3. Create a backup copy of the Hudson database and save it using the default filename in the STS folder.

4. Document the designs for all tables in the database. Include the table relationships and the field names, data types, and field sizes in the report. Export the report as a Rich Text Format file using the default filename and save it in the STS folder.

5. Suggest three strong passwords that you could use to secure the Hudson database, but do not set any passwords.

6. Create an encrypted copy of the Hudson database, using the filename **HudsonEncrypted.mdb** and saving it in the STS folder.

7. Describe a situation in which you might need to hide a table in the Hudson database (but do not actually hide the table).

8. Use the information in tblJobTitle to describe how you would assign users in specific positions at the pharmacy to groups and describe the kind of access to the database needed by each group. (Do not set user-level security in the Hudson database.)

9. Close the **Hudson.mdb** database and Access.

CHAPTER SUMMARY

This chapter presented the different ways to transform a database design into a collection of related tables in an Access database. In Level 1, you learned how to use Datasheet view, Design view, and the Table Wizard to create tables. You also learned how to create fields in a table, how to set their data types, and how to set properties that format data and ensure its accuracy. These properties included setting a field's caption, formatting values using an input mask, validating fields to ensure accurate and consistent data, and entering a default value in a field. You also learned how to create a lookup field to automate data entry in a field.

In Level 2, you learned how to populate the tables in the database by importing data from another Access database and from an Excel workbook. Importing existing data into a database saves data-entry time and reduces the risk of incorrect data, but it also is subject to problems. You learned how to troubleshoot problems, such as importing data with mismatched data types and nonmatching values into a related table's foreign key field when there are no matching values in the primary table's primary key field. You also learned how to create relationships in a database, how to create an index on a nonprimary key field, how to set a field's properties to require data entry, and how to create a composite primary key. Finally, you learned how to view related records using a subdatasheet.

In Level 3, you examined the role of the database administrator and his duties of securing and maintaining a database. The database administrator provides database maintenance, including compacting and repairing a database, scheduling and storing database backups, and documenting the database design. The database administrator is also charged with securing the database by setting a password, encrypting the database, hiding database objects, and setting user-level security for groups of users.

CONCEPTUAL REVIEW

1. Describe the three methods presented in this chapter for creating a table in Access.

2. What are the rules for naming objects in Access?

3. Write the input mask to control data entry in a field so that users can enter only three uppercase letters followed by three digits.

4. How do you validate a field and inform users of the validation rule?

5. Give three examples not presented in this chapter of how you might use a lookup field to control data entry into a table.

6. Describe how to import data from an Excel workbook into an existing table.

7. Can you set a primary key field so it accepts null values? Why or why not?

8. Can you set a nonprimary key field to accept null values? If so, give three examples not presented in this chapter of fields that might contain null values.

9. Name one advantage and one disadvantage for setting a field's Required property to Yes.

10. What are the three values for the Indexed property? Give one example not presented in this chapter of how you might use each value for a field in a table that stores data about employees.

11. How do you create a many-to-many relationship between two tables in Access?

12. What is a subdatasheet? Can you change the values in the records displayed by the subdatasheet?

13. What is DBA?

14. Describe the four ways to open an Access database.

15. What happens to a database's size and content when you compact it?

16. What is the Documenter?

17. How does encrypting a database provide security?

18. Describe the process for installing user-level security to an Access database.

CASE PROBLEMS

Case 1—Creating the Database for NHD Development Group Inc.

Information Systems

In Chapter 1, you created the database design for NHD Development Group to use at the Memories Antiques Mall in Cleveland, TN. Tim Richards, the company's chief information officer, reviewed your database design and worked to finalize it before you use Access to create the database. Figure 2.71 shows the database design that Tim approved.

Figure 2.71: Database design for NHD

tblInstructor

InstructorID
First
Last
Address
City
State
Zip
Phone
Cell
Fee

tblClass

ClassID
ClassName
Cost
Classroom
Date
Time
InstructorID
CEU

tblClass Enrollment

CustomerID
ClassID
Paid

tblEmployee

EmpID
EmpFirst
EmpLast
SSN
DOB
StartDate
EndDate
Address
City
State
Zip
JobID
Memo
Phone
Cell
Salary
HourlyRate
Review

tblCustomer

CustomerID
CustomerFirst
CustomerLast
Address
City
State
Zip
Phone
Comments
Newsletter

tblDealer

DealerID
FirstName
LastName
Address
City
State
Zip
Phone
Cell
TaxID
Comments

tblBooth

BoothID
Size
LocationType
Color
Rafters
Carpet
DealerID
Rent

tblJobTitle

JobID
Title

Tim is satisfied that the design shown in Figure 2.71 will satisfy all of the user requirements and output the data he needs to manage the mall. With the design approved, you can begin developing the database.

Complete the following:

1. Compare the database design you developed in Chapter 1 with the one shown in Figure 2.71. If necessary, change your database and table designs to match the ones shown in the figure. If you determine that you need to add or change fields in your table designs, be certain to carefully consider and then set the properties that will support the data being stored in those fields.

2. Start Access and create a new database named **Antiques.mdb** in the Case 1 folder.

3. While Tim was working with your design, he learned that the mall's manager, Linda Sutherland, already built the portion of the database related to classes. All the tables pertaining to classes are stored in the **Classes.mdb** database in the Chapter 2\Case 1 folder. Import these tables and the data they contain, but not their relationships, into the Antiques database.

4. Follow your database design to create the rest of the tables in the Antiques database using any method you choose. Be certain to specify the field names, data types, field descriptions, and field sizes as you create each table. Create validation rules and validation text, input masks, field captions, default values, and lookup fields as necessary to ensure that users enter consistent, complete, and accurate data in the tables. During the discovery phase, Tim and Linda gave you some important information that you must consider in your table designs:

   a. Tax ID numbers for dealers are unique.

   b. The valid booth locations at the mall are Inside Perimeter, Outside Perimeter, and Aisle. (On Linda's map—see Figure 1.37 in Chapter 1—booths that line the outside edge of the mall are outside perimeter booths, booths across from outside perimeter booths are inside perimeter booths, and booths on the inside rows are aisle booths.)

   c. Valid booth sizes are 8×8, 8×10, 8×12, 8×16, 8×20, 12×8, 12×10, 12×12, and 12×18.

5. After creating all of the tables in the database, create the relationships between the tables, as shown in Figure 2.71. Enforce referential integrity in each relationship and cascade updates.

6. Now that you have all the tables set up, you can import the existing data Tim and Linda provided during the discovery phase into your tables. Prior to importing this data, open the files and carefully review the data to identify and correct any compatibility errors between your table and the imported data. If you encounter errors, make the appropriate adjustments in your database. Populate the existing database tables as follows. The file you need is saved in the Chapter 2\Case 1 folder.

    a. Use Table 2.9 to enter data into tblJobTitle.

Table 2.9: Data for tblJobTitle

JobID	Title
1	Manager
2	Assistant Manager
3	Sales
4	Maintenance
5	Accounting
6	Administrative Assistant

    b. The **Memories.xls** workbook contains separate worksheets that include data for booths, dealers, and employees. Import the data into the appropriate tables in the Antiques database. You need to resolve any compatibility issues that arise when you import this data.

7. Check all your tables for accuracy and ensure that all your relationships have been established according to the design shown in Figure 2.71.

8. Set the option to compact the database when you close it.

9. Close the **Antiques.mdb** database and Access.

Case 2—Creating the Database for MovinOn Inc.

Information Systems

In Chapter 1, you created the database design for MovinOn Inc. The database will be used to manage data about the company and its operations. David Powers, the company's general manager, and Robert Iko, the company's information systems specialist, reviewed your database design and worked to finalize it. Figure 2.72 shows the database design that David and Robert approved.

Figure 2.72: Database design for MovinOn

David and Robert are satisfied that the design shown in Figure 2.72 will satisfy all of the user requirements and output the data needed to manage the business. With the design approved, you can begin developing the database.

Complete the following:

1. Compare the database design you developed in Chapter 1 with the one shown in Figure 2.72. If necessary, change your database and table designs to match the ones shown in the figure. If you determine that you need to add or change fields in your table designs, be certain to carefully consider and then set the properties that will support the data being stored in those fields.

2. Start Access and create a new database named **MovinOn.mdb** in the Case 2 folder.

3. Use the database design shown in Figure 2.72 as a guide to help you develop the database. Be certain to specify the field names, data types, field descriptions, and field sizes as you create each table. Create validation rules and validation text, input masks, field captions, default values, and lookup fields as necessary to ensure that users enter consistent, complete, and accurate data in the tables. During the discovery phase, David and Robert gave you some important information that you must consider in your table designs:

   a. Driving records for drivers are rated using the following values: A, B, C, D, or F. Users should input these values from a list.

   b. Users should be able to select the warehouse in which an employee works and the employee's position from a list of values.

   c. In tblJobDetail, the user should select the JobID, VehicleID, and DriverID from a list of values.

   d. In tblJobOrder and tblUnitRental, the user should select the CustID from a list of values.

   e. In tblStorageUnit, the user should select the WarehouseID from a list of values.

4. Check your database carefully to ensure that you have created all the tables, that you have created all the fields and set their properties, and that you have created all the necessary relationships.

5. Use the data shown in Table 2.10 to populate tblPosition.

Table 2.10: Data for tblPosition

PositionID	Title
1	General Manager
2	Warehouse Manager
3	Administrative Assistant
4	Accountant
5	Maintenance
6	Moving Assistant
7	Information Systems

6. Use the data shown in Table 2.11 to populate tblWarehouse.

Table 2.11: Data for tblWarehouse

Warehouse ID	Address	City	State	Zip	Phone	Climate Controlled?	Security Gate?
OR-1	#3 Industrial Park Way	Portland	OR	97212	(503) 551-2432	No	Yes
WA-1	8798 Warehouse Rd	Seattle	WA	98121	(206) 324-2312	Yes	Yes
WY-1	54781 Hixson Pike	Jackson Hole	WY	83001	(307) 541-3571	Yes	No

7. Populate the tables in your database using the data stored in the **MovinOn.xls** and **Job.mdb** files in the Chapter 2\Case 2 folder. Before importing the data, review each worksheet in the file and confirm that your table designs are set up correctly.

8. Set the option to compact the database when you close it.

9. Close the **MovinOn.mdb** database and Access.

Case 3—Creating the Database for Hershey College

Information Systems

In Chapter 1, you created the initial database design for the new intramural department at Hershey College. The department's manager, Marianna Fuentes, provided you with a list of data needs that you used to create the database design. Figure 2.73 shows the database design that Marianna approved.

Figure 2.73: Database design for Hershey College

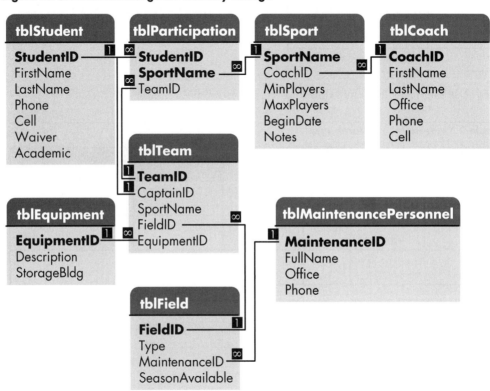

Marianna is satisfied that the design shown in Figure 2.73 will satisfy all of the user requirements and output the data needed to manage the department. With the design approved, you can begin developing the database.

Complete the following:

1. Compare the database design you developed in Chapter 1 with the one shown in Figure 2.73. If necessary, change your database and table designs to match the ones shown in the figure. If you determine that you need to add or change fields in your table designs, be certain to carefully consider and then set the properties that will support the data being stored in those fields.

2. Start Access and create a new database named **Hershey.mdb** in the Case 3 folder.

3. Follow your database design to create the tables in the Hershey database using any method you choose. Be certain to specify the field names, data types, field descriptions, and field sizes as you create each table. Create validation rules and validation text, input masks, field captions, default values, and lookup fields as necessary to ensure that users enter consistent, complete, and accurate data in the tables. During the discovery phase, Marianna gave you some important information that you must consider in your table designs:

   a. There are four storage buildings (SB-1, SB-2, SB-3, and SB-4) in which equipment is stored. In tblEquipment, a user should select equipment locations from a list of values.

   b. In tblTeam, you need to specify the court or field and equipment assigned to the team. Set up the table so that the user can select FieldIDs and EquipmentIDs from a list of values.

   c. Team captains are assigned from the pool of students. Set up the Captain field so that students are selected from a list of valid students. Store the StudentID in the Captain field.

   d. In tblSport, the user should select the CoachID from a list of values.

4. Create the relationships between all the tables, as shown in Figure 2.73. Enforce referential integrity in each relationship and cascade updates.

5. Now that you have all the tables set up, you can import the existing data you found during the discovery phase into your tables. Prior to importing this data, open the files and carefully review the data to identify and correct any compatibility errors between your table and the imported data. If you encounter errors, make the appropriate adjustments in your database. Populate the existing database tables as follows. The files are saved in the Chapter 2\Case 3 folder.

   a. The **IMDept.xls** workbook contains a collection of worksheets. Import this data into the appropriate table in your database. Be certain to check for errors and make any adjustments that are warranted.

b. The **College.mdb** database contains the records for tblField, tblTeam, and tblParticipation.

c. Use Table 2.12 to enter the data into tblSport.

Table 2.12: Data for tblSport

Sport Name	Coach ID	Minimum Players	Maximum Players	Begin Date	Notes
Basketball	18999	5	10	11/1/2008	
Football	79798	11	22	9/1/2008	
Ping Pong	18990	1		11/15/2008	
Pool	18990	1		11/15/2008	
Soccer	17893	11	22	4/18/2008	
Softball	18797	9	20	3/15/2008	
Swimming	78979	1		9/1/2008	
Tennis	78979	1		9/1/2008	
Track	79879	1		3/18/2008	
Wrestling	82374	1		11/1/2008	

6. Run the Compact and Repair utility, and then set the option to compact the database when you close it.

7. Create a backup copy of the Hershey database and save it using the default filename in the Case 3 folder.

8. Document the designs for all tables in the database. Include the table relationships and the field names, data types, and field sizes in the report. Export the report as a Rich Text Format file using the default filename and save it in the Case 3 folder.

9. What security measures do you feel are necessary for this database? Is there a good reason to invoke a password for the database? Why or why not? Keep in mind that a college must always protect the privacy of its students. Suggest three strong passwords that you could use to secure the Hershey database.

10. Create an encrypted copy of the Hershey database, using the filename **HersheyEncrypted.mdb** and saving it in the Case 3 folder.

11. Describe a situation in which you might need to hide a table in the Hershey database (but do not actually hide the table).

12. Describe how you would create groups of users in the intramural department and the kind of access to the database needed by each group. (Do not set user-level security in the Hershey database.)

13. Close the **Hershey.mdb** database and Access.

Analyzing Data for Effective Decision Making
Human Resources: Managing Employees at 4Corners Pharmacy

"The human problems which I deal with every day—concerning employees as well as customers—are the problems that fascinate me, that seem important to me."
—Hortense Odlum

Level 1

Filter and sort data to make it more meaningful
Create simple queries to answer business questions
Develop queries using comparison criteria and wildcards
Display and print query results

Level 2

Design queries that compare data from more than one table
Refine table relationships by specifying the join type
Perform calculations in queries
Customize queries and their results

Level 3

Calculate and restructure data to improve analysis
Examine and create advanced types of queries
Make decisions in a query using the immediate IF (IIF) function
Develop queries using SQL

TOOLS COVERED IN THIS CHAPTER

Action queries (update, append, delete, crosstab, and make-table)
Aggregate functions (Avg, Max, Min, Sum)
Calculated field
Comparison and logical operators
Crosstab query
Filter by Form and Filter by Selection
Find duplicates query
Find unmatched records query

Immediate IF (IIF) function
Parameter query
Query Design view
Select query
Simple Query Wizard
SQL commands (AS, FROM, GROUP BY, HAVING, ORDER BY, SELECT, WHERE)
Top Values query
Wildcard characters

3

CHAPTER INTRODUCTION

As you add data to a database, it can become increasingly difficult to find the information you need. This chapter begins by showing you how to filter data in a Microsoft Office Access 2003 database so you can retrieve and examine only the records you need. You will also learn how to sort data to rearrange records in a specified order. Next, the chapter focuses on queries, which provide quick answers to business questions such as which employees earn the highest pay rate, which employees have completed their occupational training requirements, and whether a company should continue to reimburse employees for job-related training. In Level 1, you will learn how to perform simple select queries, which specify only the fields and records Access should select. Level 2 explains how to increase the complexity of queries by using multiple tables and adding options to prepare data for forms and reports. It also explores how to make your queries interactive. Level 3 covers advanced types of queries such as those that update and add records to a table, and explains how to use the Immediate IF function to make decisions in a query and Structured Query Language (SQL) to retrieve data from an Access database.

CASE SCENARIO

Maria Garcia is the human resources manager for 4Corners Pharmacy. Her responsibilities involve hiring and firing employees and making sure they complete the necessary employment paperwork. In addition, she manages employee training, schedules periodic job reviews, and helps analyze compensation and other employee information.

**Human
Resources**

Most of the training sessions that employees of 4Corners Pharmacy attend involve mandatory certification for cardiopulmonary resuscitation (CPR) and the use of defibrillators. Maria needs a way to make sure all employees attend required classes and receive annual certification as necessary.

Until now, Maria has maintained employee and training information on printed forms that she stores in a filing cabinet. However, it is often inconvenient and time consuming to access and update these forms, especially to answer management questions that require her to analyze data. Maria plans to automate the records by using the 4Corners.mdb database to track employee and training information.

LEVEL 1

ORGANIZING AND RETRIEVING INFORMATION FROM A DATABASE

ACCESS 2003 SKILLS TRAINING

- **Build summary queries**
- **Clear a query**
- **Create a query in Design view**
- **Create select queries using the Simple Query Wizard**
- **Filter datasheet by form**
- **Filter datasheet by selection**
- **Print the results of a query**
- **Sort a query on multiple fields in Design view**
- **Sort records in a database**
- **Use date and memo fields in a query**
- **Use filter by form**
- **Use text data in criteria for a query**
- **Use wildcards in a query**

FILTERING AND SORTING DATA

Paul Ferrino, the owner of 4Corners Pharmacy, periodically reviews the wages he pays to his employees so he can budget for upcoming pay raises. He has recently increased the salaries of the two pharmacists at 4Corners, but he needs to check the hourly rates he pays to the other employees. He asks Maria to list the wages for pharmacy technicians and cashiers, ranked from highest to lowest so he can quickly see the full range of pay for nonsalaried employees.

Four tables in the 4Corners.mdb database contain employee information that Maria needs to perform her management tasks. These tables and their relationships are shown in Figure 3.1 and are described in the following list.

Figure 3.1: Relationships in the 4Corners Pharmacy database

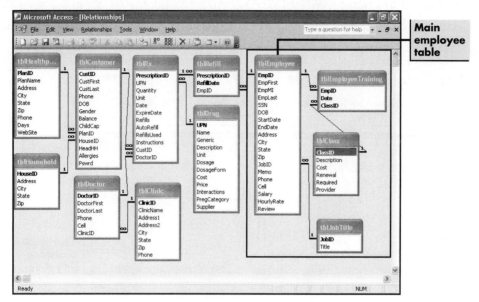

- **tblEmployee**—This table contains information about employees, including identifying information such as their ID number, name, and Social Security number, contact information such as their address and phone numbers, and employment information such as their starting date, salary or hourly rate, and job ID.
- **tblJobTitle**—This table lists the five job categories at 4Corners Pharmacy by ID number: 1—Owner, 2—Pharmacist, 3—Technician, 4—Cashier, and 5—Manager.
- **tblEmployeeTraining**—This table tracks the training classes that employees attend.
- **tblClass**—This table lists the classes employees can attend to receive required certifications or other professional training.

Maria thinks she can find the information she needs by using a filter and then sorting the results. A **filter** restricts data in a single table to create a temporary subset of records. A filter allows you to see only certain records in a table based on criteria you specify. **Sorting** records means organizing them in a particular order or sequence. You can sort records in a table regardless of whether it's filtered.

Filtering by Selection

Two tools that Access provides for filtering data are Filter by Selection and Filter by Form. **Filter by Selection** lets you select a particular field in a datasheet and then display only data that matches the contents of that field. When you filter by selection, you specify only one criterion for the filter.

Maria first wants to review employment information for pharmacy technicians only. She opens the tblEmployee table, which currently contains 24 records, and clicks the first

JobID field that contains a "3." (Recall that technicians have a JobID of 3.) Then she clicks the Filter by Selection button ▼ on the Table Datasheet toolbar. Access filters the data by selecting only those records with a "3" in the JobID field, and then displays the filtered results—eight employment records for the pharmacy technicians only. See Figure 3.2.

Figure 3.2: Using Filter by Selection to display a temporary subset of records

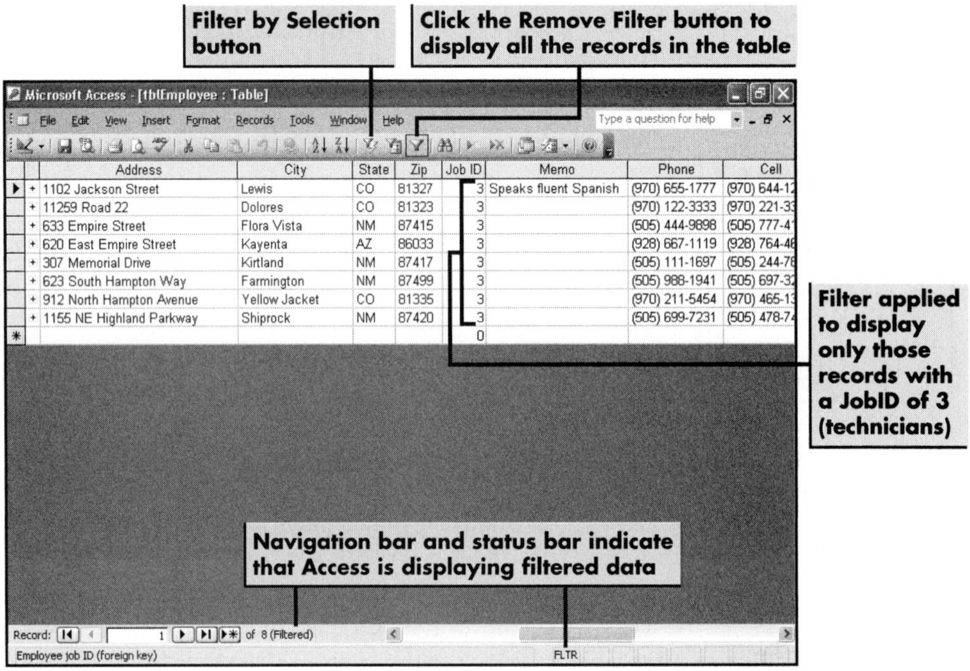

Now Maria can focus on the employment information for technicians, including their hourly rate of pay. After she prints this datasheet, she could remove the filter for displaying technician records and apply a different filter for displaying cashier records. However, she can use a different tool to display the hourly pay rates for technicians and cashiers at the same time. To accomplish that goal, she must use Filter by Form.

Filtering by Form

Whereas you specify only one criterion when you use Filter by Selection, you can specify two or more criteria with **Filter by Form**. In addition, Filter by Selection filters for records that exactly match the criterion, such as those that contain "3" in the JobID field, while Filter by Form can filter for comparative data, such as those records in which the HourlyRate field value is greater than or equal to $8.00. To enter comparative data, you use comparison operators, such as >= for greater than or equal to. You specify these criteria in a blank version of the datasheet by entering or selecting the data in one or more fields that you want to match. Access displays only those records that contain the data you selected.

Maria wants to view hourly pay rates for employees whose records contain a "3" (for technicians) or "4" (for cashiers) in the JobID field. Because she needs to specify more than one criterion, she will use the Filter by Form tool. Before doing so, however, she notes that a filter is still applied to tblEmployee because FLTR appears in the status bar (shown earlier in Figure 3.2). Maria redisplays all the records in tblEmployee by clicking the Remove Filter button ▽ on the Table Datasheet toolbar.

Next, she clicks the Filter by Form button ⊞ on the Table Datasheet toolbar. A blank version of the tblEmployee datasheet appears in the Filter by Form window. Maria clicks the JobID field to specify the first criterion for displaying records. See Figure 3.3.

Figure 3.3: Using Filter by Form to specify more than one criterion

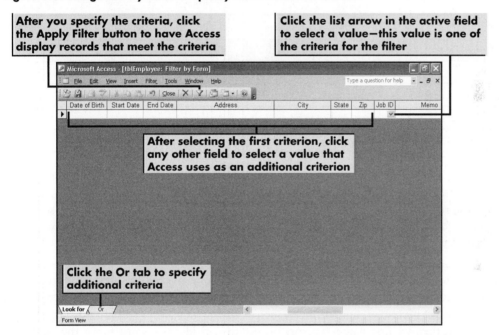

After you specify the criteria, click the Apply Filter button to have Access display records that meet the criteria

Click the list arrow in the active field to select a value—this value is one of the criteria for the filter

After selecting the first criterion, click any other field to select a value that Access uses as an additional criterion

Click the Or tab to specify additional criteria

To specify the first criterion, she clicks the list arrow in the JobID field to display all of its values, and then clicks 3 (for technician). This means that Access will display records in tblEmployee that contain a "3" in the JobID field. If Maria wanted to display a list of technicians who live in Colorado, she could also click the list arrow in the State field and then click CO. This type of criteria is called **AND criteria**—it selects records that contain *all* specified values.

However, Maria wants to view records that contain a "3" (technicians) or "4" (cashiers) in the JobID field. This type of criteria is called **OR criteria**—it selects records that contain *any* of the specified values. To enter an OR criterion, Maria clicks the Or tab. Another version of the blank tblEmployee datasheet appears in the Filter by Form window. She clicks the list arrow in the JobID field, and then clicks 4. When she clicks the Apply Filter button [icon] on the Filter/Sort toolbar, Access displays the records that satisfy any of her criteria—records that contain a "3" or a "4" in the JobID field. This is the list that Maria wants—information about the current 4Corners technicians and cashiers, including their rate of pay.

Now that Maria has filtered the tblEmployee datasheet, she needs to sort the records to rank the hourly rates of pay for technicians and cashiers.

Sorting Data to Increase Information Content

Recall that sorting records means organizing them in a particular order or sequence. Table 3.1 describes how Access sorts different types of data.

Table 3.1: Sorting types of data

Data Type	Ascending Sort Order	Descending Sort Order
Text	Alphabetic order from A to Z	Reverse alphabetic order from Z to A
Numbers and Currency	From lowest to highest	From highest to lowest
Date/Time	From earliest to latest	From latest to earliest
Yes/No	Yes values appear first	No values appear first

Sorting the data in a table or datasheet organizes the data and increases its information value. When you create a table and designate one or more fields as the primary key, Access sorts the records based on the primary key values. To change the order, you can sort the records. For example, you could sort a list of customers by state or a list of vendors in alphabetic order.

When you sort records, you select a sort field, the one Access uses first to reorder the records. For example, if you are sorting an employer list, LastName might be the sort field. You can select more than one sort field, such as when you want to sort records first by last name and then by first name. To sort on multiple fields, you must move the fields in Datasheet view, if necessary, so that they are adjacent. The leftmost field becomes the **primary sort field**, meaning that Access sorts the records by this field first. For example, you could move a LastName field to the left of a FirstName field in an employee table, select both columns, and then sort in ascending order. Access would list the records in alphabetical order by last name. If two or more employees have the same last name, Access would list those employee records in alphabetic order according to their first name.

Now that Maria has filtered tblEmployee to show records only for technicians and cashiers, she can sort the records in descending order by the HourlyRate field so that the employee with the highest hourly wage appears first and the one with the lowest wage appears last. To do so, she clicks in an HourlyRate field, and then clicks the Sort Descending button [icon] on the Table Datasheet toolbar.

Although it took Maria several steps, she produced the results she needs. She prints the sorted datasheet, clicks the Remove Filter button ▼ on the Table Datasheet toolbar to turn off the filter, and then closes tblEmployee. However, she suspects there must be an easier way to produce the same results, and decides to explore queries, which can also retrieve only selected records from a table.

USING QUERIES TO ANSWER BUSINESS QUESTIONS

If you need a quick way to restrict the data displayed in one table, the Filter by Selection and Filter by Form tools are appropriate. However, recall that a filter creates a *temporary* subset of records in a single table. Although you can save a filter, if you want to reuse the filter criteria or need data from two or more tables, the easiest approach is to create a query. A **query** is a database object that stores criteria for selecting records from one or more tables based on conditions you specify. You can save a query and use it again when you want to see the results of its criteria. Queries are often used as the basis for forms and reports and they can add, update, and delete records in tables. A special kind of query can even create a table based on criteria you supply.

Although queries and filters both display records based on specified criteria, a query is more powerful than a filter. Besides saving the criteria and letting you select records from more than one table, you can also use a query to display only some of the fields in a table. (When you use a filter, you must display all of the fields.) In addition, you can create fields in a query that perform calculations, such as sums and averages.

The following list summarizes the capabilities of Access queries:

- Display selected fields and records from a table.
- Sort records on one or multiple fields.
- Perform calculations.
- Generate data for forms, reports, and other queries.
- Update data in the tables of a database.
- Find and display data from two or more tables.
- Create new tables.
- Delete records in a table based on one or more criteria.

The most common type of query is called a **select query**. Select queries allow you to ask a question based on one or more tables in a database. Access responds by displaying a datasheet containing the set of records that answers your question. You can select only the fields you want in your result. To analyze the data that you retrieve, you can also use a select query to group records and calculate sums, counts, averages, and other kinds of totals. When you save a query, you are saving the criteria that select the records you want to display. Each time you open, or run, the query, it retrieves the records that meet the criteria you specified and displays them in a **recordset**, a datasheet that contains the results of a query. Running a typical select query does not affect the records and fields in the underlying tables; it only selects records to make your data more useful.

Maria determines that she can use a select query to provide the list of hourly wages for the 4Corners technicians and cashiers that Paul Ferrino requested. Because she is still getting acquainted with the 4Corners database, the easiest way for her to create a select query is to use the Simple Query Wizard.

Using the Simple Query Wizard to Create a Query

Access provides a number of query wizards, which guide you through the steps of creating a query. The Simple Query Wizard presents a list of tables and queries in your database and the fields that they contain. You select the fields you want from one or more tables, and the wizard creates and displays the results. For example, if an employee table contains 20 fields of information, including name, address, phone number, and Social Security number, you can use the Simple Query Wizard to create a phone list that contains only the name and phone number for each employee. Although the Simple Query Wizard provides a quick way to retrieve selected records, it does have some limitations. Table 3.2 lists the advantages and limitations of the Simple Query Wizard.

Table 3.2: Advantages and limitations of the Simple Query Wizard

You Can Use the Simple Query Wizard to:	You Cannot Use the Simple Query Wizard to:
Display selected fields and records from one or more tables and queries	Update data, create tables, or delete records
Produce summary data if one or more of the selected fields are of the numeric or currency data type	Add selection criteria
Include a count of the records	Choose the sort order of the query
Specify summary grouping by day, month, quarter, or year if one or more of your fields is a Date/Time field	Change the order of the fields in a query; fields appear in the order they are added to the Selected Fields list in the first wizard dialog box

To start the Simple Query Wizard, Maria clicks the Queries button on the Objects bar in the Database window, and then double-clicks the Create query by using wizard option. The Simple Query Wizard dialog box opens, which Maria can use to select the fields she wants to display in the query results. All of the fields she needs are included in tblEmployee, so she clicks the Tables/Queries list arrow, and then clicks tblEmployee. See Figure 3.4.

Figure 3.4: The Simple Query Wizard dialog box

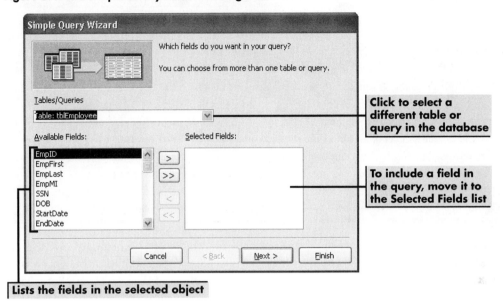

Click to select a different table or query in the database

To include a field in the query, move it to the Selected Fields list

Lists the fields in the selected object

To make the results easy to read, Maria decides to list only the employee's name, job ID, and hourly rate. She double-clicks the EmpLast, EmpFirst, JobID, and HourlyRate fields in that order to move them to the Selected Fields list. These are the fields Access will include in the query results. Then she clicks the Next button to open the next dialog box in the wizard, which asks if she wants to create a detail or summary query. A detail query shows every selected field of every record. A summary query groups records and can calculate the sum, average, minimum, or maximum value in each selected field. It can also provide a count of the records in a table. Maria wants to show every field of every record, so she selects the Detail option button.

When Maria clicks the Next button, the next dialog box in the wizard opens, where she can enter a name for the query. She types qryHourlyRate as the name, and then clicks the Finish button. Access displays the results—a list of 4Corners employees showing only the employee name, job ID, and hourly pay rate.

Best Practice

Using Prefixes in Database Object Names

When prompted to save a query, be certain to use the "qry" prefix in the query name. Naming objects with a prefix that identifies the object type is particularly important with queries because it distinguishes those objects from tables. (A query recordset looks exactly like a table datasheet.) The query wizards, however, usually suggest using a table name as the start of the query name, even if the table name uses the "tbl" prefix. Using the "qry" prefix helps you distinguish queries from tables, which is especially helpful when you are using one or the other as the basis for a new form or report.

How To

Create a Detail Query with the Simple Query Wizard

1. To create a detail query with the Simple Query Wizard, click Queries on the Objects bar in the Database window, and then double-click the Create query by using wizard option.
2. Click the Tables/Queries list arrow and then select the table or query you want to use as the basis for the query. From the Available Fields list, select the fields you want to include in the query. Use the Select Single Field button [>] to select the fields one by one; use the Select All Fields button [>>] to select them all at once. If you want to include fields from more than one table or query, click the Tables/Queries list arrow again, select another table or query, and then select the fields you want to include. Click the Next button. If a selected field contains a numeric value, the next dialog box asks if you want a detail or summary query.
3. Click the Detail option button to show all the records. Click the Next button.
4. Name the query using the "qry" prefix, and then click the Finish button.

Maria can now achieve the results she wants by sorting the results of the query. She selects the JobID and HourlyRate fields and then clicks the Sort Descending button on the Query Datasheet toolbar to sort the records first by JobID and then by HourlyRate. The records with a JobID of 5 appear first, followed by the records with a JobID of 4, sorted from highest to lowest by HourlyRate. The records with a JobID of 3 appear next, also sorted from highest to lowest by HourlyRate. The records with no HourlyRate value appear at the top and bottom of the list because employees with a JobID of 5 are managers and receive a salary. Similarly, employees with a JobID of 2 are pharmacists, and JobID 1 is the owner; they all receive salaries, not hourly wages. See Figure 3.5.

Figure 3.5: The sorted results of the qryHourlyRate query

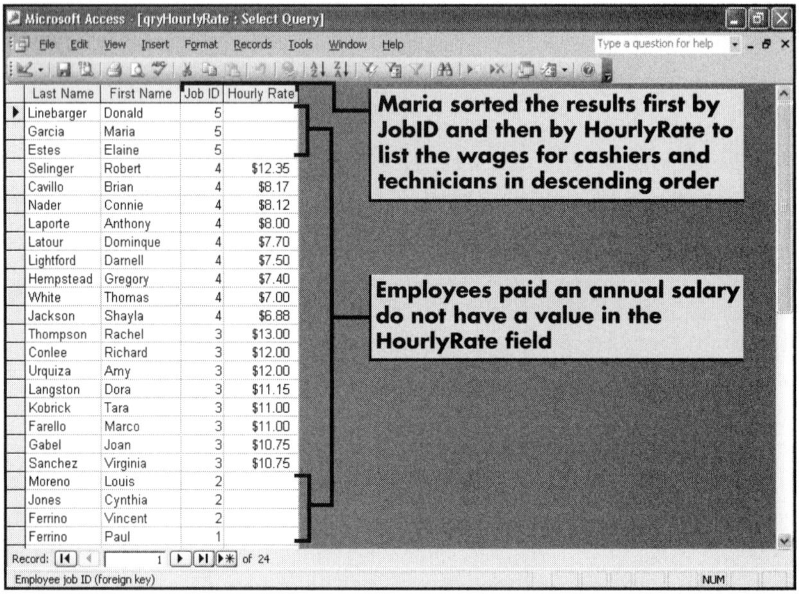

Last Name	First Name	Job ID	Hourly Rate
Linebarger	Donald	5	
Garcia	Maria	5	
Estes	Elaine	5	
Selinger	Robert	4	$12.35
Cavillo	Brian	4	$8.17
Nader	Connie	4	$8.12
Laporte	Anthony	4	$8.00
Latour	Dominque	4	$7.70
Lightford	Darnell	4	$7.50
Hempstead	Gregory	4	$7.40
White	Thomas	4	$7.00
Jackson	Shayla	4	$6.88
Thompson	Rachel	3	$13.00
Conlee	Richard	3	$12.00
Urquiza	Amy	3	$12.00
Langston	Dora	3	$11.15
Kobrick	Tara	3	$11.00
Farello	Marco	3	$11.00
Gabel	Joan	3	$10.75
Sanchez	Virginia	3	$10.75
Moreno	Louis	2	
Jones	Cynthia	2	
Ferrino	Vincent	2	
Ferrino	Paul	1	

Although using the Detail option with the Simple Query Wizard displays all the employee records, even for employees other than technicians and cashiers, creating a query allows Maria to increase the information content of the results by displaying only relevant fields and sorting the records. She shows the query results to Paul Ferrino, noting that the records at the top and bottom of the list are for salaried employees. Paul looks over the list, mentioning that he appreciates the sort order so that he can quickly analyze the range of pay for nonsalaried employees. He wonders if she could provide this information in a more accessible format, listing only the highest and lowest hourly pay rates. Including the average pay rate would also help him analyze the wages. Maria decides to explore the summary option in the Simple Query Wizard to produce the results Paul requests.

Including Summary Statistics in a Query for Data Analysis

Recall that a summary query groups records and can calculate the sum, average, minimum, or maximum value in each selected field. It can also count the records in a table or query.

Maria starts the Simple Query Wizard again so she can use it to create a summary query. In the first dialog box (shown earlier in Figure 3.4), she clicks the Tables/Queries list arrow and then selects qryHourlyRate. She can create the new query by modifying qryHourlyRate and then saving it with a different name. Instead of listing the employee name and job ID for each record, she only wants to summarize the hourly pay rate data. She double-clicks HourlyRate so it becomes the only field in the Selected Fields list. When she clicks the Next button, the next dialog box asks if she wants to create a detail or summary query. This time, she chooses to create a summary query, and clicks the Summary Options button to select the statistics she wants Access to calculate for the HourlyRate field. See Figure 3.6.

Figure 3.6: Creating a summary query with the Simple Query Wizard

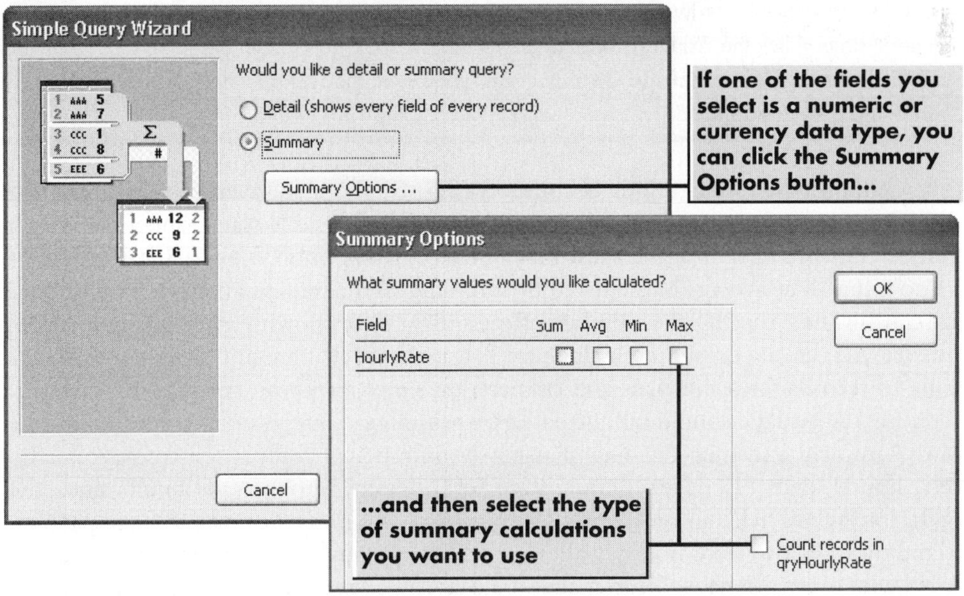

Maria selects the Avg, Min, and Max options because Paul wants to analyze the pharmacy's pay structure by examining the average, lowest, and highest hourly wages, and then completes the wizard, naming the new query qryHourlyRateSummary. The results, shown in Figure 3.7, include the average, minimum, and maximum calculations for the values in the HourlyRate field.

Figure 3.7: Summary statistics in the qryHourlyRateSummary query

How To

Create a Summary Query with the Simple Query Wizard

1. To create a summary query with the Simple Query Wizard, click Queries on the Objects bar in the Database window, and then double-click the Create query by using wizard option.

2. Click the Tables/Queries list arrow and then select the table or query you want to use as the basis for the query. From the Available Fields list, select the fields you want to include in the query. Use the Select Single Field button (>) to select the fields one by one; use the Select All Fields button (>>) to select them all at once. If you want to include fields from more than one table or query, click the Tables/Queries list arrow again, select another table or query, and then select the fields you want to include. Click the Next button. If a selected field contains a numeric value, the next dialog box asks if you want a detail or summary query.

3. Click the Summary option button, and then click the Summary Options button to open the Summary Options dialog box.

4. Click the check boxes for the summary values you want to calculate on each field that contains numeric data. Click the Count records in check box to count records in the table or query that contains numeric data. Click the OK button and then click the Next button.

5. Name the query using the "qry" prefix, and then click the Finish button.

As she examines the results, Maria becomes concerned about the average value, recalling that in the records for salaried employees, the HourlyRate field is blank. She is not sure if qryHourlyRateSummary is using these blank fields as zero or null values. (Recall that nulls have no value.) The average is calculated by summing all the values in the HourlyRate field and then dividing that by the number of records (24, as shown earlier in Figure 3.5). However, the calculation should include only those fields that are not blank—these fields belong to records for technicians and cashiers, the employees who receive hourly wages. Therefore, the average should be calculated by summing only the nonblank values in the HourlyRate field and then dividing that by the number of records for employees who receive hourly wages (17). If the HourlyRate field contains zero instead of null values, the AvgOfHourlyRate fields in qryHourlyRateSummary will not reflect the average pay rate for employees who receive hourly wages—it will erroneously include the zero values for salaried employees. Maria wants to make sure that the query does not include the records for salaried employees, and realizes she needs to create a query using a method that allows her more options than the Simple Query Wizard. She needs to use selection criteria to display only records for technicians and cashiers, and then calculate summary statistics using those records. To accomplish this, she must work in Query Design view.

Best Practice

Verifying Calculation Results

After Access calculates a value, examine the results to make sure the value makes sense in the context of the data. Many database developers use a calculator to check the results by hand to make sure the calculations they use in queries are working correctly. For this reason, most developers prefer to test their queries and other objects with only a few sample records and simple data so they can easily determine whether their results are correct.

Creating a Query in Design View

Recall from Table 3.1 that the Simple Query Wizard does not allow you to use selection criteria when creating a query, set the sort order of the results, or change the order of the fields displayed in the results. If you need to perform any of these tasks, create a query in Design view instead of using a wizard. In Design view, you can still create queries that accomplish the same goals as the Simple Query Wizard, such as displaying selected fields and records from one or more tables and calculating summary statistics.

When you create a query in Design view, you work in a window similar to the one shown in Figure 3.8

Figure 3.8: The Select Query window in Design view

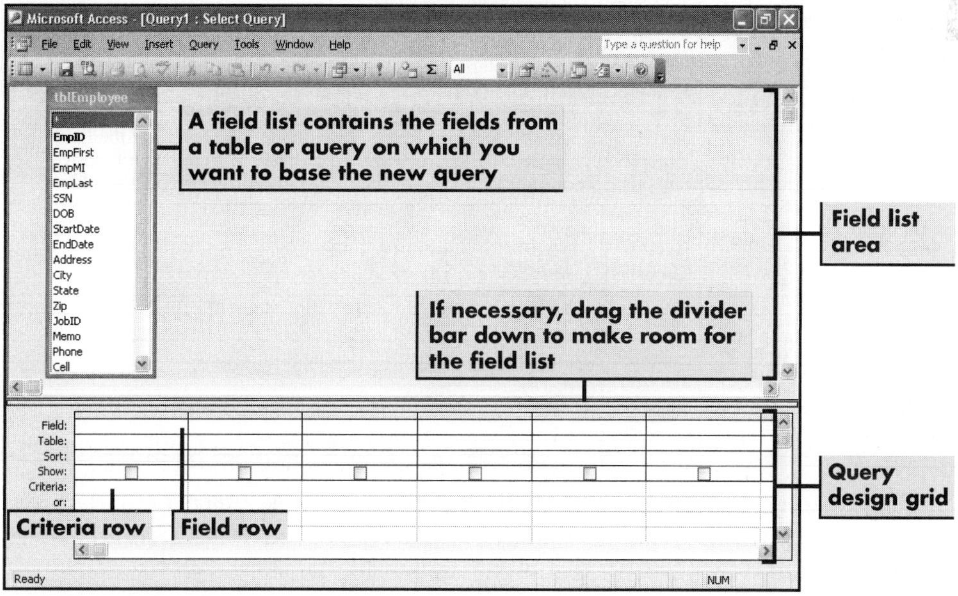

The Select Query window in Design view has two sections: an area for field lists at the top of the window and the design grid below it. You add the tables you need for the query to the top part of the window; they appear as field lists. You can resize the field lists as necessary to display all the fields and the complete field names. You add the fields you want in the query to the design grid by dragging the field from the field list to the design grid or by double-clicking the field name.

For each field you add to the design grid, you can specify criteria by typing an expression in the Criteria row. For example, to select only employees with a JobID of 3, type 3 in the Criteria row for the JobID field. Typing the value you are looking for as a criterion is why Access calls its query approach **query by example (QBE)**.

Table 3.3 describes the tools and features of query Design view.

Table 3.3: Query Design view tools

Feature or Tool	Description
Field list	Contains the fields for a selected table or query.
Design grid	Provides a grid for the fields and record selection criteria you want to use in the query.
Field row	Displays the field name in the design grid.
Table row	Displays the name of the table that contains the current field.
Sort row	Specifies ascending or descending sort order for the field. Sorting is from left to right. Fields do not need to be next to each other to be included in the sort.
Show row	When the Show box is checked, displays the field in the results. When the Show box is unchecked, the query uses the field to establish criteria, but does not display the field in the results.
Criteria row	Specifies the criteria for including or eliminating the record for the field. When one or more criteria are specified in this row, all criteria must be true for the query to display a record in the results.
or row	Specifies OR criteria for including or eliminating the record for the field. When one or more criteria are specified in this row and the Criteria row, any criteria can be true for the query to display a record in the results.
Datasheet view button	Click to display the query results.
Query Type button	Click the list arrow to select the type of query you want to run.
Run button	Click to run the query and display the results.
Show Table button	Click to select tables and add them to the field list area.
Totals button	Click to add a Total row to the design grid and perform calculations with the values in a field.

Maria is ready to design a query that will display the names of 4Corners technicians and cashiers only, their job IDs, and their hourly pay rates. The query will also sort the list in descending order first by the JobID field and then by HourlyRate.

To create this query, Maria double-clicks the Create query in Design view option in the Database window. The Select Query window opens in Design view and then the Show Table dialog box opens, listing the tables in the 4Corners database. All of the fields Maria needs are in the tblEmployee table, so she double-clicks tblEmployee to display its field list in the field list area, and then she clicks the Close button to close the Show Table dialog box.

Next, she adds the four fields she needs to the design grid. In the tblEmployee field list, she double-clicks EmpLast, EmpFirst, JobID, and HourlyRate in that order to add them to the design grid.

Her next task is to specify the criteria for displaying records only for technicians and cashiers. To do so, she must use multiple criteria, as she did when she used Filter by Form.

Creating Queries with Multiple Criteria

Most queries involve more than one criterion. You can represent AND criteria—multiple conditions that must all be true—by entering the conditions in the same Criteria row in the query design grid. For a record to be included in the results of the query, it must meet all criteria specified in the Criteria row. For example, if you want to display information about cashiers who live in Colorado, you enter "3" in the Criteria row for the JobID field and "CO" in the Criteria row for the State field.

To specify OR criteria—conditions that allow more than one alternative condition to be true—you use the "or" row of the query design grid. If the conditions apply to the same field, you enter the first condition in the Criteria row for the field, and then enter each additional condition in an "or" row for that field. The query selects records that meet all the criteria in the Criteria row, or those that meet all of the criteria in an "or" row. For example, if you want to display information about employees who live in Arizona or New Mexico, you can enter "AZ" in the Criteria row and "NM" in the "or" row for the State field. You can also type all the conditions separated by the Or operator in the same Criteria cell, as in "AZ" Or "NM".

If the conditions apply to different fields, you also enter the first condition in the Criteria row for one field, and then enter each additional condition in an "or" row for the other fields. For example, if you want to display information about employees who live in Colorado or Phoenix, you can enter "CO" in the Criteria row for the State field and "Phoenix" in the "or" row for the City field.

Best Practice

Understanding Or Criteria

In querying, *"or means more."* A query with criteria in more than one row of the query design grid is likely to return more results than the more restrictive AND criteria, in which two or more conditions must be true.

Now, Maria can specify the criteria for displaying records only for technicians and cashiers. Because she wants to display records that include 3 or 4 in the JobID field, she will use OR criteria. Recall that Maria could do this earlier when she used Filter by Form, but not when she used the Simple Query Wizard. She clicks in the Criteria row of the JobID field and then types 3 to set the criteria for displaying records only for cashiers. To include an OR criterion, she clicks in the "or" row of the JobID field and then types 4 to set the criterion for also displaying technician records. See Figure 3.9.

Figure 3.9: Setting criteria for the query in Design view

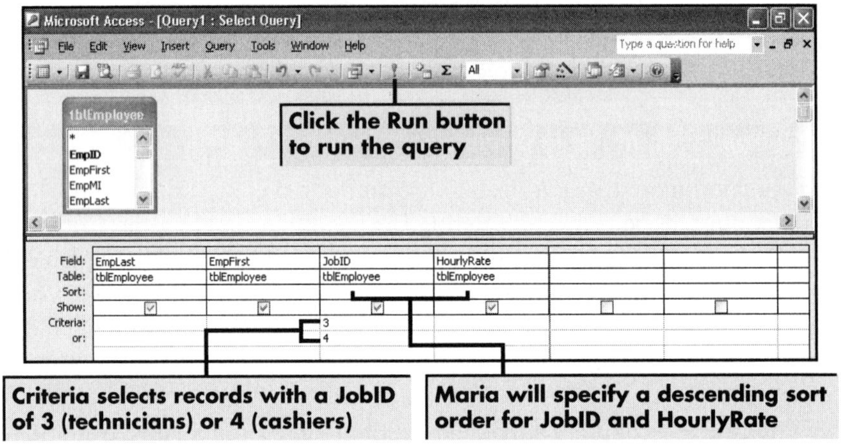

Maria's only remaining task is to sort the records the query displays so that the records for cashiers appear first, sorted from highest to lowest by hourly pay rate. Then she wants the records for technicians to appear, also sorted from highest to lowest by hourly pay rate.

Specifying Sort Order in Queries

Query results appear in the same order as the data from the underlying tables unless you specify a sort order when you design the query. Sort order is determined from left to right, so the primary sort field must appear to the left of any other sort field on the grid. You might want to sort on one or more additional fields to determine the order of records that all have the same primary sort order value. Fields do not need to be next to each other to be included in a sort within a query. You can choose ascending or descending sort order.

For example, to sort employee records alphabetically by name, you could place the EmpLast field to the left of the EmpFirst field in the query design grid. If you specify an ascending sort order for both fields, Access sorts the records in alphabetic order by last name. If two employees have the same last name, Access sorts those records according to the names in the EmpFirst field. For example, if one employee is named Arthur Johnson and another is named Tyrone Johnson, Access sorts Arthur before Tyrone.

The main reason to specify a sort order for a query is that it is saved as part of the design with the other query settings. After you run a query, you might decide to sort the data in one or more columns as you examine the data in Datasheet view. This sort order is not saved as part of the query design. Recall also that multiple columns must be adjacent to sort on more than one field in Datasheet view. In Design view, you can sort on more than one field even if they are not adjacent—the sort order is determined by their left-to-right placement in the design grid.

To sort the records first by JobID and then by HourlyRate, Maria must make sure that the JobID field appears in any column to the left of the HourlyRate field in the design grid. Maria clicks in the Sort row of the JobID field, clicks the list arrow, and then clicks Descending. She does the same for the HourlyRate field. She reviews her selections before she runs the query.

Running a Query

After you establish the criteria you want for a query, you click the Run button ![] on the Query Design toolbar to display the results. Access displays a datasheet of records that meet the criteria you specified in the design grid. Note that although the datasheet looks like a set of records in a table, and you can often enter and change data from the query datasheet, the data is still actually stored in the underlying tables that were used to create the query. When you save a query, you save only the design, not the values from the tables displayed in the results. When you run the query again, Access reapplies the criteria saved in the design grid to the data in the underlying tables to produce the query results. If the data in the query fields has changed, these changes appear when you rerun the query.

Maria saves the query as qryHourlyRateAnalysis. She is ready to run her query, so she clicks the Run button ![] on the Query Design toolbar. Access runs the query and displays the results in Datasheet view. See Figure 3.10.

Figure 3.10: Results of the query in Datasheet view

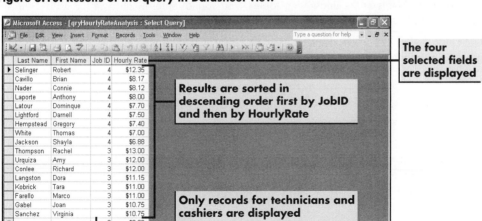

Best Practice

Referring to Query Results

Results from a query are not new tables. The original tables and queries used to create the query do not change when you run a select query. A query recordset contains "columns" and "rows" because they are not necessarily records or fields in any table. As you will see later, you can create a new column with a calculated value that does not appear in the underlying tables in the database.

Best Practice

Working with Query Datasheets

Avoid entering or editing data in the query results. It is generally considered best practice to enter data directly into a table (or form, as you will see in Chapter 4) to make sure you enter data for all fields, not only those in the query results.

Under certain conditions, you can edit the values in the query datasheet to update the records in the underlying tables. Access lets you update table records from a query datasheet if the query is based on only one table or on tables that have a one-to-one relationship (which is rare), or if the query results contain a Memo, Hyperlink, or OLE Object field. Editing records from query results saves you a few steps if you need to correct a typographical error, for example, because you don't need to close the query datasheet and then open the table datasheet to make a change.

Access might also let you update table records from a query datasheet if the query is based on two or more tables that have a one-to-many relationship. Fields you cannot update include the primary key field for the table on the "one" side of the relationship, unless you've enabled cascading updates when you set referential integrity for the relationship.

You can add records using the query datasheet only if you include a primary key or foreign key field in the query. One exception is a summary query—because it displays calculations based on the contents of the underlying tables, you cannot enter or change the data itself. If you try to enter a record or change data in a query that does not include a primary or foreign key for the underlying tables, you will receive an error message similar to the one shown in Figure 3.11, which indicates a data integrity error.

Figure 3.11: Entering or changing data in the datasheet of query results

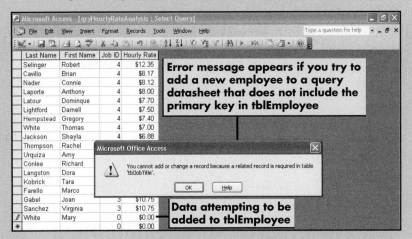

Now that Maria knows how to work in Design view, she can modify the qryHourlyRateSummary query so it uses only hourly pay rates for technicians and cashiers in its average calculation. She opens the query in Design view, adds the JobID field to the design grid, and enters the same criteria she used to select records only for technicians and cashiers in qryHourlyRateSummary—she enters 3 in the Criteria row of the JobID field and 4 in the "or" row.

If Maria runs the query now, she will probably receive an error—the three fields that calculate the average, minimum, and maximum values summarize the values in all the selected employee records, while the JobID field selects each employee record that matches the criteria. Access can't run a query that shows summary values in one row of the query results, and then uses two or more rows to display detail information. To solve this problem, Maria can use the JobID field in the query design grid to specify criteria, but not show the JobID field in the query results. She can remove the check mark from the Show box in the JobID field to indicate that it should not appear in the query results. Figure 3.12 shows the modified query design for qryHourlyRateSummary and the results, which verify that the original query calculated the average hourly rate correctly.

Figure 3.12: Revised qryHourlyRateSummary that calculates statistics for technicians and cashiers only

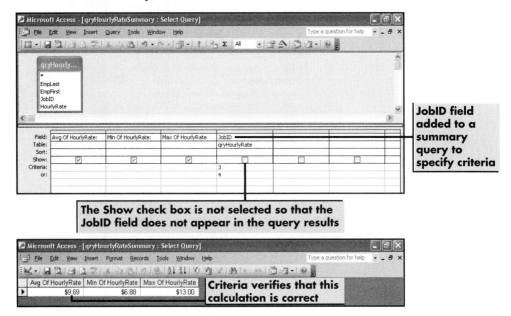

Maria has another problem she wants to work on next. Paul asked Maria to look into the possibility of scheduling at least one employee in the pharmacy who is fluent in Spanish for all shifts. She thinks she can create a query that uses broader criteria than the exact match criteria she's used so far to help with Paul's scheduling request.

ENHANCING QUERY CRITERIA TO IMPROVE DATA ANALYSIS

When you specify the criteria for a query, you are setting conditions that determine which records Access should display in the query results. Recall that to define a condition for a query, you enter the criterion in the Criteria row of the query design grid. If you enter a value, Access displays records that have an exact match of that value in the appropriate field. For example, when Maria entered 3 in the Criteria row of the JobID field, Access selected records in tblEmployee with the value 3 in the JobID field. Specifying a single criterion that Access must match exactly means you can pinpoint the records you want to select. However, suppose you want to select records for employees who earn between $8.00 and $9.00 per hour. If you know that the wages range from $8.00 to $9.00 in $.10 increments, for example, you could specify "8.00" as the first criteria, "8.10" as the next OR criteria, "8.20" as the next OR criteria, and so on, up to "8.90." Specifying 10 OR criteria is inefficient and can slow the query if the data source contains many records. In addition, this method of specifying multiple OR criteria is only possible if you are already familiar with the data in the database. If you don't know all the wage values, the criteria you specify will only retrieve some of the appropriate records. Instead of specifying exact criteria in such a case, you can expand the criteria by using wildcards or comparison operators.

Using Wildcards for Inexact Query Matches

Suppose you want to use a criterion such as a name, but do not know the spelling, or want to display records with values that match a pattern, such as phone numbers that all begin with a certain area code. In these cases, you cannot specify an exact match. Instead, you can use a **wildcard character**, a placeholder that stands for one or more characters. Use wildcard characters in query criteria when you know only part of the criteria, want to search for a value based on some of its characters, or want to match a pattern. Table 3.4 summarizes the wildcards you can use in queries.

Table 3.4: Wildcard characters used in queries

Symbol	Purpose	Example
*	Match any number of characters	Ab* to locate any word starting with Ab
?	Match any single alphabetic character	J?n finds Jan, Jon, and Jen
#	Match any single digit in a numeric field	(970) ###-#### finds phone numbers that have 970 area codes 1/##/08 finds dates during January 2008
[ ]	Match any single character listed within the brackets	J[eo]n finds Jen and Jon but not Jan
!	Match any character not within the brackets	J[!eo] finds Jan but not Jen or Jon
-	Match any one of a range of characters within the brackets; letters must be in ascending order	A[d-p] finds aft, ant, and apt, but not act and art

As you enter data in Memo fields, try to use the same keywords throughout the memos so that you can easily retrieve records later. Be certain to use wildcards when you specify the keyword as a query criterion to select records that contain characters before and after the keyword. For example, to discover how many employees speak Spanish at 4Corners Pharmacy, Maria could type *Spanish* in the Criteria row of the Memo field. The asterisk (*) wildcard character on either side of the criterion means Access selects records that contain text or other values before and after "Spanish" in the Memo field, such as those that include "Speaks Spanish fluently" and "Knows some Spanish." If Maria specifies Spanish without the asterisks, Access selects records that contain only the word Spanish in the Memo field.

Wildcards can help you match a pattern. For example, if you want to display the employees who started working in 2004, you could use */*/2004 or *2004 as the criterion in the StartDate field. Wildcards can also help you overcome data-entry errors. For example, if want to retrieve records for employees who live in Dolores, Colorado, which is often misspelled as Delores, you could specify D?lores as the criterion in the City field. In these ways, using wildcards can make your queries more powerful, allowing you to retrieve data without using criteria that demand an exact match.

Access inserts the word "Like" for criteria with wildcards, quotation marks around text, and pound signs around dates you enter, as in Like "*Spanish*" or Like #12/*/2008#.

Maria is ready to turn to Paul's scheduling request. Because many of the pharmacy's clientele speak Spanish, he wants to schedule at least one Spanish-speaking employee for each shift. If an employee speaks Spanish (or any other language besides English), it is noted in the Memo field of tblEmployee. Because this field has a Memo data type, which allows for lengthy text or combinations of text and numbers, it is often best to use wildcards in criteria that involve Memo fields.

To create this query, Maria double-clicks the Create query in Design view option in the Database window. The Select Query window opens in Design view, followed by the Show Table dialog box. All the fields she needs are in tblEmployee, so she double-clicks tblEmployee to display its field list, and then closes the Show Table dialog box. She adds the EmpLast, EmpFirst, JobID, and Memo fields to the design grid by double-clicking each one in that order. She selects EmpLast before EmpFirst because she plans to sort the records alphabetically by last name; the sort order will then be clear to anyone viewing the query results. She types *Spanish* in the Criteria row for the Memo field. The asterisks are necessary so that Access selects records that contain Spanish anywhere in the field. When she presses the Enter key, she notices that Access adds the word Like and inserts quotation marks around Spanish. See Figure 3.13.

Figure 3.13: Entering a query criterion using wildcards

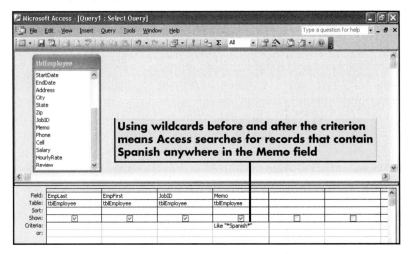

Maria saves the query as qrySpeakSpanish, runs the query, and finds three employees who speak Spanish, noting that none of them are pharmacists and that one no longer works at 4Corners. See Figure 3.14. She plans to talk to Paul Ferrino about hiring more Spanish-speaking employees; she cannot currently meet the goal of scheduling a Spanish-speaking employee for each shift. Because queries do not save the data, but rather the design, criteria, and sort order, Maria can use this query in the future to periodically update the list.

Figure 3.14: Results of a wildcard search for Spanish-speaking employees

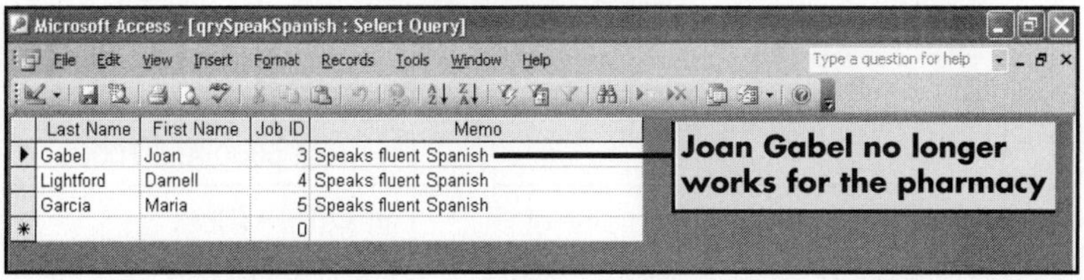

She notices that Joan Gabel is listed as an employee who speaks Spanish. However, Joan no longer works at 4Corners. Maria needs to solve the problem of maintaining data about employees who no longer work for the pharmacy. In the 4Corners database, she included records for past employees so she wouldn't lose the data about them. Eventually, the pharmacy will discard or archive printed information about previous employees, and the database will contain only current records. Maria needs a way to exclude the past employees from her queries.

Using Comparison Operators to Refine Query Criteria

In addition to entering a criterion that exactly matches a single value or using wildcards to match a pattern, you can use criteria that match a range of values. In this case, you use **comparison operators**, which compare the value in a field with a range of values in a criterion. If the value is within the range, data from the record is included. For example, you might want to know if an employee was hired after a particular date, such as June 1, 2007. Using a date as the criterion would only display those employees hired on that date. Instead, you can use a comparison operator to specify a range of dates, such as >= #6/1/2007# in the StartDate field to display employees who started working on June 1, 2007 or later. (Recall that Access requires pound signs around date values used in query criteria.) Table 3.5 shows the comparison operators used to specify a range of values.

Table 3.5: Comparison operators

Operator	Description	Examples
<	Less than	<500 <#1/1/2008#
<=	Less than or equal to	<=500 <=#12/31/2007#
=	Equal to	=500 ="CO"
>=	Greater than or equal to	>=500 >=12.75
>	Greater than	>500 >#12/31/2007#
<>	Not equal to	<>500 <>"CO"

205

Table 3.5: Comparison operators (cont.)

Operator	Description	Examples
Between...And	Include values within the specified range (inclusive); always use with dates	Between #1/01/2007# And #1/31/2007# Between 5000 And 10000
In	Include values within the specified list	In("CO","AZ")
Is	Include records in which the field contains a null, not null, true, or false value, as specified	Is Null, Is Not Null Is True, Is False
Like	Include values matching the specified pattern	Like "*Spanish*"

When Maria queries the 4Corners database for employee information, she needs to use a comparison operator in the criteria so that the query excludes employees who no longer work for 4Corners Pharmacy. These are employees whose records include a value in the EndDate field. For example, Joan Gabel stopped working for 4Corners in 2004. The EndDate field in her employee record contains the date value 5/31/2004, the last date of her employment. Maria considers using the Not comparison operator because it excludes records that contain a specified value. However, if she uses Not #5/31/2004# as the criterion in the EndDate field, the query excludes only Joan Gabel's record, and not those of other past employees. She could use the In operator with Not to list the EndDate values of all the past employees, as in Not In(#5/31/2004#,#6/15/2005#), but that requires her to find and possibly update these values each time she runs the query.

Maria reexamines the fields in the tblEmployee field list, trying to find a fresh approach to solve her problem. Instead of excluding employees with a value in the EndDate field, perhaps she could focus on selecting only those employees who do not have a value in the EndDate field. Instead of a value, the EndDate field for current employees is blank, or null. She could use the Is operator with null, as in Is Null, in the EndDate field to select current employees only.

Best Practice

Understanding Null Fields

Access has a special character called a null that indicates a field contains no value, or is blank. Nulls are different from a space or zero character, and can be used in expressions to check whether a field contains a value. To do so, you can use *Is Null* or *Is Not Null* as a criterion. Is Null selects records in which the specified field does not contain a value. Is Not Null selects records in which the specified field contains any type of value.

Maria modifies qrySpeakSpanish by adding the EndDate field to the design grid. Then she enters Is Null as its criterion to select only those records in which the EndDate field is blank, effectively eliminating former employees from the query results. She also clears the Show check box for the EndDate field because she does not want to display this field in the query results. She saves the modified query, and then runs it. Figure 3.15 shows the design and results of this query.

Figure 3.15: Only EndDate fields with null values are displayed

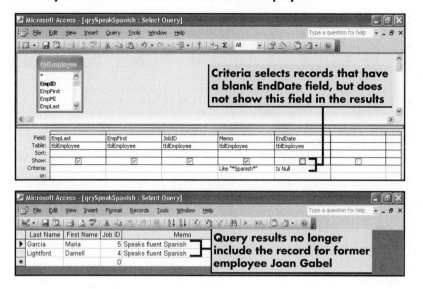

Now that Maria has refined her query for displaying current Spanish-speaking employees, she can turn her attention to solving a different problem. Paul Ferrino wants to reward long-term employees because he knows that they increase the efficiency, consistency, and quality of the pharmacy and its services. He also knows that hiring and training employees can be a drain on profits, and employee turnover can erode morale. He is considering presenting substantial bonuses to each employee who has worked at the pharmacy for more than five years. In addition, he has asked Maria to schedule a celebration later this year to acknowledge these employees and their contributions to the pharmacy. Maria needs to produce a list of employees who have worked at 4Corners Pharmacy for at least five years, or since January 1, 2003.

To produce this list, Maria can create a query that includes the StartDate field and uses the less than or equal to comparison operator (<=) to select records in which the start date is January 1, 2003 or earlier.

Because she needs to use the same tblEmployee field list as in qrySpeakSpanish, which is still open in Datasheet view, Maria switches to Design view and **clears the grid** to start with the same field list but a blank grid. To do this, she clicks Edit on the menu bar, and then clicks Clear Grid. She adds the EmpLast, EmpFirst, StartDate, and EndDate fields, and uses <=#1/1/2003# as the criterion in the StartDate field. She also decides to sort the records in ascending order by the values in the StartDate field so she and Paul can easily see who has worked for the pharmacy the longest. Finally, Maria uses the Is Null criterion in the EndDate field and removes the check from the Show box so this field does not appear in the query results. She saves the query as qryStartDate, and then runs it. Figure 3.16 shows the design and results of this query.

Figure 3.16: Using comparison operators with dates

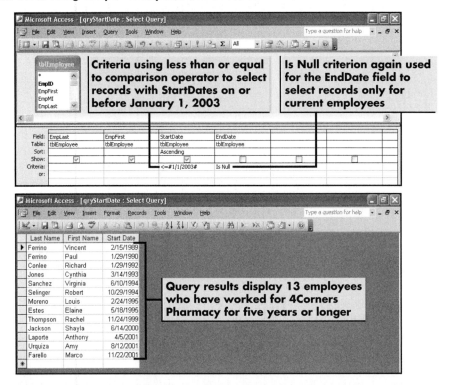

Clearing the Design Grid to Create or Modify a Query

When you are working with a query in Design view, you can clear the design grid by clicking Edit on the menu bar and then clicking Clear Grid. You can then create a query using the field lists that are already open in the field list area. Be certain to save the new query with a different name by clicking File on the menu bar and then clicking Save As so you don't overwrite the original query. You might also clear the grid when you don't plan to save the current query, but want to continue working in Design view, or the query is not producing the results you expect and want to try different criteria.

Before continuing her work with queries, Maria decides to print the results of all the queries she's created so far so that she can show them to Paul later.

VERIFYING AND PRINTING QUERY RESULTS

Before you distribute a query to others or use it as the basis for decisions, verify its results. Use your business knowledge to determine whether the results adequately answer the question you intended to answer. For example, if you want to list all the employees who have worked for your company for at least five years, but the query displays those who were hired within the last five years, you probably used the wrong comparison operator in the query criteria, such as the greater than operator (>) instead of the less than or equal to operator (<=).

Best Practice

Correcting Errors in Queries

If your query does not return any results, it might have a number of problems. Perhaps the underlying tables do not contain any matching data. Perhaps you have entered the criteria incorrectly. If you run a complex query that does not return any results when you know it should, revise the query so it specifies only one condition, and then run the query. If that works, add another condition and run the query again. As you build your query, you will probably see which additional condition is causing the problem.

If you receive an error similar to "Can't evaluate expression," look for a typographical error in the query criteria. An error similar to "Type mismatch" probably indicates that you have tried to perform mathematical operations on a Text or Date/Time data type value. An error similar to "Enter Parameter Value" usually indicates that you have misspelled a field name or have modified the table structure without changing the query to reflect the changes.

After you verify the query results, you can print the query datasheet. Although Access users usually print query results in the form of a report, which is more attractive and accessible than a datasheet, printing a query datasheet can help you and others review the query results and verify its accuracy or answer a quick question. It is good practice to check the format of the datasheet in Print Preview before printing so you can modify column widths and orientation for best results.

Modifying Query Datasheets

Access provides a number of formatting options to help you improve the appearance of a query or table datasheet. You set these formatting options when you are working in Datasheet view. (They are not available in Design view.) Table 3.6 describes the most common options you can use to format datasheets you print or view. You can open most of the dialog boxes noted in Table 3.6 by clicking Format on the menu bar and then clicking the appropriate option. You can also use tools on the Formatting (Datasheet) toolbar to achieve the same results.

Table 3.6: Formatting options for query and table datasheets

Format Option	Effect	Access Tool to Use
Font	Change font, font style, and size	Font dialog box
Datasheet	Change cell effects to flat, sunken, or raised Change background and gridline colors Show or hide gridlines	Datasheet Formatting dialog box
Row Height	Set row height	Row Height dialog box
Column Width	Set column width or click the Best Fit button	Column Width dialog box
Hide Columns	Hide a column	Hide Columns command on the Format menu
Unhide Columns	Unhide a column	Unhide Columns dialog box
Freeze Columns	Set columns to display and print even if you scroll to the right	Freeze Columns command on the Format menu
Unfreeze All Columns	Unfreeze columns previously frozen	Unfreeze All Columns command on the Format menu
Subdatasheet	Expand, collapse, or remove subdatasheets	Subdatasheet command on the Format menu

Note that you can resize the column widths in any datasheet by double-clicking the line between field names to resize the columns to their best fit. If you have too many columns or they are too wide to fit on a single page in portrait orientation, you can use the Page Setup dialog box to change the page orientation to landscape.

Maria formats qryStartDate by increasing the size of the font and resizing the columns so that each is wide enough to display all the data it contains. She clicks the Print Preview button 🔲 on the Query Datasheet toolbar to view the effects of her changes. To print the results, she clicks the Print button 🖨 on the Query Datasheet toolbar.

Steps To Success: Level 1

Kim Siemers, human resources manager at Hudson Bay Pharmacy, is ready to use the Hudson database to extract information that will help her manage employees. She asks for your help in filtering table data and creating queries, especially those that use criteria to select the information they need. As you create and save the new queries, be certain to use the "qry" prefix as part of the naming convention. Also consult your instructor for instructions about submitting your results.

Note: To complete the following steps, you must have completed the Steps to Success for Levels 1 and 2 in Chapter 2.

Complete the following:

1. Start Access and open the **Hudson.mdb** database from the STS folder.

2. Kim needs quick answers to three questions. First, she needs to know how many pharmacists are listed in the tblEmployee table. Filter the data in the tblEmployee table to answer Kim's question. How many records are displayed?

3. Next, Kim wants to know how many records in tblEmployee are for pharmacists, owners, or managers. Refilter the data in tblEmployee to answer Kim's second question. How many records are displayed?

4. Finally, Kim wants to know who was the first employee hired by Hudson Bay Pharmacy, and who was the most recent. Organize the data in tblEmployee so that you can easily answer Kim's question. Who was the first employee hired by the pharmacy? Who was the most recent?

5. To help Kim call employees when she needs a substitute, create an alphabetical phone list of Hudson Bay employees and their phone numbers. Save the query as qryEmpPhoneList.

6. Kim is planning to meet with Joan Gabel, the owner of Hudson Bay Pharmacy, to review the wages paid to employees so they can budget for upcoming pay raises. Kim wants to check the hourly rates paid to employees. List the wages for employees who are paid according to their hourly rate, ranked from highest to lowest to display the full range of pay for current, nonsalaried employees. Also include information that clearly identifies each employee. Save the query as qryHourlyRate.

7. Kim mentions that a summary of the hourly rate information would also be helpful as she prepares for her meeting. List only the highest, lowest, and average pay rates for nonsalaried employees. Make sure that the average calculation does not include zero values for salaried employees. Save the query as qryHourlyRateAnalysis.

8. Kim wants to schedule employees so that at least one who speaks Spanish is working each shift. Produce a list of current employees at Hudson Bay Pharmacy who speak Spanish. Save the query as qrySpeakSpanish.

9. To prepare for employee reviews, Kim asks you to produce a list of all employees who have been reprimanded at least once. (*Hint*: Look for keywords in the Memo field.) Save the query as qryReprimand.

10. Kim has analyzed employment data and discovered that those who have been working for one to three years are most likely to accept employment elsewhere. Kim asks you to identify employees who started working between January 1, 2005 and January 1, 2007, ranked so the most recent start date is first. Save the query as qryStartDate.

11. Format one of the queries you created for Hudson Bay Pharmacy to make it easier to read, and then print one page of the results.

12. Close the **Hudson.mdb** database and Access.

LEVEL 2

CREATING MORE COMPLEX QUERIES

ACCESS 2003 SKILLS TRAINING

- **Add a calculated field to a select query**
- **Add a table to the Design view query grid**
- **Build summary queries**
- **Change join properties**
- **Create a find duplicate query**
- **Create a find unmatched query**
- **Create a query in Design view**
- **Create a top values query**
- **Create and run a parameter query**
- **Create calculated fields**
- **Create queries using wizards**
- **Create queries with AND conditions**
- **Create queries with OR conditions**
- **Include criteria in query for field not in results**
- **Use aggregate functions in queries to perform calculations**
- **Use computed fields and sort the results**
- **Use the AVG function in a query**

EVALUATING DATA USING SPECIAL TYPES OF QUERIES

In addition to the Simple Query Wizard, Access provides other query wizards that help you evaluate and verify the data stored in a database. For example, you can use the Find Duplicates Query Wizard to retrieve duplicate records in a table, which is especially useful if the table contains data for a mailing list or if you have imported records from another source. Table 3.7 lists query wizards other than the Simple Query Wizard and describes their purpose.

Table 3.7: Wizards for specialized queries

Query Type	Purpose	Example
Find Duplicates	Locate duplicate records in a table or query	Identify the same employee who is entered multiple times with different IDs
Find Unmatched	Locate records with no related records in a second table or query	Identify employees who have not taken any training classes

In this section, you will learn how to use query wizards to answer complex business questions, analyze data, and maintain the integrity of your database.

Now that Maria Garcia is familiar with the 4Corners database, she wants to use it to automate many of her human resources tasks. First, she wants to help employees determine how they can share rides to work. To conserve gasoline and other vehicle maintenance costs, employees have asked Maria to help them coordinate car pools. Parking near the pharmacy is limited, so Paul Ferrino is also encouraging employees to organize car pools. Employees who live in the same city can contact each other and share a ride to work. Maria's next task is to create a car pool list identifying those employees who live in the same city.

Using Queries to Find Duplicate Records

One select query wizard that Access offers besides the Simple Query Wizard is the **Find Duplicates Query Wizard**, which searches for duplicate values in the fields you select. For example, you might have accidentally entered the same employee or customer name twice with two different IDs. Newly transferred data from a spreadsheet or other source to an Access table also often contains duplicate information, as does a database that was not set up correctly. In these cases, you can use the Find Duplicates Query Wizard to identify duplicate records. Be certain to examine the records the wizard identifies to determine that they indeed contain duplicate data. You can then edit the data in the table as necessary.

Besides using the Find Duplicates Query Wizard to identify and then repair data errors, you can also use the wizard to improve business operations. For example, you can find customers who live in the same city so you can coordinate sales calls, identify vendors who supply the same products or services so you can compare costs, or find employees enrolled in the same training session so you can notify them about a schedule change.

The Find Duplicates Query Wizard is designed to identify records that contain the same information in a particular field, even if you don't know all or part of the duplicated values. If a table of employee data contains five records with "Springfield" and three records with "Ashton" in the City field, the wizard selects all eight records. To select records containing the same value that you specify, however, set criteria to select those records. For example, if you want to retrieve the records for employees who live in Springfield, use "Springfield" as the criterion in the City field. The query then selects five employee records.

Maria wants to identify employees who live in the same city so they can create car pools and share rides to work. Because 4Corners Pharmacy is located in southwestern Colorado on the border of the four states of Arizona, Colorado, New Mexico, and Utah, employees live in many surrounding cities. Maria can use the Find Duplicates Query Wizard to create a list of employees who live in the same city. She can post this list so that employees can form car pools.

To accomplish this task, Maria starts the Find Duplicates Query Wizard by clicking the Queries button on the Objects bar in the Database window, clicking the New button on the Database window toolbar, and then double-clicking Find Duplicates Query Wizard. The first dialog box in the wizard opens, shown in Figure 3.17.

Figure 3.17: First dialog box in Find Duplicates Query Wizard

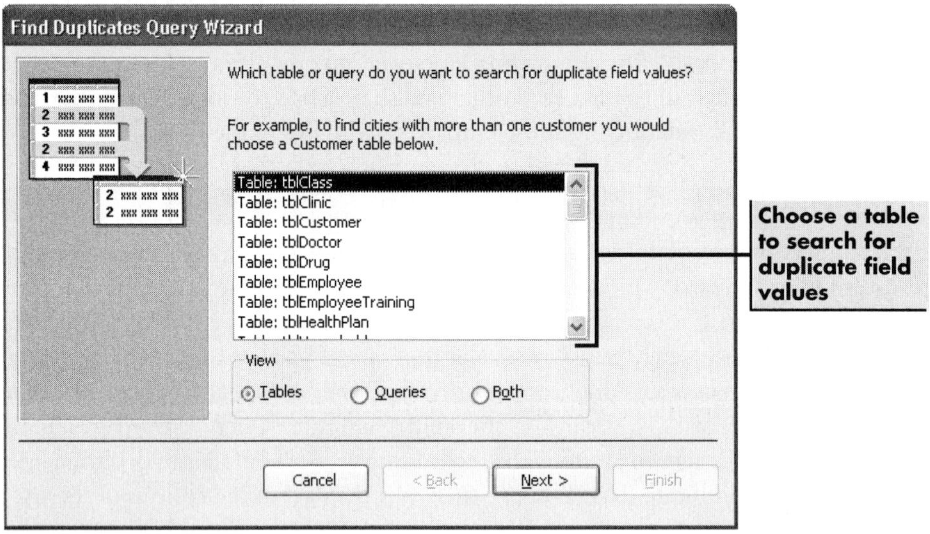

Because the tblEmployee table contains employee addresses, she clicks tblEmployee and then clicks the Next button.

The next wizard dialog box asks her to identify the fields that might contain duplicate information. Maria double-clicks City and State in the Available fields box to add them to the Duplicate-value fields box. She includes State because cities with the same name might be located in more than one state. See Figure 3.18.

Figure 3.18: Select field or fields that might contain duplicate information

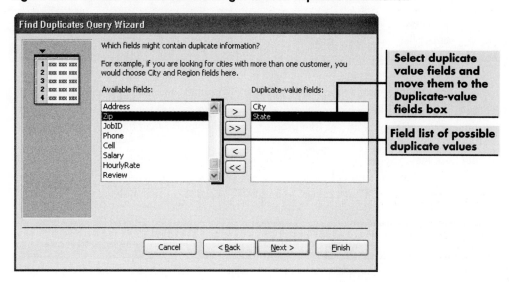

When she clicks the Next button, the third dialog box in the wizard opens, asking if she wants the query to show fields in addition to those with duplicate values. Maria selects the EmpFirst, EmpLast, Address, Phone, and Cell fields so the list will have all the information employees need to share rides, and then clicks the Next button. She names the query qryDuplicateCities, and clicks Finish. The results are shown in Figure 3.19.

Figure 3.19: Results of the Find Duplicates Query Wizard

City	State	Last Name	First Name	Address	Phone	Cell
Aneth	UT	White	Thomas	322 South Cripple Creek Avenue	(435) 167-9745	(435) 134-9462
Aneth	UT	Selinger	Robert	9411 Clarkston Avenue	(435) 243-4289	(435) 474-3497
Dolores	CO	Ferrino	Paul	133 South Washington	(970) 344-2616	(970) 445-2974
Dolores	CO	Ferrino	Vincent	1109 Siesta Shores Drive	(970) 348-5466	
Dolores	CO	Linebarger	Donald	1998 SE First Avenue	(970) 357-5546	(970) 487-6522
Dolores	CO	Farello	Marco	11259 Road 22	(970) 122-3333	(970) 221-3333
Flora Vista	NM	Sanchez	Virginia	633 Empire Street	(505) 444-9898	(505) 777-4125
Flora Vista	NM	Moreno	Louis	403 North Madison Street	(505) 599-6412	(505) 621-4477
Kayenta	AZ	Kobrick	Tara	620 East Empire Street	(928) 667-1119	(928) 764-4632
Kayenta	AZ	Laporte	Anthony	620 East Empire Street	(928) 667-1119	(928) 764-5211
Kayenta	AZ	Nader	Connie	1645 Johnny Cake Ridge Road	(928) 477-3145	(928) 397-6869
Lewis	CO	Estes	Elaine	801 Airport Road	(970) 541-8765	(970) 555-7655
Lewis	CO	Gabel	Joan	1102 Jackson Street	(970) 655-1777	(970) 644-1222
Lewis	CO	Latour	Dominque	56 East Pioneer Road	(970) 147-8458	(970) 239-6487
Pleasant View	CO	Jones	Cynthia	755 Cherry Street	(970) 344-7212	(970) 445-1498
Pleasant View	CO	Garcia	Maria	707 Cherry Street	(970) 344-8241	(970) 447-5465
Shiprock	NM	Langston	Dora	1155 NE Highland Parkway	(505) 699-7231	(505) 478-7411
Shiprock	NM	Lightford	Darnell	1309 Mesa Avenue	(505) 744-3147	(505) 775-1678

Only employees with the same city and state are listed

Avoiding Duplicate Records

If you expect duplicates to be a problem, the best way to solve the problem is to use good database design. For example, the 4Corners database allows only one person to be listed as the head of household in the HeadHH field in tblCustomer, and addresses are listed only once in a separate table named tblHousehold. The tblCustomer and tblHousehold tables share a common field, HouseID, which allows the two tables to be used in queries. By setting a criterion that HeadHH must be Yes, the problem of duplicates is eliminated by good design.

You could use the same technique with employees, but it would be difficult to designate one employee as head of the household. Although some employees might form a household, many might be roommates only. Most mailings to employees need to be sent individually for privacy reasons as well.

Using Queries to Find Unmatched Records

Another useful query wizard is the Find Unmatched Query Wizard. This type of select query compares the records in two specified tables or recordsets, and finds all the records in one table or query that have no related records in a second table or query. For example, you could find all customers who have not ordered any products, or vendors who provide services you no longer use. Identifying these unmatched records means you can then contact inactive customers to solicit business or delete records for vendors who no longer serve your needs. Note that the Find Unmatched Query Wizard requires that the two tables being compared have a common field.

At 4Corners Pharmacy, Paul Ferrino has set a store policy that all employees must maintain certifications in adult, infant, and child CPR and in defibrillator use. One of Maria's new responsibilities is to monitor training to make sure employees are enrolling in the required certification classes. This information is stored in the tblEmployeeTraining table. However, Maria is concerned that some employees might not have completed any training, and would therefore not have a record in tblEmployeeTraining. To identify these employees, she can use the Find Unmatched Query Wizard.

To start the query, Maria clicks Queries on the Objects bar of the Database window. She clicks the New button and then double-clicks Find Unmatched Query Wizard. The first dialog box opens, as shown in Figure 3.20.

Figure 3.20: Find Unmatched Query Wizard opening dialog box

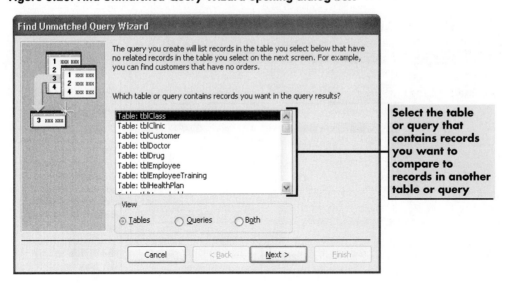

Maria wants to produce the names of employees who have not enrolled in any training classes. She therefore selects tblEmployee because it contains the employee records, which include employee names. She clicks the Next button, and the dialog box shown in Figure 3.21 opens.

Figure 3.21: Selecting the related table to compare records

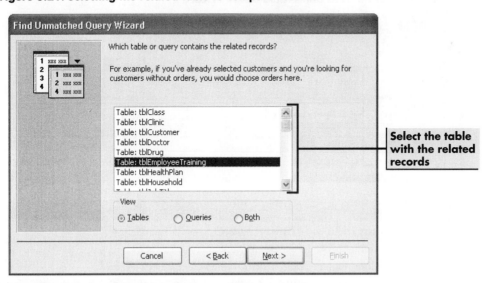

Maria selects tblEmployeeTraining and clicks the Next button because she suspects that this table might not contain records for all the employees in tblEmployee. She knows that both tables must have a common field so that the query can compare the records; tblEmployee and tblEmployeeTraining share the common field EmpID. See Figure 3.22.

Figure 3.22: Identifying the field to relate the two tables or queries

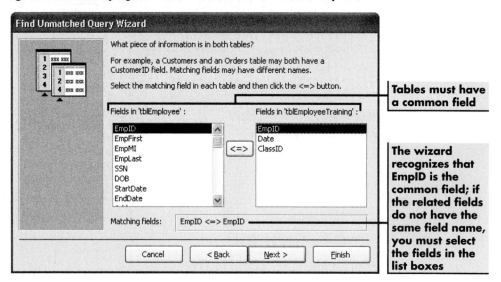

Figure 3.23: Results of the Find Unmatched Query Wizard

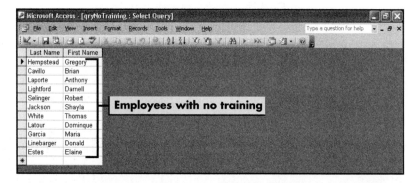

She clicks the Next button, and the next dialog box asks what other fields she wants to see in the query results. She decides to include EmpLast and EmpFirst in the results so she can easily identify the employees. Then she clicks the Next button, saves the query as qryNoTraining, and clicks the Finish button. The results are shown in Figure 3.23.

How To

Create a Query Using the Find Unmatched Query Wizard

1. Click Queries on the Objects bar in the Database window.

2. Click the New button and then double-click Find Unmatched Query Wizard.

3. Double-click to select the table or query that has the records you want in your query results. Click the Next button.

4. Double-click to select the table or query with the related records. Click the Next button.

5. If necessary, click the matching field in each table. Access identifies the common field if the fields have the same name in each table. Click the Next button.

6. Double-click the fields you want to display in the query results, and then click the Next button.

7. Name the query and then click the Finish button.

Maria finds 11 employees who have no matching records, meaning these employees need to schedule certification training as soon as possible. As she writes a note to remind herself to notify these employees, Paul Ferrino asks her to perform another task for him. He wants to identify the five best nonsalaried employees, those who have been rewarded for extraordinary customer service or other contributions to the pharmacy. He is considering developing a program that encourages employee excellence, and he might start by recognizing these five employees. Maria considers how to provide this information. She could pull out the file folders for all nonsalaried employees and scan the printed employee reviews to find citations for special service. However, this would be time consuming and error-prone; she would have to read carefully to make sure she doesn't overlook relevant information. She recalls that Paul regularly rewards employees for their performance by increasing their wages. Maria can use the 4Corners database to identify the top five wage earners—these are the same employees who provide the best service to the pharmacy.

Limiting the Records in the Query Results

Sometimes, showing all the data in a query provides more detail than you need, especially if the query selects many records that match your criteria. Limiting the results to only a few records often aids analysis. For example, schools need to identify students in the top 5% of their class. A bookstore might want to list the top 10 best-selling books, while a national business might want to increase advertising in the three regions with the fewest sales. To limit the number of records in the query results, you can create a Top Values query, which sorts and then filters records to display the specified number of records that contain the top or bottom values. You can apply the Top Values limitation to any query by using the Top Values list box on the Query Design toolbar. You indicate the number of records you want the query to display by entering or selecting an integer, such as 10 (to display the top or bottom 10 records), or a percentage, such as 25% (to display the top or bottom 25% of records). To indicate whether you want to select records with the top or bottom values, set a sort order for the field—Descending to display the records with the highest values, or Ascending to display the records with the smallest values.

Maria wants to identify the top five current wage earners at 4Corners Pharmacy. She creates a query in Design view using the EmpFirst, EmpLast, HourlyRate, and EndDate fields from tblEmployee. She uses the Is Null criterion in the EndDate field to select records only for current employees, and then removes the check mark from the Show box so the End-Date field doesn't appear in the results. Then she clicks in the Sort row of the HourlyRate field and specifies a Descending sort order. To limit the records to the top five values in that field, she clicks the arrow on the Top Values list box All ▼ and then clicks 5. She saves the query as qryTop5HourlyRates, and then runs the query. Figure 3.24 shows the design and results of qryTop5HourlyRates.

Figure 3.24: Top Values query design and results

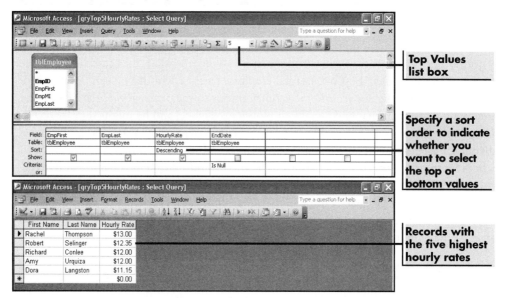

Maria can give the results of qryTop5HourlyRates to Paul to support his plans for an employee excellence program. Before she can return to the problem of tracking employee certification training, a pharmacy technician calls to say he can't work later today because of illness. Maria needs to find another pharmacy technician who can work for him. Instead of pulling out an employee phone list and searching for technicians as she's done before, Maria decides to create a query that will help her schedule employees when someone calls in sick or otherwise misses work. She'd like a way to generate a list of employees in a job category so she can quickly call others with the same job and find a substitute. She can create a query that selects employee information, including name and phone number, and uses the job ID as the criterion for selection. The problem she faces, however, is that the job ID will change depending on who is missing work. If a cashier calls in sick, for example, Maria needs to run the query using 4 as the criterion. If she needs a substitute for a pharmacy technician, she'll use 3 as the criterion. She needs to create a query that requests the criterion before it runs—then she can enter 3 or 4 as appropriate, and generate a list of employees in a particular job category.

Using Parameter Values in Queries

When you need to run a query multiple times with changes to the criteria, you can enter a **parameter value**. Parameter values are a phrase, usually in the form of a question or instruction, enclosed in square brackets, such as [Enter a job ID:] or [What job category do you want to select?]. The parameter value serves as a prompt to the user to enter a value.

To create a parameter query, you enter a parameter value as the criterion for a field, such as the JobID field. When you run the query, it opens a dialog box displaying the prompt you specified and allowing you to enter a value. For example, the dialog box might display "What job category do you want to select?" and provide a text box in which you can enter 3 or 4. When you click OK or press Enter, the query continues. Your response is then used as a criterion for the query. The benefit of a parameter query is that it is interactive—you can run the same query many times and specify different values each time.

Maria decides to create a parameter query by specifying a parameter value in the JobID field of tblEmployee. She begins creating the query in Design view using tblEmployee. She chooses EmpLast, EmpFirst, JobID, EndDate, Phone, and Cell as fields for the query. In the Criteria row for JobID, she types the prompt [What job classification do you want?], including the required square brackets. She sorts the data in alphabetical order by last name, and removes the check mark in the Show box for the JobID field because all employees in the results will have the same JobID. She remembers to include the EndDate criterion Is Null and to remove the check mark in its Show box. She saves the query as qrySubstituteList, and then runs it to make sure the Enter Parameter Value dialog box appears. Figure 3.25 shows the design of qrySubstituteList, the dialog box that appears when running the query, and the results.

Figure 3.25: Parameter query to allow user input when the query is run

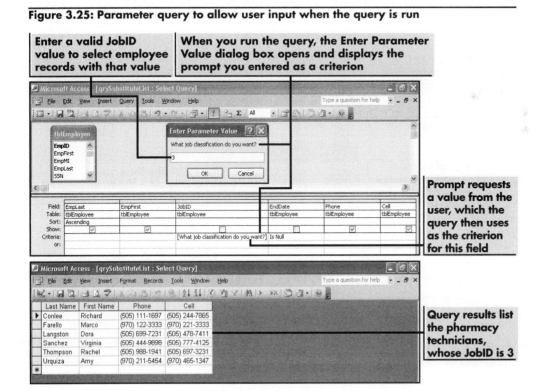

Enter a valid JobID value to select employee records with that value

When you run the query, the Enter Parameter Value dialog box opens and displays the prompt you entered as a criterion

Prompt requests a value from the user, which the query then uses as the criterion for this field

Query results list the pharmacy technicians, whose JobID is 3

When Maria runs the query from the Database window, first the Enter Parameter Value dialog box appears, in which she can enter the job ID of the job for which she needs a substitute. When she clicks the OK button, the results will display a list of employees in that job category.

When you enter the parameter value prompt as a criterion in Design view, Access assumes you want users to enter a value with the default data type, which is Text. If the required value is of a different data type, you can use the Query Parameters dialog box to specify the parameter's data type. Because many parameter queries work without specifying the data type, you should try the query first without specifying the data type to see if it runs correctly.

How To

Specify the Parameter's Data Type

1. Open a query in Design view. In the Criteria row for the field whose criterion will change each time the query runs, type the prompt you want to appear in the Enter Parameter Value dialog box. Be certain to type the prompt within square brackets.

2. Copy the text of the parameter prompt without including the square brackets. (Select the text and then press Ctrl+C to copy it.)

3. Click Query on the menu bar and then click Parameters. The Query Parameters dialog box opens.

4. Click in the first open line of the Query Parameters dialog box, and then press Ctrl+V to paste the prompt. You can also type the prompt instead.

5. Click in the corresponding Data Type text box, click the list arrow, and then click the appropriate data type. See Figure 3.26.

Figure 3.26: Changing the data type of a parameter value

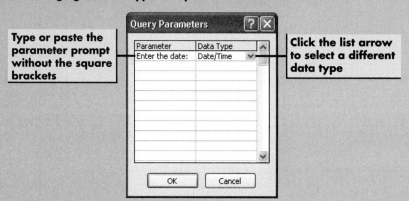

6. Click the OK button.

Best Practice

Testing a Parameter Query

As you create a parameter query, test it by using fixed criteria and then add the parameter prompts. You can then switch between the Design view and Datasheet view without stopping to enter one or more parameters. After you have tested the query, replace the fixed criteria with the prompt for the Enter Parameter Value dialog box.

Maria now has time to revisit the training issues for the pharmacy's employees. She needs to know which employees need to attend training classes to keep their certifications up to date. To investigate this problem fully, she needs to analyze data from tblEmployee and tblEmployeeTraining.

ANALYZING DATA FROM MORE THAN ONE TABLE

Often, data from more than one table is required to answer a question. In fact, the most powerful advantage of creating queries is that they let you combine records from two or more tables to display only the information you need. For example, Maria needs data from both tblEmployee and tblEmployeeTraining to answer questions about employee certification training. Although you can use the Simple Query Wizard to select fields from more than one table or query, you must work in Design view to specify criteria for selecting records from multiple tables. Figure 3.27 shows the field lists for two tables in Design view for a select query.

Figure 3.27: Join line for related tables in Query Design view

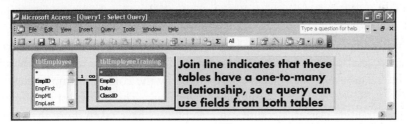

Notice that a line connects the EmpID fields in the two tables. Recall that this line represents the relationship between the primary key in tblEmployee and a foreign key in tblEmployeeTraining that you created when you established referential integrity in Chapter 2. If tables are related, you can select fields from those tables and use them together in queries. The lines between tables link the primary key, the field designated with a "1," in a table called the **primary table** to the foreign key, the field designated with an infinity symbol (∞), in a table called a **related table.** The primary table is on the "one" side of the relationship, and the related table with the foreign key is on the "many" side of the relationship. For example, in tblEmployee, the EmpID field is the primary key. Each employee has only one ID and only one record in tblEmployee, but can take many classes.

By including the EmpID in the tblEmployeeTraining table, the two tables are linked by EmpID, and fields from both tables can therefore be used in a query. This linking of tables using their primary and foreign keys is called a **join** of the tables.

If you have not already established a relationship between two tables, Access creates a join under the following conditions: each table shares a field with the same or compatible data type and one of the join fields is a primary key. In this case, Access does not display the "1" and "many" symbols because referential integrity is not enforced.

If the tables you want to use in a query do not include fields that can be joined, you must add one or more extra tables or queries to link the tables that contain the data you want to use. For example, suppose Maria needs to display a list of classes taken by pharmacists only, and wants to include the ClassID and Date fields from tblEmployeeTraining and use the JobID field from tblJobTitle to set the criterion. The tblEmployeeTraining and tblJobTitle tables are not related and do not share any common fields. She must add a table to the query that is related to tblEmployeeTraining and tblJobTitle, which is tblEmployee. Then tblEmployee serves as a bridge between the two unrelated tables so that Maria can produce a list of classes taken by pharmacists.

Note that if your query includes related tables, the values you specify in criteria for fields from the related tables are case sensitive—they must match the case of the values in the underlying table.

Maria wants to start investigating employee training by producing a list of employees who have taken certification classes, including the date and class ID. To do so, she needs fields from two tables: tblEmployee and tblEmployeeTraining. She starts creating a query in Design view, selecting the field lists for tblEmployee and tblEmployeeTraining. To the query design grid, she adds the EmpLast and EmpFirst fields from tblEmployee and the Date and ClassID fields from tblEmployeeTraining. She notes that the tables have a one-to-many relationship, and that they are linked by the common EmpID field. Maria saves the query as qryEmployeeClasses, and then runs it. The results list employees who have attended training classes. Because some employees have taken more than one class, they are listed more than once. See Figure 3.28.

Figure 3.28: Query using fields from two tables

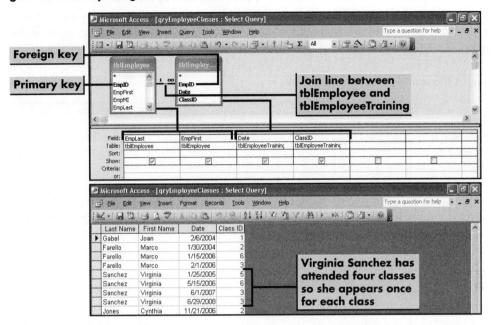

Maria can use this list herself, but she needs a similar list that includes the class description instead of the class ID. She'll post this list on the employee bulletin board as a reminder about the certification classes. Now that she's created qryEmployeeClasses, she can save time by using it as the basis for a new query that lists class descriptions. The qryEmployeeClasses query already has fields from tblEmployee and tblEmployeeTraining, including ClassID. However, neither table contains the Description field, which provides a description or title of each class. Because only tblClass contains that field, she needs to include the tblClass table in the new query to list class descriptions instead of class IDs.

You can use queries as the source of the underlying data for another query in place of one or more tables. For example, you might want to restrict the records you select by using a Top Values query or you might have already saved a query with the fields and criteria you want as the start for a new query. When you use the Show Table dialog box to select the objects to query, you can click the Query tab or the Both tab to choose queries as well as tables for field lists. Queries do not have primary keys or defined relationships the way tables do, but a line connects a field in a query used as a field list if the field names are the same in the other table or query.

Maria starts creating a query in Design view. When the Show Table dialog box opens, she clicks the Both tab to show tables and queries, and then adds qryEmployeeClasses and tblClass to the query. Because she wants to list employee names, the date they attended a class, and the class description, she double-clicks EmpLast, EmpFirst, and Date in the qryEmployeeClasses field list and Description in the tblClass field list to add these fields to the query design grid, and sorts the EmpLast field in ascending order. She saves the query as qryEmployeeClassesDescription, and then runs it. The results now include the descriptions of the classes instead of the ClassIDs, which is more meaningful to the employees who will view the list. See Figure 3.29.

Figure 3.29: Joining a query and a table

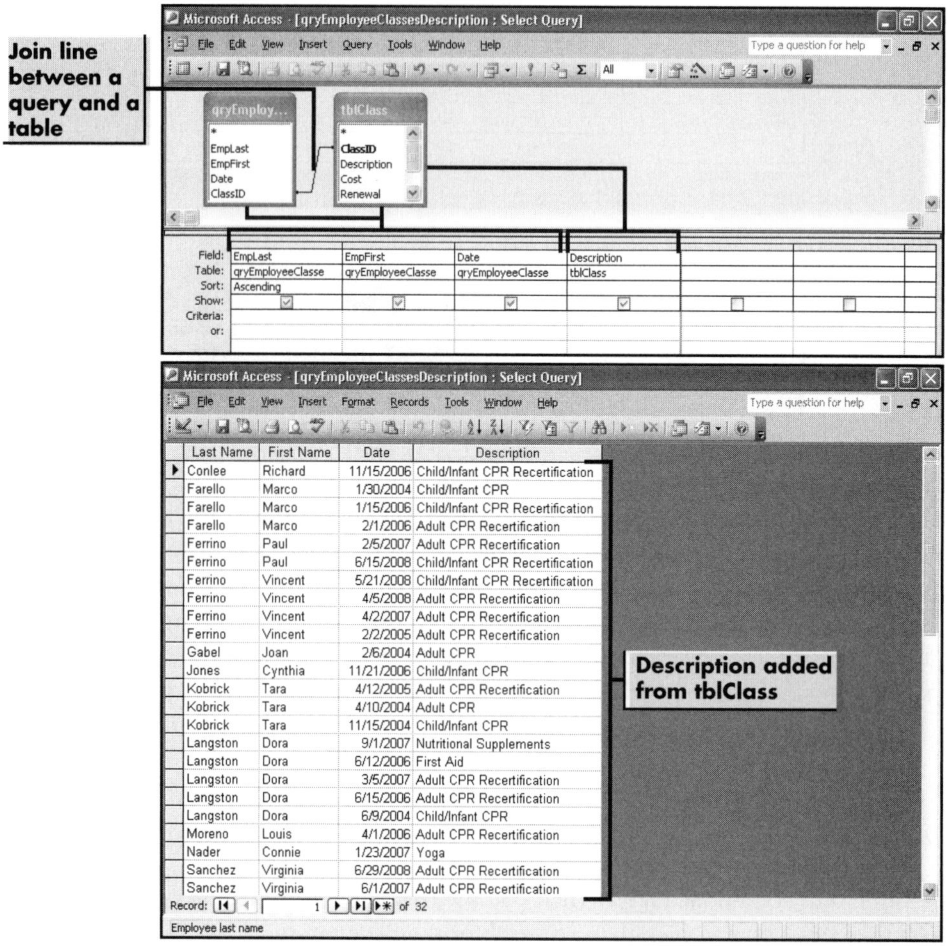

Join line between a query and a table

Description added from tblClass

Note that when you create queries based on more than one object, you should not use any table or query that does not have a common field with at least one of the other tables or queries. If the tables in a query are not joined to one another, Access cannot associate one record with another, so it displays every combination of records between the two tables. The data from a query created with unrelated tables therefore contains many extra records, often producing nonsensical results. For example, suppose Maria tried to produce a list of employee names and class descriptions by including EmpLast and EmpFirst from tblEmployee and Description from tblClass. The tblEmployee and tblClass tables are not related and contain no common fields. When Maria runs the query, Access would simply list the 24 current employees in the EmpLast and EmpFirst columns of the results, and the descriptions for all eight classes contained in tblClass in the Description column. The results would contain 192 rows of information, or 8 × 24—each employee name listed eight times for each class, regardless of whether the employee attended the class. See Figure 3.30.

Figure 3.30: Unrelated tables show no join line and give meaningless results when queried

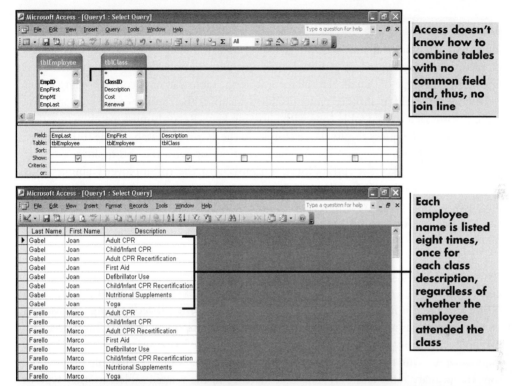

Access doesn't know how to combine tables with no common field and, thus, no join line

Each employee name is listed eight times, once for each class description, regardless of whether the employee attended the class

Verifying that Your Query Results Make Sense

When you examine the results of a query, be certain to verify that they make sense for your data and your business. One quick check is to note the number of rows in the query datasheet. Queries created using unrelated tables often contain many more rows than you expect. If you combine a large customer list of 100 customers, for example, with many purchases for each customer, you expect hundreds of rows in the results. However, if you list customers who live in a few specified cities, you expect the list to contain fewer than 100 customers. As a general rule, when the query results include a high number of rows, check to make sure the field lists have join lines and that the results seem plausible.

As Maria examines the results of qryEmployeeClassesDescription, she realizes it would provide more information if she could include the employees who have not attended any training classes—these are the employees who need to schedule training as soon as possible.

She already used the Find Unmatched Query Wizard to create qryNoTraining, which identifies employees who have not attended any training classes. Ideally, the list she posts on the employee bulletin board will include these employees and those who have attended training—some might need to update their certification. She decides to find out if she can refine the query to list all employees and their training information, even if they have not attended a class.

Refining Relationships with Appropriate Join Types

Tables with a relationship (and a common field) can be joined in two ways, and each affects the records a query selects. The most common type of relationship for select queries is an **inner join**. This type of join displays all records in one table that have corresponding values in the common field in another table. Usually, this joins the records of the primary table to the records of a related table (one with a foreign key). Records must match before they are displayed in the query results. For example, in the 4Corners database, the tblEmployee table is on the "one" side of a one-to-many relationship with the tblEmployeeTraining table. The primary key for tblEmployee is EmpID. In the tblEmployeeTraining table, EmpID is a foreign key. When these tables are related with an inner join, a query displays only those records that have a matching EmpID value—all the records in tblEmployee that have a matching record in tblEmployeeTraining, or all the employees who have attended training classes.

If you want to display all the records of one table regardless of whether a corresponding record is stored in a related table, use an **outer join**. For example, an employee record in tblEmployee might not have a corresponding record in tblEmployeeTraining because not every employee has attended a training class. An outer join query using tblEmployee and tblEmployeeTraining would list all employees regardless of whether they have attended a training class. This type of outer join applies when you want to show all the records from the primary table and only data that matches in the related table. Another type of outer join shows all the records from the related table and only data that matches in the primary table. Figure 3.31 shows an inner join, while Figures 3.32 and 3.33 show the two types of outer joins.

Figure 3.31: Inner join

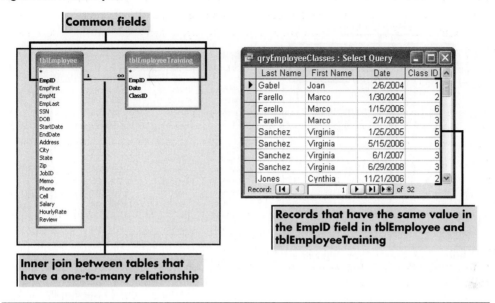

Common fields

Records that have the same value in the EmpID field in tblEmployee and tblEmployeeTraining

Inner join between tables that have a one-to-many relationship

Figure 3.32: Left outer join

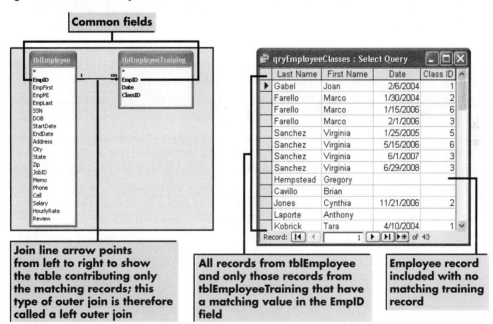

Common fields

Join line arrow points from left to right to show the table contributing only the matching records; this type of outer join is therefore called a left outer join

All records from tblEmployee and only those records from tblEmployeeTraining that have a matching value in the EmpID field

Employee record included with no matching training record

Figure 3.33: Right outer join

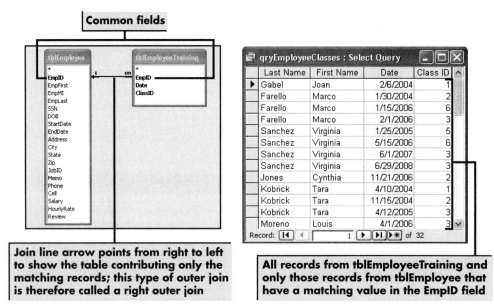

Join line arrow points from right to left to show the table contributing only the matching records; this type of outer join is therefore called a right outer join

All records from tblEmployeeTraining and only those records from tblEmployee that have a matching value in the EmpID field

The two types of outer joins are often designated as left or right, depending on the placement of the field lists in Design view for the query and whether you want the one on the right or the left to show all its records. Left outer joins include all of the records from the table on the left, even if there are no matching values for records in the table on the right. Right outer joins include all of the records from the table on the right, even if there are no matching values for records in the table on the left. Changing the position of the field lists in the query reverses the right/left designation for the join.

To produce a list of all employees and their training information, even if they have not attended a class, Maria needs fields from tblEmployee and tblEmployeeTraining, the same fields she used to create qryEmployeeClasses. She opens qryEmployeeClasses in Design view so she can modify it, and saves it as qryAllEmployeeClasses. By default, this query uses an inner join between tblEmployee and tblEmployeeTraining. To change the join type, she double-clicks the join line. The Join Properties dialog box opens, shown in Figure 3.34.

Figure 3.34: Using the Join Properties dialog box to change the join type

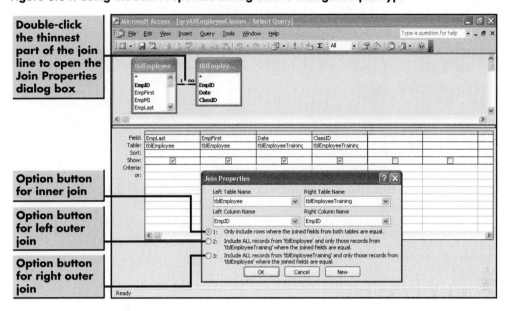

Double-click the thinnest part of the join line to open the Join Properties dialog box

Option button for inner join

Option button for left outer join

Option button for right outer join

The first option, "Only include rows where the joined fields from both tables are equal" is for an inner join. The second option, "Include ALL records from 'tblEmployee' and only those records from 'tblEmployeeTraining' where the joined fields are equal" is exactly what Maria wants. This type of outer join selects all the records from tblEmployee, even if there are no matching records in tblEmployeeTraining. In other words, it lists all the employees and the classes they've taken; if an employee has not attended a class, this outer join query lists the employee name, but leaves the Date and ClassID fields blank. The third option, "Include ALL records from 'tblEmployeeTraining' and only those records from 'tblEmployee' where the joined fields are equal" would select all the records from tblEmployeeTraining, even if there are no matching records in tblEmployee. If a class were scheduled, for example, but no employees were recorded as attending it, the results would include the Date and ClassID of that class, but no data in the EmpLast and EmpFirst fields.

Maria clicks the option button for the second option to create a left outer join, runs the query, and then saves it using the same name. The results are shown earlier in Figure 3.32.

This query, however, has the same problem as qryEmployeeClasses—it lists classes by ID number, not by the more meaningful description. Maria wants to display the Description column in the query results, not the ClassID column. Recall that tblClass contains the Description field, not tblEmployeeTraining. If she starts creating a query and uses fields from tblEmployee and tblClass, the query will not produce the results she wants because the tables are not related—they contain no common field. That means a query cannot retrieve records from these two tables as if they were one larger table, and will not produce meaningful results. Instead, she can use a third table to link tblEmployee and tblClass. The tblEmployeeTraining table is linked to tblEmployee by the common EmpID field, and is also linked to tblClass by the common ClassID field. She starts creating a query in Design view, adds the field lists for tblEmployee, tblEmployeeTraining, and tblClass to the query window, and then adds the EmpLast, EmpFirst, and Description fields to the design grid so she can list all employees and any classes they have attended. She decides to sort the records in ascending order by last name.

By default, the tables are related using inner joins. She double-clicks the join line between tblEmployee and tblEmployeeTraining to open the Join Properties dialog box, and then reviews the options for joining the two tables:

- Option 1 for an inner join is selected by default. It only includes records that contain the same value in the common field that links the tables.
- Option 2 is for an outer join that selects all records from the tblEmployee table and only those records from tblEmployeeTraining that contain matching EmpID fields.
- Option 3 is for an outer join that selects all records from the tblEmployeeTraining table and only those records from tblEmployee that contain matching EmpID fields.

Given that she wants to list all employees in the query results, she selects Option 2 to include all records from tblEmployee. The join line now includes an arrowhead pointing from tblEmployee to tblEmployeeTraining. She tries running the query, but receives an error message indicating that the query contains an ambiguous outer join. She also needs to specify the properties for the join line between tblEmployeeTraining and tblClass.

She double-clicks the join line between tblEmployeeTraining and tblClass, rereads the options in the Join Properties dialog box, and realizes that she needs to select Option 3 to include all records from tblEmployeeTraining and only those records from tblClass that contain matching ClassID fields. The join line includes an arrowhead pointing from tblEmployeeTraining to tblClass. She saves the query as qryEmployeeTraining, and then runs it. The query with outer joins produces the results she wants, shown in Figure 3.35.

Figure 3.35: Maria finally has the results she wants—all employees and descriptions of classes

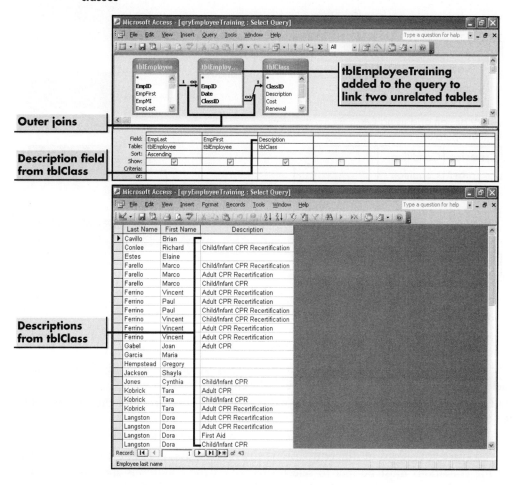

Now that Maria has produced the list she wants, she needs to review the classes that employees have attended. 4Corners requires a few classes, such as Defibrillator Use and CPR, and she wants to determine how many employees are complying with the policy. All required classes must be completed annually. Until now, it has been difficult for Maria to track compliance with the certification policy—employees postpone classes when they are busy, and she suspects that many certifications have lapsed.

Using Logical Operators to Specify Multiple Conditions

Some queries require one or more **logical operators**, which are used to test values that can only be true or false. You have already used the logical AND and OR in filters and queries when you want to combine criteria by comparing conditions. Figure 3.36 shows how the logical AND and OR operators work in the query design grid.

Figure 3.36: Using the logical operators AND and OR in query selection criteria

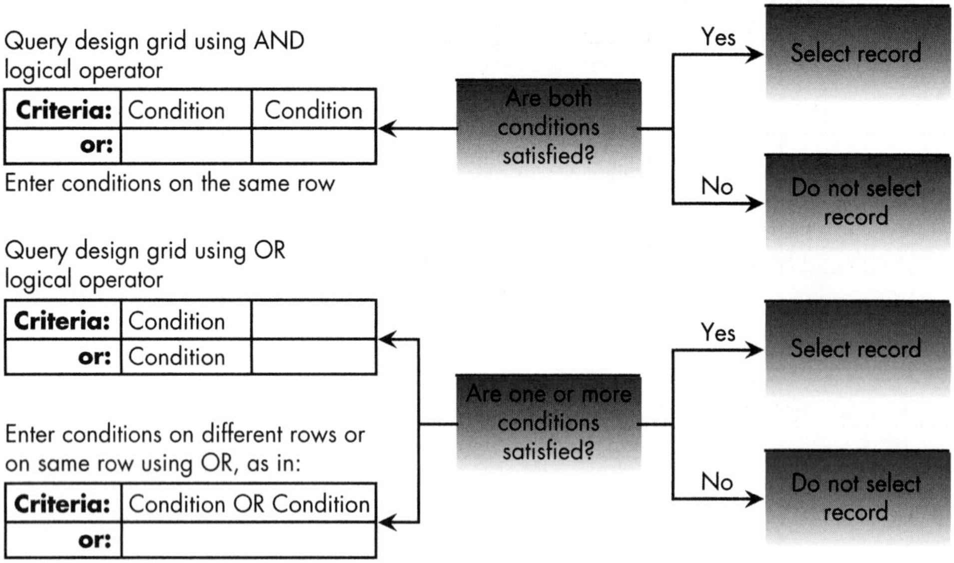

Recall that if you place conditions in separate fields in the same Criteria row of the design grid, all conditions in that row must be met to select a record. For example, if you want to select pharmacy technicians (JobID 3) who live in Colorado, enter "3" in the Criteria row for the JobID field, and "CO" in the Criteria row for the State field. You can combine the AND logical operator with the Like comparison operator to set conditions for the same field. For example, if you want to identify all the employees who are scheduled for a review in October 2008, enter the following condition in the Criteria row for the Review field: Like "10*" And Like "*2008".

If you place conditions in different Criteria rows in the query design grid, at least one of the conditions must be met to select a record. If the conditions apply to the same field, you can enter each condition separated by OR in the Criteria row. For example, if you want to select employees who live in Colorado or those who live in Utah, enter the following condition in the Criteria row for the State field: "CO" OR "UT".

The **NOT** logical operator excludes values that don't meet the criterion. For example, if you enter NOT 3 in the Criteria row for the JobID field, the query results show all employees except for pharmacy technicians. The NOT logical operator is often combined with the In comparison operator, as in NOT In("CO","UT"), which selects employees who do not live in Colorado or Utah. (Table 3.5 describes the comparison operators, including In and Like.)

Table 3.8 lists the logical operators you can use in an Access query and the results they return.

Table 3.8: Logical operators

Operator	Description	Examples	Results
AND	Logical AND	A AND B	Record selected only if both criteria are true
OR	Inclusive OR	A OR B	Record selected if any one of the rows of criteria is true
NOT	Logical NOT	NOT A	Record selected if it does not meet the condition

You can combine the logical and comparison operators to retrieve the records you need. For example, if you want to identify all the technicians and cashiers (JobIDs 3 and 4) who are scheduled for a review in October 2008, enter the following conditions in the query design grid:

	JobID	Review
Criteria:	3	Like "10*" And Like "*2008"
or:	4	Like "10*" And Like "*2008"

The qryEmployeeTraining query produces a list that includes employees and the classes they've attended and employees who have not attended any classes. Maria wants to base a new query on qryEmployeeTraining to check to see if employees taking required classes are up to date on their certifications in Adult CPR, Child/Infant CPR, and Defibrillator Use. Each type of certification needs to be renewed at different intervals, so she needs to set the criteria carefully to produce the results she needs.

Maria decides to save qryEmployeeTraining as qryUpToDate and then modify it in Design view. The query already includes field lists for tblEmployee, tblEmployeeTraining, and tblClass, with outer joins specified so that all employees are listed in the results, even if they have not attended a class. The EmpLast and EmpFirst fields from tblEmployee and the Description field from tblClass already appear in the query design grid. To determine whether an employee's certification is up to date, she needs the Date field from tblEmployeeTraining. To determine whether a particular class is required for certification, she needs to include the Required field from tblClass. She also decides to include ClassID from tblClass to make setting up the criteria easier—all she will have to do is specify the ID of the class rather than the long description. She adds the three fields—Date, Required, and ClassID—to the design grid. She clears the Show check boxes for ClassID and Required because she doesn't need to see the contents of these fields in the results.

Next, she will specify the criteria for selecting information about only the classes required for certification. Pharmacy employees must take the five classes listed in Table 3.9.

Table 3.9: Required classes for pharmacy employees

ClassID	Description	Renewal in Years
1	Adult CPR	0
2	Child/Infant CPR	0
3	Adult CPR Recertification	1
5	Defibrillator Use	1
6	Child/Infant CPR Recertification	1

The first two classes—Adult CPR and Child/Infant CPR—are the comprehensive classes employees take to receive CPR certification for the first time. Employees complete these comprehensive classes only once, and do not need to renew them. Instead, they need to complete classes with IDs 3 and 6, which are refresher courses for recertification. ClassID 5 provides certification for defibrillator use, and must be taken every year.

First, Maria adds a criterion to determine which employees are current in their Adult CPR certification. These employees would have completed the Adult CPR or the Adult CPR Recertification classes (ClassIDs 1 or 3) in the past year. She can use the logical operator OR to select employees who have completed ClassID 1 or 3, so she types "1 Or 3" in the Criteria row for the ClassID field.

To narrow the criteria and select only those employees who have taken these courses in the past year, Maria can use the Between...And comparison operator, which you use to specify two Date fields. She needs to specify the time period from January 1, 2008 to December 31, 2008, so she types "Between #1/1/2008# And #12/31/2008#" in the Criteria row for the Date field. (Recall that you use pound signs on either side of date values entered as criteria.)

Finally, she enters "Yes" as the criterion for the Required field to make sure the class is required. She runs qryUpToDate to test the results. See Figure 3.37.

Figure 3.37: Multiple criteria for listing employees who are up to date in their Adult CPR certification

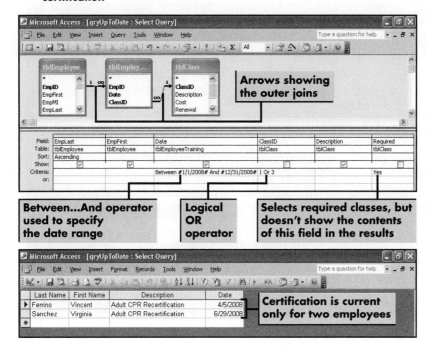

The results show that only two employees are currently certified in Adult CPR. Because these results seem accurate, Maria can continue adding criteria to the query for the other classes, starting with Child/Infant CPR. She knows that data on a second criteria row means that as long as all criteria on either line are true, records that satisfy one or the other line of criteria will be included. She types "2 Or 6" as the second criterion for the ClassID field to identify employees who have current Child/Infant CPR certification. Now, the results will include any employee who has completed Adult or Child/Infant CPR classes.

She also needs to specify the time period for the second ClassID criterion. If she doesn't, the results will include employees who have completed Adult CPR certification this year and those who have completed Child/Infant CPR certification at any time. To select only employees who have completed Child/Infant CPR in the past year, she copies the Between #1/1/2008# And #12/31/2008# criterion from the first criteria row to the second. She also enters "Yes" as the second criterion for the Required field. The three conditions on the second criteria row are three AND conditions—a record must contain all of the criteria to appear in the query results. She enters the third criteria for the Defibrillator Use class— Between #1/1/2008# And #12/31/2008# as the criterion for the Date field, "5" as the criterion for the ClassID field, and "Yes" as the criterion for the Required field. Maria saves the query with the same name—qryUpToDate—and then runs it. See Figure 3.38.

Figure 3.38: Results of modified qryUpToDate query with two rows of criteria

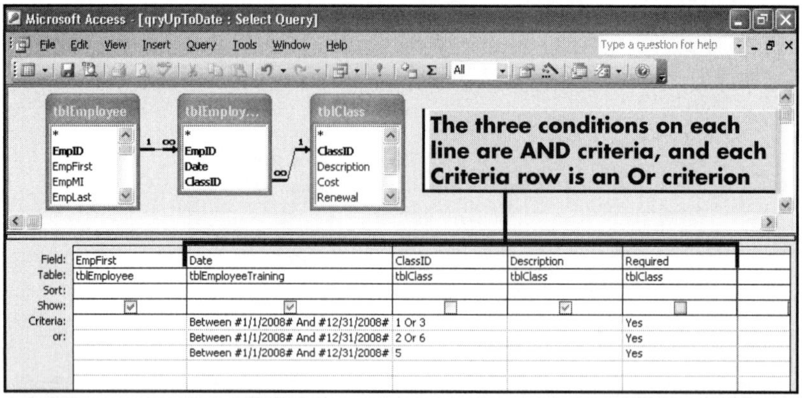

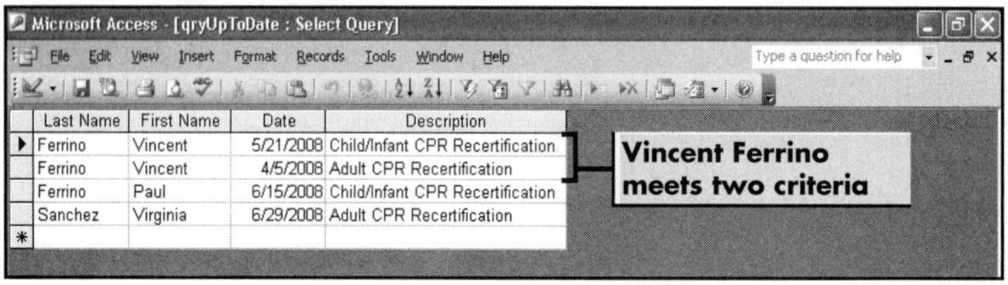

The results now include four records, but only Vincent Ferrino is completely up to date on CPR certifications. Even he needs to take the Defibrillator Use class again. As she suspected, employees have been postponing certification classes, and many no longer have current CPR certifications.

As she examines qryUpToDate in Design and Datasheet view, Maria realizes that using specific dates in the Date field criteria can cause problems. The query shows who has up-to-date certifications now, but if employees complete their requirements in the next three months, the query won't reflect that information. To allow her to enter a range of dates when she runs the query instead of changing the criteria in Design view each time she runs the query, she can change the fixed dates to parameter values. She replaces the fixed dates in the Date field with prompts for beginning and ending dates, so that Between #1/1/2008# And #12/31/2008# becomes Between [Beginning date?] And [Ending date?]. When she runs the query, it stops to ask for beginning and ending dates and waits for user input. This will make the query much more flexible in the future. See Figure 3.39.

Figure 3.39: Prompts for parameter values instead of fixed dates

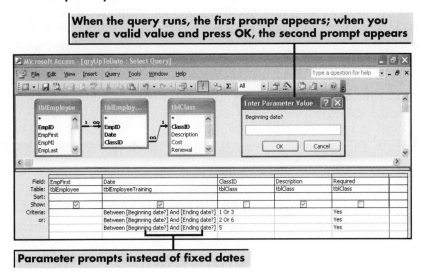

When the query runs, the first prompt appears; when you enter a valid value and press OK, the second prompt appears

Parameter prompts instead of fixed dates

As she finishes qryUpToDate, Paul Ferrino returns and asks Maria to take another look at the hourly rate analysis. The two queries she created list the hourly rates paid to part-time employees (qryHourlyRateAnalysis) and the minimum, maximum, and average hourly rates (qryHourlyRateSummary). Paul wants to improve these results so they list these statistics by job ID, not by employee name. He also wants to know how many years each employee has worked at 4Corners Pharmacy—he is reviewing plans for retirement accounts and needs to set eligibility rules if he decides to offer a plan.

PERFORMING CALCULATIONS WITH QUERIES

So far, you have worked with queries that retrieve and sort records based on criteria. More complex queries often need to include statistical information or calculations based on fields in the query. For example, you can calculate the sum or average of the values in one field, multiply the values in two fields, or calculate the date three months from the current date. Any information that can be derived from fields in a table or query should be calculated in a query rather than included as data in a table. For example, if you want to know the age of an employee or customer, calculate the age in a query rather than include the age as a field in a table. Over time, the age would become obsolete;calculating it each time you need it ensures that the age is current.

The types of calculations you can perform in a query fall into two categories: predefined and custom calculations. Predefined calculations, also called totals, compute amounts for groups of records or for all the records combined in the query. The amounts predefined calculations compute are sum, average, count, minimum, maximum, standard deviation, and variance. You select one totals calculation for each field you want to calculate.

A custom calculation performs numeric, date, and text computations on each record using data from one or more fields. For example, you can multiply each value in one field by 100. To complete a custom calculation, you need to create a calculated field in the query design grid.

When you display the results of a calculation in a field, the results aren't actually stored in the underlying table. Instead, Access performs the calculation each time you run the query so that the results are always based on the most current data in the database.

Calculating Statistical Information

Recall that you can use the Summary options in the Simple Query Wizard to calculate statistical information such as totals and averages in query results. You can also use Design view to set up these calculations. To do so, you use **aggregate functions**, which are arithmetic and statistical operations you apply to records that meet a query's selection criteria. You can group, or aggregate, the records so that your results are for records in each group that meet the selection criteria. Table 3.10 lists the aggregate functions you can use in Access.

Table 3.10: Aggregate functions

Aggregate Function	Operation
Avg	Average of the field values for records meeting the criteria within each group
Count	Number of records meeting the criteria in each group
Max	Highest field value for selected records in each group
Min	Lowest field value for selected records in each group
Sum	Total of the field values for the selected records
StDev	Standard deviation for the selected records
Var	Statistical variance for the selected records
First	Returns the value from the first row encountered in the group; results may be unpredictable because the result depends on the physical sequence of the stored data
Last	Returns the value for the last row encountered for the group; results may be unpredictable because the result depends on the physical sequence of the stored data
Expression	Allows you to create an expression to use as criteria for selecting records
Where	Indicates column has criteria in selecting records

You can calculate all types of totals by using the Total row in the query design grid. You add this row to the grid by clicking the Totals button Σ on the Query Design toolbar. You can then click the Totals list arrow in a field to select an aggregate function for the calculation you want to perform on the field. To show the calculation results for a particular field, you select Group By in the Total row. For example, because Maria wants to calculate statistics for each job ID, she can group the records on the JobID field.

Maria needs to calculate the minimum, maximum, and average hourly rates for each job ID. She creates a query in Design view, adding the JobID and HourlyRate fields from the tblEmployee table to the query design grid and setting criteria to display only records for technicians and cashiers. Because she wants to calculate three types of statistics on the HourlyRate field, she adds that field to the design grid two more times. Then she clicks the Totals button Σ on the Query Design toolbar to specify the aggregate functions and group options she wants to use—Max for the first HourlyRate field, Min for the second, and Avg for the third.. She names the query qryMaxMinAvgHourlyRate, and then runs it. See Figure 3.40.

Figure 3.40: Using aggregate functions in a query

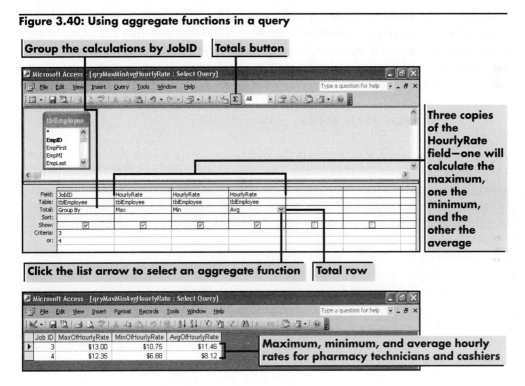

As hourly rates change, Maria can run this query again to recalculate the statistics and produce updated results for Paul.

Next, Maria can determine how long each employee has worked at 4Corners Pharmacy. She knows that she can calculate the number of days of service by subtracting the current date from the value in the StartDate field. Then she can convert the number of days to years. The aggregate functions do not perform this type of calculation. Instead, she needs to create a calculated field in a query.

Creating Calculated Fields in a Query

You can use a query to perform a calculation for immediate use or to include the calculation later when you create a report or form based on the query. You specify the calculation by defining an expression that contains a combination of database fields, constants, and operators. An **expression** is an arithmetic formula used to make the calculation. You can use the standard arithmetic operators (+, -, *, and /) in the expression. If an expression is complex, use parentheses to indicate which operation should be performed first. Access follows the order of operations precedence: multiplication and division before addition and subtraction. If the precedence is equal, Access works from left to right. For example, if you use 5 + 6 * 100, the result is 605. If you use (5 + 6) * 100, the result is 1100. It's a good idea to check your formula with a calculator to make sure it is working correctly.

To perform a calculation in a query, you add a field to the query design grid called a **calculated field**. Where you would normally insert the field name from a table or query, you type an expression. For example, suppose you want to calculate the wages employees earn if all hourly rate employees receive a 10% bonus. In the query design grid, you could enter an expression in a blank field such as the following:

Wage with Bonus: ([HourlyRate]* 1.10)

In this expression, Wage with Bonus is the name you specify for the field. Field names in the expression are enclosed in square brackets. The calculation ([HourlyRate]*.10) computes the bonus as 10% of the value in the HourlyRate field. This bonus is added to the value in the HourlyRate field to calculate the total wages including bonus. When the query is run, the expression uses values from the records that meet the criteria you specify to make the calculation.

To type a complete expression, you often need more space than is provided by the field box in the query design grid. In this case, you can open the Zoom dialog box, which provides a large text box for entering expressions or other values.

Some database developers use the **Expression Builder** when they need to build complex expressions or when they are not familiar with the field, table, and query names in the database. This database tool, shown in Figure 3.41, allows you to work with lists of objects such as tables and queries as well as constants, functions, and common operators to help you construct the expression for your calculation. You can click a field name or operator and then paste it into the expression you are building. You type any constant values that need to be part of the expression.

Figure 3.41: Using the Expression Builder to create an expression for a calculated field

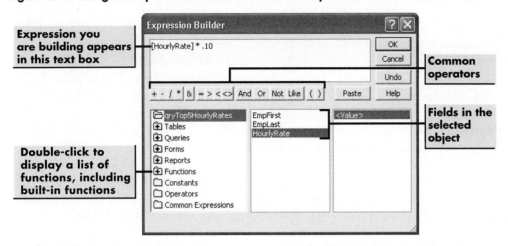

Maria needs to calculate how long each employee has worked for 4Corners Pharmacy. Paul will use this information as he reviews retirement account plans and sets eligibility rules. Maria needs to calculate the years of service each employee has provided 4Corners, and decides to use a calculated field in a query to do so. In the calculation, she needs to subtract the value in the StartDate field from today's date. She could create a parameter query that prompts her to enter today's date and then uses that value in the calculation. However, that means she would enter today's date 24 times, which seems unnecessarily repetitive. Instead, she can use the Date function to retrieve today's date.

When you are creating expressions, you can use a **function** to perform a standard calculation and return a value. The Date function is a built-in function, meaning it is provided with Access, and has the following form: **Date( )**. To use today's date in an expression, type Date( ) instead of a fixed date value. The calculation then stays current no matter when you run the query. The Date function can also be used in query criteria.

Maria creates a query in Design view, using the EmpLast, EmpFirst, and StartDate fields from tblEmployee. Even former employees might be eligible for the retirement plan, so Maria does not include the EndDate field and criteria to eliminate former employees from the query results. To make room for typing an expression and create a calculated field, she right-clicks the Field row in the first empty column, and then clicks Zoom on the shortcut menu to open the Zoom dialog box. She types "Years of Service:" as the name for the calculated field. The expression should subtract the value in the StartDate field from today's date to calculate the number of days of service. Then the expression should divide that result by 365 to calculate the years of service. Rather than using a fixed date for today's date, she will substitute Date( ) so that Access retrieves this value each time the query runs. She types the following expression into the Zoom box:

```
Years of Service: (Date() - [StartDate]) / 365
```

"Years of Service" is the name that will appear as the datasheet column heading. The colon (:) separates the name from the calculated expression. The first part of the expression—Date()—is the Access function for calculating today's date. Next comes the subtraction operator followed by [StartDate], which is the name of the StartDate field enclosed in square brackets. You use square brackets around field names to distinguish them from function names or other types of values. Including Date() – [StartDate] in parentheses means that Access subtracts the value in the StartDate field from today's date before performing the second part of the calculation, which is to divide that value by 365, the approximate number of days in a year. (This number is approximate because it doesn't account for leap years.) Dividing by 365 converts the days to years.

She clicks the OK button to close the Zoom dialog box, saves the query as qryYearsOfService, and then runs it. The results calculate the approximate years of service, but display a number with many digits after the decimal point. See Figure 3.42.

Figure 3.42: Using a calculated field in a query

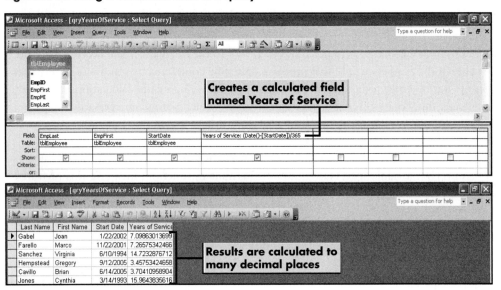

To change the format and number of decimal places for the calculated field, Maria switches to Design view, right-clicks the Years of Service field, and then clicks Properties on the shortcut menu to display the list of properties for the field. Table 3.11 describes the properties you can set for fields in a query.

Table 3.11: Field properties

Property	Description
Description	Provide information about the field.
Format	Specify how numbers, dates, times, and text are displayed and printed. You can select a predefined format, which varies according to data type, or create a custom format.
Decimal Places	Specify the number of decimal places Access uses to display numbers.
Input Mask	Specify an input mask to simplify data entry and control the values users can enter in a field as you do when designing a table.
Caption	Enter the text that appears as a column heading for the field in query Datasheet view.
Smart Tags	Assign an available Smart Tag to the field.

Maria uses the Format and Decimal Places properties to specify the format of the field values. She selects Standard as the Format and 1 for Decimal Places. She closes the property list, sets a descending sort order for the calculated field to better interpret the results, and then saves and runs the query again. She resizes each column in the resulting datasheet to its best fit. See Figure 3.43. (Your results will vary depending on the current date.)

Figure 3.43: Formatting a calculated field

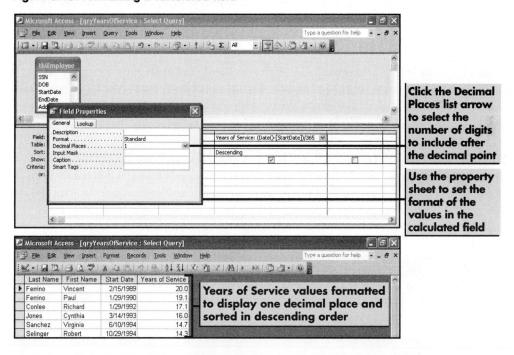

Click the Decimal Places list arrow to select the number of digits to include after the decimal point

Use the property sheet to set the format of the values in the calculated field

Years of Service values formatted to display one decimal place and sorted in descending order

Including approximate results is appropriate for Paul's purpose now—he is only reviewing retirement plans and needs to know how many people would be eligible. Considering that Paul might need precise values after he selects a plan, Maria consults the database developer, Donald Linebarger, to see if he can suggest a more accurate way to calculate the date. He gives Maria the following expression, which accounts for leap years when it calculates years of service and has the advantage of formatting the result, and explains the parts of the expression.

```
Years of Service: DateDiff("yyyy",[tblEmployee]!
     [StartDate],Now())+ Int(Format(Now(),"mmdd")
          <Format([tblEmployee]![StartDate],"mmdd"))
```

- **Years of Service**—Specifies the name of the calculated field.
- **DateDiff("yyyy",[tblEmployee]![StartDate],Now())**—The DateDiff function calculates the difference between two date values, which are defined as arguments within parentheses following the function name. The arguments are separated by commas. The "yyyy" argument specifies the interval of time between the two date values as years. The [tblEmployee]![StartDate] argument defines the first date as the value in the StartDate field of tblEmployee. The Now() argument retrieves the current date and time as stored in your computer system. In other words, this DateDiff function calculates the number of years between the value in StartDate and today, taking leap years into account.
- **Int(Format(Now(),"mmdd")<Format([tblEmployee]![StartDate],"mmdd"))**—This part of the expression verifies that the results are shown as whole numbers. The Int function removes any fractional part of the result, and returns only the integer part.

Maria copies the formula into the Years of Service field, and then runs the query to test it. The dates are in whole numbers and, Donald assures her, it also takes leap years into account. She doesn't save qryYearsOfService with the new formula because she doesn't need it yet, but she does note the expression so she can use it later.

As she looks over the results of qryYearsOfService, she considers fine-tuning the results to display employee names as full names instead of as separate last name and first name values. Doing so will make the printed datasheet more appealing and easy to use for Paul. Furthermore, if Paul decides to institute a retirement plan, she will need to develop a report based on qryYearsOfService, in which a full name will be even more well received.

Best Practice

Using Calculated Fields

Values that can be derived from other fields generally should not be stored as separate fields in a database. For example, in a product orders table, rather than store quantity ordered, unit price, and total price in three fields, use a calculated field to derive the total price from the quantity and unit price (Quantity*UnitPrice, for example). Age data would become outdated if you entered it directly. If you plan to use a calculation in a form or report, you should create a query to perform the calculation and then use the query as the basis for the form or report.

Concatenating in Queries

When you create field names for a table, you usually want to store data in separate fields for common values such as first name, last name, city, state, and zip code. Sorting or querying on a field containing a last name value is faster than on a field containing first and last name. However, when using the data in a mailing label or report, you might want to present these common values together to save space and improve readability. In the same way that you can add two or more numbers to obtain a result, you can also add text data, such as first name and last name, to display the full name. To do this, you create a calculated field that combines the values in other fields. Combining the contents of two or more fields is called **concatenation**.

You use the concatenation operator (&) for concatenating, not the plus sign (+), or addition operator, which is reserved for adding numbers. Specify spaces that naturally fall between words or other characters by enclosing the spaces in quotation marks. For example, you could use the following expression to concatenate the EmpFirst and EmpLast fields, displaying the first name and last name separated by a space:

```
[EmpFirst]& "" & [EmpLast]
```

Maria wants to combine the contents of the EmpFirst and EmpLast fields in qryYearsOfService so that a single field displays the first and last name. She opens qryYearsOfService in Design view, deletes the contents of the EmpLast field so that the column is blank, and then deletes the EmpFirst field. In the first column, she types the following expression to specify "Name" as the field name and displays the first name and last name separated by a space:

```
Name: [EmpFirst]& " " & [EmpLast]
```

She saves her changes and runs the query. Figure 3.44 shows the final design and results of qryYearsOfService.

Figure 3.44: Concatenated field for employee names

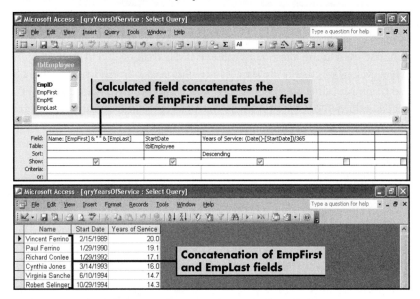

Steps To Success: Level 2

Hudson Bay Pharmacy is ready to create more complex queries to analyze employee data. Kim Siemers is the human resources manager for Hudson Bay, and asks for your help in creating queries that extract the employee information she needs from their database. As you create and save the new queries, be certain to use the "qry" prefix as part of the naming convention. Also consult your instructor for instructions about submitting your results.

Complete the following:

1. Start Access and open the **Hudson.mdb** database from the STS folder.

2. Kim wants to identify employees who live in the same neighborhood in Edmonton so they can create car pools and share rides to work. In Edmonton, the postal codes roughly correspond to neighborhood. Prepare a list of employees who live in the same neighborhood so that Kim can create a list of employees who can share rides to work. Name the query qryDuplicatePostalCodes.

3. A new policy at Hudson Bay Pharmacy is that all employees must acquire and maintain certifications in adult, infant, and child CPR and in using defibrillators. Kim asks you to identify employees who have not completed any certification training. Save the query as qryNoTraining.

4. Kim also needs to list all employees and the classes they have taken. The results should include current employees who have not attended training as well as those who have. Save the query as qryEmployeeTraining.

5. Kim also needs to identify employees whose CPR or defibrillator certification has expired, depending on the time period she specifies. Show all employees whose Adult CPR, Child/Infant CPR, or Defibrillator Use certification has expired in any specified time period. Save the query as qryUpToDate.

6. Joan Gabel, owner of Hudson Bay Pharmacy, wants to identify the five current non-salaried employees who are earning the highest wages per hour. These are the five employees who have been working for the pharmacy the longest or who have regularly received raises for their work. List the top five wage earners of all the current non-salaried employees. Save the query as qryTop5HourlyRates.

7. To prepare for employee reviews, Kim needs to calculate the minimum, maximum, and average hourly rates for each job category. Provide this information for her, saving the query as qryMaxMinAvgHourlyRate.

8. Joan is considering offering life insurance as an employee benefit, and needs to know the current age of all employees. Provide this information for her. Be certain to provide an appropriate name for the column with the result and to show the ages in descending order. Include the job title and format the results so that they include one decimal place. Also show the first name and last name together. Save the query as qryEmployeeAge.

9. Kim asks you to provide one other statistical analysis. Show the average age of employees by job title. Save this query as qryAvgEmployeeAge.

10. Close the **Hudson.mdb** database and Access.

LEVEL 3

EXPLORING ADVANCED QUERIES AND QUERIES WRITTEN IN STRUCTURED QUERY LANGUAGE

ACCESS 2003 SKILLS TRAINING

- **Create a crosstab query**
- **Create a make-table query**
- **Create a new SQL query**
- **Create a query in Design view**
- **Create and run a delete query**
- **Create and run an update query**
- **Include all fields in an SQL query**
- **Sort an SQL query**

ANALYZING QUERY CALCULATIONS

In this level, you will learn about more advanced queries. You will learn how to use the Crosstab Wizard to create a crosstab query, one of the most useful queries for preparing data for further analysis. You will also learn how to create action queries, which are those that change or move many records in one operation. There are four types of action queries: append, update, delete, and make-table. You use these types of queries to add records to one table from another, change values in a field based on criteria, delete records based on criteria, or make a new table. You will also learn how to use the IIF function to make decisions in a query and to write queries in Structured Query Language (SQL), which is the language Access uses to query, update, and manage its databases.

Crosstab queries are a special type of Totals query that performs aggregate function calculations on the values of one database field and allows you to determine exactly how your summary data appears in the results. You use crosstab queries to calculate and restructure data so that you can analyze it more easily. Crosstab queries calculate a sum, average, count, or other type of total for data that is grouped by two types of information—one as a column on the left of a datasheet and another as a row across the top. You might think of a crosstab query rotating the data to present repeating fields as columns so your data appears in a spreadsheet-like format. Figure 3.45 compares a select query and a crosstab query.

Figure 3.45: Comparing a select and crosstab query

Year	Class	Total Cost
2004	Adult CPR	$60.00
2004	Child/Infant CPR	$45.00
2004	Defibrillator Use	$25.00
2005	Defibrillator Use	$25.00
2006	Child/Infant CPR	$15.00
2006	First Aid	$15.00

This select query only groups the totals vertically by year and class, resulting in more records

Class	2004	2005	2006	Total Cost
Adult CPR	$60.00			$60.00
Child/Infant CPR	$45.00		$15.00	$60.00
Defibrillator Use	$25.00	$25.00		$50.00
First Aid			$15.00	$15.00

This crosstab query displays the same information, but groups it both horizontally and vertically so the results are easier to analyze

Create a crosstab query when you want to take advantage of one of the following benefits:

- You can display a large amount of summary data in columns that are similar to a spreadsheet. The results can be easily exported for further analysis in a program such as Microsoft Office Excel 2003.
- You can view the summary data in a datasheet that is ideal for creating charts automatically using the Chart Wizard.
- You can easily design queries to include multiple levels of detail.

Crosstab queries work especially well with **time-series data**, which is data that shows performance over time for periods such as years, quarters, or months.

Creating a Crosstab Query

You create a crosstab query using a wizard to guide you through the steps, or on your own in Design view. If you want to work in Design view, it's best to start with a select query that includes numeric values or summary calculations. You can then create a crosstab query manually by clicking Query on the menu bar and then clicking Crosstab Query. This method adds a Crosstab row to the design grid. Each field in a crosstab query can have one of four settings: Row Heading, Column Heading, Value, or Not Shown. Table 3.12 explains the four settings, which also helps you answer the questions the Crosstab Query Wizard asks.

Table 3.12: Crosstab field settings

Crosstab Field Setting	Explanation
Row Heading	You must have at least one row heading, and you can specify more than one field as a row heading. Each row heading must be a grouped value or expression, with the expression containing one or more of the aggregate functions (such as Count, Min, Max, or Sum). The row heading fields form the first column on the left side of the crosstab.
Column Heading	Only one field can be defined as the column heading, and this must also be a grouped or totaled value. These values become the headings of the columns across the crosstab datasheet.
Value	Only one field is designated as the value. This field must be a totaled value or expression that contains one of the aggregate functions. The value field appears in the cells that are the intersections of each row heading value and each column heading value.
Not Shown	You can use other fields to limit the results. If you include a field in the query design grid, and then click the (Not Shown) option in the Crosstab cell and Group By in the Total cell, Access groups on the field as a Row Heading, but doesn't display the row in the query's results.

Although you can create crosstab queries manually, if you want Access to guide you through the steps and show samples of how the crosstab results will look based on your selections, use the Crosstab Query Wizard instead.

Although the Crosstab Query Wizard can generate a crosstab query from a single table, a single table usually doesn't contain the data necessary for the Crosstab Wizard. For instance, you might want to analyze employee training costs over time. You can retrieve cost data from tblClass, but you need tblEmployeeTraining to include the dates of the training. To prepare the data for the Crosstab Query Wizard, you often need to create a query first. This query should contain data that you want to include as the rows, column headings, and values in the crosstab query. For example, each row might be a class that employees might take, the column headings the dates grouped by years, and the values the sum of the class costs per year.

A few years ago, Maria met with Paul Ferrino, and they decided that all health-related training would be reimbursed by 4Corners Pharmacy. The policy has been in effect since 2004. In preparation for the training budget, Maria wants to analyze the annual cost of training to determine whether Paul wants to continue the policy. She could create a Totals query that would calculate the total cost of training, but that would not display the cost per year. She decides to create a crosstab query to help with this analysis.

Maria starts by creating a select query with only the fields she needs in the crosstab query—Description and Cost from tblClass and Date from tblEmployeeTraining. She does not need any fields from tblEmployee because she is only interested in summary data for the costs by year for classes. She saves this query as qryTrainingCostAndDate.

She then starts the Crosstab Query Wizard and selects qryTrainingCostAndDate as the basis for the Crosstab query. See Figure 3.46.

Figure 3.46: First dialog box of the Crosstab Query Wizard

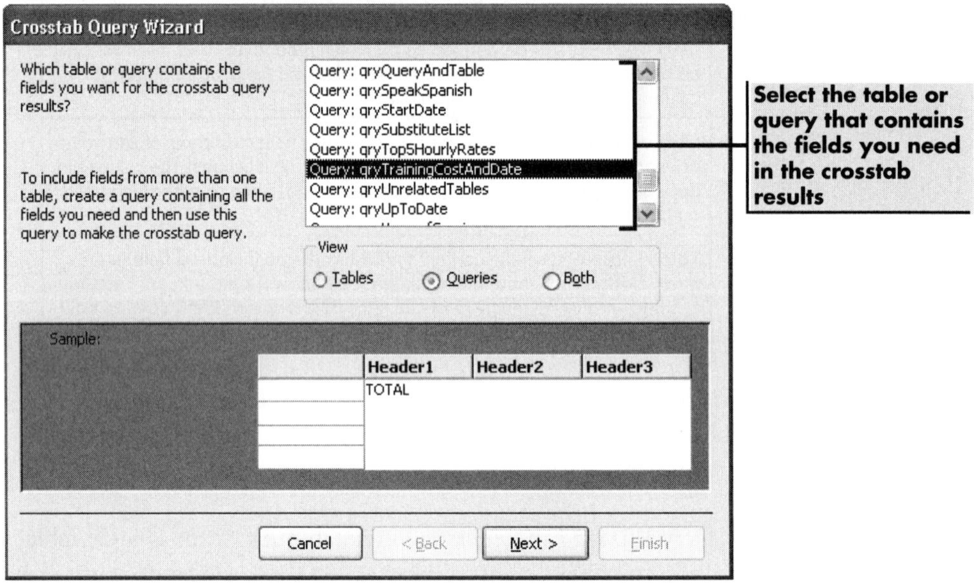

For the row headings, she selects Description because she wants to see the costs for each class. See Figure 3.47.

Figure 3.47: Select only one field for row headings

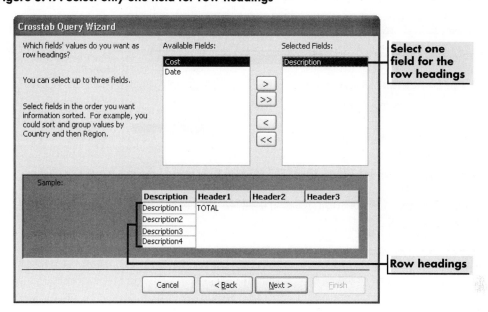

Figure 3.48: Select the column headings

Maria wants to analyze the data by year, so she chooses Date for column headings. Because she is interested in annual cost, she chooses Year as the interval. See Figure 3.48

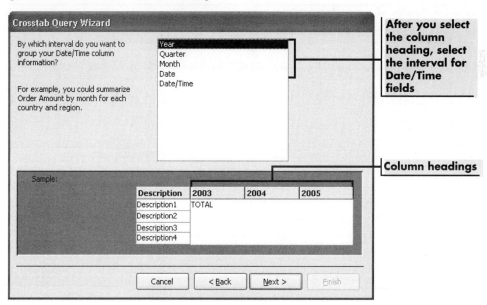

She wants the total cost for classes as the value, so she chooses Cost as the field and Sum as the function. See Figure 3.49.

Figure 3.49: Select the value to calculate

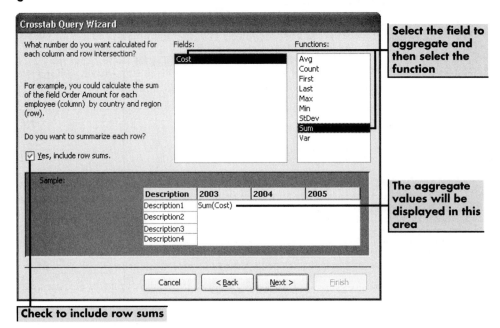

Check to include row sums

She names the query qryClassCostAnalysis and then runs it. See Figure 3.50. The results clearly compare the total annual costs of training classes and the annual costs per class.

Figure 3.50: Results of a crosstab query

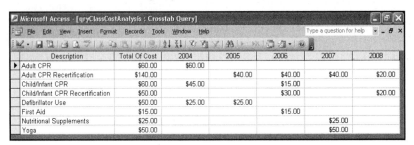

Description	Total Of Cost	2004	2005	2006	2007	2008
Adult CPR	$60.00	$60.00				
Adult CPR Recertification	$140.00		$40.00	$40.00	$40.00	$20.00
Child/Infant CPR	$60.00	$45.00		$15.00		
Child/Infant CPR Recertification	$50.00			$30.00		$20.00
Defibrillator Use	$50.00	$25.00	$25.00			
First Aid	$15.00			$15.00		
Nutritional Supplements	$25.00				$25.00	
Yoga	$50.00				$50.00	

Maria next needs to remove obsolete data from the database. She is interested in removing records for classes employees have completed and for which their certification has already been updated. In addition, she must currently remember to exclude previous employees when she is querying the 4Corners database, and wants to archive those employee records in a table separate from tblEmployee. Rather than manually deleting out-of-date class records and reentering previous employee data in a new table, she plans to use action queries to automate these tasks.

MODIFYING DATA USING QUERIES

In addition to the select and crosstab queries, Access provides a number of query types that perform an action on the data in a database: the update, append, delete, and make-table queries. These **action queries** let you modify data in a table, add records to or delete records from a table, or create a new table based on expressions you enter and criteria you set. Table 3.13 lists the purpose of each type of action query and provides an example of how it might be used.

Table 3.13: Access action queries

Query Type	Purpose	Example
Append	Add records from one table to another table with the same structure based on a criteria	Add records of employees no longer with the pharmacy to a separate employee history table to archive the records while removing them from a table of current employees
Delete	Delete records from a table based on a criterion	Delete the employees from the current employee table after the records of past employees have been appended to an employee history table
Make-table	Create a table from the results of a query	Create the history table of past employees the first time you decide to remove past employees from tblEmployee
Update	Change the contents of a field based on a criterion	Change values for hourly wage of all hourly employees to reflect a negotiated raise in a job category

Best Practice

Backing Up Your Database Before Using Action Queries

Because action queries permanently change the data in a database, you should always back up the database before performing an action query. To do so, open the database you want to back up, click Tools on the menu bar, point to Database Utilities, and then click Back Up Database. If you are working in a network environment that allows multiple users to work in the database simultaneously, the other users should close the database while you create the backup.

Maria wants to delete old classes for employees after the certification time has expired. She needs to set criteria that select only obsolete class records in tblEmployeeTraining, and then wants Access to delete the records. While discussing her problem with Donald Linebarger, database developer, he suggests that she archive the obsolete data in a new table before she deletes it from tblEmployeeTraining. If she later needs the data for another query or report, she can retrieve it from the archived table. He suggests the general procedure shown in Figure 3.51 for archiving obsolete data.

Figure 3.51: Process for archiving data

Back up the database first—this is a must.

↓

Create a select query to set up the criteria for selecting the obsolete records. Test it to make sure it selects the correct records. Then convert it to a make-table action query to create a table to store the obsolete records. Run the query to create the new table. You don't need to save this query because you only need it once to create the table.

↓

Modify the new table to add a primary key. This prevents you from adding duplicate records in the future.

↓

Create a select query that will select obsolete records and then test it. Convert it to an append action query and save it without running it. Use the query when you want to move obsolete records to another table. Use parameters to make it more general, if necessary. Save and run this query on a regular basis or as needed.

↓

Regularly check the history table to make sure the records have been successfully appended before the next step.

↓

Create a delete action query to delete the obsolete records from the original table. Run this query only after the append query as needed.

Archiving Data with Make-Table Queries

As its name suggests, a **make-table query** creates a table from some or all of the fields and records in an existing table or query. When you create a new table based on an existing one, Access does not delete the selected fields and records from the existing table. Keep in mind that the new table reflects the data as it appeared when you created the table; changes you subsequently make to the original table are not reflected in the new table.

When you use a make-table query, you usually create a select query first that contains the necessary fields and selection criteria, and then run the query to make sure the results contain the data you want. When you are sure that the query is working properly, you can change the query type to make-table. When you run the make-table query, Access creates a table containing the table structure and records that meet the criteria you established. Access asks for a new table name and adds this table to the list of available tables in the database. Be sure to change the default name of any table created with a make-table query to include the tbl prefix.

Best Practice

Using Make-Table Queries

Make-table queries are often used to create **history tables** for accounting applications. These tables contain records that need to be saved or archived, but are no longer needed in the tables used for current activities in the database. Make-table queries are also frequently used by developers who inherit poorly designed tables in a database. The developer can choose those fields that should be part of new and well-designed tables as the fields in the make-table queries. If necessary, fields from multiple tables can be combined in a query first, and then the new table can be created from the fields in the query. This way, the developer doesn't need to reenter data, but the data from the tables and queries used in the make-table queries remain in the database until they are removed manually or with a Delete query.

You can also use a make-table query to create a table to export to other Access databases. For example, you could create a table that contains several fields from tblEmployee, and then export that table to a database used by the accounting or payroll personnel.

Maria backs up the database before beginning the tasks that Donald outlined. She plans her next task—creating a select query—by considering the goals of her query and the criteria she should use. She wants to select the following classes in which employees earn certification: Adult CPR (class ID 1), Child/Infant CPR (class ID 2), Adult CPR Recertification (class ID 3), or Child/Infant CPR Recertification (class ID 6). In addition to classes 1, 2, 3, or 6, Maria wants to select all of the classes attended on or before January 1, 2005 because certification achieved in these classes is now out of date. She briefly considers setting parameters so that she can specify the date each time she runs the query. However, she realizes that she does not need to save the make-table query—after she runs it to create a table of obsolete employee training records, she can add subsequent obsolete records to it using an append query, not a make-table query.

Maria creates a select query that contains all of the fields in tblEmployeeTraining. She adds all the fields by double-clicking the field list title bar, and then dragging the selection to the design grid. She types <=#1/1/2005# in the Criteria row for the Date field and then types In(1,2,3,6) as the criteria for the ClassID field. Before converting the query to a make-table query, she runs the query to make sure it selects the correct data—it selects seven records from tblEmployeeTraining, all containing obsolete data.

To convert the select query to a make-table query, she returns to Design view, clicks the list arrow on the Query Type button 🔲 on the Query Design toolbar, and then clicks Make-Table Query. The Make Table dialog box opens, in which Maria enters tblEmployeeTrainingHistory as the name of the new table, and specifies that Access should save it in the current database.

She clicks the OK button, and then clicks the Run button 🔲 on the Query Design toolbar to run the query. Access displays a message indicating that she is about to paste seven rows into a new table. She clicks the Yes button to confirm that she wants to create the table. To verify that the query created the table as she planned, she closes the make-table query without saving it, opens tblEmployeeTrainingHistory in Datasheet view, and sees the seven records for obsolete classes as she expected. However, when she opens the table in Design view, she notices that the new table doesn't have a primary key. She also notices that the captions are missing, as are other property settings for the fields.

Best Practice

Modifying Tables Created with Make-Table Queries

When you use a make-table query to create a new table, only the field name and data type are included in the new table. You lose other property settings, such as captions, formats, and decimal places. Furthermore, the new table doesnt inherit the primary key from the original table. If you plan to use the data for reports or queries in the future, you should add a primary key and correct any important field properties such as default formats for Date/Time fields. Adding the primary key also prevents you from adding duplicate rows.

Maria creates the composite primary keys for the new table and adds captions to match the old table. She also opens tblEmployeeTraining and notes that the seven obsolete records are still stored in tblEmployeeTraining. She will have to delete these records later. Her next step is to create an append query to continue to archive obsolete training records in tblEmployeeTrainingHistory.

Adding Records to Tables with Append Queries

An **append query** is another type of action query that allows you to select records from one or more tables by setting criteria and then add those records to the end of another table. The selected records also remain in the original tables. Because the table to which you add records must already exist (as opposed to a make-table action query that creates a table), you can define field properties and primary keys in advance. You can also use an append query to bring data from another source into your database, even if some of the fields in one table don't exist in the other table. For example, the tblEmployee table has 19 fields. If you import a table named tblPersonnel, for example, and it includes only 10 fields that match the 19 in tblEmployee, you could use an append query to add the data from tblPersonnel in the fields that match those in tblEmployee and ignore the others.

Maria remembers that she needs to add obsolete records for the Defibrillator Use class to tblEmployeeTrainingHistory. She can create an append query for adding obsolete training records from tblEmployeeTraining to tblEmployeeTrainingHistory. Again, she considers the goals of her query and the criteria she should use. As with the make-table query, she can use all of the fields in tblEmployeeTraining and similar criteria. However, because she will continue to use this query, she can use parameter values that prompt for the Date and ClassID field values. For the Date field, she uses the following criterion:

```
<=[Enter the date before which certification is out of date:]
```

If she were entering a fixed criterion for the ClassID field, she would enter "In(1,2,3,5,6)" to select the required certification classes. To convert this criterion to a parameter prompt, she can still use the In comparison operator and substitute a parameter value for each ClassID value, as follows:

```
In([Enter the ID of the first certification class:],
    [Enter the ID of the second certification class:],
       [Enter the ID of the third certification class:],
          [Enter the ID of the fourth certification
              class:], [Enter the ID of the fifth
                 certification class:])
```

This criterion will work even if she wants to select fewer than five classes—she can specify "5," for example, and then click the OK button on the Enter Parameter Value dialog box without entering a value the next four times it opens.

When she runs the select query, a dialog box opens and prompts her for the date. After she enters 1/1/2006 to test the query, five other dialog boxes open and prompt her for the five class IDs. When she is sure her query returns the results she wants, she saves it as qryAppendObsoleteClasses. She then converts it to an append query by clicking the list arrow on the Query Type button 🔲 on the Query Design toolbar and then clicking Append Query. The Append dialog box opens, in which Maria enters tblEmployeeTrainingHistory as the name of the table to which she wants to append the data, and specifies that this table is in the current database. See Figure 3.52.

Figure 3.52: Creating an append query

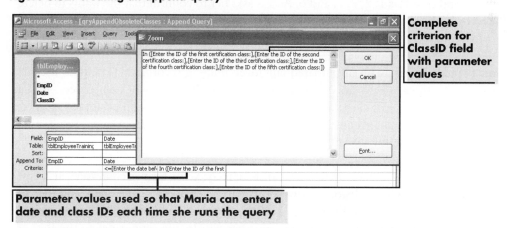

Complete criterion for ClassID field with parameter values

Parameter values used so that Maria can enter a date and class IDs each time she runs the query

She clicks the OK button, saves the query, and then runs it, entering 1/1/2005 as the date criterion and 5 as the class ID so that Access adds the obsolete Defibrillator Use class record to tblEmployeeTrainingHistory. Next, she needs to delete the obsolete records from tblEmployeeTraining because they are now archived in tblEmployeeTrainingHistory.

Removing Records from Tables with Delete Queries

A **delete query** removes information from a table based on the criteria you specify. As with other action queries, you create a select query first to specify the criteria, test it, and then convert the select query to a delete query. When you run the query, all records meeting your criteria are permanently removed from the table. You usually run a delete query after you use an append query to add those same records to a history table and have verified that you appended the correct records before you delete them in the original table.

Because a delete query permanently removes records from a table, be certain to back up the database and preview the data before you convert the select query to a delete query and run the query. Also, if your query uses only the primary table of two tables in a one-to-many relationship, and you've set up cascading deletes for that relationship, running a delete query might delete records in related tables, even if you do not include them in the query. In other words, with cascading deletes, deleting records from the "one" table also deletes records from the "many" table.

Now that Maria has created the tblEmployeeTrainingHistory table and checked to make sure it contains the obsolete training data, she can delete those records from tblEmployeeTraining. First, she backs up the database. She then creates a select query and sets up criteria to remove the obsolete records. Again, she uses the same parameter values she used in the append query, qryAppendObsoleteClasses, so she can enter the oldest date and the class IDs when she runs the query. She tests the query first to make sure it selects the right records. Next, she clicks the list arrow on the Query Type button 🔲 on the Query Design toolbar, and then clicks Delete Query to convert the select query to a delete query. She saves the query as qryDeleteObsoleteClasses and then runs it, entering 1/1/2005 as the date and class IDs 1, 2, 3, 5, and 6. Access asks her to confirm that she wants to delete the records. When she clicks the Yes button, Access permanently deletes the eight obsolete records from tblEmployeeTraining.

Now that Maria has archived outdated employee training records, she wants to use the same process to create a history table containing records for previous employees. Recall that she included previous employees in tblEmployee because she didn't want to lose their data, but needed to enter criteria to eliminate former employees from query results that listed information about current employees.

She creates and runs a make-table query to store records for former employees in a new table named tblEmployeeHistory. However, when she creates a delete query and tries to delete these records from tblEmployee, a message appears indicating that Access cannot delete the records due to key violations. In other words, she cannot delete the former employees from tblEmployee because that table is maintaining relationships with other tables. When Don Linebarger designed the database, he did not set cascading updates or deletes for employees. The tblEmployeeTraining and tblRefill tables include the EmpID field, which is a foreign key to tblEmployee. If the relationships in these tables allowed cascading deletes, deleting records for previous employees in tblEmployee would also delete the refill records for prescriptions that the previous employees refilled, which is inappropriate. Maria has already created queries that include the Is Null criterion in the EndDate field of tblEmployee, and she must remember to set this criterion in other queries so the results do not include previous employees.

Maria meets with Paul Ferrino to review all of the hourly rate analyses. Paul has been reviewing the results, and decides to give all technicians a 3% raise effective immediately. Maria could calculate the new hourly rates by hand and then update the table, but she can use an update query instead to automatically change the HourlyRate value for pharmacy technicians.

Updating Data with an Update Query

An **update query** changes the values of data in one or more existing tables. It is very useful when you must change the values of a field or fields in many records, such as raising salaries by 3% for all employees within a particular job category. Rather than change each value by editing the individual records, you can create an expression to update all the values based on a criterion you set.

How To

Create an Update Query

1. Back up the database before creating and running an action query.
2. Create a select query that includes only the field or fields you want to update and any fields necessary to determine the criteria for the update.
3. Enter the criteria and run the query to verify that the results contain the appropriate records and values and that the criteria are correct.
4. Click the Query Type button 🗃 on the Query Design toolbar, and then click Update Query to convert the select query to an update query.
5. In the Update To row for the fields you want to update, enter the expression or value you want to use to change the fields. If necessary, right-click the cell and then click Zoom on the shortcut menu to use the Zoom dialog box to enter the expression.
6. Run the query. Accept the modifications by clicking the Yes button.

Maria needs to change the values in the HourlyRate field for pharmacy technicians so they reflect the 3% raise Paul Ferrino has approved. She needs to update the records in the tblEmployee table to reflect these pay increases, and knows that an update query is the easiest way to change a number of records at the same time based on criteria. First, she backs up the 4Corners database to protect its data before performing an action query. She also notes a few wage rates for technicians so she can check the results with her calculator. For example, Virginia Sanchez currently earns $10.75 per hour. Three percent of $10.75 is about $.32, so Virginia's salary after the raise should be $11.07.

In the 4Corners database, Maria creates a query in Design view using tblEmployee and its JobID, EndDate, and HourlyRate fields. She specifies "3" as the criterion for JobID to select only pharmacy technicians, and Is Null as the criterion for EndDate so that the query selects only current employees. She also unchecks the Show box so the EndDate field does not appear in the results.

After she runs this query to make sure it selects only current pharmacy technicians, she clicks the Query Type button on the Query Design toolbar and then clicks Update Query to convert the select query to an update query. A new row named Update To appears in the design grid, in which Maria enters the following expression to increase the technicians' HourlyRate by 3%:

$$[HourlyRate]*1.03$$

When she clicks the Run button on the Query Design toolbar, a warning appears, reminding her that action queries are not reversible. See Figure 3.53.

Figure 3.53: Creating and running an update query

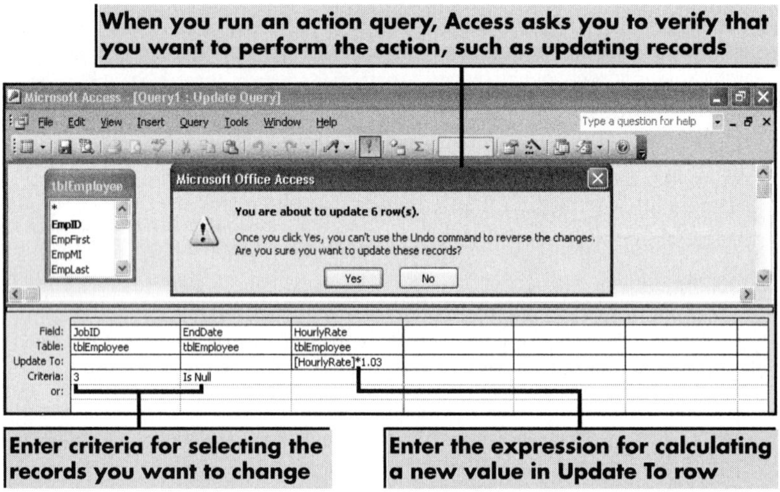

When you run an action query, Access asks you to verify that you want to perform the action, such as updating records

You are about to update 6 row(s).
Once you click Yes, you can't use the Undo command to reverse the changes. Are you sure you want to update these records?

Enter criteria for selecting the records you want to change

Enter the expression for calculating a new value in Update To row

She clicks the Yes button to update the records. Maria closes the update query without saving it, checks the new rate for Virginia Sanchez, and verifies that she now makes $11.07 per hour—a 3% raise. She doesn't save the query because she doesn't want to run it by accident and give the technicians another 3% raise.

Paul also wants to encourage employees to maintain their employment at 4Corners—low turnover saves the pharmacy training time and costs and is strongly associated with excellent service. He has decided to award a $500 bonus to employees who have worked at 4Corners for at least five years, and a $1,000 bonus to employees who have worked at least 10 years. How can Maria set up criteria that display a $1,000 bonus for some records that meet one condition and a $500 bonus for other records that meet a different condition? To do so, she needs an expression that assigns one of two values to a field based on a condition, one that, in effect, makes a decision and takes different actions depending on the outcome.

MAKING DECISIONS IN QUERIES

One of the most powerful tools available in programming languages is the ability to make a decision based on more than one condition. You do so using an IF statement, a programming statement that tests a condition and takes one action if the condition is true and another action if the condition is false. In Access, you can use the IIF function, also called an Immediate IF, Instant IF, and Inline IF, to perform the same task. The format for an IIF function statement is as follows:

```
IIF(condition to test, what to do if true, what to do if false)
```

For example, to determine which employees receive a $1,000 bonus, you can use an IIF function that tests the following condition:

IIF(you've worked for the pharmacy for 10 or more years, get $1,000 bonus, get no bonus)

You can interpret this expression as "If you've worked for the pharmacy for 10 or more years, you receive a $1,000 bonus; otherwise, you do not receive a bonus." You can also nest IIF functions by using a second IIF statement to test another condition if the first condition is false. For example, to determine which employees receive a bonus and how much the bonus should be, you can use a nested IIF function that tests the following conditions:

IIF(you've worked for the pharmacy for 10 or more years, get $1,000 bonus, IIF(you've worked for the pharmacy for more than 5 years, get $500 bonus, get no bonus))

You can interpret this expression as "If you've worked for the pharmacy for 10 or more years, you receive a $1,000 bonus; if you've worked for the pharmacy for five or more years, you receive a $500 bonus; otherwise, you do not receive a bonus."

You can use an IIF function to return a value or text. Enclose the text in quotation marks. For example, the following IIF statement checks to see if the value in the OrderAmt field is greater than 1,000. If it is, it displays "Large." If the value is not greater than 1,000, it displays "Small."

```
IIF(OrderAmt > 1000, "Large", "Small")
```

How To

Use the Immediate IF Function in Expressions

1. Create or open a query in Design view.

2. In a calculated field, as criteria, or in the Update To row of an update query, enter an expression beginning with IIF.

3. Within parentheses, enter the condition to test, the action to take if the condition is true, and the action to take if the condition is false.

4. As you type the expression, remember that each left parenthesis must have a right parenthesis to match. If you have one IIF, you need one set of parentheses. If you nest IIF statements, count the IIFs and make sure the parentheses on the right match the number of IIFs.

5. Test your results by clicking the Datasheet view button ▦ .

Maria plans the expression that assigns a bonus to an employee depending on their years of service. She can use this expression in a query that includes a calculated field for determining an employee's years of service to 4Corners Pharmacy. The first condition selects employees who have worked for the pharmacy for 10 or more years and assigns a $1,000 bonus to those employees. The IIF statement for this part of the expression is as follows:

```
IIF([Years of Service]>=10,1000,
```

This statement can be interpreted as "If the value in the Years of Service field is greater than or equal to 10, return the value 1,000." After the second comma in that statement, Maria inserts an expression that the query should perform if the first condition is false—in other words, if the value in the Years of Service field is not greater than or equal to 10. The second condition is as follows:

```
IIF([Years of Service]>=5,500,
```

This statement can be interpreted as "If the value in the Years of Service field is greater than or equal to 5, return the value 500." After the second comma in that statement, Maria inserts an expression that the query should perform if the first and second condition are false—in other words, if the value in the Years of Service field is not greater than or equal to 5: **0))**

This part of the expression returns the value 0 if the first and second conditions are false—if employees have worked at 4Corners Pharmacy for less than five years. The two parentheses complete the first and second condition. Maria will include the complete expression in a new calculated field named Bonus. The complete entry is as follows:

```
Bonus: IIF([Years of Service]>=10,1000,IIF([Years of
    Service]>=5,500,0))
```

Maria is ready to create the query that includes employees who are eligible for a bonus and lists the bonus they should receive. In Design view, she opens qryYearsOfService, the query she created earlier to calculate years of service for each employee. She saves the new query as qryBonus, and adds a calculated field named Bonus to the query. She then enters the IIF statement, shown in Figure 3.54.

Figure 3.54: Using an Immediate IF in an expression

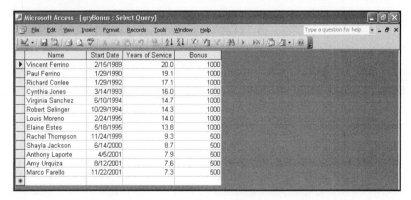

When she runs the query, the results include many employees who are not eligible for bonuses and two who no longer work for 4Corners. She realizes that she only wants to display employees who are eligible for bonuses, so she adds the criterion >5 to the Years of Service field. Then she adds the EndDate field to the query design grid, enters Is Null as the criterion, and unchecks the Show box. Figure 3.55 shows the results—current employees who are eligible for a bonus.

Figure 3.55: Employees who are eligible to receive a $500 or $1,000 bonus

Name	Start Date	Years of Service	Bonus
Vincent Ferrino	2/15/1989	20.0	1000
Paul Ferrino	1/29/1990	19.1	1000
Richard Conlee	1/29/1992	17.1	1000
Cynthia Jones	3/14/1993	16.0	1000
Virginia Sanchez	6/10/1994	14.7	1000
Robert Selinger	10/29/1994	14.3	1000
Louis Moreno	2/24/1995	14.0	1000
Elaine Estes	5/18/1995	13.8	1000
Rachel Thompson	11/24/1999	9.3	500
Shayla Jackson	6/14/2000	8.7	500
Anthony Laporte	4/5/2001	7.9	500
Amy Urquiza	8/12/2001	7.6	500
Marco Farello	11/22/2001	7.3	500

CUSTOMIZING QUERIES USING STRUCTURED QUERY LANGUAGE

Access was designed as a database management system (DBMS) for small businesses or departments within large businesses, not a DBMS for large, enterprise systems that must run at high performance levels. Creating basic database objects such as queries, forms, and reports is easy for Access users, as you have discovered, but users of enterprise DBMSs generally do not have the same access to database objects. Their interaction is usually to query the enterprise system and import the data to a program such as Access for further analysis. To do so, they must use a common query language that their DBMS and Access can both interpret.

Structured Query Language (SQL—usually pronounced "sequel" but more properly pronounced "ess-cue-ell") is the common query language of most DBMSs, including Access. You can use SQL to query, update, and manage relational databases such as Access. When you create a query in query Design view, Access translates the entries and criteria into SQL statements. You can view these statements by switching from Design view to SQL view. Parts of the SQL statements are the same as the entries you make in query Design view. For example, when you use a field name in a calculation, you enclose it in square brackets in Design view or SQL view. The two views are similar enough that some SQL developers use the query design grid in Access to develop the basic SQL code before adding specialized features.

For example, Figure 3.56 shows the qryHourlyRate query in Design view and SQL view. Recall that this query lists all nonsalaried employees and their hourly pay rates.

Figure 3.56: qryHourlyRate in Design view and SQL view

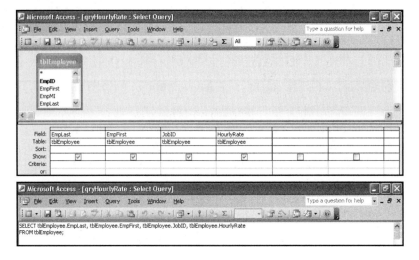

The SELECT statement defines what data the query should retrieve from the database and how it should present the data. For example, SELECT tblEmployee.EmpLast indicates that the query should select data from the EmpLast field in the tblEmployee table. The FROM statement defines the database objects that contain this data. For example, FROM tblEmployee indicates that all the data is stored in tblEmployee. SELECT and FROM are keywords in SQL; they have special meaning in SQL. To make it easy to identify the keywords in SQL code, Access displays them in all uppercase letters. An SQL statement usually begins with a keyword, which serves to define a command or clause in the expression.

Exploring the Components of an SQL Query

Table 3.14 lists the common keywords you can use to construct SQL statements. SQL code isn't required to follow a particular format, but Access and most developers place each statement on a separate line to make the SQL code easy to read. All of the wildcards, comparison operators, and logical operators you learned about in this chapter are also available in SQL.

Table 3.14: Common SQL keywords

SQL Term	What Follows the Term	Example
SELECT	List the fields you want to display. They will appear in the results in the order you list them. Note that field names with no spaces or special symbols do not require square brackets around them, but it is good practice to use the square brackets for consistency. Separate the field names with commas.	SELECT tblEmployee.EmpLast Display the EmpLast field from tblEmployee
FROM	List the table or tables involved in the query. Separate the table names with commas, and use square brackets around table names that include a space or special symbol.	FROM tblEmployee Use the tblEmployee table in the query
WHERE	List the criteria that apply. If more than one table has a field with the same name, you need to "qualify" your conditions with the name of the table followed by a period.	WHERE ((tblEmployee.JobID)=3) AND ((tblEmployee.EndDate) Is Null)) Select records in which the value in the JobID field of tblEmployee is 3 and the value in the EndDate field is null
GROUP BY	Group records with identical values in the specified fields into a single record, usually to calculate summary statistics.	GROUP BY tblEmployee.JobID Group the results by records in the JobID field
HAVING	List the conditions for selecting grouped records, connected by AND, OR, or NOT.	HAVING ((tblEmployee.JobID)=3 Or (tblEmployee.JobID)=4)) Select records that have the value 3 or 4 in the JobID field of tblEmployee
ORDER BY	Specify sorting specifications; for descending order, insert DESC after a sort field.	ORDER BY tblEmployee.EmpLast Sort the records by the EmpLast field in tblEmployee
AS	Use with calculated columns to specify the name of the resulting calculation.	[EmpFirst] & " " & [EmpLast] AS Name Concatenate the contents of the EmpFirst and EmpLast fields and display the results as the Name field
; (semicolon)	Use to end every SQL command, because it is required in some versions of SQL.	N/A

Maria wants to explore SQL view in case she needs to modify queries to include more flexibility or power than Design view can offer. One task Paul asked her to complete is to create a query similar to qryTop5HourlyRates that displays the top three salaries paid to employees. She can open qryTop5HourlyRates in SQL view and then modify it so that it selects the three records that have the highest values in the Salary field instead of the five records that have the highest values in the HourlyRate field.

Maria opens qryTop5HourlyRates in Design view, clicks the list arrow on the View button ▦ on the Query Design toolbar, and then clicks SQL View. The query appears in SQL view. See Figure 3.57.

Figure 3.57: SQL view of qryTop5HourlyRates

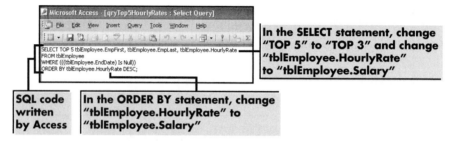

Maria takes some time to interpret the SQL statements in this view:

- **SELECT   TOP   5   tblEmployee.EmpFirst,   tblEmployee.EmpLast, tblEmployee.HourlyRate**—Display the EmpFirst, EmpLast, and HourlyRate fields from tblEmployee, and select the top five records in the field specified in the ORDER BY clause.
- **FROM tblEmployee**—Use only the tblEmployee table in the query.
- **WHERE ((tblEmployee.EndDate) Is Null))**—Select only those records in which the value in the EndDate field is null.
- **ORDER BY tblEmployee.HourlyRate DESC;**—Sort the results in descending order by the values in the HourlyRate field, and then end the query.

To change this query to select the records with the top three values in the Salary field, Maria changes "TOP 5" in the SELECT statement to "TOP 3." She also changes "tblEmployee.HourlyRate" in the SELECT statement to "tblEmployee.Salary." She doesn't need to change the FROM statement because she still wants to select records only from the tblEmployee table, nor does she need to change the WHERE statement— she only wants to display salaries of current employees. However, she does need to change the ORDER BY statement so that it sorts records by the Salary field instead of HourlyRate. That change also means the query selects the three records with the highest values in the Salary field. She completes these changes, saves the query as qryTop3Salaries, and switches to Design view, which reflects the changes she made in SQL view. Finally, she runs the query to view the results. See Figure 3.58.

Figure 3.58: Three views of qryTop3Salaries

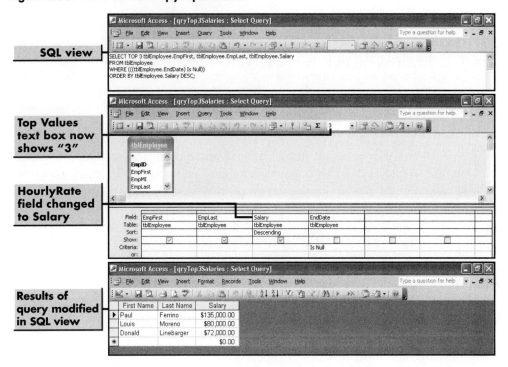

SQL view

Top Values
text box now
shows "3"

HourlyRate
field changed
to Salary

Results of
query modified
in SQL view

As you create or modify SQL statements in SQL view, Access makes corresponding changes in the query design grid in Design view. After you create a query in SQL view, you can modify it in Design view. Access reformats your SQL code so it looks like an Access-generated SQL command. Access SQL code always uses the qualified field names even if you only have one table in your query, not all fields will be enclosed in square brackets, and there might be extra parentheses in the criteria. While you are learning how to create SQL queries, you can change from SQL view to Design view to Datasheet view to gauge the effect of your SQL statements in the other views.

Steps To Success: Level 3

Kim Siemers, human resources manager for Hudson Bay Pharmacy, needs to analyze statistical data for the pharmacy and to archive obsolete records. She asks for your help creating crosstab queries and action queries that modify the data in the Hudson database. As you create and save the new queries, be certain to use the "qry" prefix as part of the naming convention. Also consult your instructor for instructions about submitting your results.

Complete the following:

1. Start Access and open the **Hudson.mdb** database from the STS folder.

2. Kim is preparing the human resources budget for Hudson Bay Pharmacy, and needs to analyze the annual cost of training to determine how much to budget for training classes. She asks you to provide summary data for the costs by year for classes. The results you create should clearly compare the total annual costs of training classes and the annual costs per class. Save the query as qryClassCostAnalysis.

3. Kim needs to remove obsolete data from the Hudson database. First, she asks you to identify all employees who no longer work for Hudson Bay Pharmacy. She then wants you to create a new history table with that data. Name the history table tblEmpHistory. Save the query as qryEmpHistory.

4. Kim also wants to remove records for classes employees have completed and for which their certification has already been updated. She asks you to select classes in which employees earn certification—Adult CPR, Adult CPR Recertification, Child/Infant CPR, and Child/Infant CPR Recertification—and that they attended before January 1, 2007 because certification achieved in these classes is now out of date in Canada. Create a history table that contains this data, and name the table tblEmployeeTrainingHistory. Name the query qryEmployeeTrainingHistory.

5. Kim checked your results, and realizes that tblEmployeeTrainingHistory should also include obsolete data for Defibrillator Use classes. Add the obsolete training records for Defibrillator Use classes to tblEmployeeTrainingHistory. Because Kim will continue to use this query for other classes as they become outdated, set up the query so that it prompts her for the necessary criteria before running. Defibrillator Use certifications before 1/1/08 are no longer valid. Save the query as qryObsoleteClasses.

6. Verify that tblEmployeeTrainingHistory includes all the obsolete classes. Delete the now archived records from tblEmployeeTraining. As with qryObsoleteClasses, Kim will continue to use this query to remove obsolete records after they've been archived. Set up the query so that it prompts her for the necessary criteria before running. Save the query as qryDeleteClasses. Make sure the total number of records you deleted is the same as the number of records in tblEmployeeTrainingHistory.

7. Kim recently met with Joan Gabel, owner of Hudson Bay Pharmacy, who authorized a 5% raise for all current pharmacy technicians. Update the employee records for pharmacy technicians so that their pay rate includes this 5% raise. Save the query as qryTechnicianRaise.

8. Kim also says that current employees are eligible for participation in a 401(k) retirement plan after one year. Identify each employee by full name and show whether they

are eligible for the plan with a column stating "Eligible" or "Not Eligible" in the results. Save the query as qryRetirement.

9. Kim is meeting with Joan later today, and needs to report which salaried employees earn the top three salaries. Create a query in SQL view that lists all employees who earn the top three salaries. Be certain to separate the SQL terms to make it more readable. Save the query as qryTop3Salaries.

10. Close the **Hudson.mdb** database and Access.

CHAPTER SUMMARY

In this chapter, you learned how to retrieve data from a database so that you can examine only the information you need. Level 1 showed you how to filter data by form and by selection to create a temporary subset of records, and how to sort data to rearrange records in a specified order. Level 1 also introduced queries, explaining how to create select queries using the Simple Query Wizard, including those that provide summary statistics, or Design view, which is necessary when you need to use multiple criteria. In addition to multiple criteria, queries you create in Design view can include wildcards and comparison operators.

Level 2 focused on more complex queries and specialized query wizards. You learned how to create special types of queries that find duplicate records or unmatched records. You also learned how to create Top Value queries that limit the records in query results and parameter queries that pause before running so that users can enter values that the query uses as criteria. In addition, Level 2 explored refining relationships with appropriate join types and using logical operators to specify multiple conditions. It also explained how to perform calculations in a query by using aggregate functions and by creating calculated fields.

Level 3 covered advanced types of queries, including crosstab queries, which present data to facilitate statistical analysis. In addition, it showed you how to create action queries, including those that create tables, and add, update, or delete records in a table. Level 3 also explained how to create a calculated field with an Immediate IF function that makes decisions in a query. Finally, Level 3 introduced Structured Query Language (SQL), the language Access uses to query its databases.

CONCEPTUAL REVIEW

1. When is it appropriate to use Filter by Selection and Filter by Form?

2. What restrictions does the Simple Query Wizard have for creating queries?

3. Why is it important to use the naming prefix "qry" for all saved queries?

4. Why is it not a good idea to add records to a table from a query datasheet?

5. What is the difference between entering multiple criteria for a query on one line of the design grid versus entering criteria on two or more lines?

6. What query wizards are available other than the Simple Query Wizard? For what do you use these types of queries?

7. What is the purpose of an outer join?

8. What role does "null" play in a field?

9. When should you use the Expression Builder?

10. What is a history table and why would a database designer include one or more in the design?

11. What is the difference between a query written in the query design grid and one written directly in SQL?

12. Describe a situation in which the IIF function would be appropriate.

13. What is the difference between an update query and an append query?

14. Why do many people run a delete query after running a make-table or append query?

15. Name an advantage that crosstab queries offer that other types of queries do not.

CASE PROBLEMS

Case 1—Managing Customer Information for NHD Development Group Inc.

Marketing

After creating the tables and relationships for the Antiques database, you meet with Tim Richards, the chief information officer for the NHD Development Group, and Linda Sutherland, the manager of the antique mall. As you review the database, Linda makes a few requests. When she tracked sales for a month, she found that repeat customers accounted for 60% of her revenue. She therefore wants to use the Antiques database to increase marketing efforts to her current customer base. First, she wants to extract information about her customers, such as a list that organizes customers by city and another that provides customer names and phone numbers. She also needs to retrieve information about the antique and restoration classes the mall offers to determine which customers enroll in the classes. Then she could provide information in the classes about items that might interest those customers. She asks for your help filtering data and creating queries that extract the information she needs.

Complete the following:

1. Open the **Antiques.mdb** database from the Case 1 folder.

2. Many of the mall's customers live in Cleveland or Collegedale, Tennessee, and Linda is debating whether to place an ad in their community newspapers or to send post-cards advising these customers about upcoming sales. If she sends more than 50 postcards, mailing costs will exceed advertising rates.

   Show Linda a quick way she can produce a temporary list of customers who live in Cleveland or Collegedale, with all the customers in Cleveland listed first. Is it more economical to send these customers postcards or to advertise in the community newspapers?

3. To increase repeat business, Linda wants to call customers and let them know when new collectibles arrive at the mall. She wants to produce a list of her customers and their phone numbers. To track the customers effectively, this telephone list should also include the customer's ID number.

   a. Create a list that includes the ID numbers, last names, first names, and phone numbers of all the customers.

   b. Because Linda expects to refer to this list by customer name, sort the list by last name.

   c. Save the query as qryPhoneList.

4. Linda is planning to create a brochure for the mall, and wants to highlight the number of booths within the mall. She wants to advertise that the mall has fifteen 8×8 booths, five 12×10 booths, and so on. Because Linda has recently reworked the booth divisions and expects to make additional changes in the future, she wants to list how many booths of each size the mall currently has. Name the query qryBoothSize.

5. Linda wants to promote the classes that will be offered in February. She will be placing an ad in the local newspaper, and wants to include the class list in the ad. She asks you to create a list of all the February classes sorted by date and by time. Be sure the list includes information readers are most interested in, such as the name of the class, the date and time, and the class fee. Name the query qryFebruaryClasses.

6. When Linda reviews the list of February classes, she thinks that the dates would be more meaningful if they spelled out the day of the week, using a format such as "Saturday, February 5, 2005." Linda asks you to modify the class list to display long dates. (*Hint*: In Design view, right-click the date field, click Properties, click the Format property's list arrow, and then click Long Date.)

7. Linda also needs a list of classes that she can use in the mall when customers and others inquire about the classes. When people call for information about the classes, they often want to know when the classes will be held. Linda also wants to use this list to call enrollees in case of a cancellation. Linda considers a person officially enrolled only when they have paid for the class.

    a. Create a list that includes the class ID and other information that callers want to know about the classes. Test your results.

    b. Modify the list so that it also includes information Linda needs to call customers and determine whether a customer is enrolled in a class. To help her find the information she needs, sort the list first by class and then by whether the customer has paid.

    c. Save the query as qryClassListing.

8. To manage the classes and instructors, Linda needs a summary of class enrollment. In addition to the names of the class and instructor, she needs to know the number of students enrolled in each class and the total of the class fees that have been paid. Save this query as qryClassEnrollment.

9. Unless at least five people are enrolled in a class, the class will be canceled. However, Linda wants to review the list of classes that are likely to be canceled to see if she can encourage some of her customers to take these classes. Modify qryClassEnrollment to include only those classes that have fewer than five customers enrolled. Save this query as qryClassDeletions.

10. Linda explains that the primary reason she offers the classes is to have people visit the mall. She has observed that most people come early for the classes and wander around the mall before the class begins. The classes are, therefore, part of her marketing strategy for the mall and she wants to protect this endeavor. One problem she wants to solve is that customers sometimes sign up for classes, but do not attend them. If class attendance is low, instructors have moved their classes to a different antiques mall. Classes with high fees seem to have the lowest attendance. Linda asks you to create a list that shows customers who have signed up for classes with a fee greater than $25 but have not paid. Provide information Linda needs so she can call the customers and request their payment, and sort the list so she can easily find customers by name. Name the qryUnpaidClassesOver25.

11. Linda often receives calls asking whether any of the dealers carry military memorabilia. She asks you to create a list of the dealers who sell such items. She will use this list to call dealers and to find other information about the memorabilia, such as discounts offered. Name this query qryMilitaryMemorabilia.

12. Close the **Antiques.mdb** database and Access.

Case 2—Retrieving Employee Information for MovinOn Inc.

Human Resources

3

Now that you have worked with Robert Iko at the MovinOn moving and storage company to develop the design for the MovinOn database, he explains that their most pressing task is to serve the needs of the human resources department. Darnell Colmenero is an administrative assistant responsible for many human resources tasks, and asks for your help extracting information from the MovinOn database. Although an outside company processes payroll for MovinOn, Darnell and others maintain complete employment information and strive to meet management's goal of recruiting and retaining skilled, qualified employees who are well trained in customer service. Having employees working in three warehouses in three states has made it difficult to track employee information, and the potential merger and expansion means that human resources must take advantage of the MovinOn database to maintain and retrieve employee information. Darnell asks for your help in filtering data and creating queries that provide the information that he needs.

Complete the following:

1. Open the **MovinOn.mdb** database from the Case 2 folder.

2. The truck drivers for MovinOn are a special type of employee, and their data is stored in a table separate from the rest of the employees because of driving certification requirements. Drivers are certified to drive trucks with a specified number of axles, and MovinOn must be certain that a driver is certified to drive a particular truck.

   a. When Darnell meets with David Bower, the general manager, he learns that only drivers who have a driving record of "A" or "B" are allowed to drive the large trucks (those with four axles or more). He asks you to identify the drivers qualified to drive the four-axle trucks. Because he will use the list you create to call drivers when he needs a substitute, include the phone numbers and driving record for each driver. Save the query as qry4AxleDrivers.

   b. Darnell also learns that he must immediately review drivers who have a driving record lower than "A" or "B." Those drivers who have a record of "C" will be put on notice, and those with a record "D" or "F" can be terminated immediately. List the drivers with these low driving records, and sort the list so that Darnell can easily determine the driving record of each driver. Because he can enroll long-term drivers in a training program, he also needs to know when each driver started working for MovinOn and whether the driver is still employed. Save the query as qryDriversWithLowRecords.

   c. If drivers have been terminated because of their driving record, Darnell wants to include them in an additional list. Create this list for Darnell, and include all relevant employment information. Save this query as qryDriversForTermination.

Chapter Exercises

3. Darnell is completing a small business certification form for the U.S. Department of Labor, and needs quick answers to some basic questions about employees. Answer the following questions:

    a. In what states do the MovinOn employees reside?

    b. How many employees live in each state?

    c. Who is the oldest employee? Who is the youngest?

    d. Who makes the highest salary?

    e. Who is paid by salary? Who is paid by hourly rate?

    f. Who is paid the lowest hourly rate?

    g. Are there any positions for which there are no employees?

    h. How many types of jobs are offered at MovinOn? How many people are employed in each type of job?

4. When MovinOn hires employees, Darnell must process the employees by informing them about company policies and making sure they complete required printed forms. Darnell sometimes spends an entire day with a new employee. He wants to know when he was able to process more than one new employee in a day—he can then look over the forms and his training notes to discover how he can work more efficiently. He asks you to produce a list of employees who were processed on the same day. Because he files the forms he wants to review by Social Security number, include this information in the list. Name the query qryDuplicateStartDates.

5. David Bowers is considering providing bonuses to long-term employees. Darnell asks you to list the 10 employees who have worked for MovinOn the longest. Name the query qryLongestEmployment.

6. To prepare for a payroll, Darnell must provide a list of employees that includes their salary or hourly pay rate. The list must also include Social Security numbers and employee IDs so that an outside firm can properly process the payroll. Produce an employee list that provides this information, and sort it so that it's easy to find an employee by name. For those employees who are on a salary, the list should show their monthly wage. Save the query as qryPayroll.

7. Darnell sometimes needs to contact the warehouse managers, accountants, administrative assistants, and other employees at the warehouse where they work. Create a contact list that he can use to phone employees, and that contains enough information to identify employees, their positions, and their warehouses along with the warehouse phone number. Because Darnell might eventually use this list as the basis for a report, the employee's name should appear as one full name, with the last name first. Save the query as qryEmployeeContact.

8. When you show qryEmployeeContact to Darnell, he realizes that it would be more helpful if he could specify a particular warehouse before producing the list, and then see the contact information only for the employees who work in that warehouse. Create a query that meets these needs, saving it as qryEmployeeContactByWarehouse. Test this query with valid and invalid warehouse information.

9. MovinOn knows that having a workforce of long-term employees improves customer service and avoids the high expense of training new employees. Darnell wants to know if one warehouse is more effective at retaining employees than another. He asks you to do the following:

    a.   Create an employee list that calculates the number of years each employee has worked for MovinOn.

    b.   Organize the list by job title within each warehouse.

    c.   Save the query as qryEmployeeLongevity.

10. MovinOn wants to offer hourly pay rates that are competitive with other moving companies in the Pacific Northwest. To identify nonsalaried employees who might be eligible for a raise in pay, Darnell asks you to do the following:

    a.   Identify employees at each warehouse who earn less than $12.00 per hour. Do not include salaried employees in the list.

    b.   Let users specify a particular warehouse, and then see information only for the employees who work in that warehouse.

    c.   Save the query as qryEmployeeLowWage.

11. Darnell learns that the manager of the Oregon warehouse has decided to give his hourly employees a 10% raise. He asks you to list all the employees who work in the Oregon warehouse, and show the old rate along with the new rate after a 10% increase to their hourly pay rate. The increase applies only to hourly employees. Save the query as qryOregonRateIncrease.

12. Close the **MovinOn.mdb** database and Access.

Case 3—Managing Equipment and Preparing for Games in the Hershey College Intramural Department

Operations Management

Recall that you are working on a database for the intramural department at Hershey College, under the direction of Marianna Fuentes. The department is preparing for its first semester of operation and needs to set up teams for each sport, manage the equipment and fields for each sport, keep track of coaches and team captains, and allow students to sign up for the sports offerings.

Marianna has interviewed the rest of the intramural staff to determine the data needs of the department. She has prepared a list of those needs. Your next task is to create lists that meet the operational needs of the department. For each list, Marianna asks you to name the columns so that it is clear what each column contains.

Complete the following:

1. Open the **Hershey.mdb** database from the Case 3 folder.

2. Review the tables that you created in Chapter 2. Keep in mind that you will use the existing data to test the database. When the database has been fully designed, the department staff will enter real data in place of the test data you have provided.

3. The intramural staff often needs to contact students who have enrolled in an intramural sport. Create a phone list the staff can use. Marianna states that they usually use the cell phone number to contact students, but they want to have both the land line and the cell phone numbers on the contact list. The list should be ordered so that it is easy to find a student by name. Name the query qryStudentContact.

4. Because the intramural department staff members serve as coaches in addition to their other responsibilities, the staff needs to schedule their time carefully. In particular, they need to monitor people who coach more than one sport. Marianna asks you to list coaches who are assigned to more than one sport and to identify the sports to which each coach is assigned. Name the query qryCoachesWithMultipleSports.

5. Before students can participate in a sport, they must provide a liability waiver and academic approval form. One staff member is assigned to calling students who are missing a required form. Marianna asks you to create a list, including all phone numbers, of students who are missing one or both of the required forms. The list should also identify the missing form. Name the query qryMissingApprovals.

6. For the next staff meeting, the department needs a list of coaching assignments. Coaches often want a quick reference to their sport, the maximum and minimum numbers of players on each team, and the date the teams start playing. Name the query qryCoachingAssignments.

7. The staff also needs to know how many sports each coach is assigned to coach for each quarter of the year. They ask you to provide this information in the form of a spreadsheet, with the coaches' names appearing for the rows of the table and the quarters appearing as the columns. The rest of the information indicates the number of sports each coach is assigned to in each quarter. Name the query qryCoachingPerQuarter.

8. Recall that students must sign a waiver of liability and maintain academic approval before they can play an intramural sport. The department wants to have a list showing students and these two ratings. If a student has submitted a signed waiver and academic approval forms, indicate that they are approved to play. If the student has not submitted both forms, indicate that they are not approved to play. Organize the list so that those with approval are grouped at the beginning. Save the query as qryApprovalStatus.

9. In some cases, students who have academic approval but not a signed liability form can play intramural sports. However, students who do not have academic approval cannot participate in intramural sports. At the beginning of each semester, the department receives a list of students who are not approved to play sports. The staff records that information in the student table. They also want to remove from the table the students who do not have academic approval. Marianna asks you to identify students who do not have academic approval, isolate them in a separate table, and then remove them from the student table, which should contain only those students who have been academically approved. Name the queries qryUnapprovedStudents and qryDeleteUnapprovedStudents as appropriate.

10. All of the students who have signed up to play a sport have been assigned to a team. Provide a list of teams and the students assigned to those teams. Name the query qryTeamAssignments.

11. The staff also needs a way to track students in the future in case someone signs up for a sport and is not assigned to a team. Provide a way for the staff to track these students. Name the query qryStudentWithoutTeam.

12. To manage the teams, the coaches need a list of teams and their student captains. The captain names for this list are most useful as full names, with the last name appearing first. Name the query qryTeamCaptainAssignments.

13. If a sports field is available in the spring, it is also available in the summer. In other words, a field that is recorded as available only in the spring is actually available in the spring and summer, and a field that is recorded as available in the fall and spring is actually available in the fall, spring, and summer. Marianna wants to know if you can easily update the data to reflect this information. Name the query qrySeasonChange.

14. Provide at least two additional lists that would be helpful to the intramural staff. Create at least one by modifying an existing query in SQL view.

15. Close the **Hershey.mdb** database and Access.

Collecting Data with Well-Designed Forms

Operations Management: Managing Daily Operations at 4Corners Pharmacy

"Making good decisions is a crucial skill at every level."
—Peter Drucker

LEARNING OBJECTIVES

Level 1

Design forms for efficient data entry
Create simple forms for data entry and editing
Develop a consistent user interface

Level 2

Create multitable forms
Improve navigation on forms
Control form printing

Level 3

Improve usability of forms
Place calculations on forms
Develop advanced forms

TOOLS COVERED IN THIS CHAPTER

AutoForm
AutoFormat (predefined and custom)
Calculated field
Combo box (for locating a record)
Command button
Control Wizards
Find tool
Form properties
Form Wizard
Subform control
Tab control
Tab order

CHAPTER INTRODUCTION

This chapter focuses on automating the important process of acquiring the data needed for the day-to-day operation of a business. Although developers often add data to databases by importing it from other sources, such as previous database files and spreadsheets or by entering data directly into table datasheets for testing, most users of Microsoft Office Access 2003 database applications enter and edit data using custom forms. In contrast to a datasheet, forms can show only one record at a time and provide many advantages to database users. You can design electronic forms to match familiar paper ones, grouping fields to facilitate rapid data entry. You can also show related records on the same form by using a main form and one or more subforms, making it easy for users to view and enter related data.

Forms also offer flexibility for users and designers. You can create forms from a single table, multiple tables with a common field, or a query. Because forms can contain all the fields for a table or just a few, they can consist of one or many pages (or screens), depending on the number of fields you choose. You can design all the forms in a database to create a consistent look and feel, and include buttons that facilitate navigation, allow the user to move from one form to another, or print the current record. To provide security, you can restrict each user to work with data in a particular view, such as one that allows users to view but not change the data.

Throughout this chapter, you will learn how to use forms to acquire data. Level 1 examines the data-entry process and explores creating simple forms. Level 2 explains how to create forms with subforms, improve navigation, and modify forms to facilitate rapid and accurate data entry. Level 3 covers more complex forms that contain data from multiple tables and provide additional navigation options. You will also learn to customize forms by modifying their properties.

CASE SCENARIO

Of all employees at 4Corners Pharmacy, technicians will interact with the new database application the most frequently. Rachel Thompson, a pharmacy technician, will work with the 4Corners database to create custom electronic forms so that the technicians can enter information directly into the database. To facilitate a smooth transition to the new system, she wants to make the forms easy to use and, if appropriate, similar to the paper forms they now use. Rachel has been working for 4Corners Pharmacy for many years and has a good idea of how the pharmacy operates. Naturally, her main interests are to automate the process of registering new customers and their prescriptions and processing refills.

Operations Management

Rachel also plans to develop custom forms so that they allow data entry and editing for every table in the database and so that they share a similar look and feel. Because the pharmacy can be very busy with phone orders and walk-in traffic, she must make sure that the forms facilitate rapid and accurate data entry.

LEVEL 1

DEVELOPING SIMPLE FORMS TO FACILITATE DATA ENTRY

ACCESS 2003 SKILLS TRAINING

- **Add a title to a form**
- **Add controls to a form**
- **Align controls**
- **Create auto forms**
- **Create forms using the Form Wizard**
- **Format controls**
- **Modify labels**
- **Move controls**
- **Resize controls**
- **Use AutoFormats**
- **Use subdatasheets**

DESIGNING FORMS FOR EFFICIENT DATA ENTRY

An electronic **form** is an object you use to enter, update, and print records in a database. Although you can perform these same tasks with tables and queries, forms present records in a format that makes data easy to enter and retrieve. Most database users interact with a database solely through its forms. They use forms to enter and update all the data in the database because forms provide better readability and control than tables and queries. In this way, the forms become the user interface of the database. Their design should, therefore, suit the way users enter or view data.

Well-designed forms let people use a database quickly, guiding them to find what they need. They should be easy to read and understand. Visually appealing forms make working with the database more pleasant and effective. Following are generally accepted guidelines for designing electronic forms:

- **Provide a meaningful title**—The title should clearly state the purpose or content of the form.
- **Organize fields logically**—Group related fields and position them in an order that is meaningful and logical for the database users. If users are more familiar with a printed form that is being converted to an electronic form, organize the fields on the electronic form to match its printed counterpart.
- **Use an appealing form layout**—Use few colors, fonts, and graphics to maintain a clean design that focuses on the data. Align fields and labels for readability. Use a consistent style for all forms in a database.
- **Include familiar field labels**—Identify each field with a descriptive label that names the field clearly.

- **Be consistent with terminology and abbreviations**—If you use a term, instruction, or abbreviation in one part of the form, use the same term or abbreviation as appropriate in another part of the form and in other forms.
- **Allow for convenient cursor movement**—Set up the fields on a form so that users can enter data in a logical and convenient order and find information easily later.
- **Prevent and correct errors**—Use techniques such as providing default values or list boxes to reduce user errors by minimizing keystrokes and limiting entries. Prevent users from changing and updating fields such as calculated fields, and allow them to correct data entered in other fields.
- **Include explanatory messages for fields**—If a field is optional, clearly mark it as such.

Figure 4.1 compares a well-designed form with a poorly designed one.

Figure 4.1: Comparing a well-designed form with a poorly designed form

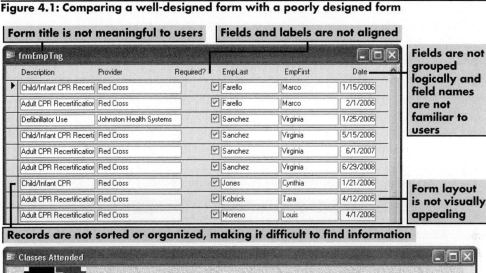

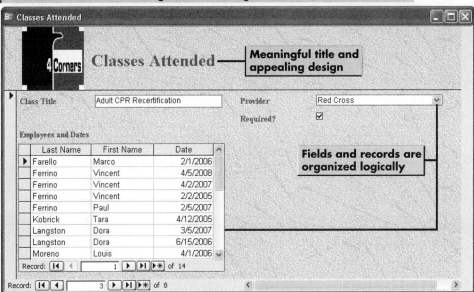

The top form is clearly difficult to use. It looks cluttered, disorganized, and unappealing. The well-designed form on the bottom is attractive and logically organized, enhancing the user experience of working with the form.

Before you create forms using Access, you should sketch the form design on paper, meeting with users and other database developers as necessary to determine content and an effective design. You should also verify database integrity, test tables and relationships, and examine and enter sample data, which are discussed in the following sections.

Verifying Database Integrity

Paul Ferrino, the owner of 4Corners Pharmacy, has read about problems with accuracy in databases. Because the purpose of the new 4Corners database is to provide timely data for decision making and to increase productivity in the pharmacy, he wants to make sure that employees can use the system to enter data accurately and efficiently. Before implementing the new database application, he also wants to make sure that it will be well received by the employees and that, after a short training period, it will speed up the daily operations of the pharmacy. He asks Rachel Thompson, a pharmacy technician, to design the data-entry forms so that they are complete, consistent, appealing, and easy to use.

Rachel starts by examining all 12 tables in the 4Corners database. These tables and their relationships are shown in Figure 4.2 and are described in the following list.

Figure 4.2: Tables and relationships for the Pharmacy database

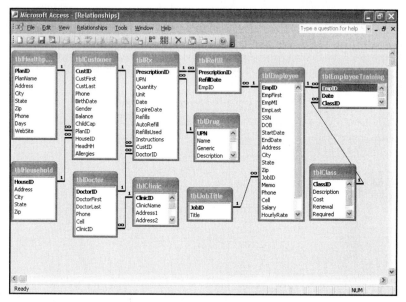

- **tblEmployee**—This table contains information about employees, including identifying information such as their ID number, name, and Social Security number, contact information such as their address and phone numbers, and employment information such as their starting date, salary or hourly rate, and job ID.
- **tblJobTitle**—This table lists the five jobs performed at 4Corners Pharmacy by ID number: 1—Owner, 2—Pharmacist, 3—Technician, 4—Cashier, and 5—Manager.
- **tblEmployeeTraining**—This table tracks the training classes that employees attend.
- **tblClass**—This table lists the classes employees can attend to receive required certifications or other professional training.
- **tblRefill**—This table tracks which employee refills a particular prescription and when.
- **tblCustomer**—This table contains information about the customers, including their ID number, name, phone, birth date, gender, and health plan ID. Each customer is assigned a household ID and information about whether they are the designated head of household for mailing purposes. The table also contains information for the pharmacist, including known allergies and preference for child-proof caps on prescription bottles, and indicates any unpaid balance on the customer's account.
- **tblHealthPlan**—This table lists the ID and name of the customer's health plan as well as the address and phone number. Also included are the number of days allowed per prescription and a hyperlink to the plan's Web site in case the pharmacy needs additional information.
- **tblHousehold**—Each customer is assigned to a household. This table includes the household ID and address so it is entered only once for each household. Unrelated customers with the same address, such as roommates, are assigned their own household ID.
- **tblDoctor**—This table contains information about doctors who write prescriptions that 4Corners Pharmacy fills. The table includes the name, phone numbers, additional phone contact (often a nurse or secretary), and the ID of the clinic with which the doctor is affiliated.
- **tblClinic**—Doctors are affiliated with one clinic. This table contains the clinic name, address, and phone number.
- **tblRx**—This table lists each prescription that the pharmacy fills, including the prescription number (called an ID), the UPN (a numeric code assigned by the drug companies), and other details about the prescription.
- **tblDrug**—This table contains information about the drugs used in the prescriptions, such as the UPN, drug name, dosage and dosage form, cost and price, and any known interactions.

Accurate data is a major goal in every database. Unintentional data-entry errors range from a typo in an address to an incorrect customer ID. Some errors can be prevented by the design of the database itself, such as entering job titles only once in the tblJobTitle table, not many times in the tblEmployee table. These are the types of errors that Rachel tests first. For example, she notes that addresses are entered only once for each customer in the tblHousehold table. Employees can verify the address with the customer when they enter this data to ensure its accuracy. Rachel also notes that all IDs are created with an

AutoNumber field type so they are arbitrary and sequential. In the forms she designs, she needs to prevent manual data entry in those fields.

Rachel examines each table in Design view to verify that field properties, such as input masks and validation rules, are in place to only allow entry of data in the proper format and within appropriate ranges. In the table datasheets, she enters test dates and phone numbers to make sure that all formats, input masks, and validation rules are working properly. She also tests referential integrity rules by trying to enter the same ID number for two records. For example, the medications listed in the tblDrug table are identified by UPN number, such as 102 for ampicillin. When Rachel tries to use 102 in the UPN field for a different drug, she receives an error message explaining that she cannot make that change because it would create duplicate values in the primary key. This ensures that each drug in tblDrug has a unique UPN.

She also tries to enter mismatching data on the many side of one-to-many relationships. For example, the tblEmployee and tblRefill tables have a one-to-many relationship— one employee can refill many prescriptions. The EmpID field in tblEmployee contains values 1–28. When Rachel enters a new refill in the tblRefill table and uses "30" as the EmpID, she receives an error indicating that she cannot add that record because a related record is required in tblEmployee. This indicates that the tables are maintaining referential integrity—only a valid employee can enter a prescription refill. After Rachel verifies that the database is designed to prevent critical data-entry errors, she deletes the test data.

Best Practice

Testing Tables and Relationships

It is much easier to test all relationships, data integrity rules, input masks, and other field properties before creating forms. If you import data from a spreadsheet, edit the data in table Datasheet view to make it compatible with your new application. For example, you might need to adjust the customer and prescription ID numbers to match the new scheme. If your database design needs further modification, complete the redesign before spending substantial time developing forms (and reports). Modifying forms (and reports) to accommodate a change in database design involves a considerable amount of work. For example, changing data types of fields and adding or removing fields from tables all require changing the forms that include those fields.

Examining and Entering Data

You can enter data into records using a table's Datasheet view or using a form that includes fields from one or more tables. Datasheet entry is efficient when you need to enter many records at the same time, especially if you routinely work with the same documents. You might also use a datasheet to quickly enter sample data for testing, especially in a table on the "one" side of a one-to-many relationship. The primary table must contain data before you can enter data in the related table, the one on the "many" side of the one-to-many relationship. However, most Access database applications use forms for data entry after the database is released for regular business use. Activities such as taking telephone orders or looking up product or customer information is more efficient and accurate with forms. For example, unlike tables, forms can include calculations so you can provide grand totals and list boxes so you can select correct items. You can also use forms to enhance the appearance of your data, making it easier to find the piece of information you need.

Rachel notes that all the tables in the 4Corners database contain data, which Don Linebarger added by importing records or entering them directly in the tables. When the 4Corners database is used every day in normal business operations, however, employees will use forms to enter data. For example, when customers order prescriptions by phone or walk-in customers request prescription refills, a pharmacy technician will open a prescription or refill form as appropriate to enter the necessary data.

When she examines the tblCustomer table, Rachel sees an expand indicator **+** to the left of the records. When she clicks the one for Ted Sabus, the prescriptions Ted received appear in a subdatasheet containing records from tblRx. (Recall that a subdatasheet is a datasheet nested in another datasheet and displays records from a related table.) If necessary, Rachel could edit or enter data in the subdatasheet to update prescription data in tblRx. The subdatasheet appears because tblCustomer is on the "one" side of a one-to-many relationship with tblRx established in the Relationships window. Records for a particular customer in tblRx are linked to that customer in tblCustomer by their common field, CustID. See Figure 4.3.

Figure 4.3: Examining data before creating forms

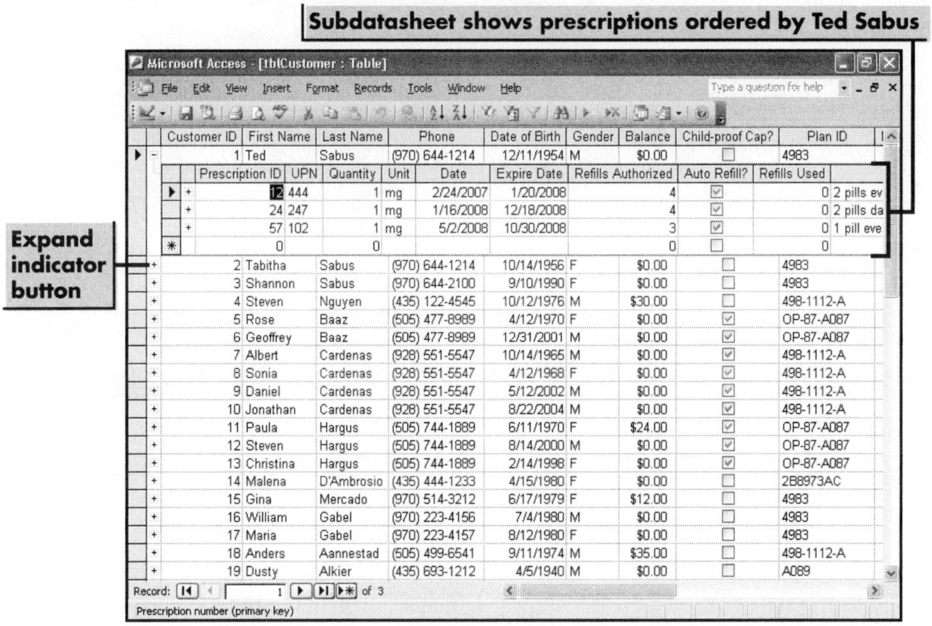

Customer ID	First Name	Last Name	Phone	Date of Birth	Gender	Balance	Child-proof Cap?	Plan ID
1	Ted	Sabus	(970) 644-1214	12/11/1954	M	$0.00	☐	4983

Prescription ID	UPN	Quantity	Unit	Date	Expire Date	Refills Authorized	Auto Refill?	Refills Used	
12	444	1	mg	2/24/2007	1/20/2008	4	☑	0	2 pills ev
24	247	1	mg	1/16/2008	12/18/2008	4	☑	0	2 pills da
57	102	1	mg	5/2/2008	10/30/2008	3	☑	0	1 pill eve
0		0				0	☐	0	

Customer ID	First Name	Last Name	Phone	Date of Birth	Gender	Balance	Child-proof Cap?	Plan ID
2	Tabitha	Sabus	(970) 644-1214	10/14/1956	F	$0.00	☐	4983
3	Shannon	Sabus	(970) 644-2100	9/10/1990	F	$0.00	☐	4983
4	Steven	Nguyen	(435) 122-4545	10/12/1976	M	$30.00	☐	498-1112-A
5	Rose	Baaz	(505) 477-8989	4/12/1970	F	$0.00	☑	OP-87-A087
6	Geoffrey	Baaz	(505) 477-8989	12/31/2001	M	$0.00	☑	OP-87-A087
7	Albert	Cardenas	(928) 551-5547	10/14/1965	M	$0.00	☑	498-1112-A
8	Sonia	Cardenas	(928) 551-5547	4/12/1968	F	$0.00	☑	498-1112-A
9	Daniel	Cardenas	(928) 551-5547	5/12/2002	M	$0.00	☑	498-1112-A
10	Jonathan	Cardenas	(928) 551-5547	8/22/2004	M	$0.00	☑	498-1112-A
11	Paula	Hargus	(505) 744-1889	6/11/1970	F	$24.00	☑	OP-87-A087
12	Steven	Hargus	(505) 744-1889	8/14/2000	M	$0.00	☑	OP-87-A087
13	Christina	Hargus	(505) 744-1889	2/14/1998	F	$0.00	☑	OP-87-A087
14	Malena	D'Ambrosio	(435) 444-1233	4/15/1980	F	$0.00	☐	2B8973AC
15	Gina	Mercado	(970) 514-3212	6/17/1979	F	$12.00	☐	4983
16	William	Gabel	(970) 223-4156	7/4/1980	M	$0.00	☐	4983
17	Maria	Gabel	(970) 223-4157	8/12/1980	F	$0.00	☐	4983
18	Anders	Aannestad	(505) 499-6541	9/11/1974	M	$35.00	☐	498-1112-A
19	Dusty	Alkier	(435) 693-1212	4/5/1940	M	$0.00	☐	A089

Rachel also notices that when she clicks the PlanID field, a list arrow appears so she can select the health plan ID. The HouseID field also has a list arrow that lets her display a list of valid household IDs and their corresponding addresses. When Rachel opens tblCustomer in Design view and examines the PlanID and HouseID fields, she finds that these are both defined as lookup fields, which streamline data entry by listing only valid choices for a field.

CREATING SIMPLE FORMS FOR DATA ENTRY AND EDITING

As with other database objects such as tables and queries, Access provides many ways to create a form, including two options for creating simple forms. Use an AutoForm Wizard to create a form that contains all the fields from a table or query arranged in a common format. Use the Form Wizard to have Access guide you through the steps of creating a form, letting you select options such as including some or all of the fields in a table or query, including fields from more than one table, and using a particular layout and style.

As Rachel continues entering test data in the tables in the 4Corners database, she discovers that data entry is easy in the tables on the "one" side of a one-to-many relationship, but takes more time for the tables on the "many" side of the relationship. In this case, she must switch among tables to make the data match in the related tables. To facilitate data entry, she plans to develop forms for all the tables in the database and to find a way to link related tables on the forms. The first form she wants to create is for tblCustomer. Because she wants to include all the fields in a basic columnar format, she decides to create the customer form using an AutoForm Wizard.

Best Practice

Determining User Screen Resolutions
Before you begin creating forms, survey your users to determine the screen resolution they typically use on their computer monitors. When designing forms, you should set the display properties on your computer to match the lowest resolution that your users have set. A screen resolution of 800 × 600 is safest. Only if all users of the database have screen resolutions of 1024 × 768 or higher should you design forms at this higher resolution. Designing forms at the proper resolution ensures that users don't need to scroll from left to right to work with the complete form. If scrolling from left to right is unavoidable, you can a split the form into multiple pages, as you will learn to do later in this chapter.

Creating a Form Using an AutoForm Wizard

Rachel is ready to create a form based on the tblCustomer table. Because she knows that other employees use an 800 × 600 screen resolution, she decides to design her forms using the same resolution so that everyone in the pharmacy can use the forms effectively. With tblCustomer open in Datasheet view, she clicks the New Object: AutoForm button 🔲 on the Table Datasheet toolbar. Access creates a form by arranging all the fields in tblCustomer in a columnar format, and displays the first record in the form window.

Access also converts the subdatasheet into a **subform**, which contains the fields from tblRx just as the subdatasheet does. See Figure 4.4. Note that the structure of the data in the table is reflected in the structure of the form. For example, the fields appear in the same order and the field names in the form match those in the table's datasheet.

Figure 4.4: AutoForm for tblCustomer

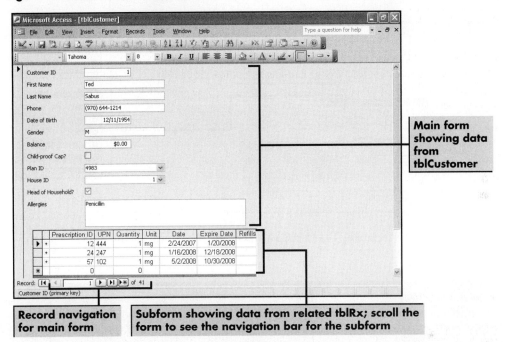

Main form showing data from tblCustomer

Record navigation for main form

Subform showing data from related tblRx; scroll the form to see the navigation bar for the subform

To move from one field to the next, Rachel presses the Tab key. To move from one record to another, she clicks the buttons on the navigation bar at the bottom of the main form. As she does, the data in the subform changes. For example, when she clicks the Next Record button ▶ on the navigation bar to view the next customer record, which is for Tabitha Sabus, the subform displays information about the prescriptions Tabitha has received. Rachel can also use the Tab key in the subform to move from one field to the next, and the buttons in the subform's navigation bar to move from one record to another. The subform provides the method Rachel sought to link related tables on a form.

Rachel notices that the PlanID and HouseID fields have list arrows in the form, just as they do in the tblCustomer table. As before, Rachel can click the list arrows to select a valid health plan ID or house ID. See Figure 4.5.

Figure 4.5: Selecting valid health plan and household entries from list boxes

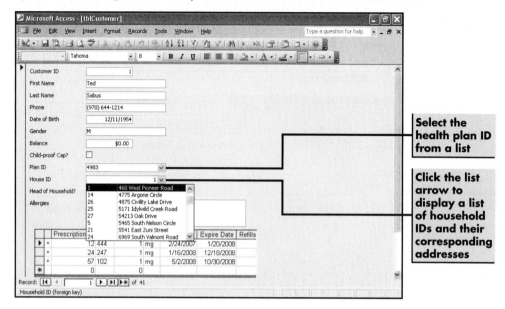

Rachel closes the form, saving it as frmCustomer. She uses "frm" as the prefix to identify the object as a form.

How To

Create a Form Using an AutoForm Wizard
1. Click the Forms button on the Objects bar in the Database window.
2. Click the New button on the Database window toolbar. The New Form dialog box opens.
3. Click AutoForm: Columnar, AutoForm: Tabular, or AutoForm: Datasheet to select an AutoForm Wizard.
4. Click the list arrow, and then select the table (or query) you want to use as the source of data for the form.
5. Click the OK button. The AutoForm Wizard creates the form and displays it in Form view.

Or

1. Open a table in Datasheet view. This table provides the fields and data for the form.
2. Click the New Object: AutoForm button 🖼 on the Table Datasheet toolbar. Access creates a form based on the most recent format you selected for creating a form.

Now Rachel is ready to create forms for the other tables in the 4Corners database.

Using the Form Wizard

Next, Rachel wants to create a form for the tblDoctor table. When she examines tblDoctor, she finds it includes the DoctorID, DoctorFirst, DoctorLast, Phone, Cell, and ClinicID fields, in that order. She thinks it would be more helpful to list the ClinicID field right after the DoctorID field on the form—technicians often associate doctors with clinics. Because she wants to change the order of the fields on the form, she can't use an AutoForm Wizard again—that feature places all the fields from a selected table (or query) on a form in the same order as they appear in the table. Instead, she can use the Form Wizard, which lets you specify field order. Rachel also wants to use a more appealing design for the form, and the Form Wizard lets her specify a particular layout and style for the form.

Rachel opens the New Form dialog box by clicking the Forms button on the Objects bar in the Database window, and then clicking the New button on the Database window toolbar. She clicks Form Wizard, and then selects tblDoctor as the table containing the source data for the form. See Figure 4.6.

Figure 4.6: Starting the Form Wizard

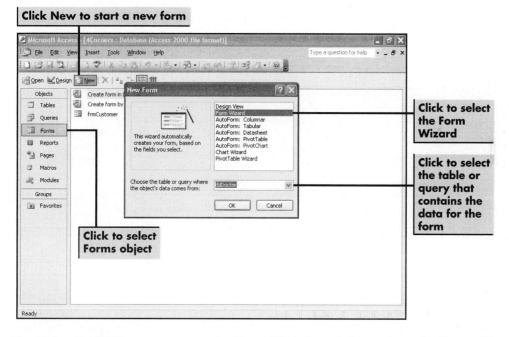

Click New to start a new form

Click to select the Form Wizard

Click to select the table or query that contains the data for the form

Click to select Forms object

She clicks the OK button to start the Form Wizard, and then selects the DoctorID, ClinicID, DoctorFirst, DoctorLast, Phone, and Cell fields from the tblDoctor table in that order. See Figure 4.7.

Figure 4.7: Select the fields you want to show on the form

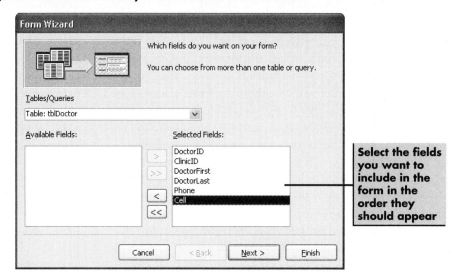

Select the fields
you want to
include in the
form in the
order they
should appear

She selects the Columnar layout and Expedition style, which uses colors and design that are appropriate for the pharmacy's location in the southwest. Then she saves the form as frmDoctor and opens it in Form view. See Figure 4.8.

Figure 4.8: Completed form for the tblDoctor table

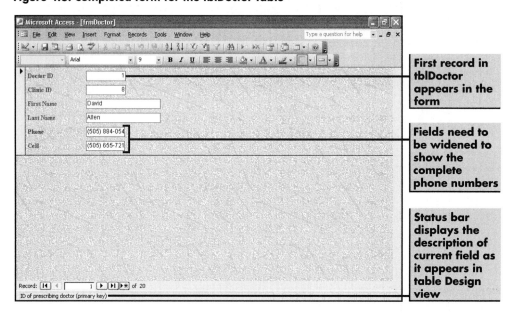

First record in
tblDoctor
appears in the
form

Fields need to
be widened to
show the
complete
phone numbers

Status bar
displays the
description of
current field as
it appears in
table Design
view

The completed form contains all the fields in tblDoctor listed in the order she selected them in the Form Wizard. Later, she needs to widen the Phone and Cell text boxes so they display the complete phone numbers.

How To

Create a Form Using the Form Wizard

1. Click the Forms button on the Objects bar in the Database window.
2. Click the New button on the Database window toolbar. The New Form dialog box opens.
3. Click Form Wizard.
4. Click the list arrow, and then select the table (or query) you want to use as the source of data for the form.
5. Click the OK button. The first dialog box in the Form Wizard opens, asking which fields you want on your form.
6. From the Available Fields list, select the fields you want to include in the form. (When you are creating data-entry forms for adding data to a table, add all fields to the form.) Use the Select Single Field button ⟨ > ⟩ to select the fields one by one; use the Select All Fields button ⟨ >> ⟩ to select them all at once. Click the Next button.
7. Select a layout for the form. A sample of the selected layout appears in the preview box of the dialog box. Click the Next button.
8. Select a style for the form. A sample of the selected style appears in the preview box. Click the Next button.
9. Type the name of the form, using "frm" as the prefix to identify the object as a form. Click the Finish button. The completed form opens in Form view.

Rachel has now created two forms—one based on tblCustomer and another on tblDoctor—that look different from each other. Before she creates other forms for the 4Corners database, she wants to determine an appropriate design for the forms and then make sure that all the forms share this design.

DEVELOPING A CONSISTENT USER INTERFACE

Recall that forms serve as the user interface of a database because most people use forms to enter and retrieve data. If all the forms in your database share the same design, they present a consistent user interface, which means users can learn how to use the forms once and apply what they learn to all the forms in the database.

Rachel thinks that the Columnar layout and Expedition style work well for the frmDoctor form—this design organizes the fields logically, and makes the form appealing and easy to read and use. Because the user interface of the 4Corners database application will comprise the forms, they should share the same design and work in a consistent way. Rachel therefore needs to change the format of frmCustomer to match frmDoctor.

Rachel also wants to display a title on all the 4Corners Pharmacy forms so that users can immediately identify the purpose of the form. To change the design and add a title to frmCustomer, she needs to work in Design view by clicking the View button ⌧. As she makes changes in Design view, she can click the View button ⊞ to switch to Form view and evaluate the effects of her changes. See Figure 4.9.

Figure 4.9: frmCustomer in Design view

Click the View button to toggle between Design view and Form view and see the effect of your changes

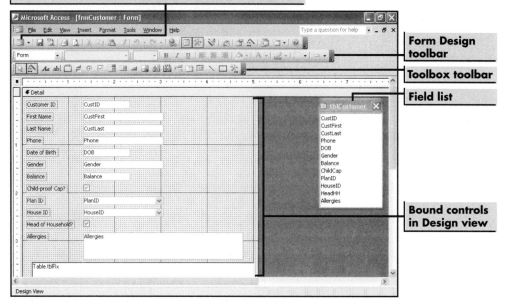

Form Design toolbar

Toolbox toolbar

Field list

Bound controls in Design view

Understanding the Importance of Consistent Style and Layout

Most developers design their forms so they share a color scheme, fonts, and general layout. Because users expect to find similar features in the same location on each form, consistency in design simplifies data entry. Follow the guidelines for designing effective electronic forms, listed earlier in this chapter in the "Designing Forms for Efficient Data Entry" section, and apply them consistently to your forms to present a unified, professional interface.

Examining a Form in Design View

The data in most forms comes from the tables and queries in the database. A form's **record source** is the underlying object that provides the fields and data in the form. A data-entry form is usually a **bound form** that displays data from the fields in its record source. (**Unbound forms** do not have a record source; they are usually designed to help users navigate through a database.) Other information on the form, such as the title, page number, calculations, and graphics, are stored in the form's design.

You link a form to its record source by using design elements called **controls**, which are small objects such as text boxes, buttons, and labels that let users interact with the form.

When you work with a form in Design view, you manipulate its controls. Forms can contain the three types of controls described in Table 4.1. Understanding when to use the various types of controls makes it easier to create and modify forms.

Table 4.1: Controls for forms

Control Type	Purpose	Examples
Bound control	Displays the field names and data from a table or query	Text boxes, combo and list boxes, subforms, and object frames for graphics that are OLE fields such as pictures or drawings
Unbound control	Displays data from sources other than a table or query	Text box that displays the results of a calculation or a label that displays the current date and time
Unbound static control	Displays text, lines, shapes, and other graphics	Labels such as the title for the form, rectangles that group related fields, or a logo or other graphic used to make the form more attractive

To place a control on a form, you use the Toolbox toolbar. Table 4.2 lists the Toolbox tools commonly used on forms.

Table 4.2: Toolbox tools for forms

Tool	Tool Name	Use the Tool to:
	Bound Object Frame	Create a bound OLE object stored in an Access database table such as a picture stored in an OLE Object data type field.
	Check Box	Create a check box control that holds on/off, yes/no, or true/false data.
	Combo Box	Create a combo box control that contains a list of potential values for the control and lets you type text or select a table or query as the source of the values in the list. You can also use the combo box to find a record.
	Command Button	Display a button you can associate with an action, such as finding a record, printing a record, or applying a form filter.
	Image	Display a static graphic image on the form. This object becomes part of the form, not part of the data from an underlying table or query.
	Label	Display text, such as titles or instructions; an unbound control.
	Line	Draw a line to enhance the appearance of the form.
	List Box	Create a list of values for the control either by typing values or specifying a table or query for the source.
	Option Button	Display an option button control bound to a yes/no field.
	Option Group	Group toggle buttons, option buttons, or check boxes. You can only select one button or check box in a group.
	Page Break	Add a page break between the pages of a multipage form.
	Rectangle	Draw a rectangle to enhance the form's appearance.

Table 4.2: Toolbox tools for forms (cont.)

Tool	Tool Name	Use the Tool to:
	Subform/Subreport	Embed another form in the current form. If the forms have a related field, Access maintains the link between the two forms.
	Tab Control	Create a series of tab pages on a form. Each tab page can contain a number of other controls that display information from another table or query.
	Text Box	Display a label attached to a text box that is bound to a field in an underlying table or query or contains a calculated value.
	Toggle Button	Display a toggle button control bound to a yes/no field. Similar to a Check Box.
	Unbound Object Frame	Add an object from another application such as a Microsoft Excel spreadsheet. The object becomes part of the form, not part of the data from an underlying table or query. You can add pictures, sounds, charts or slides to your form.

The Form Design toolbar contains a number of useful tools for designing forms. These are summarized in Table 4.3.

Table 4.3: Important buttons on the Form Design toolbar

Button	Button Name	Click to:
	Field List	Display the field list from the record source for the form
	Toolbox	Open the Toolbox toolbar if it is not open
	AutoFormat	Apply an AutoFormat or customize an AutoFormat
	Properties	Display the properties for the selected object
	Build	Start the Expression, Macro, or Code builder

Because Rachel wants to modify frmCustomer so it matches the design of frmDoctor, she needs to work in Design view. In the Database window, she switches to Design view by right-clicking frmCustomer and then clicking Design View. The Form window in Design view includes a **Detail** section for the main body of a form, which displays records and usually contains all the bound controls. In the form Rachel is creating, the Detail section contains all the fields in the tblCustomer table, with one record per page.

All forms have a Detail section, but some also include a form header, form footer, page header, and page footer. Figure 4.10 shows a blank form with these sections.

Figure 4.10: Blank form in Design view with typical sections

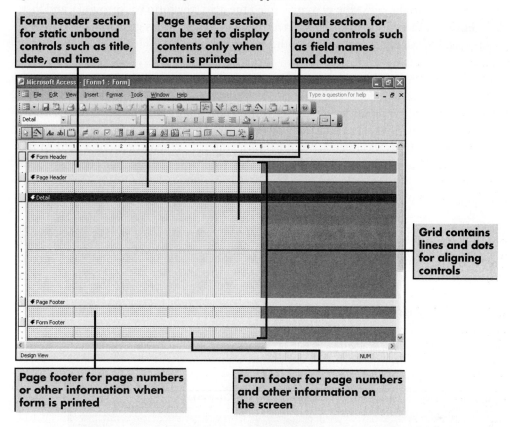

Form header section for static unbound controls such as title, date, and time

Page header section can be set to display contents only when form is printed

Detail section for bound controls such as field names and data

Grid contains lines and dots for aligning controls

Page footer for page numbers or other information when form is printed

Form footer for page numbers and other information on the screen

A **form header** displays information that always appears on the form, even when the records change. Form headers appear at the top of the screen in Form view and at the top of the first page when the form is printed. If you want to include a title on your form, you usually place it in the form header. A **form footer** also displays information that always appears on a form, but at the bottom of the screen in Form view and the bottom of the last page when the form is printed. Form footers often contain instructions for using the form or a button to perform an action, such as printing the form.

Page headers and **footers** display information at the top or bottom of every page, respectively, and appear only when you print the form by default. However, you can change the form properties to always display the page header or footer, only in Form view, or only in Print Preview and when printed. (The same is true for form headers and footers.) Page headers are useful for column headings, dates, and page numbers. Page footers are often used to display summaries and page numbers.

Forms created with the Form Wizard have a form header and footer by default, but those created with an AutoForm Wizard do not. Because frmCustomer was created using an

AutoForm Wizard, Rachel must open the form header and footer before she can add a title to the form. She right-clicks the gray area called the **grid** (the form background), and then clicks Form Header/Footer on the shortcut menu. Because it has gridlines and dots, the grid is useful for aligning controls and other items on the form.

If you need to add a field to the form, you can drag it from the field list and position it anywhere in the Detail section of the form. To open the field list, you click the Field List button [icon] on the Form Design toolbar. You can add more than one field to a form by selecting the fields you want in the field list and then dragging the selection to the form. To select all the fields, double-click the field list title bar. When you drag a field to the form, Access creates the appropriate type of control for the field based on its data type. For example, a field with a Number data type appears as a text box with a label, and a Yes/No field appears as a check box.

Customizing the Style of a Form

After you create a form, you can change its design by selecting a different AutoFormat. An **AutoFormat** is a predefined design you can apply to a form, and includes styles such as Expedition and options such as font, color, and border. Access has a number of AutoFormats designed for forms. To make the design of frmCustomer consistent with frmDoctor, Rachel applies the Expedition style to the form by clicking the AutoFormat button [icon] on the Form Design toolbar, and then double-clicking Expedition. Access applies that design to frmCustomer. See Figure 4.11.

Figure 4.11: Expedition AutoFormat applied to frmCustomer

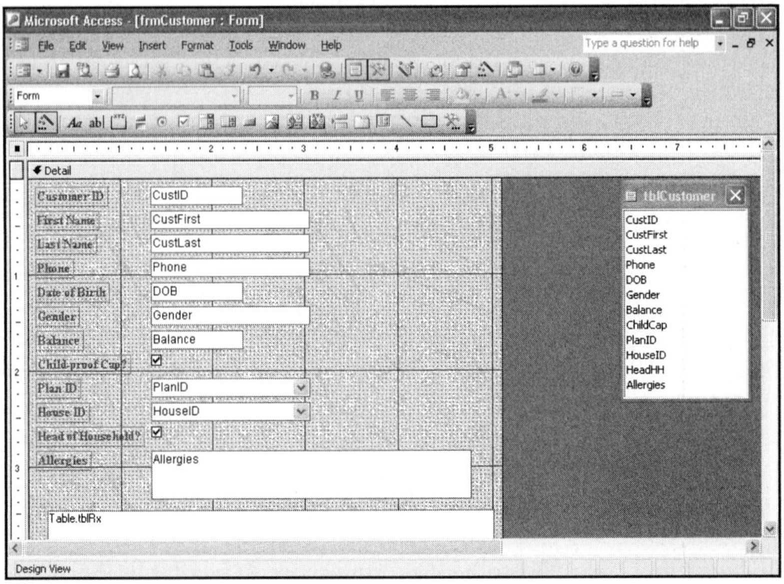

Add a Style to a Form with AutoFormat

1. Open the form in Design view.

2. Click the AutoFormat button 🔲 on the Form Design toolbar. The AutoFormat dialog box opens.

3. Select a style from the list of available styles.

4. Click the OK button to apply the style.

Besides using the same colors and fonts on each form, Rachel also wants to include an informative title. To do so, she'll work with the Label control on the Toolbox toolbar.

Adding a Title to a Form

Rachel wants to add a title to the Form Header section so that the title always appears at the top of the form. Because she created frmCustomer using an AutoForm, she must open the form header and footer by right-clicking the form in Design view, and then clicking Form Header/Footer. If she had created frmCustomer using another method, the form would already show these sections. To open or enlarge the form header or form footer, Rachel drags the bottom of the section bar to increase the height of the section. Next, Rachel creates a title by clicking the Label button **Aa** on the Toolbox toolbar. When the pointer changes to ⁺A she uses it to draw a box in the form header and then types "Customer Data Entry Form" in the box. When she checks this label in Form view, she discovers that the text is very small, so she returns to Design view to change the font. She right-clicks the new label and then clicks Properties on the shortcut menu. The label's property sheet opens. See Figure 4.12.

Figure 4.12: Properties of a label

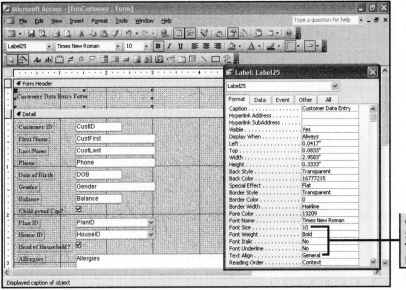

The property sheet lists all the settings you can select or enter to modify the appearance and behavior of the label. You can view a description of each property by clicking the property and then pressing the F1 key. Table 4.4 lists some common properties for labels.

Table 4.4: Common label properties

Property	Description
Back Style	Select Transparent (default) to make the background of the label transparent; in other words, the color of the form behind the control is visible. Select Normal and then set a background color if you want to change the color of the label background.
Back Color	If you want a background color for the label, specify the numeric value of the color or click the Build button [...] to use the Color Builder to select a color from a palette.
Special Effect	Specify whether the label should appear as flat (default), raised, sunken, etched, shadowed, or chiseled.
Border Style	Specify whether the label's border should appear as transparent (default), solid, dashes, short dashes, dots, sparse dots, dash dot, dash dot dot, or double solid.
Border Color	If you set a nontransparent border style, set the border color of the label by specifying the numeric value of the color or clicking the Build button [...] to use the Color Builder to select a color from a palette.
Border Width	If you set a nontransparent border style, set the width of the border to hairline (default) or to 1–6 points.
Font Size	Specify the point size of the label text.
Font Weight	Specify the font weight of the label text, such as normal or bold.
Font Italic	Specify whether the label text appears as italic.
Text Align	Specify the alignment of the text within the label.

Although Rachel could use the Formatting (Form/Report) toolbar to change the font, she also wants to use a special alignment only available in the property sheet. She uses the property sheet to increase the font size to 14 and set the TextAlign property to Distribute to space the characters evenly across the width of the label.

Best Practice

Using Undo to Reverse Changes
The Undo button [ ] on the Form Design toolbar can keep track of the last 20 changes you make to a form. When you click the list arrow on the Undo button, you can scroll down the list of actions you recently performed. If you select an action in the list, you undo all the actions since you performed that action. As you modify a form, make liberal use of the Undo button and switch between Design view and Form view often to view the changes.

To complete her changes to frmCustomer, Rachel widens the background of the form to 8 inches, and then widens the tblRx subform so that it shows as many fields as possible. In Form view, she resizes the subform's columns to their best fit. She switches between

Design and Form views and uses the Undo button  on the Form Design toolbar as necessary until she is satisfied with the result.

Best Practice

Using Unbound Controls for Titles

The label that contains the title for the form is an unbound control, so it only shows the title text—it is not bound to data in the record source. A common mistake for new database developers is to use the Text Box button ab instead of the Label button Aa on the Toolbox toolbar to create a title. However, a text box looks like a field in Form view. If you add a text box to the form header, for example, and then enter the title in the text box, an error message such as #Name? appears in the text box in Form view. This is because a text box is a bound control and Access expects that it is bound to data in the underlying table.

Saving a Custom Style as an AutoFormat

As Rachel finishes modifying frmCustomer, she realizes that she wants to use the same type of title on all the forms in the 4Corners database. She can create a custom AutoFormat that includes the style she defined for the title label. Then she can apply the custom AutoFormat to all existing and new forms using the Form Wizard or the AutoFormat button. She saves the form, and switches to Design view. She opens the AutoFormat dialog box, and then clicks the Customize button to create an AutoFormat named 4Corners Pharmacy. See Figure 4.13.

Figure 4.13: Creating a custom AutoFormat

Click to create a custom AutoFormat based on the design of the current form

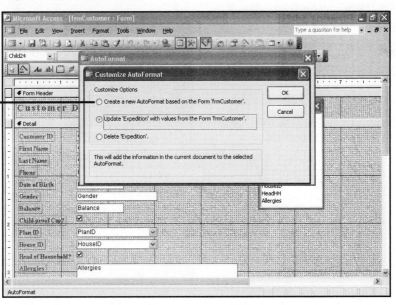

She clicks the first option button, and then clicks the OK button to create a new AutoFormat based on frmCustomer. She enters "4Corners Pharmacy" as the name for the new AutoFormat, and then she closes the frmCustomer form.

How To

Create a Custom AutoFormat

1. In Design view, open the form you want to use as the basis for the AutoFormat.
2. Make all changes to the form that you want to apply to the new AutoFormat. For example, you can change the background color, select the title font and size, and apply special effects.
3. Click the AutoFormat button 🔲 on the Form Design toolbar. The AutoFormat dialog box opens.
4. Click the Customize button. The Customize AutoFormat dialog box opens.
5. Click the Create a new AutoFormat based on the Form 'FormName' option button, and then click the OK button. (The label for this option button changes depending on the current form.)
6. Enter a name for the new AutoFormat, and then click the OK button. The new AutoFormat appears in the list of styles in the AutoFormat dialog box.

Rachel uses the Form Wizard to create a form for the tblHousehold table and applies the new custom AutoFormat to frmHousehold. She also creates forms based on tblClinic, tblDrug, tblEmployee, tblEmployeeTraining, tblClass, and tblJobTitle, using all the fields from each table. She includes a descriptive title for each form and then applies the 4Corners Pharmacy AutoFormat to each form. She replaces the "tbl" prefix with the "frm" prefix when naming the forms. For example, she saves the form based on tblClinic as frmClinic. Now she is ready to develop more complex forms than frmCustomer and frmDoctor.

Steps To Success: Level 1

To ease data entry, the Hudson Bay Pharmacy wants to create a form for each table in the Hudson database. Anne Lessard is an experienced pharmacy technician at Hudson Bay Pharmacy, and is coordinating efforts to develop the automated forms in the Hudson database. She asks for your help in creating the forms and developing a consistent form design. As you save the new forms, be certain to use the "frm" prefix as part of the naming convention. Also consult your instructor for instructions about submitting your results.

Complete the following:

1. Start Access and open the **Hudson.mdb** database from the STS folder.

2. Anne asks you to prepare for creating forms by examining the tables and relationships in the database, noting any subdatasheets and lookup fields used in the tables. Then test the relationships and verify that the field sizes and data types are appropriate. Enter test dates and phone numbers to make sure that all formats, input masks, and validation rules are working properly.

3. Anne's goal is to create a data-entry form for each table in the Hudson database. She asks you to start by creating a form that contains all the fields from tblCustomer. Navigate through the records in the main form and note the changes in the subform. Also navigate the records in the subform. Then save the form as frmCustomer.

4. Next, create a form based on the tblDoctor table that lists the ClinicID field right after the DoctorID field. Select a layout and style that make the form easy to read and use. Add an appropriate title, and save the form as frmDoctor.

5. Anne wants to use a consistent form design so that the look and feel of the Hudson database provides a uniform user interface. She approves of the design, style, and contents of frmDoctor, and suggests that you use them as the basis for creating and formatting the other forms. First, you need to modify frmCustomer so that it is similar to frmDoctor. Add an appropriate title to frmCustomer and then format and resize it as necessary.

6. Apply the same AutoFormat to frmCustomer that you used for frmDoctor.

7. Create a custom format based on the design of frmCustomer and name it "Hudson."

8. Create forms that Hudson Bay Pharmacy employees can use to enter data in the following tables:

- tblClass
- tblClinic
- tblDrug
- tblEmployee
- tblEmployeeTraining
- tblHousehold
- tblJobTitle

Save each new form with a name that replaces the "tbl" prefix with the "frm" prefix. Make sure the forms present a consistent user interface along with the other forms you've created for Hudson Bay Pharmacy.

9. Close the **Hudson.mdb** database and Access.

LEVEL 2

CREATING FORMS THAT USE FIELDS FROM MORE THAN ONE TABLE

ACCESS 2003 SKILLS TRAINING

- Add a Combo box
- Add command buttons
- Add controls to a form
- Align controls
- Create a form in Design view
- Create a subform using queries
- Create forms using the Form Wizard
- Format controls
- Modify labels
- Modify the properties of a form
- Move controls
- Resize controls
- Use combo boxes

ADDING A SUBFORM TO AN EXISTING FORM

As you have already seen, a subform is a form embedded in another form. The primary form is called the main form, and its underlying table usually has a one-to-many relationship with the table underlying the subform. The main form and subform are linked so that the subform displays only records that are related to the current record in the main form. For example, when the main form displays the record for a particular customer in the 4Corners database, the subform displays only the prescriptions for that customer.

If you use a wizard to create a subform, Access automatically synchronizes the main form with the subform only if the tables containing the fields for the form are related. The relationship can be one-to-one, one-to-many, or many-to-many. If you are using queries as the record source for the forms, the tables underlying the queries must be related. The subform must also have a field with the same name or compatible data type and field size as the primary key in the table underlying the main form.

A main form can have more than one subform. A subform can also contain another subform. This means you can have a subform within a main form, and you can have another subform within that subform, and so on. For example, you could have a main form that displays customers, a subform that displays prescriptions, and another subform that displays refill information.

Rachel examines and tests the frmHousehold form, which includes the HouseID, Address, City, State, and Zip fields from tblHousehold. This form is helpful because 4Corners considers that related people residing at the same address are part of a household, and designates one customer as the head of the household. Rachel wants frmHousehold to display only the names and phone numbers of the customers in each household.

Because tblHousehold and tblCustomer are linked by a common HouseID field, each record in tblHousehold includes a subdatasheet that displays related records from tblCustomer. However, the subdatasheet includes all the fields in tblCustomer, and Rachel only wants to display the fields related to the customer's name and phone number. If she re-creates frmHousehold using AutoForm, she'll create a main form with a subform that contains all the fields from tblCustomer.

How can she create a subform that includes only some of the fields from tblCustomer? Because tblHousehold and tblCustomer share a common field, one way to do this is to use the SubForm Wizard to add a subform to frmHousehold and include only selected fields from tblCustomer.

How To

Add a Subform to a Form

1. In Design view, open the form you want to modify.
2. Resize the form as necessary to make room for the subform.
3. Make sure the Control Wizards button on the Toolbox toolbar is selected, click the Subform/ Subreport button, and then click the form where you want to place the subform. The Subform Wizard starts.
4. To use selected fields from a table or query in the subform, select the Use existing Tables and Queries option button. To use a form as the subform, select the Use an existing form option button and then select the form you want to use. Then click the Next button.
5. If you are using an existing table or query, select the one you want to use as the record source, and then select the fields to include in the subform. Then click the Next button.
6. Choose which fields link your main form to the subform or define the fields yourself. Click the Next button.
   In most cases, Access determines the relationship between the main form and the new subform so you can choose from a list. If Access does not recognize the relationship, you can specify your own as long as there is a common field.
7. Enter a name for the subform using "frm" as the prefix for the name and "subform" as part of the name to identify it as part of another form.

Rachel opens frmHousehold in Design view and drags the Form Footer bar down to make room for the subform in the Detail section. Then she uses the Subform Wizard to add the CustID, CustFirst, CustLast, Phone, and HeadHH fields from tblCustomer to the subform. When the wizard asks if she wants to define the fields that link the main form to the subform herself, or choose from a list, she selects the Choose from a list option button and the option titled Show tblCustomer for each record in tblHousehold using HouseID. See Figure 4.14.

Figure 4.14: Defining the fields that link frmHousehold with a subform

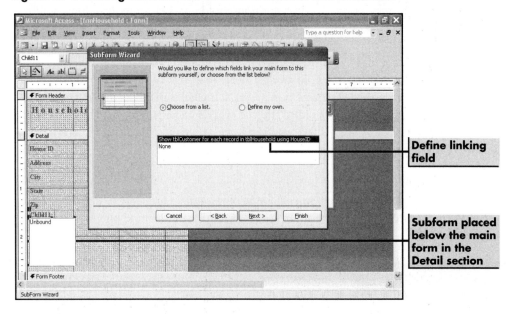

She names the subform frmCustomer subform, and then she examines the results in Form view. See Figure 4.15.

Figure 4.15: Households form after adding a subform

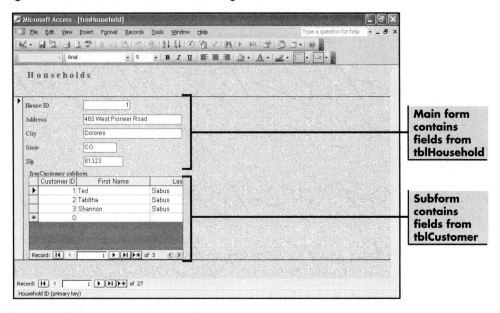

Because she needs to widen the subform so it displays all of the fields, she returns to Design view.

MODIFYING THE FORM LAYOUT

To modify a form's layout, you can move and resize its controls, including a subform. When you select a control, eight handles appear on its corners and edges. The larger handle in a control's upper-left corner is its **move handle**, which you use to move the control. You use the other seven handles, called **sizing handles**, to resize the control. To move a text box and its attached label together, you select the text box, and then move the pointer to anywhere on its border except on a move handle or a sizing handle. When the pointer changes to a 🖐 shape, you can drag the text box and its attached label to the new location.

Rachel is ready to widen the subform in frmHousehold. In Design view, she notes that she must first widen the entire form to accommodate the wider subform. She points to the right edge of the form until the pointer changes to a ✛ shape, and then drags the form so that it is 7 inches wide. To widen the subform, she clicks its border until sizing handles appear. She points to the middle-right handle until the pointer changes to a ↔ shape, and then she drags the subform border until it is 5.25 inches wide. She switches to Form view to check the results, and resizes the columns in the subform to their best fit. Figure 4.16 shows the form in Design and Form view.

Figure 4.16: Households form after modifying its layout

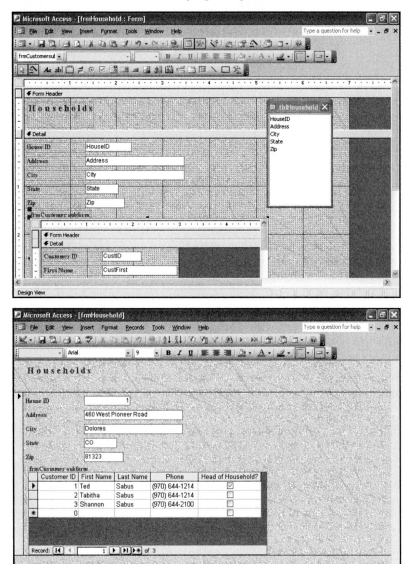

Now that Rachel is satisfied with the layout of frmHousehold, she opens frmCustomer to review its layout. She decides to move some controls so the form looks more like the paper form the pharmacy used for recordkeeping—this will help users adapt to the electronic form more quickly. She opens frmCustomer in Design view, and moves the Last Name text box and label to the right of the other controls. Then she does the same for the Date of Birth and Balance controls. See Figure 4.17.

Figure 4.17: Moving controls on a form

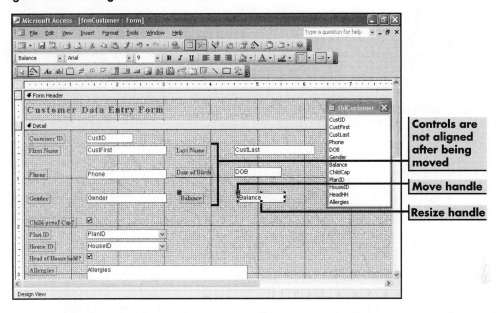

Because she moved the controls one at a time, they are not aligned. She needs to select the three controls, and then move them together so that they maintain their alignment.

How To

Move and Align Controls as a Block

1. In Design view, click a control you want to move.

2. Press and hold the Shift key and then click the additional controls you want to move. When all the controls are selected, release the Shift key. (This technique is called Shift+click.)

3. Move the pointer over a selected control until it changes to a 🖑 shape.

4. Drag the block of controls to a new location.

5. To align the selected controls, click Format on the menu bar, point to Align, and then click Top, Bottom, Left, or Right to align the controls. It might help to include other nearby controls in the selection so that they all align together.

Best Practice

Arranging Controls for Logical Data Entry

A well-designed form makes it easier to quickly add data and minimizes data-entry errors by grouping similar fields together in logical arrangements. For example, first name and last name are often grouped on the same line. The next logical line is for address, and then city, state, and zip code on another line. Matching paper forms or data-entry forms from a different application helps users accept the new application and reduces errors.

Figure 4.18: Designing the customer form to be similar to the paper form

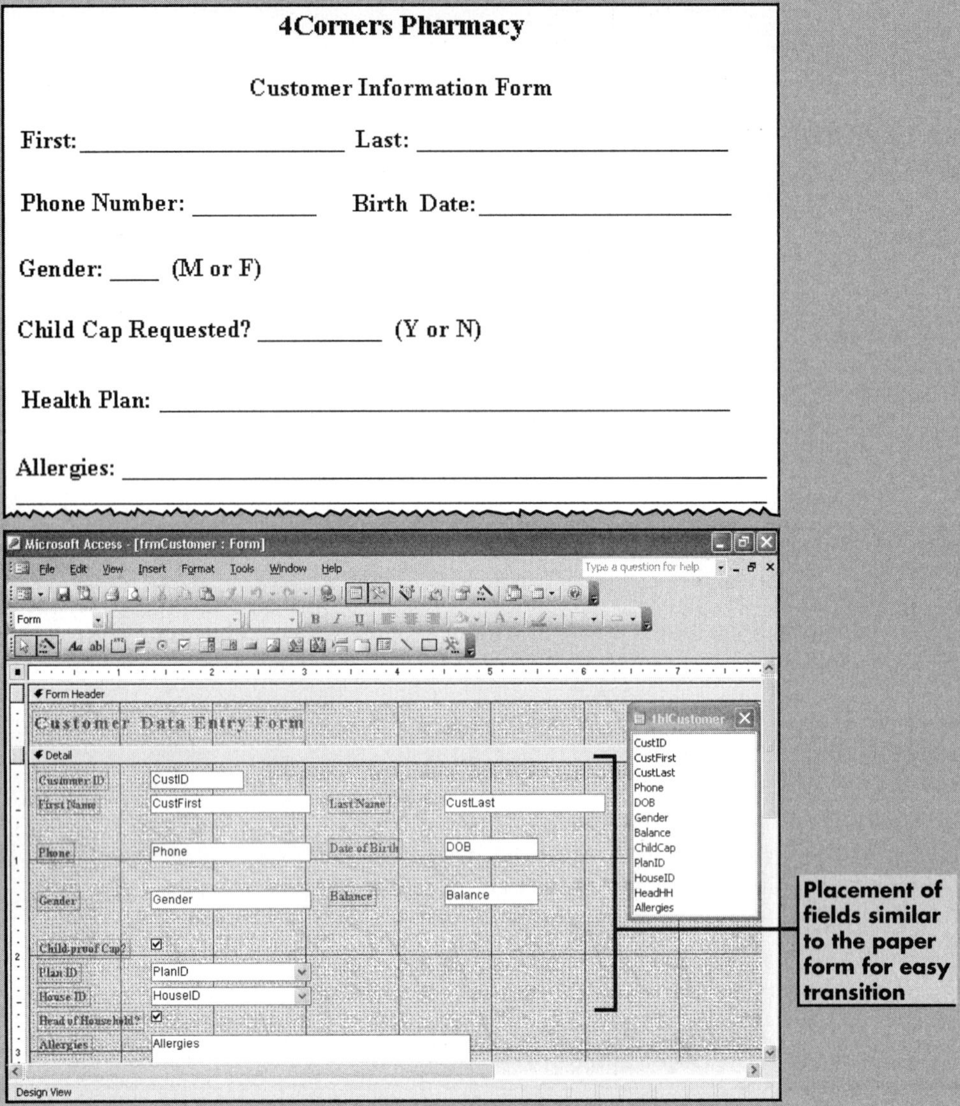

In addition to moving labels along with their text boxes, you can move them on their own. You can also modify labels in other ways, such as by editing the text they contain and resizing them. You can use any of the following techniques to modify a label:

- To edit its text, double-click a label.
- To resize a label, click the label and then drag a sizing handle to make the label larger or smaller.

- To move the label without its text box, click the label to select it, point to its move handle, and when the pointer changes to a [icon] shape, drag the label to the new location. (Note that you can do the same for moving a text box without moving its label.)
- To modify more than one label at the same time, Shift+click to select a group of labels, and then make the changes.

Rachel moves and aligns the remaining controls on frmCustomer, checking the changes in Form view. She also needs to resize some controls on the frmDoctor form—the Phone and Cell text boxes are not wide enough to display the complete phone numbers. She saves frmCustomer, opens frmDoctor in Design view, and then widens the two text boxes. Finally, she opens frmDrug in Design view, and uses good design principles to modify the form.

Now that she has modified the forms she created, she's ready to develop other forms for the database.

Creating a Form from a Query

Maria Garcia asks Rachel if she would create a form that lists the training classes 4Corners Pharmacy provides, and shows which employees have taken them. She has to schedule a number of classes and thinks this form will serve as a helpful reference when she does. She shows Rachel the query named qryEmployeeClassesDescription, which displays the class and employee information that Maria wants, and contains fields from three tables: tblEmployee, tblEmployeeTraining, and tblClass. Rachel can use this query as the basis for the form that will be a **user view** for Maria. A user view is a custom form that shows only the fields a particular user wants; it might or might not be used for data entry and, in some cases, the fields may be locked so all the user can do is look at the data.

Best Practice

Using a Query as the Basis for a Form
If you need data from multiple tables and do not want to create a complex form with a subform embedded in another subform, a query is a good way to create the necessary field list for a form. If you plan to use the form for data entry, you must include the primary keys from each table in the query. The tables must also have some common fields for the query to make sense.

Rachel uses the Form Wizard to create a form based on qryEmployeeClassesDescription. She selects all the query fields to include in the form—these are the EmpFirst and EmpLast fields from tblEmployee, Date from tblEmployeeTraining, and Description from tblClass. Because the fields come from three tables, Access asks whether she wants to view the data by tblEmployee, tblEmployeeTraining, or tblClass. Rachel pauses to think this over. If she chooses to view the data by tblEmployee, the wizard shows that EmpFirst and EmpLast will appear in the main form and Date and Description will be in the subform. If she chooses to view the data by tblEmployeeTraining, all the fields will be in the main form; Access will not create a subform. If she chooses to view the data by tblClass, the Description field will appear in the main form, and the EmpFirst, EmpLast, and Date fields will appear in the subform. Because Maria will look up this information by class and then verify which employees have taken the class, Rachel decides to view the data by tblClass. She selects a datasheet layout for the subform and the 4Corners Pharmacy style for the main form. She names the main form frmClassView and the subform frmClassView subform. In Design view, Rachel adds the title "Classes Taken" to the form header. Then she adjusts the size and placement of the other controls, and edits the subform's label text by double-clicking the label and changing it to Employees and Class Dates. Figure 4.19 shows the completed form.

Figure 4.19: User view of classes and employees

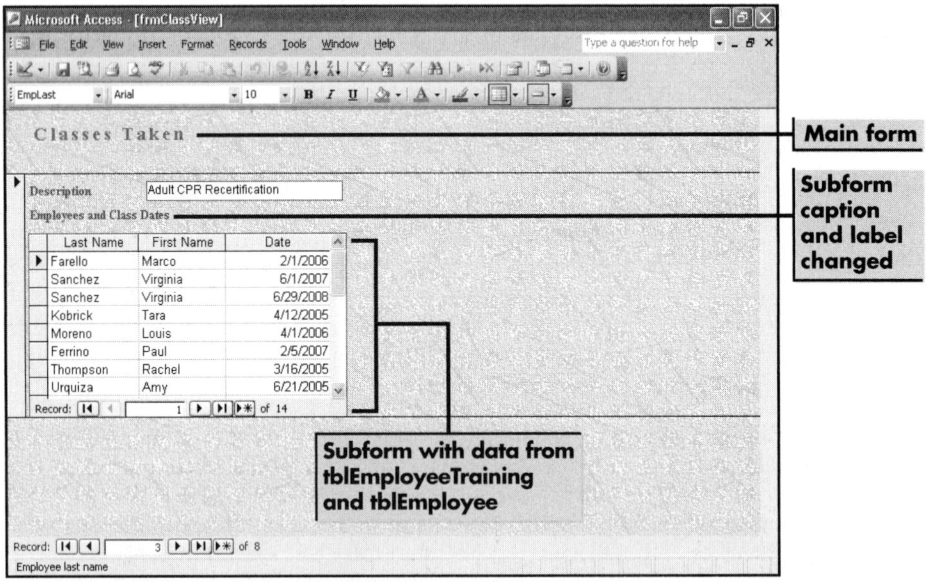

Best Practice

Creating a Form for Each Table

Every table should either have a form of its own or serve as a subform in another form. In some cases, such as to save space, you might not want to display all the fields in a table, especially on a subform. Creating a user view that contains only part of the data serves the purpose of showing only the important fields for a particular user. If you create a user view based on one or more tables, the database should still provide forms so that users can add and modify data in all the fields of all the tables.

Rachel tests the frmClassView form by trying to add a new record to the subform. However, because this user view does not include the EmpID field, the primary key in tblEmployeeTraining, Access does not allow her to add new records to tblEmployeeTraining from this form. Next, she tries to enter a new record to tblClass, which she cannot do because frmClassView does not include the primary key field (ClassID) in tblClass. She can, however, edit the value in the Description field, which could cause problems. Maria only wants to view data from this form, so Rachel modifies the form to prevent adding, editing, or deleting data by changing the Allow Edits, Allow Deletions, Allow Additions, and Data Entry form properties from Yes to No. See Figure 4.20.

Figure 4.20: Preventing additions and editing in a user view

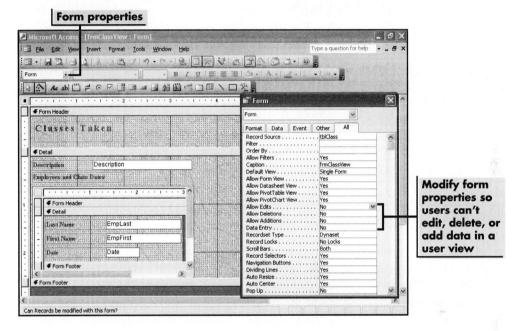

Rachel also creates a user view so that technicians can quickly view employees and their job titles without changing any employee or job information. She adds a subform to frmJobTitle that includes only the EmpID, EmpFirst, EmpLast, and Phone fields from tblEmployee, and names the subform frmEmployee subform and the completed form frmEmployeeView.

Finally, she changes the text label for the subform to "Employees." Next, Rachel wants to explore how to make the forms easier to use for all the pharmacy employees.

ADDING COMMAND BUTTONS TO A FORM

Rachel wants to make it easy for technicians and pharmacists to use the forms in the 4Corners database. She's planning to conduct a short training session and then introduce the database into the pharmacy for daily use. Rachel is becoming proficient in using Access, but not all technicians and pharmacists are. She is looking for ways to make the forms easier to use and to simplify the training process for new and existing employees so they can begin using the new application as soon as possible.

One way to make the forms easier to use is to include **command buttons** that users can click to perform common tasks. Access provides a collection of command buttons that are associated with actions such as moving to the next record in the form, adding a record, or printing a form. Command buttons can contain text, standard icons available from Access, or graphics you supply to indicate the purpose of the button. You can create a command button in Design view in two ways: by using the Command Button Wizard or by adding a button to a form and then setting its properties. Table 4.5 lists the categories of command buttons Access provides and their actions.

Table 4.5: Command button options

Category	Actions
Record Navigation	Move from one record to another and find a record using Find
Record Operations	Add, delete, duplicate, print, and undo a record
Form Operations	Open and close form, print form, apply and edit form filter, print current form, refresh form data
Report Operations	Mail report, preview report, print report, send report to file
Application	Quit application, run application, run Microsoft Excel, run Microsoft Word
Miscellaneous	Auto Dialer, print table, run macro, run query

Rachel concludes that when a form is open, users will frequently want to move to the next or previous record, add or delete a record, and close the form. She can add these five command buttons to frmCustomer that users can click to perform these tasks. After she adds the buttons to frmCustomer, she can add the same five command buttons to all the forms in the 4Corners database. She'll use the Command Button Wizard to include the buttons on the form so it guides her through the steps of creating the buttons.

She opens frmCustomer in Design view and determines that the best place to include five command buttons is along the right side of the form. She verifies that the Control Wizards button ![icon] on the Toolbox toolbar is selected—this means that the Command Button Wizard will start when she adds a command button to the form. She clicks the Command Button ![icon] on the Toolbox toolbar, and then clicks the right side of the form. The Command Button Wizard starts. See Figure 4.21.

Figure 4.21: First dialog box in the Command Button Wizard

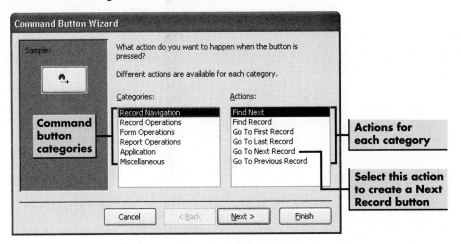

She follows the instructions in the wizard to add a Next Record button to the form. She uses the Command Button Wizard again to add the four other buttons to the form—the Previous Record, Add Record, Delete Record, and Close Form buttons. All the buttons perform the actions that correspond to their labels. See Figure 4.22.

Figure 4.22: Command buttons for typical form tasks

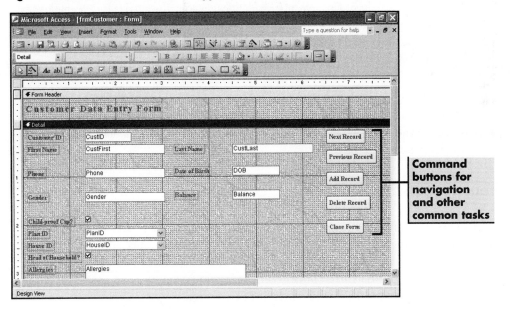

How To

Create a Command Button on a Form

1. Open a form in Design view.
2. Decide where you want to place the command buttons and move the form footer or widen the form, if necessary, to make room for the buttons.
3. Make sure the Control Wizards button ⬚ on the Toolbox toolbar is selected, and then click the Command Button button ⬚.
4. Click where you want to place the command button. The Command Button Wizard starts.
5. Click the category and then click the action you want to perform when the button is clicked. Click the Next button.
6. Click the Text option button and then type the text that should appear on the button, or click the Picture option button and then select a picture for the button. Click the Next button.
7. Enter a name for the button. This name will not appear on the form, but it should be unique. If you decide to delete the button for any reason, Access will not let you reuse the name of the deleted button. Click the Finish button. The new button appears on the form.

Best Practice

Being Consistent when Placing Command Buttons

When you are placing command buttons on forms, be certain to place them in the same order and location on all forms. Users will expect to find the buttons in the same location; inconsistency in button placement is interpreted as poor design. The goal is for all employees to be able to quickly add or edit data, not to hunt around for the appropriate button. It is especially dangerous to move the location of the Delete Record button because users might click it in error and delete records inadvertently.

Rachel also adds command buttons to frmEmployee, frmJobTitle, and frmDrug so that users can move to the next record, move to the previous record, add a record, delete a record, and close the form. To maintain a consistent user interface, she places the buttons in the same location on all the forms.

ADDING AN UNBOUND GRAPHIC TO A FORM

Rachel wants to identify the forms as belonging to 4Corners Pharmacy, so she wants to add the 4Corners logo to the forms. She'll add one to frmCustomer and then circulate that form so the managers can approve it. She opens frmCustomer in Design view, resizes the form header, clicks the Image button on the Toolbox toolbar, and then inserts the 4Corners.jpg graphic into the form header. See Figure 4.23.

Figure 4.23: Adding a graphic to frmCustomer

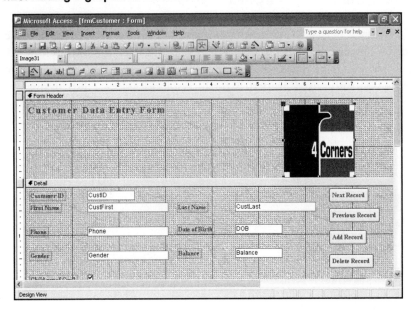

The logo needs to be smaller and moved to a better location. She clicks the image and points to the sizing handle in the lower-left corner, and then drags to make the image smaller. She can't see the entire image so she changes the Size Mode property to Zoom to fix the problem. Finally, she moves the logo to the left of the title. See Figure 4.24. Before adding the image to the forms the employees will actually be using, she'll have to check to see if there are objections.

Figure 4.24: Resizing and moving the graphic

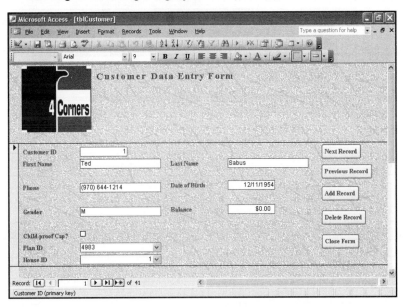

EXPLORING OTHER FORM PROPERTIES

Each form has properties that affect the entire form and other properties that affect a section of the form. To open the property sheet for a form, right-click the form selector button in the upper-left corner of the form, and then click Properties on the shortcut menu. Table 4.6 lists frequently used properties for forms and Table 4.7 lists frequently used properties for form sections. A common reason to use form properties is when you decide to base a form on a different record source from the one used to create the form. Making that simple change can prevent you from needing to start over on a new form.

Table 4.6: Common form properties

Form Property	Description
Record Source	Enter or select a table, query, or SQL statement that you want to use as the source of the data for the form.
Caption	Enter the text that you want to appear in the title bar in Form view.
Allow Edits	Select Yes or No to specify whether a user can edit saved records when using the form. You can use this property to prevent changes to existing data displayed by a form.
Allow Deletions	Select Yes or No to specify whether a user can delete saved records when using the form. You can use this property to prevent users from deleting existing data displayed by a form.
Allow Additions	Select Yes or No to specify whether a user can add records when using the form.
Navigation Buttons	Specify whether navigation buttons and a record number box are displayed on the form. You can use this property to remove the standard navigation buttons and restrict users to command buttons that you add to the form.
Height and Width	Specify the dimensions of a form.
Cycle	Specify what happens when you press the Tab key and the focus is in the last control on a bound form. The All Records option is designed for data entry, and allows the user to move to a new record by pressing the Tab key.

Table 4.7: Common form section properties

Form Section Property	Description
Force New Page	Specify whether the Detail or footer form sections print on a separate page, rather than on the current page.
Keep Together	Select Yes or No to specify whether to print a form section all on one page.
Back Color	Specify the background color for the section by entering the numeric value of the color or clicking the Build button [...] to use the Color Builder to select a color from a palette.
Special Effect	Specify whether the section should appear as flat (default), raised, sunken, etched, shadowed, or chiseled.
Display When	Select Always to display the section in Form view and when printed. Select Print Only to hide the section in Form view but display it when you print the form. Select Screen Only to display the section in Form view but not print it.

Best Practice

Including Primary Keys in Forms

If you want to use a form to add data to the underlying tables, be sure to include the primary and foreign key(s) fields in the form. Without the primary key, Access does not allow you to add new records. You can edit existing nonkey fields, however. If you do not want users to add, edit, or delete records from a form, change the properties so this is not allowed.

Most of the forms that Rachel has created so far display the form object name in the title bar in Form view. For example, "frmDoctor" appears in the title bar of the frmDoctor form. Users generally appreciate more descriptive text in the title bar, such as the title displayed in the form header. Rachel uses the property sheet for each form to change the Caption property as listed in Table 4.8.

Table 4.8: Caption properties set for 4Corners Pharmacy forms

Form Name	Caption Property
frmCustomer	Customer Data Entry Form
frmClassView	Classes Taken
frmHousehold	Households and Customers
frmDoctor	Doctor Data Entry Form
frmClinic	Clinic Data Entry Form
frmEmployee	Employee Data Entry Form
frmEmployeeTraining	Employee Training Form
frmClass	Class Data Entry Form
frmJobTitle	4Corners Pharmacy Job Titles

CONTROLLING FORM PRINTING

Rachel suspects that other employees will want to print forms and records for reference until they become familiar with the database. She therefore wants to control the form's vertical spacing on the printed page and include a date and page number on the form. Instead of using one of the forms she has already created, she uses the Form Wizard to create a sample form to test printing options based on tblEmployee, and names the form frmTestPrinting. By creating a sample form, she can avoid making changes to existing forms that might cause problems for users.

After creating the frmTestPrinting form, Rachel opens it in Design view, right-clicks a blank spot on the grid, and then clicks Page Header/Footer on the shortcut menu. The page header and footer sections open in the form. You can specify different header and footer information for the printed form and for the on-screen form. Recall that page headers and footers are a good place to display the date and page numbers on a form. You can also use the page header to include a different title in the printed version of a form, such as an invoice or order confirmation.

Access provides functions to add a date or a page number to a form. Where the date is placed depends on whether the date should be visible on the form while viewing it on the screen or only when it is printed. Keep in mind that information in the form header and footer appear only on screen in Form view, and information in the page header and footer appear only when the form is printed.

Rachel wants to include the date and page numbers in the page footer. She clicks the page footer section, opens the Date and Time dialog box, and specifies that the date should print in a dd/mm/yyyy format, such as 10/13/2008. Then she opens the Page Numbers dialog box, and chooses the "Page N" format, the "Bottom of Page [Footer]" position, and the "Center" alignment so that "Page 6" prints, for example, centered at the bottom of the sixth page. She also adds sample text to the form header and footer sections to verify that their contents appear only in Form view and do not print. See Figure 4.25.

Figure 4.25: Contents in the page header and page footer sections appear only when the form is printed

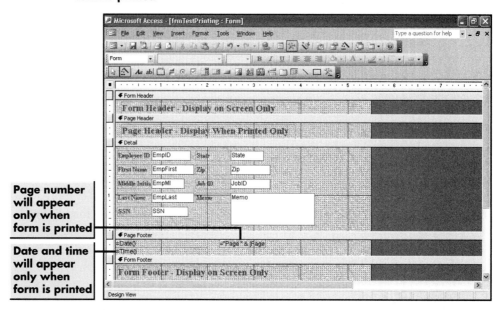

Page number will appear only when form is printed

Date and time will appear only when form is printed

How To

Insert the Date, Time, and Page Numbers
For Date and Time

1. In form Design view, click Insert on the menu bar, and then click Date and Time. The Date and Time dialog box opens.

2. Make sure the Include Date and Include Time check boxes are selected; otherwise, click to remove the check mark if you do not want to include the date or time.

3. Select the date and time formats you want to use. A sample appears at the bottom of the dialog box.

4. Click the OK button. A label containing the code =Date() appears in the page header to display the date, and a label containing the code =Time() appears to display the time.

5. Reposition the date and time label controls as necessary.

For Page Numbers

1. In form Design view, click Insert on the menu bar, and then click Page Numbers. The Page Numbers dialog box opens.

2. Select the format, position, and alignment of the page numbers.

3. Click OK. The page numbers appear as specified on the form.

Rachel also adds a page header and page footer to frmTestPrinting and displays the date and page numbers in the page footer. She adds a title for the form that will show only when printed. Now she's ready to test printing a form.

Printing a Selected Record in Form View

Rachel decides to test frmTestPrinting by printing one record in the form. First, she uses the Print Preview button 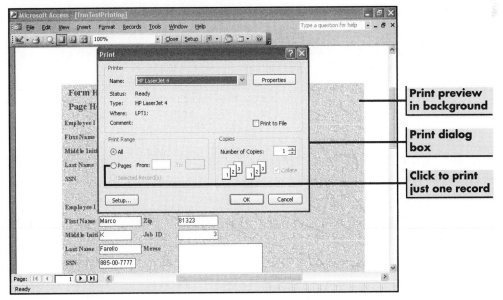 to preview the form and see how it will print. Then she uses the Print dialog box, selects the Pages option, and then enters 1 in the From and 1 in the To text boxes before clicking the OK button. See Figure 4.26. If she uses the Print button or selects the All option in the Print dialog box, Access prints all the records in the form.

Figure 4.26: Printing a record from Print Preview

Rachel reviews the printed record, and verifies that the page number and date are included on the printed page. Next, she can create the more complex forms that the pharmacists and technicians will use everyday.

Steps To Success: Level 2

Now that you have created basic data-entry forms for the Hudson Bay Pharmacy, Anne asks you to create and modify other forms to improve their appearance and ease of use. As you save the new forms, be certain to use the "frm" prefix as part of the naming convention. Also consult your instructor for instructions about submitting your results.

Complete the following:

1. Start Access and open the **Hudson.mdb** database from the STS folder.

2. As Anne and the other pharmacy technicians at Hudson Bay Pharmacy enter household information, they want to see which customers belong to a household. Knowing this information can help them make sure they have the correct address information for a customer. Modify the frmHousehold form as necessary to show the customers that belong to each household and include the phone number. Change the title to reflect your changes to the form.

3. Anne also requests a quick way to view employee names and job titles in one form. She only needs to reference the employee's name and phone number, and doesn't want to enter or change any employee or job information. She'll reference this information by job title. Create a form that meets this request, and name it frmEmployeeView. Make sure that users cannot add, delete, or modify data on the form.

4. Anne suggests that you fine-tune the form to make it more appealing and easy to use. Modify the frmEmployeeView form and its controls as necessary to display all the fields in Form view. Provide descriptive or more meaningful text labels for all the controls in the form, including the title bar.

5. She asks you to revise the frmEmployee form to meet the same goals. Organize the controls in frmEmployee in logical data-entry order. Make sure the results are aligned and attractive.

6. Revise frmDrug by using good design principles to modify the form to match the design of the other Hudson Bay forms.

7. Anne also wants to make the forms easy to use, even for employees new to the Hudson database. She asks you to include command buttons on frmEmployee, frmJobTitle, and frmDrug to allow users to move to the next record, move to the previous record, add a record, delete a record, and close the form. Be sure to place the buttons in the same location on all forms.

8. To identify the forms as belonging to the Hudson Bay Pharmacy, Anne asks you to add the logo in the **HudsonBay.jpg** file in the Chapter 4\STS folder to frmCustomer. She'll add logos to the other forms later. Make other changes to frmCustomer to make it more informative and easier to use.

9. Anne says she knows that Kim in human resources often wants to print selected records in frmEmployee, and needs to include the date on the printed copies so she can track the information. Anne asks you to modify frmEmployee to display the date and page numbers in the printed form. Make sure the title for the form shows only in Form view. Preview the form to verify that the correct information prints, while the title does not.

10. Close the **Hudson.mdb** database and Access.

LEVEL 3

CREATING FORMS FOR COMPLETING DAILY BUSINESS TASKS

ACCESS 2003 SKILLS TRAINING

- **Add a Combo box**
- **Add command buttons**
- **Add controls to a form**
- **Align controls**
- **Create a form in Design view**
- **Create a subform using queries**
- **Create calculated fields**
- **Format controls**
- **Modify a subform**
- **Modify labels**
- **Modify the properties of a form**
- **Move controls**
- **Resize controls**
- **Use a tab control to create a multi-page form**
- **Use combo boxes**

IMPROVING THE USABILITY OF FORMS

In this level, you explore using form controls as a way to speed up the process of locating a particular record. In addition, you will learn how to include a calculated control in a form, and how to create multiple-page forms and forms with multiple subforms. You will also learn about tab order, and how to control the focus in a form to skip unbound controls.

Rachel knows that the pharmacy gets very busy at times during the day and that anything she can do to decrease waiting time for customers is appreciated. One task that is currently inefficient for technicians is finding customer records—customers call for prescriptions and refills or make the request in person, and before technicians can enter prescription information, they need to find the appropriate customer record. Access provides a Find feature for finding records, but Rachel wants to see if she could develop a more efficient alternative.

Another time-consuming task is looking up the cost of a drug and its selling price. The 4Corners Pharmacy keeps track of its drug costs and periodically compares them to the selling price to make sure they are maintaining their targeted profit margin. When Rachel creates the form the pharmacists and technicians use to record prescriptions and refills, she wants to display the difference between cost and selling price for each drug. Doing so will save time for the technicians and will provide valuable tracking information for management.

Locating a Record Quickly

When a customer calls or walks into the pharmacy to request a refill, the technicians want to locate the correct customer quickly so they can enter a new prescription or process a refill. Besides navigating one record at a time, Rachel knows that Access provides two other ways to locate a record: the Find tool and the combo box control. When you use the **Find tool** with a form, you click the field in which you want to search for a particular value. Then you open the Find and Replace dialog box, and enter the value you want Access to match. Access searches for records that contain the same value in the selected field.

A combo box displays a list of values, and lets users select one from the list. As with a command button, you can use a control wizard to add a combo box to a form. Like other wizards, a control wizard asks a series of questions and then uses your answers to create a control in a form (or report). Access offers control wizards for many controls, including the Combo Box, List Box, Option Group, Command Button, and Subform/Subreport controls. To use a control wizard, the Control Wizards button ![button] on the Toolbox toolbar must be selected when you add the control to a form.

In the first Combo Box Wizard dialog box, you can specify that the combo box lists values for finding a record in the form. If you list the values in the CustID, CustLast, and CustFirst fields, for example, you can select a particular customer ID from the combo box to find the record for that customer. Table 4.9 compares using the Find tool and a combo box as ways to locate a record.

Table 4.9: Ways to locate a record

Method	Advantages	Disadvantages
Find tool	Easy to use Finds the first instance of a record containing a value that matches the criterion The Find and Replace dialog box includes a Find Next button, which locates the next record that matches the specified value Searches the entire database or only one field Matches only part of the contents of a field if you do not know the correct spelling or complete contents Starts searching with any record in the form Does not require working in Design view Searches well for a nonunique value in a field Replaces values if necessary	Can be confusing for novice users Time consuming with a large number of records May have to use the Find Next button many times to locate the record you want
Combo box on a form	Easy to use Looks for a unique record based on its primary key Creates a list using additional fields to help identify a record Lets you sort the list of values alphabetically to help you find a record quickly	Requires you to work in Design view of the form

Rachel first explores using the Find tool to locate a record. She opens the frmCustomer form in Form view and clicks the Last Name text box. This gives Last Name the **focus**, which indicates the control that is currently active and ready for user action. She clicks the Find button 🔍 on the Form View toolbar to open the Find and Replace dialog box. The dialog box requires her to type at least part of the last name she wants to locate, such as Cardenas. Because many of the customers are part of families, she might have to click the Find Next button several times to locate the record she wants. See Figure 4.27.

Figure 4.27: Using the Find tool to locate a record

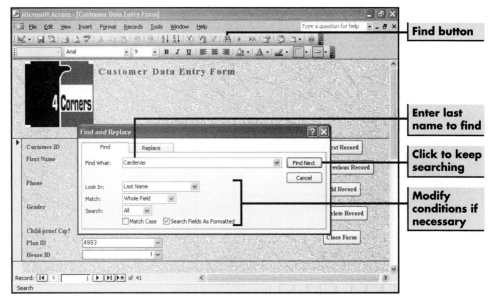

Rachel thinks the technicians and other employees will prefer using a combo box that lets them select a customer name rather than a dialog box in which they must enter a name. With frmCustomer still open, she switches to Design view and considers where to include the combo box. If she places it in the Detail section, it might be hard to find among the text boxes and command buttons. Finding a customer is probably the first task a technician will perform when adding a new prescription or a request for a refill, so the combo box needs to be easy to locate. She decides to place the combo box in the form header where it is prominent and appears to be separate from a particular record. To be consistent and use good design principles, Rachel plans to place similar combo boxes on other forms in the same place.

She clicks the Combo Box button on the Toolbox toolbar, and then clicks the right side of the Form Header section. The first dialog box in the wizard opens, as shown in Figure 4.28.

Figure 4.28: Creating a combo box to locate a unique record

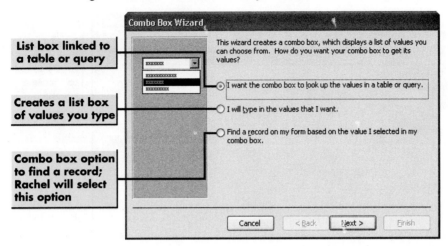

List box linked to a table or query

Creates a list box of values you type

Combo box option to find a record; Rachel will select this option

Combo Box Wizard

This wizard creates a combo box, which displays a list of values you can choose from. How do you want your combo box to get its values?

○ I want the combo box to look up the values in a table or query.

○ I will type in the values that I want.

○ Find a record on my form based on the value I selected in my combo box.

[Cancel] [< Back] [Next >] [Finish]

This dialog box provides three options for listing values in the combo box: it can look up values in a table or query, let users type a value, or let users select a value that Access matches to find a record. Rachel selects the third option to use the combo box for finding a record in the form.

Next, she selects the fields that contain the values she will use to find records. One of the fields must be a primary key field in the record source for this form, which is tblCustomer. She selects the CustID, CustLast, and CustFirst fields so that employees can easily find customer records.

Rachel completes the wizard by specifying a width for the columns of field values in the combo box list and hiding the primary key field, which does not contain information that technicians need when finding customer records. She also uses "Find a Customer" as a name for the combo box control. After she clicks the Finish button, she adjusts the width and position of the combo box control on the form. Then she tests the control in Form view. See Figure 4.29.

Figure 4.29: Using a combo box to locate a customer record

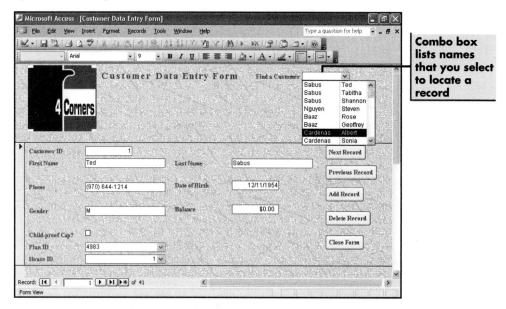

Combo box lists names that you select to locate a record

How To

Create a Combo Box to Locate a Record

1. Open a form in Design view.
2. Make sure the Control Wizards button ⟨image⟩ on the Toolbox toolbar is selected, and then click the Combo Box button ⟨image⟩.
3. Click the form where you want to position the combo box. The Combo Box Wizard starts. Be sure to leave room for the text box identifying the unbound control.
4. Click the third option button to find a record, and then click the Next button.
5. Select the primary key field and two or three other fields that will help a user to identify a record. Note that the order should be in sort order from left to right (sort on CustLast, then on CustFirst if two or more customers have the same last name). Click the Next button.
6. Modify the width of the columns of the combo box by clicking between the columns if desired to save space. Make sure the Hide key column (recommended) check box is selected if you do not want to display the primary key field values. Click the Next button.
7. Name the combo box. Because this name appears on the form, provide a name that identifies the purpose of the control, such as "Locate a Customer." Click the Finish button.
8. Modify the position of the combo box and widen the text box to display all the text, if necessary.

Rachel tests the combo box by selecting a few names to make sure they find the appropriate records. The Find a Customer combo box is working well, but she notices that the order of the customer names is not logical. She wants to investigate how to sort the contents of a combo box.

Best Practice

Including the Primary Key Field in a Combo Box List

Although you usually do not need to show the primary key field in a combo box list, you should always include this field when you are selecting fields to list in a combo box that locates a record. Access refers to the primary key as the unique identifier to use when locating the record. However, be sure to also include enough descriptive data to identify each record—arbitrary ID numbers by themselves are not helpful when your database contains many records. When you want to find records based on names, include last and first names.

Sorting the Contents of a Combo Box for Locating a Record

To make the Find a Customer combo box easier to use, Rachel wants to sort its values by name. Access sorts the contents of the combo box based on the default sort order of the record source—tblCustomer. Because the order of the underlying data in tblCustomer is based on an arbitrary ID number, the values in the combo box are sorted by the hidden CustID field. She prefers to sort the contents of the combo box first by CustLast and then by CustFirst in case two customers have the same last name. To do so, she can use the control's property sheet to specify a sort order for the record source. The Row Source property indicates how Access should provide data to the combo box, and provides a Build button [...] that she can click to open the SQL Query Builder window, which is identical to a query window in Design view and displays the fields included in the combo box. Rachel can then specify a sort order for the field values just as she can when she creates a query—by clicking in the Sort row for a field and then specifying a sort order.

Rachel opens frmCustomer in Design view, opens the property sheet for the Find a Customer combo box, and finds the Row Source property. It contains a SQL SELECT statement that specifies that Access should select the CustID, CustLast, and CustFirst fields from tblCustomer:

```
SELECT tblCustomer.CustID, tblCustomer.CustLast,
        tblCustomer.CustFirst FROM tblCustomer
```

To set the sort order of the values in the combo box list, Rachel clicks the Build button [...] for the Row Source property. The SQL Query Builder window opens, as shown in Figure 4.30.

Figure 4.30: SQL Query Builder window for setting the sort order of the combo box field values

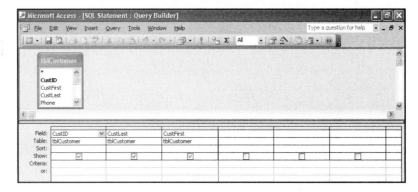

As she would do when working with a query, Rachel makes sure that the CustLast field is to the left of the CustFirst field because she wants the primary sort to be on the last name. Then she specifies an ascending sort order for both fields. She saves the settings, closes the property box, saves frmCustomer, and tests the Find a Customer combo box again. This time, it lists the customer names in alphabetic order by last name.

How To

Sort the Entries in a Combo Box

1. Open the form in Design view.

2. Right-click the combo box, and then select Properties on the shortcut menu.

3. Click the Row Source property.

4. Click the Build button [...]. The SQL Query Builder window opens, displaying the fields included in the combo box in a query design grid.

5. In the Sort row, select a sort order for the fields included in the combo box, and then click the OK button to close the window.

In addition to locating records, combo boxes are also used to speed data entry and improve data accuracy. You can create a combo box from values you type or one that looks up values in a table or query. Both improve data integrity because the user selects a value from a list rather than typing in data. You use options in the Combo Box Wizard to create these types of combo boxes as well. For lookup fields, Access creates combo boxes automatically when you create a form, as it did for the Gender and HouseID lookup fields in tblCustomer.

Rachel is finished with frmCustomer for now, so she turns her attention to frmDrug, where she wants to add a field that shows the difference between the drug's cost and its price. To do so, she needs to create a calculated field.

Adding a Calculation to a Form

Recall that you can create forms from tables or queries, and that queries can include calculated fields, which display the results of an expression that is recalculated each time a value in the expression changes. To include a calculated field on a form, most database developers create the field in a query, and then use that query as the record source for a form. In Chapter 3, you learned how to build the expression in the Field row in a new column of a query. Although most database developers recommend that you create calculated fields in a query, you can also add an unbound control that contains a calculation directly to a form.

Paul Ferrino asks Rachel to calculate the difference between the cost of a drug and its selling price. This is called gross margin. Paul wants to track the gross margin for the drugs to make sure they are maintaining their targeted profit margin.

Rachel opens the frmDrug form in Design view and moves the Cost field below the Selling price field on the form. She adjusts the width of the controls until the numbers align vertically. She inserts a horizontal line using the Line button ⬂ on the Toolbox toolbar. Then she uses the Text Box button [ab] to add an unbound control to calculate the gross margin value. For the calculation, she uses the following formula:

=[Price]-[Cost]

Note that she uses square brackets around the field names, although the brackets are not required if the field names have no spaces. She changes the label for the text box to Margin and aligns the label. She has to right-justify the calculated value so it will line up under the selling price and change its Format property to Currency and the Decimal Places property to 2. See Figure 4.31. Finally, she makes other changes that make the form appealing and easy to use, including adding the 4Corners logo to the form.

Figure 4.31: Adding a calculated field to the form

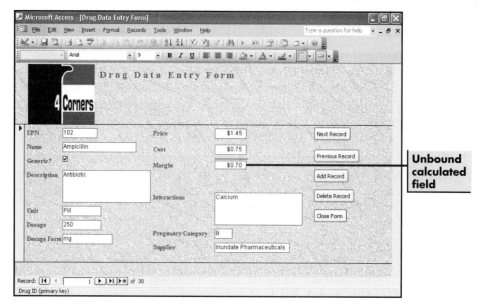

How To

Place a Calculated Field on a Form

1. Open the form in Design view.

2. Click the Text Box button `ab|` on the Toolbox toolbar.

3. Click the form where you want to place the unbound control.

4. Click again to edit the contents of the empty control.

5. Type the formula preceded by an equal sign (=).

6. Double-click the label for the control and modify its contents to make the label more descriptive.

7. To format the result of a calculation, right-click the calculated field and then click Properties to open the shortcut menu. If necessary, change the format property, such as to currency, and change the alignment of the results, such as to right-align the text.

Now that Rachel has some experience developing forms, she can work on the form that combines the main activities of the pharmacy into a central location.

STREAMLINING THE MAIN PHARMACY PROCESSES IN A COMPLEX FORM

The main purpose for the development of the 4Corners database application is to streamline the main process of the pharmacy—filling prescriptions. Paul Ferrino has put a priority on automating this business process and, if possible, making changes to the procedures in the pharmacy. Rachel expects that combining processes on a single form is part of the solution. When Donald Linebarger was developing the database, he worked with the technicians and pharmacists to understand the process necessary to fill a prescription for a new customer and a current customer. He created a process analysis by listing the steps and substeps employees perform and indicating which database objects they use to complete each task. Rachel reviews that analysis before starting to develop the necessary forms. The steps a technician and pharmacist perform are summarized in Table 4.10.

Table 4.10: Steps to filling a prescription

Step 1: Register Customer	Tables Requiring Data Input
Register customer	tblCustomer, tblHousehold, tblHealthPlan
Record prescription	tblRx
Step 2: Fill/Refill Prescription	
Check allergies and drug interactions	tblCustomer, tblDrug
Determine in-stock availability of drug	Manual at this point because database does not yet include inventory management
Fill prescription	tblRx, tblRefill, tblEmployee

Rachel develops the main pharmacy form by following the steps in the process analysis. First, however, she creates a data-entry form for tblHealthPlan and a query that displays customer and health plan information, which she names qryCustomerHealthplan. She also uses the Form Wizard to create a form that contains all the fields in tblRx, and names this form frmRx.

Step 1: Registering New Customers or Confirming Customer Identity

Step 1 in the process is usually completed by a technician. Each time a customer requests a refill for a prescription, the technician needs to enter data for a new customer or confirm the identity of the customer and verify that their information has not changed. From her analysis, Rachel decides to modify frmCustomer by adding two command buttons that allow the technician to quickly open frmHousehold and frmHealthPlan if needed. She does not need to add a button to open frmRx because data from tblRx is already included in a subform in frmCustomer. The frmCustomer form also already includes the HouseID and PlanID fields as list boxes, and employees can use these list boxes to verify household and health plan membership as necessary. They only need to open frmHousehold or frmHealthPlan if the customer is part of a new household or health plan. Rachel notices that frmHealthPlan has no form, so she creates a form and calls it frmHealthPlan. Then she uses the Command Button wizard to add two command buttons to frmCustomer— one to open frmHousehold and another to open frmHealthPlan—choosing the Form Operations category and the Open Form action in the wizard. See Figure 4.32.

Figure 4.32: Adding command buttons to open frmHousehold and frmHealthplan

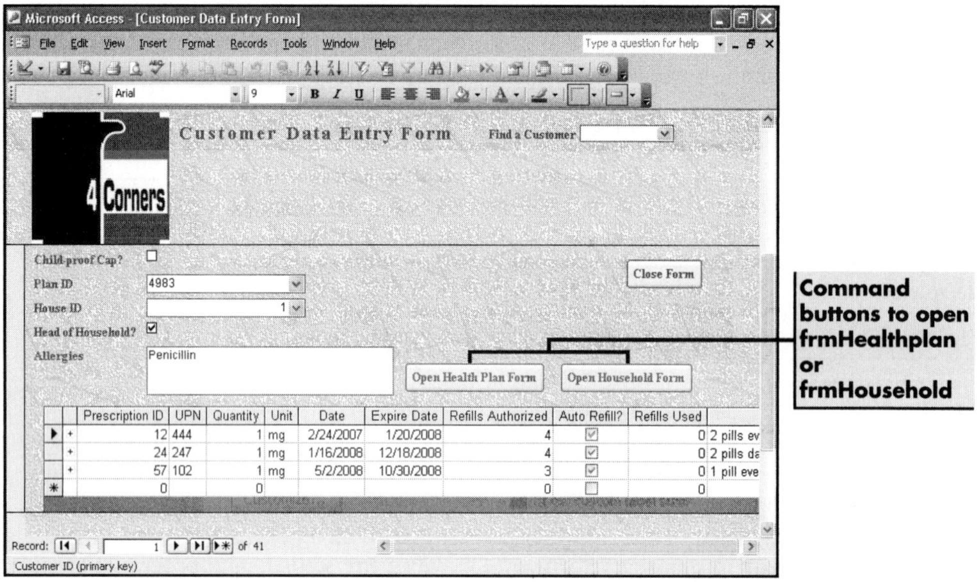

Step 2: Filling and Refilling Prescriptions

Step 2 is started by the technicians but a pharmacist must check for drug interactions and confirm instructions and dosages for each prescription. The pharmacist gives the prescription to the customer, and encourages the customer to ask questions about the prescription. Rachel consults with the pharmacists and decides that it would be most efficient to include all the prescription information on one form if possible. She decides to create the main part of the form in Design view so she can place the fields exactly where she wants them and to save space for the rest of the data. If she decides to add subforms to include data from tblDrug, tblRx, tblRefill, and tblEmployee, she'll need to do so manually. Her analysis of the necessary fields is summarized in Table 4.11.

Table 4.11: Tables and fields necessary to automate Step 2

Table	Fields to Include
tblCustomer	CustID, CustFirst, CustLast, Phone, BirthDate, ChildCap, Allergies
tblHealthplan	PlanID, PlanName, Days
tblRx	PrescriptionID, Quantity, Unit, Date, ExpireDate, Refills, AutoRefill, RefillsUsed, Instructions
tblDoctor	DoctorID, DoctorFirst, DoctorLast
tblDrug	UPN, Name, Interactions, PregCategory
tblRefill	RefillDate, EmpID
tblEmployee	EmpFirst, EmpLast

Creating Forms with Many Subforms

The focus of the form for Step 2 is the prescription to be filled, so Rachel starts by opening a blank form in Design view with tblRx as the source of the data. Rachel decides to add all the fields to the form and then to move them as necessary. The form will be crowded, so she needs to minimize the space the prescription part of the form takes. She double-clicks the title bar of the field list to select all the fields, and then drags them to the form. She arranges the fields in logical groups, according to how employees most often use them, keeping refill information together in one place and drug information together in another. She also creates a calculated field to show the refills remaining by adding a text box and then entering the following expression:

$$=[Refills]-[RefillsUsed]$$

She right-aligns the result and also right-aligns the UPN and Unit fields for improved appearance. She adds a title to the form, applies the 4Corners Pharmacy format to the entire form, and adds the 4Corners logo. She saves the form and names it frmPrimaryActivity to reflect its importance to the Pharmacy. See Figure 4.33.

Figure 4.33: The initial frmPrimaryActivity

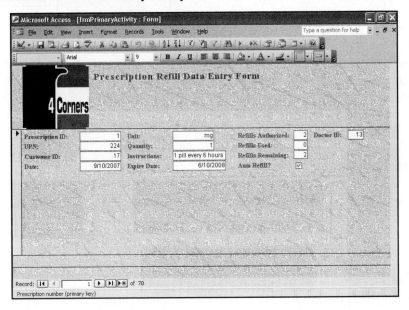

Rachel next wants to include a subform with the form that shows the refill history. To do this, she clicks the Subform/SubReport button to start the Subform Wizard, which guides her through the steps of adding a subform to the form. First, she selects qryCustomerHealthplan as the data for the subform because it has both customer and health plan fields the pharmacists want to reference. (She created this query as part of her preparation for creating the main pharmacy form.) She selects all the fields in this query.

The wizard recognizes the common CustID field that links the subform to the main form. (To link a subform to a main form, the underlying record sources must be related.)

She names the form frmCustomerHealthplan subform. To save space and prevent data errors, she changes the properties of the subform so it does not allow edits, deletions, or additions. Because each prescription has only one customer record, the subform displays only one record and, without the ability to add a new record, the new blank record does not show, which saves a line on the form. Rachel switches between Design and Form views until she positions the subform exactly. She also changes the caption of the subform to "Customer and Health Plans." Figure 4.34 shows her progress so far on the form.

Figure 4.34: The frmPrimaryActivity form with first subform

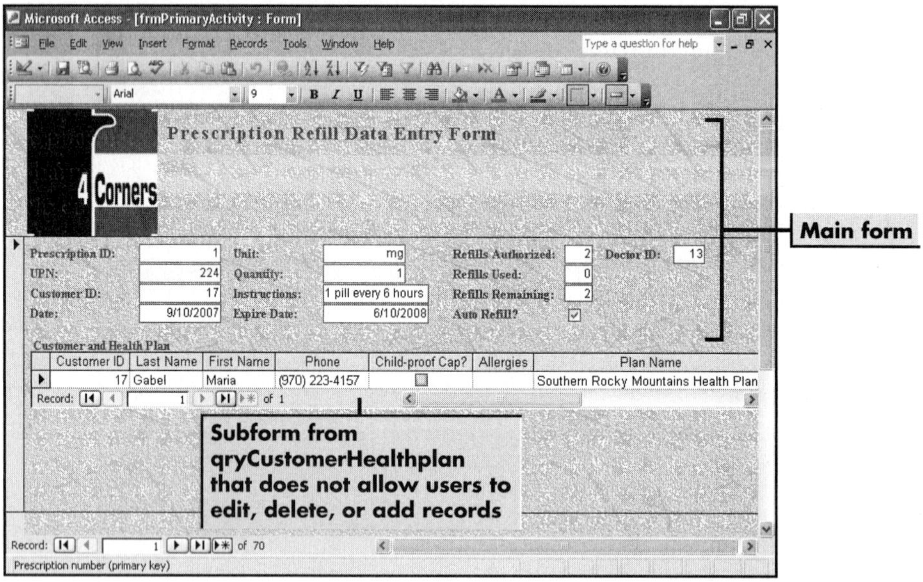

Rachel next uses the Subform/SubReport Wizard again to add the subform for the refills, using all the fields in tblRefill as the data source. Technicians need to add each refill so this subform must have add and edit capabilities. She saves the subform as frmRefill subform, changes the caption to Refills, and aligns the subform.

Then she adds a subform for the data in tblDrug including all fields except Cost, Price, and Supplier. When the wizard asks her to identify the linking field, she selects UPN, which is the common field in the main form and the subform for drug data. She changes the caption to Drug Information and modifies the properties for the subform so it does not allow additions, edits, or deletions. Because the drug information is so important, she decides to change the Default View property to Single Form, which displays all the fields in the subform using the same layout and style of the main form. Rachel adjusts and aligns the form until all fields are visible on the form, and names the subform frmDrug subform. Figure 4.35 shows the completed form.

Figure 4.35: Completed frmPrimaryActivity with three subforms

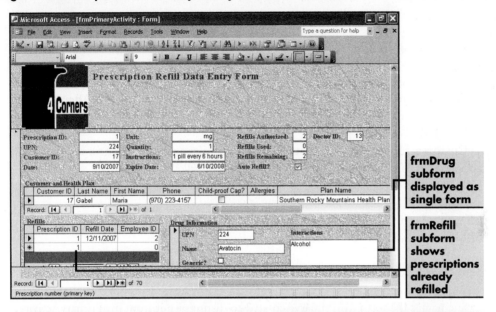

Creating Multipage Forms Using Page Break

In some applications, you might have too many fields to fit comfortably on one screen. You can continue a form onto an additional page (or pages) by placing a page break in the form 🖫 . A Page Up or Page Down key moves you from page to page.

Best Practice

Using Identifiers on Each Page of a Multipage Form

If you decide to break a form into two or more pages using the page break, users will find it easier to know where they are if you number the pages and put identifier fields on the additional pages of the forms. For example, if you are working with a form about customers, you would put bound controls for the customer first and last names on each page of the control. To keep from modifying the customer name, you can set a property to display only.

Creating Forms Using Tab Controls for Multiple Subforms

A **tab control** is another way to add multiple subforms to a form in a compact way. Each subform has a tab at the top and they are layered one on top of the other. The tabs are similar to the tabs in many Microsoft Windows applications. They are an efficient alternative to creating multipage forms using the page break control because they conserve space on the screen and allow you to add or edit data with a single form open.

Rachel and the pharmacists review frmPrimaryActivity and decide that they want more information on the form. It is not unusual for the pharmacist to call a doctor before refilling a prescription because of illegible handwriting or an expired prescription. They agree that Rachel should create a new form that includes all the subforms already created but that also has a subform from tblDoctor.

Rather than start again from scratch, she will make a copy of frmPrimaryActivity. Then she will delete the subforms and replace them with tab control subforms. She will have tabs for the customer and household query data, refills, drugs, and doctors. Then pharmacists and technicians can evaluate both and decide which form is more functional. After the form closes, she wants to see at least partial data from these tables and queries:

- **qryCustomerHealthplan**—To determine any allergies and preference for a child-proof cap as well as the days allowed for the prescription under the health plan
- **tblDoctor**—To facilitate contacting the doctor who wrote the prescription in case of questions
- **tblDrug**—To make sure the right drug, dosage, and any interactions are noted
- **tblRefill**—To add the refill date and employee information

Rachel begins by copying the frmPrimaryActivity. She right-clicks the form in the database window and clicks Copy. Then she right-clicks anywhere in the window and clicks Paste. She names the form frmPrimaryActivity2 to distinguish it from frmPrimaryActivity. She opens the form in Design view and deletes each subform by clicking it and clicking the Delete key. Next, she adds the first tab control by clicking the Tab Control button ▦. She positions the tab control cursor under the main form and clicks. Two tabs appear. She right-clicks the left tab, clicks Properties, and types Refills as the caption. She then names the next tab Customers/Health Plans. She knows she will need two more tabs, so she right-clicks a blank spot in the tab control, and then clicks Insert Page. She does this again to create all four tabs. She names the third tab Doctors, and the fourth tab Drugs.

To place the first subform, she clicks the Refills tab. Then she clicks the Subform/Subreport button. When she places the cursor over the tab, it turns black. She clicks and sees a square box that will be the subform. She selects the tblRefill for the subform and selects all the fields. The link between the main form and the refill subform is PrescriptionID. She names the form frmPrimaryActivity2Refills subform.

Next, Rachel clicks the Customers/Health Plans tab and clicks the Subform/Subreport button. She selects qryCustomerHealthplan as the data source and adds all the fields. She selects CustID as the link between the subform and the main form. She names this subform frmPrimaryActivity2CustomerHealthplan Subform.

To add the doctor information, Rachel follows the same procedure to select tblDoctor as the source and includes all but ClinicID. She links this subform on DoctorID and names the subform frmPrimaryActivity2Doctor Subform. Finally, she adds the subform for drugs using tblDrug as the data source. She selects all but Cost, Price, and Supplier fields and links on UPN. She names this subform frmPrimaryActivity2Drugs subform.

Rachel needs to modify the subform on each tab next. She decides to move each subform to the left on the tab and to change the captions to the same names as the tabs. Except for the Refills subform, she makes sure the Default View property is Single Form and sets other properties not to allow additions, edits, or deletions. She moves and aligns the controls. See Figure 4.36.

Figure 4.36: Form with tab controls

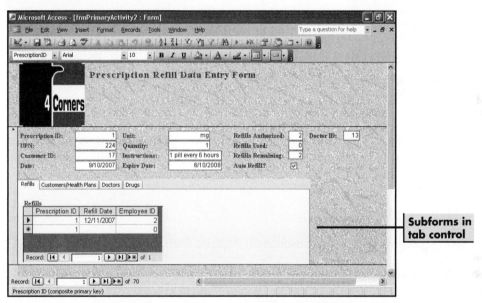

The pharmacists are delighted with the functionality of the new form. Rachel can add other tabs as they begin using the form, if necessary. Now she needs to complete a number of steps before the form is finished. She must arrange fields in logical groups, widen subforms to show all fields, and add a Find a Prescription combo box.

Changing Tab Order and Tab Stop

A form created with the AutoForm or Form Wizard places the fields in the order they appear in the table design. In many cases, that is sufficient. However, after the fields are rearranged for more logical data entry, the form needs modification to arrange the order of movement through the fields. This order is called the **tab order**.

Rachel tests each form as she modifies it by opening the form and pressing the Tab key to see if the cursor stops in each field in an appropriate order. If not, she will change the tab order until the flow from field to field is an order that facilitates data entry.

How To

Change the Tab Order on a Form

1. Open the form in Design view.
2. Right-click the form and select Tab Order on the shortcut menu. The Tab Order dialog box opens.
3. Click Auto Order. Access attempts to redo the tab order based on the location of the fields on the form. Click OK.
4. Switch to Form view to test the result. If the order is satisfactory, you are done.
5. If the order is still not satisfactory, switch to Design view, open the Tab Order dialog box again, click to select a row, and then drag it to a new position.
6. For any field you do not want to have the focus, right-click the field, click Properties, and change the Tab Stop setting to No.

Rachel has completed a full set of forms for the 4Corners database, including one data-entry form for each table in the database, and a complex form for daily use.

Steps To Success: Level 3

Anne asks you to create the primary forms that the Hudson Bay Pharmacy technicians and pharmacists will use to perform their daily activities. As you save the new forms, be certain to use the "frm" prefix as part of the naming convention. Also consult your instructor for instructions about submitting your results.

Complete the following:

1. Start Access and open the **Hudson.mdb** database from the STS folder.

2. In the frmEmployee form, add a combo box to locate an employee.

3. Sort the employee names in the combo box.

4. Add a calculated control to frmEmployee to calculate the employees' ages.

5. Modify the tab order as needed.

6. Do not allow a tab stop on the calculated field.

7. Create the main form for frmPrimaryActivity using fields from tblRx, tblRefill, tblDrug, and the qryCustomerHealthplan. (Create this query first, including six fields from tblCustomer to display the customer ID, name, phone number, child-proof cap preference, and allergy information, and the name of the health plan from tblHealthPlan.) Add the **HudsonBay.jpg** logo from the Chapter 4/STS folder to frmPrimaryActivity.

8. Make sure that the controls and subforms are aligned and attractive on the form.

9. Change the tab order to make data entry flow logically.

10. Create a tab control for frmPrimaryActivity2, as shown in Figure 4.36.

11. Add subforms to each tab and modify to show all the fields. Create the following subforms: Refills tab—frmRefillSubform, Customers/Health Plans tab—frmCustomerHealthplanSubform, Doctors tab—frmDoctorSubform, and Drugs tab—frmPrimaryActivity2DrugsSubform.

12. Add command buttons for next record, previous record, add a record, delete a record, and close the form.

13. Add a command button to open frmCustomer in case the pharmacists need more information about other prescriptions for a customer.

14. Add the **HudsonBay.jpg** logo from the Chapter 4/STS folder to frmEmployee. Size it and make sure you can see the entire image.

15. Close the **Hudson.mdb** database and Access.

4

Chapter Exercises

CHAPTER SUMMARY

This chapter presented many techniques that are useful for creating forms that can be used in data entry and editing. Although data can be directly entered in tables, forms are especially useful when the relationships between tables are complex and users need to have access to data from several related tables at a time. In Level 1, you learned about using an AutoForm Wizard and the Form Wizard to create forms. You learned about the importance of a consistent user interface and how it is best achieved. You also examined properties of forms and ways to create your own custom style and format for forms.

Level 2 moved into coverage of forms that use data from more than one table. You learned how to modify the form layout of forms and how to add subforms to an existing form. You also learned about user views created with only portions of the data for specific applications. You learned how command buttons can perform many actions and how they help with user navigation. In addition, properties of forms and printing options were discussed.

Level 3 expanded the discussion of how forms might be involved in automating and streamlining business processes for the primary activities of a business by focusing on the usability and functionality of forms. You learned how to add calculations to forms. You saw how multitable forms could be created using multiple subforms and tab controls. You also learned how to change the flow of data entry with tab stops and tab order.

CONCEPTUAL REVIEW

1. Why is it important to test your database before beginning the process of developing forms and reports?

2. When is it more appropriate to enter data in Datasheet view?

3. What are the differences between forms created with AutoForm and the Form Wizard?

4. What is the reason for working to have a consistent style and layout, especially of command buttons?

5. Explain the difference between a bound control and an unbound control.

6. What is a user view and why would you create one?

7. If you wanted to print out a selected record of a form, how would you modify the form?

8. Name two ways to locate a record rather than just moving from record to record.

9. Why would you create a calculated field on a form rather than adding a field to the table?

10. Why would you choose to use a tab control for various subforms rather than multiple pages on the form?

11. What's the difference between a tab order and a tab stop? Why use a tab stop at all?

CASE PROBLEMS

Case 1—Providing Efficient Data-Entry Forms for NHD Development Group Inc.

Operations Management

In this project, you continue working on the database for an antique mall, Memories Antiques in Cleveland, Tennessee. You have been working with Linda Sutherland, the manager of the mall, and with Tim Richards, CIO of the NHD development group, which owns this mall and several other malls across the country. Their main concern is that the database include forms that make data entry easy and efficient.

Complete the following:

1. Start Access and open the **Antiques.mdb** database from the Case 1 folder.

2. Linda has requested an easy way to browse customer data along with the classes to which customers have enrolled. She wants to also use this form to quickly mark the record when the customer has paid for a particular class. Create the requested form and save it as frmCustomersAndClasses.

3. Linda has just given you a list of three customers who have paid for one or more classes. Use your frmCustomersAndClasses to record these payments according to the following table (that is, mark them as paid).

Table 4.12: Customers who have paid

Customer	Class ID
Angela Sutherland	5
Chloe Chastaine	10
Dianne Taylor	8

4. Linda likes the form you created and asks that you create a similar form for entering all data in the database. As you discuss this task with Tim, he suggests that you provide a form for every table except the Class Enrollment table. Save each new form with a name that replaces the "tbl" prefix with the "frm" prefix. Make sure the forms present a consistent user interface along with the other forms you've created for the antiques mall.

   As you build the forms, consider the design, arrangement of fields, and general attractiveness of the form. Select the layout and style that provides the best "look" for this application. Be sure to review your work and make any modifications necessary to create an attractive and simple way to work with the data in each of the existing tables.

5. Tim suggests that you add an appropriate title to each form and also add the NHD company logo. In Design view, open each of the forms you created and add an appropriate title to the header section of the form. For example, on the customer form, you might add "Customer Data Entry Form". Make the label text large (minimum of 18 points) and bold. Also add the company logo to the form (**NHD-logo.jpg** located in the Chapter 4/Case 1 folder). Resize the graphic as necessary to fit.

6. Use each form to browse the records of the form, making sure that all the data is fully displayed in the text boxes. Make any changes that are necessary to the form.

7. Close the **Antiques.mdb** database and Access.

Case 2—Providing Data-Entry Forms for MovinOn Inc.

Human Resources

In this project, you continue working with Robert Iko, the information manager for MovinOn. Robert asks you to begin building forms that let users view and enter data. He suggests that you start by building some simple forms that will be used for entering data into the customers, drivers, employees, trucks, and warehouses tables. He also needs a few more sophisticated forms that you can base on queries or multiple tables.

Complete the following:

1. Open the **MovinOn.mdb** database from the Case 2 folder.

2. Robert states that he wants to have simple data-entry forms for each of the following tables: customers (frmCustomerData), drivers (frmDriverData), employees (frmEmployeeData), vehicles (frmVehicleData), and warehouses (frmWarehouseData). Create those forms and save them in the database using appropriate form names. As you create the forms, consider the design and layout of the form. Make selections that you feel are most appropriate for this application.

3. Open each form and view it from the perspective of the user. As you observe the form, make decisions as to what fields need to be rearranged, sized, aligned, and so on. You might even decide that a particular field doesn't need to be on the data-entry form. For example, when you are entering a customer's records, would you need the balance field for that customer? Be sure each form is attractively presented.

4. While you have been working, Robert located the logo for MovinOn (**MovinOn-logo.jpg** located in the Chapter 4/Case 2 folder). He asks you to include the logo as well as a title on each of your forms, and continue doing so to include them on all forms you create in the future.

5. When Robert reviews the employee data form, he notices a modification that would improve the look of the form. Robert thinks it would look better to remove the memo field from the form and replace it with a button that will bring up a separate form where the user can record notes about the employee. The form should display the employee's name as Last, First in a single text box along with the memo field. The form does not need to contain the company logo, but it should give the user the instruction to enter notes about the employee. Robert cautions you that the user should not be able to navigate this form and should not be able to change the name of the employee from the form.

6. The human resources department has asked that you create a form with which they can view the warehouses and the employees who work in each warehouse. This form is not to be used for data entry, rather the HR department will use it to view the employee assignments and review the salaries by warehouse. Robert has assigned you to create this form. In the main form, Robert asks that you place the pertinent data from the warehouse table. In this case, you do not need to add all the fields from the table. In the subform, Robert asks that you place data from the employees table that shows the employees for each warehouse, their position title, and what they are paid. (Note: remember that some of the employees are paid a salary and some are paid an hourly rate. For this form, you will need both fields included.) As always, check your work carefully and make any adjustments you feel are necessary. Name this form frmWarehouseAndEmployees.

7. When you present the form to Robert, he states that human resources may want to add employees from this form; he suggested that you add a command button that will open the form used for entering new employees. You should already have a form for entering employees. Create the necessary command button, making sure that it properly opens the employees form.

8. Robert tells you that the human resources department has made another request. As they reviewed employee data, they noticed that employee reviews have not been recorded in the database. Prior to the creation of this database, employee reviews were done on paper and stored in a file cabinet. Human resources plans to record their reviews directly into the database. They have requested a form they can use to enter the results of their employee review. The information will be recorded in the Review memo field with a free format (that is, the HR representative who does the review will simply write notes into this memo field). Reviews are done every three years. Your form, then, should display only those employees who have been employed more than three years. Create a query that will limit the data to employees who fit this specification, and then create a form that will properly display the employee data (all fields). Robert suggests that you use the same technique as you used on the employee form to open a separate form in which HR can record their notes about the employee. Name the form frmEmployee3YearReviews, and use a similar name for the corresponding query.

9. Close the **MovinOn.mdb** database and Access.

Case 3—Creating Data-Entry Forms for the Hershey College Intramural Department

Operations Management

In this project, you continue your work for Carla Stockman, assistant director of the intramural department at Hershey College. You have already created several tables and queries for the intramural department database. In this project, you create some forms that will be used to enter and update data. Carla has requested that you create forms for each of the tables in the database. This will allow the department staff and student workers to enter data easily and efficiently.

After you create the simple forms, Carla asks that you create some forms that will be used to assign students to teams in their chosen sport. Carla states that it would be best to show the teams at the top of the form and that it would be helpful if the teams can be browsed by sport (for example, first you see the basketball teams, then the baseball teams, and so on). She has asked that the lower portion of the form contain information related to the students who are assigned to that team.

Complete the following:

1. Open the **Hershey.mdb** database from the Case 3 folder.

2. As Carla requested, create some simple forms for entering and modifying data related to coaches, equipment, fields, maintenance personnel, sports, students, and teams. Be sure each form has an appropriate title, the Hershey College logo (**HC-logo.jpg** located in the Chapter 4/Case 3 folder), the fields are attractively arranged, and the data is fully displayed when browsing records. Carla has stated that she does not want to see just an ID on the forms. Rather, she wants to see the pertinent information related to that ID. For an example, she cites the form that will display field data. There is an ID for the maintenance personnel. Carla wants to see the name of the maintenance personnel as well as the contact information. Carla wants you to carry out this suggestion throughout the forms you create. You should decide how much additional information is important to include on each form.

3. Carla has reviewed the forms you created and is pleased with the way they look. However, she found it difficult to locate particular records. Carla has asked if you could provide a simple way for her to select the particular record she wants to view. If you can do this, she asks that you add this feature to the student, coach, and maintenance personnel forms.

4. Carla has expressed a need to see the details related to the team assignments. She wants for you to separate the data somehow so that she can view each category of detail separately. The team details would include the identity of the team (Team ID and Sport Name) along with the following categories of information:

- The coach of the team, along with the coach's contact information
- The field assigned to the team, along with the contact information for the maintenance person responsible for that field
- Equipment, description, and storage building
- The players on the team, along with their contact information

5. Carla is very pleased with what you have provided so far. She has asked for one more form that will help the staff review the coaching assignments. Carla wants to have a form that will show the coaches in one part of the form and the teams they coach in another part. She also asks you to provide a command button that the staff can click to add coaches to the database.

6. Review all your work and make appropriate changes where necessary.

7. Save your work, close the database, and close Access.

Developing Effective Reports
Accounting: Supporting Sales and Managerial Decision Making

"Nothing succeeds like reports of success."
—Sue Sanders

LEARNING OBJECTIVES

Level 1

Create and modify basic reports
Improve the information content of reports by sorting and summarizing
Create labels using the Label Wizard

Level 2

Create a custom report
Add calculations to a report
Look at Design view and properties

Level 3

Define conditional formatting rules in a report
Develop reports with subreports
Develop graphs

TOOLS COVERED IN THIS CHAPTER

AutoReport: Columnar
AutoReport: Tabular
Chart Wizard
Conditional formatting
Label Wizard
Page breaks
Queries
Report Wizard
Sorting and Grouping
Subreports

CHAPTER INTRODUCTION

So far, you have learned how to create a database with related tables, develop queries that can be used as the basis for forms and reports or for ad hoc decision making, and design forms for data entry and editing. This chapter examines another important part of database development—reports that reflect the information in the database, summarize business activities, or provide details about your data. You can use reports to format your data in an attractive and informative layout for printing, though you can also view reports on screen. Reports are often used by managers and others to determine whether their business is meeting its objectives. Reports also provide information that supports strategic decision making for the future.

5

Many of the skills you learned in previous chapters will prove useful as you begin creating reports, especially when developing queries and designing forms. Because reports are often based on data in multiple tables, database designers frequently use queries as the basis of the reports. Your proficiency with queries will therefore help you create effective reports. In addition, many form concepts and techniques apply to reports. For example, you use the same Toolbox toolbar for designing forms and designing reports.

In Level 1, you will learn three ways to create a report: using AutoReport, using the Report Wizard, and basing a report on a query. You will also learn how to sort and group data in reports and create and modify mailing labels and other types of labels. In Level 2, you will create more complicated reports, such as those that summarize performance with subtotals and percentages on grouped data. You will learn how to add controls to reports, including those that calculate subtotals and use other aggregate functions. In Level 3, you will learn how to define conditional formatting rules in a report to highlight important performance results and add subreports and graphs to reports.

CASE SCENARIO

Elaine Estes is the store manager for 4Corners Pharmacy. She watched with interest as Rachel Thompson created forms for the pharmacy. Elaine can see that many of the problems Rachel solved when designing forms are similar to those she will have as she develops reports. As the pharmacy becomes busier and the customers and managers require more feedback about their transactions, Elaine needs to prepare a number of reports to reduce response time for refills and assist in decision making and customer relations. One of Elaine's job responsibilities is to monitor the growth of the pharmacy and to report to Paul Ferrino, the owner, about how well the pharmacy is meeting its monthly and annual objectives and long-term strategic goals. Elaine decides to poll the employees and Paul Ferrino to discover what reports would be the most helpful to them. Then she can begin creating simple reports and designing more comprehensive ones with Microsoft Office Access 2003.

Accounting

LEVEL 1

CREATING SIMPLE REPORTS AND LABELS

ACCESS 2003 SKILLS TRAINING

- **Add a date to a report**
- **Add a page number to a report**
- **Align controls**
- **Check errors in a report**
- **Create a report using Report Wizard**
- **Create mailing labels**
- **Format a report**
- **Modify labels**
- **Set group and sorting options for reports**
- **Use AutoFormats**

UNDERSTANDING REPORTS

A **report** presents the information from one or more database tables in a printed format. Although you can print other Access objects, such as forms and table datasheets, reports provide the most options and advantages for printing database content—you can organize and format information to create a professional presentation, include numeric and textual data, and maintain flexibility when displaying summary information. For example, in a report that shows sales by employee, you can display the total goods sold by each employee and highlight each total as a percentage of the grand total. Typical business reports include sales summaries, purchase orders, mailing labels, invoices, and phone lists.

Access reports can use many design elements, though all should contribute to the purpose of the report and serve its audience. For example, you can combine text, calculations, charts, and graphic elements to create a report that appeals to financial managers, sales personnel, stockholders, or employees and communicates the data clearly and effectively.

Like queries and forms, reports extract information from your database. Where a query retrieves records according to criteria you specify and a form provides an easy-to-use interface for viewing and editing database information, a report lets you precisely control and organize the appearance of information that you distribute to others, usually within your organization. The power and flexibility of a report is related to its design—after you create and save a report design, you can use it again to update the contents every time you print the report.

Use a report to accomplish the following goals:

- Create a printed copy of information that you use regularly.
- Distribute information to others.
- Customize the organization and appearance of printed information, presenting data in an appealing format with graphics, lines, charts, and meaningful colors.
- Group or summarize information for reporting to others, calculating running totals, group totals, grand totals, and percentages of totals.

Many of the methods you have learned for creating forms also work for creating reports. Table 5.1 summarizes the similarities and differences between forms and reports.

Table 5.1: Comparing forms and reports

Task	Applies to Forms	Applies to Reports
Use a wizard to quickly create a report or form based on the data in tables or queries.	X	X
Create a form or report using fields from more than one table without creating a query first.	X	X
Work in Design view to place controls in sections such as the detail, page header, and page footer sections using the Toolbox toolbar.	X	X
Insert subforms or subreports that link to a common field in the main part of the form or report.	X	X
Include calculated fields to perform calculations with the values in fields.	X	X
Move, resize, and format controls.	X	X
Provide customized formats and styles.	X	X
Modify the data underlying a form or report.	X	
Group data to increase information content by showing detail and summary data together.		X

Overall, reports are primarily designed to be printed, while forms are designed to be viewed on screen. In addition, reports usually have more calculations, such as subtotals and totals. Also, although you can create reports in Design view, you view the results in Print Preview. Finally, layout and alignment are more critical with reports because variations in alignment are more obvious when printed.

Choosing the Appropriate Type of Report

Before you develop a report, determine its purpose and audience. Then you can select the appropriate type of report. For example, sales staff might use a detailed report to determine product availability, whereas management might need a summary or grouped report to analyze annual performance. Figure 5.1 shows common types of reports you can create in Access.

Figure 5.1: Examples of Access reports

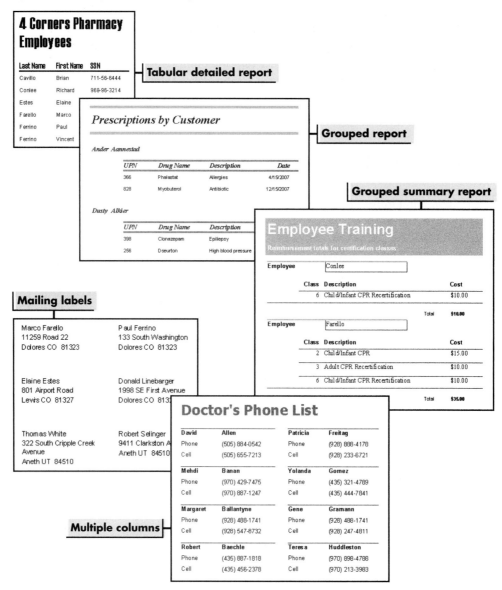

A **detailed report** lists data from a table or query, such as the tblEmployees table. A **grouped report** organizes data into groups, such as prescriptions by customer or sales by date. A **summary report** is a grouped report that calculates totals for each group and a grand total for the entire report, and doesn't necessarily include details. In a **mailing labels report**, you print names and addresses in a format suited for your mailing labels. A **multiple-column report** displays information in several columns, such as a telephone listing.

Any of these types of reports can contain other reports, called subreports, though they are most common in detailed and grouped reports. As you do with forms and subforms, you usually include a subreport when you need to display data from tables that have a one-to-many relationship. For example, a main report might take its data from tblEmployees and show the name and phone number of each employee. A subreport might take its data from tblRefill and show the prescriptions each employee refilled. Table 5.2 describes the types of reports available in Access.

Table 5.2: Types of reports available in Access

Type of Report	Description	Example
Detailed single column or columnar	• Lists field names in one column on the left side of the page with the corresponding data to the right • Can be quickly created using the AutoReport option • Seldom used for long reports because it wastes paper	Doctor report that lists the ID, name, phone numbers, and clinic for one doctor, then the ID, name, phone numbers, and clinic for the next doctor, and so on
Detailed tabular	• Lists field names in a row across the page with the corresponding data below • Can be quickly created using the AutoReport option, but might require modification to create an appealing and useful format • Best for reports with 10 or fewer fields due to space limitations on standard paper sizes • A common report format	Prescription drug report that lists the drug name, description, price, and supplier as column headings, with the data listed for each drug below the headings
Multiple columns	• Organizes field names and data in newspaper-style columns • Fits a lot of information on a single page • Used for mailing and other types of labels designed for printing on label stock • Can be quickly created using the Label Wizard, but might require modification to create an appealing and useful format	Phone list or address directory
Grouped or Summary	• Increases information content by organizing data into groups • Summarizes data within subgroups • Often has subtotals and totals for the data • Might have percentages for subgroups • Most common type of report • Simple grouped reports can be quickly created with the Columnar AutoReport or Report Wizard, but might require modification to create an appealing and useful format • More complex reports with multiple grouping levels are best designed from scratch using Design view	Employee report that lists employees by job type or a sales report that sums sales by employee

5

Level 1

Table 5.2: Types of reports available in Access (cont.)

Type of Report	Description	Example
Mailing labels	• Special kind of multicolumn report • Uses preset label formats from well-known label manufacturers • Can be quickly created using the Label Wizard if data matches preset label requirements • Number of labels per page and size determined by preset label settings or a custom design	Address labels that print on a sheet containing 12 labels
Unbound	• Unbound main report serves as a container for one or more subreports from unrelated data sources • Likely to be created from scratch using Design view to meet specific presentation requirements	Main report contains a title and two subreports, one summarizing sales by employee and the other summarizing sales by product
Chart	• Compares one or more sets of data graphically • Often added as a subreport • Can use data from a crosstab or other type of advanced query • Can be created using a form or report Chart Wizard	Main report contains pharmacist information, and chart compares the number of prescriptions filled

After you identify the purpose and audience of the report and select the appropriate type, you determine which object in your database contains the information you want to display in the report. As in a form, this object is called the record source, and can be one or more tables or queries. After you identify the record source, you are ready to create the report.

Planning Basic Reports

As store manager, Elaine Estes needs to develop reports for herself and for other managers in the pharmacy. Some of the reports provide accounting information to help Paul Ferrino, the pharmacy owner, and the other pharmacy managers. Other reports provide information to help employees to perform their jobs efficiently, such as a printed directory of employees and their phone numbers for human resources. Elaine decides to start by creating reports for various functions within the pharmacy so the managers of these areas can review the reports and comment on their usefulness and appearance. Table 5.3 lists the reports that Elaine plans to create first.

Table 5.3: First reports for the pharmacy

Category	Reports Needed
Customer relations	• Directory with information about drugs and possible interactions to post near the pharmacy counter
Daily operations	• List of health plans and the number of days allowed in each refill

Table 5.3: First reports for the pharmacy (cont.)

Category	Reports Needed
Human resource management	• List of classes approved by the pharmacy for reimbursement • Alphabetical phone list of employees • Mailing labels for employees • Employee name tags
Management decision support and long-range planning	• Physical count of drugs and their manufacturers for inventory control • Outstanding credit balances

CREATING AND MODIFYING BASIC REPORTS

Similar to forms, you can create a basic report using an AutoReport Wizard or the Report Wizard. Use an **AutoReport Wizard** to create a report that displays all the fields and records in a single table or query. For more flexibility, you can use a **Report Wizard**, which guides you through the steps of creating a report based on one or more tables or queries by asking you questions about the record sources, fields, layout, and format you want to use. You will likely use one technique or the other to create a basic report, which you can customize by modifying the layout or adding features, for example, to meet your needs.

Creating a Report Using AutoReport

When Elaine polls the 4Corners Pharmacy employees and asks what types of reports they need, Maria Garcia is the first to respond. Maria mentions that she needs a report to post on the employee bulletin board advising employees about the classes that have been approved for reimbursement. Because the report should have all the fields and records in the tblClass table, Elaine thinks that an AutoReport Wizard is a good option for quickly creating the report. Access provides two AutoReport Wizards—AutoReport: Columnar and AutoReport: Tabular. She decides to try both options to see which one presents the class information in a more accessible or useful format.

On her first try, Elaine clicks the Tables button on the Objects bar in the Database window, clicks the tblClass table, clicks the list arrow on the New Object button on the Table Datasheet toolbar, and then clicks AutoReport. Access creates a columnar report that includes all the fields from the record source, tblClass. See Figure 5.2.

Figure 5.2: Columnar report created using an AutoReport wizard

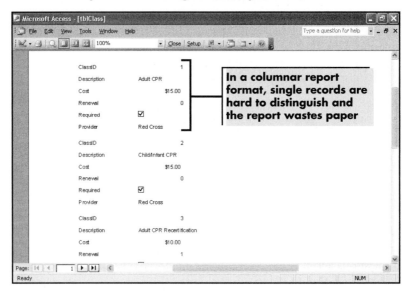

Elaine decides not to save the report because it seems hard to read, especially for employees who need quick reference to their training information.

How To

Create a Report Using an AutoReport Wizard

1. In the Database window, click the table on which you want to base the report.

2. Click the list arrow on the New Object button 📷 on the Database toolbar, and then click AutoReport. Access creates a report that includes all the fields from the record source, and applies the most recently used format.

Or

1. Click the Reports button on the Objects bar in the Database window.

2. Click the New button on the Database window toolbar. The New Report dialog box opens.

3. Click AutoReport: Columnar or AutoReport: Tabular to select an AutoReport Wizard.

4. Click the list arrow, and then select the table (or query) you want to use as the source of data for the report.

5. Click the OK button. The AutoReport Wizard creates the report and displays it in Print Preview.

Elaine wants the report to present data in a tabular format, which uses rows with column headings. The New Object button did not specify which type of AutoReport Wizard it uses—it applies the most recent report format used in the current database. Elaine can use the AutoReport: Tabular Wizard to create a tabular report instead. In the Database window, she clicks the Reports button on the Objects bar, and then clicks the New button to open the New Report dialog box. She clicks AutoReport: Tabular and selects tblClass as the record source. See Figure 5.3.

Figure 5.3: Using an AutoReport Wizard

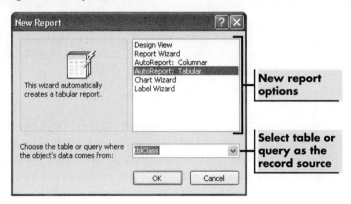

New report options

Select table or query as the record source

When she clicks the OK button, Access creates a report by arranging all the fields in tblClass in a tabular format, and displays the report in the Print Preview window. See Figure 5.4.

Figure 5.4: Results of AutoReport in Print Preview

One, two, or four pages displayed

Click the Print button to print the report

Close Print Preview with either Close button

Click the list arrow to choose different magnification if the text is hard to read

Print Preview lets you see how the report will look when printed

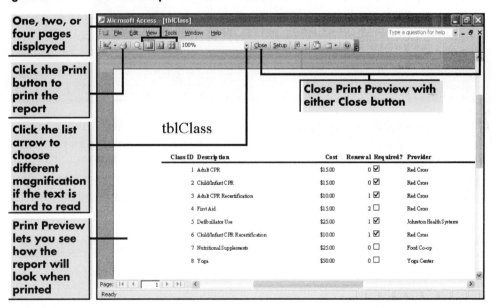

She saves this report as rptClassList and prints a copy for Maria Garcia by clicking the Print button on the Print Preview toolbar.

Best Practice

Naming Reports

Most database applications have many reports and distinguishing one from another can be difficult. In addition to using the "rpt" prefix for each report, use meaningful names that describe the contents of the reports. Although you can include spaces in field, control, and object names, most developers do not use spaces in field and control names because doing so can produce naming conflicts in some circumstances in Microsoft Visual Basic for Applications (VBA), a macro-language version of Microsoft Visual Basic that is used to program Windows applications, including Access.

In a report name, you can use an uppercase letter to start a new word, as in rptDrugList, to help make the names more readable. If you use this naming approach, you can modify the caption of the report in Design view. By default, Access uses the report name as its title, which might not be meaningful to readers of the printed report. In Design view, you can change the label containing the report title so that a more readable name appears at the beginning of the report in Print Preview. You can use the report properties to specify the report caption—this changes the text that appears in the report's title bar. For example, you could change the caption of rptDrugList to Drug List in report properties and make the same change to the title label in Design view.

Some database developers recommend using a more readable name for the report when you create it because this determines the title of the report. If you elect to use this approach, you can then change the names of the reports in the Database window to reflect the best practices for naming objects. (Right-click the report in the Database window, and then click Rename on the shortcut menu.)

Next, Elaine wants to create a report that serves as a directory of information about drugs and possible interactions. She'll post this directory near the pharmacy counter for employee and customer reference. Although she can base this report on a single table, tblDrug, the report is not a candidate for an AutoReport Wizard because she doesn't want to include all the fields in tblDrug, such as the Cost or Supplier fields. To take advantage of its greater flexibility, she decides to use the Report Wizard to create this report.

Creating a Report Using the Report Wizard

The Report Wizard provides a quick way to select only the fields you want to display in a report based on one or more tables or queries. You can also select one of several layouts and styles for the report. Even experienced Access users frequently create a report with the Report Wizard and then customize the report in Design view.

When customers pick up prescriptions at 4Corners Pharmacy, they often have questions about the medication, such as whether it's a generic drug or if it interacts with other drugs such as sedatives or alcohol. In a three-ring binder, Elaine plans to include an alphabetical listing of all drugs stocked at the pharmacy. Customers can consult this binder while they are waiting for their prescriptions, and employees can use it to answer questions.

All of the drug information is contained in the tblDrug table, but Elaine doesn't want to list the UPN (an internal drug ID), the selling price, the cost (to the pharmacy) of each drug, or the name of the supplier. Because the Report Wizard provides options for selecting fields, she decides to use it for this report. She opens the New Report dialog box, clicks Report Wizard, clicks the list arrow, and selects tblDrug. Then she clicks OK. The first dialog box in the Report Wizard opens. See Figure 5.5.

Figure 5.5: Selecting fields in the first Report Wizard dialog box

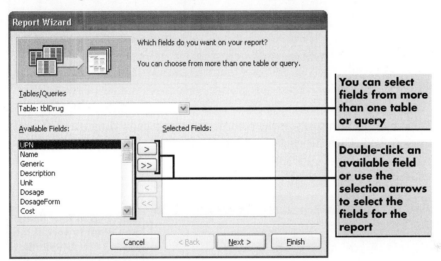

Elaine double-clicks all the tblDrug fields except the ones she does not want to include: UPN, Cost, Price, and Supplier. Then she clicks the Next button. She has the option of grouping on one of the fields but only wants to list the drugs in alphabetical order by name. See Figure 5.6. She clicks the Next button without specifying a grouping level.

Figure 5.6: Report Wizard grouping options

The next wizard dialog box asks if she wants to sort the records in the report. See Figure 5.7. Because she wants to sort the records alphabetically by drug name, she selects Name as the sort field. Then she clicks the Next button.

Figure 5.7: Selecting sorting options

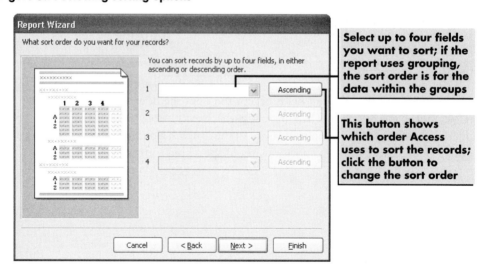

The next wizard dialog box displays layout options. Elaine selects Tabular as the layout and Portrait as the orientation. She makes sure that the Adjust field width so all fields fit on a page check box is checked so the report includes all the fields she selected on a single page. See Figure 5.8. Then she clicks the Next button.

Figure 5.8: Choosing the report layout and orientation

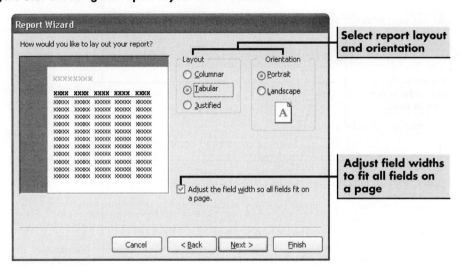

Figure 5.9: Selecting a report style

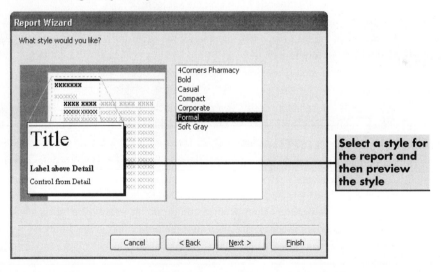

The next wizard dialog box displays formatting options. Elaine considers the possible styles, and then selects the Formal style because she is looking for a professional appearance for the report. See Figure 5.9. Then she clicks the Next button.

Finally, Elaine names the report rptDrugList, maintaining the naming convention for all Access objects that Donald Linebarger, IS manager, suggested. She clicks the Finish button and Access displays the completed report in Print Preview, as shown in Figure 5.10.

Figure 5.10: Final report created with the Report Wizard

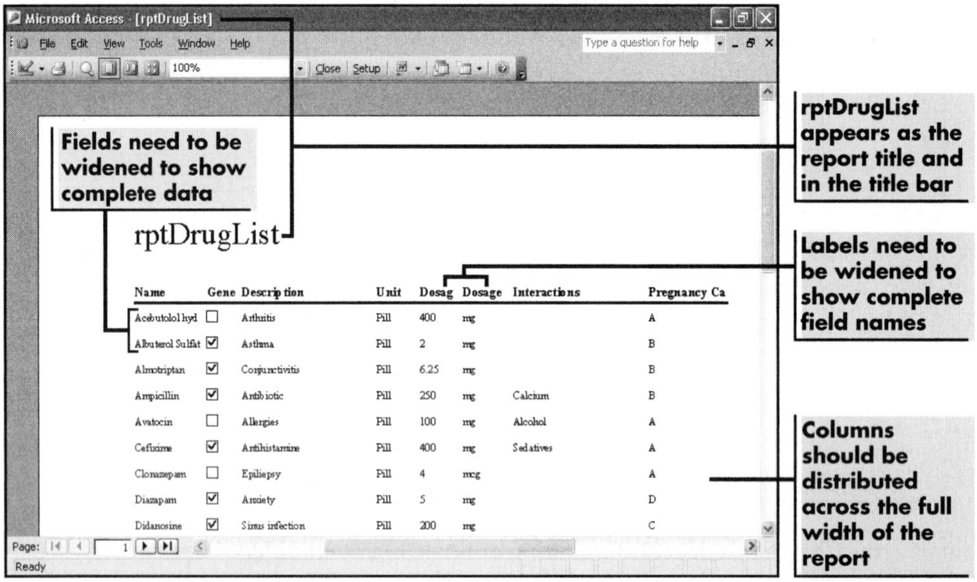

Fields need to be widened to show complete data

rptDrugList appears as the report title and in the title bar

Labels need to be widened to show complete field names

Columns should be distributed across the full width of the report

How To

Create a Report Using the Report Wizard

1. In the Database window, click the Reports button on the Objects bar.
2. Click the New button on the Database window toolbar. The New Report dialog box opens.
3. Click Report Wizard, click the list arrow, and then select the table (or query) you want to use as the source of data for the report.
4. Click the OK button. The first dialog box in the Report Wizard opens, asking which fields you want in your report.
5. From the Available Fields list, select the fields you want to include in the report. Use the Select Single Field button ⟩ to select the fields one by one; use the Select All Fields button ⟩⟩ to select them all at once. If you want to include fields from a different table or query, click the Tables/Queries list arrow, select a table or query, and then select the fields you want. Click the Next button.
6. If you are basing the report on more than one table, select the table by which you want to view the data, and then click the Next button. If you want to add grouping levels to the report, click the field by which you want to group records, and then click the Select Single Field button ⟩. If you use grouping levels, you can click the Grouping Options button to select a grouping interval. Click the Next button.
7. If you want to sort the records in the report, click the list arrow and then select the field on which to sort. By default, Access sorts in ascending order. To change this to descending order, click the Ascending button. You can sort on up to four fields. Click the Next button.
8. Select a layout for the report. A sample of the selected layout appears in the preview box of the dialog box. Make sure the Adjust the field width so all fields fit on a page check box is selected if

you want to fit all fields on a page, even if the fields must be shortened to fit. If you do not want to adjust the field widths, clear this check box. Click the Next button.

9. Select a style for the report. A sample of the selected style appears in the preview box. Click the Next button.

10. Type the name of the report, using "rpt" as the prefix to identify the object as a report. Click the Finish button. The completed report opens in Print Preview.

The title of the report that Elaine created—rptDrugList—reflects the name of the report object, but could be confusing to the customers who will refer to the report at the pharmacy counter. Some fields and labels are not wide enough to show all of the text they contain. To change the title of the report and make other revisions, Elaine must work in Design view.

Best Practice

Creating a Report from a Query

When you create a report, you can use a query as the record source. For example, when you use the Report Wizard, you can select a query as the source object in the first wizard dialog box. Many reports are created from queries because a query lets you retrieve information from more than one table and restrict the data by using criteria. Any data not meeting the criteria is not included in the report detail. If you use a parameter query as the record source, users who open the report to view or print it must first enter criteria, such as a range of dates. The report then includes only the records that meet the criteria the user entered.

All the steps in the Report Wizard work the same whether you choose multiple tables or queries as the record sources. Note that if you select fields from multiple tables, Access uses relationships you defined to build a hidden query. Access won't let you continue if you select fields from unrelated tables.

Modifying a Report in Design View

Access users often use the Report Wizard or an AutoReport Wizard to quickly generate a report that contains the basic data they want to include. Then they modify the report in Design view to customize its appearance and contents. As with forms, you can also create reports from scratch in Design view. Experienced Access users might prefer to start in Design view to place fields and other controls precisely where they want them.

As in a form, a control is a small object such as a text box that displays data or a line that separates one record from another. Table 5.4 describes the three types of controls you can add to an Access report.

Table 5.4: Report controls

Type of Control	Description	Example
Bound control	A control whose source of data is a field in the report's record source. Bound controls display values from fields in the database. The values can be any data type, such as text, dates, numbers, Yes/No values, pictures, or hyperlinks.	A text box that displays an employee's last name stored in the EmpLast field in the tblEmployee table
Unbound control	A control that doesn't have a source of data, such as a field or mathematical expression. Unbound controls are often used to display report titles, informational text, lines, rectangles, and graphics not stored in an underlying table.	A label that displays the title of a report
Calculated control	A control whose source of data is a mathematical expression rather than a field. The results of a calculated control are updated when any of the values in the expression change.	A text box that calculates the total of the values in the Price field

In Chapter 4, Table 4.2 describes the Toolbox tools you use to create form controls; you can use the same tools to create report controls.

Elaine wants to change the title of rptDrugList to one that is more meaningful to its users. With the report open in Print Preview, Elaine clicks the list arrow for the View button ⊠ ▾ and notices it lists three report views: Design View, Print Preview, and Layout Preview. Table 5.5 summarizes the options available in each view. See Figure 5.11 for examples of each view of rptDrugList.

Table 5.5: Three report views

View	Options
Design	• Modify any part of the report using the Toolbox toolbar and menu. • Use settings, controls, and other options similar to Design view for forms.
Print Preview	• View the report as it would look if printed. • Display one, two, or more pages at once. • Use the Page Setup dialog box to change the margins, page settings such as orientation, and column settings. • Use the navigation buttons to move from page to page. • Use the Zoom button to show the report using a larger or smaller magnification.
Layout Preview	• Check the font, font size, and general layout. • View all the sections of a report and a few detail records without navigating from one page to another.

Figure 5.11: Three views of rptDrugList

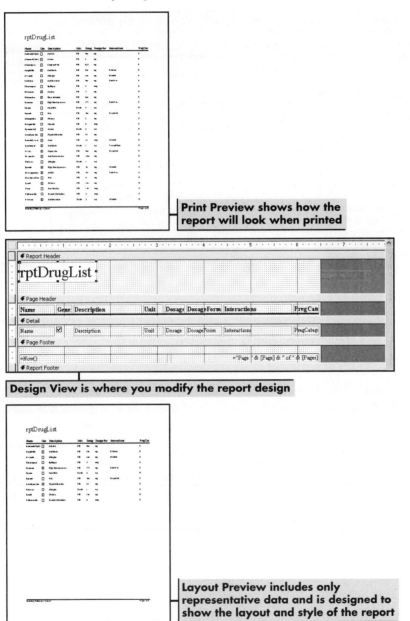

Print Preview shows how the report will look when printed

Design View is where you modify the report design

Layout Preview includes only representative data and is designed to show the layout and style of the report

Elaine will spend most of her time modifying the report in Design view and then switching to Print Preview to see the effects of changes. When she opens the report in Design view, she sees that it is divided into sections similar to those in forms. The rptDrugList report has a Report Header, Page Header, Detail, Page Footer, and Report Footer sections. See Figure 5.12.

Figure 5.12: Sections of a report in Design view

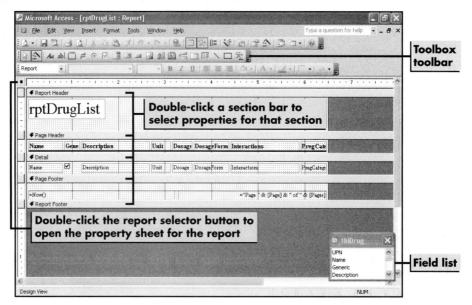

To create useful reports, you need to understand the purpose of each section. The section in which you place a control determines where and how often it appears in the printed report. An Access report can contain the following sections:

- **Report header**—This is printed once at the beginning of the report. Use the report header for information that might normally appear on a cover page, such as a logo or a title and date. The report header is printed before the page header.
- **Page header**—This is printed at the top of every page. For example, use a page header to repeat the report title on every page.
- **Group header**—This is printed at the beginning of each new group of records. Use the group header to print the group name. For example, in a report that is grouped by product, use the group header to print the product name.
- **Detail**—This is printed once for every row in the record source and includes the controls that make up the main body of the report.
- **Group footer**—This is printed at the end of each group of records. Use a group footer to print summary information for a group.
- **Page footer**—This is printed at the end of every page. For example, use a page footer to print page numbers.
- **Report footer**—This is printed once at the end of the report. Use the report footer to print report totals or other summary information for the entire report. The report footer appears last in the report design, but is printed before the final page footer.

You can customize the appearance and behavior of report sections by changing their properties. To view a property sheet for a section, double-click the section bar, such as the

Report Header bar. Table 5.6 lists common properties for sections. (You can view a description of each property by clicking a property and then pressing the F1 key.)

Table 5.6: Common section properties

Property	Description
Force New Page	Specify whether the Report Header, Detail, or Report Footer section prints on a separate page, rather than on the current page.
Keep Together	Select Yes to print a form or report section all on one page; select No to print as much of the section as possible on the current page and continue printing on the next page.
Back Color	If you want to include a background color for the section, specify the numeric value of the color or click the Build button [...] to use the Color Builder to select a color from a palette.
Special Effect	Specify whether the section should appear as flat (default), raised, sunken, etched, shadowed, or chiseled when printed.
Repeat Section	Specify whether a group header is repeated on the next page or column when a group spans more than one page or column.

The report itself also has properties that you can modify to customize the report. Table 5.7 lists common report properties that are discussed throughout the chapter.

Table 5.7: Common report properties

Property	Description
Record Source	Specify the source of the data for the report, which can be a table name, a query name, or an SQL statement.
Caption	Set the title for the report.
Width	Set the width for the report.
Picture	Select a graphic to display as the background for the report.
Picture Type	Select Embedded to store the graphic specified in the Picture property as part of the report. Select Linked to link the picture to the report. Access then stores a pointer to the location of the picture on the disk.

Best Practice

Previewing Reports Important During Report Development
Because printed reports show even minor misalignments of controls or problems with truncated data due to control width, switch from Design view to Print Preview regularly as you are creating reports. As you work on a report, also save it frequently to preserve your changes. If necessary, you can revert to a saved version of a report if you don't like your modifications. Also make liberal use of the Undo button as you work to undo your recent changes.

Because Elaine named the report rptDrugList, she has to change two properties in the report. The first is the report caption. This changes the name of the report in the title bar in Print Preview. The report header contains the title of the report in a label control, which has the same properties in Design view for a report as for a form. (See Table 4.3 in Chapter 4 for descriptions of common label properties.) To change the caption property for the report, Elaine opens the report in Design view, and then double-clicks the report selector button to open the property sheet for the entire report. She changes the Caption property to Drug List. See Figure 5.13. To change the label in the report header, she clicks it to display the label properties in the open property sheet. She changes the caption of the label to Drug List and notes that the text in the label changes accordingly. She also changes the Text Align property to Distribute, and then checks the report in Print Preview. To see the results of these changes, Elaine switches to Print Preview.

Figure 5.13: Changing the report caption and title

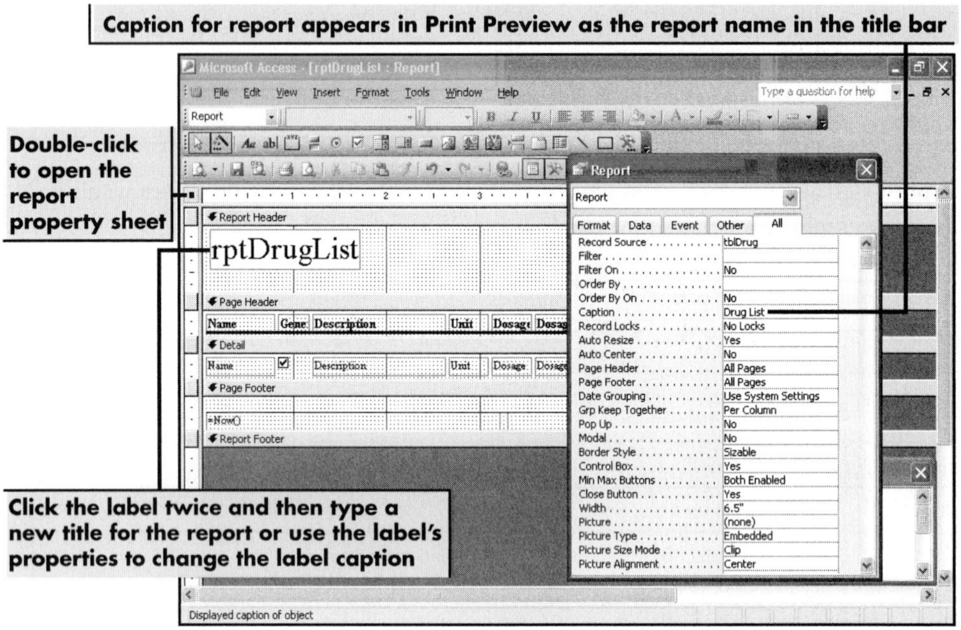

In Print Preview, some of the column headings seem crowded. To make room for the headings, Elaine can decrease the left and right margins of the page to provide more room for the column headings in the report. She makes these changes by clicking the Setup button on the Print Preview toolbar.

How To

Change Margins and Report Width

1. In Print Preview, click the Setup button. The Page Setup dialog box opens, shown in Figure 5.14.

Figure 5.14: Page Setup for report to decrease left and right margins and modify width of report

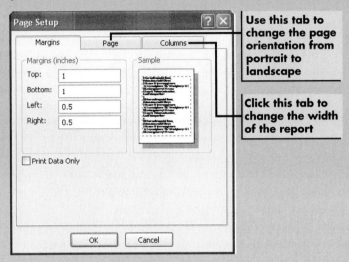

Use this tab to change the page orientation from portrait to landscape

Click this tab to change the width of the report

2. To change the margins, click the Margins tab. Most printers use minimum left and right margins of .5 inches for most reports, and .25 inches for labels.

3. To change the page orientation from portrait to landscape, click the Page tab and then click the Portrait or Landscape option button.

4. To change the width of the report, click the Columns tab. Modify the width as desired, but remember that the total of margins and report width must equal the width of the paper for the report, which is 8.5 inches for most printers. If you exceed the combined width, Access displays an error message.

In rptDrugList, margins are set to one inch by default. Elaine changes the left and right margins to .5 inches to create more room for the column headings. She clicks the Columns tab to increase the width of the report to 7.5 inches. She uses the Width text box in the Page Setup dialog box, instead of manually dragging the report border in Design view, to prevent accidentally widening the report beyond the edge of the paper.

Best Practice

Developing a Report Design Checklist

A common error made by beginning report developers is to set the width of the report plus the page margins wider than the actual width of the paper in the printer. When this happens, a blank page prints after each page of the report. Use the settings in the Page Setup dialog box and in the report's property sheet to make the total width of the report and the margins equal to the actual paper width. In Print Preview, you can also choose to view two or four pages at the same time. If doing so reveals blank pages, you know that your report is too wide for the paper.

Because a report is designed to be printed, the alignment of the headings and the spacing between lines and columns are very important. Minor variations in alignment are obvious when the report is printed, and can affect the report's readability. Incomplete field values can make the report meaningless.

If you are developing a series of reports for a database application, you should develop a checklist for the modifications you plan to make so the reports have a similar look and professional appearance. Answer the following questions as you develop your plan:

- □ Is the report in the format chosen for all reports?
- □ Does the title label caption need to be modified?
- □ Have I changed the report caption?
- □ Can I read the complete column headings or are they truncated?
- □ Does all the data in the detail area appear or is some truncated?
- □ Is the report so wide that it should use landscape orientation?
- □ Is the vertical spacing too spread out or too close?
- □ If the report has many numbers, does it use gridlines to make reading it easier?
- □ Do any extra items on the report detract from its appearance?
- □ Do any errors or blank pages appear when the report is printed?
- □ Would the data have more information content if it is grouped?
- □ Would summary data add to the information content of the report?

Elaine decides to adopt the checklist to use as she creates each report and to check for common modifications that she should make. She wants each report to reflect the professionalism of the pharmacy and to use a standard format. She re-examines the report using her checklist to evaluate its format and sees a number of modifications she needs to make. See Figure 5.15.

Figure 5.15: Additional changes to make to rptDrugList

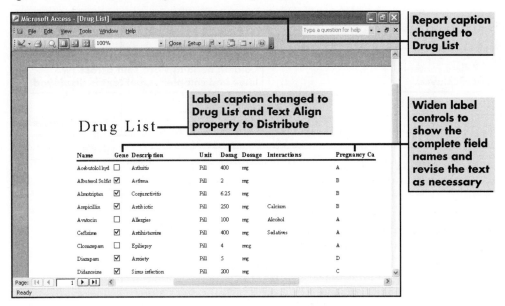

Elaine begins to modify the format of the report in Design view by clicking the label control for the Pregnancy Category label and widening it to display the complete field name. She moves the label and its text box by holding down the Shift key as she clicks to select more than one control. She also widens the Dosage Form label to display its entire text. Moving from right to left, she moves each label with its associated text box, using the Undo button on the Report Design toolbar as necessary to correct errors, and switching between Print Preview and Design view to see the effect of her changes. She decides to split the Pregnancy Category label text over two lines because the label is so much longer than the category text listed below it. She clicks after the word Pregnancy in the heading. By holding down the Shift key and pressing the Enter key, she splits the words over two lines. She does the same for the Dosage Form heading.

Elaine moves the line in the Page Header section to make more room for the two-line column heading, creating space for the rest of the fields and headings. She clicks the line and adjusts its length so it spans all the headings. She moves the labels in the Page Header section and the text boxes for the fields in the Detail section so they are distributed evenly across the form, widening text boxes as necessary. When necessary, she uses the Align and Size commands on the Format menu. Figure 5.16 shows the modified report.

Figure 5.16: Drug List report after modifications

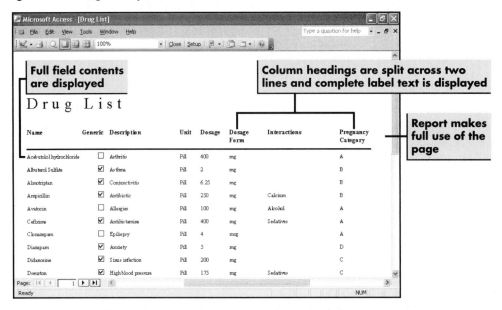

Best Practice

Modifying the Format of a Report

As you work in Design view to modify a report, keep the following suggestions in mind to enhance the format of the report:

- Decrease the left and right margins and widen the report in Print Preview using the Page Setup dialog box.
- Start modifying the layout by adjusting the rightmost label and text box. If they are readable, move both to align them with the new right margin.
- Modify the next label and text box as necessary and move them to the right.
- Continue to move labels and their text boxes to the right, making use of Print Preview and the Undo button to check and reverse your changes as necessary.
- If the report does not provide enough room for the labels in the Page Header section, click between two words in a label. Hold down the Shift key, and then press the Enter key to split the text into two lines. Increase the height of the Page Header section to accommodate the two lines.
- If you are using labels with two or more lines of text, select all the labels in the Page Header section, click Format on the menu bar, point to Align, and then click Top to align the label controls.
- Most reports use horizontal lines that must be manually widened (or shortened) if you adjust the layout of the other controls. Shift+click the lines of the report to select them and then drag a selection handle to increase their length. If it is difficult to select the lines, press the Ctrl+A keys to select all the controls on the report, and then click to deselect all but the lines.
- If the labels and text boxes do not fit in portrait orientation, use the Page Setup dialog box to change the orientation to Landscape.

Moving Detail Fields to Multiple Lines on a Report

Because the rptDrugList report is designed for customers, Elaine wants to make sure it is easy to read, even for the elderly customers. She decides to move some of the fields to a second detail line to improve spacing and to change the font for the drug names.

She increases the length of the Detail section to make room for a second row of text by dragging the Page Footer section bar down another inch or so. Then she moves Dosage, Unit, and Dosage Form fields in the Detail section under the Name field. These are commonly associated with drugs, so she deletes their labels in the Page Header section. She adjusts the size and font of the Name field to make it easier to read in the field report properties, and then adds space in the Detail section to separate each drug for readability.

How To

Move Detail Fields to Make More Space

1. In Design view, make room for additional lines in the Detail section.

2. Drag the text box for a field below another text box. For example, you could list a name on one line, move the address to a second line, and city, state, and zip to a third line. This is such a familiar format that column names are not necessary.

3. Delete the labels associated with the text boxes you moved.

4. Select the remaining labels and text boxes on the first two lines, and then move or resize them all at the same time.

5. Click Format on the menu bar, point to Align, and then click an alignment option as necessary to align the labels and text boxes vertically and horizontally.

6. Switch between Design view and Print Preview to check your work, making adjustments as necessary.

Elaine centers the report title and shows rptDrugList to Paul Ferrino, who suggests she include the pharmacy logo at the top of the report. He gives her a copy of the logo in an electronic file named 4Corners.jpg, and Elaine uses the Image button 🖼 on the Toolbox toolbar to add the pharmacy's logo to each side of the report.

The images are too big for the report so she Shift+clicks to select both images, and then drags a corner sizing handle to decrease the size of the images. Then she changes the Size Mode property for each image to Zoom. Figure 5.17 shows the report in Design view and Print Preview.

Figure 5.17: Revising a report and adding graphics

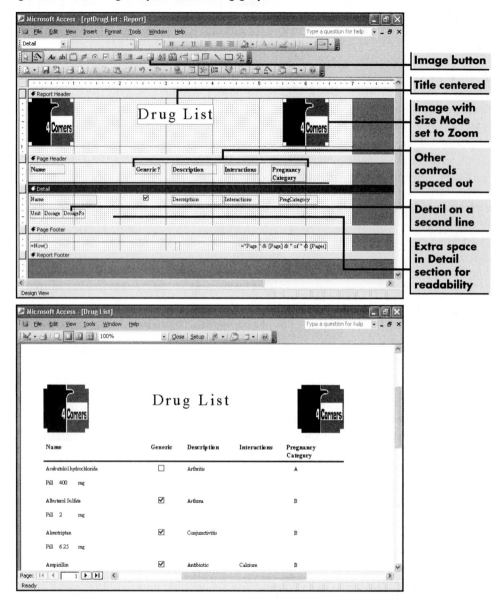

Image button

Title centered

Image with Size Mode set to Zoom

Other controls spaced out

Detail on a second line

Extra space in Detail section for readability

How To

Add an Image to a Report

1. Save the image you want to use in an electronic file on your system (preferably in the same folder where the database is located).

2. In Design view, click the Image button 🖼 on the Toolbox toolbar. Click the report where you want to place the graphic. The Insert Picture dialog box opens.

3. Navigate to where you stored the image file, and then double-click the file. Access inserts the image in the report.

4. If necessary, move the image to your desired location and resize it by dragging a corner handle. Using the corner handles maintains the proportions of the image.

5. To change the properties of the image, double-click the image. For example, change the Size Mode property to Zoom to display the entire image.

Creating a Custom Style for Reports

Elaine recalls the custom format that Rachel created to standardize the look of all 4Corners Pharmacy forms. Although Rachel standardized the forms to create a consistent user interface, Elaine could standardize the reports to create consistency in the material the pharmacy prints. Employees could then save time when developing new reports, and customers would associate a particular report format with 4Corners Pharmacy, increasing customer recognition. When Paul Ferrino shares accounting and other management reports with his banker and other investors, he will also appreciate having a set of reports with a uniform design.

Elaine switches to Design view, saves her changes to rptDrugList, and then clicks the AutoFormat button on the Report Design toolbar to create a custom AutoFormat based on the report. She saves the new AutoFormat as "4Corners Pharmacy." She can now apply the custom AutoFormat to all existing and new reports using the Report Wizard or the AutoFormat button.

Elaine needs to create two other basic reports. The first one is an alphabetical phone list of all employees' first and last names with phone and cell numbers, which she creates using the Report Wizard, naming the report rptEmployeePhoneList and applying the 4Corners Pharmacy AutoFormat. She also creates a report that shows the number of days that each health plan allows for each prescription refill. She creates this report using the AutoReport: Tabular Wizard, basing it on tblHealthPlan, and names the report rptRefillDays. She modifies this report by centering the title.

Finally, Elaine needs to create an accounts receivable report that identifies customers who have not paid in full for their prescriptions. These customers have a value in the Balance field in tblCustomer that is greater than zero. To produce this report, Elaine first creates a query called qryBalance that includes only the CustID, CustFirst, CustLast, and Balance fields from tblCustomer and uses ">0" as the criterion for the Balance field. Then she uses the Report Wizard to create a report named rptBalance based on qryBalance with the records sorted in descending order on the Balance field. She makes this report consistent with the others by applying the 4Corners Pharmacy custom format.

Creating a Grouped Report Using a Single Table

Now that Elaine has created a number of basic reports, she can concentrate on other reports. The pharmacy has not yet created a database for inventory, so the technicians do a physical count of drugs on a monthly basis. They have asked Elaine to create a report that would help them with this task and facilitate ordering drugs as needed. She decides to create a report that lists each supplier and then all the drugs alphabetically for that supplier. She plans to leave a space for the technicians to write their physical count quantity for each drug on the report.

All of the drug information she needs is contained in tblDrug, as was the information for the rptDrugList. However, this time she wants to arrange the data so that each supplier is listed once along with the drugs they supply. She could create a basic report based on tblDrug using the Report Wizard again and then sort the data first by supplier and then by drug name. This approach could create a cluttered report, and Elaine wants to find a way to organize the data but make the report easy to read.

Instead of sorting the report on two fields, Elaine can create a **grouped report**, which groups records based on the values in one or more fields. For example, to view all the drugs provided by a particular supplier, Elaine can group tblDrug records on the values in the Supplier field. Although this report might contain the same fields and values as in a standard tabular report, grouping the records makes the report more informative—she can then skim the report to find the drugs provided by a supplier. The other advantage of grouped reports is that they can calculate totals and other values for each group. For example, Elaine can calculate the number of different drugs provided by one supplier.

You can create a grouped report by using the Report Wizard to group records at the same time you create the report. You can also group records after you create a report by using the Sorting and Grouping dialog box in Design view. The Report Wizard only allows four grouping levels, but when working in Design view, you can create up to 10 grouping levels. For example, you could produce a report of doctors grouped first by their clinic and then by their specialty. To set up such a grouped report, you would assign the Clinic field to group level 1 and the Specialty field to group level 2. In other words, when you group on more than one field, the group level determines how the groups are nested.

To produce a drug physical count report, Elaine decides to create a grouped report using the Report Wizard. She bases the report on tblDrug, and selects the UPN, Name, Generic, Unit, Dosage, DosageForm, Cost, Price, and Supplier fields. By choosing to group by Supplier, all the drugs provided by a supplier will be listed under that supplier's name. She sorts each group on Name and selects Stepped as the layout. She applies the 4Corners Pharmacy AutoFormat and names the report rptPhysicalCount. See Figure 5.18.

Figure 5.18: Using the Report Wizard to created a grouped report

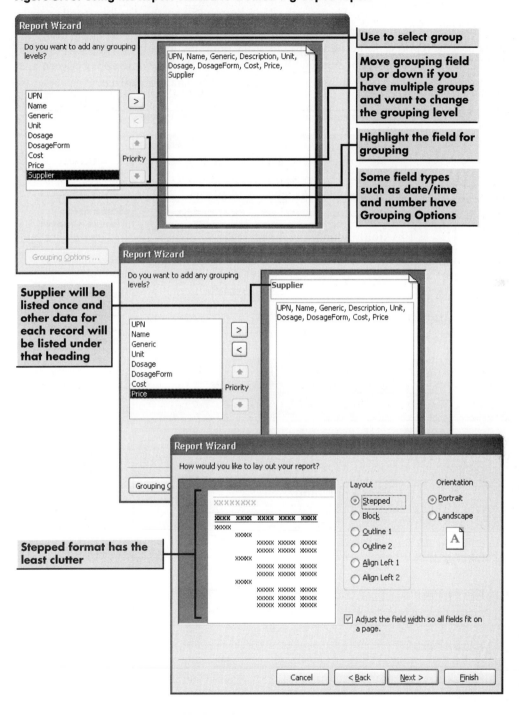

Elaine modifies the report to meet the standards she adopted and to add the unbound label control for the physical count. She uses the Line button 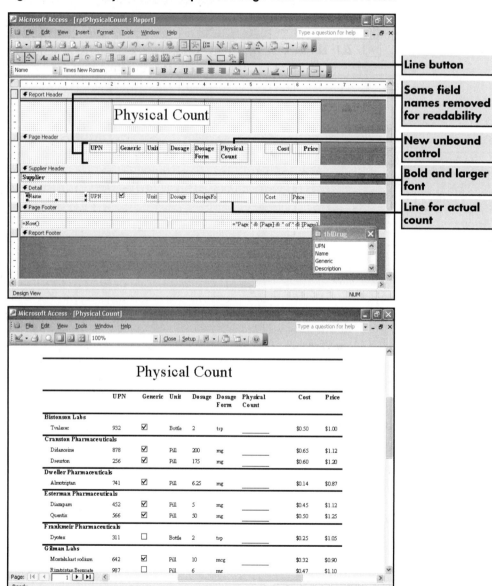 on the Toolbox toolbar to draw a line that indicates where the technicians should write their inventory count. She also changes the report caption and title to Physical Count. Figure 5.19 shows the finished report in Design view and Print Preview. Elaine notes that the only difference between a simple tabular report and one with grouping is the way the data is organized.

Figure 5.19: The Physical Count report in Design view and Print Preview

Best Practice

Formatting Groups of Alphabetic Listings

Long alphabetic listings in a report can be difficult to read. You can break up a listing into subgroups based on up to five letters of the initial word in the field. For example, in the report rptPhysicalCount, you could group on the first letter and then on Supplier. To do so using the Report Wizard, click the Grouping Options button in the second dialog box in the wizard. The Grouping Intervals dialog box opens. Click the Grouping intervals list arrow, and change the setting from Normal to 1st Letter. See Figure 5.20. You can also sort codes that are part alphabetic and part numeric using the grouping options in the Grouping Intervals dialog box.

Figure 5.20: Modifying grouping options

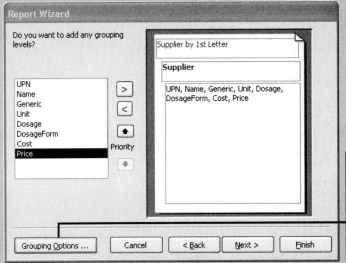

Click the Grouping Options button to open the Grouping Intervals dialog box, which you can use to group on the first letter of the group field to separate the list into alphabetic groups

In the finished report, Access inserts an "A" before all the group names that start with A, a "B" before all the group names that start with B, and so on, as shown in Figure 5.21.

Figure 5.21: Suppliers grouped by Supplier first letter and then by supplier

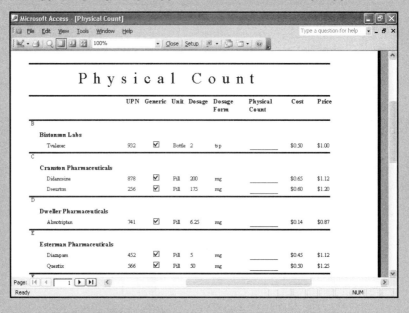

Next, Elaine needs to prepare mailing labels for the pharmacy. She occasionally needs to send tax forms to employees, and Maria Garcia also mails material to employees. Instead of re-creating the employee name and addresses in a word-processing program and using a mail merge, Elaine can extract this information already stored in tblEmployee and develop a report formatted for mailing labels that the pharmacy has in stock.

CREATING LABELS USING THE LABEL WIZARD

As you probably know, blank mailing labels are available in dozens of stock formats with or without adhesive backing and they can be used for such diverse applications as rotary cards, calling cards, shipping labels, name tags, and file folder labels. A typical mailing label looks like this:

If you store name and address information in an Access database, you can create a simple report that is formatted to look like a mailing label. The report extracts the address data from the table or query that stores the addresses, and organizes it to print a label for each address in the record source. The simplest way to create mailing labels is to use the Label Wizard. As with other types of reports, you can customize the mailing labels using Design view, changing the font, color, and layout of the label text, for example.

When you use the Label Wizard, you specify the record source for the mailing label report, and then select the type of label on which you want to print mailing information. The Label Wizard lists most common mailing label formats. One prominent label manufacturer is Avery Dennison. They developed a numbering system for each of their labels that other companies in the United States often note as an equivalent for their products. Access has built in to the Label Wizard hundreds of sizes and styles, as well as many of the common product numbers from Avery Dennison and prominent overseas manufacturers. When you specify label size, you have the option of using the English system of inches or the metric system for all measurements. You can also choose labels that are sheet fed (common today on laser and ink jet printers) or continuous (common on "tractor fed" printers that are often used for printing small quantities of labels at a time). If you need to use a label that is not included in the Label Wizard, you can also create a custom label of any size. Create a custom label when you want to print names and addresses directly on an envelope. Table 5.8 summarizes examples of label numbers and their usage.

Table 5.8: Examples of label sizes and uses

Number	Common Usage	Width in Inches
Clip Badge	Insert for clip-on name badge	2¼ × 3½
5160	White permanent laser labels, 30 per sheet, used for most bulk mailings in the United States	1 × 2⅝
5824	CD label	2 per sheet
5385	Rotary cards for Rolodex card holders	2⅙ × 4
5889	Postcards for color laser printers	4 × 6

Elaine needs mailing labels for all employees so she and other 4Corners managers can send out occasional mailings. She opens the New Report dialog box, selects the Label Wizard, and then selects tblEmployee as the record source for the labels. See Figure 5.22.

Figure 5.22: Label Wizard opening dialog box

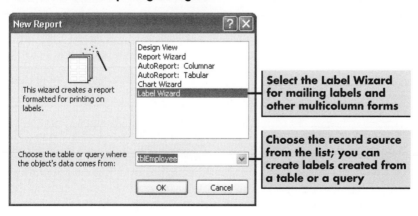

When she clicks the OK button, the first dialog box in the wizard opens. She chooses the Avery 5160 sheet feed type because the pharmacy has these in stock. See Figure 5.23.

Figure 5.23: Selecting the label size in the Label Wizard

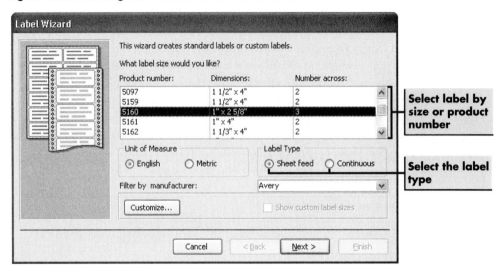

This is the most common label stock for bulk mailings because it contains 30 labels per sheet—more than most other label stock. When you preview or print Avery 5160 labels, an error message often appears indicating that some data might not be displayed. If you don't change the font, you should be able to print all of the text on the labels without modifying the label report, so you can ignore this message. Level 2 explains how to modify the label properties to avoid this message.

Next, Elaine selects the font and font weight for the label text. Although it is tempting to increase the font size to improve readability, the label stock they have won't show the entire name and address if the font is too big. See Figure 5.24.

Figure 5.24: Label text and appearance selection

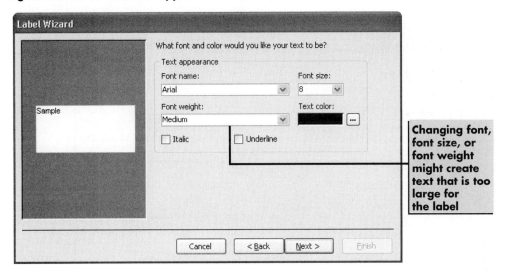

The Label Wizard lets you build a prototype of the label by selecting the necessary fields one at a time. Elaine selects the first name and then inserts a space before selecting the last name. Then she presses the Enter key to move to the next line. She selects the address and then presses Enter again. The last line of the label has city, state, and zip information. She inserts one space between each of these. See Figure 5.25.

Figure 5.25: Label prototype

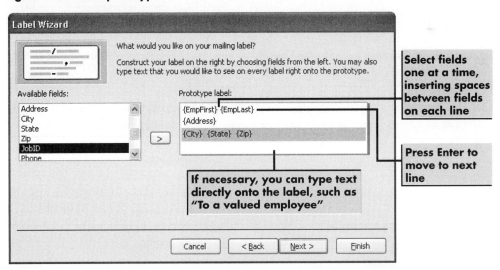

Next, Elaine specifies the sort order for the labels. She sorts on last name and then first name to organize the labels logically, and names the report rptEmpLabels. Figure 5.26 shows the final result.

Figure 5.26: rptEmpLabels in Print Preview

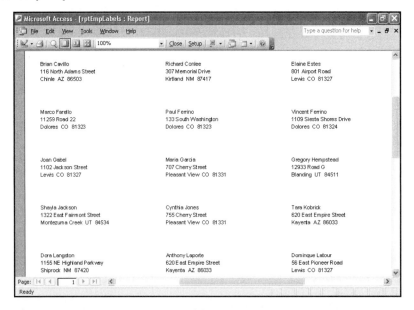

How To

Create a Label Using the Label Wizard

1. In the Database window, click Reports on the Objects bar, and then click the New button on the Database window toolbar. The New Report dialog box opens.
2. Click Label Wizard and then click the list arrow to select the table or query that contains the data for the labels. Click the OK button. The first dialog box in the Label Wizard opens, asking what label size you want to use.
3. Scroll the list to select the appropriate label by product number and size. If necessary, click the Filter by manufacturer list arrow to show product numbers and sizes for Avery labels, for example.
4. Click the Sheet feed or Continuous option button as appropriate. Click the Next button.
5. Select the font name, size, and weight for the label text. Note that the default selection is "light" font weight; you might want to change this to medium for readability. Increasing the font size or changing fonts might affect the amount of information you can fit on a label. Click the Next button.
6. The next wizard dialog box asks what you want to include on the label. In the Available fields list box, click the field you want to display on the label, such as FirstName, and then click the Select Single Field button $\boxed{>}$ to add the field to the prototype label. Continue to construct the label by adding fields to the prototype label. Press the Enter key to move to a new line. Insert spaces, additional text, commas, and other punctuation on the label manually. Click the Next button.
7. Select one or more fields on which you want to sort the labels. Sort the labels alphabetically (for first class mail) or by zip code (if you have enough to meet postal requirements for bulk mail). Click the Next button.

8. Enter a name for the label report, using the "rpt" prefix. Click the Finish button.

9. If you see an error message about the width of the labels, check your data to make sure it all appears.

Best Practice

Testing Mailing Labels Before Printing

Most mailing labels print on stock paper with no problems, but it is possible to have **print registration errors**, which affect the print alignment when you print many labels. The printing may "creep" so that the text in the second row of labels is lower than the text in the first row of labels. By the end of the page, the labels might be totally out of position on the stock. This is particularly common if you custom design a label, modify the font size, or add lines to a label in Design view and have not calculated exactly how wide and how high each label should be. If you have a large quantity of labels to print, be sure to check for possible problems before wasting label stock. Consider the following suggestions for checking:

- Print the labels on regular paper first to make sure they are printing properly.
- Print only a section of the labels at a time. For example, use the Print dialog box to print pages 1–10, then 11–20, and so on. If there are any problems, you will only waste a few sheets of label stock.

Before creating the labels, Elaine creates a query named qryEmpTitle that includes the EmpFirst and EmpLast fields from tblEmployee and Title from tblJobTitle. Then she uses the Label Wizard to create name tags for all employees that they can wear as a badge. She bases the name tag report on qryEmpTitle, and selects the Clip Badge label type. She centers the name on one line and formats the labels using a 20-point, semibold font so that the text is large enough for elderly customers to read. She also formats the job title using a 16-point, semibold font. She changes the text alignment to Center for both lines, and then saves the report as rptBadge.

Now that she is finished creating basic reports for 4Corners Pharmacy, Elaine is ready to create more sophisticated management reports.

Steps To Success: Level 1

Marie Cresson is the store manager of the Hudson Bay Pharmacy, and needs to produce information stored in the Hudson database for customers and managers. She asks for your help in creating the reports shown in Table 5.9.

5

Level 1

Table 5.9: Basic reports for Hudson Bay Pharmacy

Category	Reports Needed
Customer relations	• Directory of drugs, including possible interactions
Daily operations	• List of health plans and the number of days allowed in each refill
Human resource management	• List of classes approved by the pharmacy for reimbursement • Alphabetical phone list of employees • Mailing labels for employees • Name tags for employees
Management decision support and long-range planning	• Physical count report • Outstanding credit balances

As you save the new reports, be certain to use the name specified in the following steps, including the "rpt" prefix. Also consult your instructor for instructions about submitting your results.

Complete the following:

1. Start Access and open the **Hudson.mdb** database from the STS folder.

2. Marie wants to create a report for Hudson Bay customers that provides an alphabetical list of drugs, including information such as whether it's a generic drug or if it interacts with other drugs such as sedatives or alcohol. However, she doesn't want to list the DIN (an internal drug ID), the selling price, the cost (to the pharmacy) of each drug, the fee (dispensing fee), or the name of the supplier. Create a report that lists all drug information except information that is not appropriate for customers. Use the Hudson Bay Pharmacy logo, which is stored in the **HudsonBay.jpg** file in the STS folder. Save the report as rptDrugList.

3. Modify rptDrugList to improve its readability and enhance its appearance according to accepted standards for reports. Create a custom format based on the modified rptDrugList, and name the new AutoFormat "Hudson Bay Pharmacy."

4. Next, Marie needs to create a report for the pharmacists and technicians, which they call a daily operations report. This report shows the number of days a health plan allows for each prescription refill. Apply the Hudson Bay Pharmacy AutoFormat, and name this report rptRefillDays. Revise the report title, column headings, and fields as necessary to improve the format of the report.

5. Marie mentions that Kim Siemers, the human resources manager, needs a human resources report that shows all classes for which Hudson Bay Pharmacy will reimburse employee costs. Create this report for Kim, naming it rptClassList.

6. Modify rptClassList by applying the Hudson Bay Pharmacy AutoFormat and revising the report title, column headings, and fields necessary to improve the format of the report.

7. Marie also notes that Kim needs a human resources report that provides an alphabetical phone list for all employees. Name the report rptEmployeePhoneList. Select fields that clearly identify the employee and provide all their phone numbers.

8. Modify rptEmployeePhoneList to conform to accepted report standards, resizing and moving fields as necessary.

9. Next, Marie needs an accounting report to track customers with a balance due amount in their accounts. Create a query to provide this information, saving the query as qryBalance. Create a management report based on this query that lists the balance due amount in descending order. Name this report rptBalance.

10. Marie meets with the pharmacy technicians, who request a drug physical count report. Create a physical count report that lists drugs in alphabetical order by their supplier. Save the report as rptDrugSupplier.

11. Marie has two more requests for basic reports. First, she needs mailing labels for employees, and provides the Avery 5160 label type. Create this mailing label report, naming it rptEmpLabels.

12. Finally, create name tags for all employees that they can wear as a badge. Name the report rptBadge. Be sure the text is large and dark enough for elderly customers to read.

13. Close the **Hudson.mdb** database and Access.

5

Level 2

LEVEL 2

DEVELOPING MANAGEMENT REPORTS TO SUPPORT DECISION MAKING

ACCESS 2003 SKILLS TRAINING

- **Add a date to a report**
- **Add a field to a report**
- **Add a page number to a report**
- **Add calculated controls to a report section**
- **Check errors in a report**
- **Create a report using Report Wizard**
- **Create mailing labels**
- **Format a report**
- **Insert a picture in a report**
- **Set group and sorting options for reports**
- **Use AutoFormats**

SAM

CREATING CUSTOM REPORTS

Elaine distributed the basic reports she created to the other managers at 4Corners Pharmacy, and they have already started to use them for customer relations, daily operations, human resources, and accounting. They also discussed other reports they need to support these functional areas. Table 5.10 lists their requests for additional reports and improvements to existing reports.

Table 5.10: Additional reports suggested for the pharmacy

Category	Reports Needed
Customer relations	• On-demand report showing drug purchases during particular time periods for insurance reporting • Mailing labels for a health and wellness newsletter and coupons to send to each household • Coupons for customers with no recent refill activity • Drug refill list for all customers
Management decision support and long-range planning	• Monthly sales report

As Elaine reviews this list, she realizes that the requested reports are more complex than the first set of basic reports she created. For example, to create the customer relations report that lists drug purchases during a given period, she must find a way that users can specify which time period they want. To produce the mailing labels for the newsletters and coupons sent to each household, she must select some fields from tblCustomer and some from tblHousehold, and then select name and address information only for customers who are heads of households. To produce these results, Elaine must create **custom reports**, which are reports that require data from more than one table, have calculated fields, use summary statistics, or require parameter input at the time the report is run. Some may require more than layout modification in Design view as well.

Creating a Report Using Fields from Multiple Tables

Many of the reports that Elaine wants to create require fields from more than one table. You can use the Report Wizard to select a table and some or all of its fields in the first wizard dialog box, and then select a different table to add other fields. However, if you want to limit the records included in the report or use parameter values for the user to supply when the report is run, you need to base the report on a query.

Elaine decides to start with the mailing labels for the quarterly health and wellness newsletter, which she wants to send to all households. Regular contact with customers is a good way to have them think of the pharmacy when they need prescriptions filled. Fields to create the mailing labels for customers come from tblCustomer and tblHousehold. Because the Label Wizard lets you use fields from one table only, she must retrieve the data for this report using a query.

Elaine can specify one mailing per household because of the one-to-many relationship between HouseID in the two tables. By limiting the data to only those designated as head of household, each household will receive only one mailing. Elaine first creates the query in query Design view by selecting the CustFirst, CustLast, and HeadHH fields from tblCustomer and the Address, City, State, and Zip fields from tblHousehold. HeadHH is a Yes/No field so the criterion is "Yes" to limit the query results to heads of household. She saves the query as qryHeadHHOnly. See Figure 5.27.

Figure 5.27: qryHeadHHOnly in Design view

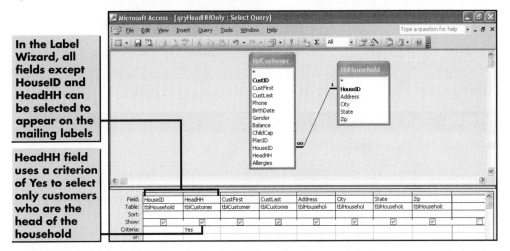

In the Label Wizard, all fields except HouseID and HeadHH can be selected to appear on the mailing labels

HeadHH field uses a criterion of Yes to select only customers who are the head of the household

When Elaine starts the Label Wizard, she uses qryHeadHHOnly as the basis for the mailing labels, selecting only the CustFirst, CustLast, Address, City, State, and Zip fields to appear on the labels. Given the large number of customers, Elaine sorts the labels by zip code to take advantage of any bulk mail cost savings. She names the labels report rptHeadHHOnly. She can also use this report to create mailing labels for the special promotion coupons she wants to send to all households. Figure 5.28 shows the mailing labels in Design view.

Figure 5.28: Design view of mailing labels

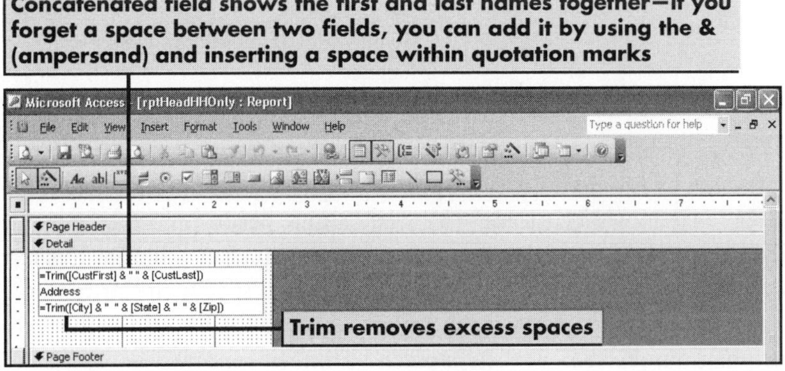

Concatenated field shows the first and last names together—if you forget a space between two fields, you can add it by using the & (ampersand) and inserting a space within quotation marks

=Trim([CustFirst] & " " & [CustLast])
Address
=Trim([City] & " " & [State] & " " & [Zip])

Trim removes excess spaces

Best Practice

Naming Queries Used as the Basis for Reports

If you require a query for a report, it is a good idea to use the same name for both the query and the report, while varying the "qry" or "rpt" prefix as appropriate. You will know the query is the basis for the report and will be less likely to delete the query.

When Elaine runs the report, she sees an error message, indicating that some data may not be displayed, and that there is not enough horizontal space on the page for the labels. This is a common error message when printing mailing labels. Before modifying the columns, Elaine previews the data to discover if any data falls outside the printing area.

It seems that the labels will print correctly, but Elaine decides to modify the labels so that pharmacy employees printing the labels do not receive the same error message each time they print.

Best Practice

Resolving Error Messages in Mailing Labels

Even when using standard mailing label layouts and fonts, you may see an error message when previewing or printing mailing labels. Before modifying column widths, check to see if the data in the labels is all printing. In many cases, no modification is necessary. Especially when using Avery 5160-compatible label stock, the Label Wizard page layout settings require a page width of 8.625 inches—more than the standard 8.5-inch standard paper size. Because this is such a common stock for mailing labels, and because your users may not want to see an error every time they print the labels, you might want to modify the width of the labels to eliminate the message.

How To

Respond to an Avery 5160-compatible Error Message

1. Open the mailing label report in Design view.
2. Hold down Shift while you click to select all the text boxes.
3. Move all text boxes one grid dot to the left.
4. Switch to Print Preview and change the left and right report margins to .25 inches and the column width to 2.583 inches. After you change the column width, you may see the column width reset itself to 2.5826.

Next, Elaine focuses on another customer relations report. Depending on their health plan, customers may need to submit a list of all prescriptions for reimbursement. Elaine wants to create a report that allows a customer to specify a time period, and then generate a list of prescriptions received during that period. Because a technician will print this report for a single customer at a time, the technicians must be able to specify the customer number and the time period before they produce the report. How can Elaine prompt the technicians to enter a customer number before they open and print the report?

Elaine recalls that parameter queries allow user input—when you run a parameter query, it displays a dialog box requesting information to be used as criteria for retrieving records. If Elaine bases the customer relations report on a parameter query, it will stop to wait for user input for each parameter requested, such as the customer number. Elaine creates the query using fields from the tblCustomer, tblRx, tblRefill, tblHealthPlan, and tblDrug tables. She also calculates the total cost of each prescription by using the Quantity, Price, and Days fields. See Figure 5.29.

Figure 5.29: Query to calculate on-demand customer drug purchases

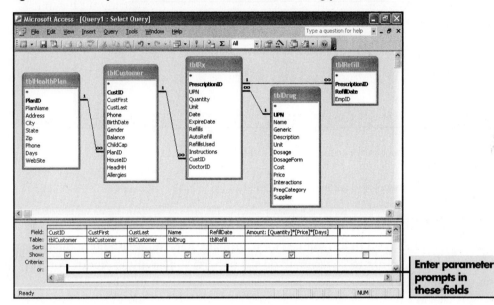

In the CustID field, she enters the parameter [Customer ID?], and in the RefillDate field, she enters the parameter "Between [Beginning Date?] And [Ending Date?]." By doing so, Access will display three dialog boxes requesting a customer number and date range. She saves the query as qryRxList, and bases a new report on this query, naming it rptRxList. She sorts the report on RefillDate. The finished report lists all prescriptions for a given time period for only one customer, as shown in Figure 5.30.

Figure 5.30: On-demand customer refill report

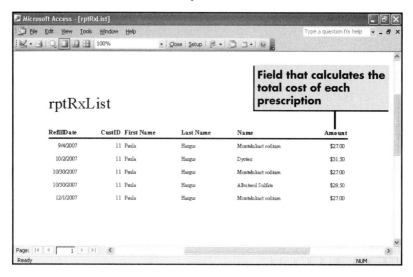

Elaine notices that the report contains several fields with repetitious data and decides to group the report so each CustID and name appears only once. She could just start over but decides to add grouping levels in Design view.

Adding or Modifying Grouping Levels to a Report

Custom reports often need to be modified for readability. Repetitious listings of the same field values make it harder to concentrate on the important data in the report. For this reason, you can add a grouping level after creating the original report. The fields that you use to sort data in a report can also serve as grouping fields. If you specify a sort field as a grouping field, you can include a group header and group footer for the group, as you can for any group. A group header typically includes the name of the group, and a group footer typically includes a count or subtotal for records in that group. You use the Sorting and Grouping button [≡] on the Report Design toolbar to select sort fields and grouping fields for a report. Each report can have up to 10 sort fields, and any of its sort fields can also be grouping fields.

Elaine wants to add a grouping level to her on-demand customer refill report to eliminate the redundant CustID and customer names. She wants to group on CustID because this is the unique field in the query. She clicks the Sorting and Grouping button [≡] on the Report Design toolbar to open the Sorting and Grouping dialog box. In the top section of the Sorting and Grouping dialog box, she can specify the sort fields for the records in the Detail section. To convert a sort field to a grouping-level field, she must select a group header or group footer for the field. For each sort field, she can use the Group Properties section of the dialog box to specify whether she wants a group header, a group footer, and other options for this field.

Elaine clicks the first line to add a grouping level, clicks the list arrow that appears, selects CustID from the list, and accepts the Ascending sort order. She decides to add a Group Header and Group Footer to the report for CustID, so she selects Yes in the text boxes for those options. Next, she adds RefillDate to the second line of the dialog box and accepts Ascending as the sort order. By not adding a group header or footer, she is only setting the sort order for RefillDate. Figure 5.31 shows the completed dialog box.

Figure 5.31: Sorting and Grouping dialog box

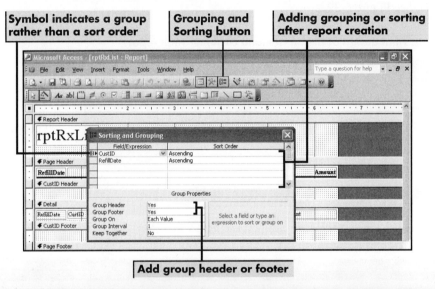

How To

Create a Grouping Level in an Existing Report

1. Open the report in Design view.

2. Click the Sorting and Grouping button [≣] on the Report Design toolbar to open the Sorting and Grouping dialog box.

3. Click the first blank row in the Field/Expression column, click the list arrow that appears, and then select the field on which you want to group records. The order of the fields determines the order for the grouping levels, so the first field determines the primary grouping level, the second field determines the secondary grouping level, and so on.

4. To change the sort order for the new group, click the list arrow in the corresponding Sort Order column, and then click Ascending or Descending.

5. In the Group Properties section, set the grouping options for the field. For example, to add a group footer for this field, click Group Footer, click its list arrow, and then click Yes.

6. Close the Sorting and Grouping dialog box.

7. Add text boxes, labels, and other controls to the new Group Header section as necessary.

In Design view for rptRxList, Elaine drags the controls for the CustID and CustName fields under the CustID Group Header so she can display them once before listing all the refills. She modifies the corresponding labels so they have larger fonts and bold type. Then she modifies the rest of the controls to improve the appearance of the report. She decides to concatenate the customer names so that the first and last name are displayed together. She deletes both CustFirst and CustLast bound controls, creates a new text box control, and then writes the formula for concatenation in the new control: =[CustFirst] & " " & [CustLast]. She changes the property of the new control to match the larger and bold font of CustID. See Figure 5.32.

Figure 5.32: Final design of the on-demand customer refill report

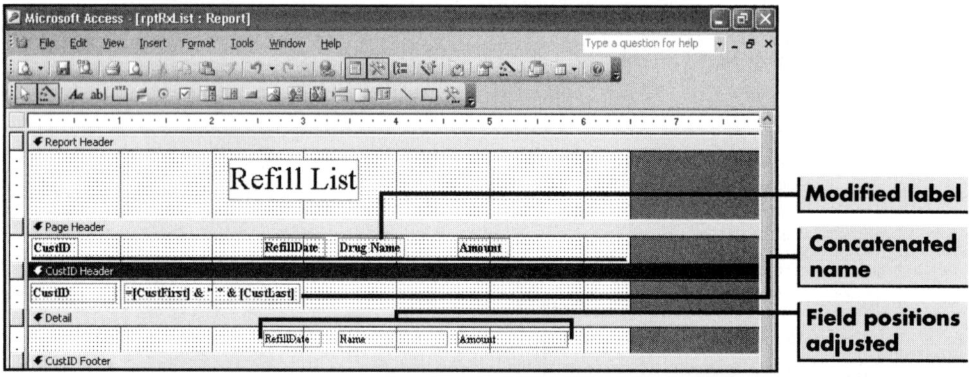

Best Practice

Avoiding #Name# Errors in Calculated Fields
If you decide to add a calculated field to concatenate names, delete any controls that will be part of the result. For example, if you plan to concatenate first and last names, remove the fields that contain this data and replace them with a new text box control. If you try to use one of the fields that will be part of the new calculation, a #Name# error appears in Print Preview because you cannot use a field in a calculation inside that field's control. This error can occur with calculated fields that concatenate the contents of other fields. If a report contains LastName and FirstName fields, for example, you might add an unbound text box to the report and then insert a concatenation calculation, such as =[FirstName] & " " & [LastName] in the new text box. However, Access will display a #Name# error in this calculated field because it contains references to other fields in the report. To avoid this error, you need to delete the controls for the FirstName and LastName fields.

Elaine tries to apply the AutoFormat to her result and discovers that the AutoFormat she defined has no formatting for group headers and footers. She can modify the AutoFormat using rptRxList and add this to the AutoFormat. See Figure 5.33. From now on, all reports with grouping will use the formats Elaine specified from rptRxList. If she later modifies the AutoFormat further, she can continue to build the AutoFormat using one of the existing reports or a new report.

Figure 5.33: Modifying custom AutoFormat with information from another report

Update AutoFormat
with sections from
another report

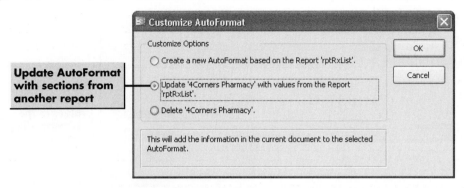

IMPROVING THE INFORMATION CONTENT OF GROUPED REPORTS

Elaine included the **group header** and **group footer** when she created the new grouping level in rptRxList. The group header section is an area on a report used to indicate the start of a new group. Any text or controls located in the group header are shown once for the group. For example, the CustID and customer name located in the group header of rptRxList are only shown once and then the detail about each refill is listed below it in the Detail section. The group footer section is shown only once at the end of any group detail. It can be used to identify the group but it is most often used to contain summary data such as subtotals for the data in the group. Recall that the Report Wizard automatically includes a group header and footer as part of the report if you specify any grouping levels. If you have no information for the group footer, whether you added it as part of a new grouping level or the Report Wizard added it, you can remove it using the Sorting and Grouping dialog box.

Tabular reports that have large amounts of data often contain more information content if the report uses grouping. The groups organize the data into smaller segments that are easier to comprehend. When you use the Report Wizard to create a grouped report, the wizard provides optional summary statistics and percentages to show more information about each group, as well as overall totals for the report.

Elaine wants to add a total for all refills for each customer in rptRxList. Because the report is already created, she wants to add the calculation to the group footer of the report. She recalls that calculated fields are unbound text box controls and that the general format is to use an equal sign followed by the calculation. She opens rptRxList in Design view and adds a text box control in the group footer section of the report. She wants a total, so she types =Sum([Amount]) in the control. Amount was created in an underlying query, so all she needs to do is add up the amounts for each refill. When she checks the report in Print Preview, she notes that the total is not formatted, so she returns to Design view and changes the Format property for the control to Currency. She also changes the label for the control to Refill Total and modifies the report further for best appearance. Figure 5.34 shows the resulting report in Design view and Print Preview.

Figure 5.34: rptRxList in Design view and Print Preview

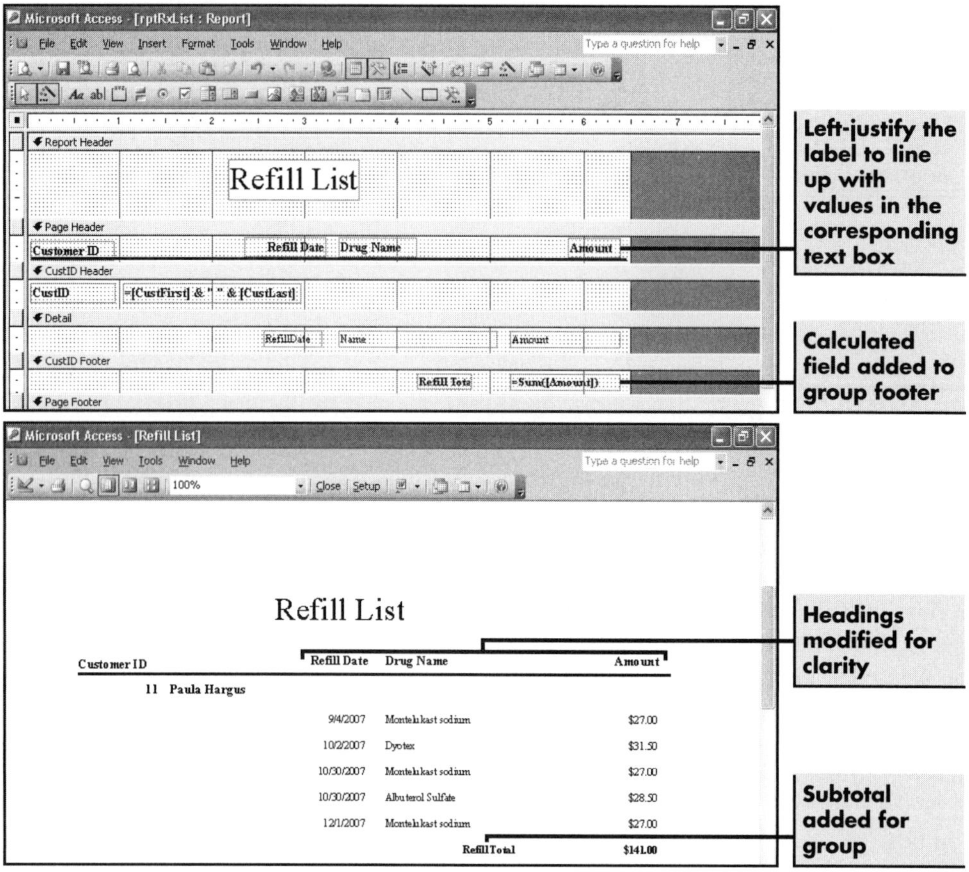

Left-justify the label to line up with values in the corresponding text box

Calculated field added to group footer

Headings modified for clarity

Subtotal added for group

The pharmacy technicians can now use the refill report to show the prescription refills each customer ordered and the total cost of each prescription.

Best Practice

Using Queries to Create Calculated Fields

You can include calculated fields on a report using a text box control. However, most developers recommend creating the calculation in a query and then using the query as the basis for the report. In the query design grid, you can use the Zoom feature to create and modify a calculation and set its format there; Design view for a report does not provide this feature. Using the query design grid is, therefore, preferable for long calculations.

If you do insert a calculated field on a report manually, you can either temporarily widen the control or right-click a control and then click Properties. You can right-click Control Source property and then click Zoom to open a larger window for creating the expression, or click the Build button ⌞...⌟ to open to the Expression Builder dialog box for help in building your expression.

When Elaine shows Paul Ferrino, the owner, her report for customers showing refills, he becomes interested in seeing the same data arranged in a different way, showing all customers in any given time period grouped by year, quarter, and month. He needs to prepare accounting statements for his banker and investors monthly, quarterly, and annually, and knows that this report will show the sales values he needs for the income statement. He also wants monthly and quarterly subtotals and a grand total for the period specified. Elaine decides to create a report that will give Paul all of these values by grouping on year, then on quarter, and finally on month. She won't show detail for each refill because Paul doesn't need it.

Best Practice

Understanding That Sometimes Less Is More

It is tempting to print every report showing all the detail. Grouping helps to break the data into subgroups and summary statistics may help to provide more information content to the user. However, it is often more effective to show only part of the data. Looking at just the top values helps the user to see only what's truly important. For example, a chart showing every drug in inventory, many of which have no sales activity in the time period, is distracting. Looking at only the most-used drugs is more helpful. Grouped reports also allow the option of printing only summary information using Sum and Avg calculations, for example. A summary report does not show any detail. For long lists of detail, such as all prescription refills for a year, the detail would be overwhelming.

Grouping on Date and Time

Accounting reports are usually prepared for monthly, quarterly, and annual time periods. Accounts receivable and sales values in particular are needed for these time periods, and grouping is a good way to facilitate creating these reports. The Report Wizard has built-in grouping options for Date/Time fields that can use the same date field for multiple time periods.

Because Paul wants to specify the time period in his accounting report, Elaine must first create a query to limit the data. To include the RefillDate and Amount fields, the query uses five tables. This is because there are no direct relationships between tblRefill, tblRx, and tblHealthPlan, which are the tables that contain the fields necessary for the report and the calculated field. To relate their fields, she must also use intermediate tables—tblCustomer and tblDrug. She adds the calculation for Amount and the parameters to allow Paul to input any dates at the time the report is run. She names the query qrySales. See Figure 5.35.

Figure 5.35: Parameter query to calculate sales and allow input of dates

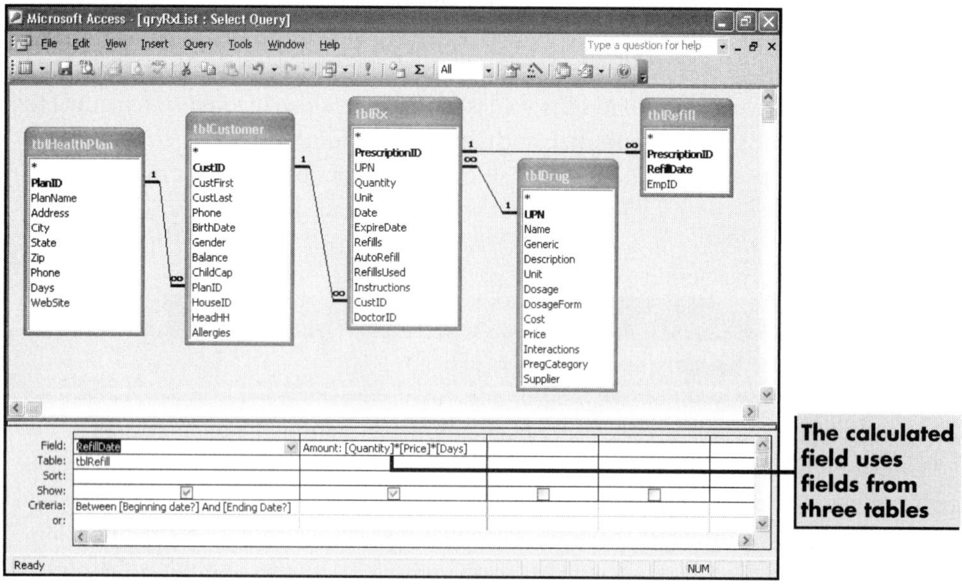

The calculated field uses fields from three tables

Elaine will base the sales report on qrySales. She decides to use the Report Wizard for the basic report because the built-in grouping level options will save her time. She knows she needs three grouping levels dealing with dates, so she selects RefillDate three times as the grouping level. The first level is grouped by Year. The second nested level is grouped by Quarter, and the innermost level is grouped by Month. See Figure 5.36.

Figure 5.36: Creating a sales report

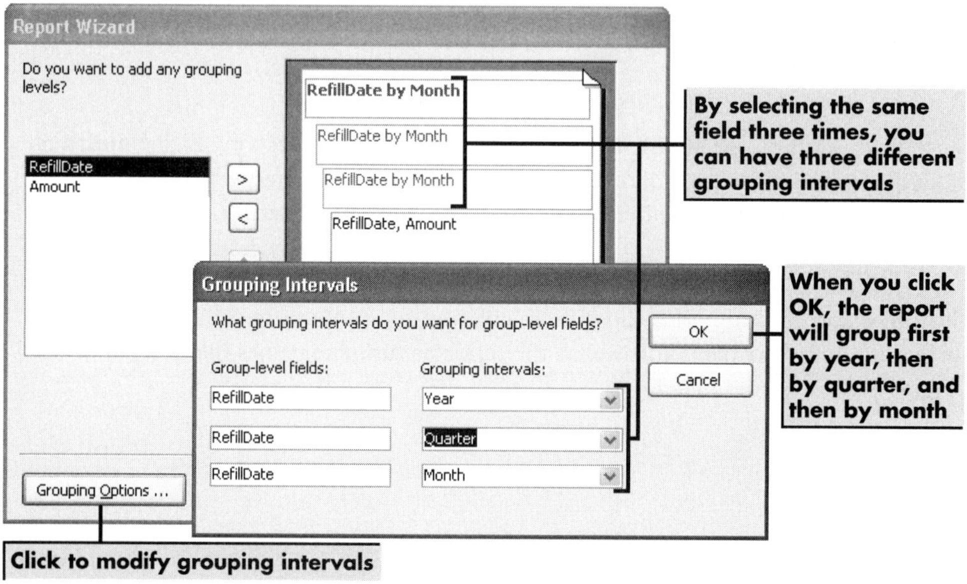

By selecting the same field three times, you can have three different grouping intervals

When you click OK, the report will group first by year, then by quarter, and then by month

Click to modify grouping intervals

Elaine needs sums on the report for each grouping level, so she clicks the Summary Options button. She selects Sum and Summary Only, and checks the Calculate Percent of total for sums check box. See Figure 5.37.

Figure 5.37: Specifying summary options

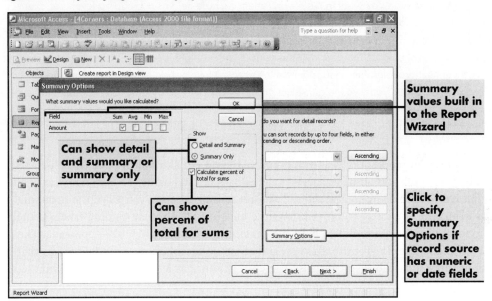

Elaine selects Stepped as the layout to stagger the three grouping levels, applies the 4Corners Pharmacy AutoFormat, and saves the report as rptSales. See Figure 5.38.

Figure 5.38: Three levels of grouping in the sales report

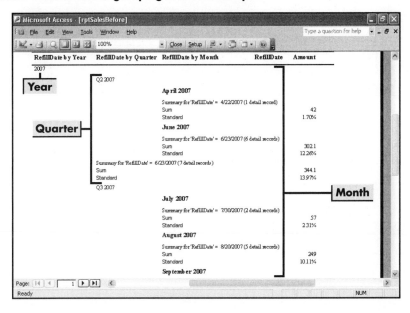

How To

Group on Multiple Time Periods

1. Start the Report Wizard and select the fields from one or more tables or queries. Then click the Next button.
2. For each time period you want in the report, select the date field as a grouping level. For example, if you want to group on year, quarter, and month, select the date field three times.
3. Click the Grouping Options button to modify the time period for each group level. The first grouping level should be the greatest time period, for example, year.
4. Select the next grouping time period within the greatest time period for the next grouping level. For example, within year, you might select group by quarter and then by month. Note that you can group on year, quarter, month, week, day, hour, and minute. Then click the Next button.
5. Continue the wizard to completion, and then click the Finish button.

Elaine thinks the report looks cluttered and confused, so she follows her checklist and modifies the report until it meets the 4Corners Pharmacy standards. To eliminate the clutter, she removes the summary labeling. She figures out that she can leave the grouping levels from year to quarter to month the same but, by putting the grouping labels in the group footer for quarter and switching the headings, she can improve the appearance and clarity of the report. She formats the year and report totals for currency and discovers that aligning the results is difficult because the currency format leaves space for parentheses around any negative values. See Figure 5.39.

Figure 5.39: Final sales report in Design view and Print Preview

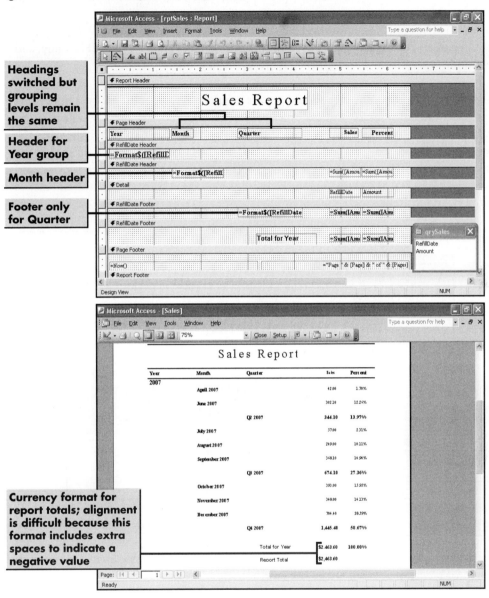

Paul is pleased with the report, and plans to use it for his next meeting with the pharmacy investors. Even as volume for the pharmacy increases, the report will continue to stay concise because it only has summary data.

To increase refill volume at the pharmacy, Elaine now wants to create labels to send to customers who have no refill activity within a specified time period. The pharmacy wants to send a coupon to attract these customers back to 4Corners Pharmacy with an offer for a discount on any new or transferred prescriptions. How can she identify these customers?

Elaine recalls that Maria Garcia mentioned using aggregate functions in a query and decides to see if any would identify the last date of a prescription refill. She knows that the labels themselves won't be any different from the household mailing labels. She decides to create the query she needs, make a copy of the mailing label report rptHeadHHOnly, and then modify the record source for the report to the new query.

To identify the households that should receive coupons, Elaine must create a query that shows only the last refill for any customer within a household. She creates a query using the HouseID and RefillDate fields from tblCustomer, tblRx, and tblRefill. She sorts the query on RefillDate in ascending order. This places the last refill for any customer at the bottom of the list. Then she clicks the Totals button **Σ** on the Query Design toolbar, and groups by HouseID. She chooses the Last aggregate function from the list box and names the query qryLastRefill. See Figure 5.40.

Figure 5.40: Identifying the last prescription date for each household

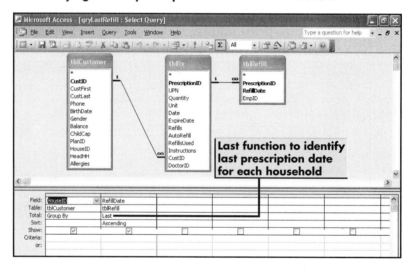

The Last function returns the value for the last row encountered for each group. (See Table 3.10 in Chapter 3 for more information about aggregate functions.) Including the Last function in the Total row for the RefillDate field means that the query will identify the last, or oldest, prescription date for each household.

It doesn't matter who in the household refilled the oldest prescription, Elaine only needs their name and address so she can send only one coupon to each household. To do this, she must create a new query to join the records from qryLastRefill with name and address information from tblCustomer and tblHousehold. She creates the query using an outer join to restrict the data and a parameter query to set the cutoff date for no refill activity. Figure 5.41 shows the query design.

Figure 5.41: qryAttractOldCustomers

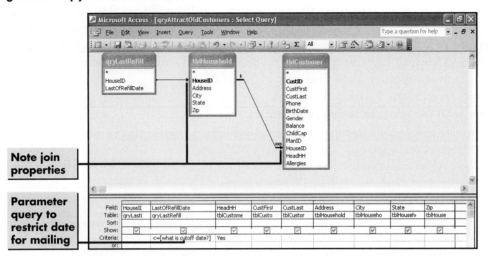

Note join properties

Parameter query to restrict date for mailing

The parameter included in the LastOfRefillDate calculated field means that users will be prompted to enter a date, and the query will select only those customers whose latest refill occurred on or before that date. The right outer join between qryLastRefill and tblHousehold means that the query will include all records in qryLastRefill and only the matching records in tblHousehold that meet the criteria. For example, if Elaine specifies 1/1/2008 as the LastOfRefillDate, the query displays only the names of addresses of household heads whose last prescription refill is on or before 1/1/2008. She tests the results of this query, using 1/1/2008 as the cutoff date, and confirms that the 10 customers the results display are heads of households. She saves the query as qryAttractOldCustomers.

Next, Elaine needs to make a copy of rptHeadHHOnly to use for the coupon mailings and revise the report so that it is based on qryAttractOldCustomers. In this way, she can create mailing labels only for household heads whose last prescription refill is on or before a specified date, and then send these customers a promotional coupon.

Changing the Record Source and Adding Fields

Report designers often need to change the source of data for a report after it is created. For example, if they base a report on a table, but then decide to limit the data using criteria or a parameter query, they can change the record source from a table to the new query. To change the record source for a report, you change the Record Source property in the report's property sheet. You can often copy an object such as a query, form, label, or macro, and then modify it for another use. This is particularly useful with reports, which often involve hours of design time. If you copy a report and then change its record source, the field list for the report also changes so that it contains all the fields in the new record source. However, you still need to delete controls on the report for fields that are not included in the current record source or add fields from the field list as necessary.

Elaine copies the mailing label report rptHeadHHOnly and names it rptAttractOldCustomers to match the name of the query that will serve as its record source. Then she opens the property sheet for the report, clicks the Record Source property, and selects qryAttractOldCustomers as the new record source for the mailing labels. See Figure 5.42. Recall that this query selects the names and addresses of household heads whose last prescription refill is on or before a specified date.

Figure 5.42: Changing the record source for the report

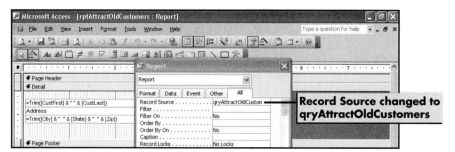

If the fields in the new record source match the fields needed for the report, you only need to change the record source. If not, you might need to remove fields that are not included in the new record source or add fields from the new record source to the report. The fields for Elaine's labels use the same fields as in qryAttractOldCustomers except for the parameter prompt that requests a cutoff date as a criterion. Elaine saves the query, and then switches to Print Preview. The Enter Parameter Prompt dialog box opens, requesting a cutoff date, and she enters 1/1/2008. The Print Preview window displays 10 mailing labels for the heads of households whose last prescription refill is on or before 1/1/2008.

Next, Elaine meets with a group of pharmacy technicians, who mention that the demand for the refill list report is high and that it is causing a bottleneck in the pharmacy. The refill report shows the prescription refills each customer ordered and the total cost of the prescription. After conferring with Paul Ferrino, Elaine decides to modify the report so it can be sent to every customer. This will provide a list of prescriptions and the associated price for each customer. Elaine and Paul anticipate that they will mail the report annually, but will review this policy after the first mailing.

To create this report, Elaine can revise rptRxList. The original report is based on qryRxList, which is a parameter query that asks for a customer ID and time period, and then lists all the prescriptions for that customer during that time. Elaine plans to change the underlying query to remove the parameter for CustID so that it lists all the customers. She will also add the name and mailing address to the report. For privacy reasons, Paul and Elaine decide to send a separate list to each customer, so she will need to print the prescription information on separate pages, with one or more pages for each customer. If she designs the report carefully, Elaine can use a window envelope to display the mailing address and save the step of printing separate mailing labels.

First, Elaine makes copies of qryRxList and rptRxList and names them qryAllCustRxList and rptAllCustRxList. Next, she modifies the query to remove the CustID parameter and to add the customer address to the query. Because address data is in tblHousehold, she adds the tblHousehold table to the field list area in Design view for qryAllCustRxList. See Figure 5.43.

Figure 5.43: Modified query for rptAllCustRxList

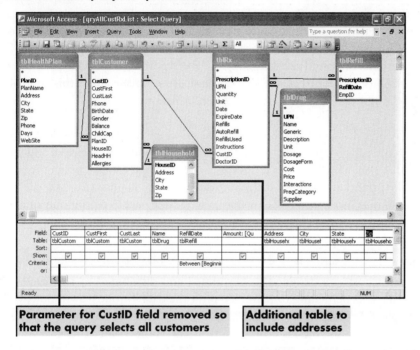

Parameter for CustID field removed so that the query selects all customers

Additional table to include addresses

Now she is ready to modify rptAllCustRxList to add address data and revise the formatting. She changes the record source for the report to qryAllCustRxList. The field list for the report now includes the additional fields from tblHousehold.

You can add a field from an underlying table or query to a report by dragging the field name from the field list. Then you can align the field's label and text box for best appearance.

Elaine opens rptAllCustRxList in Design view. Because she will send this report to each customer, she decides to move the title of the report, Refill List, from the report header to the page header so it prints on each page. She increases the size of the page header, and then moves the Refill List title label into the page header.

She also wants the three column headings—Refill Date, Drug Name, and Amount—and the line in the CustID header to print on each page so that this information appears for each customer. She selects these four controls and moves them into the page header. Now that the page header contains the report title, she no longer needs the report header, which appears on the first page of the report only. She drags the page header bar up to close the report header. Then she removes the CustID label and its text box from the CustID header because this information might be confusing to the customers.

She is ready to create an address block that will show the customer's name and address through the window in a window envelope. To place the address, she drags the Address field from the field list to the report. Access automatically creates a label for the field, but Elaine deletes it because she does not want the address block to include any labels. She decides to create a concatenated field for the city, state, and zip information to save space and improve the report's appearance, and does so by typing =[City] & " " & [State] & " " & [Zip] in an unbound text box control. The report already includes an unbound text box control for the concatenated first and last name, so she aligns this control with the ones for the address and city, state, and zip information.

Elaine measures the distance from the edge of the envelope to its address window and the distance from the edge of the report to the address block, and then uses trial and error to format the address block so that it will appear in the envelope window when the report is printed. As she prints and modifies the report design to accomplish this task, she notices that the report prints more than one customer on the same page. To print only one record per page, she needs to force a page break after each customer.

Forcing a Page Break After Each Group

Many grouped reports are designed to be printed and distributed so that each person receives only the data pertaining to them. To print the data for one person only, you can insert a Page Break control to force a page break so that data for each person prints on a separate page. You can use the Page Break button ▤ on the Toolbox toolbar to insert a page break in the group footer; each new group is then forced to print on a new page. You can also use the Keep Together setting in the Sorting and Grouping dialog box to keep a heading and at least part of the detail together.

Elaine inserts a Page Break control in the CustID footer so that the report prints data for a customer, and then starts printing the data for the next customer on a new page. She also notices that the page footer includes page numbers, which are consecutive for the entire report. She consults with Donald Linebarger, database developer, to learn if she can reset the page number to 1 after each customer record prints. He says that she can use a macro or a Visual Basic procedure, which she is not prepared to do, so she decides to simply delete the page numbers in the page footer. The page footer also includes the date, which might be useful to the customers, so she leaves that in the report. Figure 5.44 shows the final report in Design view.

Figure 5.44: Design View for rptAllCustRxList

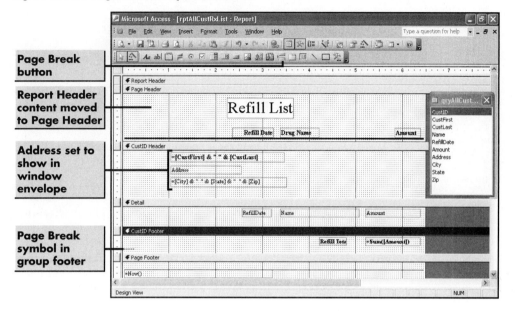

Page Break button →

Report Header content moved to Page Header →

Address set to show in window envelope →

Page Break symbol in group footer →

When Elaine prints the report, each page will list the customer's name and address, prescription refills, and total amount spent on the prescriptions.

Steps To Success: Level 2

Marie Cresson of the Hudson Bay Pharmacy needs additional reports for the other managers at the pharmacy, and asks for your help in creating the reports shown in Table 5.11.

Table 5.11: Additional reports for Hudson Bay Pharmacy

Category	Reports Needed
Customer relations	• On-demand report showing drug purchases during particular time periods for insurance reporting • Mailing labels for a health and wellness newsletter and coupons to send to each household • Coupons for customers with no recent refill activity • Drug refill list for all customers
Management decision support and long-range planning	• Annual, quarterly, and monthly sales report

Create queries as necessary to serve as the basis for the reports. As you save the new reports, be certain to use the name specified in the following steps, including the "rpt" prefix. Also consult your instructor for instructions about submitting your results.

Complete the following:

1. Start Access and open the **Hudson.mdb** database from the STS folder.

2. Marie needs to develop a customer relations report. Depending on their health plan, customers might need to submit a list of all prescriptions for reimbursement. Marie wants to create a report that allows a customer to specify a time period, and then generate a list of prescriptions received during that period. Because a technician will print this report for a single customer at a time, the technicians must be able to specify the customer number and the time period before they produce the report. Create an on-demand report showing drug purchases during a particular time period for insurance reporting for a single customer. Base the report on a parameter query named qryRxList. This report should also calculate the total cost of refill purchases. Make sure that the report uses the AutoFormat specified for Hudson Bay Pharmacy and that it is in good form. Save the report as rptRxList.

3. Marie also wants to send a health and wellness newsletter to all households each month. Create the mailing labels for the monthly newsletter that are addressed only to the head of each household. Save the mailing label report as rptHeadHHOnly.

4. Marie also wants to send promotional coupons to the head of each household whose last prescription refill is on or before a specified date. Create mailing labels to send to each household for customers with no activity in a specified time period. Name the report rptAttractOldCustomers.

5. Besides mailing labels, Marie also needs a few other customer reports. First, she asks you to create a customer telephone directory that includes all customers, their addresses, and their phone numbers listed in alphabetic order and printed in portrait orientation. Because many customers residing in the same household have different phone numbers, the phone number for each customer should be listed with the customer rather than the household. Thus, every customer must have a listing in the directory. Name the report rptCustomerPhoneList. Move the address and phone fields under the customer name fields and rearrange the report to make it more readable.

6. The next report Marie needs is a sales report with monthly, quarterly, and yearly sales summary figures. This report should allow input of any time period. Create this report for Marie, naming it rptSales. Make sure this report is in good format and shows the quarterly summary figures after the monthly figures for each quarter.

7. Finally, Marie wants to send a report to all customers listing their drug purchases. Create this report, making sure to include a page break after each customer record so that each page can be mailed to customers individually. Save this report as rptAllCustRxList.

8. Close the **Hudson.mdb** database and Access.

LEVEL 3

DESIGNING REPORTS FOR DATA ANALYSIS

ACCESS 2003 SKILLS TRAINING

- **Add a field to a report**
- **Add calculated controls to a report section**
- **Create reports with at least three sections using Report Design view**
- **Format a report**
- **Set group and sorting options for reports**

CREATING ADVANCED REPORTS IN DESIGN VIEW

Elaine has met with the management team and discussed developing more reports that would help the pharmacy. She has listed them in Table 5.12.

Table 5.12: Advanced reports for the pharmacy

Category	Reports Needed
Daily operations	• Labels for prescription bottles and containers • Customer Health plan demographics
Management decision support and long-range planning	• Contribution margin analysis • Graph showing refill activity to analyze coupon promotion effects • Margin data to export to Excel

She considers these advanced reports because they include special features such as a chart or subreport. She might start some reports using the Report or Label Wizard; after that, she will spend most of her time working in Design view. She will also start in Design view for reports over which she wants maximum layout control.

One of the most important reports Paul Ferrino has requested is a report detailing the contribution margin of the various drugs the pharmacy carries. The sales report Elaine created included information about drugs sold, which is appropriate for creating an income statement, but it doesn't include information to help with decision making about pricing. Paul asks Elaine to create a report that contains details about the volume sold of each drug and its contribution to the overall profitability of the pharmacy.

After some discussion, Paul and Elaine decide to analyze data for a user-specified time period, but will not group the data by quarters or months. Because the database does not contain the tables necessary for inventory management, which would help them calculate actual refill days, they assume that every refill is for the maximum number of days allowed under the health plan of the customer. A more sophisticated analysis would also include expenses for variable costs as well as fixed costs, but because Elaine's aim is to compare the profitability of the various drugs, she will not include variable and fixed expenses at this point.

If a drug has a high gross margin, that doesn't necessarily mean it contributes to profits—it might be a drug the pharmacy seldom sells, and then only in limited volume. Lower margin per unit of drugs might make a bigger overall contribution to gross profit due to high volume sales. This is what Paul wants to examine.

Elaine knows that she must first create a query as the basis of this report because she needs to enter parameters for the time period. She creates a query using data from tblHealthPlan, tblCustomer, tblRx, tblRefill, and tblDrug, and creates calculated fields for sales volume and contribution to profit. She clicks the Totals button Σ on the Query Design toolbar and groups by drug name. Because the time period will vary, she uses RefillDate to specify the time-period parameters. She saves this query as qryContributionMarginAnalysis. See Figure 5.45.

Figure 5.45: Query for rptContributionMarginAnalysis

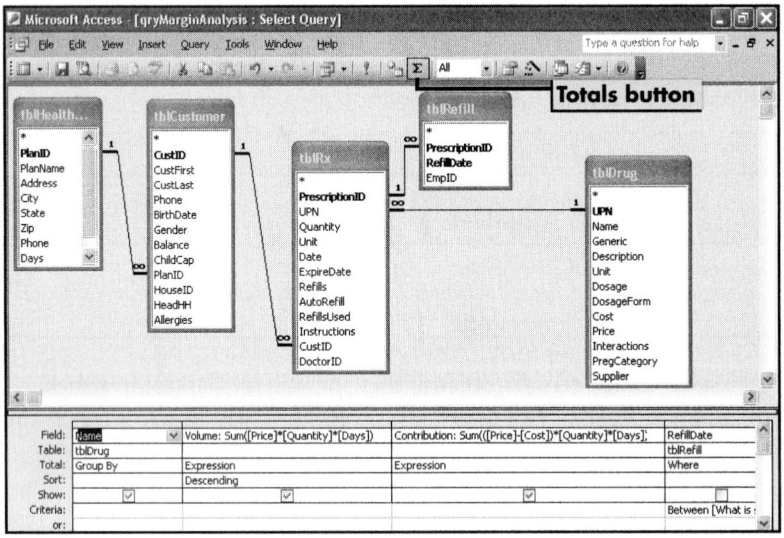

Elaine decides to create the report based on qryContributionMarginAnalysis from scratch in report Design view. She will then have complete control over its appearance and properties. Because the contribution margin analysis report is a decision support tool for Paul, she will consult with him frequently as she creates the report.

How To

Create a Report in Design View
1. Click Reports on the Objects bar in the Database window.
2. Click the New button, and then click Design View.
3. Specify the data source. If you do not specify the data source at this point, you can double-click the report properties to specify record source later.
4. Click OK. A blank report opens in Design view.

5. Add a Report header and footer if desired by right-clicking a blank spot on the report grid, and then clicking Report Header/Footer. See Figure 5.46.

Figure 5.46: Blank report open in Design view to start a new report from scratch

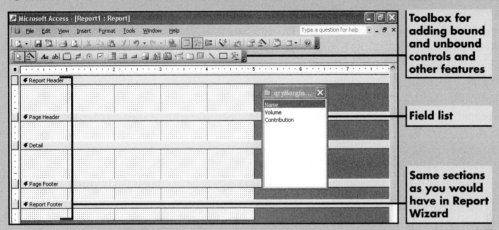

Toolbox for adding bound and unbound controls and other features

Field list

Same sections as you would have in Report Wizard

6. Create a report title if desired using a label.

7. Drag fields to the Detail section from the field list.

8. Highlight a label in the Detail section and right-click. Click Cut to separate it from its text box. Then paste it where you want it in the Page or Group Header. You can create column headings from label controls as needed if you prefer.

9. Add grouping and/or sorting in the Sorting and Grouping dialog box by clicking the Sorting and Grouping button 📇 on the Report Design toolbar. All other features in the Toolbox can be added to reports as desired in the same way they are with the Report Wizard or forms.

Best Practice

Using the Field List to Create Bound Text Boxes in Design View

When you work from Design view to create a report from scratch, you can create the text boxes used for bound controls by clicking the Text Box button 📇 on the Toolbox toolbar. Then you type the field name into the text box itself or change the ControlSource value in the control's property sheet.

However, using the field list to create a bound text box offers the following two advantages:

1. When you add a text box to a report by dragging a field from the field list, Access provides a corresponding label with the same name as the field. (If the record source defines a caption for that field, Access uses the caption instead.)

2. Using the field list also creates a bound text box that inherits many of the same properties the field has in the record source, such as a Currency format for a numeric field. If you don't use the field list to create a text box, you must set these properties in the report manually.

Elaine drags each field in qryContributionMarginAnalysis to the Detail section of the report. She moves the field labels into the Page Header section so that only the fields' text boxes remain in the Detail section. She uses commands on the Format menu to align the labels with their text boxes and to improve the appearance of the report. She clicks the AutoFormat button 📋 on the Report Design toolbar and applies the 4Corners Pharmacy AutoFormat. She also changes the label text to 10-point, semibold, modifies the labels to read Sales Volume and Gross Margin Contribution, and then uses Shift+Enter to split the labels into two lines.

Elaine right-aligns the volume and contribution labels, and then moves and aligns the labels and their text boxes. She notices the currency format makes the values harder to read, so she changes the format for both volume and contribution to Standard. She uses the Line button ＼ on the Toolbox toolbar to draw a line that separates the labels from the data.

Next, Elaine wants to include the date and page numbers on each page. She creates an unbound text box control in the page footer and deletes its label. In the control, she types =Now() to display the current date, and changes the format to show only the short date. Then she creates an unbound text box control and types ="Page "&[Page]&" of "& [Pages] to place page numbers in the page footer. Now(), [Page], and [Pages] are built-in functions. She also changes the report caption and sets the sort order for the Contribution field to descending in the Sorting and Grouping dialog box. She saves the report as rptContributionMarginAnalysis.

Best Practice

Specifying Sort Order in the Sorting and Grouping Dialog Box
Any sorting you specify in a query is overridden by the sorting you specify in the Sorting and Grouping dialog box for a report. To ensure that your data sorts the way you want it to, specify sorting criteria in the Sorting and Grouping dialog box, not the underlying query.

When Elaine shows the report to Paul, he asks if she can add totals and a running total to the report. To make room for this additional information, she changes the margin of the report, making sure that the total report width is less than 6.5 inches so she doesn't exceed the paper width of 8.5 inches. (The report width plus two one-inch margins equals the total width of the paper.)

In report Design view, Elaine creates a new label called "Running Total" and a new unbound text box with the calculation =[Contribution] to calculate the running total for the Contribution field. Then she modifies the calculated control's properties to set the Running Sum property to Over All and sets the Format property to Standard with two decimal places. (If this report grouped records, she could set the Running Sum property to Over Group.) Figure 5.47 shows the final design and Figure 5.48 shows the report in Print Preview.

Figure 5.47: Final Design view of the Contribution Margin Analysis report

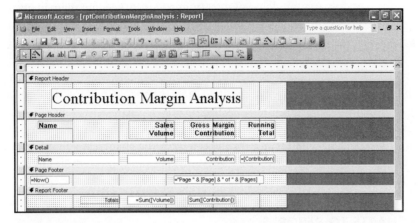

Figure 5.48: Final Contribution Margin Analysis report

Name	Sales Volume	Gross Margin Contribution	Running Total
Myobuterol	288.00	189.00	189.00
Xeroflarol	220.50	115.50	304.50
Hyometadol	202.50	105.00	409.50
Dyotex	126.00	96.00	505.50
Avatocin	168.00	90.00	595.50
Phalastat	144.00	76.50	672.00
Ampicillin	130.50	63.00	735.00
Tvalaxec	120.00	60.00	795.00
Rivastigmine tartrate	94.50	58.50	853.50
Cefixime	144.00	58.50	912.00
Clonazepam	108.00	49.50	961.50

How To

Create a Running Total

1. Create space if necessary in the report for the running total column by widening the report or reducing the left and right margins. Be sure to stay within standard page width.
2. Add a label in the page or group header for the running total field.
3. Add an unbound text box to the detail or group footer section and create the calculation by using =[*Fieldname*].
4. In the property sheet for the unbound text box, change the Running Sum property to Over Group (if you have groups and want the running total to reset at each group) or Over All.

Paul and Elaine need to study the new Contribution Margin Analysis report. They may need to raise prices on low-margin, low-volume drugs to justify keeping them in inventory; they may decide to lower prices on high-volume drugs if their margin is sufficient. Comparing margins over time provides valuable input to their decision making.

Elaine knows that charts are also helpful to decision makers. She decides to create a chart showing the number of refills over a specified time period as part of the long-range accounting information that Paul wants. As the pharmacy grows, it will increase its prescription refill volume. After sending coupons to all households and special promotions to households with no recent refill activity, Elaine can track the change in volume. Although she has no guarantee that these changes are a direct result of promotions, it might help in deciding how often to send out promotions.

ADDING CHARTS TO REPORTS

A chart compares trends in data and can summarize data more effectively than a listing showing large quantities of detail. Access charts are helpful for analyzing performance data over a **time series**, or period of time. You can use the Chart Wizard to create a chart in Access. Like other wizards, the Chart Wizard guides you through the steps of selecting an appropriate chart type and adding it to a report.

For the report that shows the number of prescriptions filled monthly, Elaine decides to graph the results using the Chart Wizard instead of listing the detailed information as text. She wants to limit the time period for the report, so she creates a parameter query for the date range. The Chart Wizard does provide a date range option, but after the range is specified, it is fixed. The parameter query can update the date range as necessary—each time Elaine or another employee opens the report, Access will ask for a data range, and then graph the prescriptions refilled within that time. The query Elaine creates uses only the field RefillDate from tblRefill because she only needs a count of prescription refills for this report. She names the query qryRefillsOverTime.

On the Database window, Elaine opens the New Form dialog box because this Chart Wizard provides more options for creating charts, selects the Chart Wizard, and specifies qryRefillsOverTime as the data source. She decides to use a Column Chart because it shows variations over a period of time. She uses months as the horizontal axis and the number of prescription refills as the vertical axis. She does not need a legend because this chart will have only one series—number of refills. See Figure 5.49.

Figure 5.49: Chart in Form view showing refills over time

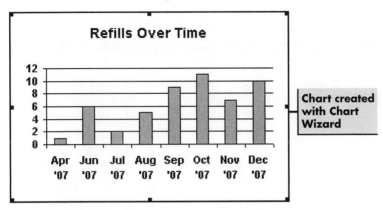

Elaine notices that there is no Y-axis label for the number of refills, and that the graph is small. She wants to improve the appearance of the chart to make it more readable and larger.

Modifying the Features of a Chart

Access uses a built-in program called Microsoft MSGraph to create charts in the Chart Wizard. After creating a chart, you can use MSGraph to modify it. Table 5.13 lists features of the graph that you can modify.

Table 5.13: Common chart features to modify

Chart Feature	Possible Modifications
Datasheet of chart values from Access-created crosstab	Number—Change format and decimal values Font—Change font, font size, emphasis, and color
Chart, X-axis, and Y-axis titles	Font, font size, emphasis, and color, as well as the alignment of the title and its orientation
X-Axis or Y-Axis	Pattern, scale, font, number, and alignment
Gridlines	Vertical and horizontal gridlines present or absent
Chart type	Change chart type
Legend	Show or hide, position
Data labels	Show data labels on graph
Data table	Show table of data used for graph

Elaine drags the lower-right corner of the chart to resize it to 6.5 inches by 3.5 inches. She double-clicks the chart to start MSGraph, and then right-clicks a blank part of the chart to display the chart options. She adds titles for the X- and Y-axes and changes the font for the X-axis. See Figure 5.50.

Figure 5.50: Datasheet view of data created by Access during Chart Wizard

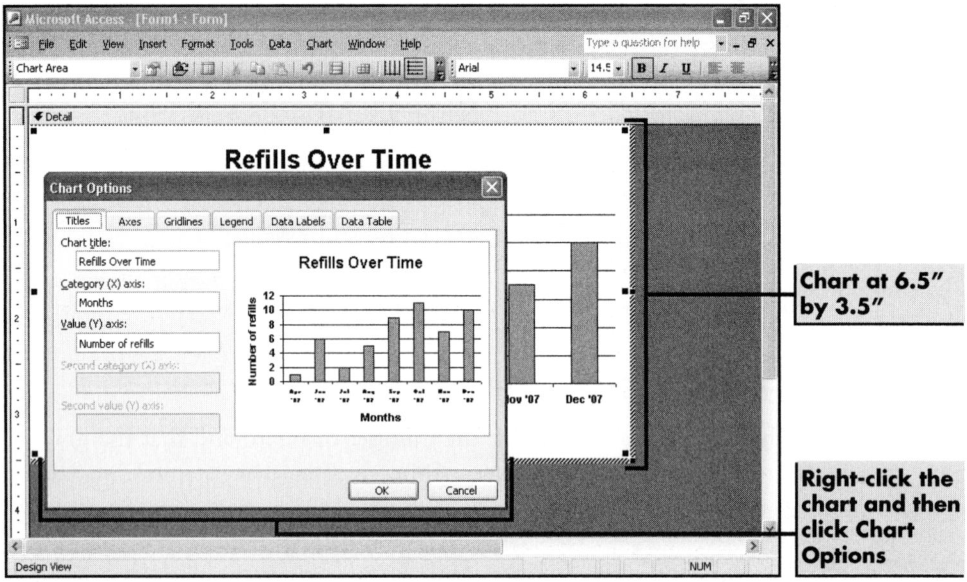

Elaine wants to save the chart created by the form Chart Wizard as a report. She opens the chart in Design view, clicks File on the menu bar, and then clicks Save As. In the Save As dialog box, she clicks the As list arrow, and then clicks Report so it will appear in the list of other reports in the Database window. She saves the report as rptRefillsOverTime.

Paul is much more comfortable analyzing numeric data in Microsoft Office Excel 2003. He asks Elaine if she could prepare data for him to examine, and perhaps chart, in Excel. Because he wants to analyze margin and pricing over time, Elaine must first create a crosstab query to provide the data he needs.

First, Elaine creates a query that includes the fields necessary for the crosstab query. Paul wants to compare the name of the drug, the margin percentage for each drug, the margin for each prescription in dollars, and the refill date. She calculates the margin percentage for each drug as [Price]-[Cost]/[Price]. Recall that Elaine and Paul are assuming that all refills are filled for the maximum period allowed. Thus, the crosstab query should also include days allowed. She creates the query using parameters for any time period so that Paul can specify this information, and names this query qryDrugMargin. Figure 5.51 shows the design of this query.

Figure 5.51: Design of margin query for the crosstab query

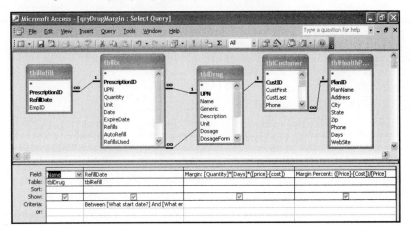

Elaine starts the Crosstab Wizard and uses qryDrugMargin as the data source. She includes Name and Margin Percent as the rows—this will list all drugs and their individual percent margin. She selects RefillDate for the columns and monthly for the time period. Sum of the Margin is the calculated value. When she tests the query, she notices that the drugs are in alphabetical order. She switches to Design view and sorts the Percent Margin column in descending order to list the drugs with the highest margin first. She considers limiting the drugs to the top 25 or 25%, but Paul wants to look at all of them for now. She saves the crosstab query as qryDrugMargin_Crosstab. Now all she has to do is export the data to Excel for Paul. Figure 5.52 shows the results of the crosstab query.

Figure 5.52: Results of margin crosstab

Name	Margin Percent	Total Of Margin	Jan	Feb	Mar	Apr	M
Oyotex	76%	$168.00		$24.00		$72.00	
Tolbutamide	73%	$39.60					
Glimepiride	72%	$39.00	$39.00				
Albuterol Sulfate	68%	$58.50					
Nvalax	67%	$36.00				$18.00	
Myobuterol	66%	$220.50				$31.50	$
Montelukast sodium	64%	$17.40	$17.40				
Rivastigmine tartrate	62%	$58.50		$58.50			
Quentix	60%	$90.00	$45.00				
Diazapam	60%	$40.20		$40.20			
Avatocin	54%	$112.50	$22.50	$67.50			
Phalastat	53%	$127.50			$25.50	$25.50	
Xeroflarol	52%	$181.50			$66.00		
Hyometadol	52%	$231.00		$21.00	$63.00		
Acebutolol hydrochloride	50%	$99.00					
Dseurton	50%	$18.00					
Levothyroxine	50%	$21.00		$21.00			
Tvalaxec	50%	$60.00	$15.00	$15.00		$15.00	
Ampicillin	48%	$210.00			$63.00		
Haloperidol	46%	$18.00	$18.00				
Clonazepam	46%	$66.00	$16.50	$16.50	$16.50		
Epronix	43%	$39.00	$19.50		$19.50		
Didanosine	42%	$28.20					
Cefixime	41%	$58.50		$58.50			

Record: |◄| ◄ | I | ► | ►| | ►* of 24

Drug name   NUM

How To

Export Data to Microsoft Office Excel for Further Analysis and Creating Charts

1. Select the query you want to export.
2. Click File on the menu bar, and then click Export. The Export Query dialog box opens.
3. Click the Save as type list arrow, and then select the appropriate data type. For example, click Microsoft Excel 97-2003.
4. Enter a name for the exported query, and then click the Export button.
5. Open the query in Excel. You will only see the data, not the underlying query.

Elaine exports the data for Paul and warns him that this data will become obsolete. She can always run the crosstab query again with new dates and then export the data. Paul should design his worksheet so that he can replace obsolete data with the new data in the future. If he decides to look at only the top margin values, Elaine can modify the underlying query to specify the top value amount or percent that Paul wants.

Beyond Calculated Fields

Elaine wants to know what proportion of the 4Corners Pharmacy customers are members of each health plan. The pharmacy might be able to negotiate with the various health plans based on the number of members patronizing the pharmacy. She could also use this data to help analyze the effect of any selling price or other limitations that health plans might want to impose. To produce this report, she needs data from tblHealthPlan and tblCustomer. Although the two tables are related on the common field PlanID, they do not use a numeric field to calculate the number of health plans or the percentage of customers that belong to each plan. She wants to use the Report Wizard for this report but needs a numeric field to take advantage of the summary options. She realizes that she must create a totals query first to count the number of customers in each plan and then use the query's numeric field in the report. She creates the query and names it qryHealthplanAnalysis. The results are shown in Figure 5.53. Elaine notes that the numbers are small because the database hasn't yet been put into production. When it is, she will have this report ready.

Figure 5.53: Count of customers in each health plan

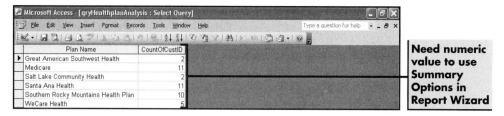

Need numeric value to use Summary Options in Report Wizard

Elaine creates the report using the Report Wizard and uses the qryHealthplanAnalysis query, which counts the number of customers in each plan, as the data source. She groups records on the PlanName field so she can perform calculations for each group, even though the data already appears in a summarized format. Because qryHealthplanAnalysis includes a numeric value, the wizard displays the dialog box containing summary options. She selects Sum because the report needs this value to calculate the percentages. She also selects the Calculate percent of total for sums check box, selects a Stepped layout, and applies the 4Corners Pharmacy AutoFormat. Following best practices, she names the report rptHealthplanAnalysis. The report still needs considerable modification to meet the professional standards of the pharmacy, however. She can move the PlanName, Count, and Percentage fields to the grouping header, delete the summary text in the group footer, modify the label for the Percentage field, and generally make the report more attractive. The modified report is shown in Figure 5.54.

Figure 5.54: Healthplan Analysis report

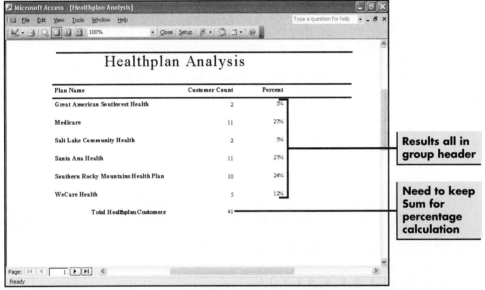

Advanced Label Formatting

Next, Elaine plans to create the labels for all prescription containers and bottles using the Label Wizard. She finds an Avery USA 4168 label (continuous) that measures 2 1/16" × 4" in the Label Wizard. This type of label can wrap around the smallest container that 4Corners Pharmacy uses. Larger containers and bottles can also use the same size label. The pharmacy needs to use a printer that can print continuous labels because the technicians will print the labels one at a time throughout the day. She plans to order the labels already printed with the logo, name, address, and phone number of the pharmacy.

Because the Label Wizard allows only one table or query as the basis for the labels, Elaine starts by creating a query with the fields she needs. She will limit the RefillDate in the query to today's date after she finishes modifying the label, when she will also add parameter values for the Prescription Number and Use by Date fields. (She can create and test a query more quickly if she uses fixed values in these fields for now.) She sorts the query on

RefillDate in descending order so the latest refill is first, and creates calculated fields to calculate the refills remaining and the total quantity in the container. She names the query as qryRxContainer.

Next, she lists the data required for the label, the table it comes from, and an approximate order for the contents of the label:

- Prescription number: tblRx
- Date of refill: tblRefill
- Date of prescription: tblRx
- Name of the prescribing doctor: tblDoctor
- Name of drug: tblDrug
- Quantity (needed to calculate total quantity) and unit of drug: tblRx
- Days: tblHealthPlan (to calculate total quantity)
- Name and address of the customer: tblCustomer and tblHousehold
- Instructions: tblRx
- Number of refills remaining and expiration date of prescription: tblRx
- Number of refills remaining: tblRx
- Use Before date: Determined by the expiration date on the drug in inventory and input when the refill is processed
- ID of employee who filled the prescription: tblRefill

Elaine is now ready to create the label for the prescription container. She uses the Label Wizard to get started but plans to modify the label significantly. Figure 5.55 shows the label in its initial layout. She saves the label report as rptRxContainer.

Figure 5.55: Layout of container label before modification

Modifying Labels in Design View

Elaine can use the properties of the controls to modify the label precisely. Remembering that many of the pharmacy's customers are elderly, she wants the prescription number, the name of the person for whom the prescription is filled, the name of drug, and the instructions to be large and bold. She also plans to use color to highlight items on the label that a technician might want to know if the customer calls to ask for a refill. Elaine uses the properties in the property sheets for the label and its controls. Figure 5.56 displays the label in its final format.

Figure 5.56: Finished container label showing test data

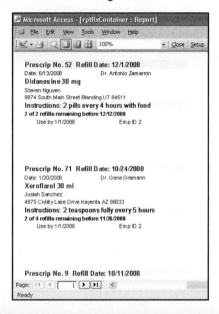

Best Practice

Changing Column Widths and Label Position

You can modify column widths in labels using the Columns tab in the Page Setup dialog box for the labels the same way you can change the settings in reports. This might be necessary for custom labels and for continuous labels positioned in tractor-fed printers to prevent label "creep" after many labels have printed due to slight misalignment of the labels.

Change the Number of Columns option to set the number of labels across the page. Left and Top margin settings determine the position for the upper-left corner of the first label. Row spacing and Height determine the number of labels that will fit vertically on a page and the vertical distance between the labels. Setting Row Spacing to 0 allows the depth of the Detail section to determine the vertical spacing of the labels. Printing on continuous labels might require more adjustments than the sheet-fed labels, so it is a good idea to test print a new label to make sure the alignment is right. Buying continuous labels in large quantities so that you don't have to put new labels into the printer avoids having to make the adjustments often.

Elaine is pleased with the labels for the prescription containers. They should save time as each prescription is filled and are designed to work with all pharmacy containers. Paul is preparing for his investor's meeting and has asked Elaine to create a report specifically for 2007 and to add a graph to the sales report to show the 2007 monthly sales.

INCLUDING ADDITIONAL DATA FOR ANALYSIS

To provide additional information on a report from a table or query, you can include a subreport, which provides information similar to that of a subform. You can also apply conditional formatting to a report so that it displays some information in a certain color, for example, if that information meets specified conditions. You might display negatives values in red, for example, or values greater than one hundred thousand in bright blue.

Adding a Subreport to a Report

As you have learned, you can link several tables with one-to-many relationships to display lots of detail in a report. Access supports grouping to help you arrange the data in a hier-archical way by nesting the groups. You can also embed **subreports** or subforms in a report including charts or unrelated data. Subreports are reports you create and then embed in another report. Access allows you to embed subforms as well. (Note that subreports can't be embedded in forms.) Because the Report Wizard does not create main reports and subreports at the same time, you must create the report (or form) you want to use as a subreport first and then add it to the main report in Design view.

After creating the form or report you want to use for the subreport or subform, you add it to the report the same way you added a subform to a form—using the Subform/Subreport button 🔳 on the Toolbox toolbar. In many cases, the subreport is linked to a field on the main part of the report, although that is not required. Linked subreports must have a common field in the main part of the report and in the subreport. Unlinked subreports allow you to combine unrelated data on one report. To create a subreport, you can use the Subreport Wizard, one of the Control Wizards Access offers in Design view of a report.

How To

Add a Subform or Subreport to a Report in Design View
1. In report Design view, create space for a subreport by increasing the size of the Detail section.
2. Make sure the Control Wizards button 🔲 on the Toolbox toolbar is active.
3. Click the Subform/Subreport button 🔳 on the Toolbox toolbar.
4. Click where you want to place the subreport. The Subform/Subreport Wizard starts.
5. Select a table, query, form, or report as the source for the subreport. Click the Next button.
6. Select the fields you want for the subreport. Click the Next button.
7. Define the link between the main form and the subform. If there is no link, select None. Click the Next button.
8. Name the subreport. This name will appear on the report. Click the Finish button.
9. Modify the subform and the rest of the report as necessary.

Paul is getting ready for the 2007 annual investors meeting for the pharmacy. He asks Elaine to combine sales data from rptSales and the chart showing monthly sales into a single report. Elaine suggests that they keep the original sales report with variable time inputs, but create this report with only 2007 data. The report will use fixed dates, but she can use it for comparison purposes next year. To create this report, Elaine must complete the following tasks:

- Copy qrySales, name it qry2007Sales, and modify it to use fixed dates for 1/1/2007 through 12/31/2007 as criteria.
- Copy rptSales, name it rpt2007Sales, and modify the record source for this report to qry2007Sales. Change the title of the report to 2007 Sales Report.
- Create a new chart using qry2007Sales as the data source and name it frm2007SalesChart. Modify the chart to add X- and Y-axes and to make it about 6.5 inches by 3 inches.

To add the new chart as a subform, Elaine opens rpt2007Sales in Design view and moves the page footer down to make room for the chart. She won't need the page numbers because this report will fit on one page, so she deletes the page numbers. She does want the date, so she moves it to the page footer. She clicks the Subform/Subreport button ▣ on the Toolbox toolbar, and then clicks in the page footer area to start the Subform/Subreport Wizard. She chooses frm2007SalesChart as the data source and accepts the default name for the subform. She deletes the subform label because the same information is in the title of the graph. Note that she has to keep the Report Total field to maintain the running totals. Figure 5.57 shows her report.

Figure 5.57: rpt2007Sales in Design view and Print Preview

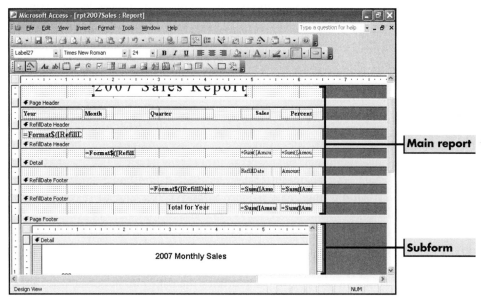

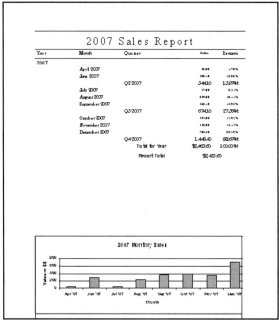

Paul has one more request of Elaine for the investors' annual meeting. He wants the rpt2007Sales report to highlight any quarter that has less than 25% or more than 50% of the total sales. Elaine suggests changing the color of the percentage value to red to show low values and blue for high values. To accomplish this, she can use conditional formatting.

Conditional Formatting for Report Values

Conditional formatting allows the developer to add formatting features such as color, bold, or larger fonts based on the values in the report. Using conditional formatting, you can change the appearance of a control on a report so that it differs from one record to another depending on whether the value in the control meets criteria that you specify. You can use conditional formatting to use a different background color, font style, or text color in a control so that its values are highlighted when they meet a certain condition. If the value of the control changes and no longer meets the condition, Access uses the default formatting for the control. You can specify up to three conditions for a field.

Elaine wants to change the format of the quarterly percentage of sales in rpt2007Sales depending on the values calculated in that field. To do this, she right-clicks the calculated field for Percent, and then clicks Conditional Formatting on the shortcut menu. She specifies that the condition is less than 25%, and changes the font color to red. For the second condition, she specifies values between 25% and 50% and leaves the font black. For the third condition, she specifies values above 50% and makes these blue. Only those values meeting the conditions will show the changes. Figure 5.58 shows the conditions Elaine sets and the resulting completed report.

5

Level 3

Figure 5.58: Setting conditional formatting for the calculated Percent field

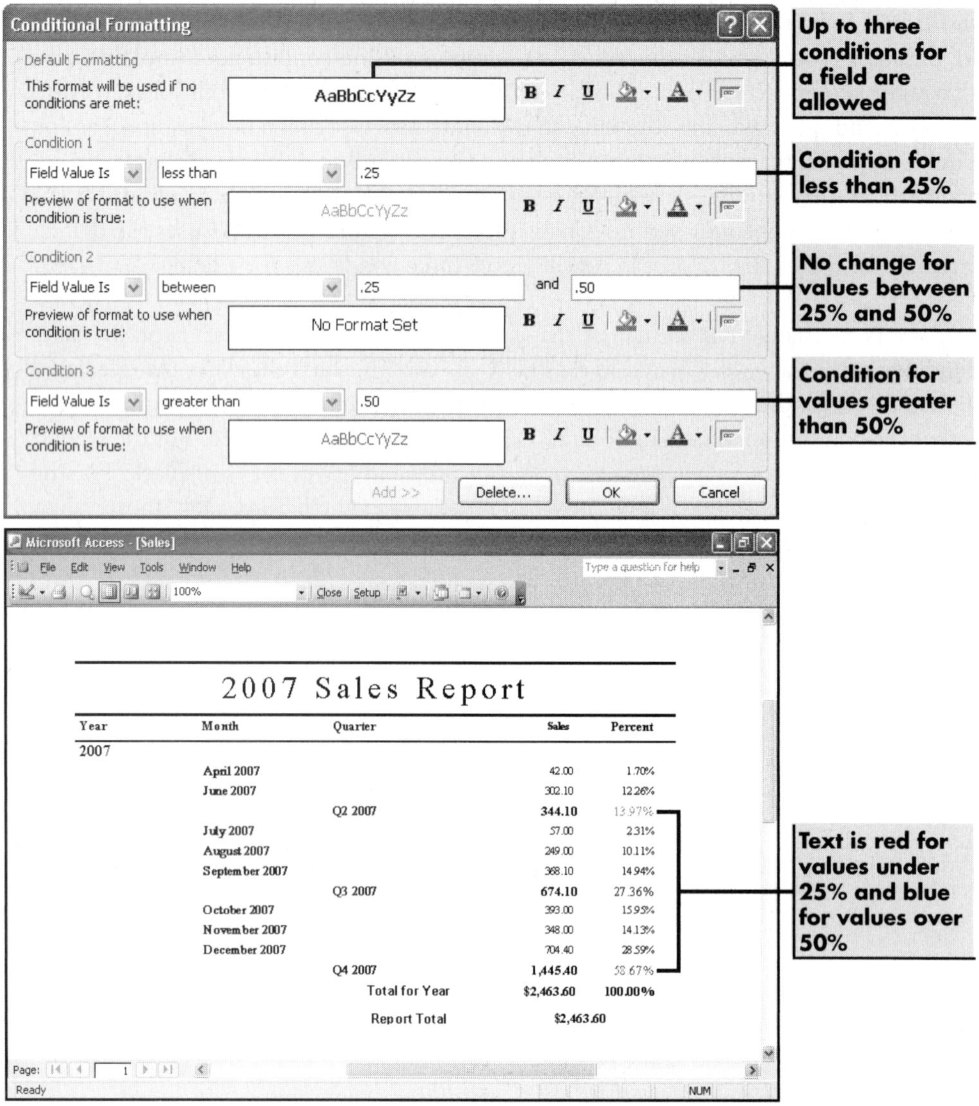

Up to three
conditions for
a field are
allowed

Condition for
less than 25%

No change for
values between
25% and 50%

Condition for
values greater
than 50%

Text is red for
values under
25% and blue
for values over
50%

Now that Elaine has created all the reports Paul needs, he is ready for the annual investor meeting.

Steps To Success: Level 3

Marie Cresson of the Hudson Bay Pharmacy needs additional reports for the other managers at the pharmacy, and asks for your help in creating the reports shown in Table 5.14.

Table 5.14: Advanced reports for the Hudson Bay Pharmacy

Category	Reports Needed
Daily operations	• Labels for prescription bottles and containers • Percentage of customers in each health plan
Management decision support and long-range planning	• Contribution margin analysis • Graph showing refill activity to analyze coupon promotion effects • Margin data to export to Excel • 2007 investor's report with graph and conditional formatting

Create queries as necessary to serve as the basis for the reports. As you save the new reports, be certain to use the name specified in the following steps, including the "rpt" prefix. Also consult your instructor for instructions about submitting your results.

Complete the following:

1. Start Access and open the **Hudson.mdb** database from the STS folder.

2. Create a report from scratch in Design view to analyze contribution margin for all drugs for any given time period. The report should include sales and gross margin subtotals by drug but no detail. Drugs should be sorted by contribution margin in descending order. Be sure the report has a date and page numbers. Add running totals to the report. Modify the report as necessary to conform to the pharmacy standards. Save the report as rptContributionMarginAnalysis.

3. Create a chart to show the monthly number of refills over a specified time period. Be sure the chart has a title and X- and Y-axes labels. Name the chart frmRefillsOverTime.

4. Prepare data for export to Excel that shows the drugs, percent margin for each drug, and the margin for each drug over monthly time increments. Name the data rptDrugMarginforExcel. Export the data in Excel 97-2003 format. Save the exported file as **qryDrugMarginforExcel.xls**.

5. Create a summary management report that shows what proportion of Hudson Bay Pharmacy customers are members of each health plan. Show both the total number of customers and the percentage of the total. Save the report as rptHealthplanAnalysis, and then modify it as necessary to meet the professional standards of the pharmacy.

6. Create labels for the prescription containers using labels that fit on a typical prescription container. Hudson Bay Pharmacy needs the same information on their prescription labels as does 4Corners Pharmacy. Name the report rptRxContainer.

7. Use copies of qrySales and rptSales as the basis for a 2007 sales report with a fixed time period of 1/1/2007 to 12/31/2007. Modify the report as necessary and name it rpt2007Sales.

8. Create a chart called frm2007SalesChart showing monthly sales and add it to rpt2007Sales as a subform.

9. In rpt2007Sales, show conditional formatting for each quarter that distinguishes between quarters contributing less than 25% to the pharmacy and those contributing more than 50% to the pharmacy.

10. Close the **Hudson.mdb** database and Access.

CHAPTER SUMMARY

This chapter presented many of the ways you might present data in a database. Because paper reports are still used extensively by management, reports must not only look professional, but must also have the maximum information content to aid in decision making. In Level 1, you learned how to create simple reports using AutoReport and the Report Wizard. You also learned how to create grouping levels in a report from a single table and how to create mailing labels using the Label Wizard. You learned how to modify the results of the Report Wizard in Design view and how to create a custom AutoFormat for all reports.

In Level 2, you learned about customizing reports using data from two or more tables or queries, about grouping issues such as summary statistics, keeping data together, and page breaks, as well as grouping on date and time or a part of a field's contents.

In Level 3, you learned about many advanced techniques for working with reports. You learned about advanced formatting in labels and the Chart Wizard for graphic representation of data, as well as how to add a subreport or subform to a report.

CONCEPTUAL REVIEW

1. What are the most popular types of reports produced by Access and why?

2. What methods can you employ to increase the information content of a report?

3. What would your checklist be to make sure your reports all met the highest standards of professionalism?

4. What other uses are there for labels besides the standard label on an envelope used for mass mailings?

5. Why would you use the Label Wizard instead of just a report for label creation?

6. What naming conventions can you suggest for a large database with many reports, beyond just naming queries and reports the same name?

7. Why do most database developers create calculated fields in a query rather than just adding them to a report?

8. When would a subreport be a better way to design a report, rather than just grouping?

9. Give an example of how conditional formatting might help with decision making.

10. Explain the difference between a sorted report and a grouped report.

11. Give an example of when you would create a summary report.

12. What can you do to change a report if you want to include fields other than those listed in the report's field list?

13. Where would you insert page numbers if you wanted them to print on every page in the report?

14. In which section would you include running totals for a report?

15. Including charts in a report is helpful when analyzing what kind of data?

CASE PROBLEMS

Case 1—Creating Effective Reports for NHD Development Group Inc.

In this project, you continue working on the database for an antiques mall, Memories Antiques in Cleveland, Tennessee. You have been working with Linda Sutherland, the manager of the mall, and with Tim Richards, the chief information officer of the NHD Development group, who owns this mall and several other malls across the country. Tim and Linda are ready to consider what types of written reports they will be able to obtain through the database. In this project, you design several reports that Tim will send to the NHD corporate headquarters about the Memories mall. His main goals are to create reports that are clear, appealing, and well organized, using a format that makes information easily accessible.

**Human
Resources**

Complete the following:

1. Start Access and open the **Antiques.mdb** database from the Case 1 folder.

2. Before you start creating reports, Tim suggests that you plan their layout and design. The reports should share a similar format and include the following elements:

- The NHD logo and name of the mall (Memories Antiques) should appear at the top of every report.
- An appropriate title should clearly state the purpose of each report.

- The bottom of every page should include the page number, total number of pages, date, and name of the person who prepared the report in the format "Prepared By: Your Name".
- Each report should show the appropriate information except for ID numbers, which are meaningful only to the mall, not to the managers at the NHD corporate headquarters.

3. To prepare annual bonuses for employees, the first report Tim needs is an employee compensation report. He'll use this report to determine an appropriate bonus amount for each employee, so it should include detailed information. To compare salaries and wages fairly, the report should group employees by position. Tim also wants the report to show summary statistics for all positions, including the sum, average, maximum, and minimum of the hourly rates. The report should also calculate the total salaries and total wages at the end of the report. Name this report rptEmployeeSalaryDetail.

4. Tim also plans to send a summary of employee compensation to his managers at NHD. Instead of including detailed employee information, this report should only summarize wages and salaries by position and provide grand totals. Like the detailed report, the summary report should include the sum, average, maximum, and minimum of the salaries for each position. Name this report rptEmployeeSalarySummary.

5. After he analyzes the salary reports, Tim will mail a bonus check to each employee. He needs a set of mailing labels that include all the information necessary to mail the check to each employee's home. He gives you a box of Avery #J8160 labels, and notes that NHD usually uses Times New Roman, 10-point bold text for mailings. Create the mailing label report for Tim, naming it rptEmployeeLabels.

6. Tim and Linda are also planning a company meeting to celebrate a successful year of business. Because Tim does not know all the employees by name, he asks you to create name tags for each employee. The name tag should show the NHD logo, and the employee name followed by their position title. He gives you a box of Avery #CB720 labels for the name tags. (*Hint*: If your copy of Access does not include label CB720, choose another label suitable for name tags.) Create the name tags for Tim, naming the report rptEmployeeNametags.

7. At the meeting, Tim plans to discuss the classes that are offered at the mall and brainstorm ideas for new classes. He believes that additional classes could boost the mall's profit significantly. He asks you to create a report showing the current class offerings, along with the name of the instructor (in the form Last, First), the number of customers who are currently enrolled and have paid, the cost of the course, and the total amount that has been received for each class. (*Hint*: You can use a query as the basis of this report.) The final page of the report should show the grand total of all collected class fees. Because this grand total is the most important calculation in the report, Tim suggests that you format it so that it stands out from the other information. Name the report rptClassEnrollment.

8. Close the **Antiques.mdb** database and Access.

Case 2—Creating Financial Reports for MovinOn Inc.

Finance

In this project, you work with Kristina Romano, an accountant in the Washington warehouse of MovinOn Inc. Kristina needs to prepare a series of financial reports to present to David Bowers, owner of MovinOn, the warehouse managers, and the accountants at MovinOn at their annual meeting. They are naturally interested in how much revenue recent jobs have generated, as well as the labor costs that offset this revenue.

Complete the following:

1. Open the **MovinOn.mdb** database from the Case 2 folder.

2. Because Kristina will discuss all the reports at the same time, she wants them to look similar and present a consistent, unified package. She suggests that you use the following guidelines as you design the reports:

- Include the MovinOn logo at the top of every report.
- Provide an appropriate title that clearly states the purpose of each report.
- Show all dollar amounts with a dollar sign and two decimal places.
- At the bottom of every page, include the page number, total number of pages, date, and name of the person who prepared the report in the format "Prepared By: Your Name".

3. Before the annual meeting, Kristina plans to mail copies of some reports to the warehouse managers. Because she will send materials to each manager at different times, she needs a way to indicate which warehouse she wants before she prints the mailing label. The label she produces should include the manager's warehouse number next to their name, along with other appropriate mailing information. Managers receive a lot of mail, so Kristina asks you to print "Important!" in red text at the top of each label. She plans to use Avery #8663 labels and asks you to create the mailing label report. (Ignore any errors you receive about the size of the labels.) Name this report rptWarehouseManagerLabels.

4. The next report that Kristina needs should show the income from recent moving jobs. MovinOn charges $.70 per mile plus $.20 per pound for each job. From this total, Kristina deducts the driver's payment to determine the net income for the moving job. Drivers receive $50 for each job plus their mileage rate (that is, the driver's rate multiplied by the number of miles plus $50). Kristina asks you to create an income report that provides the job ID, the date of the move, the driver's name and rate, the mileage and weight of the job, and the income calculations as described. At the end of the report, Kristina wants to show the total income, the total payments to drivers, and the total net income. (*Hint*: Consider creating a query as the basis for this report.) Name the report rptJobRevenue.

5. Kristina also needs a report that shows the income from the storage units. Group the information by warehouse and show the name of the renter so that it's easy to identify the renter by last name. The report should also include the rent per unit, the total rent for each warehouse, and a grand total of rent for all warehouses. Name the report rptStorageRevenue.

6. Kristina suspects that MovinOn could increase its income from storage units by encouraging more long-term rentals. Add a calculation to rptStorageRevenue that shows how long each renter has rented a storage unit. Show the figure in years with one decimal place.

7. Close the **MovinOn.mdb** database and Access.

Case 3—Creating Meaningful Reports for the Hershey College Intramural Department

Finance

In this project, you help Marianna Fuentes, assistant director of the intramural department at Hershey College, to create reports for the department. First, Marianna needs to print labels that identify the equipment. Then she needs a report of the coaches' purchases. Each coach has been given $700 to spend on each of their assigned sports. This budget is for items that are not supplied directly through the department, such as shirts, water bottles, or trophies. As coaches make their purchases, they are to submit their receipts to Marianna. Marianna has been recording the receipts in a separate database and wants that data to now be incorporated with the department database. She asks if you can import the data into the database and then generate some reports based on this data.

Complete the following:

1. Start Access and open the **Hershey** database located in the Case 3 folder.

2. Before you can create the coach purchases report, you need to import the data from Marianna's database. The database, **CoachPurchases.mdb**, is located in the Case 3 folder. The data you need is in the tblPurchaseByCoach table. Be sure you establish appropriate relationships after you have imported the tblPurchaseByCoach table.

3. Marianna needs a report that shows what each coach has spent from their $700 budget for each sport. The report should show the sport, the coach name, the purchases for that sport, and the total spent. Because this is the first year they are using a budget, the intramural staff is aware that the purchases might exceed the budget.

She also says that for each sport, you should show the percentage of the budget that has been spent, as well as the remaining amount in the budget. (*Hint*: This could be a negative number.) She also asks you to indicate those sports that have gone over budget by highlighting each of the calculated values: the total amount, the percentage of the budget, and the remaining amount in the budget. The date and time of printing should also appear near the title of the report, and the Hershey college logo should appear on all reports. Name the report rptCoachPurchasesDetail.

4. Marianna asks that you prepare another report similar to rptCoachPurchasesDetail, but it should provide a summary of the purchases. This report should contain only the total spent, percentage of budget, and remaining budget for each sport. Marianna suggests that you use a line in the report to separate the summary for each sport, and highlight the calculated values as you did in rptCoachPurchasesDetail for sports that are over their $700 budget. Finally, this report needs a page header on all but the first page. (*Hint*: Use the report's properties to specify where the page header appears.) Name this report rptCoachPurchasesSummary.

5. In addition to a textual summary, Marianna wants a visual representation of the summary report. She asks if you can add a chart that depicts the percentage of the total amount spent for each sport. She suggests a pie chart but leaves that final decision up to you. She asks that you add the chart to the end of the rptCoachPurchasesSummary summary report.

6. Provide the labels that are requested for the equipment. In addition to the data pertaining to the equipment, Marianna asks you to include the date the label was printed. The labels should be printed on Avery Label #5386, with large text that nearly fills the labels. After the labels are printed, the department will stick them onto a tag that will then be attached to the equipment. Name the report that will print the labels rptEquipmentLabels.

7. Close the **Hershey.mdb** database and Access.

Automating Database Processing
Operations: Making the Database Easier to Use

"An organization's ability to learn, and translate that learning into action rapidly, is the ultimate competitive advantage."
—Jack Welch

CHAPTER INTRODUCTION

As you add queries, forms, and reports to your database, you will need to manage access to these objects to make the database easy to use without jeopardizing the security of the data. This chapter begins by teaching you how to design and implement a user-friendly menu, called a switchboard, so that employees can work with only those parts of the database they need. You will also learn how to restrict the Microsoft Office Access 2003 menus and toolbars so that users cannot affect the design of your database. To automate repetitive tasks you perform frequently and to add more functionality to reports and forms, you will be introduced to basic macros, and then to more advanced macros, including macro groups and special macros, such as AutoExec and AutoKeys, that can save time when working with your database.

Level 1 shows you how to build a user switchboard and explores introductory concepts about macros. Level 2 discusses advanced macro topics, such as macro groups and event-driven programming. It also explains how to troubleshoot macros so that they are free of error. Level 3 covers macro conditions and using message boxes, techniques that can automate your database to a professional level.

CASE SCENARIO

In previous chapters, Don Linebarger consulted with the stakeholders of 4Corners Pharmacy and developed a database design. When he releases the 4Corners database for daily use, many employees who work with it will be new to Access. When Rachel Thompson created the electronic forms for the pharmacy, she began to develop the user interface for the database. (Recall that a user interface is what you see and use to communicate with a computer program such as Access.) Don wants to extend her work by customizing the organization of the user interface. Instead of using the Database window, which lists all of the objects in the database, Don wants to present a menu of options from which employees can select the forms and reports they use most often. Furthermore, Don needs a way to restrict access to some objects and options. For example, employees can now use the Database window to modify the design of the tables. Accidentally changing the data type of a primary key or inadvertently deleting a field in a table could cause problems in many queries, forms, and reports and even jeopardize the reliability of the data. A specialized user interface that prevents users from working in Design view would also help Don maintain the integrity and security of the database.

Operations Management

Don also wants to reduce the number of steps required to perform common tasks, such as moving from one form to another. In addition he wants to display a custom message before a record is deleted, change the format of a report or print it depending on its contents, validate the accuracy of data in a form, and make it easier to print frequently used reports.

LEVEL 1

AUTOMATING TASKS WITH SWITCHBOARDS AND MACROS

ACCESS 2003 SKILLS TRAINING

- **Add an action to a macro**
- **Create a macro**
- **Create database switchboards**
- **Modify switchboard pages**
- **Run a macro**
- **Set startup options**
- **View and test a switchboard**

UNDERSTANDING SWITCHBOARDS

A **switchboard** is a special kind of form that can appear when you open a database. It lists options for working with the tables, forms, queries, and reports in the database. When you create a switchboard, you select up to eight objects that you want to list on the switchboard. You also determine what action you want Access to take when users select an option. For example, if you want users to be able to open frmEmployee from the switchboard, you can include an Employee Form option on the switchboard. When users select this option, you can specify that frmEmployee opens to a new, blank record in Form view so that users can enter employee data.

A typical switchboard has buttons that users click to open forms, reports, and other objects; open other switchboards that list additional database objects; close the switchboard and open the Database window; or close Access. If a database contains many objects, you can create a main switchboard that includes only a few buttons, such as one labeled Forms, another labeled Reports, and one labeled Close Database. You can also create secondary switchboards, such as one listing forms and another listing reports. Using a main switchboard with secondary switchboards lets you present the objects in your database using a logical organization, as shown in Figure 6.1.

Figure 6.1: Typical switchboard design

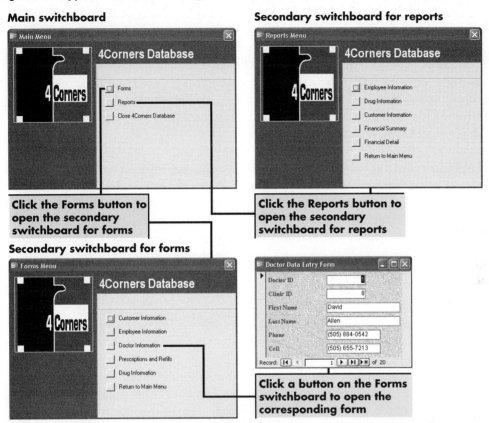

Because a switchboard serves as the user interface for a database, most switchboards include graphics and labels to provide identification and visual appeal. When you use a switchboard as the main gateway to the database, it's a good idea to set database options that restrict the menu bar to specified options and hide the toolbar to prevent users from accessing commands they could use to change the database design. In these ways, a switchboard provides an interface that is more appealing, personalized, and secure than the Database window.

Designing a Switchboard

To create a switchboard, you use the **Switchboard Manager**, a tool that helps you design and customize a switchboard. You start by creating the main switchboard, and then you add the command buttons that you want to appear on the switchboard. For each button, you specify up to three properties: the text associated with the button, the command you want Access to perform when the button is clicked, and the object associated with this button. For example, to add a button that opens the frmEmployee form, you can specify "Employee Form" as the button text, "Open Form in Edit Mode" as the command to perform, and "frmEmployee" as the associated object.

When you complete the switchboard design using the Switchboard Manager, Access creates a form with the default name Switchboard. Access also creates a table, named Switchboard Items, that contains data describing the command buttons on the switchboard.

You can create only one switchboard form for a database, but the switchboard can contain many pages, one of which is the main page, or default page, the one that appears when you open the switchboard form. In most databases, the default page contains buttons for each category of objects in the database. Most of these buttons are designed to open a secondary page listing objects in that category.

Don starts his work on the 4Corners database by reviewing its objects and planning the categories he will use to organize the objects on the pages of the switchboard. He does not want to let employees open tables from the switchboard—they can use the forms Rachel created to enter data and the reports that Elaine Estes developed to view and print information. Furthermore, he wants to prevent most employees from opening tables in Design view so they cannot modify the database design. The queries employees need are now used as the basis for forms and reports, so employees do not need to open queries from the switchboard either.

Don determines that the switchboard should only allow access to the forms and reports. However, the 4Corners database now contains dozens of forms and reports, and employees should be able to open most of them. Instead of listing each form and report on the main switchboard page, he can include one command button for forms and another for reports. When users select the button for forms, a secondary switchboard page will open. Don considers listing all the forms on this secondary page, but realizes that the list is so long, users will not be able to easily find the form they need. He decides to organize the forms into five categories: employees, customers, financial, drugs, and doctors. For example, the employee forms include frmEmployee, the main form for entering employee information, and frmEmployeeView, the form that identifies the employees in each job position. He can use the same approach and categories for the reports. For example, the financial reports include rpt2007Sales, the summary sales report for 2007, and rptBalance, the report listing outstanding customer balances. Don sketches a design for his switchboard, as shown in Figure 6.2.

Figure 6.2: Sketch of switchboard design

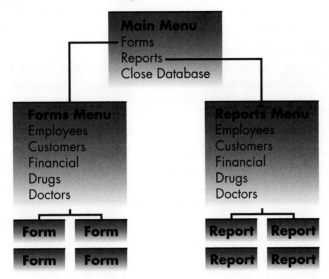

Note that the main switchboard page contains an option to close the database. Including this option means that users can perform all the work they need, and then close the database without using any other part of the Access interface.

Creating a Switchboard

Now that Don has sketched the design for the switchboard, he can create the main page and the secondary pages using the Switchboard Manager. In the 4Corners database, he opens the Switchboard Manager by clicking Tools on the menu bar, pointing to Database Utilities, and then clicking Switchboard Manager. A message asks if he wants to create a switchboard. When he clicks the Yes button, the Switchboard Manager dialog box opens. See Figure 6.3.

Figure 6.3: Switchboard Manager dialog box

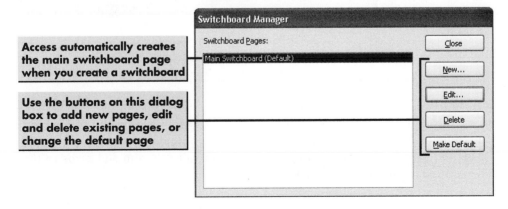

You use the five buttons on the Switchboard Manager dialog box to perform the tasks described in Table 6.1.

Table 6.1: Switchboard Manager buttons

Button	Task
Close	Close the Switchboard Manager dialog box
New	Create a switchboard page
Edit	Edit the selected switchboard page
Delete	Delete the selected switchboard page
Make Default	Make the selected switchboard page the default, or the main page

Recall that Don wants the main switchboard page to contain three options. The first option opens a secondary page listing form categories, the second opens a secondary page listing report categories, and the third closes the database. Because the options on the main switchboard page open other pages, Don must first create those secondary switchboard pages for the forms and reports. In the Switchboard Manager dialog box, he clicks the New button to open the Create New dialog box, in which he can enter the name of the secondary switchboard page. He enters Forms and then clicks the OK button. He does the same to create a secondary switchboard page named Reports. As shown in Figure 6.4, the switchboard now has three pages: the main page, one named Forms, and one named Reports.

Figure 6.4: Two new switchboard pages in the Switchboard Manager dialog box

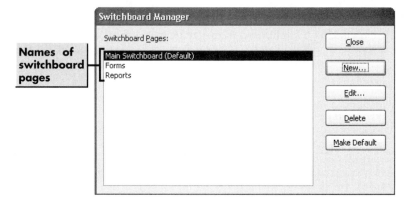

Now that he has created two secondary switchboard pages, he can edit the main switchboard by adding the options that open the secondary pages. In the Switchboard Manager dialog box, he selects the Main Switchboard (Default) item, and then clicks the Edit button. The Edit Switchboard Page dialog box opens, in which he can add items to the switchboard and change its name. See Figure 6.5.

Figure 6.5: Edit Switchboard Page dialog box

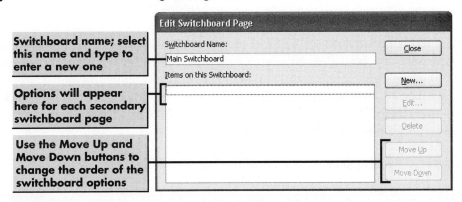

Don changes the name of the main switchboard to Main Menu. Next, he can add the options he wants to appear on the main switchboard page. He clicks the New button to open the Edit Switchboard Item dialog box. See Figure 6.6.

Figure 6.6: Edit Switchboard Item dialog box

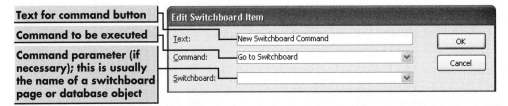

This dialog box contains three text boxes. In the Text text box, Don enters the text that he wants to appear to the right of the first command button on the main switchboard page—Forms. In the Command text box, Don can select the action, or command, he wants Access to take when users select the Forms option. Table 6.2 lists the possible switchboard commands.

Table 6.2: Switchboard commands

Command	Explanation
Go to Switchboard	Opens a secondary switchboard page
Open Form in Add Mode	Displays a new, blank record in the specified form in which you can add data
Open Form in Edit Mode	Displays the specified form in which you can edit records
Open Report	Displays the specified report in Print Preview
Design Application	Edits the switchboard
Exit Application	Closes the database
Run Macro	Runs the specified macro
Run Code	Runs the specified Visual Basic for Application (VBA) function

Because he wants the Forms option to open a secondary switchboard page, Don clicks the Command list arrow, and then clicks Go to Switchboard.

The third text box appears only if Access needs more information about the entries in the other text boxes. Its label also changes to reflect the content of the other text boxes. Because Don specified that the Forms option should open another switchboard page, this text box is labeled Switchboard. He clicks the Switchboard list arrow, and then clicks Forms—this is the switchboard page he wants to open when users select the Forms option on the main switchboard page. See Figure 6.7.

Figure 6.7: Specifying options for a switchboard item

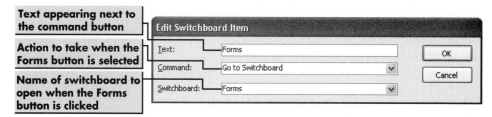

After Don clicks the OK button, he adds the option for opening the Reports switchboard page the same way—he clicks the New button on the Edit Switchboard Page dialog box, enters Reports in the Text text box, clicks the Command list arrow and selects Go to Switchboard, and then clicks the Switchboard list arrow and selects Reports.

Now he is ready to add one more item to the main switchboard page for closing the database. He clicks the New button to open the Edit Switchboard Item dialog box, enters Close 4Corners Database in the Text text box, and then clicks the Command list arrow and selects Exit Application. (This command does not require additional information.) When he clicks the OK button, three items appear in the Edit Switchboard Page dialog box. See Figure 6.8. These are the three options that will appear on the main switchboard page.

Figure 6.8: Three items to appear on the main switchboard page

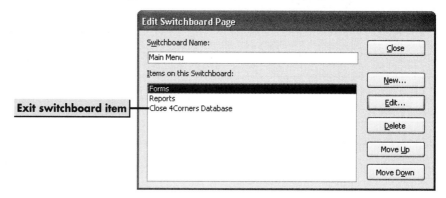

Best Practice

Having an Exit Strategy

A computer program should not only provide the information that the user requires, but should also be easy to navigate. A well-organized, user-friendly switchboard guides users through a database and helps them find the information they need. Besides organizing switchboard items into logical groups, database designers recommend that the last item in every switchboard should close the current switchboard page and open the previous one. The last item on the main switchboard page should be to close the database.

After closing all the dialog boxes, Don returns to the Database window and verifies that the 4Corners database now contains a form named Switchboard and a table named Switchboard Items. Recall that a switchboard is a special type of form. The Switchboard Item table keeps track of switchboard items, commands, and arguments and should be altered only through the use of the Switchboard Manager. Don opens the Switchboard form to see how it looks and works so far, and restores the form window so it is no longer maximized. See Figure 6.9.

Figure 6.9: Initial appearance of the main switchboard

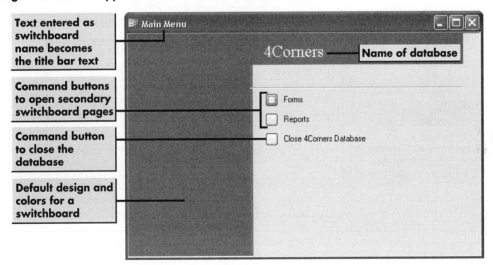

When he clicks the Forms button, another switchboard window opens that uses the same design, but includes one command button with the text "There are no items for this switchboard page." The Reports switchboard page includes the same command button. Don's next task is to create the secondary switchboard pages that the Forms and Reports buttons open. Recall that according to Don's switchboard design, the Forms button should open another switchboard page listing the five categories of forms—employees, customers, financial, drugs, and doctors. The Reports button should also open another page listing the same five categories of reports.

Don opens the Switchboard Manager dialog box, and then clicks the New button to create another switchboard page, naming it Employee Forms. He does the same to create nine other switchboard pages: Customer Forms, Financial Forms, Drug Forms, Doctor Forms, Employee Reports, Customer Reports, Financial Reports, Drug Reports, and Doctor Reports.

Each of the switchboard pages Don just created should list the forms and reports in each category, and the corresponding command buttons should open the form or report. To add the command buttons, Don must edit each switchboard page. He decides to start with the Employee Reports switchboard, so he selects that page in the Switchboard Manager dialog box, and then clicks the Edit button. This switchboard should list reports related to 4Corners employees. To add the command buttons that correspond to the employee reports, Don clicks the New button in the Edit Switchboard Page dialog box. He enters Employee Mailing Labels as the text, selects Open Report as the command, and rptEmpLabels as the report to open. He repeats this process to add buttons to open rptEmployeePhoneList and rptBadge to the switchboard. Then he adds a final button to this switchboard to return to the Reports switchboard. The complete Edit Switchboard Page for the Employee Reports switchboard is shown in Figure 6.10.

Figure 6.10: Creating a switchboard with command buttons for employee reports

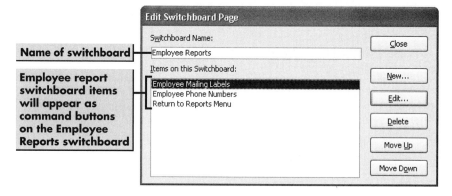

Don closes the Edit Switchboard Page dialog box, opens the Reports switchboard page for editing, and then adds an item that opens the Employee Reports switchboard. See Figure 6.11.

Figure 6.11: Adding an item to the Reports switchboard page

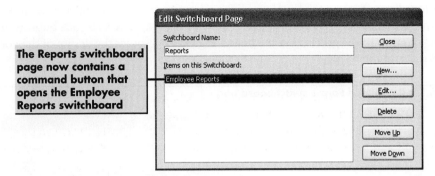

The Reports switchboard page now contains a command button that opens the Employee Reports switchboard

He edits the switchboard pages for customer reports, financial reports, drug reports, and doctor reports, adding command buttons that open the reports in each category and one for returning to the Reports switchboard. Finally, to the Reports switchboard he adds buttons that open each report and a command button that returns to the main switchboard. Figure 6.12 shows the design of the Reports switchboard and the results.

Figure 6.12: Completed Reports switchboard page

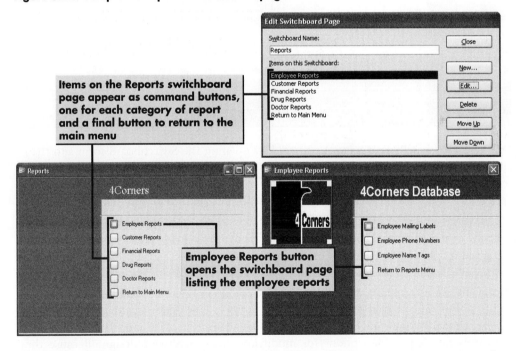

Items on the Reports switchboard page appear as command buttons, one for each category of report and a final button to return to the main menu

Employee Reports button opens the switchboard page listing the employee reports

When users click the Reports button on the Main Menu switchboard, the Reports switchboard page opens, listing the five categories of reports and one option to return to the main menu. When users click a button for a report category, such as the Employee Reports button, the appropriate switchboard page opens, listing the associated reports.

To create the Forms switchboard, Don follows the same procedure by adding command buttons for editing forms to the Employee Forms, Customer Forms, Financial Forms, Drug Forms, and Doctor Forms switchboards. To each switchboard, he also adds buttons users can click to return to the previous switchboard. Figure 6.13 shows the design of the Forms switchboard and the results.

Figure 6.13: Completed Forms switchboard page

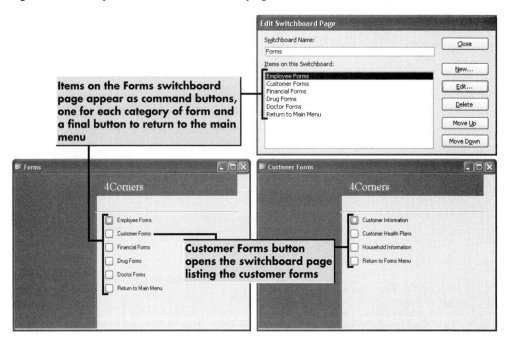

Items on the Forms switchboard page appear as command buttons, one for each category of form and a final button to return to the main menu

Customer Forms button opens the switchboard page listing the customer forms

Don tests the switchboard pages he created by opening the Switchboard form and then clicking each button, making sure that it opens the appropriate report or form, or that it returns to the previous switchboard page. When he is finished, he decides to modify the appearance of the switchboard so that it reflects the customized design of other objects in the database. In particular, he wants to add the 4Corners logo, change the title label, and change the background color of the switchboard pages.

Formatting a Switchboard

By default, Access switchboards share the same layout and design, including background colors and placement of the title. Although you use the Switchboard Manager to create the switchboard pages and add working command buttons to them, the Switchboard Manager doesn't provide options for modifying the switchboard design. Because the switchboard is a form, you can format the switchboard in form Design view. This means you can make the same kinds of changes to the switchboard that you can make to other forms, such as changing the background colors, adding and changing labels, and inserting images, lines, and other graphic elements. However, you should not change the command buttons or their properties in form Design view. Use only the Switchboard Manager to modify the contents and behavior of the switchboard. If you change the command buttons in form Design view, the Switchboard Manager cannot update the Switchboard Items table as necessary, and the switchboard will not work correctly.

Don wants to add the 4Corners logo to the switchboard, change the title label, and change the background color of the switchboard pages. He starts making these formatting changes by opening the Switchboard form in Design view and maximizing the window. See Figure 6.14.

Figure 6.14: Switchboard form in Design view

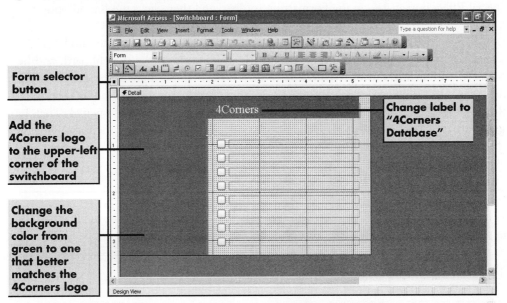

First, Don decides to add the 4Corners logo to the Switchboard form. Then he can match the background color and font as he changes the other elements in the form. He clicks the Image button 🖼 on the Toolbox toolbar and then clicks in the upper-left corner of the form. The Insert Picture dialog box opens. He navigates to the 4Corners.jpg file, and then clicks the OK button. Access inserts the logo on the form. Don adjusts i s placement so that it aligns with the title label.

The logo has two background colors—black and brick red. He decides to change the green background in the form to brick red. He right-clicks the background of the form near the logo, points to Fill/Back Color, and then clicks the brick red color square. This changes the color behind the logo, but not the color behind the title label—that color is contained in a separate shape. Don uses the same technique to change the background of the form behind the title label from green to brick red.

Don notices that the default label style for the Switchboard form includes two copies of the label text: one in white and one in gray to serve as a shadow. For the title label, he wants to use a font similar to the one used in the logo. He clicks the label to select it, and then presses the Delete key. This deletes the white copy of the label. He clicks the gray label and deletes that. Now he can add a new title to the form. He clicks the Label button Aa on the Toolbox toolbar, clicks above the command buttons on the form, and then types 4Corners Database as the new title. He formats the label so it appears in bold, Arial Narrow, 20-point text, which looks similar to the font used in the logo, and then changes the label text color to white.

When he checks the results in Form view, he decides to enhance the logo by applying a raised special effect. He returns to Design view, clicks the logo, clicks the list arrow on the Special Effect button ▣ on the Formatting toolbar, and then clicks the Raised option.

Don reviews the switchboard, and resizes the window so that it fits in the middle of the screen. He wants Access to use the current size when it opens the switchboard, and he wants to prevent users from resizing the form. To make these changes, he double-clicks the form selector button to open the property sheet for the form. First, he sets the Auto Resize property to No so that Access will not resize the form when it is opened. Then he sets the Border Style property to Dialog to prevent users from resizing the form. Finally, he saves his changes to the form and opens it in Form view. Figure 6.15 shows the completed Switchboard form.

Figure 6.15: Redesigned Switchboard form

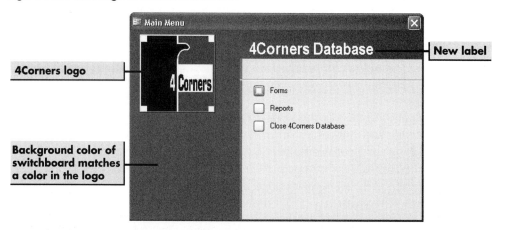

How To

Change the Format of a Switchboard
1. Open the Switchboard form in Design view.
2. To change formatting elements such as color, labels, images, and lines, use the tools on the Toolbox and Formatting toolbars as you would to change any other form.
3. To change properties such as the form's size and position, double-click the form selector button, and then change entries on the form's property sheet.

Be certain you do not change the format or the properties of the command buttons on the Switchboard form; doing so could change the switchboard so it no longer works properly.

Don shows the switchboard to Paul, who finds it a useful and attractive way for employees to interact with the 4Corners database. Now Paul wants to add a switchboard page for queries; Maria Garcia developed a few queries that are helpful on their own and do not serve as the basis for a form or report. However, recall that the Switchboard Manager does not provide commands for running queries (refer to Table 6.2). On the other hand, it does provide a command for running a macro. Don thinks this over, and realizes that he needs to create a macro that opens a query from the switchboard page.

UNDERSTANDING BASIC MACROS

A **macro** is an action or series of actions that you want Access to perform. Rather than performing a set of instructions repeatedly to perform the same task, you can save time and ensure accuracy by creating a macro that performs those actions for you. Macros automate repetitive tasks, such as opening forms, printing reports, and running queries. Macros are usually assigned to a key, key combination, or button. To run the macro, you press a key combination, such as Ctrl+Alt+F, or click a button that has been associated with the macro. In fact, the command buttons on the switchboard are associated with macros—when you click the Forms button, for example, Access performs a macro containing the action that opens the Forms switchboard page.

Macros are composed of a series of actions organized in the sequence in which they should be performed. These actions are instructions designed to manipulate database objects, such as opening a form or printing a report. Table 6.3 shows a list of commonly used macro actions.

Table 6.3: Common macro actions

Macro Action	Explanation
Beep	Plays a beep tone
Close	Closes a specified database object
FindRecord	Finds the first record that meets the specified criteria; if the action is used again, the macro finds the next record that meets the criteria
Hourglass	Changes the mouse pointer to an image of an hourglass (or another specified icon) while a macro is running
MsgBox	Displays a message box containing a warning or informational message
OpenForm	Opens a form in Form view, Design view, Print Preview, or Datasheet view
OpenQuery	Opens a select or crosstab query in Design view, Datasheet view, or Print Preview

Table 6.3: Common macro actions (cont.)

Macro Action	Explanation
OpenReport	Opens a report in Print Preview or Design view or prints a report
Quit	Closes Access
SendKeys	Sends keystrokes to Access or another active program

To create a macro, you work in the Macro window, in which you can select actions such as those listed in Table 6.3. You list the actions in the order you want Access to perform them. For example, if you want to create a macro that prints a report, closes the report, and then closes Access, you list three actions in the Macro window: OpenReport, Close, and Quit.

Best Practice

Protecting the Database from Macro Viruses

Computer viruses pose risks to computer systems and their data. Because millions of computer users are affected by viruses every year, you must protect your data from corruption by these viruses. The best line of defense is to install an antivirus program and update the virus definitions on a regular basis.

Macros are susceptible to a virus attack and can be programmed to include viruses that can harm your database. To help protect your data from the corruption caused by a virus hidden in a macro, Access lets you set the macro security level on your computer. You set the macro security level by selecting Tools on the menu bar, pointing to Macro, and then clicking Security. The Security dialog box opens, in which you can select one of three macro security levels. See Figure 6.16.

Figure 6.16: Security dialog box

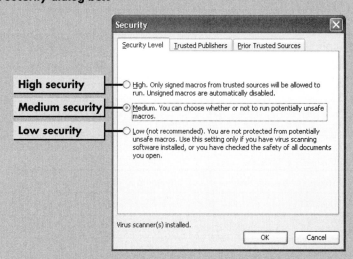

The High security level means that only macros that are digitally signed and come from a trusted source are allowed to be executed. The Medium security level indicates that you want to be prompted before any macro is run. The Low security setting allows all macros to run, but does not offer any protection. As a best practice, you should set the security level for your database to Medium or High.

Before Don can tackle the problem of adding queries to the 4Corners switchboard, Paul mentions that he is preparing for a meeting with the pharmacy's accountant, and needs to update prescription information and produce the rptContributionMarginAnalysis report for each of the past 12 months. At this point, the 4Corners database contains nearly 20 reports, and Paul thinks it will be tedious to find and generate this report 12 times. Don offers to create a macro for Paul to run the rptContributionMarginAnalysis report. He can also enhance the macro so that Access displays an hourglass while the report is being generated and sounds a beep when it is complete.

Creating a Macro

Unlike other Microsoft Office products, such as Microsoft Excel and Microsoft Word, which record keystrokes to create macros, you create an Access macro in the Macro window. To begin creating the macro for Paul's report, Don opens the Macro window by clicking Macros on the Objects bar in the Database window and then clicking the New button on the Database window toolbar. See Figure 6.17.

Figure 6.17: Macro window for creating a macro

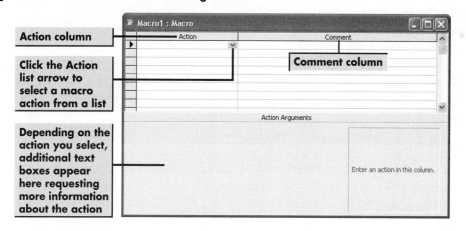

You use the **Action column** to list the actions the macro performs. To select the appropriate actions, you click the list arrow in the Action column. Access provides over 50 different actions, most of which perform multistep tasks, such as selecting a specified report and then opening it in Print Preview. Other actions are available only to macros, such as Beep, which plays a beep when the macro is finished, and Echo, which turns off screen updating while a macro is running. You can press the F1 key to open a Help window providing more information about the action. In the **Comment** column, you document the action by describing what task it performs. For example, if you select the Hourglass action, you can enter "Displays an hourglass while the report is generated." Users do not see the comment text; it only serves to explain the action to a database administrator should the macro need to be altered.

In the lower part of the Macro window is the **Action Arguments pane**, which is used to provide additional information for performing the macro action. The arguments needed vary depending on the selected action chosen. For example, if the action is Quit, the Action Arguments pane displays one text box in which you can enter or select additional information: whether to save any changed database objects before closing Access, to prompt the user to save the objects, or to close Access without saving.

Don plans to add three actions and associated arguments to the Macro window:

- **Hourglass**—This action changes the pointer to an hourglass icon while the macro runs. It has one argument that turns the hourglass icon on or off.
- **OpenReport**—This action opens a report and has five arguments: Report Name (enter or select the report you want to open), View (specify whether to print the report or to open it in Print Preview or Design view), Filter Name (enter the name of a filter you want to use to sort or restrict the records the report includes), Where Condition (enter a SQL WHERE clause that selects records for the report), and Window Mode (select how to display the report window after Access generates the report).
- **Beep**—This action plays a beep when the macro is finished, and has no arguments.

In the first row of the Macro window, Don clicks the Action column and then selects the Hourglass action. The Hourglass On argument is set to Yes by default, so he doesn't need to change that. In the next row, he selects the OpenReport action, and then selects rptContributionMarginAnalysis as the report name and Print for the View argument. The last action he selects is Beep. He saves the macro as mcrContributionMarginAnalysis, using the standard "mcr" prefix for macro objects. Figure 6.18 shows this macro in the Macro window.

Figure 6.18: mcrContributionMarginAnalysis macro

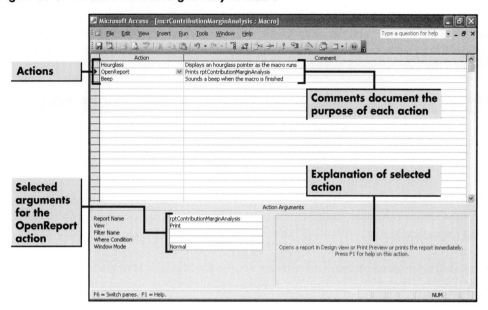

Now that Don has created and saved a macro, he can run it to make sure it performs the task it is designed to perform.

Create a Macro

1. In the Database window, click the Macros button on the Objects bar, and then click the New button on the Database window toolbar. The Macro window opens.

2. In the Action column, select the actions you want the macro to perform. Enter one action per line in the order Access should perform them.

3. Select the appropriate action arguments for each action.

4. Add comments to each action to explain its purpose.

5. Save the macro using a name that begins with the "mcr" prefix.

Choosing Tasks to Automate

Macros are designed to perform repetitive actions, so use them to automate tasks you perform often or those that combine basic tasks into a long series, making each step difficult to remember. Keep in mind that macros are restricted to the actions listed when you click a row in the Action column of the Macro window, which includes about 50 actions. You should be familiar with the most common actions (refer to Table 6.3) so you can identify tasks as suitable candidates for macros. If you want to automate a task that is not addressed in the built-in macro actions, you can use VBA, the programming language for most Microsoft Office programs, to create a program. (You will learn how to use VBA in Chapter 7.) VBA does offer advantages over using macros, such as better error-handling features and easier updating capabilities. Macros, however, are useful for small applications and for basic tasks, such as opening and closing objects. Furthermore, you cannot use VBA to assign actions to a specific key or key combination or to open an application in a special way, such as displaying a switchboard. For these types of actions, you must use macros.

Running a Macro

After you create and save a macro, you can run it in three ways:

- In the Macro window, click the Run button on the Macro Design toolbar.
- Click Tools on the menu bar, point to Macro, click Run Macro, click the Macro Name list arrow, click the name of the macro you want to run, and then click the OK button.
- In the Database window, click Macros on the Objects bar, right-click the macro name, and then click Run.

When you run a macro, Access performs the actions listed in the Macro window one after the other.

Now that the mcrContributionMarginAnalysis macro is complete, Don can use the Macro Design toolbar to run the macro. You can also use this toolbar to edit the macro and extend its functionality. See Figure 6.19.

Figure 6.19: Macro Design toolbar

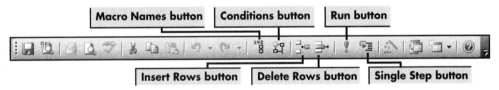

Don clicks the Run button ![Run] on the Macro Design toolbar. The hourglass pointer appears briefly, and then the Enter Parameter Value dialog box opens. Because the rptContributionMarginAnalysis report is based on a parameter query, Don must enter start and end dates to define the period the report covers. When the report opens in Print Preview, a beep plays in the computer's speakers.

As Don tests the macro by running it several times, he decides that it would be more helpful if the macro print, so he closes the report instead of opening it in Print Preview. The final Beep action can then signal that the report is finished printing. To make these changes, Don can edit the mcrContributionMarginAnalysis macro.

Editing a Macro

To edit a macro, you work with the Macro window as you did to create a macro. You can rearrange the order of the actions by dragging the action line to a new position. To insert a new action between two existing actions, right-click a row and then click Insert Rows to insert a blank row above the selected one. In the new row, click the Action column, click the list arrow, and then select the action you want to perform. To delete an action, right-click the row and then click Delete Rows.

Don wants to change the View argument of the OpenReport action so that Access prints rptContributionMarginAnalysis instead of opening it in Print Preview. He also wants to insert a Close action after the OpenReport action to close the report when it is finished printing. He opens the mcrContributionMarginAnalysis macro, and clicks the OpenReport action. In the Action Arguments pane, he changes the View argument from Print Preview to Print. Next, he inserts a row before the Beep action, clicks the list arrow in the new row, and selects Close. This action has three arguments: Object Type (select the type of object to close, or leave this argument blank to close the active window), Object Name (enter or select the name of the object to close), and Save (select whether to save the object before closing, prompt to save, or close without saving). Don selects Report as the Object Type, rptContributionMarginAnalysis as the Object Name, and Yes to save the report before closing. Then he edits the OpenReport comment and adds a comment to explain the Close action. Figure 6.20 shows the completed design of mcrContributionMarginAnalysis.

Figure 6.20: Modified mcrContributionMarginAnalysis macro

OpenReport action modified to print the report instead of opening it in Print Preview

New action added to close the report after printing

Description of Close action

Arguments for Close action

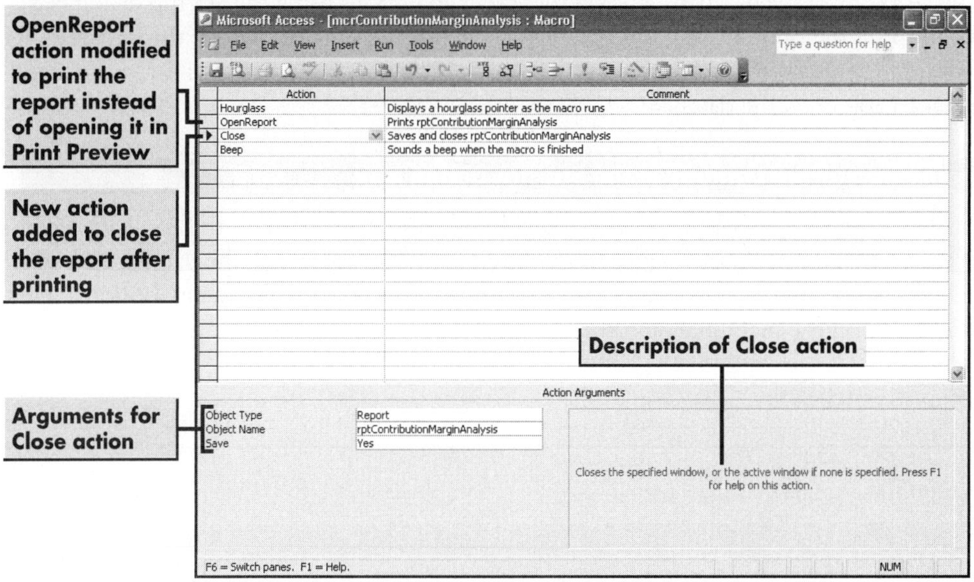

Don runs this macro several times to test it, verifying that the report prints and closes as it is designed to do. He demonstrates the macro for Paul, who plans to use it to print copies of rptContributionMarginAnalysis for his accountant.

Now that Don understands the basics of creating and using macros, he realizes that to solve the problem of including queries on the switchboard, he needs to create one macro per query—he can select the OpenQuery action to run a query, but he must specify which query to run. Even if he includes only five or six queries on the switchboard, creating five or six of the same type of macro seems unnecessarily repetitive. He decides to study more about macros to determine whether he can find a better solution.

In the meantime, Paul asks Don to address the problems of security and personalizing the 4Corners database so that users recognize it as a 4Corners application. Don can accomplish both tasks by specifying what Access does when users open the 4Corners database.

SETTING STARTUP OPTIONS

You can specify certain actions and configurations, called **startup options**, that Access performs when a database opens. For example, you can set the name that appears in the Access window title bar, prevent users from using the Database window, or specify a form to open. You can also help to secure the database by hiding toolbars and restricting access to the menu commands. Doing so means that only authorized users, such as the database manager, can work with tables and other objects in Design view or use menu commands to make a copy of the database. You set these startup options using the Startup dialog box. After you set the options, they are in effect the next time someone opens the database. If you want to bypass the startup options that you set, you can press and hold down the Shift key when you open the database.

Specifying Startup Options in the Startup Dialog Box

Recall that one of Don's goals in creating a switchboard is to hide the toolbars when Access starts and restrict the menus so that users cannot tamper with the database design. He also wants to prevent users from changing the toolbar and menu options. He clicks Tools on the menu bar, and then clicks Startup. The Startup dialog box opens. See Figure 6.21.

Figure 6.21: Startup dialog box

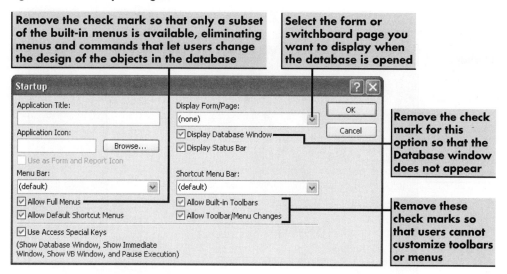

Remove the check mark so that only a subset of the built-in menus is available, eliminating menus and commands that let users change the design of the objects in the database

Select the form or switchboard page you want to display when the database is opened

Remove the check mark for this option so that the Database window does not appear

Remove these check marks so that users cannot customize toolbars or menus

Don sets the following options in the Startup dialog box:

- **Display Form/Page**—Don clicks this list arrow and then selects Switchboard. This setting specifies that the Switchboard form will open upon startup.
- **Display Database Window**—Don clicks this check box to remove the check mark. This setting specifies that the Database window will not open upon startup.
- **Allow Full Menus**—He also clicks this check box to remove the check mark. This setting eliminates menus and commands that let users change the design of the objects in the 4Corners database, and provides only a subset of the built-in menus.
- **Allow Built-in Toolbars**—He clicks this check box to remove the check mark. This setting eliminates the toolbars from all the windows in the 4Corners database.
- **Allow Toolbar/Menu Changes**—He clicks this check box to remove the check mark. This setting prevents users from customizing toolbars, menu bars, and shortcut menus.

Don clicks the OK button to close the Startup dialog box, and then tests the startup options by closing and then reopening the 4Corners database. Figure 6.22 shows the main switchboard after Don sets the startup options.

Figure 6.22: Main switchboard page after setting startup options

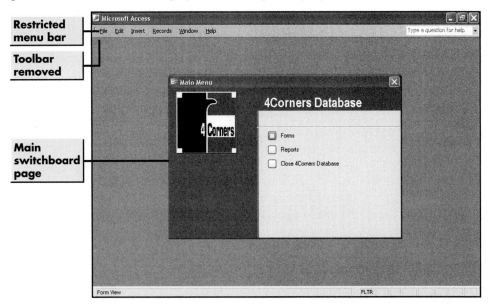

Restricted menu bar

Toolbar removed

Main switchboard page

Set Startup Options

1. Click Tools on the menu bar, and then click Startup. The Startup dialog box opens.

2. Set startup options such as selecting the form or page to display when the database opens.

3. Click the OK button.

Now that Don is satisfied with the additional security the startup options provide, he can focus on Paul's next request—to further personalize the 4Corners database.

Creating a Splash Screen

With the startup options in effect, Access displays the main switchboard page when someone opens the 4Corners database. However, Don wants to personalize the database by displaying a **splash screen**, a form that includes the name of the pharmacy and the database and provides information so that users can contact the appropriate employee for help when necessary. Don already specified that the switchboard appears when users open the 4Corners database. If he changes this option to display a splash screen form instead, the switchboard won't open, meaning users will again be on their own when navigating the database. The Startup dialog box doesn't allow you to set two objects to open in sequence. How can Don specify that when the 4Corners database opens, first a splash screen appears, and then the main switchboard opens?

Access lets you create a special macro named AutoExec that runs automatically when a database is opened. When Access starts, it checks for an AutoExec macro. If it finds a macro by this name, Access runs the macro before performing the tasks specified in the Startup dialog box. Don can create a macro named AutoExec to display a splash screen form. On this form, he can identify the pharmacy and database name to personalize the database, include his name and phone number so that users can contact him if they have questions, and display instructions for closing the splash screen window. When users follow these instructions, the main switchboard page opens.

To create the splash screen, Don reopens the 4Corners database, pressing Shift as it opens to bypass the startup options he set. Then he works in form Design view, using the same colors, fonts, and logo that he used for the switchboard. He also includes his name and phone number and instructions for closing the splash screen. To specify the size and behavior of the splash screen, he works with the form's property sheet and changes the following properties:

- **Caption**—Set to Welcome to the 4Corners database
- **Scroll Bars**—Changed from Both to Neither
- **Record Selectors**—Changed from Yes to No
- **Navigation Buttons**—Changed from Yes to No
- **Auto Resize**—Changed from Yes to No
- **Border Style**—Changed from Sizable to Dialog
- **Min Max Buttons**—Changed to None
- **Width**—Set to 6 inches

He saves the form as frmSplash, and switches to Form view. See Figure 6.23.

Figure 6.23: Initial splash screen for the 4Corners database

Now that Don has created the splash screen form, he is ready to create the AutoExec macro and specify that it opens the splash screen.

Creating an AutoExec Macro

To create an AutoExec macro, you create a macro that contains the actions you want Access to perform when the database is opened. Then you save the macro using the name AutoExec. Access looks for this macro when it starts, and runs the macro before performing the actions specified in the Startup dialog box.

Don opens a new macro in Design view, selects OpenForm as the action, and selects the frmSplash form as the argument. He saves the macro as AutoExec. See Figure 6.24.

Figure 6.24: Creating the AutoExec macro

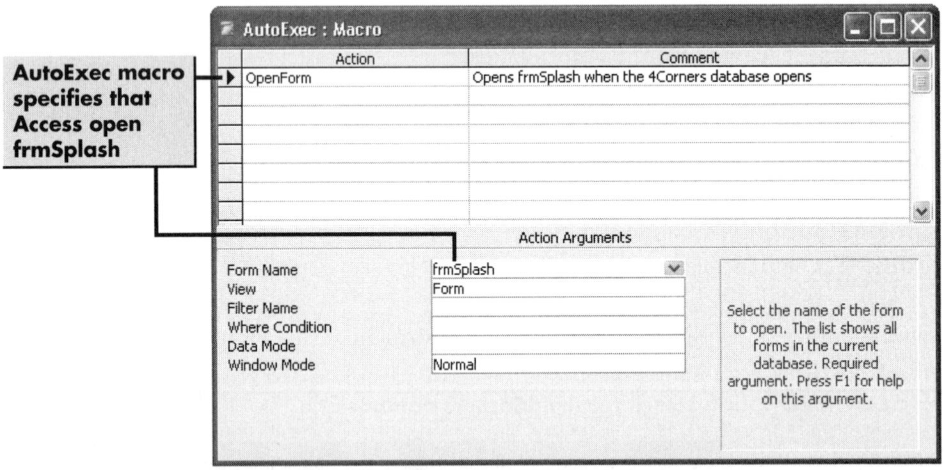

How To

Create an AutoExec Macro
1. Click the Macros button on the Objects bar in the Database window, and then click the New button on the Database window toolbar.
2. In the Action column, select the actions that Access should perform when the database is opened.
3. Select the appropriate arguments for each action.
4. Add comments to each action to explain its purpose.
5. Save the macro using the name AutoExec.
6. Close the Macro window.

Don closes Access, and then restarts it. When he opens the 4Corners database, the AutoExec macro runs and opens the splash screen form. When he clicks the Close button ⊠ on the splash screen, the main switchboard page appears with restricted menus and toolbars as specified in the Startup dialog box.

Now that Don has accomplished his goals of creating a more secure and personalized database, he is ready to solve the problem of including queries on the switchboard.

Steps To Success: Level 1

Glenn Hollander is serving as the database manager for the Hudson Bay Pharmacy, and asks for your help in extending the user interface for the Hudson database and personalizing its appearance. He also wants to automate a task that Joan Gabel, owner of the pharmacy, performs often.

Complete the following:

1. Start Access and open the **Hudson.mdb** database from the STS folder.

2. Review the objects in the Hudson database and plan the categories you will use to organize the objects on the pages of the switchboard. Glenn does not want to let Hudson Bay Pharmacy employees open tables from the switchboard—they can use the forms created earlier to enter data and reports developed earlier to view and print information. He also wants to prevent most employees from opening tables in Design view so they cannot modify the database design. The queries employees need are now used as the basis for forms and reports, so employees do not need to open queries from the switchboard either.

3. Create a switchboard for the Hudson database based on your design.

4. Test the switchboard to ensure that it is logically organized and provides all the reports and forms that employees need. Make sure that users can return to the previous switchboard from each switchboard page.

5. Glenn wants to add the Hudson logo to the switchboard, change the title label, and change the background color of the switchboard pages. Format the switchboard to meet Glenn's goals. Use the logo in the **HudsonBay.jpg** file in the Chapter 6\STS folder.

6. Joan Gabel is preparing for a meeting with her accountant, and needs to print 12 versions of the rptContributionMarginAnalysis report, one for each of the past 12 months. Automate this task for Joan. As the report prints, set Access to display an hourglass icon. When the report finishes, a beep should play. Save the macro as mcrContributionMarginAnalysis.

7. Glenn wants to set options that will help to secure the Hudson database when users open it. For example, he wants to restrict the menus so that users cannot tamper with the database design. He also needs to specify that Access opens the switchboard when it starts. Set these options for Glenn, selecting the ones that will help to secure the database and open the switchboard.

6

Level 1

8. Personalize the database by creating a splash screen, providing a way for users to close it to work with the Hudson database.

9. Glenn wants to display the splash screen first, and then open the switchboard. Create the appropriate object to meet Glenn's goals.

10. Close the **Hudson.mdb** database and Access.

LEVEL 2

CREATING ADVANCED MACROS

ACCESS 2003 SKILLS TRAINING

- **Add an action to a macro**
- **Create a macro**
- **Create the macro group for switchboards**
- **Run a macro**
- **Single step a macro**

UNDERSTANDING MACRO GROUPS

A **macro group** is two or more macros placed within the same macro file. Instead of creating several separate macros, you can combine them in a macro group. You use macro groups to consolidate related macros and to manage large numbers of macros. When you create a macro group, only its name is displayed as a macro object in the Database window, not all of the macros it contains. For example, suppose Don Linebarger wants to create a macro to open each report in the database. He would have to create over 20 macro objects. Instead, he can create one macro group named mcrReports, for example, that contains 20 OpenReport actions, one for each report in the database.

Paul Ferrino has been running the mcrContributionMarginAnalysis macro to print the rptContributionMarginAnalysis report, and wants to print a number of other reports the same way. He asks Don to create similar macros to print the four financial reports that he prints most often: rpt2007Sales, rptBalance, rptRxList, and rptSales. Rather than creating one macro for each report, Don decides that he will create a macro group to solve the problem.

Creating a Macro Group

Although macros within a group are not required to be related, it is logical to organize similar macros within a group. Doing so helps to identify the macros within a group and to later reference those macros as necessary.

Before Don creates a macro group, he plans the macros the group will contain. He needs four macros to print the four reports that Paul specified. Don can use the OpenReport action with the Print argument that he used for the rptContributionMarginAnalysis report. Each macro should also close the report after it prints. To accomplish this, he can use the Close action, which he also used in the mcrContributionMarginAnalysis macro.

To create a macro group, Don opens a new Macro window. Then he clicks the Macro Names button [xyz] on the Macro Design toolbar. Access adds the Macro Name column to the left of the Action column. See Figure 6.25.

Figure 6.25: Macro Name column

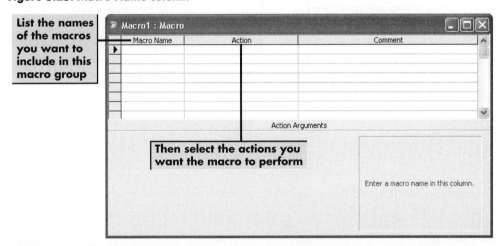

List the names of the macros you want to include in this macro group

Then select the actions you want the macro to perform

Enter a macro name in this column.

To add a macro to the group, you enter the name of the macro in the Macro Name column, which lets you distinguish individual macros in a macro group. Each macro within the group must have a unique name. Because a macro can contain many actions, the macro name tells Access where the macro begins. If a macro contains several actions, you leave the Macro Name column blank for actions added after the first one. Access performs the actions in the Action column and any actions that immediately follow it until another macro appears in the Macro Name column. To create a macro group, you name one macro and list the actions for it. Then you skip a row, name the second macro, list the actions for it, and so on. You can define the macros in any order, and you can group as many macros as you want in the Macro window.

In the first row of the Macro Name column, Don enters the name of the first macro in the group: mcr2007Sales. This macro will print and close the rpt2007Sales report, and he wants to use macro names that remind him of what the macros do. In the Action column, Don selects the OpenReport action and selects the arguments to print the rpt2007Sales report. For the second action in the mcr2007Sales macro, he selects the Close action and the appropriate arguments for closing the report. Then he includes a comment to remind him of the purpose of the macro. He repeats this procedure to create three other macros named mcrBalance (to print and close rptBalance), mcrRxList (to print and close rptRxList), and mcrSales (to print and close rptSales). He also leaves a blank line between each macro to improve readability. He saves the macro group as mcrFinancialReports. See Figure 6.26.

Figure 6.26: Creating a macro group

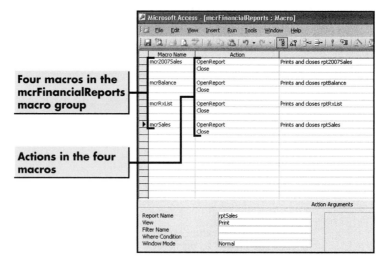

Don closes the Macro window, tests the macro group to make sure it prints, and then closes the four reports.

How To

Create a Macro Group

1. Click the Macros button on the Objects bar in the Database window, and then click the New button on the Database window toolbar.

2. Click the Macro Names button on the Macro Design toolbar. Access adds the Macro Name column to the left of the Action column.

3. In the Macro Name column, enter the name of a macro.

4. In the Action column, enter the corresponding actions for the macro.

5. Enter comments as needed in the Comment column, and set arguments as needed in the Action Arguments pane.

6. Save the macro group, using the "mcr" prefix in the object name.

Running the Macros in a Macro Group

If you click the Run button on the Macro Design toolbar to run the macros in a macro group, Access runs only the first macro in the group. To run a particular macro within a group, click Tools on the menu bar, point to Macro, and then click Run Macro. The Run Macro dialog box opens. You can click the Macro Name list arrow in this dialog box to show all of the macros in the current macro group. Select the macro you want to run, and then click the OK button.

In the Switchboard Manager and many property sheets, you can specify the name of a macro to run when appropriate. To run a macro object, you enter or select its name. To run only one macro in a macro group, you use the following special notation:

mcrGroupName.mcrMacroName

For example, the mcrReports macro group might include a macro named mcrRxList, which prints rptRxList. To specify in the Switchboard Manager that you want to run the mcrRxList macro in mcrReports and print rptRxList, you use the following notation: mcrReports.mcrRxList.

The options for running the macros in the mcrFinancialReports macro group introduce extra steps for Paul—he must first open the macro group, and then run the appropriate macro. That takes just as much work as opening and printing a report. Don investigates another way to run a macro—by assigning it to a key combination. To do so, he must create a macro named AutoKeys.

Creating an AutoKeys Macro Group

You can create an AutoKeys macro group to assign a macro action or set of actions to a key or key combination. For example, when you press the key combination, such as Ctrl+T, Access performs the action associated with that key combination. If you assign an action to a key combination that is already being used by Access (for example, Ctrl+C is the key combination for the Copy command), the action you assign can replace the default Access key assignment, though this is not recommended. The new key assignments are in effect as soon as you save the macro group and each time you open the database.

To create an AutoKeys macro group, you open a new macro group as you usually do. Click the Macro Names button ![XYZ] on the Macro Design toolbar to open the Macro Name column. In the Macro Name column, you type the key or key combination to which you want to assign one or more actions. You must use a special syntax, or notation, to enter the key combinations. Names of single keys, such as the F1 key, must be enclosed within curly braces ({}). The Ctrl key is represented by a caret (^), the Shift key by a plus sign (+), and the Alt key by a percent sign (%). (These key combinations are a subset of the syntax used in the SendKeys command, which is covered shortly.) Table 6.4 shows a partial list of key combinations.

Table 6.4: Examples of key combinations for the AutoKeys macro group

Key Combination	Macro Name Syntax
F1	{F1}
Ctrl+F1	^{F1}
Shift+F1	+{F1}
Alt+F1	%{F1}
Ctrl+Q	^Q
Ctrl+2	^2
Left arrow	{LEFT}
Backspace	{BKSP} or {BS}
Print Screen	{PRTSC}

Instead of printing the four financial reports in mcrFinancialReports by selecting and running a macro, Don can modify the mcrFinancialReports macro group to assign key combinations to each macro and then rename the macro group to AutoKeys. For example, he can assign the macro that prints and closes rptBalance to the Ctrl+B key combination. Paul can then press Ctrl+B when the 4Corners database is open to print the rptBalance report.

Don opens the mcrFinancialReports macro group in Design view. He decides to use a Ctrl key combination associated with the name of each macro. In the Macro Name column, he selects the first macro name, mcr2007Sales, and replaces it with ^7. He replaces the mcrBalance macro name with ^B, rptRxList with ^R, and mcrSales with ^A. Then he saves the macro group as AutoKeys. See Figure 6.27.

Figure 6.27: Creating an AutoKeys macro group

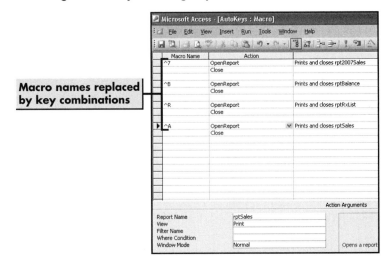

Don closes the Macro window. Paul can now use the key combinations to print and close the four financial reports.

When Don demonstrates the AutoKeys macro, Paul immediately sees how it will save him time. However, he also wants to be able to press a key combination to print and close any report he opens. Don considers how he can do this. He could add key combinations to the AutoKeys macro for every report in the database. However, that means creating over 20 unique key combinations and then asking Paul and others to use them appropriately. Furthermore, as reports are added to the database, Don will have to modify the AutoKeys macro to include these new reports. Instead, Don can use the SendKeys action in the AutoKeys macro. The **SendKeys action** sends keystrokes to Access or to another active program. Don can determine the keystrokes used to print and then close the current report from Print Preview—first you press the Alt+F keys to open the File menu, then you press the P key to print the report, and finally you press Alt+C to close the report. He can specify these keystrokes as arguments in the SendKeys action, and associate the SendKeys action with the Ctrl+P key combination.

Don opens the AutoKeys macro group in Design view, enters ^P in a blank row in the Macro Name column, and then selects the SendKeys action in the Action column. For the Keystrokes argument, he enters %FP%C, which is shorthand for Alt+F, P, Alt+C. Figure 6.28 shows the SendKeys action in the AutoKeys macro group.

Figure 6.28: The AutoKeys macro group with a SendKeys action

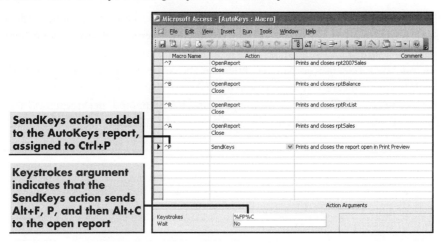

When Paul opens a report in Print Preview, he can press Ctrl+P to print and close the report.

Modifying the Switchboard to Run Macros

Now Don knows how to modify the switchboard to include queries—he can create a macro group listing macros that open the queries employees use most often. He meets briefly with the other managers, and determines that they use five queries most often: qryHourlyRateSummary, qryNoTraining, qrySpeakSpanish, qrySubstituteList, and qryYearsOfService. After he creates the macro group for these queries, Don can add a new switchboard page named Queries to the switchboard, and then specify five options that open the queries.

He creates a macro group named mcrFrequentQueries that includes five macros, one for each query. Each macro opens the specified query. A final macro closes the active window. See Figure 6.29.

Figure 6.29: Creating a macro group for the Queries switchboard page

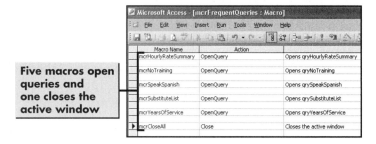

Five macros open queries and one closes the active window

Don closes the mcrFrequentQueries macro group, and then opens the Switchboard Manager. First, he creates a switchboard page named Queries. Then he edits the Queries switchboard page by adding a new item named Hourly Rate Summary. He clicks the Command list arrow, and then selects Run Macro. Then he clicks the Macro list arrow and selects mcrFrequentQueries.mcrHourlyRateSummary. (Recall that this notation refers to the macro named mcrHourlyRateSummary in the macro group named mcrFrequentQueries.) See Figure 6.30.

Figure 6.30: Creating a switchboard item that runs a macro

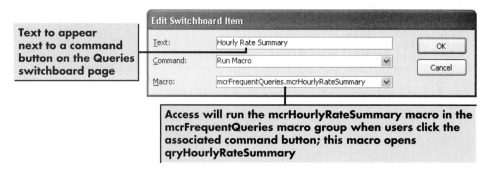

Text to appear next to a command button on the Queries switchboard page

Access will run the mcrHourlyRateSummary macro in the mcrFrequentQueries macro group when users click the associated command button; this macro opens qryHourlyRateSummary

Don clicks the OK button, and then adds items for the other four queries, for closing the Queries switchboard, and for returning to the main switchboard. Then he adds the Queries item to the main switchboard page. See Figure 6.31.

Figure 6.31: Adding queries to the 4Corners switchboard

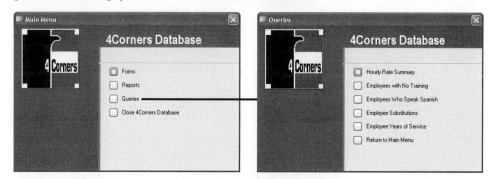

Clicking the Queries button on the main switchboard page opens the Queries switchboard page, which lists frequently used queries

The 4Corners switchboard allows employees to open all of the database objects they need.

Now that Don has gained experience with macros, learning how to assign macros to key combinations and how to use macros to create switchboard items, he wants to assign a macro to a control such as a command button. Users could then click a button on a form, for example, to open a related form and print it.

SPECIFYING CONDITIONS AND EVENTS FOR MACROS

Two powerful ways to use macros are to specify conditions for performing the macro actions and to assign a macro to a control, such as a command button. In some cases, you only want to run a macro under certain conditions. Consider the following scenario. Suppose you create a macro named mcrTravelExpenses to print a report named rptTravelExpenses, which lists travel expenses incurred by employees. This report is based on a parameter query that requests the start and end date for selecting records. In some months, such as August, employees do not submit any travel expenses. When you run the mcrTravelExpenses macro to print rptTravelExpenses and enter August 1 as the start date and August 31 as the end date, the report prints with no data. To avoid this, you could set the OpenReport action in mcrTravelExpenses to print a report only if the report contains information. To do so, you specify conditions, as shown in Figure 6.32.

Figure 6.32: Condition testing

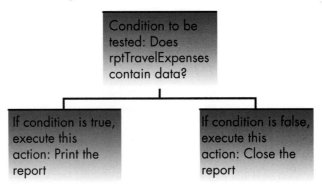

Another way to make macros more powerful is to associate them with controls, such as a command button or combo box on a form. When a user clicks the button, Access runs the macro. The technique is called **event-driven programming**, or running a macro when the user interacts with an object, such as clicking a button or moving to a specified field on a form. An **event** is a state, condition, or occurrence that Access recognizes. For example, events occur when you click a field on a form, click a command button on a switchboard page, or press a key to choose a menu command. Each event has an associated **event property**, which specifies how an object responds when the event occurs. For example, each form has an On Open event property, which specifies what happens when the form is opened. A text box on a form has an On Click property that specifies what happens when the text box is clicked. These event properties appear in the property sheets for forms, reports, and controls. By default, they do not have an initial value, meaning that the event property has not been set. In other words, when you click a text box, by default, Access takes no special action because the On Click event property for the text box has not been set.

If you set an event property value to a macro name, Access runs the macro when the event occurs. For example, you could create a macro named mcrHighestBalance that opens a form, such as one named frmSales, and then finds the record with the highest value in the Balanced Owed field. If you add a command button to a form named frmCustomer, you can open the property sheet for that command button, and then set the On Click property to mcrHighestBalance. When users click the command button on frmCustomer, Access runs the mcrHighestBalance macro to open frmSales and find the record with the highest value in the Balanced Owed field.

Paul has a new request for Don that involves specifying conditions and associating macros with events. When Paul works with the frmEmployee form, which lists all the employees in the pharmacy, he often filters the form by the JobID so that he can view only employees in a particular position. Doing so involves four steps: he opens frmEmployee, clicks the Next Record button as necessary to find the JobID he wants, clicks the JobID field, and then clicks the Filter by Form button. He must perform these four steps for each job category, and wants to automate this process somehow instead. Don considers how to fulfill Paul's request, and determines that he can place command buttons on the frmEmployee form that Paul can click to filter the records.

Assigning a Macro to a Control

A common use for macros is to create a macro or macro group that performs a series of actions, and then assign that macro to a control such as a command button. When users click the button, Access runs the macro. For example, you can add a command button to a form to execute a series of actions. First, you create the macro that specifies the actions you want to perform when someone clicks the button. Next, you add a command button to a form by opening the form in Design view and using the Command Button tool on the Toolbox toolbar. Then you attach the macro with the desired actions to the command button.

Don first designs a macro group that will filter records when executed. He opens a new Macro window and then the Macro Name column. For the first macro in the macro group, he enters mcrJobID1 and then selects the ApplyFilter action. This action has two arguments that specify how to apply the filter: Filter Name and Where Condition. You use the Filter Name argument if you are using a query to set the filter conditions. For example, if a query selected only those records from tblEmployee that included the value 1 in the JobID field, Don could enter the name of that query as the Filter Name argument. However, the 4Corners database does not include this query, and Don can use the Where Condition argument to specify the same criteria. For this argument, you can specify a condition to select records as you do in a query. Don enters the following condition in the Where Condition argument:

$$[JobID] = 1$$

This condition specifies that the macro select records in which the JobID field contains the value 1. As in a query, the field name appears in brackets. Don adds four other macros that use the ApplyFilter action and similar conditions to select employee records in the other four job categories. For example, he names the second macro mcrJobID2, selects the ApplyFilter action, and specifies [JobID]=2 as the Where Condition argument. For the final macro in the group, he adds a macro named mcrShowAll, and selects the ShowAllRecords action to remove the filters. He also adds comments to document each macro, and then saves the macro group as mcrJobID. See Figure 6.33.

Figure 6.33: mcrJobID macro for filtering employee records by Job ID

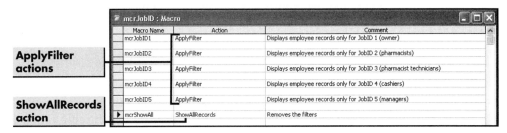

ApplyFilter actions

ShowAllRecords action

Now that Don has created the necessary macros in the mcrJobID macro group, he can add buttons to frmEmployee and assign the macros to the buttons. He opens frmEmployee in Design view, clicks the Control Wizards button 🔨 on the Toolbox toolbar to deselect it (so that the Command Button Wizard does not start), and then clicks the Command Button button ▬ on the Toolbox toolbar. He clicks in the form header to add a button to the form.

To associate the mcrJobID macro with the new button and to set other properties for the button, he right-clicks the button and clicks Properties on the shortcut menu to open its property sheet. He changes the Caption property to Job ID 1, and then clicks the Event tab to set the event properties. For the On Click property, he selects the mcrJobID.mcrJobID1 macro. See Figure 6.34.

Figure 6.34: Associating a macro with a command button's event properties

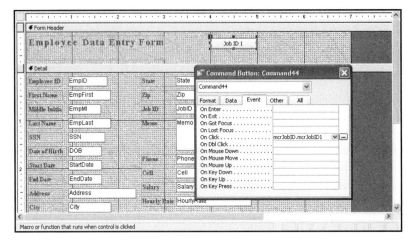

Don repeats this procedure for the four remaining job categories, adding command buttons to the form and specifying the corresponding macro as the On Click event property. He also adds a button with the caption "Remove Filter," and assigns the mcrShowAll macro to its On Click event property.

Don resizes and moves the buttons, adds a border around them and a label to identify them. Then he switches to Form view and clicks the Job ID 3 button to verify that the frmEmployee form now shows only pharmacy technicians, which are the employees with Job ID 3. See Figure 6.35.

Figure 6.35: Using a command button to filter records

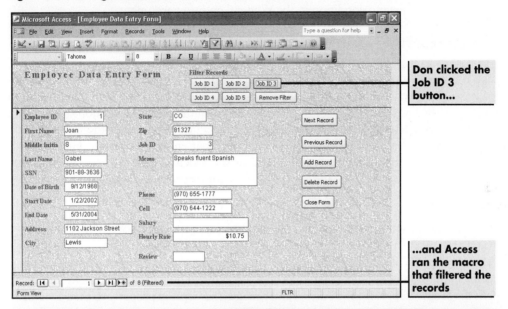

Don clicked the Job ID 3 button...

...and Access ran the macro that filtered the records

Specifying Conditions in a Macro

Don has discovered a new problem that he can solve by using a button and a macro associated with a button event. When pharmacists and technicians are working with the frmPrimaryActivity form to enter prescriptions and refills, doctors are listed according to their ID. Employees often need to call doctors for information, and need a quick way to open the appropriate record in the doctor form to find the doctor's name and phone numbers. Don decides to add a button to the prescription form that employees can click to open the doctor form and display the record for the appropriate doctor.

Don creates a macro called mcrViewDoctor. In the Action column, he selects the OpenForm action. For the arguments, he chooses frmDoctor as the Form Name, Form as the View argument, and Read Only for the Data Mode argument because he does not want the employee to change the doctor's information. For the Where Condition argument, he must construct a condition that filters the records in the frmDoctor form based on the value of the DoctorID field in the frmPrimaryActivity form. To do so, he must refer to the DoctorID field in the Where Condition argument.

When referring to controls on a form that are not currently active, Don must use the control's complete name, which includes the type of object that contains the control, the name of the object, and then the name of the control. Each part of the complete name is separated from the other using an exclamation mark (!). Following is the general form of this reference:

[Forms]![*formName*]![*controlName*]

Don enters the following condition in the Where Condition argument:

[DoctorID] = [Forms]![frmPrimaryActivity]![DoctorID]

This argument identifies the DoctorID field as a control on a form named frmPrimaryActivity. Now the mcrViewDoctor macro will open frmPrimaryActivity, and then display the record that meets the criteria specified in the Where Condition argument, the record in frmDoctor that contains a DoctorID value that matches the one for the current record in frmPrimaryActivity. In other words, if employees are working with a record in frmPrimaryActivity that displays 13 in the DoctorID field, they can run the mcrViewDoctor macro to open the appropriate doctor record, the one in frmDoctor that also contains 13 in the DoctorID field.

To run the mcrViewDoctor macro, Don will add a button to frmPrimaryActivity and then associate the mcrViewDoctor macro with the button's On Click event property. He opens frmPrimaryActivity in Design view, makes sure that the Control Wizards button is not selected in the Toolbox toolbar, and then adds a command button to the form header. He opens the property sheet for the button, and changes the Caption property to View Doctor. Then he clicks the Event tab, clicks the On Click property list arrow, and then selects mcrViewDoctor.

He saves the changes to frmPrimaryActivity, notes that the DoctorID for the first record is 13, and then tests the macro by clicking the View Doctor button. Don expects the frmDoctor form to open to the record for DoctorID 13, but something is wrong with the macro. Although the frmDoctor form does appear, no information is displayed. Don needs to troubleshoot the macro to solve the problem.

TROUBLESHOOTING MACROS

Any type of macro is prone to errors, but those containing arguments, such as the Where Condition argument, that you enter rather than select are especially error-prone. When you first run a macro, it might display a message and stop running, run using the wrong object, or cause other problems that are difficult to trace.

Three types of errors can occur during macro creation and execution. The first type of error is known as a **syntax error**, which is code that violates the macro rules established by Access. Because Access cannot interpret the syntax of the command, it displays a message in a dialog box identifying the error and the statement it cannot interpret. To repair these types of error, you must find the incorrect statement, identify the missing information or incorrect entry, and then correct the problem. Often, missing brackets or other symbols cause syntax errors.

The second type of error is known as a **logic error**, which occurs when the macro fails to produce the results you intended. This can be caused by an action placed out of sequence in the macro or incorrect action arguments.

The third type of error is a **run-time error**, which occurs when the macro tries to perform actions that are not possible to perform. For example, if a macro is designed to open a form that has been deleted, the macro cannot find the form and displays a run-time error.

The possibility of errors increases with the number of actions and conditions you include in a macro. To help you find and repair errors, Access provides several troubleshooting tools, including single stepping through the execution of the macro, using the Debug window, and printing the macro code.

Don decides to first print the macro code in the mcrViewDoctor macro to see if he can spot the problem.

Printing Macros

In Chapter 2, you learned how to print a report of selected objects in the database. One of the simplest ways for Don to debug a macro is to print it. Then he can refer to the printed copy of the macro while the macro runs or while he uses other more sophisticated debugging tools to solve the macro problem. He can choose to print the properties of the macro, its action and arguments, or the permissions by user and group. He can read through the code on the printed copy and choose the repairs to make.

To print the macro, Don can open the Documenter dialog box, which includes a tab for each type of object in an Access database. He clicks Tools on the menu bar, points to Analyze, clicks Documenter, and then clicks the Macros tab to select a macro to print. See Figure 6.36.

Figure 6.36: Documenter dialog box open to the Macros tab

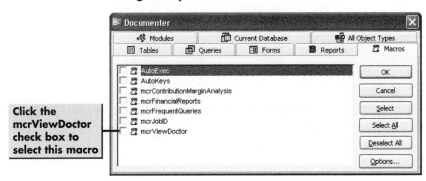

Click the mcrViewDoctor check box to select this macro

He clicks the mcrViewDoctor check box, and then clicks the Options button to select which details of the macro he wants to print: properties, actions and arguments, or permissions. He selects the Actions and Arguments check box only, and then clicks the OK button. When he closes the Documenter dialog box, a report appears in Print Preview listing the actions and arguments set for the mcrViewDoctor macro.

How To

Print a Macro

1. Click Tools on the menu bar, point to Analyze, and then click Documenter. The Documenter dialog box opens.

2. Click the Macros tab and then select one or more macros to print.

3. Click the Options button to select which details you want to print: properties, actions and arguments, or permissions. Then click the OK button.

4. Click the OK button to open the Documenter report in Print Preview.

5. Print and then close the report.

Don studies the contents of the mcrViewDoctor macro, but cannot locate the error. He decides to try another troubleshooting technique known as single stepping.

Single Stepping a Macro

Because macros execute very quickly, it is sometimes difficult to identify the action that caused the error. **Single stepping** runs a macro one action at a time, pausing between actions. You use single stepping to make sure that the actions appear in the correct order and with the correct arguments. If you have problems with a macro, you can use single stepping to find the cause of the problems and to determine how to correct them. To single step a macro, you use the Single Step button ⊞ on the Macro Design toolbar to turn on single stepping. When you turn on single stepping, it stays on for all macros until you turn it off.

With the single stepping feature turned on, macros execute one action at a time and pause between actions, displaying a Macro Single Step dialog box that shows the name of the macro, the value of any conditions, the action to be taken, and the arguments for the action. The dialog box also has three buttons you can use to perform the next action in the macro. You can run the next part of the macro by pressing the Step button or stop running the macro by pressing the Halt button. The Continue button steps into the next action and turns off the Single Step feature to perform the rest of the actions.

Don opens mcrViewDoctor in Design view, clicks the Single Step button ⊞ on the Macro Design toolbar, and then clicks the Run button ▮ on the Macro Design toolbar. Figure 6.37 shows the Macro Single Step dialog box.

Figure 6.37: Macro Single Step dialog box

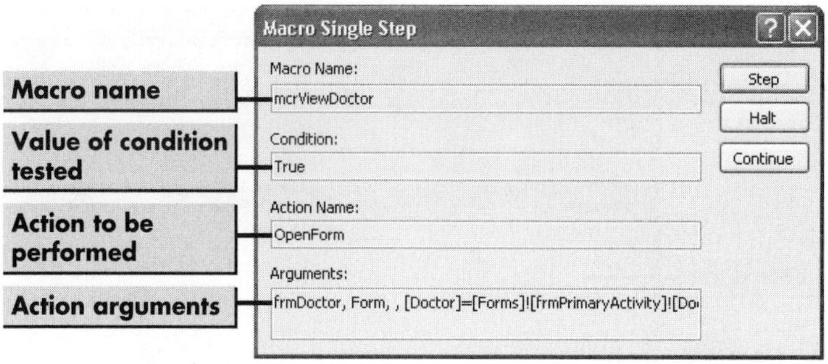

Don examines the dialog box but cannot see anything wrong in this step. He clicks the Continue button to perform the next step in the macro.

How To

Single Step a Macro

1. In the Macro window, click the Single Step button ⬛ on the Macro Design toolbar.

2. Click the Run button ⬛ on the Macro Design toolbar. If necessary, click the Yes button to save the macro. The Macro Single Step dialog box opens and Access performs the first action in the macro.

3. Click the Step button to execute the next action, click the Halt button to stop the macro, or click the Continue button to execute all remaining actions in the macro and turn off single stepping.

Because mcrViewDoctor contains only one action, Don wants to use another troubleshooting tool that will let him examine each part of the action and its arguments. He clicks the Single Step button ⬛ on the Macro Design toolbar to turn off single stepping.

Using Breakpoints and the Debug Window

When macros become more complicated, you often need to see the details of a macro action and its results. To do so, you can use the Debug window and set a **breakpoint**, which is a code you insert in the macro, signaling where you want to stop the macro. Then you can examine the values of the actions, controls, and arguments the macro is using in the Debug window. (Debugging a macro means that you are testing it and checking for errors.) The Debug window shows the macro as it appears in VBA code, which is the programming language Access uses for macros. You can examine the details of the macro code in the Debug window, which usually reveals the problems in a complicated macro. If you have already printed a macro and used single stepping to run a macro, the Debug window can help you identify values that are incorrect and are causing the macro to fail.

Don thinks the problem is with the frmPrimaryActivity form, so he closes the mcrViewDoctor macro and opens frmPrimaryActivity in Design view. Then he opens the Debug window by pressing the Ctrl+G keys. See Figure 6.38.

Figure 6.38: Debug window

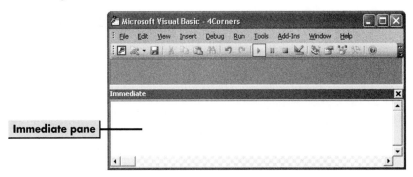

Immediate pane

The lower half of the Debug window is called the **Immediate pane**, which is used to display the current value of controls and arguments. Don can display a value by using the question mark (?) operator followed by the expression he wants to evaluate. For example, to evaluate a mathematical expression, he can enter ?4 * 5, and the Debug window will perform the calculation and show the results. To debug a macro, Don can view the values used in an action's arguments by typing the value. He wants to determine the results of the expression that he entered as the Where Condition argument for the OpenForm action in mcrViewDoctor. When he types this expression, the Debug window evaluates it and displays the results. In this way, Don can check which DoctorID value the macro is using to select a record in frmPrimaryActivity.

?Forms!frmPrimaryActivity!Doctor

When he presses the Enter key, the error message shown in Figure 6.39 appears.

Figure 6.39: Error generated

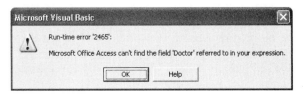

The results indicate that Access cannot find the Doctor field. Upon closer examination, Don realizes that he mistyped the field and should have entered it as DoctorID. To verify that he has identified the error, he enters the same expression, but using the correct name for the DoctorID field:

?Forms!frmPrimaryActivity!DoctorID

This time, the results are correct. See Figure 6.40.

Figure 6.40: Debug window results

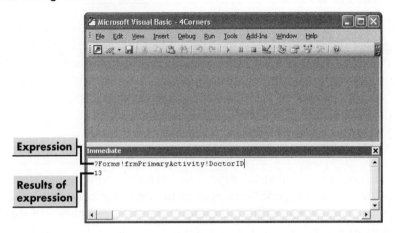

In mcrViewDoctor, Don corrects the error in the Where Condition argument to:

[DoctorID] = [Forms]![frmPrimaryActivity]![DoctorID]

He tests the macro again and this time frmDoctor opens when he clicks the View Doctor button and displays the correct doctor's information. See Figure 6.41.

Figure 6.41: Testing the View Doctor button and associated macro to find a specified record in another form

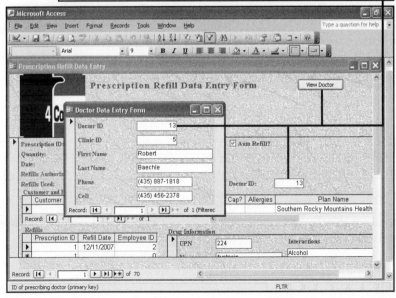

Steps To Success: Level 2

Glenn Hollander wants to continue to improve the user interface of the Hudson database, and asks for your help in creating advanced macros that Joan Gabel and others at the Hudson Bay Pharmacy can use to print reports and update the switchboard to include queries. He also wants to include buttons on forms that run macros when users click them.

Complete the following:

1. Start Access and open the **Hudson.mdb** database from the STS folder.

2. Glenn mentions that employees print four financial reports in the Hudson database the most often: rpt2007Sales, rptBalance, rptRxList, and rptSales. Provide a way to let users automatically print and close each report. Save the macro as mcrFinancialReports.

3. Instead of running mcrFinancialReports to print and close the financial reports, Glenn wants employees to be able to press a key combination and run the associated macro. Create a macro named AutoKeys that fulfills Glenn's request. Choose key combinations that are easy for employees to remember and associate with each report.

4. Glenn also wants to be able to print and close any report from Print Preview by pressing the Ctrl+P keys. Revise the AutoKeys macro to print and close any report from Print Preview.

5. Modify the Hudson switchboard so that it includes a Queries page that opens the following queries in the database: qryHourlyRate, qryNoTraining, qrySpeakSpanish, and qryUpToDate.

6. When working with frmEmployee, Joan Gabel wants to be able to display only those records that are in a particular job category. Add buttons to the frmEmployee form so that Joan can filter the records based on JobID by clicking a button. Be sure to include a button that removes the filter.

7. Glenn mentions that when pharmacists and technicians are working with the frmPrimaryActivity form to enter prescriptions and refills, doctors are listed according to their ID. Employees often need to call doctors for information, and need a quick way to open the appropriate record in the doctor form to find the doctor's name and phone numbers. Add a button to frmPrimaryActivity that employees can click to open the doctor form and display the record for the appropriate doctor.

8. Use three troubleshooting tools to test a macro you created for Hudson Bay Pharmacy. Describe the results of each tool.

9. Close the **Hudson.mdb** database and Access.

LEVEL 3

MACRO CONDITIONS

ACCESS 2003 SKILLS TRAINING

- Add an action to a macro
- Create a macro
- Run a macro

6

Level 3

EXPLORING MACRO CONDITIONS

Paul Ferrino frequently uses the rptBalance report that shows customers with an outstanding balance greater than zero, and wants to change the format of this report depending on its contents. He wants to contact customers who have outstanding balances over $25.00. He asks Don to modify the report so that any balance greater that $25.00 is placed in a rectangle and highlighted with an asterisk. Elaine Estes, the pharmacy manager, can then contact these customers and work out a payment plan.

Don considers modifying the report by using the Access conditional formatting tool, but discovers that he cannot add a rectangle or an asterisk as Paul requested using this tool. Instead, he can create a macro and specify conditions that will produce the same results.

Macro conditions are logical expressions that result in a true or false answer. Depending on the outcome of the condition, the macro can perform one set of actions or another. Using macro conditions, you can add the power and flexibility of decision making, common in computer programming, to your database without directly writing programming code. To enter macro conditions, you open the Condition column in the Macro window by clicking the Conditions button on the Macro Design toolbar. See Figure 6.42.

Figure 6.42: Condition column in the Macro window

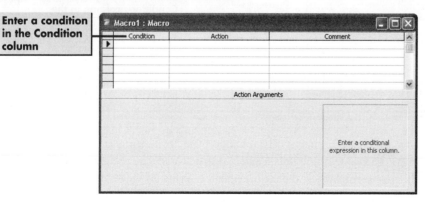

If the condition is true, Access performs the corresponding action in the Action column. When you want Access to perform more than one action if the condition is true, enter a conditional statement in the Condition column, and then select actions in the Action column in the order you want Access to perform them. In the Condition column, enter an ellipsis (…) for each subsequent action associated with the condition. The ellipsis (…) indicates that the condition extends to these actions, and Access should perform them also if the condition is true. If the condition is false, Access ignores the corresponding action, and evaluates the next action that contains a condition. You can also use an ellipsis (…) in the Condition column to indicate that Access should perform more than one action if the condition is false.

Best Practice

Displaying the Condition and Macro Name Columns by Default
If you find that you regularly use the Condition or the Macro Name column in the Macro window, you can specify that Access open these columns each time you open the Macro window. To do so, click Tools on the menu bar, and then click Options. The Options dialog box opens, as shown in Figure 6.43. On the View tab, select the Names column and the Conditions column check boxes to display these columns by default when you create or modify a macro.

Figure 6.43: View tab of the Options dialog box

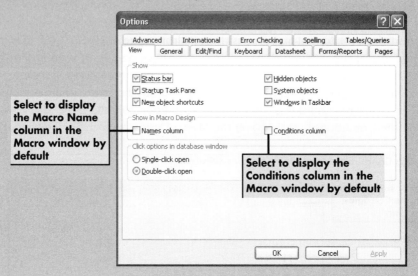

Don wants to create a macro that changes the formatting in the rptBalance report depending on the value of the Balance field. He will associate the macro with a report event so that the macro runs when the report opens in Print Preview.

First, Don redesigns the rptBalance report to include a rectangle control to outline the Balance field in the Detail section and a label that contains an asterisk. Don right-clicks the rectangle object and sets its Fill/Back Color property to Transparent. He names these two objects rectBalance and lblAsterisk, and uses their property sheets to set their Visible property to No so that these controls do not appear by default. See Figure 6.44.

Figure 6.44: Line and label properties

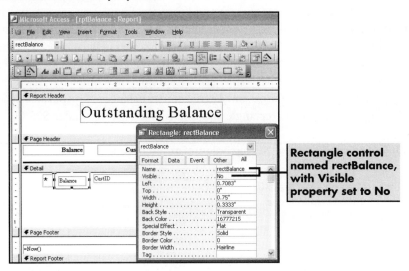

He will specify that the Visible property changes to Yes if the contents of the report meet the condition he creates in a macro. Next, he creates a macro named mcrBalanceFormat that contains a condition to test the value in the Balance field. He enters the following condition in the Condition column to test the value:

`[Balance] >= 25`

This expression determines whether the value in the Balance field is greater than or equal to 25. If this condition is true, Don wants to display the rectangle and the asterisk by setting their Visible properties to Yes. To do so, he can use the **SetValue action**, which can change the property of an object by disabling, updating, hiding, or displaying a control. The SetValue action has two arguments: Item and Expression. The Item argument specifies the control whose property you want to change, such as rectBalance or lblAsterisk. The Expression argument specifies the new value for the property, such as Yes. Don selects the SetValue action for the first control and uses the following expression as the Item argument:

`[rectBalance].[Visible]`

This notation includes the name of the control within square brackets, then a period, then the name of the property to set. In this case, Don wants to change the Visible property of the rectBalance control. For the Expression argument, Don enters Yes to indicate that if the value in the Balance field is greater than or equal to 25, Access should set the Visible property of the rectBalance control to Yes, thereby displaying a rectangle around the balance amount.

Don clicks in the second row of the Condition column, types an ellipsis (…), clicks in the second row of the Action column, selects the SetValue action again, and then enters [lblAsterisk].[Visible] as the Item argument and Yes as the Expression argument. Then he adds a second condition to specify what Access should do if the Balance amount is less than 25. He clicks in the third row of the Condition column, enters [Balance]<25 as the condition, and then enters two SetValue actions to set the Visible property of the rectangle and asterisk to No when the Balance value is less than 25. The completed macro, shown in Figure 6.45, will display a rectangle and asterisk under balances in rptBalance of $25.00 or more, but will not display the rectangle and asterisk for balances under $25.00.

Figure 6.45: Setting conditions for the mcrBalanceFormat macro

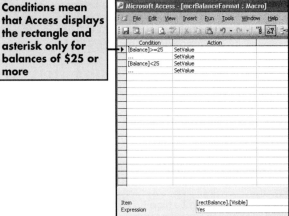

Conditions mean that Access displays the rectangle and asterisk only for balances of $25 or more

Now that the macro is complete, Don needs to associate it with a report event so that it runs when the rptBalance report opens in Print Preview.

Assigning a Macro to an Object Event

In addition to assigning a macro to a control, such as a command button, by specifying a macro name in a control's event property, you can assign a macro to an object by specifying a macro name in an event property of the object. These events fall into two categories. Report events occur to the report as a whole, such as when the report is opened or closed. Section events occur to a section of the report, such as when the section is formatted or printed. Table 6.5 shows the report events, and Table 6.6 shows the section events.

Table 6.5: Report events

Event Name	Action That Triggers the Event
On Open	When report opens but before it prints
On Close	When report closes
On Activate	When report gets focus
On Deactivate	When report loses focus
On No Data	When the record source of the report contains no data
On Page	When the report advances to the next page
On Error	When a run-time error occurs

Table 6.6: Report section events

Event Name	Action That Triggers the Event
On Format	When page layout can change
On Print	After the section is laid out but before it prints
On Retreat	After the On Format event but before the On Print event (not available in page header or footer sections)

Don can associate the mcrBalanceFormat macro with the On Format event property of the rptBalance report. This means that when Access formats the report to prepare it for Print Preview, it will also run mcrBalanceFormat, test the conditions in the macro, and then display the line and asterisk if the first condition is true. On Format is a report section event, so Don should assign the mcrBalanceFormat macro to the Detail section—that's the section that contains the line, asterisk, and Balance amount.

Don opens rptBalance in Design view, opens the property sheet for the Detail section, and then clicks the Event tab. He clicks the list arrow for the On Format event property, and then selects the mcrBalanceFormat macro from the list of available macros. He tests the macro by opening the report and verifying that all balances greater than $25 are appropriately formatted with a rectangle and an asterisk. See Figure 6.46.

Figure 6.46: rptBalance with conditional formatting created by mcrBalanceFormat

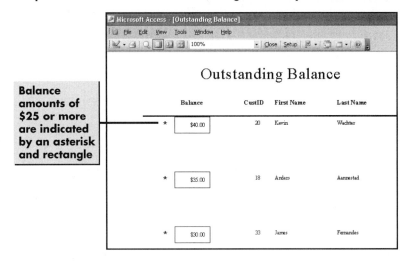

Balance amounts of $25 or more are indicated by an asterisk and rectangle

Don can also attach macros to automate some of the existing forms. To prevent employees from inadvertently deleting records, he wants to open a message box when employees try to delete a record from a form. The message will instruct them to check with a supervisor before completing the deletion. If they click the OK button, the record is deleted. If they click the Cancel button, the record is not deleted. He can accomplish this by using the MsgBox command in a macro.

Using Message Boxes with Forms

As with reports, form events can also trigger macros. Use macros with forms to validate data, set values, navigate between forms, and filter, find, and print records. Table 6.7 shows a sample list of form events.

Table 6.7: Form events

Event Name	Action That Triggers the Event
On Load	When the form loads
On Unload	When the form is closed
On Click	When the user clicks the left mouse button on any control on the form
On Dbl Click	When the user double-clicks the left mouse button on any control on the form
Before Update	Before changed data is updated
On Delete	When the user begins to delete a record but before the record is deleted
On Activate	When the form becomes the active window (receives focus)
On Timer	When a specified time interval has elapsed
Timer Interval	Before triggering the event, wait the specified amount of time (milliseconds)

When users click the Delete Record button ⊠ on the Form View toolbar to delete a record in a form, Don wants to display a dialog box asking users if they are sure they are authorized to delete the record. (The policy at 4Corners Pharmacy is that employee supervisors must approve all record deletions.) Therefore, the macro he creates must first open such a dialog box. To achieve this, Don can use the **MsgBox command**, which opens a message box and displays a warning or informational message. When you set a condition that uses the MsgBox command, you write a MsgBox statement using the following syntax:

```
MsgBox ("Message", Sum of button and icon values, "Title")
```

- **Message**—The text in quotation marks that appears in the message box, such as "Are you sure you want to delete this record?"
- **Sum of button and icon values**—The sum of the values associated with the icons and buttons you want to display in the message box. Each type of icon, such as an informational icon, or button, such as the OK button, is associated with a value. The button that you want to select by default is also associated with a value. (See Tables 6.8, 6.9, and 6.10.) You select the icons, buttons, and default button that you want, and sum their values. Then you use this sum as the second part of the MsgBox command.
- **Title**—The text in quotation marks that appears in the title bar of the message box.

Table 6.8: Type of buttons and values

Value	Type of Button
0	OK
1	OK, Cancel
2	Abort, Retry, Ignore
3	Yes, No, Cancel
4	Yes, No
5	Retry, Cancel

Table 6.9: Icon style and values

Value	Icon
0	No icon
16	Critical (white X in a red ball)
32	Warning? (blue question mark in a white balloon)
48	Warning! (black exclamation point in a yellow triangle)
64	Information (blue letter I in a white balloon)

Table 6.10: Default buttons and values

Value	Default Button
0	First
256	Second
512	Third

In the MsgBox that Don is designing, he wants to include the Yes and the No buttons (value 4) and the icon that displays a blue question mark in a white balloon (value 32). He also wants the No button—the second button—as the default (value 256). To specify this argument in the MsgBox command, he must sum the values of the buttons and icons he wants to display: 4 + 32 + 256 = 292. He can use the following command to specify the message box he wants to create, as shown in Figure 6.47.

```
MsgBox("Did you check with supervisor?", 292, "Delete?")
```

Figure 6.47: Sample message box created with the MsgBox action

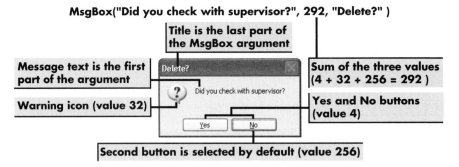

The MsgBox also returns a value depending on which button is clicked. Table 6.11 shows the values returned depending on which button is selected. Don can use these values to finish setting up the condition for the message box.

Table 6.11: Return value of buttons

Value Returned	Button Selected
1	OK
2	Cancel
3	Abort
4	Retry
5	Ignore
6	Yes
7	No

Don can create a condition that checks to see which button users click. If they click the Yes button, the MsgBox returns the value 6. If users click the No button, the MsgBox returns the value 7. The condition can check whether the value returned is equal to 7. Don creates a new macro named mcrConfirmDeletion, opens the Condition column, clicks in the first row of the Condition column, and enters the following MsgBox statement:

```
MsgBox("Did you check with supervisor?", 292, "Delete?") = 7
```

Eventually, Don will assign the mcrConfirmDeletion macro to the On Delete event of a form. If a user tries to delete a record in the form, the mcrConfirmDeletion macro will run and test the first condition in the Condition column of the macro, which is MsgBox("Did you check with supervisor?", 292, "Delete?") = 7. If this condition is true—in other words, if the user clicks the No button—the macro cancels the deletion and stops running. To specify these actions, Don clicks in the first row of the Action column and selects the CancelEvent. Then he enters an ellipsis (…) in the second row of the Condition column, clicks in the second row of the Action column, and selects the StopMacro action. Don's entries indicate that if the condition is true, the macro performs first the CancelEvent action and then the StopMacro action.

Next, Don must specify what the macro should do if the condition is false (in other words, if the user clicks the Yes button). In that case, the macro should allow the deletion. To specify that action, Don uses the SendKeys action with {ENTER} as the Keystrokes argument for the third entry in the Action column. If users click the Yes button, the mcrConfirmDeletion macro deletes the record by pressing Enter. See Figure 6.48.

Figure 6.48: mcrConfirmDelete macro

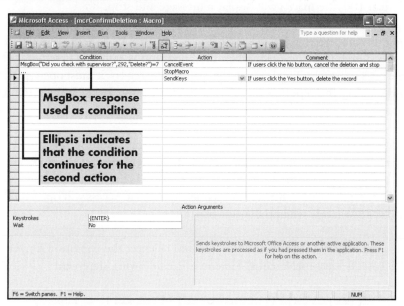

Don wants to test the mcrConfirmDeletion macro on frmCustomer so he saves and closes the macro, and then opens frmCustomer in Design view. He opens the property sheet of the form and assigns the mcrConfirmDeletion macro to the On Delete event. Now, if a user tries to delete a record by using the Delete Record button ▯ on the Form View toolbar (or any other technique for deleting a record), the macro displays the message box asking to confirm the deletion. Don tests the mcrConfirmDeletion macro by saving frmCustomer, opening it in Form view, and then trying to delete a record. The message box appears as designed, so he knows that the macro is working correctly.

Next, Paul wants a monthly report to list all the prescriptions issued for the drug Rizatriptan Benzoate. Because this drug is classified as a narcotic, Paul must provide a monthly report to the government if the quantity dispensed is greater than 100 pills. If the pharmacy dispenses fewer than 100 pills of Rizatriptan Benzoate in a month, he does not need to print the report.

Don creates a query named qryNarcotic that selects all prescriptions for Rizatriptan Benzoate (UPN 987) and displays the customer's last name and quantity of pills dispensed for a particular month and year. He creates a report named rptNarcotic that uses this query as the record source. Then he adds a text box named Total to the UPN footer to sum the quantity dispensed. When Paul opens this report, he does not know if more than 100 pills of Rizatriptan Benzoate have been dispensed. To save time, Don can create a macro to print the report only if this condition occurs.

Using Message Boxes with Reports

Don is ready to create a macro that tests the Total field in rptNarcotic to determine if it contains a value over 100. If it does, the macro will print the report. If the field contains a value less than 100, the macro will display a message and stop.

When conditions in a macro reference the name of a control from a source, such as a form or report, the source must be open when the condition is tested. Therefore, before an action in the macro tests the Total field in the rptNarcotic report, it must open rptNarcotic. Instead of displaying the report, which might be distracting, Don can hide the window while the macro tests the condition.

Don creates a macro named mcrNarcotic and opens the Condition column. He clicks in the first row of the Action column and selects the OpenReport action. He selects rptNarcotic as the Report Name argument, Print Preview as the View argument, and Hidden as the Window Mode argument. This action means that Access will open rptNarcotic but not display its window when the macro starts.

He clicks the second row of the Condition column to enter the condition for testing the value in the Total field of rptNarcotic. He enters the following statement:

```
([Reports]![rptNarcotic]![Total]) < 100
```

This statement checks whether the value in the Total field is less than 100 in a report named rptNarcotic. If the condition is true—if the Total field contains a quantity fewer than 100—Don wants the macro to display a message informing Paul that he does not need to print the report. If this condition is false—if the Total field contains a quantity of 100 or more—the macro should print the report.

To achieve this, Don must use the **MsgBox action**, which opens a message box and displays a warning or informational message. Using the MsgBox action is similar to using the MsgBox command in a condition, except that with the action, Access lets you select the arguments you need. A macro containing a MsgBox action does not continue to the next action until a user clicks the OK button, so when you add the MsgBox action to a macro, users will have as much time as they need to read and react to the message box. The MsgBox action requires four arguments: Message, Beep, Type, and Title:

- **Message**—The text that appears in the message box when it is displayed.
- **Beep**—A Yes/No argument that specifies whether a beep sounds when the message box is opened.
- **Type**—The argument that determines which icon, if any, appears in the message box to signify the critical level of the message: None (no icon), Critical (white X in a red ball), Warning? (blue question mark in a white balloon), Warning! (black exclamation point in a yellow triangle), and Information (blue letter I in a white balloon).
- **Title**—The title that appears in the message box title bar.

Don clicks in the Action column corresponding to the conditional statement he entered and selects the MsgBox action. For the Message argument, he enters Total dispensed is less than 100. For the Beep argument, he selects Yes. For the Type argument, he selects Information. Finally, for the Title argument, he enters You do not need to print the narcotic report. This means that if the Total field in rptNarcotic contains a quantity less than 100, an informational message box titled "You do not need to print the narcotic report" opens with the message "Total dispensed is less than 100."

If the condition is true, Don wants to close the hidden report and then stop the macro. In the third row of the Condition column, Don enters an ellipsis (…), and then selects the Close action, specifying Report as the Object Type and rptNarcotic as the Object Name. This means that the macro will close the rptNarcotic report if the condition entered in the first row of the Condition column is true. He also enters an ellipsis (…) in the fourth row of the Condition column because he wants to perform one more action if the condition is true—stop the macro. He selects the StopMacro action in the fourth row of the Action column. Now he can specify the action the macro should perform if the condition in the first row is false—that is, if the total dispensed is 100 or more. He selects the OpenReport action and specifies rptNarcotic as the Report Name argument and Print Preview as the View. The entire mcrNarcotic macro is shown in Figure 6.49.

Figure 6.49: mcrNarcotic macro

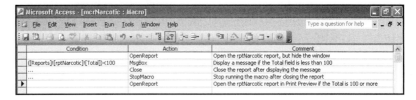

Don saves the mcrNarcotic macro, opens rptNarcotic in Design view, opens the property sheet for the report, and then assigns it to the On Open event property for the report. Now, when Paul opens this report, he will trigger the mcrNarcotic macro, which first opens the rptNarcotic report, but hides the window. The next action in the macro tests the value in the Total field. If the value is 100 or less, three actions are performed: a message box is displayed, the report closes, and the macro stops. If the value in the Total field is greater than 100, these three actions are skipped and the report opens in Print Preview so that Paul can print it.

VALIDATING DATA WITH MACROS

The most common ways to validate data are to use field properties such as input masks, validation rules, and validation text. However, those field properties have their limits. For example, you can specify only one validation rule for a field and display only one validation message. To validate data using more than one rule and more than one validation message, you can create a macro.

A typical error when entering data in forms is to attempt to enter a record using a primary key value already used in another record. Because a primary key must be unique within a table, Access indicates when you save the form that another record contains the same primary key value, and does not allow you to save the form. The validation rule and input mask control the range and the format of the primary key, but do not prevent you from entering a record with a duplicate primary key value. Only when Access attempts to save the record does it display an error message.

If you have entered many records, it might be difficult to retrace your work and find the one with the duplicate value. It would be more helpful to receive a friendly error message when you enter the duplicate primary key value in the record.

Paul has this problem with the frmDrug form. The primary key field is the UPN, which is a three-character text field. The input mask for the UPN field limits the data entry to three digits and does not use a validation rule. The input mask can ensure that users enter only three digits in the UPN field, but it does not ensure which digits they enter. Paul is finding that when a new drug is entered, employees often mistype a digit, creating an incorrect entry and possibly a duplication of a primary key. Paul feels that it would save time if employees were notified that the field value they entered was a duplicate of another primary key value. Paul speaks to Don about his concerns, and Don decides to create a macro to solve this problem.

Don begins by creating a macro named mcrDuplicateKey and opening the Condition column in the Macro window. In the first row of the Condition column, he will enter a logical expression to determine if the value entered as the UPN is a duplicate primary key. To perform this task, Don can use a domain aggregate function. Unlike aggregate functions such as Sum and Count, which are used to calculate totals, **domain aggregate functions** calculate statistics for a set of records (recordset), or **domain**, from a table or a query. Table 6.12 provides examples of domain aggregate functions.

Table 6.12: Common domain aggregate functions

Function Name	Purpose
DSum	Calculates the sum of a set of values in a specified set of records
DCount	Determines the number of records that are in a specified set of records
DAvg	Calculates the average of a set of values in a specified set of records
DVarP	Calculates the variance across a population in a specified set of records
DStDevP	Calculates the standard deviation across a population in a specified set of records

When users enter a new record in frmDrug and enter a value in the UPN field, Don wants to determine the number of records that share that value, which is the primary key. To find duplicates, he can use the DCount function to determine the number of records in a set that matches a condition. The DCount function has the following general form:

$$\text{DCount}(\textit{expression, table or query, condition})$$

- **Expression**—Represents the field for which you are counting records
- **Table or query**—Identifies the object that contains the entire recordset
- **Condition**—Limits the data to a subset of the entire recordset; a conditional expression or logical expression

For the mcrDuplicateKey macro Don is creating for frmDrug, he can use the following DCount function:

$$\text{DCount}(\text{"[UPN]", "tblDrug", "[UPN]=[txtUPN]")}$$

Note that txtUPN is the name of the control on the frmDrug form that contains the UPN number. Don will change the name of this text box to txtUPN to distinguish it from the UPN field in tblDrug. If the DCount function finds a record that matches the condition—that is, if a value in the UPN field in tblDrug is the same as the value in the txtUPN text box in frmDrug—the function returns the value of 1. Don uses the following complete condition in the mcrDuplicateKey macro:

```
DCount ("[UPN]", "tblDrug", "[UPN]=[txtUPN]") = 1
```

If this condition is true, it means that Access found a record that has the same primary key as the one being entered into the form. Don next specifies the action he wants the macro to perform if this condition is true: display an error message. In the Action column, he selects the MsgBox action and uses "You have entered a UPN for a drug already entered in this form. Press the OK button and reenter the UPN." as the Message argument. He also selects Critical as the Type argument and "Duplicate Primary Key" as the Title argument.

After displaying the message box, Don wants the macro to cancel the event that triggered the macro. He clicks in the second row of the Action column and selects the CancelEvent action, which has no arguments. If the condition is true—if a user enters a duplicate primary key value—a message box appears and the insertion point remains in the txtUPN text box of the form. If the condition is false, no action needs to be taken. The completed macro is shown in Figure 6.50.

Figure 6.50: mcrDuplicateKey macro

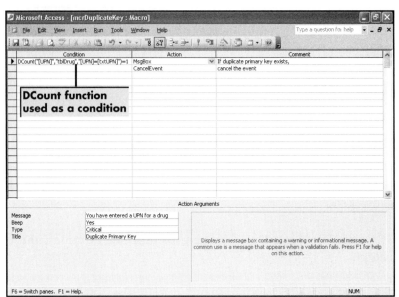

Don opens frmDrug in Design view, opens the property sheet for the UPN text box, and changes its name to txtUPN. Then he assigns the mcrDuplicateKey macro to the Before Update event property of the frmDrug form. This means that if a user enters a duplicate primary key value, the macro will run before Access updates the record. Don tests the macro by opening frmDrug in Form view, noting the UPN in the first record—102—and then attempting to enter a new record with the same UPN. When he finishes entering data for the new record, the error message shown in Figure 6.51 appears.

Figure 6.51: Duplicate key error message generated by mcrDuplicateKey

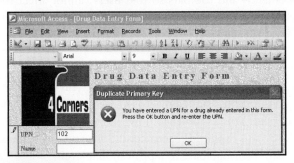

Steps To Success: Level 3

Glenn Hollander is impressed with your work with macros, and wants to continue to use them to improve the Hudson database. He asks for your help in setting macro conditions for forms and reports, displaying custom error messages, and validating data.

Complete the following:

1. Start Access and open the **Hudson.mdb** database from the STS folder.

2. Joan Gabel frequently uses the rptBalance report, and wants to display an asterisk next to balances of $20.00 or more. She also wants to display a rectangle around those balances. Modify rptBalance to display a rectangle and asterisk for balances of $20.00 or more. Name the macro you create for this task mcrBalanceFormat.

3. Create a macro that provides a custom message to the users of frmCustomer, reminding them that they should check with a supervisor before deleting a customer record from the form. Name the macro mcrConfirmDeletion.

4. Create a query that will determine what quantity of the drug Rizatriptan Benzoate has been dispensed during a particular month. Name the query qryNarcotic. Write a report based on qryNarcotic named rptNarcotic. Assign a macro to rptNarcotic so that the report prints only if the total quantity dispensed is over 100. Name the macro mcrNarcotic.

5. Using a macro, add data validation to the frmDrug form so that a user cannot add a duplicate DIN. Name the macro mcrDuplicateKey.

6. Close the **Hudson.mdb** database and Access.

CHAPTER SUMMARY

In this chapter, you learned how to design and implement a switchboard for a database. You also learned how to use the Startup dialog box to set security options such as restricting the use of the Access menus and toolbars so that users cannot affect the design of your database. You created macros to automate repetitive tasks you perform frequently and add functionality to reports and forms.

In Level 1, you designed a switchboard and then created and ran basic macros. You also set startup options and created a splash screen. In Level 2, you worked with macro groups to organize macros and then you assigned macros to events to make your forms and reports more flexible and powerful. You also learned how to troubleshoot macros so that they are free of error. In Level 3, you explored macro conditions and using message boxes, techniques that can automate your database to a professional level.

CONCEPTUAL REVIEW

1. What is a switchboard?

2. Describe the steps for using the Switchboard Manager to create a switchboard.

3. List at least three uses of a macro.

4. What is a macro group?

5. What is the function of the SendKeys action?

6. What is the function of the AutoExec macro?

7. What are some of the options you can set using the Startup dialog box?

8. Explain how macros can be used for database security.

9. What is an event? Explain how you can use macros with events.

10. Explain the purpose of macro conditions.

11. Under what circumstances would you use an ellipses (…) to set a macro condition?

12. What is the purpose of the ShowAllRecords macro command?

13. Name the techniques you can use to troubleshoot a macro.

14. Explain how a macro can be used to enhance data integrity.

15. Explain the purpose of the following macro commands:

    a.   SetValue

    b.   Beep

    c.   Hourglass

    d.   Close

    e.   Exit

    f.   OpenForm

CASE PROBLEMS

Case 1 – Providing a User Interface for the NHD Development Group Inc.

In this project, you continue working on the database for an antiques mall, Memories Antiques in Cleveland, Tennessee. Tim Richards, the chief information officer of the NHD Development Group, which owns this mall, recently reviewed the work you completed in the Antiques database. The queries, forms, and reports you created are proving to be useful to the mall staff, and are helping to streamline the mall operations. However, Tim is concerned that users who are new to Access will find it difficult to navigate the Database window and select the objects they need.

Tim asks you to create a user interface that provides an easy way to view and select queries, forms, and reports in the Antiques database. To personalize the database, he wants it to open with a window showing the company name and logo along with a command button users can click to display a series of menus. Users could then select the objects they need from these menus.

Complete the following:

1. Start Access and open the **Antiques.mdb** database from the Case 1 folder.

2. Tim wants to provide easy access to the forms and reports in the Antiques database without using the Database window. Create a switchboard that allows users to access all the forms and reports in the Antiques database. Tim suggests that you group the reports and forms on separate switchboard pages. He also reminds you to verify that the appropriate object opens when you click each entry.

6

Chapter Exercises

Management

3. Tim wants to be sure to associate the database with the mall's parent company, NHD Development Group. Include the company logo and identify Memories Antiques Mall on the main switchboard. Tim also suggests that you design the switchboard and select colors to coordinate with the company logo. (The logo, **NHD-logo.jpg**, is located in the Case 1 folder.)

4. After reviewing the switchboard, Tim realizes that it should provide an option to view the queries (lists) you created earlier. Include the queries on a separate switchboard page designed to match the ones you created for forms and reports. (*Hint:* First create macros to open each query, and then run the macros from the switchboard page.)

5. In addition to using a switchboard, Tim wants to personalize the database by displaying a splash screen when users open the Antiques database. Create a splash screen that includes the name of the mall and identifies NHD as its parent company. It should also contain the NHD logo and your name and phone number so that users can contact you if they have questions or problems with the database. (The logo, **NHD-logo.jpg**, is located in the Case 1 folder.) Finally, the splash screen should provide a command button that users can click to open the main switchboard.

6. For security, set the splash screen to appear when the database opens. Specify properties appropriate for a splash screen.

7. Carefully review your work to make sure that the switchboard and splash screen work properly and are attractive and easy to use.

8. Close the **Antiques.mdb** database and Access.

Case 2—Improving Access to Data and Reports for MovinOn Inc.

Information Systems

Previously, you created tables, queries, forms, and reports to help MovinOn streamline the recording, managing, and viewing of data in the MovinOn database. After you finish your work with the database, Dora Nettles, current administrative assistant in the Washington warehouse, will serve as the database manager. Dora is currently training employees on using the MovinOn database, and reports that some employees are not familiar with Access and don't know how to use the Database window to open the queries, forms, and reports that they need. Dora asks you to create an interface that lets users work with the data without using the Database window.

Complete the following:

1. Start Access and open the **MovinOn.mdb** database from the Case 2 folder.

2. Dora says that most employees only need to open queries, forms, and reports. Create a switchboard that provides access to all the forms, queries, and reports in the database. To create a consistent user interface, the company logo should appear on the switchboard. (The logo, **MovinOn-logo.jpg**, is located in the Case 2 folder.) The design and colors of the switchboard should coordinate with the company logo. Dora also makes the following requests to consider as you design your switchboard:

- Because this database contains many queries, group them into logical categories on separate switchboard pages. (*Hint*: Use a macro group for each set of queries.)
- Design a form that provides options to either preview or print the reports. For example, you could include two buttons for each report, one to preview and the other to print the report. The form should open when users select the Reports option on the main switchboard.

3. Dora also wants to clearly identify the database when it is opened. Create a splash screen that includes the company logo. (The logo, **MovinOn-logo.jpg**, is located in the Case 2 folder.) The splash screen should have a button that users can click to open the main switchboard for the MovinOn database. In addition, the splash screen should show the company name and contact information. Use your name and phone number as the contact information.

4. For security, set the splash screen to appear when the database opens. Specify properties appropriate for a splash screen. Do not allow users to access the Database window.

5. MovinOn is a growing company and expects to add several employees this year. Dora explains that when entering and editing employee data, users often need to find records for employees in a certain job category. On the frmEmployeeData form, provide a way to filter records to show only those employees in a specified job category. For example, users should be able to open frmEmployeeData and then select an option or click a button to view employee records only for warehouse managers.

6. Dora wants you to provide the same kind of functionality in the Driver Data Entry form that you used in the Employee Data Entry form. Modify frmDriverData so that users can filter records in three ways: view records only for drivers with an "A" driving record, view records for drivers with an "A" or a "B" driving record, or view all the records. To maintain consistency, use the same technique and design that you used in frmEmployeeData.

7. Finally, when users are working with the Customer Data Entry form, Dora wants to make it easy to locate a particular customer. Because users usually know the customer by the last name of the contact person, add a control to frmCustomerData that lets you search for a record by selecting a contact's last name. Dora wants you to keep this control separate from the data so that it stands out but is still readily available. (*Hint*: Consider placing the control in the form's header section.)

8. Close the **MovinOn.mdb** database and Access.

Case 3—Providing a User Interface for the Hershey College Intramural Department

Finance

In this project, you continue to work with Marianna Fuentes, assistant director of the intramural department at Hershey College. She has some concerns about the purchases that coaches have made and asks that you flag large purchases in the Hershey database. She wants to highlight the large purchases on screen and on the written purchases detail report.

In addition, to maintain security and make the Hershey database easier to use, Marianna does not want the staff to work directly with the objects in the Database window. Most department employees are not familiar with Access, and she wants to provide a menu system that includes options users can choose to open the queries, forms, and reports in the database.

Complete the following:

1. Start Access and open the **Hershey.mdb** database located in the Case 3 folder.

2. When you last worked with this database, you imported data pertaining to the purchases made by coaches for their assigned sport. You also created a report containing this data. Now that you have imported this data, Marianna explains that additional purchases will be entered directly in the database. Therefore, she needs an easy way to enter the purchase data. Create a form named frmPurchaseData that meets Marianna's needs. Also be sure to coordinate the design of the new form with the rest of the database.

3. Marianna is concerned that coaches are making large purchases without the proper approval. In the frmPurchaseData form, highlight purchases for $150 or more by placing the words "Large Purchase" next to the amount and drawing a box around both the amount and these words. Change the color of these elements to red.

4. To help track and prevent unauthorized large purchases, Marianna asks you to provide a way to display the coach's information in frmPurchaseData for any purchase of $150 or more. Add a button to the form that only appears for a large purchase. When users click this button, it should display the name and other relevant information for the coach who made this purchase. Users should only be able to view, not change, the coach's data. The button should not be visible when the amount is less than $150.

5. In addition to highlighting large purchases in the Purchase Data form, Marianna wants to do the same in the Purchase Detail report. Add the same words, "Large Purchase," next to purchase amounts greater than or equal to $150. Format the words in bold red text, and draw a red box around the words.

6. Recently, a coach turned in a purchase receipt, which the intramural staff recorded in the database using frmPurchaseData. Later, a staff member inadvertently deleted the record of that purchase, and no one could find the original receipt or a copy. Marianna wants to avoid this kind of problem in the future. In frmPurchaseData, provide a means to caution users when they are deleting a purchase record. The caution should ask users if they have a receipt for the purchase and then confirm that the record should be deleted. If the user verifies the deletion, remove the record.

7. Finally, Marianna wants to display a splash screen when the database is opened. Create a splash screen that includes the name of the department and the department logo. (The logo, **HC-logo.jpg**, is located in the Case 3 folder.) The splash screen should also provide a button users can click to display a menu that allows them to access the queries, forms, and reports in the Hershey database. Design the menus so they are attractive and coordinate well with the department logo. Include your name and phone number on the splash screen and on the main menus so that users can reach you if they have questions or problems with the database.

8. For security, set the splash screen to appear when the database opens. Specify properties appropriate for a splash screen. If users close the splash screen, the switchboard should appear. Do not allow users to access the Database window.

9. Close the **Hershey.mdb** database and Access.

Enhancing User Interaction Through Programming
Human Resources: Extending the Capabilities of the Database Using VBA

"I like thinking big. If you're going to be thinking anything, you might as well think big."
—Donald Trump

LEARNING OBJECTIVES

Level 1

Design, create, and test a subroutine in a standard module
Design, create, and test an event procedure
Analyze decisions using procedures
Design, create, and test a function in a standard module

Level 2

Design, create, and test a custom function in an event procedure
Use ElseIf and If statements
Verify data using event procedures
Use the Case control structure

Level 3

Troubleshoot problems in VBA procedures
Compile modules
Develop sources for learning VBA
Explore completed modules in the Northwind sample database

TOOLS COVERED IN THIS CHAPTER

Assignment statement	**If statement**
Breakpoints	**Immediate window**
Code window	**Northwind sample database**
DateDiff function	**Variables**
DateSerial function	**Visual Basic Editor**
Debug	**Watches window**
DoCmd statement	

CHAPTER INTRODUCTION

Users of professionally developed databases work with forms to maintain data and work with forms and reports to display information. In Chapters 4 and 5, you learned about the features and properties of forms and reports and learned how to customize these objects for users. In Chapter 6, you learned how to use macros to create switchboard forms and automate repetitive form and report tasks. However, you can customize and automate a database only so far by using the features and properties of forms and reports and by using macros. To fully customize and automate a database to perform more complex validity checking and to use functions and actions not available with macros, you must use Visual Basic for Applications (VBA).

This chapter introduces you to VBA and describes how to use VBA to enhance database processing for users. Level 1 compares macros with VBA and explains how to create subroutines and functions in modules. Level 2 discusses how to use VBA to verify data in more complex ways and to extend the functionality of a form. Level 3 explains how to troubleshoot VBA and how to learn more about programming a database application with VBA.

7

CASE SCENARIO

Maria Garcia, the human resources manager for 4Corners Pharmacy, has observed her staff using the new user interface and has talked with other employees about the automated tasks developed by Don Linebarger. Now that the database is close to completion, Maria meets with Don to review their interaction with the database and prepare a list of improvements they want to make to it.

Human Resources

Although the database contains all the data Maria needs, she must manually calculate some information based on the data stored in the database. For instance, the pharmacy provides special bonuses to employees with at least five but fewer than ten, and ten or more years of service based on the employee's actual annual salary or estimated annual salary for those paid an hourly rate. Thus, when Maria works with frmEmployee, the form should display estimated salaries for hourly paid employees and a message indicating the employee's tenure if it is more than five but fewer than ten or more than ten years. In both cases, the form should display information only for active employees. In addition, for each active employee, Maria wants to see the current age of the employee displayed on the form. Finally, she wants the database to help verify the accuracy of zip codes and phone area codes.

The improvements Maria needs go beyond the capabilities of standard Access objects and also go beyond what Don can do with macros. To provide the database features needed by human resources, Don needs to enhance the forms in the database by using VBA.

LEVEL 1

WRITING VISUAL BASIC FOR APPLICATIONS CODE

ACCESS 2003 SKILLS TRAINING

- **Create a Sub procedure**
- **Use Sub procedures with VB**
- **Create an event procedure with VB**
- **Create and test a Visual Basic function in a standard module**
- **Create Access modules using one or more Visual Basic routines**

UNDERSTANDING VISUAL BASIC FOR APPLICATIONS

Visual Basic for Applications (VBA) is the programming language for Microsoft Office programs, including Access. VBA has a common syntax and a set of common features for all Microsoft Office programs, but it also has features that are unique for each Microsoft Office program due to each program's different structure and components. For example, because Access has fields, tables, queries, forms, other objects, tab controls, subforms, and other controls that are unique to Access, VBA for Access has language features that support these components. In contrast, because Microsoft Excel does not have these same Access components, VBA for Excel does not support them, but VBA for Excel does support cells, ranges, and worksheets—three of the basic structures of Excel. The basic VBA skills you learn for any one of the Microsoft Office programs transfer to any other Microsoft Office program, but to become proficient with VBA for another program, you first need to master its unique aspects.

When you use a programming language, such as VBA, you write a set of instructions to direct the computer to perform specific operations in a specific order, similar to writing a set of instructions for a recipe or an instruction manual. The process of writing instructions in a programming language is called **coding**. You write the VBA instructions, each one of which is called a **statement**, to respond to an event that occurs with an object or control in a database. A language such as VBA is, therefore, called both an **event-driven language**—an event in the database triggers a set of instructions—and an **object-oriented language**—each set of instructions operates on objects in the database. Your experience with macros, which are also event-driven and object-oriented, should facilitate your learning of VBA. Although you must use macros if you need to assign actions to a specific keyboard key or key combination, or if you need to open a database in a special way, such as displaying a switchboard, you can use VBA for everything else you can do with macros. VBA provides advantages over using macros, such as better error-handling features and easier updating capabilities. You can also use VBA in situations that macros do not handle, such as creating your own set of statements to perform special calculations, verifying a field value based on the value of another field or set of fields, or dynamically changing the color of a form control when a user enters or views a specific field value.

Event-Driven Programming

An **event** is a state, condition, or occurrence that Access recognizes. For example, events occur when you click a field or command button in a form, open an object, change a field value in a form, or press a key to choose a menu option. Each event has an associated **event property** that specifies how an object responds when the event occurs. For example, each report has an On Open event property that specifies what happens when a user opens the report and triggers the Open event, and each form control has an On Click event property that specifies what happens when a user clicks the control and triggers the Click event. Event properties appear in the property sheet for forms, reports, and controls. By default, event properties are not set to an initial value, which means that no special action takes place when the event occurs.

If you set an event property value to a macro name, as you did in Chapter 6, Access runs the macro when the event occurs. You can also create a group of statements using VBA code and set an event property value to the name of that group of statements. Access then executes the group of statements, or **procedure**, when the event occurs. Such a procedure is called an **event procedure**. Access has over 60 events and associated event properties. Table 7.1 lists some frequently used Access events.

Table 7.1: Frequently used Access events

Event Name	Action That Triggers the Event
After Update	After changed data in a control or a record is updated
Before Update	Before changed data in a control or a record is updated
Activate	When a form or report receives the focus and becomes the active window
Change	When the value in a text box or combo box changes
Click	When a user clicks the left mouse button on a control in a form
Current	When the focus moves to a form record, making it the current record
Dbl Click	When a user double-clicks the left mouse button on a control in a form
Delete	When a user takes some action, such as pressing the Del key, to delete a record, but before the record is actually deleted
Got Focus	When a form or form control receives the focus
Key Down	When a user presses a key in an active form
Key Up	When a user releases a key in an active form
Load	When a form is opened and its records are displayed
Mouse Down	When a user presses a mouse button
Mouse Move	When a user moves the mouse pointer
Mouse Up	When a user releases a mouse button

7

Level 1

Table 7.1: Frequently used Access events (cont.)

Event Name	Action That Triggers the Event
Not In List	When a user enters a value in a combo box that is not in the combo box list
Open	When a form is opened, but before the first record is displayed; before a report is previewed or printed
Timer	When a specified time interval has elapsed
Undo	When a user undoes a change to a form or form control
Unload	When a form is closed

Some events apply to both forms and reports, other events apply to only forms or only reports, and still other events apply to certain types of form controls. For example, command buttons, text boxes, option buttons, and combo boxes have different uses and exhibit different behaviors, and, therefore, have different events associated with them. Table 7.2 shows some common events and whether the event applies to forms, reports, and selected form controls. For example, note that the Not In List event is unique to combo box controls, and the Delete, Load, and Timer events are unique to form objects, whereas other events are common to two or more objects/controls.

Table 7.2: Common events for selected controls

Event	Report	Form	Command Button	Text Box	Option Button	Combo Box
			Object or Control			
After Update		x		x	x	x
Before Update		x		x	x	x
Activate	x	x				
Change		x		x		x
Click		x	x	x	x	x
Delete		x				
Key Down		x	x	x	x	x
Load		x				
Mouse Down		x	x	x	x	x
Not In List						x
Open	x	x				
Timer		x				

Coding VBA

When you work with VBA, you code a group of statements to perform a set of operations or calculate a value, and then you attach the group of statements to the event property of an object or control. Access then executes (or runs or **calls**) these statements every time the event occurs for that object or control. Each group of statements is called a procedure. The two types of procedures are Function procedures and Sub procedures.

A **Function procedure**, or **function**, performs operations, returns a value, accepts input values, and can be used in expressions (recall that an expression is a calculation resulting in a single value). For example, some of the 4Corners database queries use built-in Access functions, such as Avg, Min, and Max, to calculate an average and to determine minimum and maximum values. Don can create new functions to support the unique needs of users for their database processing. For example, he might create a function to determine the number of years between two dates and then use that function to calculate employees' ages and years of service, which are calculated values that Maria wants to see in frmEmployee. In the case of determining an employee's age, Don uses the function with the employee's date of birth and today's date, and the function returns the employee's age, which he can display in a form or report.

A **Sub procedure**, or **subroutine**, performs operations and accepts input values, but does not return a value and cannot be used in expressions. Most Access procedures are subroutines because you need the procedures to perform a series of actions or operations in response to an event. For example, Don will create a procedure to calculate and display the estimated salary for active hourly paid employees later in this chapter.

You store a group of related procedures together in a database object called a **module**. Each module starts with a **Declarations section**, which contains statements that apply to all procedures in the module. One or more procedures, which follow the Declarations section and which can be a mixture of functions and subroutines, constitute the rest of the module. The two basic types of modules are standard modules and class modules.

A **standard module** is a database object that is stored in memory with other database objects (queries, forms, and so on) when you open the database. You can use the procedures in a database's standard modules from anywhere in the database—even from procedures in other modules. A procedure that more than one object can use is called a **public procedure**. For example, you could create a function to determine the number of years between two dates, store the function in a standard module, and then use that function to determine ages or other year difference calculations in any query, form, report, or macro in the database. All standard modules are listed on the Modules tab in the Database window.

A **class module** is usually associated with a particular form or report. When you create the first event procedure for a form or report, Access automatically creates an associated form or report class module. When you add additional event procedures to the form or report, Access adds them to the class module for that form or report. Each event procedure in a class module is a **local procedure**, or a **private procedure**, which means that only the form or report for which the class module was created can use the event procedure.

Why classify a procedure as a public or private procedure? There are two reasons for this classification. The first reason is that private procedures use internal memory more efficiently and release storage space more quickly than public procedures. Memory is an important resource in a computer and using it effectively means more efficient operations of the system. The second reason is that private procedures are protected from being called inadvertently. Some procedures can be coded as support to other procedures within a module. These support procedures might not function correctly if used by other procedures from outside the module. By classifying the support procedures as private procedures, you prevent these procedures from being used by other procedures outside the module and eliminate the possibility that an error can occur or that the application can fail.

Best Practice

Choosing Between a Function and a Subroutine

You can set an event property to one of three values: a macro name, an event procedure, or an expression. If you set the event property to a macro name, the macro runs when the event occurs. If you set the event property to an event procedure, the associated subroutine in the object's class module runs when the event occurs. Finally, if you set the event property to an expression, the expression is evaluated and results in a single value when the event occurs. By default and by design, all event procedures are subroutines. In all other cases, you should create the module as a function only if you need to calculate a single value without any other processing operations; otherwise, you should create the module as a subroutine.

Best Practice

Dividing an Application into Parts

Programming is as much an art as it is a science. Before actual coding begins, a team of system analysts usually performs an analysis and design of the system. Part of the analysts' job is to look at the large application and break it down into manageable parts and then distribute the parts to individual modules with each module assigned to specific programmers. Even when writing small VBA applications, you should write only one part of an application at a time. In this way, you focus on smaller portions of the problem at one time rather than trying to make the entire application work at once.

CREATING A SUBROUTINE IN A STANDARD MODULE

In Chapter 6, Don created a macro named mcrContributionMarginAnalysis to print rptContributionMarginAnalysis. Don also included in the macro the display of an hourglass while the report is being generated and a beep sound when the report is finished.

Table 7.3 lists the three actions in the macro and the action arguments and comment that Don set for each action.

Table 7.3: Actions in mcrContributionMarginAnalysis

Macro Action	Action Arguments	Comment
Hourglass	Hourglass On: Yes	Displays an hourglass pointer as the macro runs
OpenReport	Report Name: rptContributionMarginAnalysis View: Print Window Mode: Normal	Prints rptContributionMarginAnalysis
Beep		Sounds a beep when the macro is finished

Don wants to replace mcrContributionMarginAnalysis with a VBA procedure to accomplish the same task—printing rptContributionMarginAnalysis. This is part of Don's overall plan to replace all macros with VBA procedures, except for the simplest macros, such as those that open an object when clicking a command button on the switchboard, and for the essential macros that accomplish tasks that he cannot perform with VBA, such as the AutoKeys macro (which assigns a macro action or set of actions to a key or key combination) and the AutoExec macro (which opens the splash screen when the database opens). Don feels, as do most database developers, that the advantages of using VBA over using macros—better error-handling features and greater capabilities—outweigh the relative ease of creating macros.

Creating a New Standard Module

Don will place the procedure in a standard module because the procedure will print rptContributionMarginAnalysis but it will not interact with the report or cause changes to the report in any way. Thus, the procedure will exist externally to the report and will not be part of its class module. Also, because the procedure does not return a value, Don will create the procedure as a subroutine instead of as a function.

Using the actions in mcrContributionMarginAnalysis as a guide, Don creates a new standard module by opening the 4Corners database, clicking the Modules tab in the Objects bar of the Database window, and then clicking the New button. To begin a new procedure in the module, Don clicks the list arrow on the Insert Module button on the Standard toolbar, clicks Procedure, types "PrintReport" in the Name text box, makes sure the Sub and Public options buttons are selected, and then clicks the OK button. Figure 7.1 shows the Visual Basic window with the new subroutine in the Code window.

Figure 7.1: Starting a new subroutine in the Code window

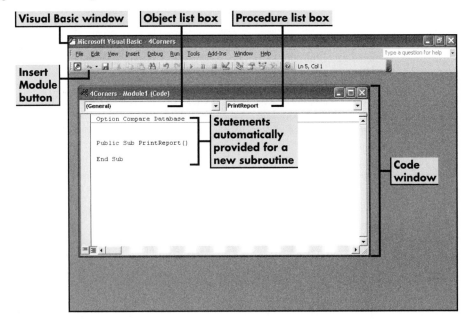

The program you use to create and modify VBA code is called the **Visual Basic Editor** (**VBE**, or **editor** for short), and the **Visual Basic window** is the program window that opens when you use VBE. The **Code window** is the window in which you create, modify, and display specific VBA procedures. You can have as many Code windows open as you have modules in the database. In the Code window, the Object list box indicates the current control ("General" means there is no current control), and the Procedure list box indicates the procedure name (PrintReport) for the procedure you are viewing or editing.

How To

Create a Subroutine in a New Standard Module

1. Click Modules in the Objects bar of the Database window.
2. Click the New button.
3. Click the list arrow on the Insert Module button ![button], click Procedure, type the subroutine name in the Name text box, click the Sub option button, click the Public option button, and then click the OK button.
4. Type the statements between the Sub and End Sub statements.
5. Click the Save button, type the module name in the Module Name text box, and then click the OK button.

A horizontal line in the Code window visually separates each procedure in the module. Don's subroutine begins with a **Sub statement** and ends with an **End Sub statement**. The Sub statement includes the **scope** of the procedure (private or public), the name of the procedure (PrintReport), and an opening and a closing parenthesis.

Notice the Option Compare statement in the Declarations section above the horizontal line. The **Option Compare statement** designates the technique Access uses to compare and sort text data. The default method "Database," as shown in Figure 7.1, means that Access compares and sorts letters in normal alphabetical order, using the language settings specified for Access running on your computer.

Creating a Subroutine

Don types the statements in his procedure between the Sub and End Sub statements. He replaces each of the three actions in the mcrContributionMarginAnalysis macro with an equivalent action in the procedure using the **DoCmd statement**, which executes an action in a procedure. For example, to run the Hourglass macro, Don types the following VBA statement:

```
DoCmd.Hourglass True
```

DoCmd, an Access object, is separated from Hourglass, a method, by a period or dot; and True is an argument with the effect of the statement being to change the mouse pointer to an hourglass pointer. You use False instead of True to change the hourglass pointer back to the standard mouse pointer. Note that a **method** is an action that operates on specific objects or controls.

Similarly, Don uses the DoCmd.Beep statement to sound a beep at the end of the procedure and the DoCmd.OpenReport statement to print rptContributionMarginAnalysis. The Beep method does not have any arguments, but the OpenReport statement needs arguments to name the report, to identify which view to use for the report (the acViewNormal argument constant prints the report immediately), and to identify which window type to use for the report (the acWindowNormal argument constant uses the default Report window).

Figure 7.2 shows the complete set of statements that Don enters for the PrintReport subroutine.

7

Level 1

Figure 7.2: Completed PrintReport subroutine

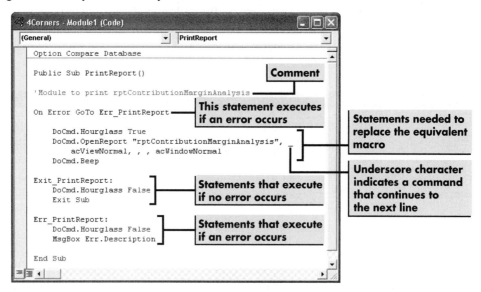

The first statement after the Sub statement is a comment that explains the procedure's purpose. You can include comments anywhere in a VBA procedure to describe what the procedure or a statement does to make it easier for you and other programmers to identify the purpose of statements in the code. You begin a comment with the word Rem (for "Remark") or with a single quotation mark ('). VBA ignores anything following the word Rem or the single quotation mark on a single line. Comments appear in green in the Code window.

Best Practice

Documenting VBA Code

Different people can use different approaches to solving a problem, so you should use comments in a VBA procedure to explain the purpose of the procedure and to clarify any complicated programming logic used. Most companies have documentation standards that specify the types of comments that should be included in each procedure. These standards typically require comments that identify the name of the original creator of the procedure, the purpose of the procedure, and a history of changes made to the procedure by whom and for what purpose.

The statement On Error GoTo Err_PrintReport after the comment line is processed only if an error occurs with one or more of the three DoCmd statements. What type of error can occur? The rptContributionMarginAnalysis report is based on a parameter query in which the user must enter start and end dates to define the period the report covers. If a user types an illegal date, an error occurs, and the On Error statement is executed. When the On Error statement executes, the next statement processed is the line with Err_PrintReport as a line label because the On Error statement contains GoTo Err_PrintReport—that is, go directly to the Err_PrintReport line label. A **line label** is a statement that serves as the starting point for a block of statements in a procedure; a line label begins at the start of a line and ends with a colon. Don used another line label, the Exit_PrintReport statement, to serve as the start of a section of statements consisting of the two statements that follow.

What happens if the procedure prints the report successfully, that is, the DoCmd statements complete without an error? Access changes the hourglass pointer back to the standard mouse pointer (the first DoCmd.Hourglass False statement), and then the procedure ends (the Exit Sub statement). On the other hand, if an error occurs, Access changes the hourglass pointer back to the standard mouse pointer (the second DoCmd.Hourglass False statement), and then Access displays a message box containing a description of the error that occurred (the MsgBox Err.Description statement).

The underscore character at the end of the line that begins "DoCmd.OpenReport" indicates a statement that continues to the next line. Entering the statement on one line would extend the statement far to the right and possibly require scrolling left and right to view parts of the statement. In these cases, you can split a statement across two or more lines by typing the underscore character to signal that the statement continues on the next line. If you try to go to the next line without completing a statement and without typing the underscore character, you receive an error message.

Best Practice

Indenting Statements in Procedures

VBA does not require statements to be indented in procedures. However, all experienced programmers indent statements to make procedures easier to read and maintain. Except for beginning comments and line labels, it is best to indent all lines equally within a procedure. Pressing the Tab key once indents the line four spaces to the right, which is a sufficient amount of indentation, and pressing the Shift + Tab key combination moves the insertion point four spaces to the left. Later in this chapter, you will see statements that are indented more, but always in multiples of four spaces, and you will learn why the additional spacing is necessary.

To run the procedure, Don clicks the Run Sub/UserForm button ▶ on the Standard toolbar. The hourglass pointer appears, the Enter Parameter Value dialog box opens, Don enters a start date of 1/1/2007, clicks the OK button, enters an end date of 12/31/2007, clicks the OK button, a beep sounds, the report prints, and then the pointer changes back to its standard shape. Don also runs the procedure and enters an illegal start date. Instead of printing the report, Access displays a message box that explains an illegal value was entered.

Don has finished his work with the procedure, so he saves the module by clicking the Save button 🖫 on the Standard toolbar, types bas4CornersGeneralProcedures in the Module Name text box, presses the Enter key, and then clicks the Close button on the Visual Basic window to close the window and return to the Database window. The bas4CornersGeneralProcedures module appears on the Modules tab of the Database window.

Don now turns his attention to the enhancements requested by Maria. He begins by writing a procedure to display the estimated annual salaries for employees who are paid an hourly rate.

CREATING AN EVENT PROCEDURE

When Maria uses frmEmployee, she wants to view each employee's annual salary. For salaried employees, the Salary field value represents the annual salary. However, for active, hourly paid employees, the form displays the hourly rate but not an annual salary. For these employees, Don needs to multiply the hourly rate by 2,080, which is the product of 40 hours per week and 52 weeks per year.

Based on the requirements, Don adds a text box with an associated label to frmEmployee. The label will have the caption "Est Salary," and the text box will be filled with the results of the calculated estimated salary. Maria wants to view the two controls only for active, hourly paid employees, so the controls should be invisible for inactive employees and for active salaried employees. Likewise, the calculation should be performed only when the two controls are displayed. Further, Maria wants the estimated salary for hourly rates $12 or more per hour to be in green font and in all other cases to be in blue font. Don and Maria agree that the estimated salary label and text box should be displayed to the right of the Salary text box and below the Close Form command button. Figure 7.3 shows where Don adds the controls.

Figure 7.3: Planning the estimated salary enhancement to frmEmployee

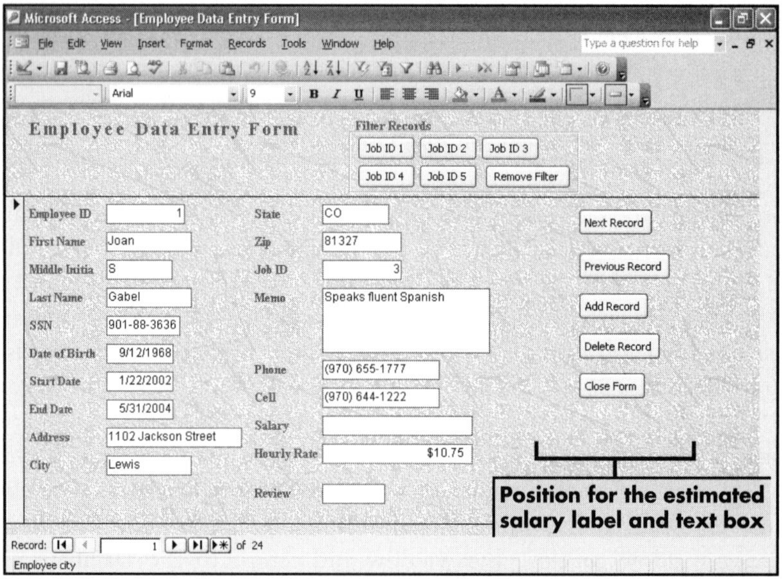

Designing an Event Procedure

Maria's enhancement applies only to frmEmployee, so Don adds a procedure to the form's class module. Each time Maria navigates to a record, Don wants the procedure to run for the current record. Thus, Don associates the procedure with the form's On Current event property, which is triggered when the form's Current event occurs. (The Current event occurs when the focus moves to a record, making it the current record.)

First, Don adds a text box control to frmEmployee in Design view. Because the procedure must decide when to make the text box control visible, both the label and text box must have meaningful Name property values. The procedure will use these names when setting the controls to visible or invisible. Don sets the label's Name property to EstSalary_Label, the label's Caption property to Est Salary, and the text box's Name property to EstSalary. Don then resizes and repositions the controls, as shown in Figure 7.4.

Figure 7.4: Text box and associated label added to form

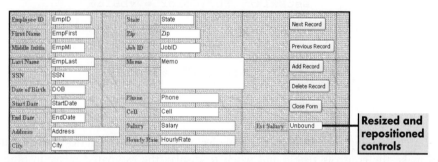

To add the event procedure, Don opens the property sheet for the form, clicks the On Current text box, clicks its list arrow, clicks [Event Procedure], and then clicks the Build button [...] to the right of the On Current text box. The Code window opens in the Visual Basic window and contains the Private Sub and End Sub statements for the new event procedure. The event procedure name, Form_Current, means the Current event for the form control.

Don writes the procedure statements he needs before he types them in the event procedure, so that he can review them and make sure they will accomplish what Maria wants, accurately and without error. Don's design for the event procedure is as follows:

```
Private Sub Form_Current()
     'For active employees paid an hourly rate
     '    display their estimated salaries
     If IsNull(EndDate) And IsNull(Salary) _
          And Not IsNull(HourlyRate) Then
          EstSalary = HourlyRate * 2080
          EstSalary.Visible = True
          EstSalary_Label.Visible = True
          If HourlyRate >= 12 Then
               EstSalary.ForeColor = vbGreen
          Else
               EstSalary.ForeColor = vbBlue
          End If
     Else
          EstSalary.Visible = False
          EstSalary_Label.Visible = False
     End If
End Sub
```

The key statements in the event procedure involve deciding when to perform the calculation and make the controls visible and when to display the estimated salary in blue or green font. For these statements, Don uses one of VBA's decision-making statements, the If statement.

Making Decisions Using the If Statement

One portion of Don's procedure must determine whether to display the estimated salary in blue or green font. He creates a decision-making statement to make this determination. A decision-making statement executes a group of statements based on the outcome of a condition. In the simplest decision-making statement, Access executes a group of statements if the condition is true and executes nothing if the condition is false. You can also create a decision-making statement that executes a second group of statements if the condition is false; in this case, only one set of statements is executed—the true-statement group executes only if the condition is true, and the false-statement group executes only if the condition is false. When the procedure needs to make a decision, you need to identify the condition to test. In this case, Don's condition is "is the hourly rate $12 or more?" If the condition is true, the procedure sets the text box font color to green. If the condition is false, the procedure sets the text box font color to blue. Don can use the comparison operators shown in Table 7.4 to test conditions in procedures.

Table 7.4: Comparison operators and how to use them in conditions

Operator	Meaning	Example
<	Less than	txtTotal < 7
<=	Less than or equal to	txtBill <= 10.50
>	Greater than	EmpAge > 21
>=	Greater than or equal to	StartDate >= #01/01/2008#
=	Equal to	txtName = "Jones"
<>	Not equal to	TestAnswer <> "yes"

Note that text fields and controls, which contain values such as names and addresses, are enclosed in quotation marks, and that dates are enclosed in pound signs (#).

After Don identified the condition that the program must test, he wrote the VBA statement that supports what he wants to accomplish. To test one condition that results in one of two answers, Don uses the **If statement**, which tests a condition and follows one of two paths depending on the outcome of the condition. The general form of a VBA If statement is:

```
If condition Then
    true-statement group
[Else
    false-statement group]
End If
```

Access executes only the true-statement group when the condition is true and only the false-statement group when the condition is false. In the general form of the If statement, the bracketed portion is optional. Therefore, you must omit the Else and its related false-statement group when you want Access to execute a group of statements only when the condition is true. Don's If statement is:

```
If HourlyRate >= 12 Then
    EstSalary.ForeColor = vbGreen
Else
    EstSalary.ForeColor = vbBlue
End If
```

The statement contains one condition (HourlyRate >= 12), one statement (EstSalary.ForeColor = vbGreen) in the true-statement group, and one statement (EstSalary.ForeColor = vbBlue) in the false-statement group. Given an HourlyRate field value greater than or equal to 12 (the condition is true), the estimated salary font is set to green; otherwise, the font is set to blue. Notice that statements in the true-statement group and the false-statement group are indented to make the procedure more readable.

Statements such as EstSalary.ForeColor = vbGreen are assignment statements. An **assignment statement** assigns the value of an expression—the color constant value vbGreen, in this case—to a control or property—the text color, or ForeColor property, for the EstSalary control, in this case.

Because a property is associated with a control, you use the general form of ControlName.PropertyName to specify a property for a control. An assignment statement such as EstSalary.ForeColor = vbGreen, for example, assigns a value to the EstSalary control's ForeColor property. A control's **ForeColor property** determines the control's foreground, or font, color. The expression in this assignment statement uses a built-in color constant named vbGreen. **Color constants** are predefined VBA names that have values that represent the system color value for the color in the constant name. Other color constants you can use are vbBlack, vbRed, vbYellow, vbBlue, vbMagenta, vbCyan, and vbWhite.

Best Practice

Using the End If
For If statements that do not require the false-statement group, you can omit the Else part of the If statement. For If statements that have no false-statement group and only one statement in the true-statement group, you can omit the End If part of the If statement and place the statement immediately after the Else part of the If statement as follows:

```
If HourlyRate >= 12 Then EstSalary.ForeColor = vbGreen
```

However, changing business requirements frequently necessitate changes to procedures, and programmers who change the procedures in the future are usually not the same programmers who originated the procedures. Better programmers keep the future in mind when writing procedures, and write procedures so that they can be easily maintained. One such technique is to use the End If part of the If statement even when there is no false-statement group and only one statement in the true-statement group. Not only does this make the statements stand out more clearly to anyone reading the procedure, it also makes it easier to add additional statements to the true-statement group should new requirements arise that require a programmer to add more commands.

Don's procedure has another, more complicated, If statement that determines whether Access should calculate the estimated salary and make the label and text box visible. Just as you can use the And, Or, and Not operators in queries, you can use these same operators in VBA If statements to test multiple conditions. The statement uses the **IsNull function**, which returns a True value when the field or control is null and False when it is not. Don's If statement is as follows:

```
If IsNull(EndDate) And IsNull(Salary) _
      And Not Is Null(HourlyRate) Then
```

For the If statement to be true, all three conditions must be true because And operators connect each separate condition. Only if the EndDate is null (the employee is an active employee and has no ending employment date), the Salary is null (the employee is not a salaried employee), and the HourlyRate is not null (if null, the hourly rate has not yet been stored for the employee, so you have no hourly rate upon which to base the calculation) does Don want to calculate the estimated salary, make the two controls visible, *and* determine the font color for the estimated salary. In this case, the eight lines following the two-line If statement are the true-statement group. When one or more of the conditions is false, the two statements following the second Else constitute the false-statement group and are executed—the two controls are hidden.

Note that Don could have entered the If statement on one line without the underscore (_) character, as follows:

```
If IsNull (EndDate) And IsNull(Salary) And Not Is Null(HourlyRate) Then
```

Best Practice

Properly Matching Clauses in Embedded If Statements

The End If clause terminates an If statement. You can embed, or nest, If statements within other If statements, and each embedded If statement is terminated by its own End If clause. When you have an If statement with a false-statement group, the Else clause terminates the true-statement group and marks the beginning of the false-statement group. You must make sure in procedures that you match Else and End If clauses with the correct If clause. Else and End If clauses match up with the most previous If clause that has not already been paired with its Else and End If clause. That is, the matching first occurs with the embedded If statement. Although you can nest If statements for several levels, experienced programmers avoid deep nesting because it is too easy to make errors when designing and writing such complicated procedures. Also, other programmers have difficulty understanding and changing them. It is best to redesign and rewrite complicated procedures to make them simpler and easier to understand and maintain.

The EstSalary = HourlyRate * 2080 assignment statement multiplies the HourlyRate field value by 2,080 and assigns the calculated value to the EstSalary control. The Visible property is set in the four remaining procedure statements—setting the Visible property to True displays the control, and setting it to False hides the control.

Testing an Event Procedure

Don types the statements in the Code window for the Current event in frmEmployee, as shown in Figure 7.5.

Figure 7.5: Current event procedure in the Code window

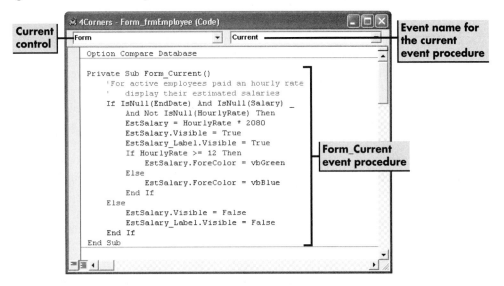

Don saves the class module, closes the Visual Basic window, and then saves his changes in Design view for frmEmployee. To test the event procedure, Don switches to Form view. The first record is for Joan Gabel, an inactive employee with an EndDate field value, so the two new controls are hidden correctly, as shown in Figure 7.6.

Figure 7.6: Testing for an inactive employee

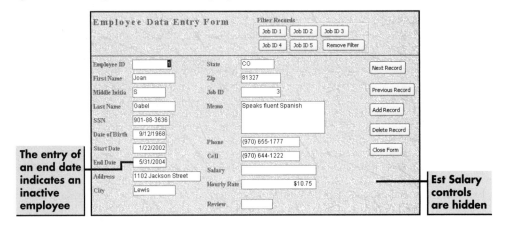

Navigating to the second record for Marco Farello, the two controls are visible because he is an active, hourly paid employee. The estimated salary is displayed correctly with a blue font because Marco's hourly rate is $11.33, which is less than $12.00, as shown in Figure 7.7.

Figure 7.7: Testing for an active employee

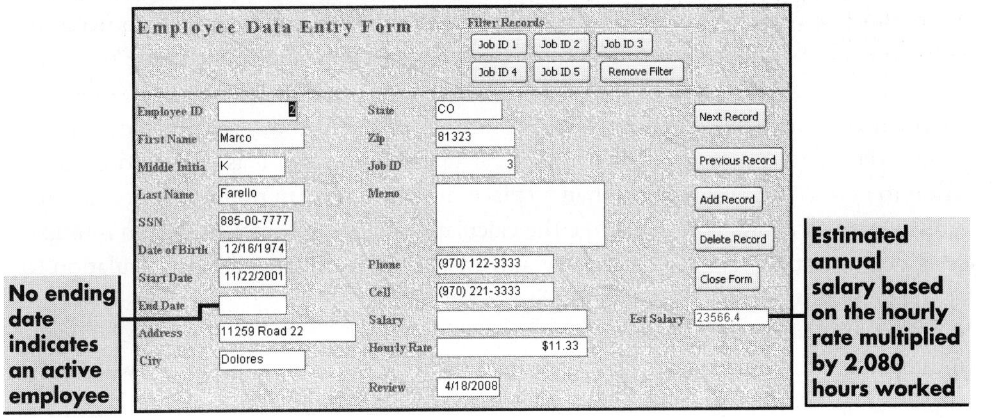

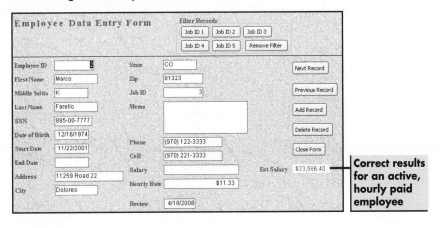

Don navigates through the other records to make sure the results are correct in the different situations. Don demonstrates the results to Maria, who approves his enhancement but wants the estimated salary values displayed in currency format similar to the salary field values. Also, because the estimated salary is a calculated control, users should not be able to change its value or tab to it, and its appearance should be different from a normal text box to distinguish it as a calculated control. To make these changes, Don switches to Design view, sets the estimated salary text box control's format to Currency, its Tab Stop property to No, its Border Style to Transparent, and its Locked property to Yes. He then saves the changes, switches back to Form view, and navigates to the second record. Figure 7.8 shows the estimated salary value for Marco Farello formatted as currency and in a text box with no borders.

Figure 7.8: Testing the event procedure

Don continues his work on the enhancement requests from Maria.

CREATING A FUNCTION

Don reviews the remaining enhancement requests and notices that two requests have a similar need. The years of service and employee age requests both require the calculation of the number of years between two dates. For the years of service request, Don needs to calculate the number of years between an employee's start date and today's date to determine the number of years of service. For the employee age request, Don needs to calculate the number of years between an employee's date of birth and today's date to determine the employee's age. When you have similar calculation requests, it is better to create a function to perform the calculation than to place the calculation in multiple places in procedures. Doing so allows you to change the calculation in one place instead of in multiple places if you need to correct an inaccuracy in the calculation or enhance the calculation to meet changing business needs, for example.

Don designs the following function to calculate the number of years between two dates:

```
Public Function YearDiff(FirstDate As Date, SecondDate As Date)
    'Determine the number of years between two dates
    YearDiff = DateDiff("yyyy", FirstDate, SecondDate)
End Function
```

A function begins with a Function statement and ends with an End Function statement. Because Don will use the function in multiple places in the database, Don designates the function as public instead of as private.

Variables

Don designs the function so that it will be supplied with, or passed, two date values, which in the function are referenced using the variable names FirstDate and SecondDate. A **variable** is a named location in computer memory that can contain a value. In programming, you use these memory locations to store and retrieve data needed to complete a calculation or for later display or use. You reference a memory location by using the variable name assigned to the location. A variable holds only one value at a time; if you store another value in a variable that already contains a value, the new value replaces the old value.

All VBA variable names, subroutine names, function names, and other names you create must conform to the following rules:

- They must begin with a letter.
- They cannot exceed 255 characters.

- They can include letters, numbers, and the underscore character (_). You cannot use a space or any punctuation or special characters.
- They cannot be the same as keywords or reserved words, such as DoCmd, Sub, Function, and IsNull, that VBA uses as part of its language.

Each variable has a data type, and the VBA variable types differ in some cases from the Access data types. Table 7.5 lists some common VBA data types.

Table 7.5: Common VBA data types

Data Type	Range
Boolean	True or False
Byte	0 to 255
Currency	–922,337,203,685,477.5808 to 922,337,203,685,477.5807
Date	January 1, 100 to December 31, 9999
Double	–1.79769313486231E^{308} to –4.94065645841247E^{-324} for negative values; 4.94065645841247E^{-324} to 1.79769313486232E^{308} for positive values
Integer	–32,768 to 32,767
Long	–2,147,483,648 to 2,147,483,647
String	0 to approximately 2 billion characters

Don assigns the Date data type to both variables in the first line of the function using the general form of the variable name As data type.

Using Functions

You use a function that you create similarly to the way you use the built-in functions in Access. For example, to calculate the total of the Balance field amounts, you use the expression Sum (Balance). The function name (Sum) is followed by the argument(s) it needs, which are enclosed in parentheses. If a function needs more than one argument, commas separate the arguments. When Access encounters a function name in an expression, Access executes the function and passes the argument values to the function. The function uses the values to perform its operations and, when the function finishes, the single value calculated by the function replaces the function in the expression.

When using the YearDiff function to calculate an employee's age, Don enters YearDiff (DOB, Date), where DOB is the employee's date of birth and Date is today's date. When the YearDiff function executes, FirstDate represents the DOB field value and SecondDate represents today's date. The YearDiff function uses the built-in **DateDiff function**, which calculates the number of time intervals between two dates; the two dates are the second and third arguments in the function. The time interval is the first argument, and "yyyy" as an argument value specifies year as the time interval. Other time interval values include "m" for month, "ww" for week, and "d" for day.

Because the database will use the YearDiff function in more than one place in the database, Don will add the function to the standard module he created earlier. He opens the bas4CornersGeneralProcedures module in Design view by returning to the Modules tab in the Database window, selecting the module, and then clicking the Design button on the Database window. He clicks the list arrow on the Insert Procedure button [image] on the Standard toolbar, clicks Procedure, types YearDiff in the Name text box, makes sure the Function and Public option buttons are selected, and then clicks the OK button. Figure 7.9 shows the function after Don enters the statements, including adding the arguments to the Function statement.

Figure 7.9: YearDiff function in the Code window

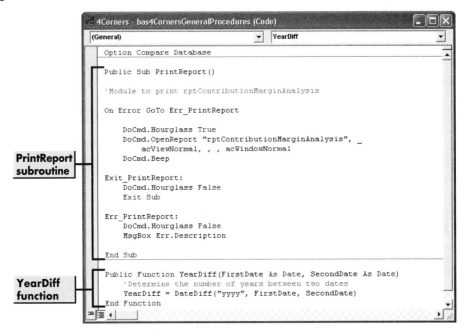

Don decides to test the YearDiff function before using it in frmEmployee for the service request and employee age request by using the Immediate window.

Testing a Function in the Immediate Window

After entering a VBA statement, the editor checks the statement to make sure its syntax is correct. Although you may have entered all procedure statements with the correct syntax, the procedure might still contain logic errors. A **logic error** occurs when the procedure produces incorrect results. For example, the YearDiff function has a logic error if you provide argument values of 3/15/2001 and 11/25/2008 and the function returns a value of 17, -1, or anything other than the correct result of 7. Even the simplest procedure can contain errors, and experienced programmers test each procedure thoroughly to ensure that it does exactly what's expected in all situations.

When working in the Code window, you can use the **Immediate window** to test VBA procedures without changing any data in the database. In the Immediate window, you can enter different values to test a procedure. To test a procedure, type the keyword "Print" or a question mark (?), followed by the procedure name and the argument values you want to test in parentheses and separated by commas. For example, to test the YearDiff function in the Immediate window using dates of 3/15/2001 and 11/25/2008, type ?YearDiff (#3/15/2001#, #11/25/2008#) and then press the Enter key. Access executes the function and prints the value returned by the function (you expect it to return 7). Note that you must enclose a string of characters within quotation marks in the test statement and a date within pound signs.

How To

Test a Procedure in the Immediate Window

1. In the Visual Basic window, click View on the menu bar, and then click Immediate Window.

2. Type a question mark (?), the procedure name, and the procedure's argument values in parentheses.

3. Press the Enter key and verify the displayed answer.

Don opens the Immediate window, tests the YearDiff function, and verifies that the displayed result of 7 is the correct answer, as shown in Figure 7.10.

Figure 7.10: Testing the YearDiff function in the Immediate window

Instead of typing the entire statement again, Don uses the arrow keys and replaces characters in the function statement and presses the Enter key after each change to the statement. After entering several pairs of dates and verifying that the function works correctly, Don changes the two dates in the function statement to ?YearDiff(#3/15/1991#, #2/25/2011#). The displayed answer of 20 is incorrect because employees who started with the pharmacy on 3/15/1991 will not celebrate their twentieth anniversary until 3/15/2011. The function is returning a year difference value that considers only the difference between the years of the two dates, but it also needs to consider the month and day portions. Don's function returns a value that either is correct or is one year more than it should be.

Don needs to modify the function so that it is accurate in all cases, and he decides to research the issue on the Web and finds a number of solutions that solve the problem. Some solutions he finds are short and complicated and others are long and simple. He finds a compromise solution that is short and only slightly complicated, incorporates it into the YearDiff function, and retests the function, which now returns correct values. Figure 7.11 shows Don's revised YearDiff function.

Figure 7.11: Revised YearDiff function in the Code window

```
End Sub

Public Function YearDiff(FirstDate As Date, SecondDate As Date)
    'Determine the number of years between two dates
    YearDiff = DateDiff("yyyy", FirstDate, SecondDate) + (SecondDate _
        < DateSerial(Year(SecondDate), Month(FirstDate), Day(FirstDate)))
End Function
```

Don's revised YearDiff function retains the same beginning of YearDiff = DateDiff("yyyy", FirstDate, SecondDate). This expression calculates the correct number of years between two dates such as 3/15/1991 and 5/15/2011—20 is the calculated result, and there are 20 years, 2 months, and 0 days between the two dates, so 20 as a person's age, for example, is correct. However, this same expression calculates the same 20 years for two dates such as 3/15/1991 and 2/15/2011, even though there are only 19 years, 11 months, and 0 days between the two dates—in this case, 19, not the calculated 20, is considered to be the person's age. To correct the YearDiff function, Don adds an expression to the function that adds zero in those situations when the original function is correct and subtracts one in those cases when the original function is incorrect. The following addition to the function accomplishes just what Don wants:

```
(SecondDate < DateSerial(Year(SecondDate), Month(FirstDate),
    Day(FirstDate)))
```

The **DateSerial function** returns a date value for a specified year, month, and day. Table 7.6 shows the results of the DateSerial function for three sets of test values. In all cases, the DateSerial function result has the month and day values from the FirstDate argument and the year value from the SecondDate argument. In other words, the result represents the birthday or anniversary for the FirstDate value in the year of the SecondDate. For all days in a given SecondDate year, the DateSerial function result is always the same.

Table 7.6: DateSerial function results for selected argument values

FirstDate	SecondDate	DateSerial(Year(SecondDate), Month(FirstDate), Day(FirstDate))	SecondDate < DateSerial Function Result
3/15/1991	5/15/2011	3/15/2011	False
3/15/1991	3/15/2011	3/15/2011	False
3/15/1991	2/15/2011	3/15/2011	True

There is one remaining new component to the YearDiff function—the SecondDate value is compared to the result of the DateSerial function using the less than operator (<). If the SecondDate is less than the DateSerial result, the comparison is True; otherwise, the comparison is False. When comparing two dates, the first date is less than a second date when the first date chronologically precedes the second date. It is interesting that Access stores a True comparison result as a zero value, and a False comparison result as a value of minus one (-1). Recall that Don's original YearDiff function gave results that were either accurate or one year more than the correct result. In the cases in which the original YearDiff function was accurate, the new version of the function adds zero, which means the result continues to be accurate. And in the cases in which the original YearDiff function was one year higher than it should be, the new version subtracts one (by adding minus one), which means that these results are correct, too. Don saves the standard module that contains the revised YearDiff function and tests its results. The revised function returns the correct results.

Best Practice

Testing the Logic of a Procedure

Experienced programmers thoroughly design procedures before entering them into the computer. However, these same programmers find logic errors in procedures they thought were flawless. The complexity of computer procedure logic is sufficiently high so that logic errors will occur. That is why it is important for programmers to test, correct, and retest every procedure until it works in all situations. Never release a new or enhanced procedure to users until you are positive it will work for them in all situations. For example, if Don had not tested the YearDiff function with several pairs of dates, he might not have identified the problem that his revised YearDiff function corrects, and users would have received incorrect results some of the time.

Best Practice

Creating Generalized Procedures

Making the YearDiff function a public function in a standard module allows it to be used in any expression in the database. Doing this also isolates any problems with the function to a single location in the database and isolates the follow-up problem correction there, too. In addition, the YearDiff function requires two dates as arguments, even though the present requirements specify that today's date (for the years of service request and for the employee age request) is always the second date passed as an argument to the procedure. Don purposely built a two-argument requirement into the function so that he could anticipate meeting future user requirements for the same function. For example, it is possible that Maria might plan a future awards banquet, in which case she needs to know which employees will have served for 20 or more years with the pharmacy as of a certain future date. In this case, Don can use the YearDiff function as written because he had the experience and foresight to anticipate how useful the function could be as a generalized procedure.

7

Level 1

Steps To Success: Level 1

Glenn Hollander is the database manager for Hudson Bay Pharmacy and asks for your help in enhancing the Hudson database. He also wants to automate a task that Joan Gabel, owner of the pharmacy, performs often.

Complete the following:

1. Start Access and open the **Hudson.mdb** database from the STS folder.

2. Review mcrContributionMarginAnalysis and mcrBalanceFormat. Replace each macro with a VBA procedure, and then test each procedure.

3. Design and create an event procedure that calculates and displays the profit (price less cost) for a drug in frmDrug. Use red font for profits more than five cents and blue font for all others.

4. Create a public function named YearDiff in a standard module that accurately calculates the number of years between two dates, and then test the function.

5. Create a public function named MonthDiff in a standard module that accurately calculates the number of months between two dates, and then test the function.

6. Close the **Hudson.mdb** database and Access.

LEVEL 2

USING CUSTOM FUNCTIONS AND VERIFYING DATA

ACCESS 2003 SKILLS TRAINING

- **Create an event procedure with VB**
- **Create and test a Visual Basic function in a standard module**

ENHANCING AN EVENT PROCEDURE TO USE A CUSTOM FUNCTION

Don continues his work on enhancing the database. He still needs to work on two of Maria Garcia's outstanding requests, both of which can use the YearDiff function he already created. The first request is to add functionality to frmEmployee so it displays a message for active employees who have worked at the pharmacy for at least five years but fewer than ten years or for ten or more years, so it is easier for Maria to keep track of salary increases for all employees. The second request is to add functionality to the same form so it displays the current age of all active employees, so Maria can watch for employees nearing retirement age.

Don could design VBA solutions for both requests at the same time because the requests involve the same form, use the same function, apply only to active employees, and are relatively simple in concept and design. However, he decides to tackle them individually, starting with the years of service request. Designing the requests individually lets Don concentrate on a single problem at a time, reducing the chance of introducing flaws into the design and subsequently implementing a VBA solution that does not work properly. After implementing the VBA solutions individually for the two requests, Don can always review them and combine them later, if appropriate.

The years of service request must use the YearDiff function to determine the difference in years between the employee's start date and today's date and display a message for employees with ten or more years of service and employees with at least five but fewer than ten years of service. After conferring with Maria to understand and confirm her requirements, Don maps out how he must modify the form and what additional VBA procedure logic he must create. His notes after meeting with Maria are as follows:

- Add a text box named YearsOfService to frmEmployee to the right of the StartDate text box, and set its Border Style property to Transparent, Tab Stop property to No, and Locked property to Yes. In the text box, display a message in frmEmployee depending on the years of service for each employee with at least five but fewer than ten years of service and for employees with ten or more years of service. Use the YearDiff function to determine an employee's number of years of service based on the start date and today's date. For employees with ten or more years of service, display "10+ years" in a blue font; for employees with fewer than ten but more than five years of service, display "5+ years" in a blue font. Delete the label from the text box control because the positioning of the text box and its displayed message make the text box self-explanatory. Deleting the label will reduce clutter on an already crowded form.
- Add the VBA statements to frmEmployee's Current event procedure, which already contains statements to calculate and display the estimated annual salary for hourly employees, because the procedure statements must be executed every time the focus changes to a new record, making it the current record.
- Design decision-making logic in the VBA procedure for frmEmployee to include only active employees (active employees are designated by an end date without a value) who have a start date, which is required for the years of service calculation.
- Design additional decision-making logic in the VBA procedure based on the years of service calculation to make the text box control visible and to display one of two messages; otherwise, the text box control should not be visible.

Based on the design requirements, Don writes the following VBA procedure statements to add to the form's Current event procedure:

```
'For active employees, display a message for those
'    with at least five but less than ten or ten or
'    more years of service
If IsNull(EndDate) And Not IsNull(StartDate) Then
    If YearDiff(StartDate, Date) >= 10 Then
        YearsOfService = "10+ years"
        YearsOfService.Visible = True
    ElseIf YearDiff(StartDate, Date) >= 5 Then
        YearsOfService = "5+ years"
        YearsOfService.Visible = True
    Else
        YearsOfService.Visible = False
    End If
End If
```

How To

Add and Change Statements in a Procedure
1. Open the object that contains the event procedure in Design view.
2. Click the Code button 🔲 on the toolbar.
3. To add a new procedure, module, or class module, click Insert on the menu bar in the Code window, and then click Procedure, Module, or Class Module.
4. To edit existing statements, scroll the Code window to the desired statement, and then make the necessary changes.
5. Click the Save button 🔲 on the Standard toolbar, and then close the Visual Basic window.

Using an ElseIf Statement in an If Statement

After three opening comment lines to describe the purpose of the set of VBA statements, Don's design uses an If statement (If IsNull(EndDate)) to select only active employees with a StartDate field value (Not IsNull(StartDate)). For each employee record that passes this test (meaning that both conditions are true), it is necessary to determine whether the employee has either five but fewer than ten years of service (display the message "5+ years") or ten or more years of service (display the message "10+ years"), using the expression YearDiff(StartDate, Date) to determine the accurate number of years of service. Note that Date is an argument in the YearDiff function that actually uses the **Date function**, which returns the current computer system date, so that the employee's start date and today's date are the arguments to the YearDiff function.

The ElseIf statement is equivalent to an Else clause followed immediately by an If statement. Figure 7.12 shows the syntax for an ElseIf clause on the left and an Else clause followed by an If statement on the right.

Figure 7.12: Comparing an ElseIf clause to an Else...If clause

ElseIf clause	Else...If clause
| ```
If condition Then
    true-statement group 1
ElseIf condition Then

    true-statement group 2
Else
    false-statement group

End If
``` | ```
If condition Then
    true-statement group 1
Else
    If condition Then
        true-statement group 2
    Else
        false-statement group
    End If
End If
``` |

The choice of which If statement version you use is a matter of personal preference, although the ElseIf version requires one less End If statement at the end and is not as deeply indented, which makes the code more readable for some programmers.

Best Practice

Arranging the Order of Condition Testing

Does it matter in which order you check whether the employee has more than five years but fewer than ten years of service, versus ten or more years of service? Don's design first tests for ten or more years of service and, for those employees for which the condition is true, executes the two following assignment statements and then proceeds with the next statement after the End If. For all other employees, the condition with the ElseIf clause executes and, for those employees with at least five years but fewer than ten years of service, the design executes the two following assignment statements and then proceeds with the next statement after the End If. Finally, for all employees with fewer than five years of service, the design executes the statement following the Else clause, setting the Visible property for the text box to False.

On the other hand, if the design first tests for employees with five or more years of service, then the condition is true for both employees with five or more years of service and for employees with ten or more years of service. Thus, both sets of employees would have the text box message set to "5+ years" and the Visible property for the text box set to True, and then the statement following the End If would be executed. In other words, the design would never result in the display of the "10+ years" message.

Therefore, the order of condition testing is critical. You must place the conditions in order from least inclusive (for example, employees with ten or more years of service) to most inclusive (for example, employees with at least five but fewer than ten years of service). Placing the conditions in the wrong order will cause the statements following the ElseIf clause never to execute; only the statements following the initial If condition and following the Else condition execute.

Don spots an inefficiency in his design. The YearDiff function is used twice—once in the second If statement and again in the ElseIf clause. For those employees with ten or more years of service, only the first function call executes, but both function calls execute for all other employees. Executing the function twice takes more computer time than if he uses an assignment statement, such as Service = YearDiff(StartDate, Date), and then replaces the two uses of the function with the following statements:

```
If Service >= 10 Then
ElseIf Service >= 5 Then
```

Don corrects the design inefficiency by adding the assignment statement for the Service variable and modifying the two conditions. He also adds a declaration statement (Dim Service As Integer) immediately following the comment lines. You use the **Dim statement** to declare variables and their associated data types in a procedure. Figure 7.13 shows the completed procedure.

Figure 7.13: Completed procedure to determine an employee's years of service

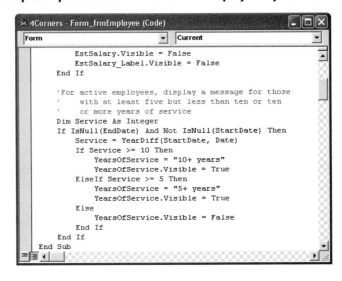

Don tests the enhancement and verifies that it works correctly for all conditions tested in the VBA statements. Figure 7.14 shows the YearsOfService text box for the record for Virginia Sanchez, who is an active employee with more than ten years of service. The message "10+ years" appears correctly.

Figure 7.14: Testing the procedure to determine an employee's years of service

Message is displayed correctly for an employee with 10 or more years of service

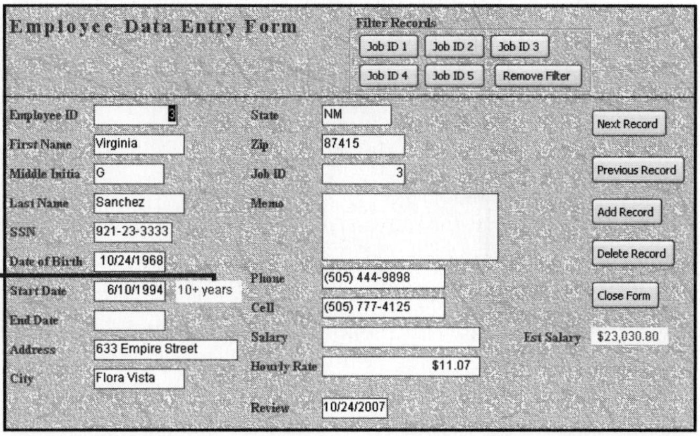

Next Don turns his attention to designing the VBA statements to calculate and display the age of active employees. Don's form modifications and VBA statements must address the following:

- Add a text box named Age and an associated label named Age_Label to frmEmployee to the right of the DOB field text box. Set the text box's properties similar to the YearsOfService calculated control. The associated label should display "Age" as its caption.
- Add VBA statements to the form's Current event procedure.
- Design decision-making logic in the VBA procedure to include only those employees who are active (designated by an end date without a value) and who have a date of birth, which is required for the age calculation.
- Use the YearDiff function to determine an employee's age based on the date of birth and today's date.
- Neither the text box nor the label should be visible for inactive employees or employees without a date of birth value.

Figure 7.15 shows the VBA procedure statements Don adds to the form's Current event procedure to calculate and display the age of active employees.

Figure 7.15: Procedure to calculate an active employee's age

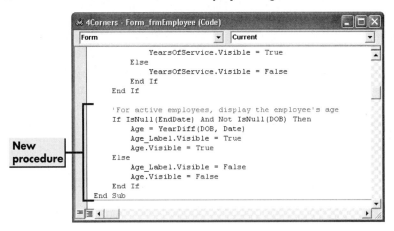

Why do the Visible properties have to be set to either True or False each time the statements execute? When the routine executes, it does not remember the settings of the Visible property made the last time the routine was executed and, thus, you have to set them each time to ensure they are correct for this employee.

Don tests the enhancement and verifies the test results. Figure 7.16 shows the form with the record for Anthony Laporte displayed. Anthony has worked at the pharmacy for more than five but fewer than ten years and is 32 years old as of May 1, 2008.

Figure 7.16: Testing the procedure to display an active employee's age

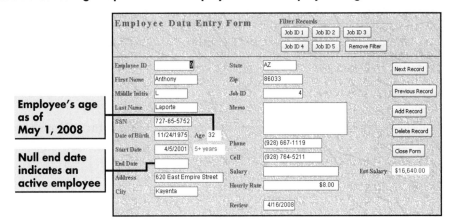

Combining the VBA Statements for Separate Enhancements

Both of Don's enhancements involve the form's Current event. Further, the VBA statements display the controls only for active employees. Why doesn't Don combine the VBA statements as much as possible or, at the very least, enter the VBA statements for both enhancements at the same time and test them together? Experienced programmers find that it is easier to test enhancements separately because errors are isolated to the single added enhancement, making it easier to find any problem and correct it. After an enhancement is entered and completely tested, the programmer enters the next enhancement and tests it, this time knowing that any problems detected apply to this enhancement.

After entering and testing all enhancements, should you consolidate code? For example, Don's completed Current event contains the estimated salary enhancement, the years of service enhancement, and the current age enhancement. All three enhancements apply only to active employees, so he could review the three separate sets of statements, find three If statements that include testing the EndDate field value for a null value, and combine the three sets so that only one If statement tests the EndDate field value. If he chooses not to combine the sets of statements, each enhancement remains implemented as a separate set of statements, which makes it easier to understand the event procedure and modify it in the future. Also, each set of separate statements is simpler than if combined because combining the statements intermingles them into one more-complicated set. The main argument for combining the enhancements is to make the event procedure execute faster. If Don combines the enhancements, he might reduce the number of conditions tested, which results in less time needed to process the event procedure. As a general rule, you should keep the enhancements separate until execution speed becomes a critical factor.

7

Level 2

Don decides not to combine the three separate enhancements in the form's Current event procedure. Next, Don will implement the enhancements Maria requested to verify zip codes and phone area codes. He begins by designing the zip code enhancement.

VERIFYING DATA WITH VBA

Maria often makes typing errors when entering Arizona zip codes, whose first three digits range between 850 and 865, and New Mexico zip codes, whose first three digits range between 870 and 884, because she tends to transpose the first two digits. She wants Don to create a procedure to verify that Arizona and New Mexico zip codes are in the correct range when she updates the Zip field in frmEmployee. For this procedure, Don uses an event procedure attached to the Before Update event for frmEmployee. The **Before Update event** occurs before changed data in a control or a record is updated in the database. Don uses the form's Before Update event for this new procedure because he wants to find data-entry errors for Arizona and New Mexico zip codes and alert users to the errors before the database is updated.

Designing the Field Validation Procedure to Verify Zip Codes

The subroutine that Don designed for frmEmployee to verify Arizona and New Mexico zip codes uses several of the statements from Don's previous designs:

```
Private Sub Form_BeforeUpdate(Cancel As Integer)
    'Verify the first three digits of zip codes
    '    in Arizona and New Mexico
    Dim ZipFirstThree As Integer
    If Not IsNull(State) And Not IsNull(Zip) Then
        ZipFirstThree = Val(Left(Zip, 3))
        Select Case State
            Case "AZ"
                If ZipFirstThree < 850 Or ZipFirstThree > 865 Then
                    MsgBox "AZ zip codes must start 850 to 865"
                    GoTo CommonProcessing
                End If
            Case "NM"
                If ZipFirstThree < 870 Or ZipFirstThree > 884 Then
                    MsgBox "NM zip codes must start 870 to 884"
                    GoTo CommonProcessing
                End If
        End Select
    End If
Exit Sub
CommonProcessing:
    DoCmd.CancelEvent
    Me.Undo
    Zip.SetFocus
End Sub
```

The Sub and End Sub statements begin and end the subroutine. As specified in the Sub statement, the subroutine executes when the form's Before Update event occurs. Within parentheses in the Sub statement, Cancel As Integer defines Cancel as a parameter with the Integer data type. When an event occurs, Access performs the default behavior for the event. For some events, such as the Before Update event, Access executes the attached event procedure or macro before performing the default behavior. Thus, if you detect something is wrong and you do not want the default behavior to occur, you can cancel the default behavior in the event procedure or macro. For this reason, Access automatically includes the Cancel parameter for the Before Update event, which you can use to cancel the default behavior.

After two lines of comments, the next statement, Dim ZipFirstThree As Integer, declares the integer variable named ZipFirstThree. The subroutine assigns the first three digits of the zip code (the Zip field) to the ZipFirstThree variable, and then uses the variable when verifying that Arizona and New Mexico zip codes begin in the correct range.

The procedure should not attempt to verify records that contain null field values for the State field and the Zip field. To screen out these conditions, the procedure uses the procedure statement, If Not IsNull(State) And Not IsNull(Zip) Then, which pairs with the last End If statement. The If statement determines whether both the State and Zip fields are not null. If both conditions are true, Access executes the next statement in the procedure. If either condition is false, Access executes the paired End If statement, and the following Exit Sub statement ends the procedure without the execution of any other statement.

The procedure statement, ZipFirstThree = Val(Left(Zip, 3)), uses the built-in Val and Left functions to assign the first three digits of the Zip field value to the ZipFirstThree variable. The **Left function** returns a string containing a specified number of characters from the left side of a specified string. In this case, the Left function returns the leftmost three characters of the Zip field. The **Val function** returns the numbers contained in a specified string as a numeric value. In this case, the Val function returns the leftmost three characters of Zip as an integer value.

Using the Case Control Structure

The statements from the Select Case State statement to the End Select statement are an example of a control structure. A **control structure** is a set of VBA statements that work together as a unit. One control structure Don has already used is the If statement, a decision-making or conditional control structure. The **Case control structure** is another conditional structure; it evaluates an expression—the value of the State field, in this case—and then performs one of several alternative sets of statements based on the resulting value (or condition) of the evaluated expression. Each Case statement, such as Case "AZ" and Case "NM", designates the start of a set of alternative statements. Note that you can use a Case Else statement as the last Case statement, if you need to include a false-statement group.

For the Before Update event procedure, the Select Case State statement evaluates the State field value. For State field values equal to AZ (Arizona zip codes), the Case "AZ" statement marks the beginning of the statement group that executes for Arizona, and the statement group's end occurs with the next Case statement. For State field values equal to NM (New Mexico zip codes), the Case "NM" statement marks the beginning of the statement group that executes for New Mexico, and the statement group's end occurs with the End Select statement. For zip codes other than those for Arizona and New Mexico, neither Case statement is true, so execution proceeds to the End Select statement, then the following End If statement, and finally the Exit Sub statement, so that control returns to the form for normal processing.

Because valid Arizona zip codes start with the values 850 through 865, invalid numeric values are less than 850 or greater than 865. The next VBA statement, If ZipFirstThree < 850 Or ZipFirstThree > 865 Then, is true only for invalid Arizona zip codes. When the If statement is true, the next two statements execute. When the If statement is false, nothing further in the procedure executes, Access performs the default behavior, and control returns to the form for normal processing. A similar If statement detects and acts on invalid New Mexico zip codes.

The MsgBox statement displays an appropriate error message in a message box that remains on the screen until the user clicks the OK button. The message box appears on top of frmEmployee so the user can view the changed field values in the current record. After the user clicks the OK button in the message box, the GoTo CommonProcessing statement then causes execution to proceed to the CommonProcessing label to execute the three statements that follow the label.

Recall that the DoCmd statement executes an action in a procedure. The DoCmd.CancelEvent statement, the first statement following the CommonProcessing label, executes the CancelEvent action. The **CancelEvent action** cancels the event that caused the procedure or macro containing the action to execute. In this case, Access cancels the Before Update event and does not update the database with the changes to the current record. In addition, Access cancels subsequent events that would have occurred if the Before Update event had not been canceled. (You will learn more about these subsequent events in Level 3.) For example, because the form's Before Update event is triggered when you move to a different record, the following events are triggered when you move to a different record, in the order listed: Before Update event for the form, After Update event for the form, Exit event for the control with the focus, Lost Focus event for the control with the focus, Record Exit event for the form, and Current event for the form. When the CancelEvent action executes, all these events are canceled and the focus remains with the record being edited.

The Me.Undo statement executes next. The **Me keyword** refers to the current object, in this case frmEmployee. **Undo** is a method that clears all changes made to the current record in frmEmployee, so that the field values in the record are as they were before the user made current changes.

Finally, the Zip.SetFocus statement executes. **SetFocus** is a method that moves the focus to the specified object or control. In this case, Access moves the focus to the Zip field in the current record in frmEmployee, making it the current control in the form.

Testing the Field Validation Procedure to Verify Zip Codes

Don opens the property sheet for frmEmployee and sets the form's BeforeUpdate property to [Event Procedure] to open the Code window in the Visual Basic window. Figure 7.17 shows the VBA procedure statements that Don enters.

Figure 7.17: Procedure to verify employee zip codes

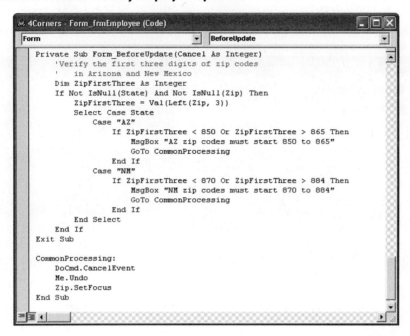

```
4Corners - Form_frmEmployee (Code)

Form                          ▼    BeforeUpdate                    ▼

    Private Sub Form_BeforeUpdate(Cancel As Integer)
        'Verify the first three digits of zip codes
        '   in Arizona and New Mexico
        Dim ZipFirstThree As Integer
        If Not IsNull(State) And Not IsNull(Zip) Then
            ZipFirstThree = Val(Left(Zip, 3))
            Select Case State
                Case "AZ"
                    If ZipFirstThree < 850 Or ZipFirstThree > 865 Then
                        MsgBox "AZ zip codes must start 850 to 865"
                        GoTo CommonProcessing
                    End If
                Case "NM"
                    If ZipFirstThree < 870 Or ZipFirstThree > 884 Then
                        MsgBox "NM zip codes must start 870 to 884"
                        GoTo CommonProcessing
                    End If
            End Select
        End If
    Exit Sub

    CommonProcessing:
        DoCmd.CancelEvent
        Me.Undo
        Zip.SetFocus
    End Sub
```

Don saves the procedure, closes the Visual Basic window, saves the form, and then switches to Form view to test the zip code validation procedure, changing AZ and NM zip codes to valid and invalid values, and changing other state zip codes in a similar way, making sure each record ends up with its original zip code. Note that changing a zip code and then moving to another field on the form does not trigger the procedure; only by navigating to another record does the form's Before Update event occur and cause the procedure to execute. Figure 7.18 shows the message box that opens when Don changes the zip code for record 3 from a valid value of 87415 to an invalid value of 97415 and clicks the Next Record button.

Figure 7.18: Testing the procedure to verify employee zip codes

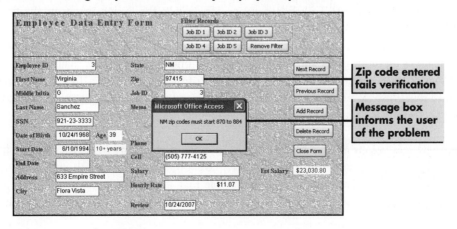

After Don clicks the OK button, the Before Update event is canceled, the changes to the record are canceled, and the focus moves to the text box for the Zip field. Don will add the zip code verifications for other states at a later time.

Best Practice

Using an Event Procedure for a Control or for a Form

Don designed the zip code verification procedure to trigger when the form's Before Update event occurs. Not only is there a Before Update event for each form, but there is also a Before Update event for each control on a form. Why didn't Don design the procedure to use the Before Update event for the Zip field or for the State field? That is, why not trigger the procedure when a user enters or changes an employee's zip code? The reason for not using the Before Update event for the Zip field is that users can enter and change data in any order on a form. It's possible that an employee moves from Arizona to Colorado, for example, which would require the user to change both the State field value and the Zip field value. If the user changes the Zip field value before the State field value and Don used the Before Update event for the Zip field, the procedure would determine that the zip code is invalid and would undo all changes made to the record, even though the user *intended* to change the State field value next. When you need two or more fields as part of the validation process, you should use the form's Before Update event. However, the downside to using the form's Before Update event in this situation is that *all* changes made to the record are undone, not just the fields involved in the event procedure's validation process. The phone area code validation procedure that Don designs next shows an alternative validation approach that could be used instead that doesn't have this drawback.

Designing the Field Validation Procedure to Verify Phone Area Codes

Maria has a similar need to validate the area codes for employees. Don designs a procedure to validate the phone area codes for Arizona and New Mexico and will add the statements to validate the other phone and cell phone area codes at a later time.

How will the design for this procedure be the same as the procedure to validate zip codes, and how will it be different? To validate phone area codes, the design first tests the first three digits of the phone number, just as the procedure for zip codes tests the first three digits of the zip code. Note that phone numbers are displayed as (###) ###-####, but the Phone field has an input mask and only the ten-digit phone number is actually stored in the database, which means that the design needs to test the first three digits. The new procedure must display a message for invalid phone area codes, similar to the procedure that displays a message for invalid zip codes.

Because new regulations allow people to keep their phone numbers when they move, an employee living in one state might legitimately have a phone number with an area code that is assigned to a different state. So it is possible that the phone number is valid even though it has a different area code than the ones assigned to the state. The zip code rules stipulate that a state *must* have specific zip codes, but the phone number rules stipulate that a state is assigned specific area codes but could also have other area codes. The zip code procedure prevented users from entering invalid zip codes, but the phone number procedure must allow users to use any area code. For this procedure, the message can suggest a potential error, but must accept any phone area code entry, regardless of the person's state of residence.

Don's procedure to verify Arizona and New Mexico phone area codes is as follows:

```
Private Sub Phone_BeforeUpdate(Cancel As Integer)
     'Verify the phone area code for Arizona and New Mexico
     Dim PhoneFirstThree As Integer
     If Not IsNull(State) And Not IsNull(Phone) Then
         PhoneFirstThree = Val(Left(Phone, 3))
         Select Case State
             Case "AZ"
                 If Not (PhoneFirstThree = 623 Or
                    PhoneFirstThree = 928) Then
                     MsgBox "AZ phone area codes should be 623 or 928"
                 End If
             Case "NM"
                 If Not (PhoneFirstThree = 505) Then
                     MsgBox "NM phone area codes should be 505"
                 End If
         End Select
     End If
End Sub
```

The design considers only records with State and Phone field values that are not null. If the procedure detects a potential error with the first three digits of the phone number, the procedure displays an informative message in a message box and lets the user decide whether the value is valid. Also, the Before Update event for the Phone field triggers the procedure, meaning that any change to the Phone field value causes the procedure to execute. If, for any reason, there is a possibility that a user could modify Phone field values and then modify State field values and in that update sequence cause a potential error, you should consider making the procedure a public procedure in a standard module and triggering the standard module for the Phone field's Before Update event and for the State field's Before Update event.

Don opens the property sheet for the Phone field in frmEmployee, sets the field's BeforeUpdate property to [Event Procedure], and then clicks the Build button to open the Code window in the Visual Basic window. Figure 7.19 shows the VBA procedure statements that Don enters.

Figure 7.19: Procedure to verify employee phone area codes

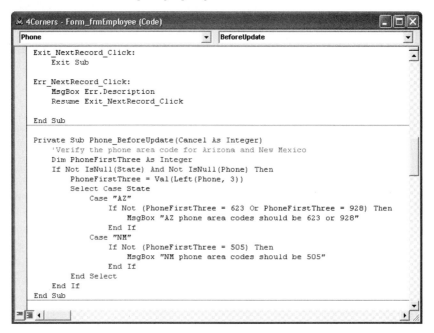

Don saves the procedure, closes the Visual Basic window, saves the form, and then switches to Form view to test the phone area code validation procedure, changing AZ and NM area codes to valid and invalid values, and changing other state area codes in a similar way, making sure each record ends up with its original phone value. Note that changing a phone area code value and then switching to another field on the form triggers the procedure. Figure 7.20 shows the message box that opens when Don changes the phone area code in record 3 from a valid value of 505 to a potentially invalid value of 605.

Figure 7.20: Testing the procedure to verify employee phone area codes

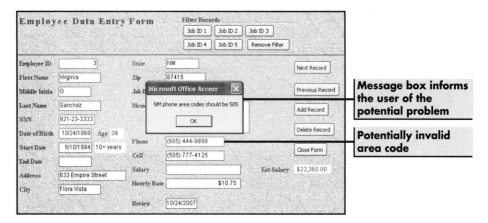

After Don clicks the OK button, the focus returns to the field in the record that Don navigated to after making the phone area code change. He changes the area code back to 505 and finishes his testing.

Steps To Success: Level 2

Glenn Hollander wants you to continue to automate the Hudson database by adding functionality to four existing forms. He wants to enhance frmEmployee to make it easier to identify an employee's current age and the age at which the employee began working at the pharmacy. He also wants to enhance frmPrimaryActivity and frmPrimaryActivity2 to make it easier to identify the number of months since a customer's last refill and to alert the pharmacist when a customer has no refills remaining. Finally, Glenn wants to enhance frmClinic to ensure that users enter valid phone area codes and postal codes when entering the record for a new clinic.

Complete the following:

1. Start Access and open the **Hudson.mdb** database from the STS folder.

2. The frmEmployee form has an approximate calculation for an employee's age. Replace the expression that calculates an employee's age with an expression that calculates the employee's exact age, displaying the calculated age for every employee record. Change the properties of the text box for the calculated control, so that it has the properties of a calculated control instead of a normal text box. (*Hint:* Because you need to use the Date function, and not the field named Date, the expression must use Date().)

3. Below the employee's age and to the right of the employee start date in frmEmployee, add a calculated field that displays the employee's age at the time he or she started working at the pharmacy.

4. For frmPrimaryActivity and frmPrimaryActivity2, add a calculated field that displays the number of months between the prescription date and the expiration date, using blue font for the calculated field. Display the calculated field only when both source dates are not null.

5. For frmPrimaryActivity, add a calculated field without its associated label that displays the message "Call the customer" if the number of refills used is zero, and that displays the message "Call the doctor" if the number of refills used equals the number of refills authorized, displaying both messages with red font.

6. For clinics in Edmonton, validate the postal code values in frmClinic, which must start with either T5 or T6, and the phone area codes, which should be 780. Prevent updates to the record only if the postal code field value is invalid.

7. Close the **Hudson.mdb** database and Access.

LEVEL 3

TESTING AND EXPLORING VBA

ACCESS 2003 SKILLS TRAINING

- **Create an event procedure with VB**
- **Create and test a Visual Basic function in a standard module**

TROUBLESHOOTING VBA PROCEDURES

As an experienced systems analyst and information systems specialist, Don knows that learning to troubleshoot and handle the errors that can occur when coding a program in VBA or any other programming language is a critical part of learning the language. As you have already seen, several types of errors can occur when working with VBA code. These errors are grouped into the general categories of syntax, compilation, logic, and run-time errors.

A **syntax error** occurs when a VBA statement violates the language rules for the statement, such as a misspelling, an incorrect sequence of keywords, or a missing parenthesis. Syntax errors are detected immediately when you complete the statement and move to another statement. An error message opens and explains the error, and the statement is highlighted until you correct the error. For example, if you try to go to the next line in the Code window and do not complete a statement, you receive the error shown in Figure 7.21.

Figure 7.21: Syntax error message

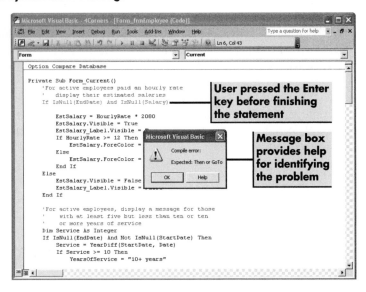

At this point, you can either return to the previous line and continue typing the statement, or type an underscore character on the previous line to indicate that the statement continues to the next line. Often, as is the case in Figure 7.21, it is up to the programmer to determine the cause of the error because the error shown in the message box does not specifically tell you that you didn't type an underscore character; it only tells you that something it expected is missing. The types of syntax errors that you receive as you are typing statements are usually only typing errors, and with practice and experience, you can identify the problem quickly and solve it.

A **compilation error** occurs when you translate procedures into a form the computer can understand. The process of translating modules from VBA to a form the computer understands is called **compilation**; you say that you **compile** the module when you translate it. When you run a procedure for the first time, Access compiles it for you automatically and opens a dialog box only when it finds syntax errors in the procedure. If it finds an error, Access does not translate the procedure statements. If no errors are detected, Access translates the procedure and does not display a confirmation. Sometimes compilation and syntax errors are not identified until you actually run the procedure. For example, Figure 7.22 shows the bas4CornersGeneralProcedures module in the Code window. When Don typed the YearDiff function, he accidentally typed "DateDiff" as "DataDiff." The compiler did not highlight this misspelling as a syntax error. However, when he attempted to navigate to the second record in frmEmployee, the Code window opened and a message box displayed the message "Compile error: Sub or Function not defined." After clicking the OK button, the compiler highlighted the YearDiff function in yellow and selects "DataDiff" as the potential source of the error.

Figure 7.22: Compilation error identified

In this case, Don can quickly spot the problem and select and retype the function name to DateDiff. In other cases, he might need to spend more time analyzing the problem to find its solution. In the meantime, frmEmployee is locked until he stops the debugger by clicking the Reset button ▣ on the Standard toolbar. After stopping the debugger, he can correct the error and save the module, and return to the current object. A good way to avoid encountering compilation errors in the database object at run time is to compile the module before you save it. In response, Access compiles the procedure and all other procedures in all modules in the database. It is best to compile and save your modules after you make changes to them, to ensure that they do not contain compilation errors.

How To

Compile a Module
1. Click Debug on the menu bar in the Visual Basic window.
2. Click Compile.
3. Correct any errors identified by the compiler.
4. Save the module.

If you do not compile each module in the database, each procedure is compiled the first time it is executed by you (or worse, a user), and debugging of the procedure proceeds at this point. To prevent compilation errors at run time, you should use the Compile command on the Debug menu to compile them as your last step before saving the module. If the compiler reports an error, you can correct it; if the compiler does not report any problems, you can save the module knowing that it compiles correctly.

Although you might have entered all procedure statements with the correct syntax and compiled the module with no errors, the procedure might still contain logic errors. You learned in Level 1 that a logic error occurs when the procedure completes and produces incorrect results. For example, Figure 7.23 shows frmEmployee with the record for Marco Farello displayed. On May 1, 2008, Marco should be 33 years old. However, the form displays his age as -34.

Figure 7.23: Logic error in a procedure

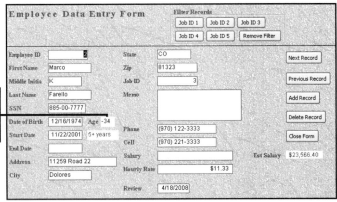

A person cannot have a negative age; the procedure does not produce the correct result

Figure 7.24 shows the Code window for the form. The module does not have any syntax errors and compiled correctly. However, the programmer transposed the arguments in the YearDiff function, resulting in a logic error and an incorrect result in the form.

Figure 7.24: Identifying a logic error in the Code window

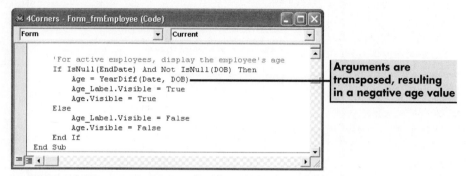

Changing the YearDiff function to YearDiff(DOB, Date) corrects the logic error, and Marco's age is correctly displayed as 33 in the form. As you learned in Level 1, it is critical to test as many situations as possible to discover and correct logic errors in your procedures. The result might display correctly in 19 of 20 records, but the last record might alert you to a logic error that you need to correct.

An **execution error**, or **run-time error**, occurs when a procedure executes and stops because it tries to perform an operation that is impossible to perform. For example, the procedure might try to open an object that does not exist or that has been deleted, or divide a value by zero in a calculation.

USING THE DEBUGGER TO CORRECT ERRORS

The source of any error in a procedure can be difficult to debug. To help you to debug a procedure, you can use the commands on the Debug menu in Visual Basic. Setting a **breakpoint** in a procedure lets you run the subroutine or function up until the line on which you set the breakpoint. When a breakpoint is set, the procedure halts execution at that point and displays the module screen. Using one or more breakpoints in a procedure is a good way to isolate the place at which the procedure stops producing the anticipated result.

How To

Set a Breakpoint

1. Click in the gray margin area to the left of the statement on which you want to set the breakpoint. The breakpoint changes the statement to a maroon background and a maroon dot appears in the margin to the left of the statement, as shown in Figure 7.25.

Figure 7.25: Setting a breakpoint

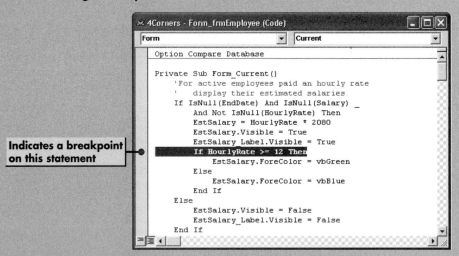

Indicates a breakpoint on this statement

2. Save the module and then open the object that uses the procedure that you are testing. When Access encounters a breakpoint, the Code window opens and a yellow arrow appears in the margin to the left of the statement that contains the breakpoint.

When a procedure is executing and the statement that contains the breakpoint is executed, the procedure halts and the VBA code is displayed. You can use the mouse pointer to get more information about the procedure. For example, pointing to a variable name displays a ScreenTip with the value contained in the variable at the point that the procedure halted. Often, you can use the ScreenTip to isolate a problem in a function or its arguments to identify the cause of an error. You can also execute the procedure one statement at a time to try and identify the cause of an error by clicking Debug on the menu bar, and then clicking Step Into. When you use the Step Into command, the procedure executes the next statement and stops. Clicking Debug on the menu bar and then clicking Step Out executes the current subroutine or function and then halts. By setting breakpoints and stepping in and out of procedures, you can often identify the exact cause of an error. When you identify the error, clicking the Reset button ■ stops the debugger so you can fix the problem, recompile the module, and then save the module. When you no longer need the breakpoints, click Debug on the menu bar, and then click Clear All Breakpoints.

Identifying Errors Using the Watches Window

Another useful tool that you can use to debug a procedure is the Watches window. The **Watches window** shows the current value of a specified variable that you set by clicking Debug on the menu bar, and then clicking Add Watch. The Add Watch dialog box opens, in which you enter the variable name that you want to watch. Figure 7.26 shows the Add Watch dialog box, which is set to watch the Service variable in the procedure.

Figure 7.26: Add Watch dialog box

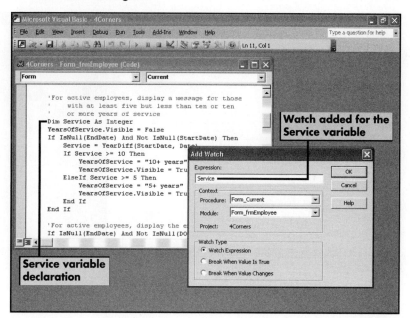

After clicking the OK button in the Add Watch dialog box and setting the variable to watch, the Watches window opens at the bottom of the Visual Basic window. Figure 7.27 shows the Watches window with the Service variable as the watch expression and after setting a breakpoint in the Current procedure for the statement after the assignment statement for the Service variable. "<Out of context>" in the Value column in the Watches window appears for the watch expression when Access is not executing the procedure that contains the watch expression. The Service variable is a variable that is local to the Current procedure and has a value only when the On Current event procedure executes.

Figure 7.27: Watches window

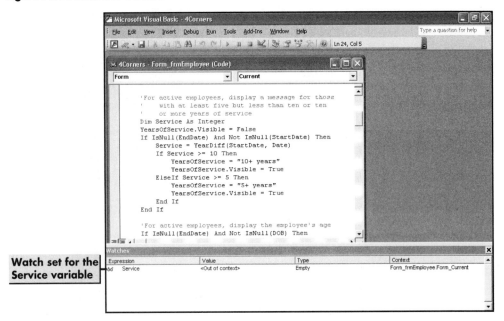

Watch set for the
Service variable

The current value of the specified variable appears in the Watches window as you step through a procedure. After switching to frmEmployee in Form view and navigating to the second record, Figure 7.28 shows that the Service variable is assigned the value of 6, which is correct for a start date of 11/22/2001 and using 5/1/2008 as today's date. Repeatedly using the Step Into command, or pressing the equivalent F8 key, executes the statements in the procedure and continues to display the Service variable in the Watches window. When the procedure ends, the Value column for the Service variable again displays the "<Out of context>" message in the Value column.

Figure 7.28: Watches window after a breakpoint

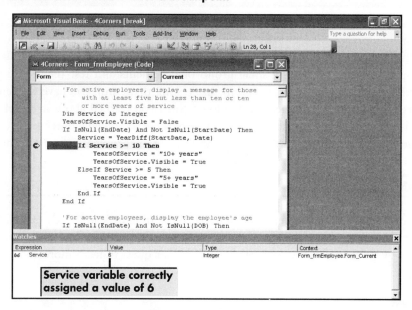

Service variable correctly assigned a value of 6

Instead of setting a breakpoint in the procedure, when you add a watch expression you can specify in the Add Watch dialog box (see Figure 7.26) that you want to see the value of the watch expression by breaking when the value of the watch expression changes or when the value is true.

Best Practice

Troubleshooting VBA Errors

When VBA procedure errors of any type occur, you must find where the error occurred, what caused the error, and then fix the error. Finding the location of the error is easy for syntax, compilation, and run-time errors because Access highlights the statement that caused the error. Fixing syntax and compilation errors is also easy because the highlighted statement is the location and cause of the error, and you must correct the statement itself. Fixing run-time errors is more difficult because the highlighted statement is not always the cause of the error; the execution of previous statements in the procedure might have set up an error situation that became evident only when the highlighted statement executes. In many ways, troubleshooting logic errors is the most difficult because you have to find the location of the error, find what caused the error, and determine how to fix the error. Having a set of tools to use for troubleshooting, such as breakpoints and watch expressions, is critical for troubleshooting success, as is having a solid understanding of VBA and an inquisitive open mind.

Building Procedures Slowly to Isolate Problems

Another way to prevent problems in your procedures is to build them slowly using small groups of statements so you can prove them to be correct as you go. It is easier to correct problems in small groups of statements than it is to try to debug a long procedure. If you use this approach, you can write a small group of statements and test them, and then continue adding statements to the procedure and testing them until you have written the entire procedure. Using the Immediate window, which you learned about in Level 1, is also a good way to check your statements as you write them. If you encounter an incorrect result in the Immediate window, you can stop and debug the problem before continuing.

EXPLORING VBA

VBA is a powerful but complicated language that takes time to learn. Even experienced VBA programmers are learning something new about the language every day. It is important to know what resources are available to you in your quest to learn more about VBA and what it can do.

Using the Northwind Sample Database

As you become more proficient at coding VBA procedures, you will often find that it is very efficient to reuse code that you have included in different modules. You can also use the sample Northwind database that is installed with Access to study existing procedures to understand what they accomplish and the logic used to arrive at the results. You can load the Northwind database by clicking Help on the menu bar in Access, pointing to Sample Databases, and then clicking Northwind Sample Database. The Northwind database contains a variety of simple and complex VBA procedures. You can view the effects of these procedures by using them in the sample database. Microsoft encourages you to copy and use the procedures in this database as a way to learn and use VBA more quickly. If you have time, you should open the Northwind database and study its objects and the logic of the VBA procedures it contains. You can also review the objects in the Northwind database to explore new ways to display and program the various controls on forms and reports and to see how data is validated.

Best Practice

Avoiding Problems with Reusing Code from Other Sources

Creating your first few VBA procedures from scratch is a daunting task. To get started, you should take advantage of the available resources that discuss various ways of designing and programming commonly encountered situations. These resources include, but are not limited to, the Northwind database, Access VBA books and periodicals, Web sites that provide sample code, and Access Help. These resources contain sample procedures and code segments, often with commentary about what the procedures and statements accomplish and why. However, when you create a procedure, you are responsible for knowing what it does, how it does it, when to use it, how to enhance it in the future, and how to fix it when problems occur. If you simply copy statements from another source without thoroughly understanding them, you won't be able to enhance or fix the procedure in the future. In addition, you might overlook better ways to accomplish the same thing—better because the procedure would run faster or would be easier to enhance. In some cases, the samples you find might be flawed, so that they won't work properly for you. The time you spend researching and completely understanding sample code will pay dividends in your learning experience to create VBA procedures.

Using Help to Learn More About Programming and VBA

Access Help contains valuable information about VBA. For example, you can learn more about events in Access Help by typing "What are events?" in the Type a question for help text box on the menu bar, clicking the "Order of events for database objects" link in the Search Results list, and then clicking the Show All link. See Figure 7.29.

Figure 7.29: Access Help about the ordering of events

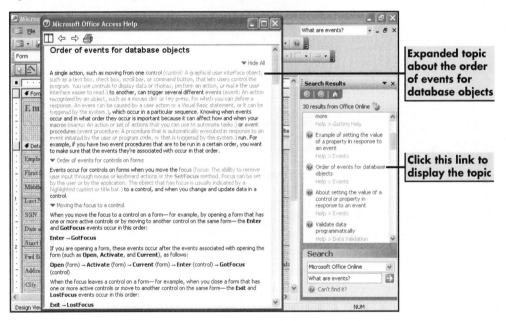

Reading the individual topics gives excellent background about events and the order in which they occur for various objects and controls. Other links in the Search Results list give sample code for situations such as validating data (the "Validate data programmatically" link and the "About validating data programmatically" link), setting property values (the "Set the value of a property in response to an event" link), and navigating forms (the "Navigate between controls, records, and form pages programmatically" link).

If you type "VBA" in the Type a question for help text box on the menu bar, Access displays another list of helpful topics, such as when to use macros or VBA (the "Should I use a macro or Visual Basic?" link), how to change the display of VBA (the "Change the display of your Visual Basic code" link), and how to copy samples (the "Copy Visual Basic code examples from Help to the Code window" link).

A different collection of Help topics about VBA is available when the Visual Basic window is the active window. Figure 7.30 shows the Table of Contents when you click Help on the menu bar of the Visual Basic window, click Microsoft Visual Basic Help, and then click the Microsoft Access Visual Basic Reference link.

Figure 7.30: Visual Basic Help Table of Contents

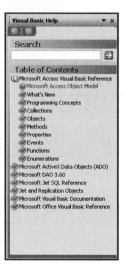

Expanding a topic in the Table of Contents—for example, the Events topic—displays an alphabetized list of elements for that topic—for example, the Activate event, AferDelConfirm event, and so on appear when you click the letter A in the list.

You can type search criteria in the Search text box to display a list of Visual Basic Help topics that satisfy the search criteria. For example, Figure 7.31 shows the list of topics that appears when you use MsgBox as the search criteria.

Figure 7.31: Visual Basic Help for MsgBox search criteria

Clicking the "MsgBox Function (Visual Basic for Applications)" link displays a full description about the MsgBox function, as shown in Figure 7.32, including how to control which buttons to display in the message box and how to identify which button the user clicked in the message box.

Figure 7.32: MsgBox function help

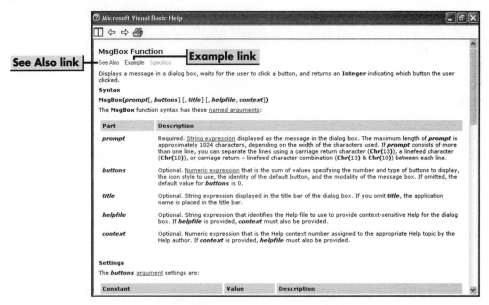

Many topics have a "See Also" link that displays a list of related topics and an Example link that displays a code segment related to the topic. Figure 7.33 shows the VBA code segment that appears when you click the Example link for the MsgBox function topic.

Figure 7.33: MsgBox function help example

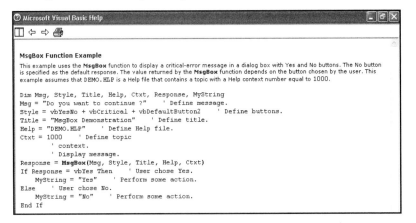

When you need to learn more about a specific VBA function, event, object, or other element, you should first use the help available with Microsoft Access and with Visual Basic and use the sample VBA in the Northwind database. If you need more information or help, take advantage of the multitude of books, periodicals, and Web sites that focus on the use of VBA in Microsoft Access.

Steps To Success: Level 3

Complete the following:

1. Start Access and open the **Hudson.mdb** database from the STS folder.

2. Sometimes the information you need about a VBA topic is found in Access Help and other times it's found in Visual Basic Help. Which of the two Help systems contains a topic named "Debug your Visual Basic code?" Some of the links in this topic cover material, such as breakpoints and watch expressions, that were discussed in this chapter. For the debugging topics that were not covered in this chapter, create a document using any word-processing program that names and describes each of these techniques.

3. Find sample code in the Northwind database or use Help to learn how to display a message when a required field is left blank. Create and test a VBA event procedure that displays a message when the employee last name in frmEmployee is left blank.

4. Canadian postal codes consist of six characters with a required format of letter, digit, letter, digit, letter, and digit. Find sample code in the Northwind database or use Help to learn how to verify Canadian postal codes. Use a make-table query to create a copy of tblEmployee as tblEmployeeCopy and then use a Form wizard to create a form, named frmEmployeeCopy, for the new table. (*Note:* Do not create a copy of

the table; you must use a make-table query. Do not save the make-table query in the database.) Create and test a VBA event procedure that verifies Canadian postal codes in frmEmployeeCopy.

5. In the Help system, find the "Improve Visual Basic code performance" topic and copy and paste the contents into a Word document. For each performance tip that you don't understand, research it and then add material to further explain and clarify the tip.

6. Close the **Hudson.mdb** database and Access.

CHAPTER SUMMARY

In this chapter, you learned how to enhance a form using VBA procedures in ways that are not possible using only the tools provided with Access. In Level 1, you learned how to create a subroutine in a standard module, how to create an event procedure, how to code control structures in VBA that add decision making to a procedure, how to assign values to variables, and how to create and test a function. You also learned how to correct problems in procedures.

In Level 2, you learned how to create a custom function to solve a problem in a specific database object. You also learned how to code procedures that can verify data entry by validating the user's entry against a predefined list of acceptable values.

In Level 3, you explored different methods for troubleshooting logic, compilation, run-time, and syntax errors in procedures. You learned how to use breakpoints to isolate logic and syntax problems and explored different ways to isolate problems. You also explored the Northwind sample database that is installed with Access and used the Access Help and Visual Basic Help systems to learn more about general programming basics and coding in VBA.

CONCEPTUAL REVIEW

1. Why is VBA an event-driven and object-oriented language?

2. What is an event property?

3. What is an event procedure?

4. Why would you choose to use a function instead of a subroutine?

5. When would you choose to use a standard module?

6. What is the difference between a private procedure and a public procedure?

7. When would you choose to use a class module?

8. Which statements begin and end a subroutine?

9. Describe the general syntax of the If statement.

10. What is a variable? How do you declare a variable in a procedure?

11. What is the Dim statement? When do you use it?

12. When does the Before Update event occur?

13. What is a control structure and when do you use it?

14. Describe the following types of errors and give an example of each type: syntax, compilation, logic, and run-time.

15. What does it mean to compile a module?

CASE PROBLEMS

Case 1—Enhancing Employee Data for NHD Development Group Inc.

Human Resources

Linda Sutherland, manager of the Memories Antique Mall in Cleveland, Tennessee, has been using the database to manage data about dealers, employees, classes, instructors, customers, and booths. She has transferred most of her manual systems to the database and has been very pleased with the database. Linda asks if you can make it easier to print the two reports that she frequently prints, rptEmployeeSalaryDetail and rptEmployeeSalarySummary, because she sends these reports to the NHD corporate offices on a quarterly basis.

Another change that Linda asks you to make is to hide the Hourly Rate controls for salaried employees and to hide the Salary controls for hourly employees in frmEmployeeData. In the same form, Linda mentions that she needs a way to monitor personnel reviews for employees with regard to having advance notice to schedule them and a reminder when they are past due. You tell Linda that she might benefit from having a reminder on frmEmployeeData to indicate how many months remain until the employee's next review date, and a reminder for employees who have not had their reviews when the scheduled date has passed. Linda wants the overdue reminder to appear in red, bold font and the number of months until the next review to appear in blue, bold font. She also wants you to hide the review date when the review is overdue so it does not display a negative number, and to hide the review date for inactive employees.

Complete the following:

1. Start Access and open the **Antiques.mdb** database from the Case 1 folder.

2. Create a new standard module named basAntiquesGeneralProcedures and add two procedures to it. The first procedure should print rptEmployeeSalaryDetail, and the second procedure should print rptEmployeeSalarySummary.

3. Open frmEmployeeData. Hide the Salary controls for hourly employees and the Hourly Rate controls for salaried employees.

4. Create a text box control below the Review controls with the caption "Months Until Next Review" and the name ReviewMonths_Label, and a text box with the name ReviewMonths. In the ReviewMonths text box, add a calculated field that accurately displays the number of months between the current date and the employee's next review date. Format the ReviewMonths value in a blue, bold font.

5. If the value in ReviewMonths in frmEmployeeData is less than zero, hide the ReviewMonths and ReviewMonths_Label controls and display the message "Review is overdue!" in a bold, red font. (*Hint:* Set your computer's system clock to the year 2008 or later to test the procedure.)

6. Hide the ReviewMonths and ReviewMonths_Labels controls in frmEmployeeData when the value in the Review field is null.

7. Save and test your procedures and make sure that your changes to frmEmployeeData work correctly.

8. Close the **Antiques.mdb** database and Access.

Case 2—Enhancing Data Entry and Verifying Data for MovinOn Inc.

Human Resources

David Bowers, general manager of MovinOn, met with his warehouse managers to discuss the progress you have made in developing the MovinOn database. Because MovinOn recently adopted a pension plan for all employees, the managers want to inform employees when they are fully vested in the plan, which happens after five years of service. David asks if you can add a message to the form that indicates when an employee is fully vested based on the length of service. He also wants you to add a control that calculates an employee's years of service. For active employees, he wants you to hide the End Date field; for inactive employees, he wants you to hide the Review field. Finally, to help with data entry, the warehouse managers want to verify phone and cell phone area codes entered into frmEmployeeData.

Complete the following:

1. Start Access and open the **MovinOn.mdb** database located in the Case 2 folder.

2. Add a new control to frmEmployeeData that uses a function to accurately calculate the years of service for each active and inactive employee. Set the control's properties so users cannot change it or tab to it, and so its border is transparent.

3. Add a label control to frmEmployeeData in the appropriate position on the form, using the name Vested_Label and the caption "Fully Vested." The message should appear on the form when an active or inactive employee has five or more years of service. Display the message in red font. (*Hint:* Set your computer's system clock to the year 2008 or later to test the procedure.)

4. For active employees, hide the End Date controls in frmEmployeeData. For inactive employees, display the End Date controls in a bold, red font.

5. For hourly employees, hide the Salary controls; for salaried employees, hide the Hourly Rate controls.

6. Verify phone area codes for employee phone numbers in frmEmployeeData. For employees living in Oregon, the valid area codes are 541, 503, and 971; for employees living in Washington, the valid area codes are 425, 360, 206, 509, and 253; for employees living in Wyoming, the valid area code is 307. Warehouse managers should be able to enter phone area codes not included in the lists.

7. Verify cell phone area codes for employee cell phone numbers in frmEmployeeData. The valid cell phone area codes are the same as the ones for regular phone numbers. Warehouse managers should be able to enter phone area codes not included in the lists.

8. Save and test your procedures and make sure that your changes to frmEmployeeData work correctly.

9. Close the **MovinOn.mdb** database and close Access.

Case 3—Enhancing the Database for Hershey College

Operations Management

Marianna Fuentes, assistant director of the intramural department at Hershey College, is concerned about the purchases that coaches have made and asks that you "flag" large unapproved purchases in frmPurchaseData with a message box indicating that the purchase requires her approval, and to put a message on the form when the amount exceeds $100. Marianna is also finding transposed phone area codes in the database. Because the college is located in an area with only one phone area code, she asks if there is a way to ask the user to confirm the entry of telephone and cell phone numbers when they do not begin with the 717 area code.

Complete the following:

1. Start Access and open the **Hershey.mdb** database located in the Case 3 folder.

2. Open frmPurchaseData and replace the form's On Current macro with a procedure that displays the message "Please see Marianna Fuentes for approval" in a message box when the amount exceeds $100. In addition, display the message "Needs Approval" to the right of the Amount text box in red font when the amount exceeds $100.

3. Write the procedures to verify the phone area code and cell phone area code in each form that uses these fields.

4. Find sample code in the Northwind database or use Help to learn how to use the InputBox function to obtain data from a user.

5. After you have read the information related to the InputBox function, consider how you might use it to replace the message box you created in Step 2. Write a proposal of how you might use the InputBox function in this form and why you would choose to use it.

6. Marianna has learned that there are sometimes discrepancies in the way people enter data. For example, in frmFieldData, users might enter the season as "Fall" or "FALL." Marianna wants to change all entries entered into the SeasonAvailable field to upper-case letters. Use Help to learn how to use the UCASE function, and then change the values in the SeasonAvailable field to uppercase. Marianna might decide to use this function in other places in the database.

7. Use Help to learn about the CurrentUser method, and then use this method to display the name of the current user when frmStudentData is opened. Use Help to learn where this method name comes from. How else might you use the CurrentUser method?

8. Close the **Hershey.mdb** database and Access.

Integrating a Database with a Web Site
Marketing: Expanding Customer Service Using the Internet

> *"A business has to be involving, it has to be fun, and it has to exercise your creative instincts."*
> —Richard Branson

LEARNING OBJECTIVES

Level 1

Plan and create a data access page

Customize the record navigation bar in a data access page

Add command buttons to a data access page

Change a data access page to read-only

Apply a theme to a data access page

Level 2

Write scripts for command buttons

Work in Microsoft Script Editor

Use functions to perform actions in a Web page

Secure a data access page by writing a script that accepts a password entry

Work with events

Level 3

Understand how to use XML data in a business

Understand the requirements for creating well-formed XML documents

Import XML data into an Access database

Understand how to use schema files to format XML data

Export data from an Access database into an XML document

TOOLS COVERED IN THIS CHAPTER

Command Button Wizard
Microsoft Script Editor
Page Wizard

CHAPTER INTRODUCTION

You have learned how to display data stored in a database in queries, forms, and reports. You can also display data stored in a database in a Web page. A Web page that you create in Access is called a data access page. When you create a data access page, you connect the Web page to the database so that the data users see in the Web page reflects the current state of the data. When used in a Web site, data access pages can provide users with the ability to search the database and update it using their Web browser. In this way, you control a user's access to the database and provide a method for users to make changes without needing to start Access or use any tools such as Datasheet view or a switchboard. Because a data access page is a Web page, you can publish it on a local area network, on which user access is restricted through the security controls that exist on the network, or on a Web server that the public can access. You can also set the page's properties to control how users access the data—you might want to set properties to let them make changes or set properties that restrict their ability to update the database.

A data access page might include command buttons that perform certain actions as the user interacts with the page. These actions are performed by scripts that Access includes in the page or that you might write to perform a certain function. In Level 2, you will learn more about scripts and use them to enhance a Web page.

Finally, in Level 3, you will learn about Extensible Markup Language (XML), a markup language that developers can customize to facilitate data exchange between systems and organizations. Access 2003 supports importing and exporting of XML data.

CASE SCENARIO

With the development and maintenance work on the database almost complete, Paul Ferrino wants to focus Don Linebarger's attention on developing a Web site for 4Corners Pharmacy. Paul wants the Web site to promote good health. He also thinks it would be advantageous to provide some data from the database on the Web site. His primary interests are to provide information about drugs, such as drug interactions and prices. Don responds by telling Paul that he can build Web pages in the database using the information already stored in tblDrug. Paul asks Don to proceed, and also to look for other ways to enhance the Web site with Web pages that display data from the database.

Marketing

Don also received an e-mail message from Elaine Estes, the pharmacy's manager. One of the health plans that the pharmacy works with has requested a list of prescriptions filled for the plan's customers. Elaine indicated in her message that the health plan wants to receive the data in electronic format so it is easy to import into the system. Because Elaine is not familiar with the health plan's system or the capabilities of the 4Corners database, she refers the request to Don and asks him to contact the health plan directly to discuss the best way to transmit the requested data.

LEVEL 1

USING A DATA ACCESS PAGE TO DISPLAY DATA FROM THE DATABASE

ACCESS 2003 SKILLS TRAINING

- **Create data access pages using the Page Wizard**
- **Use data access pages (dynamic HTML documents)**

UNDERSTANDING HOW THE INTERNET WORKS

The **Internet** is a large, worldwide collection of computers that are connected together in various ways to form a large computer network. You are probably already familiar with the Internet and use it to transfer files from one computer to another, to send e-mail messages, and to participate in online forums or chats. The **World Wide Web** (or the **Web**) is a subset of the computers connected to the Internet that host Web sites. Most companies operating in today's economy have some sort of online presence to market their businesses and conduct online sales. A Web site is stored on a **Web server**, which is a computer that is connected to the Internet and runs special software to store and manage a Web site. A Web server accepts requests from other computers that are connected to it and shares its resources, which include Web pages and other files.

Each Web server that is connected to the Internet has a unique address, called a **Uniform Resource Locator** (**URL**). A URL includes the transfer protocol to use to transfer the file and the domain name of the computer. If the URL includes information about a specific file to open from the Web server, the URL also includes a pathname of the directory that contains the file and the name of the file, including its filename extension. Figure 8.1 shows a URL and its different parts.

Figure 8.1: Parts of a URL

The **transfer protocol** is the set of rules that computers use to send and receive files from other computers. The transfer protocol used to send and receive Web pages is **Hypertext Transfer Protocol** (**HTTP**), which includes http:// as the first part of its URL. Because this is the most commonly used transfer protocol on the Internet, most Web browsers add it automatically to a URL that you type into the browser's address bar when you type a domain name. Another commonly used transfer protocol on the Internet is **File Transfer Protocol** (**FTP**), which includes ftp:// as the first part of its URL and is used to transfer files between computers.

Most Web pages are written in a language called **Hypertext Markup Language** (**HTML**), which includes a set of codes or **tags** that describe how to format the content in the document. Because Web pages are written in HTML, they are also called **HTML documents**. To view the pages stored in a Web site, you must use a **Web browser**, such as Microsoft Internet Explorer, Mozilla Firefox, or Netscape Navigator, to read the tags in an HTML document and display the Web page content according to the standardized rules defined for those tags. HTML documents also include **hyperlinks**, which are tags that include instructions that point to another location in the same document, to a new location in the same Web site, or elsewhere on the Internet.

Web pages are generally classified into two categories—static and dynamic. A **static Web page** displays information that is current at the time the page was created or last saved. A static Web page at 4Corners Pharmacy might provide a map with the location of and directions to the pharmacy. The content of a **dynamic Web page** is based on the user's interaction with the Web site. At 4Corners Pharmacy, for example, a dynamic Web page might display a list of prescriptions sold to a specific customer within the past 30 days or 12 months. In this case, the user would enter her name and other identifying information using the Web page, indicate the desired time frame for the prescription history, and click a button to search the Web site for data matching the request. The Web server would respond by generating a dynamic Web page that includes the customer's name and pre-scription history. If the customer fills a new prescription and requests a new prescription history, the Web server responds to the same request from the customer by generating a new Web page that includes the existing information and the new information. Because the Web page is generated based on the current data in the database, the data in the page is always current.

HTML was designed to create static Web pages. As companies and organizations found new ways to use the Internet for their business operations, they needed ways to extend HTML to do new things. Although you can use HTML to create static Web pages, it does not have the functionality to create dynamic ones. You can learn how to use other lan-guages, such as VBScript, JavaScript, ASP.NET, CGI, and PERL, to add the necessary programming instructions to HTML documents to create dynamic Web pages. (You will learn how to use one of these languages, VBScript, in Level 2 of this chapter.)

Processing Requests from Clients

Most networks, including the Internet, connect two broad categories of computers to each other in a network called a client/server network. A **client/server network** connects computers called **client computers** to a main computer called a **server**. The clients send requests to the server, which responds by sharing its resources, including files, programs, and connected devices such as printers. When you connect to the Internet and use the Web browser on your computer to open a Web site, your computer becomes a **Web client**. At any time, a Web server might have many Web clients connected to it. The server might store Web sites, databases, and other files that the Web clients need. When a Web client connects to a Web server, such as one used by 4Corners Pharmacy, it might send a request for information about specific drugs or a prescription history. The server responds to the request by returning the answers to the Web client in the form of a Web page. Some Web servers must be very powerful to handle the number of requests from clients. For example, the servers at eBay and Amazon.com receive and process millions of requests each day. To handle such a volume, server computers are quite powerful in terms of their memory capacity and processing capability. Many organizations use a Web server to process Web pages and a separate server to process database requests. Figure 8.2 shows how the computers in a client/server network work together.

Figure 8.2: Sample client/server network

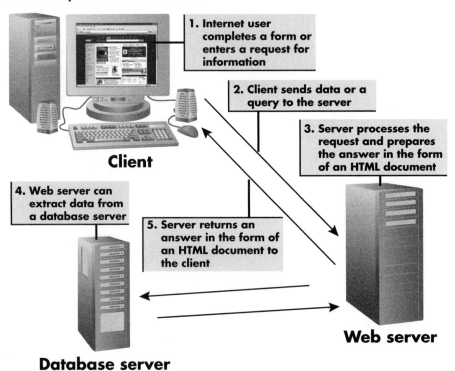

It is important to understand this client/server environment because it is an important key to understanding the way Access works with Web pages. To create dynamic Web pages, the database that contains the data in the pages must be stored on the server. When an Internet user completes an online form or enters a query into a search field to locate a product and then clicks the Submit button, the data from the form or the query is sent to the server. The server receives the request and then executes a server-side script to process the form or to find the product in the database. The result is formatted as an HTML document and sent back to the client that requested it. The client's browser displays the result in the form of a Web page.

PLANNING A DATA ACCESS PAGE

A **data access page** is a dynamic Web page that you can open with a Web browser and use to view or change the data stored in an Access database. Don can create data access pages in the 4Corners database that make it possible for customers and employees to view data in the database without using Access. Figure 8.3 shows a data access page that displays the fields and field values from the database object on which it is based, and also includes a record navigation bar that you can use to browse, add, change, filter, or delete records.

Figure 8.3: Data access page viewed in Internet Explorer

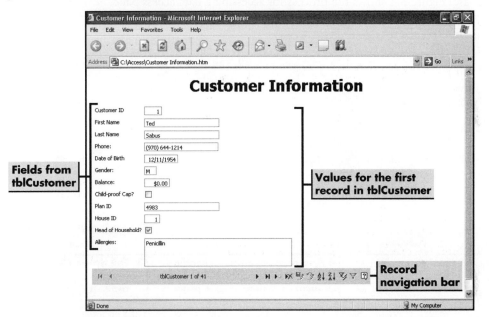

When you use Access to create a data access page, you are actually creating two items. The first item is a page object in the database that contains instructions for connecting the database object on which the data access page is based to the second item, which is the HTML document. The HTML document is stored outside the database and contains HTML tags to format the data access page. When you create a data access page in Access, Access uses a **connection string** to specify the disk location of the HTML document and the database name to which the page is connected. A connection string is written using an **absolute path**, which is a path that provides an exact location for a file within a computer's entire directory structure, and not as a **relative path**, which is a path that describes the location of a file relative to the location of the current document. The path from the HTML document to the database becomes part of the data access page. If you move the HTML document to another location, Access does not update the reference to that location in the connection string. For this reason, it is important to check the page objects in a database carefully to make sure that the connection strings include the correct absolute path to the HTML document. If you move an HTML document for a data access page, you can change the path to the HTML document by changing the absolute path in the ConnectionString property of the page object in the database. (You will learn more about connection strings in Level 2.)

When you open a data access page in a Web browser, you can sort and filter records based on the values in a particular field and use the buttons on the record navigation bar to view the records in the database object on which the data access page is based. If the data access page is created so as to accept changes, deletions, and additions, any changes you make to an existing record are made in the database object on which the data access page is based. In addition, using a data access page to delete or add a record also updates the database. Figure 8.4 shows the process for accessing a data access page.

Figure 8.4: Accessing a data access page

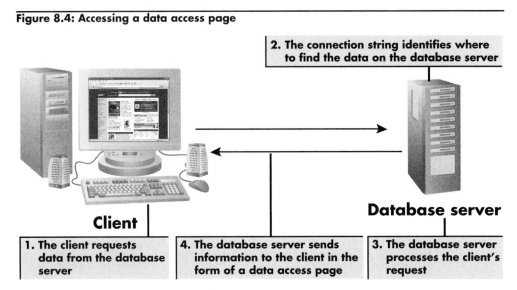

2. The connection string identifies where to find the data on the database server

Client

Database server

1. The client requests data from the database server

4. The database server sends information to the client in the form of a data access page

3. The database server processes the client's request

Don knows that data access pages are useful when he needs to provide access to the data in a table or query using a Web browser, but he also knows of several issues that he must consider before using this technology in the 4Corners Web site. The first and most important issue is the Web browser that is used to view the data access page. About 90% of Internet users use Internet Explorer, the browser that is installed with the Microsoft Windows operating system. The remaining 10% of Internet users use other browsers, including Firefox, Navigator, and Opera. Data access pages that Don creates using Access are designed to work with Internet Explorer version 5.01 and Service Pack 2 or higher, and will not function well or at all if they are accessed by other browsers. Although Don believes that most of the pharmacy's customers and all of the pharmacy's employees have Internet Explorer, he does need to consider the potential problems that people will encounter if they try to use a data access page using a browser other than Internet Explorer. Don can include information in the data access page to inform users that the page functions best when viewed using Internet Explorer if he sees from the Web site's server statistics that users are trying to open it with other browsers.

The second issue that Don must consider when planning to use a data access page is whether the Web server can process the scripts in the data access page that define the database connection. The server on which the data access page is stored must be compatible with the code that Access inserts in the page to produce the dynamic content. When he selects the Web server for the pharmacy, Don needs to ensure that it is capable of processing data access pages and then test the pages thoroughly to make sure that the connection strings and pages work as expected.

Before creating the data access page, Don needs to determine the database object on which to base the data access page. If he chooses a table, he can select all or some of the fields in the table to include in the data access page. He can also base the data access page on a query, in which case he must create and save the query in the database before creating the data access page. The first data access page that Don wants to create displays data about the classes that employees must take to fulfill their professional certifications and other recreational classes provided through the pharmacy. The data access page will include all of the fields from tblClass, so he will base the data access page on tblClass and not on a query.

Now that Don has decided on the content to include in his data access page, he is ready to create it using Access.

CREATING A DATA ACCESS PAGE WITH THE PAGE WIZARD

Similar to other database objects, Don can use Design view or a wizard to create a data access page. Because the page he needs to create is simple, he decides to use the Page Wizard to create it. He starts Access and opens the 4Corners database, clicks the Pages object in the Database window, and then double-clicks the Create data access page by using wizard option. The Page Wizard starts. Don uses the Tables/Queries list arrow to select tblClass, and then clicks the Select All Fields button >> to include all of the fields in the data access page. See Figure 8.5.

Figure 8.5: Choosing the object and fields for the data access page

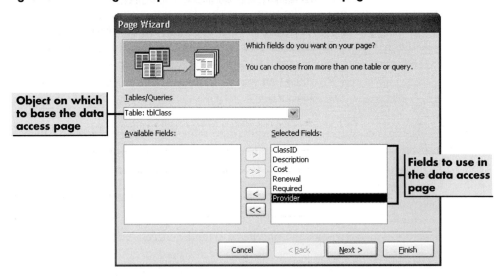

Object on which to base the data access page ⟶ (Tables/Queries — Table: tblClass)

Fields to use in the data access page ⟶ (Selected Fields: ClassID, Description, Cost, Renewal, Required, Provider)

Don clicks the Next button. The second dialog box asks if he wants to add any grouping levels to the data access page. Don does not need to group the records, so he clicks the Next button to open the dialog box in which he can select a sort order. Don wants to sort the records using the ClassID field, so he clicks the list arrow and chooses this field. He clicks the Next button to display the final dialog box. See Figure 8.6.

Figure 8.6: Adding a title to the data access page

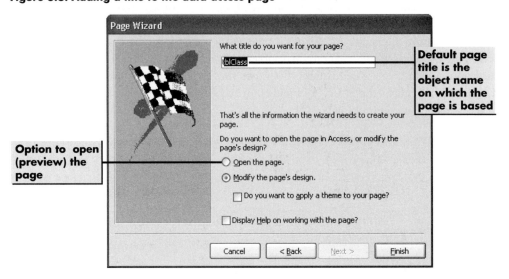

Default page title is the object name on which the page is based

Option to open (preview) the page

The default page title for a data access page is the name of the object on which it is based. Don changes the page title to "Class Information" so it will appear in the browser's title bar when viewed by users, clicks the option button to open the page, and then clicks the Finish button. The data access page appears in Figure 8.7.

Figure 8.7: Class Information data access page created by the Page Wizard

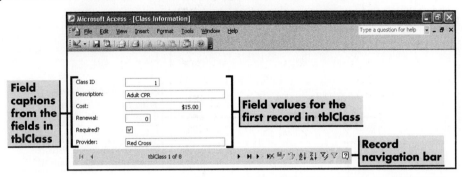

The data access page displays the field captions and field values for each field in tblClass and the record navigation bar. The **record navigation bar** contains buttons that let users change the view of the data displayed by the page in many ways without affecting the records in tblClass. For example, Don clicks the Cost field, and then clicks the Sort Descending button on the record navigation bar. The records are sorted so that the most expensive class—Yoga—appears as the first record in the data access page. See Figure 8.8.

Figure 8.8: Records sorted in descending order by class cost

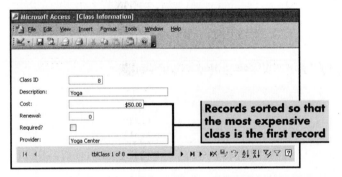

Don can also filter the records to display only those records with a specific value in a field. For example, to view only those records with Renewal values of 1 (for one year), he can use the record navigation buttons to scroll through the records until he finds a record with the value 1 in the Renewal field, click the Renewal field, and then click the Filter by Selection button on the record navigation bar. When he does this, the data access page displays only those records that contain the value 1 in the Renewal field, as shown in Figure 8.9.

Figure 8.9: Records filtered based on a renewal value of 1

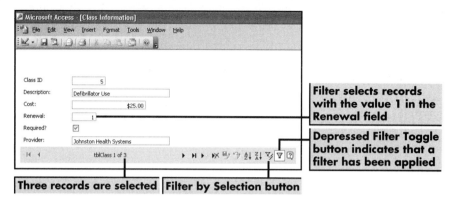

Filter selects records with the value 1 in the Renewal field

Depressed Filter Toggle button indicates that a filter has been applied

Three records are selected | Filter by Selection button

Because Don applied a filter to select the records with a Renewal value of 1, the Filter Toggle button ▼ is depressed to indicate that a filter has been applied. Clicking ▼ removes the filter and displays all of the records again.

Don does not need to make any adjustments to the page, so he saves it as an object in the database by clicking the Save button 🔲 on the Page View toolbar. The Save As Data Access Page dialog box opens and displays a filename using the title Don used when he created the page. In this case, the default filename is Class Information.htm. When Don clicks the Save button, the message box shown in Figure 8.10 opens to remind Don that the connection string contains an absolute path.

Figure 8.10: Message box with connection string reminder

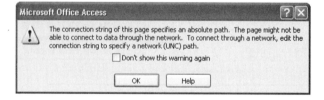

Don wants the message to be displayed each time he saves a data access page, so he does not select the check box to disable the message, and then he clicks the OK button. Access saves the Class Information page object in the database and the Class Information.htm Web page in the folder Don specified.

Don can view the Class Information page in a browser by clicking the list arrow for the View button on the Page View toolbar, and then clicking Web Page Preview. Because Don's computer has browsers other than Internet Explorer installed on it, a message box opens and reminds him that data access pages can be viewed only in Internet Explorer. He clicks the Yes button to open the page in Internet Explorer. Because the page contains scripts and his computer's operating system is Windows XP, the browser issues a warning asking if he wants to allow blocked content. He clicks the Information Bar, clicks the Allow Blocked Content option in the menu, clicks the Yes button to run the active content, and then Internet Explorer displays the page. See Figure 8.11. Notice that the page title appears in the browser's title bar.

Figure 8.11: Class Information page in Internet Explorer

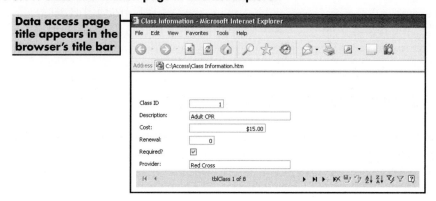

Now pharmacy employees can use the page to browse the classes that they can take. In addition, if information about a class changes, Don or Maria can use this page to make the necessary changes. For example, Don just learned that the cost of the Adult CPR class has increased from $15 to $18. To make this change, he could open tblClass in Datasheet view. Because the data access page is already open, he selects the value $15.00 in the Cost field for this record, types 18, and then presses the Tab key to move to the next field. The data type for the Cost field is Currency, and the value 18 changes to $18.00, as shown in Figure 8.12.

Figure 8.12: Using a data access page to change a record

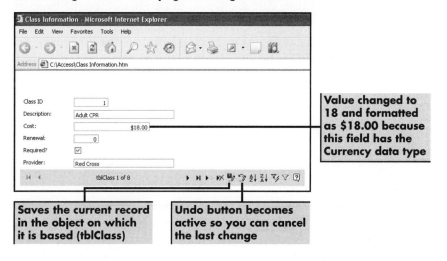

When you change a record using a data access page, the Save button on the record navigation bar becomes active to remind you to save the record. The Undo button also becomes active; clicking this button lets you undo the change you made. Don clicks to save the record, which updates the data in tblClass.

Don can also use the New button on the record navigation bar to add a record to tblClass using the data access page, and he can use the Delete button to delete the currently displayed record from tblClass. Clicking the Help button opens the Microsoft Access Data Access Pages Help window and provides help for using and working with data access pages.

Don is satisfied with the Class Information page, so he closes the browser and then closes the page in Access. Next, he needs to create the data access page to display information about the different drugs sold through the pharmacy. Because customers will use this page, he wants to make sure that the page has a professional appearance, the information provided is easy to read and understand, and customers cannot make changes to the database. He decides to create the page in Design view instead of using the Page Wizard to maintain tighter control over the page's appearance and format.

CREATING A DATA ACCESS PAGE IN DESIGN VIEW

Don's next task is to create a data access page that customers can use to learn more about the drugs sold through the pharmacy and prescribed to them. Most of the information that Don needs already exists in tblDrug, so he will base the data access page on this table. Because Don does not want to provide customers with access to drug cost and supplier information, he will exclude these fields from the data access page.

Don starts by double-clicking Create data access page in Design view on the Pages object in the Database window. A message box opens and warns Don that he cannot open a data access page created using Access 2003 in Design view with previous versions of Access. This message is not a concern for Don because the pharmacy is only working with the latest version of Access. He clicks the OK button and Figure 8.13 shows Design view for a data access page.

Figure 8.13: Design view for a data access page

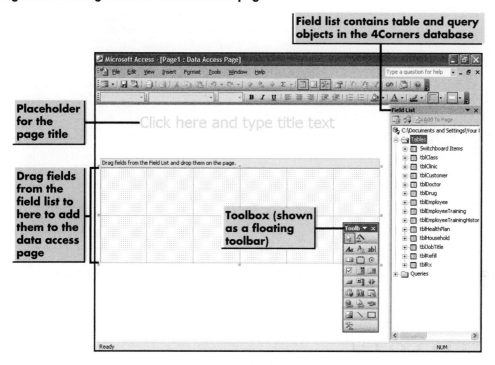

Field list contains table and query objects in the 4Corners database

Placeholder for the page title

Drag fields from the field list to here to add them to the data access page

Toolbox (shown as a floating toolbar)

The Toolbox, which is a floating toolbar in Figure 8.13, includes tools for working with data access pages in Design view. The field list, which appears on the right side of the window, includes the table and query objects in the 4Corners database. You can drag the Toolbox and field list around the screen as necessary to move them out of the way as you are designing the data access page, you can close them, or you can dock the Toolbox like you would a toolbar. Don docks the Toolbox below the other toolbars to prevent it from obscuring the content of the data access page.

Adding Fields to a Data Access Page

The first thing that Don does in Design view is move the fields he plans to use from the tblDrug object to the data access page. He could use fields from different objects, but in this case, his plan only includes fields from tblDrug. He begins by clicking the expand indicator **+** for tblDrug. He double-clicks the UPN field to add it to the design grid, which also adds a record navigation bar to the navigation section, and then continues double-clicking the fields in tblDrug, except for the Cost and Supplier fields, which he will not include. The data access page now includes 10 controls, arranged in a columnar layout, as shown in Figure 8.14.

Figure 8.14: Fields from tblDrug added to the data access page

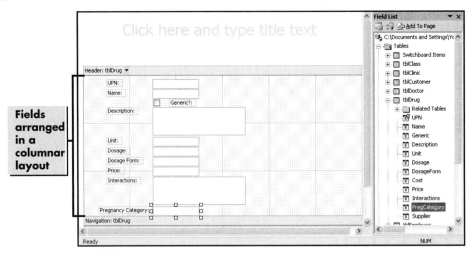

Fields arranged in a columnar layout

As is the case when creating a form or report, Access automatically creates controls that are bound to the fields you add to a data access page. Moving controls in Design view for a data access page is similar to moving and resizing controls in Design view for forms and reports. Don moves the Generic, Dosage, Dosage Form, and Pregnancy Category labels and controls, resizes the text box controls for the UPN, Name, Unit, Dosage, Dosage Form, Price, and Pregnancy Category fields, and aligns the text box labels on the right side. Don reduces the height of the header section by dragging its bottom border up to below the Interactions field. The revised data access page is shown in Figure 8.15.

Figure 8.15: Data access page after resizing and rearranging the controls

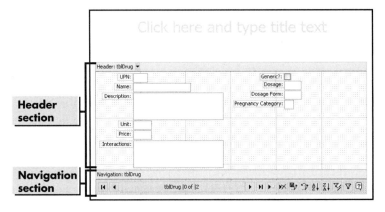

Header section

Navigation section

Similar to forms and reports, data access pages are divided into sections. Most data access pages have header and navigation sections. The **header section** displays the data from the database object(s) on which the data access page is based. The **navigation section** contains the record navigation bar, which Access creates automatically. The two other sections, which do not appear in Figure 8.15, are the caption section and footer section. The **caption section** might contain text boxes and other controls to display captions. It appears above the group header and cannot be used for bound controls. The **footer section** is used to display values and to calculate summary values for groups of records. You can display and hide the different sections of a data access page by clicking the list arrow next to the header section name and then clicking the section to display or hide. For example, you might want to view just the head of the household information without seeing the individual household members.

Customizing the Record Navigation Bar

The record navigation bar contains buttons that let users scroll through, sort, filter, add, save, and delete records. Table 8.1 identifies the buttons on the default record navigation bar, along with their class names and descriptions.

Table 8.1: Record navigation bar buttons and functions

Button	Button Function
First	Displays the first record
Previous	Displays the previous record
Recordset label	Displays the table or query name on which the data access page is based, the current record number, and the total number of records in the current dataset
Next	Displays the next record
Last	Displays the last record
New	Clears the data access page and accepts data entry of a new record
Delete	Deletes the current record
Save	Saves the current record
Undo	Cancels the last change
Sort Ascending	Sorts the data in ascending order based on the selected field
Sort Descending	Sorts the data in descending order based on the selected field
Filter by Selection	Filters the data and displays matching records based on the value in the current field
Filter Toggle	Removes or applies a filter
Help	Opens the Microsoft Access Data Access Pages Help window

In some cases, Don might want to retain the default record navigation bar because it includes the necessary tools for interacting with the data displayed in the data access page. However, in other cases, he might want to remove buttons to prevent users from accessing certain functions. For example, if Don does not want a user to be able to delete a record displayed by the data access page, he can right-click the record navigation bar in the navigation section, and then point to Navigation Buttons on the shortcut menu. The menu that opens, which appears in Figure 8.16, includes check marks to the left of each button on the record navigation bar.

Figure 8.16: Navigation Buttons menu

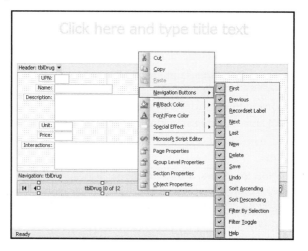

To remove the Delete button, Don clicks the Delete option on the shortcut menu. Access removes the Delete button and organizes the remaining buttons on the record navigation bar to reflect the deletion of a button. To prevent users from adding new records to tblDrug and saving changes to records, Don also removes the New, Undo, and Save buttons from the record navigation bar.

In other situations, Don might decide to replace the *entire* record navigation bar with buttons that he creates and defines. The Visibility property for an object controls the display of the object. Three options—inherit, visible, and hidden—control the visibility of the record navigation bar. Don changes the property to hidden, which hides the record navigation bar in Page view. However, the record navigation bar is still visible in Design view.

How To

Change the Visibility Property of the Record Navigation Bar

1. In Design view, select the record navigation bar.

2. Click the Properties button 🖻 on the Page Design toolbar to open the Navigation properties dialog box for the object.

3. Click the All tab.

4. Scroll to the Visibility property, select the text in the Visibility text box, and then type "hidden" to hide the record navigation bar, or type "inherit" to display it.

Even though the record navigation bar still appears in Design view, when Don views the data access page in Page view, the record navigation bar is hidden, as shown in Figure 8.17.

Figure 8.17: Hidden record navigation bar in Page view

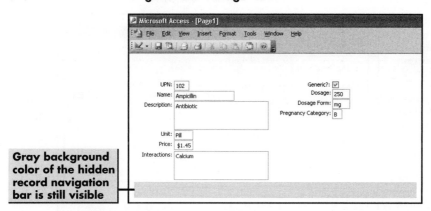

Gray background color of the hidden record navigation bar is still visible

Don wants to change the gray background color of the navigation section to transparent so customers cannot see it. He returns to Design view, clicks the navigation section to select it, clicks the list arrow for the Fill/Back Color button on the Formatting toolbar, and then clicks Transparent in the menu. The background color of the navigation section changes to transparent, which means that regardless of the background color used in the page, users will not see it.

Now that Don has hidden the record navigation bar, he needs to add user-defined buttons so that customers can scroll through the drug records in the data access page. To do this, Don increases the height of the navigation section to make room for the command buttons that he adds. With the navigation section still selected, he uses the mouse pointer to drag the bottom edge of the data access page down approximately one-half inch. Then he selects the record navigation bar and drags it to the bottom of the page.

Adding Command Buttons to a Data Access Page

Don can add the command buttons that will let customers scroll through the records by programming them or by using the Control Wizard. With the Control Wizards button on the Toolbox selected, he clicks the Command Button button on the Toolbar to select it, and then clicks the upper-left corner of the navigation section. The Command Button Wizard starts, as shown in Figure 8.18.

8

Level 1

Figure 8.18: Command Button Wizard dialog box

Preview of the command button using the current selections

Categories of predefined actions

Command button in the navigation section

Specific actions

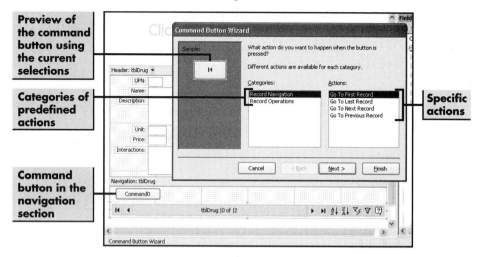

The Command Button Wizard includes different categories of predefined actions that you can use in a data access page. Don's command buttons must provide the functionality to navigate the records, so he selects the Record Navigation category. The first button will move to the first record, so he selects the Go To First Record action and clicks the Next button to open the dialog box shown in Figure 8.19.

Figure 8.19: Formatting the command button

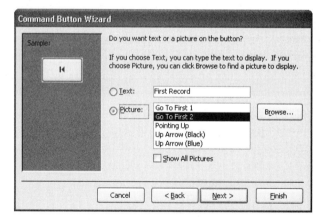

In this dialog box, Don selects the option button to include text or a predefined picture on the command button. The Sample section on the left side of the dialog box provides a preview of the button as Don creates it. He wants the button to display the text "Move First," so he selects the Text option button, selects the default text in the text box, and then types "Move First." After making these changes, the Sample section displays the command button with text on it. Don clicks the Next button to open the next dialog box, which requests a name for the command button. To make things easy, Don uses the name "cmdMoveFirst" for the command button, and then clicks the Finish button. The wizard closes and the command button uses the new caption. Don wants the buttons to have equal sizes with the default height and a width of one inch. With the cmdMoveFirst command button selected, Don clicks the Properties button [icon] on the Page Design toolbar, and then changes the Width property to 1 inch. Don adds the other command buttons to the data access page, using the names cmdMovePrevious, cmdMoveNext, and cmdMoveLast, and resizes them to 1-inch widths. Figure 8.20 shows the command buttons after Don aligned them on their top edges.

Figure 8.20: Command buttons added to navigation section

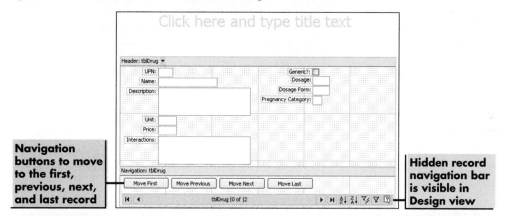

Navigation buttons to move to the first, previous, next, and last record

Hidden record navigation bar is visible in Design view

After doing this work, Don saves the data access page by clicking the Save button [icon] on the Page Design toolbar. In the Save As Data Access Page dialog box, Don types Drugs.htm as the filename for the HTML document. He changes to Page view to preview the page, which appears in Figure 8.21. He uses the command buttons to scroll through the records in the page, which are sorted in ascending order by the values in the UPN field.

Figure 8.21: Data access page with command buttons and hidden record navigation bar

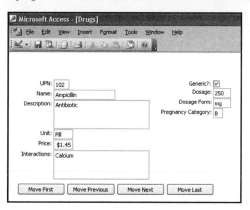

Changing a Data Access Page to Read-Only

Even though he hid the record navigation bar, Don needs to make sure that customers cannot use the keyboard or mouse to change the records in tblDrug. To prevent users from making changes, Don changes the page so that the page will not permit users to add, delete, or edit records displayed by the page.

How To

Prevent Additions, Deletions, and Changes in a Data Access Page

1. In Design view, click the list arrow on the header section, and then click Group Level Properties on the shortcut menu.

2. Change the AllowAdditions property to False to prevent users from adding records.

3. Change the AllowDeletions property to False to prevent users from deleting records.

4. Change the AllowEdits property to False to prevent users from editing records.

After changing the page properties to prevent updates, Don changes to Page view and attempts to change the data in the page. The properties he set work correctly and he is not able to make any changes. However, as Don uses the command buttons to scroll through the records in the page, he decides that the list of drugs is too long and that users need a way to find a specific drug in the list. He decides to change the Name text box to a list box so users can select the desired drug from a list.

Adding a List Box to a Data Access Page

Don changes the text box control for the Name field to a list box so customers can select the drug they need from a list of drugs arranged in alphabetical order, instead of using the command buttons to scroll through the drugs until they find the one they need.

How To

Change a Text Box Control to a List Box Control

1. In Design view, right-click the text box control that you want to change to open the shortcut menu.

2. Click Group Filter Control on the shortcut menu.

Don changes to Page view, clicks the Name list arrow, and the drugs from tblDrug appear in the list box (see Figure 8.22). To select a drug and display its information, customers can click the drug they need from the list.

Figure 8.22: Name field changed to a list box

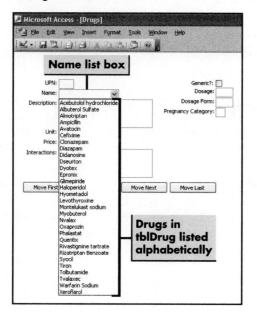

As Don examines the drug list, he realizes that the list box might not be wide enough to accommodate longer drug names that might be added to tblDrug in the future. To correct this problem, he returns to Design view and increases the width of the Name list box by selecting the list box control, and then dragging the middle-right sizing handle to the right. After changing back to Page view, he clicks the list box again and sees that the complete drug names are visible in the list.

When you change a text box control to a list box control, any command buttons in the page stop working because the list box control becomes the page's navigation. Clicking a command button results in a message box indicating that the command is not available. To correct this problem, Don needs to either hide or delete the command buttons. He decides to hide them so he can use them later if he redesigns the data access page. He changes to Design view, selects all four command buttons, and then uses the Properties dialog box to change their Visibilty properties to hidden. Figure 8.23 shows the data access page with the resized Name list box and the hidden command buttons.

Figure 8.23: Revised Drugs page

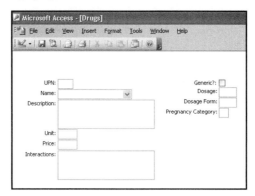

Now that the data access page displays the correct data and the records in tblDrug are protected from changes by customers, Don can work on the appearance of the data access page.

Applying a Theme to a Data Access Page

Because customers will access the Drugs page over the Internet, Don wants to make sure that the page has a professional appearance and is easy to read. An easy and quick way to format a data access page is to apply a theme to it. A **theme** is a predefined collection of design elements that format the text, objects, and page with coordinated fonts, colors, backgrounds, and other design elements. The themes installed on different computers vary because users can add and create new themes using the Microsoft Office CD or the Microsoft Office Online Web site. The names of the themes appear in the Choose a Theme list box and a preview of the selected theme appears in the sample box. Because the Drugs page does not have a theme applied to it, its current theme is "(No Theme)," as shown in Figure 8.24.

Figure 8.24: Theme dialog box

Installed themes

Sample styles for the selected theme

How To

Apply and Remove a Theme

1. To apply a theme to a page, change to Design view, click Format on the menu bar, and then click Theme. The Theme dialog box opens.

2. Preview the installed themes by clicking each one in the Choose a Theme list box, and then viewing the sample in the dialog box.

3. If desired, include vivid colors, active graphics, and/or a background image in the theme by adding check marks to the Vivid Colors, Active Graphics, and Background Image check boxes.

4. If desired, click the Set Default button to use the selected theme for all pages created in the current database.

5. Click the OK button.

6. To remove a theme from a page, use the Theme dialog box to select the (No Theme) theme, and then click the OK button.

Best Practice

Choosing an Appropriate Theme for a Data Access Page

The different themes that you can apply to a Web page reflect different styles. Some themes are professional and include fonts used in business correspondence, such as Times New Roman, and subdued but complementary colors. Other themes are wild and include bright colors and more casual fonts, such as Comic Sans. The different themes also use different styles for bullet characters, command buttons, and different hyperlinks. Most Web designers suggest formatting Web pages to reflect the audience for which they are intended. In addition, most Web designers avoid using dark page backgrounds because they might make the page difficult to read. Some Web sites follow accessibility standards for disabled users who might have difficulty seeing certain color combinations and smaller font sizes or reading Web page content by using programs that "speak" the content for visually impaired users. You can learn more about Web page design and accessibility standards by searching the Web for "Web content accessibility" or a similarly worded search string. The World Wide Web Consortium (W3C) sets standards for accessibility, and other Web sites provide tools that analyze online content for compliance with the W3C standards.

When you use data access pages in a Web site, it is important that the pages match the formatting and style of other Web pages in the Web site, even if those pages were created using a program other than Access. Customers expect all Web pages to have the same presentation so they can easily identify the pages as belonging to a particular site. One way to ensure consistency is to format all pages using the same theme. You can also include the organization's logo in Web pages to associate the page with the organization. When Web pages in a single Web site use different styles and formats, customers might feel as though they are viewing a different Web site when they are not. One way to ensure a consistent appearance is to use Access to set a default theme for all Web pages it creates. You can set a default theme by selecting a theme, and then clicking the Set Default button in the Theme dialog box. When additional pages are created, Access automatically applies the default theme to the pages.

The Romanesque theme uses a light background picture and Times New Roman and Book Antiqua fonts, and conveys a professional appearance. Don selects the Romanesque theme and applies it to the page, as shown in Figure 8.25.

Figure 8.25: Romanesque theme applied to data access page

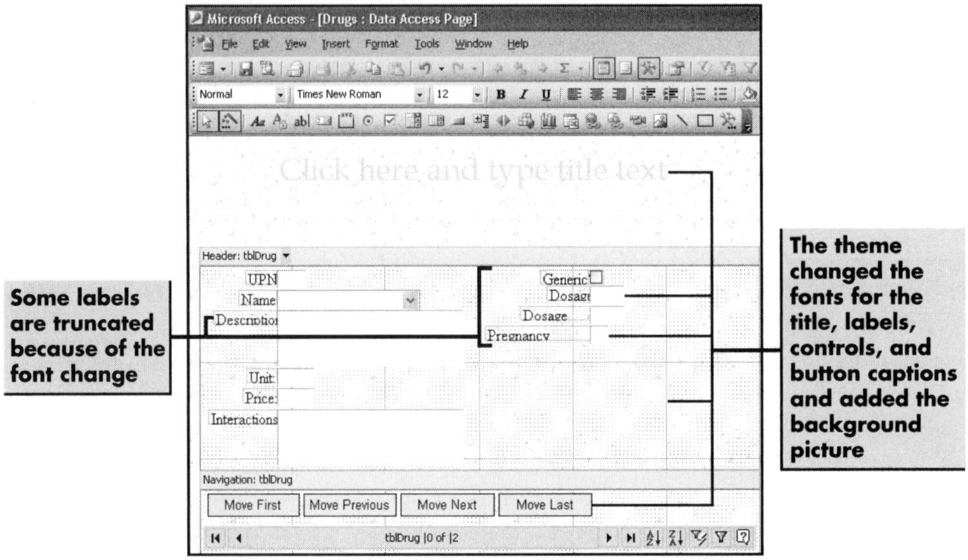

Because the theme uses fonts and font sizes different from the ones used when no theme is applied, the text in the labels changes to 12-point Times New Roman font. Some of the text in the labels no longer fits in the text box controls. To fix this problem, Don presses and holds the Ctrl key and clicks each label on the page, and then changes the font size to 10 points. To distinguish the labels from the values in the text boxes, he also changes the labels to bold. After making this change, he rearranges the labels and text boxes on the page so that the text in each label is correctly aligned and fully displayed, and then he moves the controls to make the necessary room for the labels. Don changes to Page view. Figure 8.26 shows the data access page after making these changes.

Figure 8.26: Resized labels and revised fonts in Page view

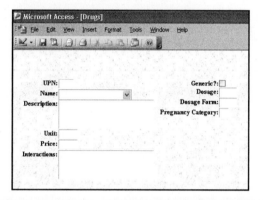

Adding a Title to a Data Access Page

The page title that Don used when he saved the page will appear in the browser's title bar when a customer views the page. However, Don knows that using a descriptive page title in the page itself is a good way to identify the page's contents. He changes back to Design view, clicks the title placeholder text ("Click here and type title text") at the top of the page, and then types "Drug Information for Customers." The Romanesque theme applies 24-point, bold, Book Antiqua font to the title. Don saves the page and then previews it in Internet Explorer to check its appearance and function. Don likes the page's new appearance, but realizes that customers will need some directions for using the page. He also wants to include a note about using Internet Explorer to view the page. Don returns to Design view, adds the note below the page title, and then saves and previews the page again. Figure 8.27 shows the completed page.

Figure 8.27: Resized labels and revised fonts

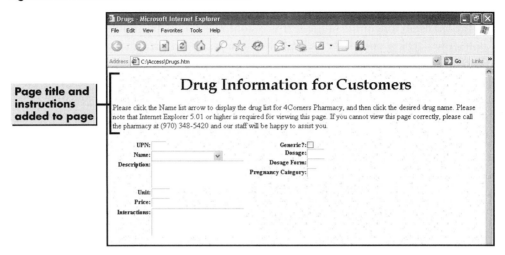

Best Practice

Testing a Data Access Page

The final step in creating any Web page is to test it in multiple browsers and using different computers that are running different operating systems and that use different monitors. Although HTML is generally interpreted in the same way by different browsers, there are some differences that you must test for and correct. For example, some computers cannot display colors in the same way because the operating systems running on them or the monitors attached to them cannot display the color used in the page. A color that looks red on your PC might be displayed as pink on a Macintosh computer or on a computer with a very old monitor. To prevent problems displaying colors, when they select colors, most developers use a browser-safe color palette, which is a palette of 216 colors that are displayed consistently on all computers. To learn more about using colors in Web pages, use any search engine to search using the key terms "browser-safe colors."

Other computers might not have the correct browser to display a data access page. In these cases, the script that Access adds to the page should help the user to view the page correctly. Some Web servers include log files that identify the browser version that accesses the Web site's pages. You can examine these logs to determine which browsers and operating systems your customers use to view the site. If you find that the majority of your target audience uses a browser or operating system that does not support data access pages, you might consider including the content of the data access pages in HTML documents that do not use scripts so your audience can still access the content.

Steps To Success: Level 1

As private insurance becomes more affordable and available in Canada, Joan Gabel knows that it will be important to provide information to the pharmacy's customers and potential customers about the health insurance policies that the Hudson Bay Pharmacy accepts. Joan wants to provide this information in a Web page and publish the page on the pharmacy's Web site. She wants you to make sure that customers can view the data about health insurance companies, but that they cannot make any changes to the database.

Joan also just finished several employee performance reviews and wants to use a data access page to change the hourly rate to give some employees raises. She asks you to create a Web page that lets her complete this work. You'll store this page on the company's intranet and not on the company's Web site.

Complete the following:

1. Start Access and open the **Hudson.mdb** database from the STS folder.

2. Create a data access page based on tblHealthPlan that will satisfy Joan's goal of providing information about health insurance carriers to customers. Exclude the Days field from the data access page and sort the records in ascending order by the plan name. Make sure that customers cannot add, delete, or change records using the data access page. The page should include command buttons for navigating to the first, previous, next, and last records.

3. Apply an appropriate theme, a page title, and a note with instructions for using the page to the data access page.

4. Save the HTML document as **Health Insurance Companies.htm** in the STS folder, and then test the page in a Web browser.

5. Create a data access page for Joan to use to update the salary information for active hourly employees. She wants to view employee records with the employee ID, first name, last name, hourly rate, and job title for each employee. Joan wants to sort the employee records by the employee's last name. Save the HTML document for the data access page as **Salary Increase.htm** in the STS folder.

6. Add an appropriate page title and theme to the page.

7. Change the RecordsetLabel property to Employee.

8. Change the hourly rate for Catherine Adams-Cook to $9.25 and change the hourly rate for Christine Sullivan to $9.00.

9. Use the data access page to determine how many employees earn $9.00 per hour and to determine the number of technicians working at the pharmacy.

10. Close the **Hudson.mdb** database and Access.

LEVEL 2

USING SCRIPTS TO EXTEND THE FUNCTIONALITY OF DATA ACCESS PAGES

ACCESS 2003 SKILLS TRAINING

- **Create data access pages using the Page Wizard**
- **Use data access pages (dynamic HTML documents)**

USING SCRIPTS IN WEB PAGES

Don included a message in the Drugs page telling customers that they need Internet Explorer 5.01 or higher to view the page. For customers without the correct version of Internet Explorer, he provided the pharmacy's phone number so they can still obtain the information they need. When he created the data access page, Access did something similar by including a script in the page to determine if the user's browser can run the active content in the page. For example, if you open the Drugs page in Firefox, it looks like Figure 8.28.

Figure 8.28: Data access page displayed in Firefox

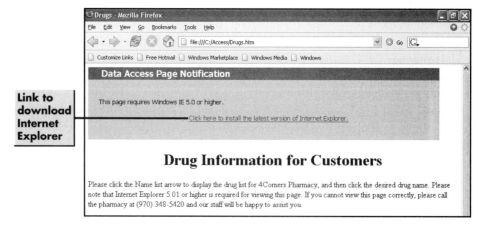

Access included a script in the data access page to test the user's browser to determine if it supports data access pages. The script includes a link in the page for the user to install the correct browser. Figure 8.29 shows part of the HTML document for the Drugs.htm data access page. The script that Access included to check the browser used to open the page begins with the opening <SCRIPT> tag and ends with a closing </SCRIPT> tag (which is not visible in the figure).

Figure 8.29: HTML document for the Drugs page

Script that checks the user's browser

```
Source of: file:///C:/Access/Drugs.htm - Mozilla Firefox
File  Edit  View

<SCRIPT language=Javascript id=MSODSC_Validation>
validateBrowser();

function validateBrowser() {
        strVers=navigator.appVersion
        strName=navigator.appName
        strPlat=navigator.platform
        intIndex1=strVers.indexOf("MSIE");
        intIndex1=intIndex1+5
        intIndex2=strVers.lastIndexOf(";");
        intVer=strVers.substring(intIndex1, intIndex2);
        intVer=parseInt(intVer)
        if (strName=="Microsoft Internet Explorer" && strPlat=="Win32" && intVer>="5") {
        validateOWC();
        }
        else {
            strMsgGetIE="<TABLE cellSpacing=0 cellPadding=0 width='95%' border=0
height='8'><TR>"
            strMsgGetIE+="<TD bgColor='#336699' height=25 width=15> </TD><TD
bgColor='#666666' width=500px><FONT face=Tahoma "
            strMsgGetIE+="size=4 color=white><b> Data Access Page
Notification</B></FONT></TD></TR>"
            strMsgGetIE+="<TR><TD bgColor='#cccccc' width=15> </TD><TD
bgColor='#cccccc' width=500px><BR>"
            strMsgGetIE+="<p><font face='Tahoma' size='2'>"
            strMsgGetIE+="This page requires Windows IE 5.0 or higher.</p>"
            strMsgGetIE+="<a
href='http://www.microsoft.com/isapi/redir.dll?Prd=Office&Sbp=Access&Pver=10&Ar=DPdesigner&Sba=IE
align='center'>"
            strMsgGetIE+="Click here to install the latest version of Internet
Explorer.</a></font></p><br></TD></TR></TABLE>"
            document.write(strMsgGetIE)
```

Access generates the required code for some scripts, sometimes without you even knowing about it. For example, the navigation command buttons that Don included in the Drugs data access page use scripts to move to the first, previous, next, and last records in tblDrug. He didn't need to do anything to write the scripts—the Command Button Wizard added them automatically, based on the options he selected when he created the command buttons.

Although you can take additional courses to learn how to write scripts to do various tasks in Web pages, you can perform some sophisticated tasks by learning how to write some simple statements in a scripting language. A **scripting language** is a programming language that you use to write code that an interpreter executes. When you include a script in a Web page, the script is referred to as an **embedded script** because it is embedded in the HTML document that contains it. When a Web browser reads the opening <SCRIPT> tag in the HTML document, one of two things happens:

1. The browser runs the script.

2. The browser determines that it cannot run the script because it lacks an interpreter for the language in which the script is written. In this case, the browser cannot execute the code contained between the <SCRIPT> and </SCRIPT> tags and either displays it in the Web page or ignores it.

When a browser can interpret the script, the browser's interpreter translates the code in the script into an executable format so it can perform the actions contained in the script. Older versions of some Web browsers might not be compatible with recent versions of scripting languages. The script that Access inserted in the Drugs data access page that checks the user's browser to determine if the browser supports data access pages is written in JavaScript, which is a common scripting language used in Web pages, because nearly all browsers include an interpreter for executing its code. Don's note in the page provides instructions for people using very old browsers that cannot process the script that Access added. Two common scripting languages that are used to enhance Web pages are VBScript and JavaScript—VBScript was originally developed for Internet Explorer and JavaScript was originally developed for Navigator. Currently, only Internet Explorer has an interpreter that can execute scripts written in VBScript, which is why data access pages work only in that browser.

When a browser encounters the opening <SCRIPT> tag in an HTML document, most developers include the language attribute to identify the scripting language used to write the script. In some cases, the language attribute might also identify the version of the scripting language. For example, the opening <SCRIPT> tag for a script written in JavaScript might be <SCRIPT language=Javascript>. Most Web browsers, including Internet Explorer, Firefox, and Navigator, load the HTML document and then interpret the script. For browsers that can interpret the scripting language, the browser's interpreter executes the contents of the script. When a browser cannot interpret a script, it simply displays the code for the script in the Web page, as if it were text. To prevent this from happening, most developers include the lines for the scripts that will not work for all browsers within the HTML comment tags (<!-- and -->) to prevent browsers that cannot interpret the script from displaying the script's code in the Web page. In this case, the browser simply treats the lines of code in the script as a comment and ignores the script.

In addition to programming command buttons to move through records in a data access page, scripts might cause text to scroll across the page, display the current date or the date a page was last updated, or validate data that a user enters into a form. Most developers include scripts in the head section of the HTML document so the browser can load them before displaying the Web page's content, which is contained in the body section of the HTML document. For some scripts, such as ones associated with a specific command button or form object (such as a text box into which a user enters his name or phone number), the developer might include the script with the object instead of in the head section. An HTML document can contain one or more scripts to add functionality and dynamic content to a Web page. The compatible browser loads each script as it encounters it, interprets the actions, and then executes the contents.

Although he is satisfied with the Drugs page and the list box for finding drugs, Don knows that the pharmacy will be adding many more records to tblDrug over time. As the list of drugs in the table increases, the list box in the Drugs data access page will become too large for customers to scroll through all of the drug names to find the one they are looking for. Most customers will expect the page to include a way to search for the desired drug. To add this functionality to the page, Don needs to write a script that lets customers find a drug by typing its name in a dialog box. When the user clicks the Find button in the data access page, the browser should open a dialog box and request the drug name. The user enters the drug name in a text box, and then clicks the OK button to close the dialog box. If a matching drug record is stored in tblDrug, the data access page displays the drug information. If there is no matching drug record in tblDrug, the browser displays a message box indicating that no drug was found.

ADDING A COMMAND BUTTON TO THE PAGE AND STARTING THE SCRIPT EDITOR

Microsoft Visual Basic Scripting Edition, or **VBScript**, is a scripting language that you can use to enhance the functionality of a Web page. Unlike JavaScript, only Internet Explorer can interpret the commands in scripts written using VBScript—this is why users of the Drugs page and other data access pages need to use Internet Explorer to view them. To enhance the data access page with a find feature, Don opens the Drugs data access page in Design view. Because the page cannot contain a list box and command buttons, he deletes the Name list box control from the page and then uses the field list to add it back as a text box control. Then he changes the font of the Name label to match the style of other labels in the page and increases the width of the text box control so it will accommodate the longest drug name. He also changes the Visibility property for the command buttons in the navigation section to inherit so they are visible on the page again.

Don's next task is to add a "Find" command button to the data access page. Instead of creating a new command button, Don copies the cmdMoveLast command button, pastes it on the page, and changes the properties of the new button to use "Find" as the label and "cmdFind" as the command button name.

How To

Copy and Paste a Command Button and Set Its Properties
1. In Design view, right-click the command button that you want to copy, and then click Copy on the shortcut menu.
2. Click the Paste button 🖻 on the Page Design toolbar.
3. If necessary, move the new command button to the correct location on the data access page and resize it.
4. Click the command button to select it, and then click the Properties button 🖺 on the Page Design toolbar.
5. Click the Other tab.
6. Change the Id property to the desired command button name.
7. Change the InnerText property to the desired button label.

After creating the Find command button and setting its properties, Don clicks the Microsoft Script Editor button 💿 on the Page Design toolbar to open the Microsoft Script Editor window for the Drugs data access page. See Figure 8.30. **Microsoft Script Editor** is the program that Access uses to create and edit scripts written in VBScript.

Figure 8.30: Microsoft Script Editor window

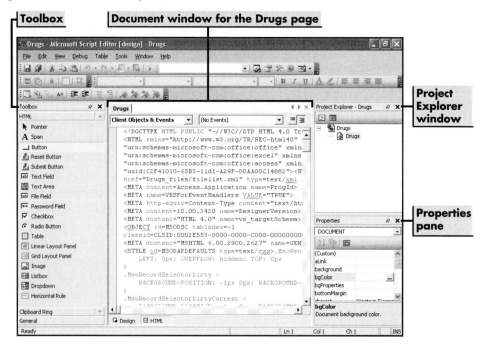

The Script Editor includes several panes to work with scripts. The **Toolbox** on the left side of the window includes the objects that you can place on a data access page, similar to the Toolbox that you see in Design view for a data access page. The HTML document for the Drugs data access page appears in the center pane, which is called the **document window**. You can use the scroll bars on the document window to view the HTML tags and scripts in the data access page. The list boxes on top of the document window let you select objects and events. The Object list box contains the objects in the data access page that you created, such as cmdFind and the labels for the text box controls. When you select an object using the Objects list box, the Event list box lets you choose the event to associate with the object. For example, clicking a command button with the Object list box displays the events associated with command buttons. By default, the entire HTML document is displayed in the document window. You can view only the scripts by clicking the Script Only View button ▤ on the document window. Clicking the Full HTML View button ▤ on the document window displays the full HTML document, including the HTML tags and scripts. Choosing the view is a matter of personal preference; in some cases, you might want to view only the scripts and in other cases, you might want to see the full HTML document.

The **Project Explorer window** in the upper-right pane lets you choose between the open HTML documents in Script Editor. The **Properties pane** includes properties that you can set for a data access page, such as the page's background color or default scripting language. Because Don does not need to switch between open projects, set any page properties, or add any controls to the page, he closes the Toolbox, Project Explorer, and Properties panes by clicking their Close buttons so he can view more of the HTML document for the data access page. He also clicks the Script Only View button ▤ to see only the scripts in the page. Figure 8.31 shows the Script Editor window after making these changes. The script in the document window is the one that Access created to identify the user's browser when the page is loaded.

Figure 8.31: Script Only view of the Drugs page

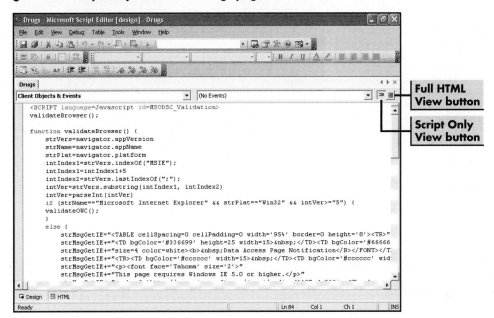

The scripts in the Drugs page identify the user's browser when the page is loaded, and provide the instructions for the four command buttons in the navigation section of the data access page. Each script begins with the opening <SCRIPT> tag and ends with the closing </SCRIPT> tag. The scripts for the command buttons were written in Javascript.

WRITING THE SCRIPT FOR THE FIND COMMAND BUTTON

Because Don already created the cmdFind command button in the data access page, he begins by selecting the cmdFind object using the Object list box. When you are learning to write scripts, it is easier to use the tools in Design view to create the objects and controls on the page, and then use the Script Editor to write the scripts that execute their functions. Don clicks the Object list arrow, and then clicks cmdFind in the list box. When he clicks the Event list arrow, he sees the events for command buttons. Don wants to trigger the script when the user clicks the Find button, so he chooses the onclick event. The Script Editor starts a new script in the document window, inserts the opening and closing tags, and includes attributes in the opening <script> tag to identify the scripting language (vbscript), the object (cmdFind), and the event (onclick). The Script Editor also adds the opening and closing HTML comment tags inside the opening and closing script tags, and then positions the insertion point between them. This structure ensures that browsers that cannot interpret the script do not display the code for the script and ignore it. See Figure 8.32.

Figure 8.32: Script for the cmdFind command button

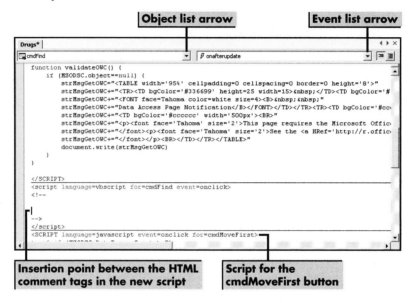

Notice that the different scripts in the page are separated by horizontal lines and that each script is enclosed within its own set of <SCRIPT> tags.

Don has already completed the first step in writing a script—he chose the onclick event so that the script is executed when the user clicks the Find button in the page. Now he needs to write the script to execute the actions that accept the customer's input (the drug name) and search tblDrug for a matching drug. Don needs to declare a variable to store the drug name entered by the customer. He chooses the variable name "strDrugName" because it is easy to associate with the user's entry, which is a string. He uses a Dim statement to declare the variable, and types the following first line of the script:

Dim strDrugName

Unlike VBA, VBScript does not require you to declare variables before using them. Although you can use a Dim statement to declare a variable, omitting the Dim statement results in the data type being assigned when a variable receives an initial value. Similar to VBA, variable names should include a prefix to indicate the variable type; in this case, Don used "str" to indicate that the variable stores a string.

Next, Don needs to use a function to open the dialog box into which the customer enters the drug name. VBScript includes many functions that you can use to enhance a data access page. Table 8.2 identifies some common functions that you might use in your data access pages.

Table 8.2: VBScript functions

Function (Arguments)	Description
Date	Returns the current system date.
DateDiff(interval, date1, date2)	Calculates the specified *interval* between the values specified as *date1* and *date2*. Some common intervals are day (d), month (m), year (yyyy), hours (h), minutes (n), or seconds (s).
FormatCurrency(expression)	Returns *expression* in currency format.
FormatPercent(expression)	Returns *expression* as a percentage.
InputBox(prompt[,title])	Displays the message *prompt* in a dialog box with the optional *title* and a text box into which the user enters a value, and then returns the contents of the text box.
IsNumeric(expression)	Tests *expression* and returns the value True if the expression is a number or the value False if the expression is not a number.
LCase(string)	Returns a *string* that has been converted to lowercase letters. If the string is null, the value null is returned.
Left(string,length)	Returns the specified number of characters in *length* from the left side of the value *string*.
Len("string")	Returns the number of characters in *string*.
LTrim("string")	Returns a copy of *string* with any space characters removed from the left side of the string. If the string is null, the value null is returned.
MsgBox(prompt[,buttons][,title])	Displays the message *prompt* in a dialog box with the optional *title*, waits for the user to click a button specified as *buttons*, and then returns the value of the button the user clicked. Some commonly used *buttons* values are 0 (the default, OK), 1 (OK and Cancel), and 4 (Yes and No).
Now	Returns the date and time using the computer's system date.
Right(string,length)	Returns the specified number of characters in *length* from the right side of the value *string*. If the string is null, the value null is returned.
RTrim("string")	Returns a copy of *string* with any space characters removed from the right side of the string.
Time	Returns the time using the computer's system time.
Trim("string")	Returns a copy of *string* with any space characters removed from the left and right sides of the string.
UCase(string)	Returns a *string* that has been converted to uppercase letters. If the string is null, the value null is returned.

Because Don needs the user to input the name of the drug to find, Don decides to use the InputBox function. This function requires a prompt that contains the message to display in the dialog box. Don also decides to include an optional title for the dialog box. Because

8

Level 2

he only needs to include the OK and Cancel buttons in the dialog box, which is the default if no buttons value is supplied, he does not need to specify a buttons value. He enters the following statement in the script:

```
strDrugName=InputBox("Enter a drug name to find","Find Drug")
```

When the browser interprets this statement, it opens a dialog box with the title "Find Drug" and a message to instruct the user on what to do ("Enter a drug name to find"). The user enters the drug name in the text box, and then clicks the OK button to submit the value. The value entered in the text box is stored in the variable named strDrugName.

Best Practice

Increasing Your Scripting Knowledge
Although you can use the information provided in Level 2 of this chapter to write some simple scripts, mastering a scripting language requires an understanding of basic programming concepts and skills, and the rules (syntax) of the language. Microsoft Script Editor installs a Help system that includes tutorials and detailed code examples for completing tasks with a script. If you need more information about scripts, you can start Help by clicking the Microsoft Script Editor Help button 🔘 on the Standard toolbar in the Script Editor.

Next, Don must create a variable to store a recordset of the data and write the statement to connect the recordset to the data access page. A **recordset** is a snapshot of the records in a table or query that is used to view or update the data. Don creates a clone of the data in tblDrug so that he can search and manipulate the data and then display it on the data access page. He adds the statements to the script to perform this task, as shown in Figure 8.33.

Figure 8.33: Creating a recordset for tblDrug

In the Set statement, MSODSC.DataPages(0) refers to the data connection source of the data access page. MSODSC (Microsoft Office Data Source Control) is the reference to the object that describes the data. The index, 0, refers to the first page opened; in this case, it is the only page that is opened.

Next, Don needs to add a statement to locate the drug in the Name field of tblDrug using the value stored in strDrugName. He uses the recordset Find command, which searches the recordset for a matching record. The command Don uses is:

```
rsDrug.Find "Name= '" & strDrugName & "'"
```

The Find statement includes a condition that concatenates the statement with the value entered by the customer and stored in strDrugName. The user-entered value is enclosed in single quotation marks because it is a string. For example, if the customer enters the drug name Tiron, the statement is concatenated as follows:

$$Name='Tiron'$$

If the Find command locates the record the customer requested, the script must note its position in the recordset so it can display the drug information in the data access page. When the Find command locates the first record in the recordset that matches the user-entered drug name, it creates a record pointer in the recordset called a **bookmark**. If the Find command does not find a matching record, the end-of-file marker is set to True. Don uses the following If statement to check for the end-of-file marker and display either an error message indicating that no matching record was found or the record at the bookmark. If no matching record is found, Don uses the MsgBox function to let the customer know that no record was found. The MsgBox function appears in the If statement and is called when there is no match. The MsgBox function that Don uses displays the message "No drug found." in a dialog box with the title "Search Complete." The value 0 in the function includes the OK button in the dialog box, which the user clicks after reading the message.

```
If (rsDrug.EOF) Then
    MsgBox "No drug found.",0,"Search Complete"
Else
    MSODSC.DataPages(0).Recordset.Bookmark=rsDrug.Bookmark
End If
```

If the If statement reaches the end of the file without finding a matching record, the MsgBox function displays the message. Otherwise, the Else statement displays the record marked by the bookmark. Figure 8.34 shows the script for the Find command button.

Figure 8.34: If statement added to cmdFind command button script

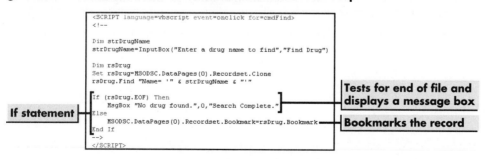

Don can test the script by clicking the Save button 🖫 on the Standard toolbar, and then switching to Access and viewing the Drugs data access page in Page view. He clicks the Find button and the InputBox function opens the dialog box shown in Figure 8.35.

Figure 8.35: Testing the Find button

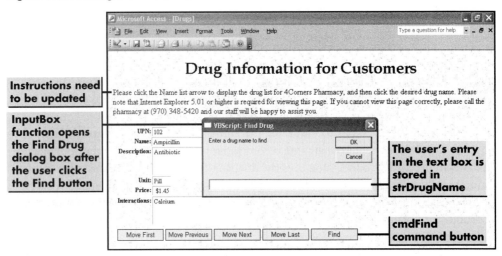

The InputBox function adds the title "Find Drug" to the dialog box and creates the message "Enter a drug name to find." Don types the drug name Tiron in the text box, and then clicks the OK button. The dialog box closes, the If statement locates the record with the drug name Tiron in the recordset, and the data access page displays the drug information for the selected drug. The page correctly located an existing drug. However, Don realizes that the instructions he added to the page are now incorrect. He changes to Design view and updates the page instructions so customers know how to use the Find button.

Don wants to try the Find button again, but this time he wants to test the page to make sure that the script correctly handles the situation in which no matching drug is found. He clicks the Find button again, enters "Don" in the text box, and then clicks the OK button. Figure 8.36 shows the Search Complete dialog box that opens, indicating that no drug was found.

Figure 8.36: Testing the Find button when no matching record is found

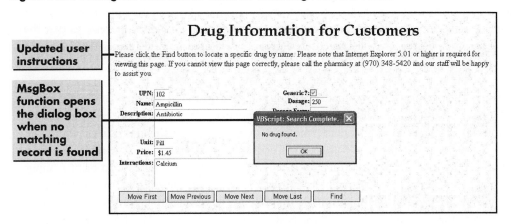

The page works correctly in Page view. Don also tests the page in Internet Explorer and finds that it works correctly. He makes a note to himself to test the page again after publishing it on the Web site to ensure that customers will not have any problems using the page. The Drugs page is complete.

If Don adds a field to tblDrug in the future, and wants to display the new field in the Drugs data access page, he needs to reset the database connection so the new field will appear in the field list in Design view.

How To

Refresh the Fields in the Data Source for a Data Access Page

1. Open the data access page in Design view. If necessary, display the field list.
2. Click the Page connection properties button 🗔 on the field list. The Data Link Properties dialog box opens.
3. Click the Build button to the right of the Select or enter a database name text box, browse to the drive or folder that contains the database file, and then double-click the database file.
4. Click the Test Connection button to reset the connection string, and then click the OK button to close the message box.
5. Click the OK button to close the Data Link Properties dialog box.
6. If necessary, click the Refresh field list button 🔃 on the field list. New fields in an existing table or query, or new tables or queries, will appear in the field list.

SECURING A DATA ACCESS PAGE BY REQUIRING A LOGIN PASSWORD

When Don first created tblHousehold, which stores data about households, and tblCustomer, which stores data about the people living in each household, he entered a small number of records into each table. When the pharmacy started using the database, the staff had to import and create new household and customer records as customers came to the store. Because this initial time of data entry was conducted in a fast-paced, live environment, Don is concerned about data accuracy. He created these tables to ensure accurate data by using input masks and other validation techniques. However, he realizes that the pace at which customer data was entered probably resulted in a few errors that he could not prevent.

Elaine Estes mentions to Don that she needs to send a letter to customers of the pharmacy who have been taking Oxaprozin, an anti-inflammatory drug that has been recalled. She wants to make sure that customers who have been prescribed this drug know about the recall and also to ask them to contact their doctors to make other arrangements for medication to control their conditions. Don tells Elaine that it will be easy to print mailing labels for customers who have been prescribed Oxaprozin and agrees to complete this work right away. However, as Don considers the request, he realizes that another priority is to make sure that the data in the database is accurate.

The pharmacy staff verifies customer addresses and other information each time they fill a prescription. In addition to this oral verification, Don wants to use a data access page so customers can verify their information online and then contact the pharmacy with any updates. Don is reluctant to let customers change their own data because of the risk of them changing important data, such as their customer or household numbers. To prevent anomalies from entering the database, he decides to create the data access page so that customers can only view their information, and then to ask them to inform the pharmacy of any changes by phone or by sending an e-mail message.

Managing Passwords for Customers

Before creating the Customer Verification data access page, Don needs to consider several issues. First, he needs to make sure that customers can view only their own information using the page. In other words, Ted Sabus should not be able to view the data for Cesar Lopez and vice versa. Don can create the data access page so it prevents users from being able to navigate the records in tblCustomer and tblHousehold, but he needs a way to display the data for Ted Sabus only when Ted properly identifies himself to the database. To accomplish this first goal, Don needs to assign customers login passwords and store them with the customer's record. The original design of tblCustomer did not include a field to store the customer's password. Don subsequently changed the customer information form (see Figure 1.2 in Chapter 1) that all new customers use to provide their personal information to the pharmacy so it contains a space for the pharmacy to assign the customer a unique, eight-character password. The password is included on the inside page of the customer's pharmacy receipt and is printed with a reminder to customers to verify the information the pharmacy stores about them. Existing customers will see their assigned passwords on their next pharmacy orders.

The next task Don needs to complete is to add a field to tblCustomer to store the customer's password. Don knows that the word "Password" is a reserved word in some programming languages so he chooses the name "Pwd" for the new field. He opens tblCustomer in Design view, creates a Text field with eight characters and named Pwd, creates an index on the Pwd field so it prevents customers from having duplicate passwords, and then saves the table design. Then he uses a program that generates strong passwords to assign a password to each customer in the database. Strong passwords are usually seven or more characters that consist of strings of random letters, characters, and symbols. For example, the password generator issued the password j79IKL9z for Ted Sabus. The password generator will issue passwords to new customers and store them in the Pwd field.

Adding a Login Control to the Data Access Page

The next task is for Don to create a query that selects the customer and household information for each customer. He creates and saves qryCustVertification using the Query Wizard. This query selects the CustFirst, CustLast, Phone, DOB, Gender, ChildCap, HeadHH, Allergies, and Pwd fields from tblCustomer and the Address, City, State, and Zip fields from tblHousehold.

Next, Don starts the Page Wizard and selects qryCustVerification as the data source for the data access page. He rearranges and resizes the fields on the data access page in Design view. To prevent people from seeing the customer's password, Don deletes the label for the Pwd field, and then changes the Visibility property of the Pwd text box control to hidden. He also adds a title to the page and a note indicating its use; applies the Romanesque theme to the page; changes the page to read-only by setting the group level AllowAdditions, AllowDeletions, and AllowEdits properties to False; and saves the page using the name Customer Verification. Figure 8.37 shows the data access page.

Figure 8.37: Customer Verification data access page

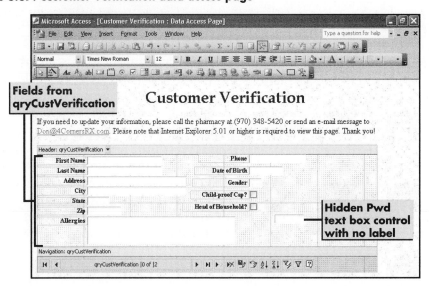

Now Don needs to work on restricting access so customers can view only their own records. He can do this by adding a login control to the navigation section. The login is successful if the customer's password entry matches the hidden password in the header section. If the login is successful, the data access page will display the customer's record. If the login is unsuccessful (the password the customer entered does not match the one in the database), the browser will display a message. Don increases the height of the navigation section, changes the Visibility property of the record navigation bar to hidden and drags it to the bottom of the navigation section, and changes the background color of the navigation section to transparent. He adds a text box control to the navigation section, changes the label text to "Please enter your password:", and changes the Id property for the text box control to txtPwd. Next, he turns off the Control Wizards by clicking the ▨ button on the Toolbox, uses the Command Button button ▨ to add a command button to the right of the text box control, and changes its Id property to cmdLogin and its InnerText property to "Login." Figure 8.38 shows the data access page after making these changes.

Figure 8.38: Login added to navigation section

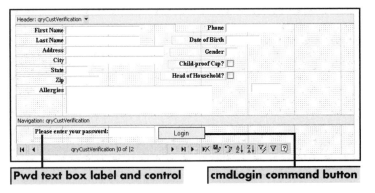

WRITING THE SCRIPT FOR THE LOGIN COMMAND BUTTON

Don needs to write a script for the Login command button that executes after the user enters a password in the text box control and clicks the Login button. The script filters the records in qryCustVerification to locate the one with a matching password stored in the Pwd field. If the passwords match, the page displays the record; if the passwords do not match, the browser opens a dialog box indicating that the login failed.

Don clicks the Microsoft Script Editor button ▨ on the Page Design toolbar to start the Script Editor and changes to Script Only view. The only script in the page is the one that checks the user's browser when the page is loaded. He uses the Object list box to select the cmdLogin object and the Event list box to select the onclick event. The Script Editor starts a new script in the head section of the HTML document and adds the opening and closing tags to it.

Don enters the following statements to create a recordset named rsCust and searches it for a matching password entered into the txtPassword text box:

```
Dim rsCust
Set rsCust=MSODSC.DataPages(0).Recordset.Clone
rsCust.Find "Pwd = '" & txtPwd.value & "'"
```

These statements compare the user's entry in the txtPwd text box control with the values in the Pwd field in the rsCust recordset. If the script does not find a matching password, the end-of-file marker is set to True and the browser displays an error message. If the end-of-file marker is set to False, a match was located and a filter identifies the customer's record. Don inserts an If statement to test the end-of-file marker, as shown in Figure 8.39.

Figure 8.39: Script for the cmdLogin command button

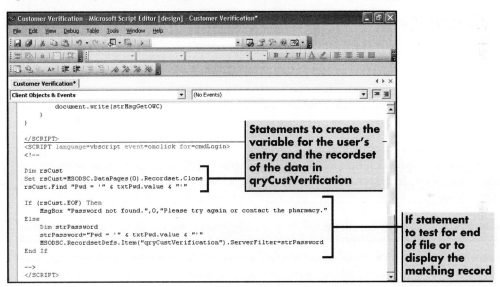

If the end-of-file marker is True, it means that no match was found; the browser executes the true portion of the If statement and displays a dialog box indicating that the password was not found. If the end-of-file marker is False, the Else statement creates a variable named strPassword, concatenates the user's entry in the text box control, and compares it to the password stored in tblCustomer. The next statement sets the filter. Remember that the records are stored on a server and transmitted to the client so the filter needs to be set on the server side so it transmits only the appropriate records. The property to set a server-side filter is **ServerFilter**. The filter is applied to qryCustVerification, which is the data source for the data access page. To set the filter, Don uses the data connection to connect to qryCustVerification. MSODSC refers to the current data connection source. RecordsetDefs.Item is the collection of objects on the data access page with qryCustVerification being the record source for the page. The ServerFilter property specifies the criterion for retrieving records from the database stored on the Web server and placed on the data access page.

Don saves the script and views the data access page in Page view. The first record in the query appears in the page before he enters a password. See Figure 8.40.

Figure 8.40: Testing the Customer Verification data access page

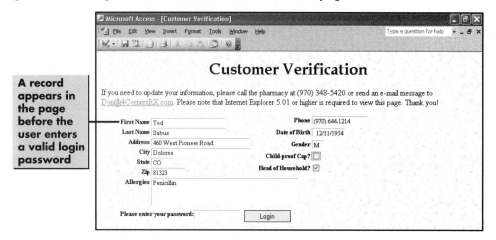

A record appears in the page before the user enters a valid login password

This result is not desirable because any customer who opens this page will be able to view the data for the first record in the query. To solve this problem, Don needs to set the page so that it originally returns no records, thereby displaying the data access page without any data. To accomplish this goal, Don needs to write a script that is executed when a browser loads the page.

Setting the Window Onload Event

When you need to execute a script when the user opens the page in a browser, you can write a script for the window onload event. The browser executes the statements in the window onload event when it loads the data access page for the first time. Don writes the script for the window onload event by using the Object list box to select the window object and by using the Event list box to select the onload event. The Script Editor starts a new script in the document window and adds the opening and closing tags for the script. Don also sets a filter to contain no records by using a criterion of zero. Figure 8.41 shows the window onload event.

Figure 8.41: Creating the window onload script

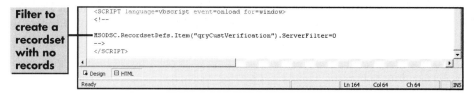

Filter to create a recordset with no records

Don tests the page again and it is still not functioning correctly. Now when Don types a password into the txtPassword text box, the program responds with a no password found message, even though Don knows that there is a password in the table matching the one he typed. The problem is that the server filter was set to no records when the page loaded. The program is trying to match the password Don typed in the txtPwd text box in the records of the currently set filter. Because there are no records in the current filter, the program cannot find a match. To fix this situation, the server filter must be removed before the search can begin. The easiest way to remove a server filter is to change the filter criterion in the window onload event from 0 to 1, which sets the filter to all records, as follows:

```
MSODSC.RecordsetDefs.Item("qryCustVerification").ServerFilter=1
```

Don tests the program again and discovers that it still has a flaw. If a user types an incorrect password, the dialog box opens and indicates that no matching password was found. However, a record is displayed in the form, as shown in Figure 8.42.

Figure 8.42: Incorrect password entered

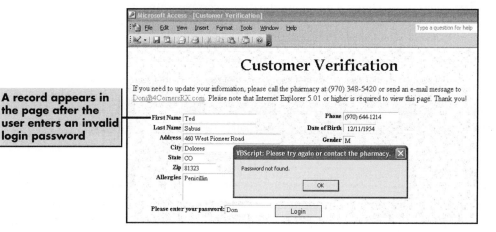

A record appears in the page after the user enters an invalid login password

To fix this problem, Don changes the filter in the window onload event back to 0 so the recordset contains no records when the browser loads the page. When he makes this change, no records are transmitted from the server to the client and, therefore, no records are displayed when an incorrect password is entered. Then he adds the filter to the beginning of the If statement, so no records are loaded before the browser processes the statement. If the If statement does not find a matching record when the customer enters a password, the browser displays the "Password not found." message and does not load a record into the page. If the If statement finds a matching record, the browser displays the matching record in the page. Figure 8.43 shows the completed scripts for the cmdLogin command button and the window onload event.

Figure 8.43: Completed scripts for the Customer Verification data access page

```
<SCRIPT language=vbscript event=onclick for=cmdLogin>
<!--

MSODSC.RecordsetDefs.Item("qryCustVerification").ServerFilter=1

Dim rsCust
Set rsCust=MSODSC.DataPages(0).Recordset.Clone
rsCust.Find "Pwd = '" & txtPwd.value & "'"

If (rsCust.EOF) Then
    MSODSC.RecordsetDefs.Item("qryCustVerification").ServerFilter=0
    MsgBox "Password not found.",0,"Please try again or contact the pharmacy."
Else
    Dim strPassword
    strPassword="Pwd = '" & txtPwd.value & "'"
    MSODSC.RecordsetDefs.Item("qryCustVerification").ServerFilter=strPassword
End If

-->
</SCRIPT>
<SCRIPT language=vbscript event=onload for=window>
<!--

MSODSC.RecordsetDefs.Item("qryCustVerification").ServerFilter=0
-->
</SCRIPT>
```

Don saves his work and tests the page in Internet Explorer. He types the passwords of several existing customers in the Pwd text box, and each one displays the correct record in the data access page. Figure 8.44 shows the data access page after accessing the record for Jennifer Ramsey.

Figure 8.44: Record is displayed after entering the correct password

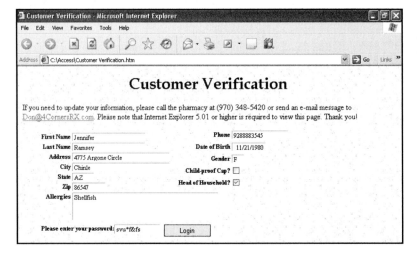

He also types his name in the Pwd text box to simulate a customer entering an invalid password. Figure 8.45 shows the browser after entering an incorrect password. The If statement checks to the end of the file and cannot find a matching password, so the dialog box opens and indicates to the customer that the password was not found and to contact the pharmacy for assistance.

Figure 8.45: No record is displayed after entering an incorrect password

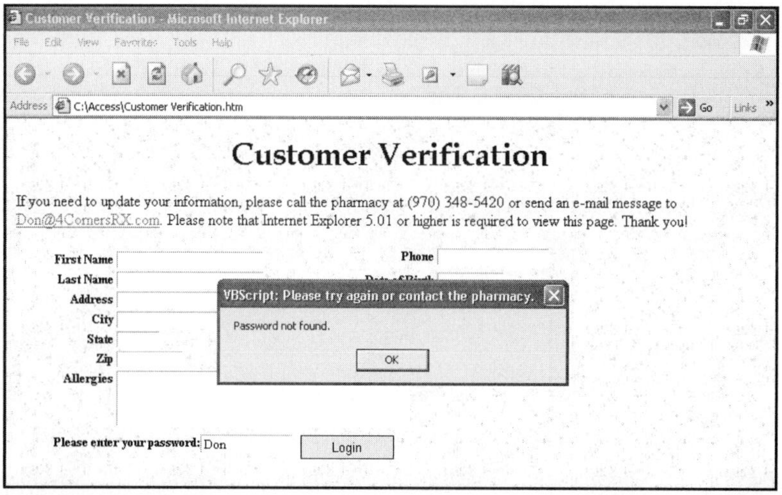

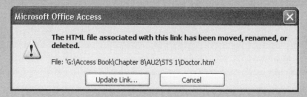

(Figure 8.45 — Internet Explorer browser showing "Customer Verification" page with a "VBScript: Please try again or contact the pharmacy." message box reading "Password not found." and an OK button. Address bar shows C:\Access\Customer Verification.htm. Password field contains "Don" with a Login button.)

Best Practice

Changing a Connection String to a Database

When you create a data access page in a database, you create a page object in the database and an HTML document that is stored outside the database. Both objects are connected to the database using a connection string. The connection string describes the type of database (such as Microsoft SQL Server or Access), the database password (if one exists), and the location of the database on the system. When you save a data access page, the connection string stores the database location using an absolute path. If you move either the database or the HTML document after creating them, the dialog box shown in Figure 8.46 opens when you try to open the page object in the database because the connection string points to the old file location.

Figure 8.46: Message box that opens after moving an HTML document

(Figure 8.46 — Microsoft Office Access message box: "The HTML file associated with this link has been moved, renamed, or deleted." File: 'G:\Access Book\Chapter 8\AU2\STS 1\Doctor.htm' with "Update Link..." and "Cancel" buttons.)

If you encounter this dialog box, click the Update Link button, and then browse to and select the HTML file for the data access page. After clicking the OK button, you might see a Microsoft Internet Explorer message box that tells you that the Microsoft Office Web Components could not open the database stored in the connection string. If this problem occurs, click the OK button to close the message box, and then open the page object in Design view. (Another message box might open to tell you that Access could not find the database; if this problem occurs, click the OK button to close the message box.) Right-click the data access page to open the shortcut menu, and then click Page Properties. Click the Data tab in the Properties dialog box, and then click the Build button ▐...▌ for the ConnectionString property. The Data Link Properties dialog box shown in Figure 8.47 opens.

Figure 8.47: Data Link Properties dialog box

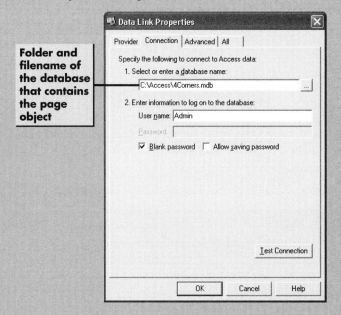

Folder and filename of the database that contains the page object

Now you need to change the connection string to include the revised database location. Click the Build button to open the Select Access Database dialog box, and then browse to and select the database. After clicking the Open button, click the Test Connection button in the Data Link Properties dialog box. When the test connection succeeds, you correctly updated the connection string. Click the OK button to close the open dialog boxes, and then save the page object. Now the data access page will work correctly.

It is important to be aware of how to change a connection string because publishing a database that contains page objects to a Web server requires you to update the links. If you do not update the links, the Web pages will display error messages when users try to use them.

Steps To Success: Level 2

Joan Gabel wants you to enhance the Health Insurance Companies page you created for the Hudson Bay Pharmacy Web site. She likes the page, but is concerned that as more records are added to the table, it might take a long time for customers to navigate through the records to find the desired company. She thinks that customers would appreciate having a Find button in the page that lets them search for insurance companies by the plan name.

Joan also wants to create a page that employees can use to update their personal data. She wants to store this page on the company's intranet and restrict access so that employees must use a password to view and change their data. Employees should not be able to view or change their employee ID number, SIN, date of birth, start date, end date, job ID, memo, salary/hourly rate, or review date.

Complete the following:

1. Start Access and open the **Hudson.mdb** database from the STS folder.

2. Open the Health Insurance Companies data access page and add a button that lets customers search for a health plan by name.

3. Create the page that lets employees update their personal information using the information Joan provided. Save the HTML document as **Employee Information.htm** in the STS folder.

4. Change the database to store employee passwords, and then add the password qU5%jhi9 to Joan Gabel's record. Change the Employee Information page so that employees must provide a password to view and change their data, add a title and user instructions, and then save the page.

5. Open the page in a browser, and then change Joan Gabel's cell phone number to 780-480-0010. (*Note:* Do not type the literal characters.)

6. Close the **Hudson.mdb** database and close Access.

LEVEL 3

IMPORTING AND EXPORTING XML DATA

ACCESS 2003 SKILLS TRAINING

- **Export Access data as XML**
- **Export data from tables**
- **Import XML documents into Access**

EXCHANGING DATA ACROSS BUSINESS ENTERPRISES

Most organizations design and maintain databases to operate companies in many types of industries. Don designed the database for 4Corners Pharmacy to match the unique needs of this specific pharmacy. The tables and other objects that he created in the database are unique to 4Corners Pharmacy and might not be appropriate for use by another business. As information technology and systems continue to become more sophisticated, many businesses look for ways to simplify and automate their business functions. For example, most major shippers in the United States use the Internet to supply customers with tracking information about packages. Previously, customers had to call the shipper to get these package shipment details. The replacement of the telephone representatives with a Web page automated the process and made information more available to customers.

Don knows that the employees at 4Corners Pharmacy will spend a lot of time on data entry and updates to maintain data about customers, drugs, refills, and other business operations. As new drugs are introduced, the pharmacy staff must add new records to the database. Don knows that some of the data about drugs that the staff needs is standardized in the pharmaceutical industry and is probably available in an electronic form from the drug suppliers or wholesalers that sell them. If Don can find a way to obtain data from the supplier or wholesaler and convert it into a format that is compatible with tblDrug in the 4Corners database, the pharmacy will benefit in two ways. First, the data will be accurate because it is not retyped by a member of the pharmacy staff; and second, the pharmacy staff will not need to spend time entering standardized data about drugs.

After doing some research, Don learns that the wholesaler from which the pharmacy purchases most of its drugs maintains a database of the individual drugs, but this data is not stored in an Access database. Despite this difference, if Don can find a way to work with the data and import it into tblDrug, he will save a lot of time and ensure data accuracy.

Don also wants to automate the process for confirming a customer's enrollment with a particular health plan. Currently, employees at the pharmacy confirm customer health plan enrollment information and other information, such as pharmacy co-payments, deductibles, and plan exclusions (drugs not covered by the customer's plan), by calling the health plan company and speaking with a representative, who verifies and confirms the customer's information using the health plan's database. Because most pharmacies and health plan companies would benefit from electronic exchanges of data, it is likely that Don can find a way to exchange data with the health plan companies as well.

UNDERSTANDING XML

HTML is very efficient in creating Web pages. The language is simple to learn, the files do not require a lot of disk space, and the documents can be created using a simple text editor. Because of its relatively small file size, HTML is an ideal choice for the Web because the pages download from the server to the client very quickly. Another important factor in the success of the Web is that most Web browsers, regardless of the operating system on which they are installed, read and interpret HTML tags in the same way. It is this interoperability that makes it possible for users with different computers, monitors, operating systems, and browsers to view Web pages without worrying much about the compatibility issues that exist in many other programs.

As the Internet grew, businesses saw great value in sharing data through the Web. Although HTML is an efficient way to construct Web pages, it has limitations when it comes to sharing data. One of these limitations is that HTML is not extensible. "Not extensible" means that the HTML language consists of a set of tags, and you cannot customize the tags for a specific use.

Another deficiency of using HTML to describe data is that the language was designed to define the format and content of the page, but not to validate or control the actual page content. Because the structure and content of an HTML document are so closely interwoven, it is often difficult to separate the formatting instructions from the content. For businesses to efficiently share data, they must be able to separate the content of the document from the formatting instructions. For example, Don might design a simple Web page that displays information about a drug. The HTML document on the left in Figure 8.48 defines the formatting instructions for the Web page shown on the right.

Figure 8.48: HTML document and resulting Web page

```
<html>
<head>
<title>4Corners Pharmacy</title>
</head>
<body>
<table border="1" width="214" align="center">
  <tr>
    <td width="137">
    <p align="left">UPN</td>
    <td width="61">102</td>
  </tr>
  <tr>
<td width="137">Drug Name</td>
<td width="61">Ampicillin</td>
  </tr>
  <tr>
    <td width="137">Description</td>
    <td width="61">Antibiotic</td>
  </tr>
  <tr>
    <td width="137">Price</td>
    <td width="61">$1.45</td>
  </tr>
  </table>
</body>
</html>
```

UPN	102
Drug Name	Ampicillin
Description	Antibiotic
Price	$1.45

Web page

HTML document

As you can see, the actual data displayed in the Web page is only a small portion of the HTML document. If Don wants to share the data in the HTML document with another organization, he needs to locate the data in the HTML document and separate it from the HTML tags that define its format in the Web page. Because the HTML language combines content and formatting instructions, the actual data is difficult to identify.

Extensible Markup Language (XML) is a markup language that is similar to HTML, but that includes features that let developers customize data to facilitate sharing data with other programs. XML has other uses besides being a common format for sharing database records. Businesses can use XML to exchange Web services and documents. For example, a traveler might use an airline Web site to purchase a ticket and reserve a car at his destination. In this case, the airline sends the car rental reservation to the agency that will actually rent the car to the traveler. The airline and the car rental agency might not use the same system to track customer data. However, their systems must be able to exchange data to process a customer's requests. The airline can convert the data to XML and send it to the car rental agency, which can then import it into its database. XML is becoming a standard for sharing information and data across the Internet.

After designing the structure of the data, a developer can construct a set of tags to describe the data. As the name implies, XML is extensible because it does not have a fixed set of tags. The tags are created and defined by the developer. For example, the data in the Web page shown in Figure 8.48 could have been stored in the XML document shown in Figure 8.49.

Figure 8.49: XML document containing drug information

```
<?xml version="1.0" encoding="UTF-8" standalone="yes"?>
<tblDrug>
    <UPN>102</UPN>
    <Name>Ampicillin</Name>
    <Description>Antibiotic</Description>
    <Price>1.45</Price>
</tblDrug>
```

The XML document shown in Figure 8.49 includes only the data in the Web page shown in Figure 8.48; the XML document does not include any formatting instructions that tell the browser *how* to display the data. The XML developer still needs to use HTML to tell the browser how to format the data. When you use XML and HTML together, the HTML defines the format of the data and the corresponding XML document contains the data to display in the page. If the data in the XML document changes, the Web developer needs to change only the XML document to update the Web page. Because of this flexibility, Web developers can use XML documents to create the equivalent of dynamic Web pages without linking them to a database. Figure 8.50 shows an HTML document that includes references to an XML document. The HTML tags format the Web page and identify the data that the XML document provides.

Figure 8.50: HTML document with XML references

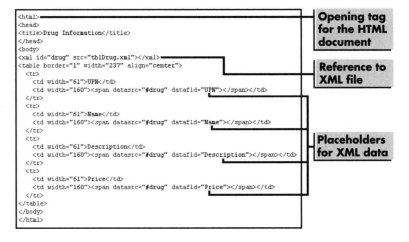

Don is confident that XML can provide the opportunity he is seeking to increase data accuracy and decrease data-entry time when adding new drugs to the database. Access 2003 fully supports importing and exporting of XML data. With proper planning, Don can work with the supplier's information systems department to share data between systems that might not otherwise be compatible.

8

Level 3

CREATING WELL-FORMED XML DOCUMENTS

Similar to HTML documents, Web developers must follow rules for coding XML documents. Some programs, including Access, output data into XML format, making it unnecessary for a person to mark up the content. Although many products code XML documents using a graphical user interface (GUI), all that is required for a person to write an XML document is a text editor, such as Notepad. When properly constructed, an XML document is called a **well-formed document** when it meets the established guidelines set forth by the World Wide Web Consortium for how data is defined and described in XML.

Also similar to HTML documents, an XML document includes three sections that define the document. These three sections are the prolog, the document body, and the epilog. The **prolog** is an optional section that provides information about the XML document, the **document body** contains the content of the XML document, and the **epilog** is an optional section that might contain comments.

Creating an XML Declaration

The prolog usually includes an **XML declaration** (which identifies the document as being written in XML), and might also include comments about the document or its creator and a document type declaration. The syntax of the XML declaration is:

```
<?xml version="versionNumber" encoding="encodingType"
    standalone="yes"/"no" ?>
```

The XML declaration begins with <?xml, which indicates that the document contains XML statements. The versionNumber value identifies the version of the XML specification used to write the code; the current version is 1.0. The encodingType value indicates the language coding scheme (also called a character set) used to create the document. The character set makes it possible for XML to be written in many languages; the character set value for English is UTF-8. When the encodingType value is omitted, the default character set is English. The standalone value ("yes" or "no") indicates how to process the XML document. A value of "yes" indicates that the XML is complete and requires no external files for processing; a value of "no" indicates that external files are necessary to process the document.

The XML declaration for a standalone XML document written using the English character set is as follows:

```
<?xml version="1.0" encoding="UTF-8" standalone="yes" ?>
```

This statement specifies that the document conforms to version 1.0 of the XML standard, uses the English character set, and does not require any external documents to define its data.

Best Practice

Using Comments in an XML Document
Just like in other programs, you can use comments in an XML document to identify the page's author, to describe the page's contents, or to leave notes for future developers. The syntax for a comment in an XML document is as follows:

```
<!-- comment -->
```

Because XML is extensible and developers can create many user-defined tags, XML developers recognize the vital importance in documenting their code so it is easy to understand and maintain when enhancements are made to the page in the future. Most developers suggest including documentation comments at the beginning of an XML document to describe the data the file contains and descriptions of its elements.

Using Elements and Attributes to Define Data in an XML Document

In an XML document, an **element** defines the data, just like a field describes the data in a database table. Although the developer creates the element names used in an XML document, the element names must be written to conform with established standards for naming elements. These rules are as follows:

- Element names are case sensitive; for example, the element names Drug and drug are not the same.

- Element names must begin with a letter or underscore character, cannot contain spaces, and cannot begin with the letters "xml."
- Element names must appear within angle brackets (< and >). Elements have opening and closing tags, similar to HTML. The closing tag includes a forward slash character (/).

For example, the following statement uses the Name element to store the drug named "Epronix:"

```
<Name>Epronix</Name>
```

Elements are usually nested within other elements to describe the relationship of data in the XML document. For example, a complete drug description might be as follows, with the Name, UPN, and Price elements nested within the tblDrug element:

```
<tblDrug>
    <Name>Epronix</Name>
    <UPN>412</UPN>
    <Price>1.50</Price>
</tblDrug>
```

An **attribute** is used within an element to describe a characteristic of the element and supply additional information. The general syntax of an attribute is as follows:

```
<elementName attribute="value">data</elementName>
```

Attribute names have the same syntax as element names. An example of an attribute within an element is as follows, in which the UPN attribute further describes the drug name "Epronix:"

```
<Name UPN="412">Epronix</Name>
```

There is no standard for using attributes versus using the equivalent element, but XML developers generally use attributes to describe data that is used by XML and that does not need to be viewed using a browser.

Creating the Root Element

In an XML document, the developer creates a **root element** to enclose the contents of the entire XML document. An XML document can contain only one root element that is user defined to describe the data. All other elements within an XML document must be nested within the root element. For example, in the following XML document, all of the elements are nested within the root element named <Supplier>:

```
<?xml version="1.0" encoding="UTF-8" standalone="yes" ?>
    <Supplier>Vacer Labs
        <tblDrug>
            <Name>Epronix</Name>
            <UPN>412</UPN>
            <Price>1.50</Price>
        </tblDrug>
        <tblDrug>
            <Name>Levothyroxine</Name>
            <UPN>289</UPN>
            <Price>1.40</Price>
        </tblDrug>
    </Supplier>
```

IMPORTING XML DATA INTO A TABLE

With proper planning, Access can import data from an XML document into a database table. After discussing the 4Corners database structure with the wholesaler's information systems department, Don receives an XML document with the corresponding information about two new drugs that the pharmacy will soon stock. See Figure 8.51.

Figure 8.51: XML data to import into tblDrug

```
  <?xml version="1.0" encoding="UTF-8" standalone="yes" ?>
- <wholesaler>
  - <tblDrug>
      <UPN>998</UPN>
      <Name>Accessillin</Name>
      <Description>Antibiotic</Description>
      <Cost>2.95</Cost>
      <Supplier>TJR Labs</Supplier>
    </tblDrug>
  - <tblDrug>
      <UPN>997</UPN>
      <Name>Exceldrin</Name>
      <Description>Pain</Description>
      <Cost>0.85</Cost>
      <Supplier>TJR Labs</Supplier>
    </tblDrug>
  </wholesaler>
```

He compares the XML file he received with tblDrug to ensure that the elements in the XML document match the fields in the table. The XML document does not contain all the data that the pharmacy stores about drugs, but it does supply the drug's UPN value, name, description, cost, and supplier. Don checks to make sure that the element names match the field names in the table. If the element names differ from the field names, Access imports the XML data into a new table instead of appending the XML data into an existing table.

Importing XML data into an existing table is similar to the process of importing data from a spreadsheet or other file. After verifying the contents of the XML document, Don imports the data stored in tblDrug.xml into tblDrug in the 4Corners database. He does not need to import the document structure because he already verified that the structure of the XML data matches the existing table structure.

How To

Import Data from an XML Document into an Existing Table
1. Click File on the menu bar, point to Get External Data, and then click Import.
2. In the Import dialog box, click the Files of type list arrow, and then click XML.
3. Browse to and select the XML file, and then click the Import button. The Import XML dialog box opens.
4. Click the Options button. The Import Options section lets you choose how to import the data: Structure Only (which creates an empty table in the database), Structure and Data (which creates a table in the database with the data in the XML document), or Append Data to Existing Table(s) (which adds the data in the XML document to an existing table). Depending on the XML document structure, there might be more than one table in the Tables list. Figure 8.52 shows the elements stored in tblDrug.xml.

Figure 8.52: Import XML dialog box

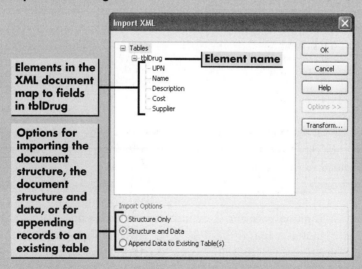

Elements in the XML document map to fields in tblDrug

Options for importing the document structure, the document structure and data, or for appending records to an existing table

5. Click the appropriate option button in the Import Options section, and then click the OK button.

Figure 8.53 shows tblDrug with the records Don imported from the tblDrug.xml file. The pharmacy staff can enter the appropriate information into the other fields as necessary to complete the record entries.

Figure 8.53: XML data imported into tblDrug

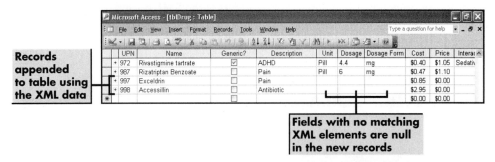

Records appended to table using the XML data

Fields with no matching XML elements are null in the new records

Using an XML Schema File to Describe Data

If the XML document contains all of the data that you need to import into a new table in the database, choosing the Structure and Data option button in the Import XML dialog box creates the table structure and imports the data in one action. By default, the elements in the XML document are imported as Text fields in the database. However, you can use an XML schema to describe the imported data so that the table structure is created using the data types available in Access. A **schema** is a file that describes the elements used in one or more XML documents and their relationships to other elements. Because a schema is a separate file, a developer must write it to include the necessary content to describe the elements in the XML document that contains the data to import. Schema files are text files and use the filename extension .xsd. The XML document that uses the schema file includes a reference to it in the prolog.

The syntax of a schema file to define data for an Access database is as follows:

```
<?xml version="1.0" encoding="UTF-8" ?>
    <xsd:schema xmlns:xsd="http://www.w3.org/2001/XMLSchema"
        xmlns:od="urn:schemas-microsoft-com:officedata">
        document structure specifications
    <xsd:schema>
```

xmlns stands for **XML namespace** and is defined as the address that defines the schema specifications used. The first xmlns is the W3C XML specification, and the second is the validation rules for a Microsoft Office document. The document structure specifications define the structure of the data, such as names and data types, just as the field properties define the characteristics of fields in an Access table.

You can define a simple data type in the document specification using the <element> tag as follows:

```
<xsd:element name="Name" type=od:jetType="data type" />
```

In this statement, name is the field name and od:jetType is the Access data type. For example, Don could define the Name field in tblDrug as follows:

```
<xsd:element name="Name" od:jetType="text" />
```

Table 8.3 lists some common Access data types and their jetType equivalents.

Table 8.3: Commonly used Access data types and jetType equivalents

Access Data Type	jetType Equivalent
Text	text
Date/Time	datetime
Number (single)	single
Number (double)	double
Yes/No	yesno

To declare several data properties, the developer must define a **complex type element** that contains one or more attributes. The syntax of a complex data type declaration is as follows:

```
<xsd:element name="name">
      element declarations
</xsd:element>
```

For example, the schema definition for the UPN field, which was defined in Access as a Text field with three characters in tblDrug, is written in the XML schema files as follows:

```
<xsd:element name="UPN" od:jetType="text">
     <xsd:maxLength value="3"/>
</xsd:element>
```

Table 8.4 describes some commonly used attributes that you can define in a schema definition.

Table 8.4: Attributes commonly used in schema definitions

Attribute	Description
maxLength	Specifies the field length.
name	Specifies the field name.
jetType	Specifies the data type.
maxOccurs	Specifies the maximum number of times an item can occur in a document.
minOccurs	Specifies the minimum number of times that an item can occur in a document. A value of zero indicates that the item is optional.

8

Level 3

Figure 8.54 shows part of the schema file that describes XML data that Don might use to define the data he imports into tblDrug. Notice that the schema defines the fields in the table and the table's primary key.

Figure 8.54: XML schema file for tblDrug

```
<?xml version="1.0" encoding="UTF-8"?>
<xsd:schema xmlns:xsd="http://www.w3.org/2001/XMLSchema"
xmlns:od="urn:schemas-microsoft-com:officedata">
<xsd:element name="dataroot">
<xsd:complexType>
<xsd:sequence>
<xsd:element ref="tblDrug" minOccurs="0" maxOccurs="unbounded"/>
</xsd:sequence>
<xsd:attribute name="generated" type="xsd:dateTime"/>
</xsd:complexType>
</xsd:element>
<xsd:element name="tblDrug">
<xsd:annotation>
<xsd:appinfo>
<od:index index-name="PrimaryKey" index-key="UPN " primary="yes" unique="yes" clustered="no"/>
<od:index index-name="drugID" index-key="UPN " primary="no" unique="no" clustered="no"/>
</xsd:appinfo>
</xsd:annotation>
<xsd:complexType>
<xsd:sequence>
<xsd:element name="UPN" minOccurs="0" od:jetType="text" od:sqlSType="nvarchar">
<xsd:simpleType>
<xsd:restriction base="xsd:string">
<xsd:maxLength value="3"/>
</xsd:restriction>
</xsd:simpleType>
</xsd:element>
<xsd:element name="Name" minOccurs="0" od:jetType="text" od:sqlSType="nvarchar">
<xsd:simpleType>
<xsd:restriction base="xsd:string">
<xsd:maxLength value="30"/>
</xsd:restriction>
</xsd:simpleType>
</xsd:element>
<xsd:element name="Generic" minOccurs="1" od:jetType="yesno" od:sqlSType="bit"
od:nonNullable="yes" type="xsd:boolean"/>
<xsd:element name="Description" minOccurs="0" od:jetType="memo" od:sqlSType="ntext">
<xsd:simpleType>
<xsd:restriction base="xsd:string">
```

To use a schema with an XML document, Don would define the schema version he wants to use to validate the file and specify the location of the .xsd file. He would place this definition at the beginning of the XML file as part of the root element, using the following syntax:

```
<rootName xmlns:prefix="URI"
xsi:SchemaLocation="URI">
```

The URI in the statements is a **Uniform Resource Identifier** that identifies a resource used in the schema definition. The following statements represent the code Don could use to link his schema for tblDrug to the XML file:

```
<dataroot xmlns:od="urn:schemas-microsoft-com:officedata"
xmlns:xsi="http://www.w3.org/2001/XMLSchema-instance"
xsi:SchemaLocation="tblDrug.xsd">
```

The od="urn:schemas-microsoft-com:officedata" entry references Microsoft Office products and the "http://www.w3.org/2001/XMLSchema-instance" identifies the schema language version used. After defining a schema file, Don can import the XML data into a new Access table that has the correct field names and field properties defined for each field based on the information the schema file provides for each element in the XML document.

EXPORTING AN ACCESS TABLE TO AN XML DOCUMENT

Access can also export data stored in a table or query to an XML document. When you use Access to export data, you can choose to export the data (in an XML file), the schema (an XSD file), or a stylesheet for the data (an XSL file). Access creates the XML document and the XML schema files automatically. Exporting data into an XML file is similar to the process that you might use to export data into a spreadsheet or other document type.

Elaine received a request from one of the insurance carriers with which the pharmacy works, and forwards this request to Don. Southern Rocky Mountains Health Plan is conducting a general audit of its systems and needs to reconcile its records with the prescriptions filled by its customers. Southern Rocky Mountains Health Plan uses a database management system that is not compatible with Access; however, after discussing the company's data needs with Don, the lead information systems specialist has determined that the DBMS the health plan uses can import the pharmacy's data using XML.

After determining that the health plan can process XML data, Don inquired about the exact data that it needs. He creates a query to select the first name, last name, date of birth, and plan ID for each customer, and the UPN, quantity, and date of each prescription for customers with the plan ID for Southern Rocky Mountains Health Plan. Because the health plan does not need the PlanID, he selects the option to exclude this field from the query results. He saves the query as qrySRMHP in the 4Corners database, and runs it. Figure 8.55 shows the query results.

Figure 8.55: Prescription records for customers of Southern Rocky Mountains Health Plan

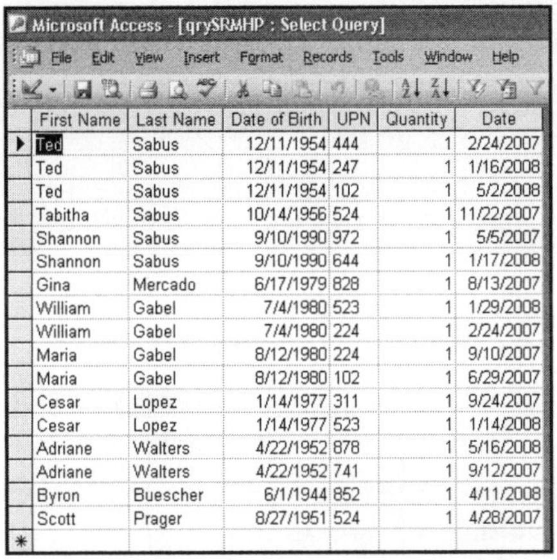

First Name	Last Name	Date of Birth	UPN	Quantity	Date
Ted	Sabus	12/11/1954	444	1	2/24/2007
Ted	Sabus	12/11/1954	247	1	1/16/2008
Ted	Sabus	12/11/1954	102	1	5/2/2008
Tabitha	Sabus	10/14/1956	524	1	11/22/2007
Shannon	Sabus	9/10/1990	972	1	5/5/2007
Shannon	Sabus	9/10/1990	644	1	1/17/2008
Gina	Mercado	6/17/1979	828	1	8/13/2007
William	Gabel	7/4/1980	523	1	1/29/2008
William	Gabel	7/4/1980	224	1	2/24/2007
Maria	Gabel	8/12/1980	224	1	9/10/2007
Maria	Gabel	8/12/1980	102	1	6/29/2007
Cesar	Lopez	1/14/1977	311	1	9/24/2007
Cesar	Lopez	1/14/1977	523	1	1/14/2008
Adriane	Walters	4/22/1952	878	1	5/16/2008
Adriane	Walters	4/22/1952	741	1	9/12/2007
Byron	Buescher	6/1/1944	852	1	4/11/2008
Scott	Prager	8/27/1951	524	1	4/28/2007

After verifying that the query selected the correct records, Don needs to export it as an XML document. You have three options for exporting Access data into XML format. The first option creates the XML data in an XML document. You might use this XML document later to import the data into Text fields in a new table in another database. You also could use the XML document to append the data into an existing table if the field names match the element names. If Don exports a table that has other tables related to it, he could specify which of the tables to export. If Don uses this option, Access exports all the fields from the selected table. By creating the query first and then exporting it, Don has more control over which fields to export.

The second option creates an XML schema file that defines the fields and field properties using the table or query that contains the original data. Saving the schema in a separate file makes it possible for one or more XML documents to use the schema. Embedding the schema in the exported XML document makes the schema available only for the current XML document; it cannot be used by other XML documents. The other option on the Schema tab lets you include primary key and index information in the schema. If the XML data is to be used to create a new table, including this information helps to construct the table properly. If the XML data will be used to append data into an existing table, this information does not need to be included because the primary key and index information already exist in the table's structure.

The third option is to create an **Extensible Style Language (XSL)** file. An XSL file, also called a presentation file in Access, is a stylesheet that can be used to format the XML data and transform the XML file to HTML format.

The health plan wants to receive an XML document and an XML schema file, so Don selects these export options.

How To

Export an Access Table or Query as an XML Document
1. Open the table or query in Datasheet view.
2. Click File on the menu bar, and then click Export. The Export dialog box opens.
3. Browse to the location in which to save the file.
4. Click the Save as type list arrow, click XML, and then click the Export All button. The Export XML dialog box opens. See Figure 8.56.

Figure 8.56: Export XML dialog box

Select the check box(es) to export the data, schema, and/or presentation files

5. Click the Data (XML), Schema of the data (XSD), and/or Presentation of your data (XSL) check boxes to select the file(s) that you want to create.

6. If necessary, click the More Options button to select additional options for how to export the data, how to create the schema file, or how to create the stylesheet. Figure 8.57 shows the options for exporting data.

Figure 8.57: Data tab in the Export XML dialog box

Options for creating a schema file

Object that contains the data to export

Use this text box to specify the folder and filename to contain the exported data

Figure 8.58 shows the options for exporting the schema file.

Figure 8.58: Schema tab in the Export XML dialog box

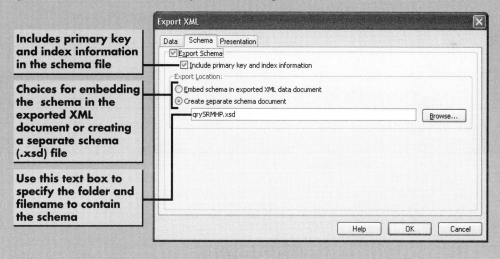

Includes primary key and index information in the schema file

Choices for embedding the schema in the exported XML document or creating a separate schema (.xsd) file

Use this text box to specify the folder and filename to contain the schema

7. Click the OK button.

After completing the export process, Don examines the files that Access created. Figure 8.59 shows part of the XML document in a text editor.

Figure 8.59: XML document for qrySRMHP

qrySRMHP.xml - Notepad

File Edit Format View Help

```
<?xml version="1.0" encoding="UTF-8"?>
<dataroot xmlns:od="urn:schemas-microsoft-com:officedata"
xmlns:xsi="http://www.w3.org/2001/XMLSchema-instance"
xsi:noNamespaceSchemaLocation="qrySRMHP.xsd" generated="2005-04-19T15:02:51">
<qrySRMHP>
<CustFirst>Maria</CustFirst>
<CustLast>Gabel</CustLast>
<DOB>1980-08-12T00:00:00</DOB>
<UPN>224</UPN>
<Quantity>1</Quantity>
<Date>2007-09-10T00:00:00</Date>
</qrySRMHP>
<qrySRMHP>
<CustFirst>William</CustFirst>
<CustLast>Gabel</CustLast>
<DOB>1980-07-04T00:00:00</DOB>
<UPN>523</UPN>
<Quantity>1</Quantity>
<Date>2008-01-29T00:00:00</Date>
</qrySRMHP>
<qrySRMHP>
<CustFirst>Cesar</CustFirst>
<CustLast>Lopez</CustLast>
<DOB>1977-01-14T00:00:00</DOB>
<UPN>311</UPN>
<Quantity>1</Quantity>
<Date>2007-09-24T00:00:00</Date>
</qrySRMHP>
<qrySRMHP>
<CustFirst>Ted</CustFirst>
<CustLast>Sabus</CustLast>
<DOB>1954-12-11T00:00:00</DOB>
<UPN>444</UPN>
<Quantity>1</Quantity>
<Date>2007-02-24T00:00:00</Date>
</qrySRMHP>
<qrySRMHP>
<CustFirst>Adriane</CustFirst>
<CustLast>Walters</CustLast>
<DOB>1952-04-22T00:00:00</DOB>
<UPN>878</UPN>
<Quantity>1</Quantity>
```

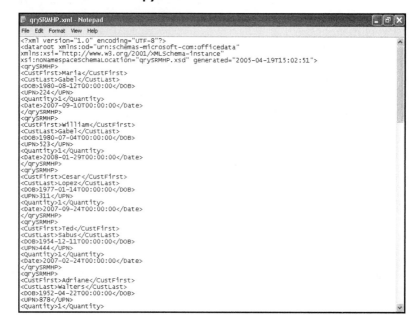

Figure 8.60 shows part of the XML schema file in a text editor.

Figure 8.60: XML schema for qrySRMHP

qrySRMHP.xsd - Notepad

File Edit Format View Help

```
<?xml version="1.0" encoding="UTF-8"?>
<xsd:schema xmlns:xsd="http://www.w3.org/2001/XMLSchema"
xmlns:od="urn:schemas-microsoft-com:officedata">
<xsd:element name="dataroot">
<xsd:complexType>
<xsd:sequence>
<xsd:element ref="qrySRMHP" minOccurs="0" maxOccurs="unbounded"/>
</xsd:sequence>
<xsd:attribute name="generated" type="xsd:dateTime"/>
</xsd:complexType>
</xsd:element>
<xsd:element name="qrySRMHP">
<xsd:annotation>
<xsd:appinfo/>
</xsd:annotation>
<xsd:complexType>
<xsd:sequence>
<xsd:element name="CustFirst" minOccurs="0" od:jetType="text" od:sqlSType="nvarchar">
<xsd:simpleType>
<xsd:restriction base="xsd:string">
<xsd:maxLength value="30"/>
</xsd:restriction>
</xsd:simpleType>
</xsd:element>
<xsd:element name="CustLast" minOccurs="0" od:jetType="text" od:sqlSType="nvarchar">
<xsd:simpleType>
<xsd:restriction base="xsd:string">
<xsd:maxLength value="30"/>
</xsd:restriction>
</xsd:simpleType>
</xsd:element>
<xsd:element name="DOB" minOccurs="0" od:jetType="datetime" od:sqlSType="datetime"
type="xsd:dateTime"/>
<xsd:element name="UPN" minOccurs="0" od:jetType="text" od:sqlSType="nvarchar">
<xsd:simpleType>
<xsd:restriction base="xsd:string">
<xsd:maxLength value="3"/>
</xsd:restriction>
</xsd:simpleType>
</xsd:element>
<xsd:element name="Quantity" minOccurs="0" od:jetType="longinteger" od:sqlSType="int"
type="xsd:int"/>
```

Steps To Success: Level 3

Karl Fujikawa, a pharmacist at Hudson Bay Pharmacy, just informed you that the pharmacy has been awarded several long-term contracts with a private insurer in the Edmonton area. Because the National Insurance Company (NIC) insures employees at some of Edmonton's largest employers, it wants to make sure that the pharmacy has the correct data when employees begin filling prescriptions under the company's various health plans. NIC sent you an XML document that contains data that you can import into the Hudson database.

Joan Gabel, the pharmacy's owner, has also been talking with NIC about providing a prescription drug benefit to the pharmacy's full-time employees. She negotiated a good rate and now needs to send NIC a list of full-time employees and some basic information about them, including their full name, address, date of birth, start date, and phone number. Because the Hudson database is not compatible with the NIC's system, she needs you to provide her with an XML file to send to NIC. NIC will use this data to contact employees so they can complete the required paperwork to add themselves and their families to the health plan.

Complete the following:

1. Start Access and open the **Hudson.mdb** database from the STS folder.

2. Compare the structure of tblHealthPlan with the **tblHealthPlan.xml** document that NIC sent and that contains the health plan information that you need to import into the database. (The tblHealthPlan.xml file is saved in the Chapter 8 folder.) If necessary, change the XML document so you can import its data into tblHealthPlan, save the XML document, and then append the records in tblHealthPlan.xml into tblHealthPlan.

3. Export the data for full-time employees as described by Joan into an XML document named **HBPEmployees.xml** in the STS folder. The company wants to receive an XML document and a schema that includes primary key and index information.

4. Close the **Hudson.mdb** database and close Access.

CHAPTER SUMMARY

In this chapter, you learned how to work with technologies that make it possible to view and change data stored in a database using Web pages. In Level 1, you learned how to connect a Web page to a database and how to use data access pages to view and change data in the database object on which the page is based. You also learned how to customize the navigation options that you provide to users and how to prevent users from making changes. Finally, you learned how to apply a theme to a data access page.

In Level 2, you learned how to enhance the functionality of a data access page by writing scripts to perform certain tasks. You used functions to open dialog boxes and display messages to users as they interact with the page. You also learned how to program a command button so it searches the database for matching records entered by users. Finally, you learned how to restrict a user's access to a data access page by creating a password and writing a script to compare the user's password entry with the one stored in the database.

In Level 3, you learned some basic information about using XML to share data with and between applications. You learned some general syntax, how to create well-formed XML documents, and the basic parts of an XML document and how to write an XML declaration. You also imported XML data into Access by appending data to an existing table and exported data from an Access object into an XML document.

CONCEPTUAL REVIEW

1. What is the difference between a client computer and server computer?

2. What is the difference between a static Web page and a dynamic Web page? How do you create dynamic Web pages in Access?

3. What information is stored in a connection string? When might you need to change a connection string, and how would you do so?

4. What is the difference between an absolute path and a relative path? Why is it important to understand these concepts when working with data access pages?

5. What are the sections in a data access page, and what information does each one contain?

6. How do you replace a record navigation bar with command buttons? Why would you do so?

7. Why are scripts embedded in a Web page? How do you prevent a browser that cannot execute the script from displaying the script in the Web page?

8. What is a recordset bookmark?

9. What is a server filter?

10. What two deficiencies of HTML does XML solve?

11. What is a well-formed document? Which organization controls XML standards?

12. What are the three sections of an XML document, and what information does each one contain?

13. Write the XML declaration for a document coded in English and with the default standalone value.

14. What is important about the root element in an XML document?

15. What is a schema?

CASE PROBLEMS

Case 1—Creating Data Access Pages for NHD Development Group Inc.

As you continue consulting with Tim Richards, the chief information officer for NHD Development Group, he tells you that NHD wants to publish some of the Memories Antique Mall's database information on the mall's Web site. He wants to include Web pages in the Web site that let customers view information about the mall's classes and let potential dealers examine the mall's available booth space.

Management

Tim wants you to include the class information in a Web page so customers can see information about the classes the mall offers so that they cannot change any of the information in the database. In the future, he might want to accept online registration and payment, but currently he only wants to include the mall's phone number for registration purposes. Tim also wants to include the mall's vacant booths in a separate Web page so dealers can get information about the available booth spaces for lease. Potential dealers should not be able to view information about rented booth space, nor should they be able to change any of the information they view. Tim wants dealers to be able to sort the vacant booth data by booth size.

Tim did not specify an exact presentation for the pages that he needs, except to indicate that both pages should include the NHD logo.

Complete the following:

1. Start Access and open the **Antiques.mdb** database from the Case 1 folder.

2. Create the Web page to display the information about classes offered by the mall. Following Tim's request, be certain that the page does not accept changes to existing data, deletions, or additions. The page should include navigation options so customers can browse the records in tblClass. Arrange the fields in an appropriate way and resize and reorganize the controls as necessary to ensure accurate data presentation. Make sure that the page includes a title and the NHD logo (saved as **NHD-logo.jpg** in the Chapter 8 folder), and that the page uses an appropriate page theme. Save the HTML document as **Classes.htm** in the Case 1 folder.

8

Chapter Exercises

3. Preview the Classes page in Internet Explorer and browse the records. As you view the records, determine if any of the fields need to be moved or resized so that all the data is fully displayed. If you need to make any changes, save the page.

4. Create the page to display booth data for only those booths that are currently vacant (not rented). After adding the controls to the page, rearrange and resize them as necessary to ensure the best presentation of data. Set the page's properties so that page users cannot change, delete, or add records, but so that users can navigate from one record to another. Format the page to match the Classes page, include the NHD logo, and add an appropriate title and user instructions. Save the HTML document as **Vacant Booths.htm** in the Case 1 folder.

5. Create a filter in the Vacant Booths page that lets dealers browse vacant booths by booth size.

6. Preview the Vacant Booths page in Internet Explorer and browse the records by each available booth size. As you view the records, determine if any of the fields need to be moved or resized so that all the data is fully displayed. If you need to make any changes, save the page.

7. Linda Sutherland, the mall's manager, wants to be able to use a data access page on the mall's local area network to change booth data, so she can update the database from any computer in the mall that is connected to the network. Because only Linda and other office staff will use this page, she wants to be able to update, add, and delete records in tblBooth. Design a Web page that lets Linda update tblBooth and save the HTML document as **Booth Information.htm** in the Case 1 folder. Linda asks you to format the page so it has the same appearance as the Web pages you created for Tim.

8. Use Internet Explorer and the Booth Information page to rent booth A-07 to an existing dealer, Karen Kline, who has the dealer ID 4577.

9. Linda asks you to add a new booth in the mall. The booth ID is A-21, the booth size is 8 × 8, and the location is on the mall's outside perimeter. The booth's color is green and it has rafters and carpet. The booth's monthly rent is $110.

10. Rent booth A-21 to Karen Kline.

11. Carefully review your work, make any necessary changes, and then save your work.

12. Close the **Antiques.mdb** database and Access.

Case 2—Creating Data Access Pages for MovinOn Inc.

Management

Dora Nettles will manage the MovinOn database after you complete it. In anticipation of this responsibility, she reviews the database to become familiar with all of its objects and structure. Dora just returned from a meeting with the managers at the three warehouses in which they discussed the plans for expanding the business into other regions. The managers are excited about the expansion and want to make sure that customers can get the information they need about the services MovinOn offers.

To work toward that goal, David Bowers, MovinOn's general manager, hired a Web site developer. In addition to providing general company and operations information on the Web site, David also wants to provide customers with information that is stored in the MovinOn database. Dora suggests including information about the warehouses and available storage units on the Web site. Because this information needs to be current, Dora suggests using data access pages instead of static HTML documents. She wants customers to be able to browse the data for each warehouse and the storage units they contain.

Dora also suggests using the company's private intranet to make it easier for managers to view complete job order information and customer contact data. Having this information in a Web page should make it easier for managers and employees to make last-minute changes to customer data and to view the active jobs.

Complete the following:

1. Start Access and open the **MovinOn.mdb** database from the Case 2 folder.

2. Create a data access page that displays warehouse and storage information. Dora and David did not request a specific "look" for the page except that they want to include the company logo on all pages, and for the color and style of the page to coordinate attractively with the logo. Dora suggests that you include the warehouse information at the top of the page and the units in each warehouse in a list at the bottom of the page. (*Hint:* Group the page using the warehouse data.) Dora also reminds you that she does not want the user to be able to alter any of the data. Save the HTML document as **WarehouseAndUnits.htm** in the Case 2 folder.

3. Dora reviewed the WarehouseAndUnits page and asks you to make a few modifications. First, she wants to display five units to make the list more manageable. She suggests that you keep the record navigation bar for browsing the unit data but remove all buttons except for the ones that let customers navigate the data. However, for the warehouses, Dora wants to replace the record navigation bar with buttons that let customers view the first, last, next, and previous warehouse. Finally, she wants customers to see the expanded data about units when the page is loaded, instead of having to click the expand indicator. (*Hint:* Change the ExpandedByDefault property to True for the warehouse group.)

8

Chapter Exercises

4. Save your changes to the WarehouseAndUnits page, and then test it in a browser.

5. Create the page that will display job order information. (*Note:* Make sure that the page displays job order information, and not job detail information.) Dora wants to include the job order data and the contact information for the customer that placed the order. Dora asks you to add borders around the pickup location, destination location, and customer information to visually separate this data in the page. Dora wants users to be able to update existing data and add new records, but she does not want users to be able to delete any information. Save the HTML document as **JobOrders.htm** in the Case 2 folder.

6. Dora wants users to be able to display the information for a job by entering the job ID. She asks you to add this functionality to the JobOrders page.

7. Dora wants to create an employee contact page for the intranet to make it easier to contact a specific employee. She wants to include the employee ID, last name, first name, warehouse ID, warehouse phone number, phone number, and cell phone number for each employee. Page users should not be able to change, add, or delete records using this page. Dora also wants you to include a button on the page that lets the user search for a specific employee by entering the employee's last name. Save the HTML document as **Employee.htm** in the Case 2 folder.

8. Carefully review your work, make any necessary changes, and then save your work.

9. Close the **MovinOn.mdb** database and close Access.

Case 3—Creating Data Access Pages for Hershey College

Marketing

In this project, you continue to work with Marianna Fuentes, assistant director of the intramural department at Hershey College. Recently, Hershey College enhanced the college Web site and created a subsite for the intramural department to use. Marianna is excited about the exposure that the Web site will give to the department. She asks you to create a Web page for the site that lists all the sports offered, along with their start dates and assigned coaches. By linking this page to the database that stores this information, Marianna knows that the information in this page will be current and might reduce the number of phone calls she receives from students who are trying to contact their coaches. This page should include information about each sport the department offers, the coach for each team and his or her contact information, and each sport's starting date. Marianna stresses that this page should be read-only and, as such, it should not accept changes from users.

Marianna has not specified any particular format or appearance for the page and decides to leave that to your discretion. However, she does want all the pages in the Web site to be neat and attractive, and to include the college logo.

In addition to creating the page for the college Web site, Marianna also has two requests for pages that she wants to post on the college intranet so that only she and authorized staff members can access them. The first page for the intranet needs to show detailed information about the established teams, including the team ID, sport name, and start date; the field ID, maintenance liaison and his or her contact information; and the equipment ID and details. She also wants to include each team member's name in this page.

The second page should include all student records and indicate the student's eligibility status for participating in intramural sports. The staff will also use this page to determine whether a student has signed the required waiver for participation and is eligible to participate, and to change a student's status when necessary. Marianna remembers that there might be an existing query that you can use to create this page.

Complete the following:

1. Start Access and open the **Hershey.mdb** database from the Case 3 folder.

2. Follow Marianna's instructions to create the page for the college Web site, which lists the sports offered, along with their start dates and assigned coaches. In talking with Marianna, you discovered that she doesn't want to use the default record navigation bar in this page, but instead wants to use command buttons with labels that will allow the user to view the first, previous, next, and last records. Marianna also wants to make it easy for students to find information about a specific sport by searching for a sport name. She also wants you to include a note in the page that tells students to contact the coaches directly if they are interested in a particular sport. She wants the coach's name listed in the format "Stone, Sharon" in a single text box. Save the HTML document as **SportAndCoach.htm** in the Case 3 folder.

3. Follow Marianna's instructions to create the team detail page for the intranet. She wants to include information about the team, field, and equipment at the top of the page and the first and last names of the team members at the bottom of the page. The team members should be visible with the team, field, and equipment detail. She wants the list of players to be displayed at the same time as the team details (that is, she does not want to have to expand the list), and she wants all the players listed together below the team details. She asks that you somehow visually separate the team detail from the list of players on the team. Save the HTML document as **TeamDetails.htm** in the Case 3 folder.

4. Follow Marianna's instructions to create the student eligibility page for the intranet. Marianna also wants to be able to search for a particular student's record either by entering the student's last name or by entering the student's ID. Save the HTML document as **ApprovalStatus.htm** in the Case 3 folder.

5. The academic dean just contacted Marianna and requested a copy of the data showing the approval status of all students who have enrolled in the intramural program. Marianna knows that the dean's office uses a database and suggests that the data be provided in such a way that it can be easily imported. She reminds you that you already have a query that shows the approval status and suggests that you create an XML document from this query. Save the XML document and a separate schema file as **StudentApprovalStatus.xml** in the Case 3 folder.

6. The office staff is busy trying to get the new department up and running. The coaches frequently change their contact data and a staff member must make the coaches' changes in the database. Marianna wants you to create another page for the intranet for coaches to use to update their contact data. The coaches should not be able to add or delete records but they should have the ability to edit their own record, with the exception of their ID number. Marianna wants you to protect the coaches' information using a password that you assign to each coach. Create this page and save the HTML document as **CoachContactUpdate.htm** in the Case 3 folder. When you are finished, preview the page in a browser, and then change Jean Epperson's last name to Stringfield and save the change.

7. One of the faculty members, Lynn Scott, has agreed to do some coaching for the intramural department. Her contact information is stored in the faculty database. Larry Tinsley, the college's database administrator, does not want to provide public access to this information. Instead, he agrees to provide Lynn's contact information to the intramural department in an XML document. Import the data from the **NewCoach.xml** file located in the Chapter 8 folder. Be sure to check tblCoach to ensure that the data was properly imported.

8. Carefully review your work, make any necessary changes, and then save your work.

9. Close the **Hershey.mdb** database and close Access.

Glossary

A

absolute path A path that provides an exact location for a file within a computer's entire directory structure.

Action Arguments pane The lower portion of the Macro window that provides additional information for performing a macro action.

Action column A column in the Macro window that lists the actions the macro performs.

action query A special type of query that performs actions on a table, such as changing the contents of a field, adding records from one table to another table, deleting records from a table, or making a new table based on criteria.

aggregate functions The arithmetic and statistical operations such as Avg, Sum, Min, Max, StDev, and Var. You can apply aggregate functions to groups of data to calculate results for each group.

Allow Built-in Toolbars A startup option that lets you show or hide built-in toolbars when Access starts.

Allow Full Menus A startup option that lets you show complete menus and all commands or only a subset of menus and commands when Access starts.

Allow Toolbar/Menu Changes A startup option that allows or prevents users from customizing toolbars, menu bars, and shortcut menus.

analysis The process of collecting, organizing, and transforming data into information that can be used to support decision making.

AND criteria The conditions that must all be true for Access to select a record.

append query A type of query that selects records from one or more tables and then adds those records to the end of another table.

artificial key A primary key that is created when no natural key exists.

assignment statement A statement that assigns the value of an expression to a control or property.

attribute A part of an XML element that describes a characteristic of the element to supply additional information.

AutoExec A special macro that runs automatically when a database is opened.

AutoFormat A predefined design you can apply to a form or report.

AutoKeys A macro group that assigns an action or set of actions to a key or key combination.

AutoNumber The Access data type that generates a unique number in a field to produce unique values for each record in a table.

AutoReport Wizard A Report Wizard that creates a report displaying all the fields and records in a single table or query.

B

back up The process of creating a copy of a database that can be restored in the event of a loss.

base table (underlying table) The table on which a query, form, report, or data access page is based.

Beep A macro action that plays a beep sound.

Before Update event The event that occurs before changed data in a control or record is updated in the database.

bookmark A pointer used to mark the position of a record within a recordset.

breakpoint A code inserted into a macro or VBA procedure signaling where to stop the macro.

C

Calculated field A field in a query, form, or report containing an expression that is calculated from the data.

calls The term used in a programming language to describe the process of executing statements when an event occurs.

CancelEvent action An action that cancels the event that caused a procedure or macro containing the action to execute.

candidate key A field or collection of fields that could function as a table's primary key, but that was not chosen to do so.

Caption property A field property that determines how the field name is displayed in database objects.

caption section The part of a data access page that might contain text boxes and other controls to display captions.

cascade deletes An option that allows Access to delete related records in related tables when the primary record in the primary table is deleted.

cascade updates An option that allows Access to update the appropriate foreign key values in related tables when a primary key value in the primary table is updated.

Case control structure A conditional structure that evaluates an expression and then performs one of several alternative sets of statements based on the resulting value (or condition) of the evaluated expression.

chart A graphic representation of data that is helpful for analyzing trends, especially changes during a period of time.

class module A module associated with a particular form or report in a database.

Clear the Grid A query option that lets you show the field lists in the query design window, remove all fields, criteria, and sort order from the design grid.

client computer In a client/server network, a computer that sends requests to a server, which responds by sharing its resources, including files, programs, and connected devices such as printers.

client/server network A network configuration that connects client computers to a server.

Code window The Visual Basic Editor window in which you create, modify, and display specific VBA procedures.

coding The process of writing instructions in a programming language.

color constant A predefined name in VBA that represents a system color value.

Command button An unbound control that users click to perform common tasks, such as moving to a different record or closing a form.

Comment column A column in the Macro window that documents a macro action.

common field A field that appears in two or more tables and contains identical data that is used to relate the tables. The common field is called a primary key in the primary table and a foreign key in the related table.

compact To reorganize the data and objects in a database by reassigning and deleting unused space. Compacting a database usually reduces its file size.

compilation error An error that occurs when you translate VBA procedures into a form the computer can understand.

compilation The process of translating modules from VBA to a form the computer understands. You say that you compile the module when you translate it.

complex type element An element in an XML document that contains one or more attributes.

composite primary key (composite key) A primary key composed of two or more fields.

concatenation The process of combining the contents of two or more fields, such as a first and last name, into one string.

conditional formatting The process of applying formatting features such as color, bold, and font size based on whether the values in a report or form meet criteria that you specify.

connection string A path indicating the disk location of the HTML document and database name to which a data access page is connected.

control A small object such as a text box, button, or label that lets users interact with a database object.

control structure A set of VBA statements that work together as a unit. The If statement is an example of a control structure.

crosstab query A type of totals query that performs aggregate function calculations on the values of one database field and allows you to determine how your summary data appears in the results.

Currency The Access data type that formats numeric values with a dollar sign and two decimal places.

custom report A report that requires data from more than one table, includes calculated fields, uses summary statistics, or requires parameter input when the report is opened or printed.

D

data access page A dynamic Web page that you can open with a Web browser and use to view or change the data stored in the database object on which the data access page is based.

data consumer The person who transforms data into information by sorting, filtering, or performing calculations with it.

data duplication The process of creating repeated records in a database, which leads to wasted space and inconsistent and inaccurate data.

data Raw information, including words, images, numbers, or sounds.

data redundancy An undesirable effect of storing repeated data in fields in a table that wastes space and results in inconsistent and inaccurate data. Data redundancy is often avoided by creating additional tables.

data type A field property that determines how to store the data in the field.

database A collection of one or more tables.

database administration (DBA) The group that is responsible for designing, maintaining, and securing a database.

database administrator The person who designs, maintains, and secures a database.

database management system (DBMS) A system that creates and defines a database; a software program that creates and accesses the data in a database.

Database window The main control panel for an Access database.

datasheet A view of data that displays fields in columns and records in rows.

Datasheet view An Access view that displays the records in a table or query in rows and fields in columns.

Date function A VBA function that returns the current computer system date.

Date/Time The Access data type that stores dates or date and time combinations.

DateDiff function A VBA function that calculates the number of time intervals between two dates.

DateSerial function A VBA function that returns a date value for a specified year, month, and day.

Declarations section The first part a VBA module that contains statements that apply to all procedures in the module.

decrypt (decode) The process of canceling the encryption of data in a database.

Default Value property A field property that enters a default value into a field; can be used for all field types except AutoNumber.

delete query A query that removes records from a table based on criteria you specify.

deletion anomaly The problem that occurs when a user deletes data from a database and unintentionally deletes the only occurrence of that data in the database.

Description property A property of a field used to document its contents.

design grid (Table Design grid) The top pane in Table Design view that includes the Field Name, Data Type, and Description columns; each row in the Table Design grid represents a field in the table.

Design view The window that lets you define the fields and properties for a table, query, form, report, or data access page.

Detail The main section in a form or report that displays data from the underlying data source.

detailed report A report that lists each row of data from a table or query.

determinant A field or collection of fields whose value determines the value in another field.

Dim statement In a VBA procedure, the statement used to declare a variable and its associated data type.

discovery phase The first step in planning a database, which includes gathering all existing data, researching missing and incomplete data, and talking with users about their data output needs.

Display Database Window A startup option specifying whether to display the Database window when Access starts.

Display Form/Page A start-up option specifying which form or page to open when Access starts.

DoCmd statement The VBA statement that executes an action in a procedure.

document body The section of an XML document that contains the content of the XML document.

document window The window in Script Editor in which you view and change the HTML document for a data access page.

Documenter An Access tool that produces a report of selected objects in a database and their relationships.

domain A set of records, a recordset.

domain aggregate function A function that calculates statistics for a domain from a table or a query.

dynamic Web page A Web page whose content changes based on a user's interaction with the Web page.

___

E

element In an XML document, an element defines the data.

embedded script A script that is embedded in an HTML document.

encrypt (encode) A process that converts data in a database into a format that is readable only by Access.

End Sub statement The last line of a subroutine.

entity integrity A guarantee that there are no duplicate records in a table, that each record is unique, and that no primary key field contains null values.

epilog The optional section of an XML document that might contain comments.

event A state, condition, or occurrence that Access recognizes, such as clicking a command button or opening an object.

event property The property associated with an event that specifies how an object responds when the event occurs.

event-driven language A programming language, such as VBA, in which a set of programming instructions are triggered by an event in the database.

event-driven programming The computer programming code that executes when a user interacts with an object.

expression An arithmetic formula that performs a calculation in a query, form, or report.

Expression Builder A tool to assist in developing complicated expressions for calculated fields that shows the fields, functions, and other objects available in Access.

Extensible Markup Language (XML) A markup language that is similar to HTML, but that includes features that let developers customize data to facilitate sharing data with other programs.

Extensible Style Language (XSL) A presentation file used to format XML data and that can be used to transform the XML file to HTML format.

___

F

field (column) A single characteristic of an entity in a database. For example, fields that describe a customer might include first name, last name, address, city, and state.

Field Properties pane The lower pane of Table Design view that displays the field properties for the selected field.

Field Size property A property of a field that limits the number of characters to store in a Text field or the type of numeric data to store in a Number field.

File Transfer Protocol (FTP) The protocol used to transfer files between computers over a network.

Filter by Form An Access feature that lets you specify two or more criteria when filtering records.

Filter by Selection An Access feature that lets you select a field in a datasheet and then display only data that matches the contents of that field.

filter One or more conditions that restrict data in a single table to create a temporary subset of records.

Find An Access tool that searches a recordset for a record that matches a specified criterion.

first normal form (1NF) A database table that does not contain any repeating groups.

flat file database A simple database that contains a single table of information.

focus The control on a form that is currently active and ready for user action.

footer section The part of a data access page that displays values and calculates summary values for groups of records.

ForeColor property The property for a control that determines the control's foreground (font) color.

foreign key The common field in the related table between two tables that share a relationship.

form A database object based on a table or query and used to view, add, delete, update, and print records in the database.

form footer The lower part of a form. It displays information that always appears on a form but at the bottom of the screen in Form view and the bottom of the last page when the form is printed.

form header The upper part of a form. It usually contains static text, graphic images, and other controls on the first page of a form.

function (Function procedure) In a programming language, a function performs operations, returns a value, accepts input values, and can be used in expressions.

functional dependency A column in a table is considered functionally dependent on another column if each value in the second column is associated with exactly one value in the first column.

G

grid The gray background on a form or report that displays dots and grid lines to help with aligning controls.

group footer A section of a report that is printed at the end of each group of records. Often used to print summary information such as subtotals for a group.

group header A section of a report that is printed at the beginning of each group of records. Often used to print the group name.

grouped report A report that organizes one or more records into categories, usually to subtotal the data for each category. The groups are based on the values in one or more fields.

Groups bar The part of the Database window that can be used to organize database objects and create shortcuts for working with them.

H

header section The section of a data access page that displays the data from the database object(s) on which the page is based.

history table A table of data containing archived records.

Hourglass A macro action that changes the pointer to an hourglass while the macro runs.

HTML document A text file containing HTML tags that format the content of a Web page.

Hyperlink (data type) The Access data type that displays text that contains a hyperlink to an Internet or file location.

hyperlink (Internet) A tag in an HTML document that points to another location in the same document, to a new location in the same Web site, or to elsewhere on the Internet.

Hypertext Markup Language (HTML) A markup language used to create Web pages.

Hypertext Transfer Protocol (HTTP) The transfer protocol used to send and receive Web pages.

I

If statement In a programming language, the statement that tests one condition that results in one of two answers and that follows a set of instructions depending on the outcome of the condition.

Immediate pane The part of the Debug window that you use when debugging macros and that displays the current value of controls and arguments.

Immediate window The part of the Code window in Visual Basic Editor that is used to test VBA procedures without changing any data in the database.

index A list maintained by the database (but hidden from users) that associates the field values in the indexed field with the records that contain the field values.

information Data that is organized in some meaningful way.

input mask A property of a field that applies a predefined format to field values.

Input Mask Wizard An Access wizard that guides you through the steps of creating an input mask and lets you enter sample values to ensure the correct results.

insertion anomaly The problem that occurs when a user cannot add data to a database unless other data has already been entered.

Internet A large, worldwide collection of computers that are connected together in various ways to form a large computer network.

IsNull function A VBA function that returns the value True when the field or control is null and the value False when it is not.

J

join A relationship between tables and the properties of that relationship. The relationship is shown by a join line in the Relationships window in Access. Tables that are joined have a common field with the same or compatible data type and the same field values.

junction table An intermediary table created to produce a many-to-many relationship between two tables that do not share a one-to-one or one-to-many relationship.

L

Left function The VBA function that returns a string containing a specified number of characters from the left side of a specified string.

line label A VBA statement that serves as the starting point for a block of statements in a procedure. A line label begins at the start of a line and ends with a colon.

literal character A character that enhances the readability of data but is not necessarily stored as part of the data, such as a dash in a phone number.

logic error In a programming language, the error that results when a procedure produces an incorrect result.

Lookup field A field that provides a list of valid values for another field, either using the contents of another field or values in a list.

Lookup Wizard The Access wizard that allows you to set field properties to look up data in another table or in a list of values created for the field.

M

macro An action or series of actions that you want Access to perform.

macro condition A logical expression that results in a true or false answer.

macro group Two or more macros stored in the same macro file.

mailing labels report A type of multicolumn report used to print names and addresses in a format suited for sending mail through the postal service. Labels can also be used for other purposes such as name badges.

many-to-many relationship (M:N) A relationship between tables in which each record in the first table matches many records in the second table, and each record in the second table matches many records in the first table.

Me keyword A VBA keyword that refers to the current object.

Memo The Access data type that stores long passages of alphanumeric data.

method An action that operates on specific objects or controls.

Microsoft Script Editor The program that Access uses to create and edit scripts written in VBScript.

module (Access) An object that contains instructions to automate a database task, such as verifying the data entered into a field before storing it in the database.

module (VBA) A group of related procedures saved in a database object. A module begins with a Declarations section and includes one or more procedures.

move handle The larger handle in a control's upper-left corner that you use to move the control.

MsgBox action A macro action that opens a message box and displays a warning or other information.

MsgBox command A command you can use in a macro condition to specify what action the macro should take depending on the state of the message box.

multiple-column report A report that displays information in several columns, such as a telephone listing or mailing labels.

N

natural key A primary key that details an obvious and innate trait of a record, such as an ISBN code for a book.

navigation section The part of a data access page that contains the record navigation bar.

nonkey field A field in a table that is not part of a table's primary key.

normalization A process that reduces the chance of deletion, update, and insertion anomalies in a database.

Null value A field value that is unknown, unavailable, or missing.

Number The Access data type that stores numbers that are used in calculations.

O

object-oriented language A programming language, such as VBA, that includes a set of instructions that operate on objects in the database.

Objects bar The part of the Database window that contains buttons to access objects so they can be created, opened, designed, and viewed.

OLE object The Access data type that identifies files that were created in another program and then linked to or embedded in the database.

one-to-many relationship (1:M) A relationship between tables in which one record in the first table matches zero, one, or many records in the related table.

one-to-one relationship (1:1) A relationship between tables in which each record in one table matches exactly one record in the related table.

Open Exclusive mode A method of opening an Access database that locks out all users except for the current user from opening and using the database at the same time.

Open Exclusive Read-Only mode A method of opening an Access database that locks out all users except for the current user, but the current user can only view the data in the database.

Open mode A method of opening an Access database that lets multiple users open and use the database at the same time; it is the default option for opening a database.

Open Read-Only mode A method of opening an Access database that lets multiple users open the database, but users cannot write any information to the database and are limited to viewing existing data only.

OpenReport A macro action that opens a report.

Option Compare statement In a subroutine, the Option Compare statement designates the technique used to compare and sort text data. The default method, Database, means that letters are compared and sorted in normal alphabetical order.

OR criteria The criteria that select records that match any of the specified values.

orphaned The term used to describe a record whose matching record in a primary or related table has been deleted.

P

page footer A section of a report or form that appears at the end of every printed page.

page header A section of a report or form that appears at the top of every printed page.

parameter value A prompt used in a query to allow user input when the query is run. The value the user enters is then used as the criterion for that field.

partial dependency The situation in which a field is dependent on only part of a composite primary key.

password A collection of characters that a user types to gain access to a file.

permission The rules that specify the level of access in a database for a user or group of users.

personal ID (PID) In a database that uses user-level security, a string value with 4 to 20 characters that identifies a user.

primary key A field or combination of fields that creates a unique value in each record in a table.

primary sort field The field used to sort the records first, which must appear to the left of any other field. Additional fields used to further sort the records must appear to the right of the primary sort field.

primary table In a one-to-many relationship, the table that is on the "one" side of the relationship.

print registration error An error that causes misaligned printed items.

private procedure (local procedure) A procedure in a class module that can be used only by the form or report for which it was created.

procedure (event procedure) A group of statements in a programming language that are executed when an event occurs.

Project Explorer window The window in Script Editor that lets you choose between open HTML documents for different data access pages.

prolog An optional section in an XML document that provides information about the XML document, including the XML declaration.

Properties pane The window in Script Editor that includes properties that you can set for a data access page.

public procedure A procedure that more than one database object can use.

Q

query A database object that stores criteria for selecting records from one or more tables based on conditions you specify.

query by example (QBE) Creating a query by entering the values you want to use as criteria for selecting records.

R

record (row) Collectively, the values in each field in a table for a single entity.

record navigation bar A toolbar that contains buttons that let users change the view of the data displayed by a data access page.

record source The underlying table or query object that provides the fields and data in a form.

recordset (query) A datasheet that contains the results of a query.

recordset (Script Editor) A snapshot of the records in a table or query that is used to view or update the data by a script.

referential integrity A rule that if the foreign key in one table matches the primary key in a second table, the values in the foreign key must match the values in the primary key. When the database does not enforce referential integrity, certain problems occur that lead to inaccurate and inconsistent data.

related table In a one-to-many relationship, the table that is on the "many" side of the relationship.

relational database A database that contains tables related through fields that contain identical data, also known as common fields.

relative path A path that describes the location of a file relative to the location of the current document.

repeating group In an incorrectly designed database table, a field that contains more than one value.

report A database object that presents the information from one or more database tables or queries in a printed format.

report footer A section of a report that is printed once at the end of the report. The report footer appears last in the report design but is printed before the final page footer.

report header A section of a report that is printed once at the beginning of the report. The report header is printed before the page header.

Report Wizard A wizard that guides you through the steps of creating a report based on one or more tables or queries by asking you questions about the record sources, fields, layout, and format you want to use.

Required property The property of a nonprimary key field that requires users to enter a value in the field.

root element The topmost user-defined element in an XML document. An XML document can contain only one root element.

run-time error (execution error) An error that occurs when a procedure executes and stops because it tries to perform an operation that is impossible to perform.

S

schema A file that describes the elements used in one or more XML documents and their relationships to other elements.

scope In a subroutine, the scope indicates the procedure as public or private.

scripting language A programming language that is used to write code that an interpreter executes.

second normal form (2NF) A database table that is in first normal form and that does not contain any partial dependencies on the composite primary key.

select query A query that selects data from one or more tables according to specified criteria, and displays the data in a datasheet.

SendKeys action A macro action that sends keystrokes to Access or to another active program.

server In a client/server network, the computer that processes requests from client computers and shares resources, such as files and printers.

ServerFilter A property used to set a server-side filter.

SetFocus method A VBA method that moves the focus to the specified object or control.

SetValue action A macro action that can change the property of an object by disabling, updating, hiding, or displaying a control.

single stepping Running a macro one action at a time, pausing between actions.

sizing handle A small square that appears on the corners and edges of a selected control and that lets you resize the control.

sort To arrange records in a table or query in a particular order or sequence.

splash screen A form that opens when an application begins, often listing information such as the name of the application and programmers and contact information.

standard module A database object that is stored in memory with other database objects when the database is opened. Standard modules can be used from anywhere in the database.

startup options A set of actions and configurations that Access performs when a database opens.

statement A VBA instruction that responds to an event that occurs with an object or control in the database.

static Web page A Web page that displays information that is current at the time the page was created or last saved.

strong password A password that contains at least seven characters consisting of combinations of uppercase and lowercase letters, numbers, and symbols.

Structured Query Language (SQL) The common query language of most DBMSs, including Access. A query created in SQL can run in most database programs.

Sub statement The first part of a subroutine that includes the scope of the procedure (private or public), the name of the procedure, and an opening and closing parenthesis.

subdatasheet A datasheet that displays records from related tables in Table Datasheet view.

subform A form that appears within another form and is usually used to display related data.

subreport A report that appears within another report and is usually used to display related data.

subroutine (Sub procedure) In a programming language, a subroutine performs operations and accepts input values, but does not return a value and cannot be used in expressions.

summary report A type of grouped report that calculates totals for each group and a grand total for the entire report, and doesn't necessarily include details.

surrogate key A computer-generated primary key that is usually invisible to users.

switchboard A special kind of form that appears when you open a database and lists options for working with tables, forms, queries, and reports.

Switchboard Manager A tool that helps you design and customize a switchboard.

syntax error An error that occurs when a VBA statement violates the language rules for a statement, such as a misspelling, an incorrect sequence of keywords, and a missing parenthesis.

T

Tab control A control you can add to a form that contains a subform on each page of the control. Users can move between the control pages by clicking the tabs.

tab order The order in which you move from one control to another in a form when you press the Tab key. The tab order determines the order for data entry.

table (entity, relation) A collection of fields that describe one entity, such as a person, place, thing, or idea.

Table Wizard An Access wizard that includes sample tables for business and personal needs with fields that you can select and modify to create your own tables.

tag A code used in an HTML document that describes how to format the content in the document.

Text The Access data type that stores up to 255 alphanumeric characters that are not used in calculations.

theme A predefined collection of design elements that format the text and objects in a Web page with coordinated fonts, colors, backgrounds, and other design elements.

third normal form (3NF) A table that is in second normal form and the only determinants it contains are candidate keys.

time-series data The data that shows performance over time for periods such as years, quarters, or months.

Toolbox A toolbar in Design view for forms, reports, and data access pages that lets you add controls to the object.

transfer protocol A set of rules that computers use to send and receive files from other computers.

transitive dependency The situation that occurs between two nonkey fields that are both dependent on a third field; tables in third normal form should not have transitive dependencies.

U

unbound control A text box that displays the results of a calculated field, a label such as the title of a form, or a logo or other graphic used to make the form more attractive. It is unbound because it is not based on an underlying table or query.

unbound form An Access form with no record source, such as one containing instructions to help users navigate through a database.

Undo In VBA, a method that clears all changes made to the current record so that the field values in the record are as they were before the user made current changes.

Uniform Resource Identifier (URI) In an XML document, the address that identifies a resource used in the schema definition.

Uniform Resource Locator (URL) The unique address that identifies a Web server that is connected to the Internet. The URL includes the transfer protocol to transfer the file, the domain name of the computer, and an optional pathname and filename.

unnormalized data Data that contains deletion, update, or insertion anomalies.

update anomaly The problem that occurs when, due to redundant data in a database, a user fails to update some records or updates records erroneously.

update query A query that changes the values of data in one or more existing tables based on criteria.

user view A form that shows only the fields a particular user wants or is allowed to see. It might not allow data entry or deletions.

user-level security A type of database security that establishes specific levels of access to the database objects for individual groups of users.

V

Val function The VBA function that returns the numbers contained in a specified string as a numeric value.

validation rule A rule that compares the data entered into a field by a user against one or more valid values that the database developer specified.

Validation Rule property A property of a field that specifies the valid values that a user can enter into the field.

Validation Text property A property of a field that displays a predefined message if a user enters an invalid value into the field.

variable A named location in computer memory that can contain a value.

VBScript Short for Microsoft Visual Basic Scripting Edition, a scripting language that you can use to enhance the functionality of a Web page.

Visual Basic Editor (VBE, editor) The program used to create and modify VBA code.

Visual Basic for Applications (VBA) The programming language for Microsoft Office programs, including Access.

Visual Basic window The program window that opens when you use Visual Basic Editor (VBE).

W

Watches window The VBA window that is used to debug a procedure by showing the current value of a specified variable while the procedure is executing.

Web browser A program that reads the tags in an HTML document and displays the content as a Web page according to the standardized rules defined for those tags.

Web client A computer that uses a Web browser to connect to a Web site.

Web server A computer that is connected to the Internet and runs special software to store and manage a Web site.

well-formed document An XML document that is written to meet the established guidelines set forth by the World Wide Web Consortium for how data is defined and described in XML.

wildcard character A placeholder that stands for one or more characters. Common wildcards are the asterisk (matches any number of characters), question mark (matches any single alphabetic character), and pound sign (matches any single digit in a numeric field).

workgroup ID (WID) In a database that uses user-level security, the unique character string of 4 to 20 characters that identifies a workgroup.

workgroup information file In a database that uses user-level security, the file that defines user groups, usernames, and user passwords.

World Wide Web (Web) A subset of the computers connected to the Internet and that host Web sites.

X

XML declaration The part of an XML document that identifies the document as being written in XML and that might also contain comments about the document or its creator and a document type declaration.

XML namespace (xmlns) An address that defines the schema specifications used in an XML document.

Y

Yes/No The Access data type that stores one of two values, such as yes or no, true or false, or on or off.

Index

Some of the exercises in this book require that you begin by opening a Data File. Follow one of the procedures below to obtain a copy of the Data Files you need.

Instructors

- A copy of the Data Files is on the Instructor Resources CD under the category Data Files for Students, which you can copy to your school's network for student use.

- Download the Data Files via the World Wide Web by following the instructions below.

- Contact us via e-mail at reply@course.com.

- Call Course Technology's Customer Service Department for fast and efficient delivery of the Data Files if you do not have access to a CD-ROM drive.

Students

- Check with your instructor to determine the best way to obtain a copy of the Data Files.

- Download the Data Files via the World Wide Web by following the instructions below.

Instructions for Downloading the Data Files from the World Wide Web

1. Start your browser and enter the URL www.course.com.
2. When the course.com Web site opens, click Student Downloads, and then search for your text by title or ISBN.
3. If necessary, from the Search results page, select the title of the text you are using.
4. When the textbook page opens, click the Download Student Files link, and then click the link of the compressed files you want to download.
5. If the File Download dialog box opens, make sure the Save this program to disk option button is selected, and then click the OK button. (NOTE: If the Save As dialog box opens, select a folder on your hard disk to download the file to. Write down the folder name listed in the Save in box and the filename listed in the File name box.)
6. The filename of the compressed file appears in the Save As dialog box (e.g., 3500-8.exe, 0361-1d.exe).
7. Click either the OK button or the Save button, whichever choice your browser gives you.
8. When a dialog box opens indicating the download is complete, click the OK button (or the Close button, depending on which operating system you are using). Close your browser.
9. Open Windows Explorer and display the contents of the folder to which you downloaded the file. Double-click the downloaded filename on the right side of the Windows Explorer window.
10. In the WinZip Self-Extractor window, specify the appropriate drive and a folder name to unzip the files to. Click Unzip.
11. When the WinZip Self-Extractor displays the number of files unzipped, click the OK button. Click the Close button in the WinZip Self-Extractor dialog box. Close Windows Explorer.
12. Refer to the Read This Before You Begin page(s) in this book for more details on the Data Files for your text. You are now ready to open the required files.

Macintosh users should use a program to expand WinZip or PKZip archives. Students, ask your instructors or lab coordinators for assistance.